12th International Conference on Axiomatic Design (ICAD 2018)

MATEC Web of Conferences Volume 223 (2018)

Reykjavik, Iceland
9 - 12 October 2018

Editors:

E.C.N. Puik
J.T. Foley
D.S. Cochran
M.L. Betasolo

ISBN: 978-1-5108-7408-4

Printed from e-media with permission by:

Curran Associates, Inc.
57 Morehouse Lane
Red Hook, NY 12571

Some format issues inherent in the e-media version may also appear in this print version.

Printed by Curran Associates, Inc. (2018)

For additional information, please contact EDP Sciences – Web of Conferences at the address below.

EDP Sciences – Web of Conferences
17, Avenue du Hoggar
Parc d'Activité de Courtabœuf
BP 112
F-91944 Les Ulis Cedex A
France

Phone: +33 (0) 1 69 18 75 75
Fax: +33 (0) 1 69 28 84 91

contact-edps@webofconferences.org

Additional copies of this publication are available from:

Curran Associates, Inc.
57 Morehouse Lane
Red Hook, NY 12571 USA
Phone: 845-758-0400
Fax: 845-758-2633
Email: curran@proceedings.com
Web: www.proceedings.com

TABLE OF CONTENTS

edp sciences

MATEC Web of Conferences

Statement of Peer review

In submitting conference proceedings to MATEC Web of Conferences, I certify to the Publisher that I adhere to the **Policy on Publishing Integrity** of the journal in order to safeguard good scientific practice in publishing.

1. All articles have been subjected to peer review administered by the proceedings editors.
2. Reviews have been conducted by expert referees, who have been requested to provide unbiased and constructive comments aimed, whenever possible, at improving the work.
3. Proceedings editors have taken all reasonable steps to ensure the quality of the materials they publish and their decision to accept or reject a paper for publication has been based only on the merits of the work and the relevance to the journal.

Title, date and place of the conference

12th International Conference on Axiomatic Design
October 9-12, 2018
Reykjavík University, Reykjavík, Iceland

Proceedings editor(s):

Erik C. N. Puik
Joseph T. Foley
David S. Cochran
Mirzi L. Betasolo

Date and editor's signature

2018 October 8

Design of a low-cost loading/unloading mechanism for processing stations in an automated production environment

Georg Egger[1,*], *Michael* Riedl[1], *Erwin* Rauch[2], and *Dominik T.* Matt[1,2]

[1]Fraunhofer Italia, Automation and Mechatronics Group, 39100 Bolzano, Italy
[2]Free University of Bozen-Bolzano, Italy

Abstract. A loading/unloading mechanism was designed using the axiomatic design method. The mechanism is a standardized part of a smart factory currently implemented at Fraunhofer Italia research institute on behalf of the DeConPro research project, and as such is specified to fit any processing station. The mechanism is used in conjunction with an automated transport system, which carries standardized transport boxes on rails. The transport systems stop at the processing stations and shall be grabbed by the mechanism subject of this publication and dragged into the processing station, where. Also, the transport boxes must be fixed onto the shuttles of the transport system avoiding drops while moving, which is also part of the design exercise. Inside the processing station, the transport boxes shall be further movable in both directions perpendicular to the direction of the mechanism movement. The mechanism shall build compact especially in depth, and shall also be optimised in cost, as it is a recurring item in all processing stations. The resulting FR/DP decomposition lead to an decoupled design matrix up to second level, which allowed for choosing the right engineering sequence of the functions. The axiomatic design procedure helped considerably in finding the best concept for holding and handling the box. The further engineering steps benefit also considerably by the anticipated trade-off between alternatives for actuator types.

1 Introduction

Today, Industry 4.0 and cyber-physical production systems (CPPS) is an omnipresent buzzword in both traditional manufacturing and mass production and several research projects at Fraunhofer Italia are dedicated to this topic. Among other projects, Fraunhofer Italia is working on currently on a small-scale factory, which shall serve as a sandbox for applying decentralized control schemes to control the dynamic nature of production. Physically, the research infrastructure will consist of:

- an autonomous transport system as the common means for accessing all modules
- a laser cutting machine as a example for an digital production module
- an assembly station for a demonstration of the capabilities of a modern cooperative robotic arm
- a quality check module for automated routine checks
- a delivery station

The parts and the material is moved in so-called intelligent work-piece carriers (IWC), which are standardized containers and all handling operations will be designed around them. Hence, common to all modules is their interface to the transport system. As this is a recurring element, the impact on the overall system cost is of interest and was selected as worthy to be prototyped. Se Figure 1 for a conceptual illustration of the problem.

There are several ways of designing such a mechanism and it is easy to get lost among the number of requirements. In the past, the authors have made several successful experiences in using the Axiomatic Design method to structure and solve design problems in the field of assembly system design [1] [2] [3].

For this purpose, the axiomatic design method was selected as a systematic approach finding an answer to the principal design questions. See [4] and [5] for the definition of axiomatic design.

The remaining content of the paper is organised in the following chapters:

Chapter 2: Customer attributes The boundary conditions and expectations to the product are listed. In the absence of an external customer, the CAs are identified through a self-interview.

Chapter 3: Identification of Cs and n-FRs Among the CSs, contraints and non-functional requirements are identified. In particular the maximum accelerations are treated in detail.

Chapter 4: FR/DP decomposition This chapter holds the definition of FR0/DP0 and the first and second level decomposition. The decomposition adheres to the first axiom, the selection of appropriate physical implementations follows axiom 2.

*e-mail: georg.egger@fraunhofer.it

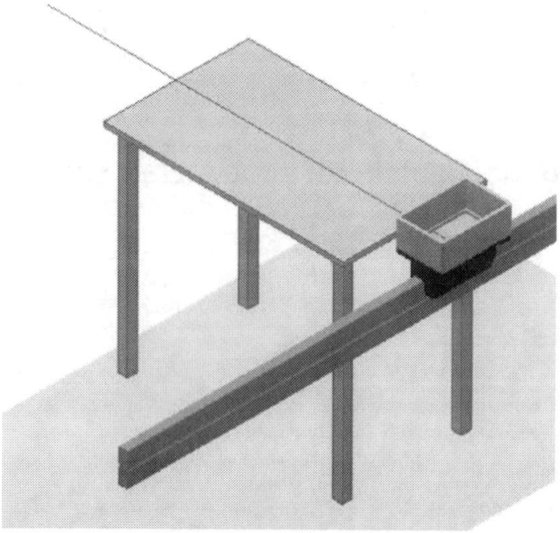

Figure 1. The design task comprises the supporting structure on the shuttles (blue) and the mechanism, which shall be integrated with the table-like object. The direction of movement is along the axis shown on the table.

Chapter 5: Discussion The approach to the problem is recapped, the benefits and limitations of the work is addressed.

Chapter 6: Outlook Planned follow-up activities on this topic.

2 Customer attributes

In the current application, there is no customer, as the mechanism is designed for the purpose of a research project. Hence the CAs are interpreted as user needs.

CA1 the transport boxes are 300 mm x 200 mm box Auer EG 32/12 HG (see Figure 2) filled no higher than 300 mm. The boxes are to be positioned in the longitudinal direction on the shuttles, that is when the long side is parallel to the trajectory of the shuttles;

CA2 the boxes are brought on rail-based transport shuttles, which will stop at the given position quite precisely (1 mm or better);

CA3 the supporting structure holding the boxes on the shuttles shall be designed according to the needs of the mechanism;

CA4 the boxes shall not fall off the shuttles while being moved.

CA5 unlike on the shuttles, there is electrical power and compressed air available on the stationary side;

CA6 the mechanism shall be able to grab boxes, drag them up to 500 mm away from the shuttle (orthogonal to the rails) and to release them;

CA7 once retracted, the boxes shall be free to move in orthogonal to the mechanism movement (parallel to the rails);

CA8 compact build, particularly in depth;

CA9 the boxes are limited to 3 kg in mass, which can be assumed to be equally distributed throughout the volume envelope;

CA10 the shuttles move no faster than 55 m/min;

CA11 the shuttles accelerate from 0-30 m/min in 0.5 s or slower, depending on the load;

CA12 the curves on the track shall have a radius of at least 220 mm; and

CA13 there are more shuttles than stations.

3 Identification of constraints and non-functional requirements

The following constraints have been identified from the customer attributes:

C1 as container, Auer EG 32/12 HG [6] shall be used. The box with content weights max 3 kg and the mass can be assumed equally distributed;

C2 the longitudinal orientation of the boxes shall correspond to the movement of the shuttles on the rails;

C3 the shuttles will stop with a position accuracy of 1 mm;

C4 compressed air and electrical power is available on the stationary side, no active power source available on the shuttles;

Figure 2. The stackable Euro container EG 32/12 HG from Auer Packaging GmbH, which shall be used by the mechanism. The container features two handling holes on each lateral face, which may be used for grasping the box.

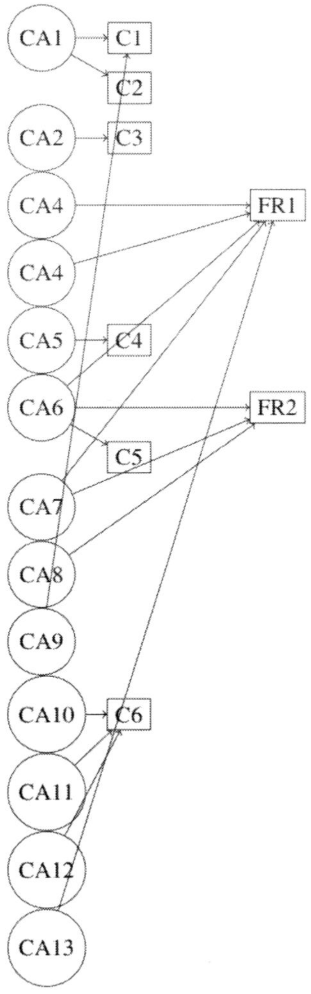

Figure 3. Assignment of customer attributes (CA) to constraints (C) and functional requirements (FR).

C5 the translation shall be 500 mm orthogonal to the rails on the same plane; and

C6 the maximum speed of the shuttles is is 55 m/min.

3.1 Determining the accelerations acting on the box

The maximum acceleration, that acts on the boxes while on the shuttle, can be derived from CA10, CA11, and CA12.

Two cases are to be distinguished:

- Longitudinal direction (starting and stopping)
- Transversal direction (moving through curves)

In the case of longitudinal acceleration, the shuttle accelerates from zero to 30 m per minute (CA10) in 0.5 seconds (CA11). The acceleration is assumed to be constant:

$$a_{linear} = \frac{\Delta v}{\Delta t} = \frac{30\,\mathrm{m\,min^{-1}}}{0.5\,\mathrm{s}} = \frac{30\,\mathrm{m}}{60\,\mathrm{s}\cdot 0.5\,\mathrm{s}} = 1\,\mathrm{m\,s^{-2}} \quad (1)$$

The longitudinal direction of the box corresponds to the longer side of the box W (from CA1).

For the transversal acceleration, the shuttle travels with maximum speed through a curved element. Centrifugal forces act on the box and its content. Assuming a circular-shaped curve with radius r_{min}, the worst case acceleration is given by:

$$a_{circular} = \frac{v_{max}^2}{r_{min}} = \frac{\left(\frac{55\,\mathrm{m\,min^{-1}}}{60\,\mathrm{s\,min^{-1}}}\right)^2}{0.22\,\mathrm{m}} \sim 3.8\,\mathrm{m\,s^{-2}} \quad (2)$$

4 FR/DP decomposition

The top level functional requirements and design parameters are defined as follows:

FR0 box handling for rail-based transport system

DP0 linear actuator with forklift mechanism

In the first level of the decomposition, two FR/DP pairs are identified:

FR1 hold and release of the transport boxes

DP1 frame and forklift

FR2 move the box perpendicular to the rails

DP2 linear actuator

The further decomposition is given in the following sub-chapters.

4.1 FR1/DP1: Hold and release of the transport boxes

There are numerous ways of holding the box on the shuttle, as requested by CA4. There are active ways, requiring the presence of some sort of energy source (primarily electrical or mechanical) on the shuttle, and passive ones, where the power required to overcome the locking mechanism is provided by the stationary side. Both ways, there is a strong coupling to the release mechanism on the stationary side.

The FR/DP pair can be decomposed further:

FR1.1 fix the boxes firmly on the transport shuttle

DP1.1 frame

FR1.2 release of the boxes

DP1.2 forklift

The partial design matrix shows a decoupled design, where the function of the box release (FR1.2) depends on the fixation device (DP1.1) and the design of the release mechanism (DP1.2).

$$\begin{Bmatrix} FR_{1.1} \\ FR_{1.2} \end{Bmatrix} = \begin{bmatrix} X & 0 \\ X & X \end{bmatrix} \begin{Bmatrix} DP_{1.1} \\ DP_{1.2} \end{Bmatrix} \quad (3)$$

4.1.1 FR/DP 1.1: Fix the boxes firmly on the transport shuttle

CA5 restricts the types of holding and release mechanisms to passive ones, which limits the possibilities significantly. In order to minimise the coupling factor between fixation and movement as much as possible, a simple interface is sought and found in a simple frame, embracing the base of the box. The introduction of this frame makes it impossible for the box to slip off the shuttle, the box however might tilt when sufficient acceleration is applied. The contained weight and speed of the boxes allow this frame to have a rather limited height. The maximum allowed height can be found by observing Figure 4, where a represents in one case the constant acceleration and in the other the centrifugal acceleration. Both forces F_A and F_G can be composed in components acting along the line - defined by the center of rotation on the border of the frame and the center of gravity of the box - and perpendicular to it (direction of rotation). In the latter direction, both forces act in a contrary sense and the equilibrium point can be seen as the critical point corresponding to the tolerable acceleration.

The decomposition of F_A and F_G in the direction of rotation (see Figure 4) yields:

$$a \sin\theta = g \cos\theta \tag{4}$$

where g is the gravitational constant and a is the acceleration. For the angle θ one can find:

$$\tan\theta = \frac{\frac{H}{2} - h}{\frac{W}{2}} = \frac{H - 2h}{W} \tag{5}$$

Given a certain maximum acceleration a_{max} the step height h must be at least:

$$h \geq \frac{1}{2}\left(H - \frac{gW}{a_{max}}\right) \tag{6}$$

It can be seen, that the minimum required h might as well be negative. In this case, the acceleration is not sufficient to lift the weight of the box at all.

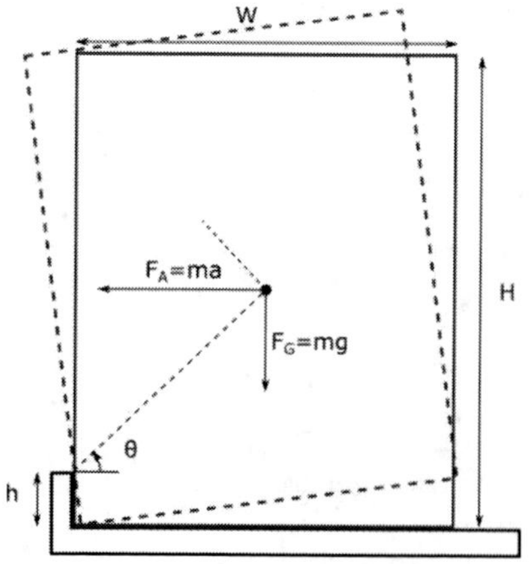

Figure 4. Acceleration of the box around the border frame.

C6 gives the numerical values for the worst case accelerations. Table 1 shows the results of the minimum height calculations. From the numerical values can be readily seen that the worst case is the circular motion.

Even in the worst case, the required minimum height for tilting is negative, which means that any height of the embracing frame will prevent falling off.

4.1.2 FR/DP 1.2: Release of the boxes

The box is supposed to be dragged over the table, perpendicular to the orientation of the rails. Before the box can be dragged, it must be raised above the edge of the supporting frame (FR/DP 1.1), in order to be released from the fixation.

Fundamentally, there are two approaches to this: the rise from the frame is performed by the shuttle or by the stationary side. The complexity seems manageable for both parties, but as CA5 states, there is no power available on the shuttles. Hence it is simpler allocating this function to the stationary side, also because there are more shuttles than stations in the system (CA13).

Another CA to be considered is CA7: Once retracted, the boxes must be able to move in the direction parallel to the rails (orthogonal to the linear actuator, see also Figure 6).

The process of releasing the box is hence twofold: First, release the box from its fixation on the shuttle and second, once retracted, release it from the mechanism and allow for movement parallel to the rails. As illustrated in Figure 7, there are two ways of performing this operation, the characteristics are discussed in Table 2.

Among the two possibilities the authors preferred option b), whose drawbacks could be overcome by design.

Table 1. Results minimum height calculation

Scenario	a_{max}	W	h_{min}
Linear	1 m s^{-2}	300 mm	-1.35 m
Circular	3.8 m s^{-2}	200 mm	-0.1 m

Figure 5. For estimating the order of magnitude of the deflection of a potentially feasible fork design, the displacement of a U-shaped aluminium profile has been carried out. The width of the sheet metal is 2 mm, its length width 30 mm and the height 6 mm. The worst case deflection amounts to less than 2 mm over a length of 200 mm, which is sufficient to cover the width of the transport box [6].

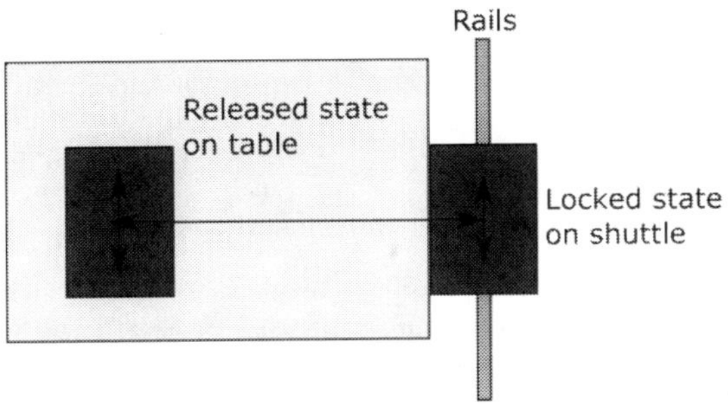

Figure 6. Longitudinal and orthogonal directions of movement.

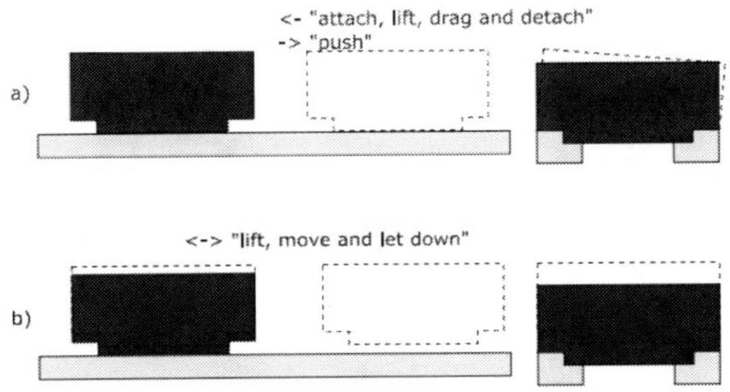

Figure 7. Design options for fetching the box. Option a) implies a hook mechanism, most conveniently engaging with the centering holes on the on the lateral sides of the box, in order to get hold to the box and to lift it. Option b) implies a forklift-like mechanism and grooves in the table for lowering the forks below the table surface.

Table 2. Comparing box fetching options

Option	Characteristics
a)	• requires hook/grip mechanism on the moving part • depends on stop position accuracy of the shuttle • weight is carried by the table during drag phase, but lifting and gripping mechanism must be dimensioned to support half of the weight of the box • friction between box and table must be overcome by a linear actuator and might result in a consumption of the boxes plastic material • operation is asymmetric
b)	• requires forklift on the moving part of the mechanism • is more robust against stop position of the shuttle • requires grooves in the table for lowering the fork into • the mechanism must carry the full weight of the box • limited friction and hence no material consumption • operation is symmetric

Figure 8 shows the resulting design concept. A displacement analysis has been carried out, in order to determine an adequate material strength of the fork, see Figure 5 for result. The bending of less than 2 mm over the whole length shall be covered in the tolerances of the travel distance of the lifting device.

Figure 8. Lifting device carrying the box with volume envelope of its content.

The rationale was guided by choosing the more simple option (axiom 2). The following thoughts were considered:

- the clamping of the box laterally required precise knowledge of the centering holes on the box. Inaccurate stopping position of the shuttles and/or potential obstructions represent unnecessary additional risk;
- even with option b), there is a way to transfer the weight of the box to the table surface through wheels; and
- compensating friction with motor power is inefficient.

4.2 FR/DP 2: Linear actuator

For the translatory movement on the stationary side, plenty of options exist, as both electric and pneumatic energy is available. The choice of the actuator type is not the only design parameter, there is also the choice of the placement of the actuator, which has great impact on complexity and performance.

The FR/DP pair can be decomposed furthermore:

FR2.1 actuator type

DP2.1 belt-type

 https://doi.org/10.1051/matecconf/201822301001

FR2.2 placement

DP2.2 below the table

The partial design matrix shows an uncoupled design.

$$\begin{Bmatrix} FR_{2.1} \\ FR_{2.2} \end{Bmatrix} = \begin{bmatrix} X & 0 \\ 0 & X \end{bmatrix} \begin{Bmatrix} DP_{2.1} \\ DP_{2.2} \end{Bmatrix} \tag{7}$$

4.2.1 FR/DP 2.1: Actuator type

Pneumatic cylinders can be found often in industrial automation. Among their benefits is their simplicity in construction hence reduced cost, sturdiness in operation, achievable speed, self-guided, suitability for explosive atmospheres and hygienic-sensitive applications. Among the drawbacks there is the difficulty in controlling the position and the speed of the piston in between the final positions, limited force (hydraulic cylinders as an alternative), need for compressed air, noise. The actual force and piston speed depend on the pressure and flow rate of the compressed air. Figure 9 shows a pneumatic cylinder of suitable length. For implementation, electrically controlled valves, a pressure regulator, and magnetic limit switches are required, which neutralizes the cost-benefit of the actuator, if not shared with other cylinders.

Lead screw actuators (electric cylinders) are used similarly to pneumatic cylinders. Their popularity for certain is due to the relatively simple interfaces: 2 wires are sufficient for controlling the motor, reversing the polarity reverses the direction of movement. Internal limit switches bring the motor to a stop when it reaches the final positions. By measuring the current, the load on the motor can be easily monitored and overload can be avoided by electrical fuses. Due to the lead screw principle, the actuator is self-locking. Intrinsic to the operating principle is however also the slow operation of the piston. Similar to a pneumatic cylinder the device requires significant volume when fully extracted, therefore the available stroke length is rather confined.

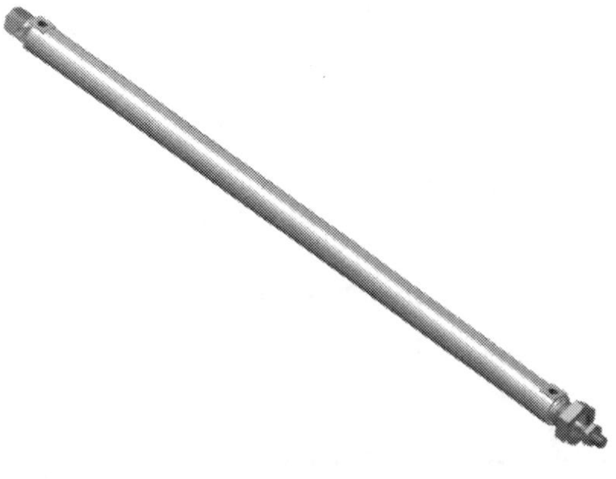

Figure 9. Festo DSNU [7] pneumatic cylinder in 500 mm length with 25 mm piston diameter. The cylinder is shown in the retracted state. When the piston is extended, the overall length almost doubles.

The Linear-Mech UBA-0 [8] is an example of a lead screw actuator with motor assembly for loads up to 420 N and linear speeds of up to 500 mm/s. The device can be equipped with mechanical and/or magnetic limit switches and with an encoder for position feedback.

Direct drive linear motor technology has been around for decades, it's implementation has however been limited due to the associated complexity. Linear motors are electrical motors where the windings are laid out on a linear axis. The windings are powered and driven by power electronics, which can be controlled to a good precision just from the stator side. The dynamics of such a system can be impressive, which comes at the price of complexity and power consumption. Linear motors can be found in applications with extraordinary dynamic requirements, particularly in spatially limited environments.

The LDC-series of Allen-Bradley [9] is a commercial example of such a device. It delivers up to 10 m/s. A single rail is available with lengths of up to 600 mm, several rails can be connected to cover larger distances. The rails require individual high-voltage power supplies and the maximum actuation force depends strongly on the employed cooling technique.

Rack and pinion drives are used for more than 100 years to transform rotation in linear motion by the use of a sprocket (the pinion) and a geared track (the rack). The transmission ratio is determined by the gear ratio, which can be adapted to the needs of the application either directly or in a wider range through gears like worm or epicyclic gear boxes. A linear actuation mechanism must provide sufficiently strong guidance between the elements whilst allowing them to move in the desired direction easily, otherwise the pinion is likely to slip or the friction to be overcome is too high.

Wittenstein produces many rack and pinion drive components with planetary gearboxes [10]. The portfolio of their value line starts with loads of 100 kg and the maximum speeds are given to about 2-7 m/s. The application is mainly in industrial machinery.

Rigid chain actuators use interlocking chain elements in order to resist to both drag and compression. As a consequence, the rigid chain actuator behaves similarly to a rack and pinion actuator, while occupying less space in the retracted state. As a consequence rigid chain actuators can be found in cases where rack and pinion actuators would obstruct useful space. Rigid chain actuators are available in different sizes.

A chain actuator can be seen as a special type of a rack and pinion drive. A pinion drives an interlocking chain, which is resistant to both drag and compression in at least one direction and can often be found in window opening mechanisms. For example, Windowmaster WMU 836 [11] is a 300 N model and operates at up to 11 mm/s. The device is tested to 10000 movements over its lifetime.

Belt driven actuators can be found in many space-confined applications, where precisely controlled movements are required. The use of timing belts (synchronous belts) ensures linearity in between final positions, and hence by simply controlling the revolutions of an electrical motor the position is defined. The motion is smooth and depending on the mobile mass also reasonably fast. Belt drives are used with medium travel distances, limited mainly by the elasticity of the belt on the upper side and the dimensions of the sprockets on the lower side.

A belt driven linear axis uses a timing (synchronous) belt and sprockets, interconnected by stiff rails, which guide a sled. The motor can be directly connected or through a gearbox. An example is the Igus drylin E series entry-level model [12], which features a directly connected NEMA23 stepper motor and is capable of up to 2 m/s for a load of 100 N.

With many options available, the best option can be selected by performing a trade-off in the sense of axiom 2 of the axiomatic design theory. The constraints of the particular application have been taken into consideration and included in the qualitative weighting of the individual options (see Table 3). Promising options are pneumatic and electrical cylinders, however as the spatial demands are stringent, the length of the cylinders in the extracted state represents an issue. Among the other options, the belt actuator fits best in the set of requirements and is selected as a baseline. Having considered the loads which are to be expected, a stepper motor was selected as the active unit. Other options would have considered servo motors or induction motors, which however need encoders, which would drive up the cost and complexity unnecessarily.

4.2.2 FR/DP 2.2: Placement

The placement of the linear actuator is relevant, as it might obstruct the movement of the box. There are 3 fundamental options:

1. lateral to the perpendicular movement of the box
2. above the volume envelope of the box (crane-like)
3. below the table surface

The first option, however, restricts the further movement of the box to the side of the mechanism and hence is not compliant to CA7. Also, it is not in the spirit of CA8, as it occupies additional area in the working plane. Hence the lateral placement is rejected.

Two options remain, above the volume envelope, or below the table. It seems straightforward that the option below the table is less complex, as the overhead option would require structural elements in another plane over the boxes and their contents, which so far was not required. It is noteworthy, that this choice is independent of the release mechanism (DP1.2), even though other release principles could have a coupling.

We have seen that the placement of the linear actuator below the table seems reasonable. As a consequence, the motion must, however, be transferred to the top of the table. This requires a slot in the table along the direction of the linear axis, and a fin transfers the force to the top (Figure 10 and Figure 11).

Table 3. Summary of linear actuator options

Option	Speed	Load	Volume	Interfaces	Cost	Sum
Pneumatic cylinder	+	0	-	+	0	+
Lead screw	-	+	-	+	+	+
Linear motor	+	-	+	-	-	-
Rack and pinion	0	+	0	0	-	0
Rigid chain	-	-	+	+	0	0
Timing belt	+	0	+	0	0	++

4.3 Design matrix

The complete design matrix follows from the decompositions in the previous chapters:

$$\begin{Bmatrix} FR_0 \\ FR_1 \\ FR_{1.1} \\ FR_{1.2} \\ FR_2 \\ FR_{2.1} \\ FR_{2.2} \end{Bmatrix} = \begin{bmatrix} X &&&&&& \\ & X &&&&& \\ && X &&&& \\ && X & X &&& \\ &&&& X && \\ &&&&& X & \\ &&&&&& X \end{bmatrix} \begin{Bmatrix} DP_0 \\ DP_1 \\ DP_{1.1} \\ DP_{1.2} \\ DP_2 \\ DP_{2.1} \\ DP_{2.2} \end{Bmatrix} \quad (8)$$

The overall design matrix is decoupled, with off-diagonal coupling only for FR1.2 between DP1.2 and

Figure 10. The final concept for the linear actuator integrated in the table. The fin transfers the motion to the top of the table, all active elements can be placed below the level where the boxes are handled.

Figure 11. The table top has been removed and the rails, the stepper motor, the timing belt, the sprockets and various support brackets are revealed..

DP1.1. The resulting dependency can be managed by sequentially engineering the FR1.1 (fix box on shuttle) and then FR1.2 (release). Other than this, there are no couplings to be considered.

5 Discussion

At the begin of the design process, the authors thought of the problem as a single function: The idea was to perform the lifting and movement with a single actuator. The actuator would push and drag a fork-like construction, guided by lateral slots. Those slots would vary in height over the stoke length of the actuator, and control so the height and angle of the fork. At first glance, the initial idea appeared simple, because it could fulfil the requirements with just a single actuator. Looking at the approach more in detail, it turned out that the concept was more complex as expected if feasible at all: The lifting and putting down at the shuttle requires two different profiles of the slots, otherwise the fork would hit the box when trying to fetch the box from the shuttle. Different profiles require some sort of switch, which is de facto another function, so the appealing single function was proved infeasible. Furthermore the required steepness of the slots profile was also questionable, as the whole amount of lifting must occur in a narrow range of the actuator stroke, resulting in an oversized actuator with respect to the mass of the box.

The difficulties with the first design attempt lead the authors to the application of axiomatic design, which rapidly lead to the decomposition into two primary functions: Hold/release, and linear movement of the box. The result of the axiomatic design application is a decoupled design matrix, which means that the functions shall be developed in sequence in order to avoid unnecessary iterations, the hold/release function first, then the movement.

Both functions can be adjusted independently from each other. An example for a possible adaptation could be the change of the transport system to a faster one. The dynamics of it could require the fixation of the boxes also in the height dimension, so the forklift solution to release them would no longer be feasible. These aspects are covered by FR/DP 1.1 and 1.2 and as long as the other constraints remain the same, the FR/DP 2 remain entirely unaffected.

The physical solution as result of the axiomatic design process is however determined to a large degree by the boundary conditions of the application, particularly the transport box, transport system characteristics and volume envelope of the material. For example, the given application requires to release the boxes once they reach their final position on the table (CA7). This might not be the case elsewhere, which would allow for a simpler principle of grasping (i.e. dragging instead of lifting). Hence care must be taken when transferring the results to a different application.

6 Outlook

The work has shown that by applying axiomatic design methodology in a design phase of a coupled system has lead to a robust design concept. The design concept will now further engineered to more detailed technical specifi-

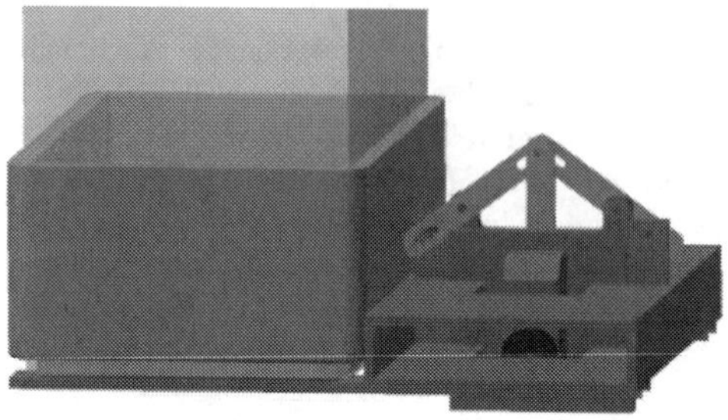

Figure 12. The final concept of the lifting actuator in the lowered state. Through a rod, the force required to lift the box is transferred. Via a symmetrical lever design, the force required to lift the box is applied to both sides of the fin, which should help to prevent wedging. Also visible, the wheels which run on the table top surface.

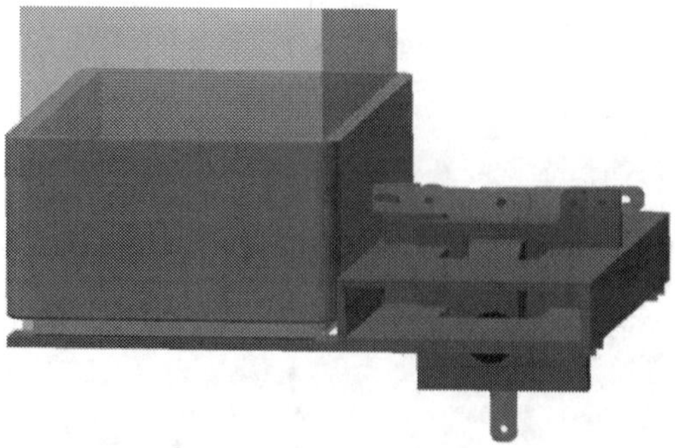

Figure 13. The lifting mechanism in the raised state. The rod connecting to the bottom of the plate connects to a cylinder, which is mounted below the table. This way, no active elements must be placed above the table surface.

cations. The testing of the prototype is scheduled for the end of 2018.

This paper has been supported by funding from the European Regional Development Fund ERDF 2014-2020 under the grant agreement with project DeConPro FESR1017 (CUP B56J16001730001).

efre · fesr
Südtirol · Alto Adige
Europäischer Fonds für regionale Entwicklung
Fondo europeo di sviluppo regionale
EUROPEAN UNION

AUTONOME PROVINZ BOZEN SÜDTIROL
PROVINCIA AUTONOMA DI BOLZANO ALTO ADIGE

References

[1] D.T. Matt, *Design of a scalable assembly system for product variety*, in *Assembly Automation* (2013), Vol. 33, pp. 117–126, iSSN: 0144-5154, doi: 10.1108/01445151311306627

[2] D.T. Matt, *Application of Axiomatic Design principles to control complexity dynamics in a mixed-model assembly system: A case analysis*, in *International Journal of Production Research* (2012), Vol. 50, pp. 1850–1861, iSSN: 0020-7543, doi: 10.1080/00207543.2011.565086

[3] D.T. Matt, *Template based production system design*, in *Journal of Manufacturing Technology Management* (2008), Vol. 19, pp. 783–797, iSSN: 1741-038X, doi: 10.1108/17410380810898741

[4] N.P. Suh, *The principles of design* (Oxford university press, 1990)

[5] N.P. Suh, *Axiomatic design: Advances and Applications* (Oxford university press, 2001)

[6] Auer Packaging GmbH, *Euro container EG 32/12 HG product page* (2018), `https://www.auer-packaging.com/Euro-containers-solid/EG-3212-HG.html`

[7] Festo, *Standard cylinders DSNU/DSNUP/DSN/ESNU/ESN, ISO 6432 catalogue*, `https://www.festo.com/cat/en-gb_gb/data/doc_engb/PDF/EN/DSNU-ISO_EN.PDF` (2015)

[8] Linear-Mech S.r.l., *UBA 0 ball screw linear actuator*, `http://www.linearmech.it/linearmech/azienda/azienda/documenti_prodotti/uba0_eng.pdf`

[9] Rockwell Automation Inc., *Allen-Bradley Kinetix Linear Motion Specifications MP-Series, LDAT-Series, LDC-Series, LDL-Series*, `http://literature.rockwellautomation.com/idc/groups/literature/documents/td/knx-td002_-en-p.pdf` (2018), KNX-TD002B-EN-P

[10] Wittenstein, *alpha Linear Systems Product Catalogue*, `https://www.wittenstein.de/download/alpha-linear-systems-en.pdf` (2018)

[11] WindowMaster A/S, *WMU 836 chain actuator 300N product sheet* (2018), `https://www.windowmaster.com/Admin/Public/DWSDownload.aspx?File=%2fFiles%2fFiles%2fPDF%2fdatablade%2fWMU_836-n_data_UK-13.pdf`

[12] igus GmbH, *drylin E electric linear axes and linear drives with motor* (2018), toothed belt axis size 1040

 https://doi.org/10.1051/matecconf/201822301002

Human Design Parameters for Safety of Products and Systems

Kenji Iino[1,*], and *Masayuki* Nakao[1]

[1]The University of Tokyo, Hongo, Bunkyo-ku, Tokyo, 113-0033, Japan

Abstract. Designers spend much efforts in defining their products and systems, planning how they work during normal operation. Design assisting tools like Design Matrices in Axiomatic Design (AD) or Design Record Graphs (DRG) are available to the designer in search for ways to improve their work. Majority of accidents, however, take place during irregular operations like maintenance when interlocks are often bypassed and automatic processing are switched to manual. System safety is then in the hands of human operators. A number of past AD studies have addressed safety in products and systems, however, design parameters (DPs) have been physical parts or structures. This paper shows assignment of human actions, like, "reading the quantity display," "making judgement," or "pressing a control button," as DPs in axiomatic design. Such human DPs play important roles during maintenance, nevertheless, designers often leave out safety evaluation of their designs in this maintenance mode. When a human DP fails to meet its functional requirement (FR), the product often faces failure and the system often heads into an accident. Identifying human DPs in products or systems thus alerts maintenance phase workers about actions that are critical for safety. Most accidents take place with excessive dependence on human DP of memory.

1 Introduction

1.1 The Water Faucet Problem

Often used as the first example in teaching Axiomatic Design (AD), we are all familiar with the hot and cold water faucet problem [1]. The two functional requirements (FR) are to adjust FR1: the water temperature, and FR2: the water flow rate to ideal ranges.

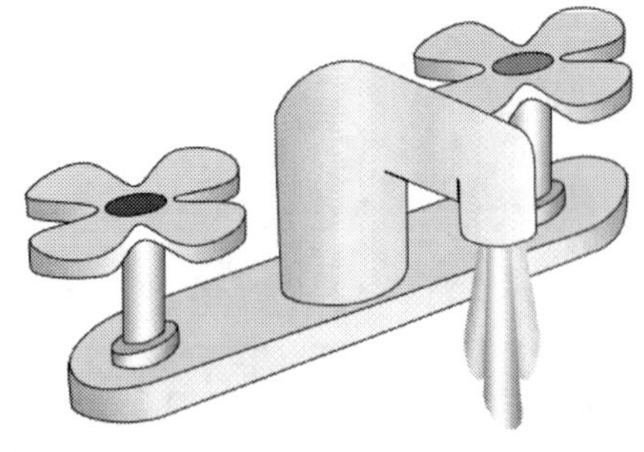

Fig. 1. Simple hot and cold water faucet

The design equation in this case shows a clear interference for the two design parameters, DP1: turning the hot water knob and DP2: turning the cold water knob. The design is coupled.

$$\begin{Bmatrix} \text{temperature} \\ \text{flow rate} \end{Bmatrix} = \begin{bmatrix} X & X \\ X & X \end{bmatrix} \begin{Bmatrix} \text{hot water knob} \\ \text{cold water knob} \end{Bmatrix} \quad (1)$$

Equation (1) shows the design equation of the system and Fig. 2, the Design Record Graph (DRG).

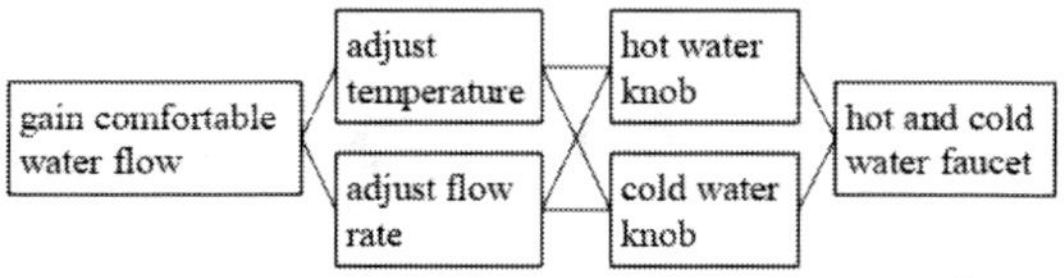

Fig. 2. DRG of the simple hot and cold water faucet

This problem is ideal for first teaching the concept of AD, however, a closer look reveals that the formulation has completely left out human factors. They are the operator sensing the water temperature with hands, the flow rate also with hands and possibly assisted with the water flow sound through the ears, making the judgement of which handle to turn in which direction by how much, and actually applying torque to the handles.

In this section, we will first show how the design equation changes with the inclusion of human interaction in reaching the desired FRs with the water faucet problem. We will then discuss a better design faucet and its problem when human factors come in play and yet another improvement common in Japan.

The second section discusses how designers often leave out human factors in their design. The problem is designers are concerned only about their designs in operation and not much thoughts are given to maintenance phases. Section 3 then explains a recent fatal industrial accident and applies AD analysis with human factor. Section 4 shows how our AD analysis

* Corresponding author: kiino@sydrose.com

with human factor can identify serious risks with designs, followed by our conclusions in Section 5.

1.2 The Water Faucet Problem with Human Factor

Fig. 2 shows the human interaction with the water faucet. The user has two active things to do; one is to adjust the hot water knob rotation, and the other is to adjust the cold water knob rotation. The user also has to sense the water flow rate and water temperature. In addition to sensing the flow rate with the feel of water falling on the hand, the user's eyes and ears receive visual and audible signals to help judging if the flow rate is ideal or not. The hand is the only practical receptor for the water temperature sensing.

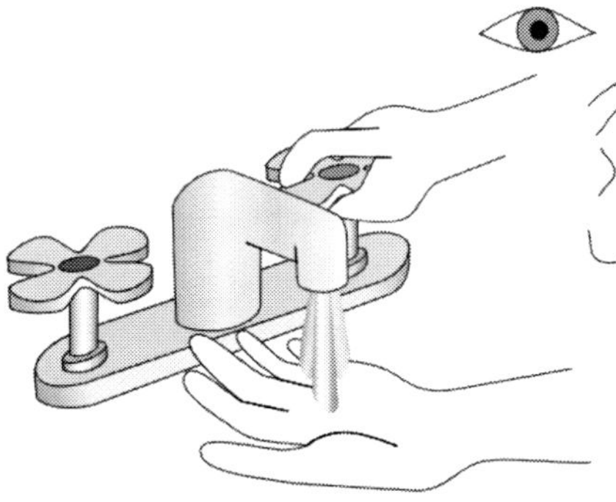

Fig. 3. Human adjusting hot and cold water faucet

Fig. 4 shows the DRG of this system. The user human and the water faucet system works together for obtaining a comfortable water flow. Equation (2) is the design equation.

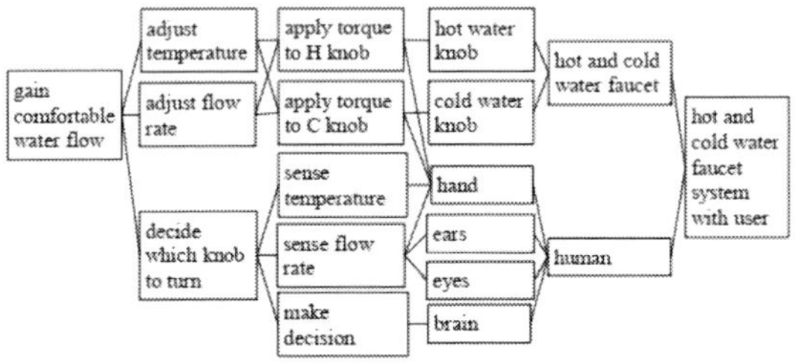

Fig. 4. DRG for human adjustment of hot and cold water faucet

$$\begin{Bmatrix} \text{apply torque to H knob}\\ \text{apply torque to C knob}\\ \text{sense temperature}\\ \text{sense flow rate}\\ \text{make decision} \end{Bmatrix} = \begin{bmatrix} X & 0 & X & 0 & 0 & 0\\ 0 & X & X & 0 & 0 & 0\\ 0 & 0 & X & 0 & 0 & 0\\ 0 & 0 & X & X & X & 0\\ 0 & 0 & 0 & 0 & 0 & X \end{bmatrix} \begin{Bmatrix} \text{hot water knob}\\ \text{cold water knob}\\ \text{hand}\\ \text{ears}\\ \text{eyes}\\ \text{brain} \end{Bmatrix} \qquad (2)$$

The interference in Eq. (1) seems to be removed in Eq. (2), however, it is present in higher level of the DRG in Fig. 4, among the temperature and flow rate adjustment FRs and the torque application to H and C knobs FRs.

1.3 The Single Lever Solution

A solution known to have removed the interference with double knob design is the swivel lever design shown in Fig. 5. The lever has a spherical opening on its bottom that mates a spherical joint so the user can turn it up and down latitude-wise to change only the water flow rate and sideways longitude-wise to change only the water temperature. The design has a common name of single handle water faucet.

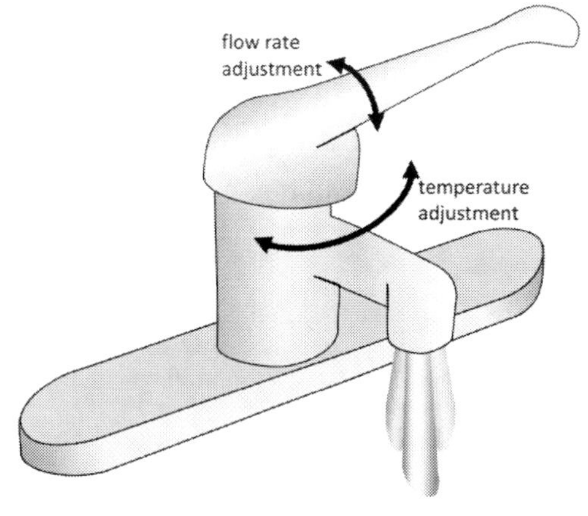

Fig. 5. Single handle solution for hot and cold water faucet

Figure 6 shows the DRG for the single handle design with human interaction. Note that the interference in Fig. 4 is now gone.

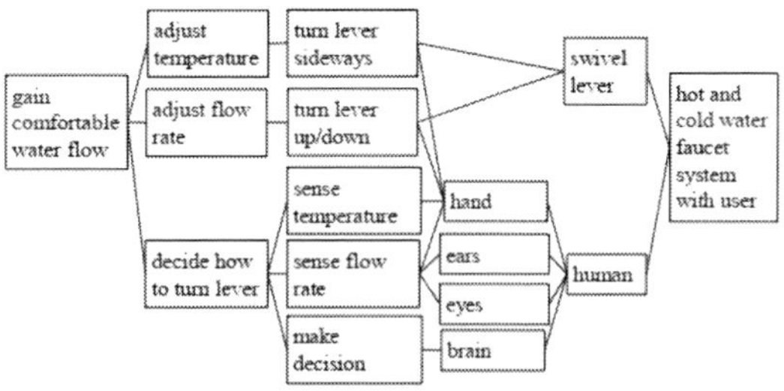

Fig. 6. DRG for swivel lever hot and cold water faucet

The single handle design, therefore, is theoretically a superior design, however, one of the authors, Iino often faced troubles using them. One reason is the 2 degrees of freedom (DOF) that the lever has in contrast to the 1 DOF for each of the hot or cold knob.

Increasing or decreasing the flow rate of hot or cold water with a knob is fairly clear with the simple right-hand rule; turn it counter-clockwise to increase the flow. With the swivel lever design, at an arbitrary point when the water is flowing, the user can rotate the lever into any direction to change the flow rate, temperature, or both at the same time. The operation, thus, burdens the brain in deciding how to turn the lever to change the conditions of the flowing water.

Another bothering factor is the non-standard directions for changing flow conditions with single lever water faucets. Probably in the US, the latitude-wise up and down convention is; turn it up to increase the flow and down to decrease it. It is reasonable because when the seating of the spherical joint wears, gravity on the lever will tend to lower the lever, i.e., the direction of shutting the water flow off.

In Japan, however, many of the early designs worked the other way, i.e., to lift the lever to shut the water off. Unaware of this difference, Iino often had the problem of pushing the lever down, thinking that was the direction to shut the water off, and getting a gush of water in the wash basin and a splash of water on his pants.

The reason for this failure is the brain making a wrong decision. Fig. 6 shows this factor in the DRG by drawing human factors in it. A brain makes its decision based on logic, however, oftentimes, quick decisions are reached based on experience and habits.

1.4 Independent Control Solution

Figure 7 shows a solution often seen in public baths at hot spring resorts in Japan. It has an independent knob for water temperature control and a separate one for switching the flow to go to the showerhead or faucet and moving the mark further away from the neutral position increases the flow rate.

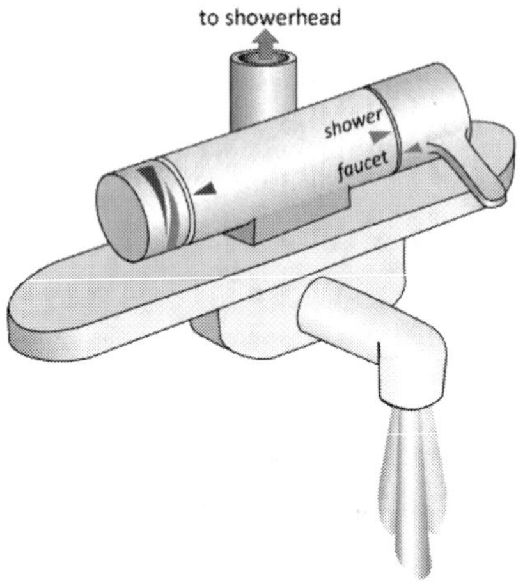

Fig. 7. Independently controlled shower/faucet

Reference [1] actually hints this solution as the first uncoupled solution to the coupled double knob design. The DRG (Fig. 8) for this design is clean without interference.

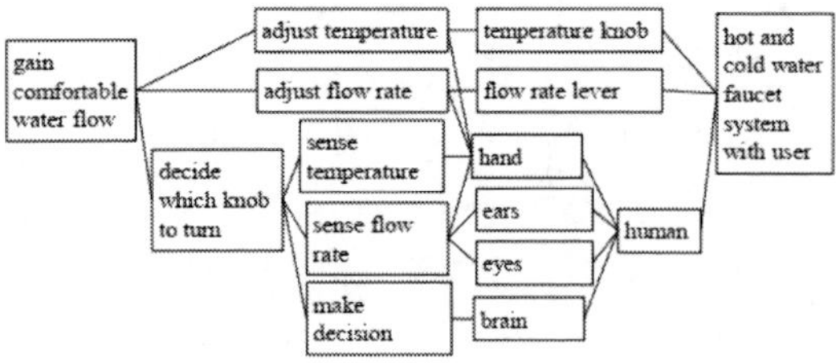

Fig. 8. DRG for independently controlled shower/faucet

2 Human Factor Evaluation

2.1. Designers Forgetful of Human Factor

We earlier pointed out that designers often leave out reliance on human operation from their design concepts [2]. Let's take a simple example of a flashlight to revisit this claim. Figure 9 shows parts of our flashlight to analyse and Fig. 10, a typical DRG of the flashlight by a designer when asked to draw a function-structure diagram (DRG) for it.

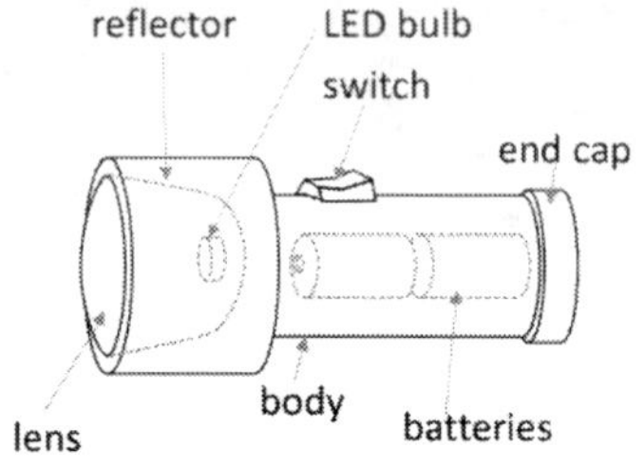

Fig. 9. Flashlight and its parts

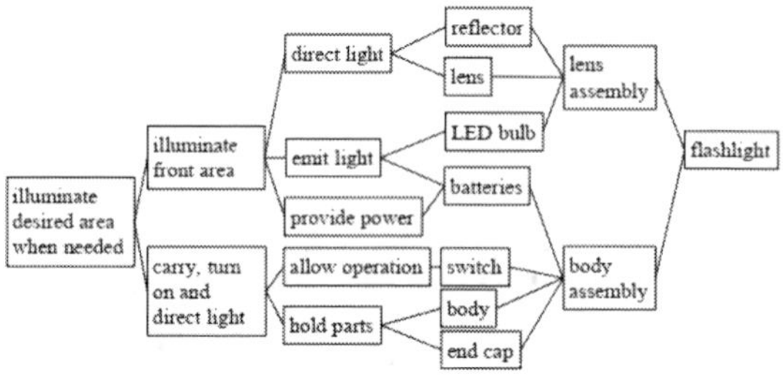

Fig. 10. Flashlight and its parts

Note in Fig. 10 that it is so easy to forget that the user has to turn the switch ON and direct the flashlight in the direction the user wants to illuminate. The user has to know how to push the switch to turn the light on and to move the arm and hand carrying the flashlight so the illuminated area matches the desired area.

2.2 Human Factor during Maintenance

Even simple products like a flashlight go out of order and we have to fix them unless we want to dispose it and go through the trouble of getting a new one.

A common failure of a flashlight is its batteries losing power and failure of the lightbulb. The lightbulb failure is now rare with LEDs, however, they were common with incandescent lightbulbs up until just a few years ago.

Now the user has a number of tasks to perform:

(1) Find and purchase the right replacement part,
(2) Open the end cap or lens assembly,
(3) Remove the failed part,
(4) Place the new part in place,
(5) Close the assembly back to the original state,

https://doi.org/10.1051/matecconf/201822301002

and in addition for protecting the global environment, we now have to know where to dispose the old batteries instead of tossing them into the garbage bin.

Figure 11 added human factors for the common battery replacement operation. Note that body parts, eyes, hands, and the brain are involved in every step.

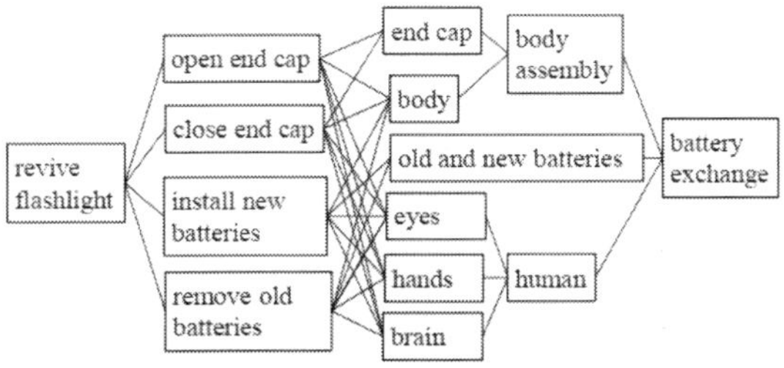

Fig. 11. Battery exchange operation of a flashlight

Although rare, a common failure of the battery exchange operation was to insert the batteries in the wrong direction, i.e., to reverse the positive and negative poles of the batteries. Surprisingly, the mistake could go unnoticed for some incandescent models, however, not with flashlights using LED lightbulbs.

To help the user insert batteries in the right orientation, many tools that require battery exchange have battery symbols printed inside the battery sockets so the users will not reverse the orientation. Mistakes that some people make come from the brain making the wrong decisions about orientation of batteries.

3 A Fatal Accident Case

3.1 Ethylene Plant Gas Quenching Line

On December 21, 2007, a fire broke out at Ethylene Plant 2 in Kashima Plant of Mitsubishi Chemical Corporation in Ibaraki Prefecture. Four employees of a contractor company lost their lives with this accident.

The accident took place after the decoking process of a furnace was finished. The furnace was a thermal decomposition furnace for ethylene production and refinement from crude gasoline, kerosene, and other material. Decoking removes coke (carbon residue) from the processing tubes using high-pressure water jet. During normal thermal decomposition, the furnace discharges exhaust gas for reprocessing. The gas discharge line has a quencher box after it leaves the furnace. Figure 12 shows a simplified outline of the furnace, gas discharge line, and its quencher.

Figure 13 is the quenching oil line configuration during normal operation. A ring-shaped spacer is in place. Figure 14 shows the DRG elements for this configuration. This is probably how far a plant designer will take the design concept. The design matrix for the elements in Fig. 14 will show a clean uncoupled design.

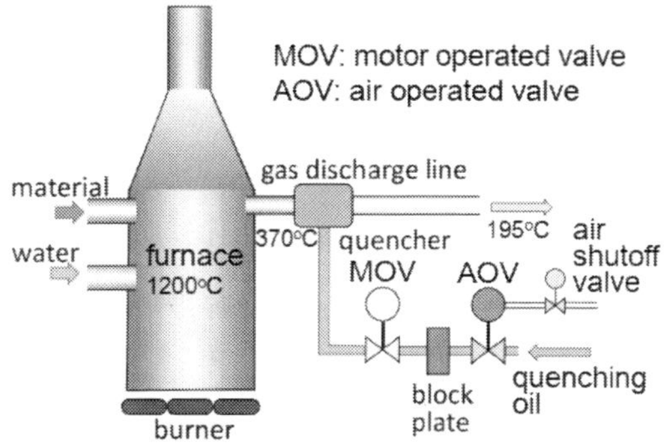

Fig. 12. Ethylene plant furnace and gas discharge line

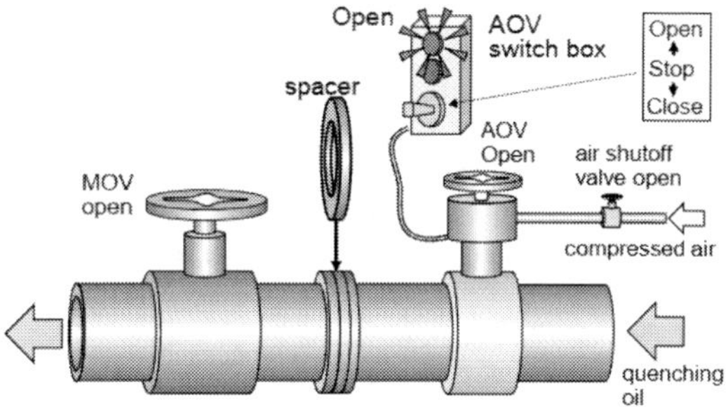

Fig. 13. Quenching oil control during normal operation

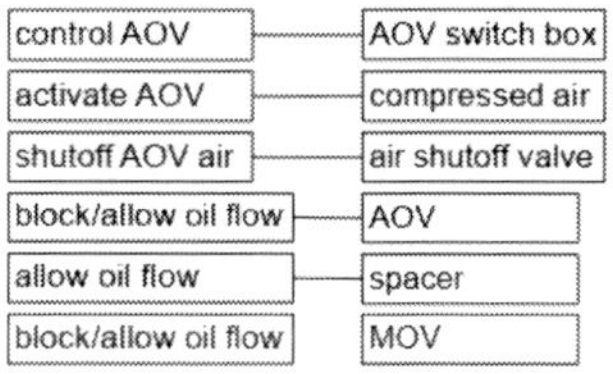

Fig. 14. DRG elements of the quenching oil line

During the maintenance of the furnace tubes, a block plate is inserted in place for the spacer so the quenching oil has no chance of reaching the quencher. The process of exchanging the spacer with the block plate had double protection against accidental quenching oil leakage. The air shutoff valve was closed so the air-operated valve (AOV) will not accidentally open and even the AOV itself was locked so that it will not open during the exchange as Fig. 15 shows.

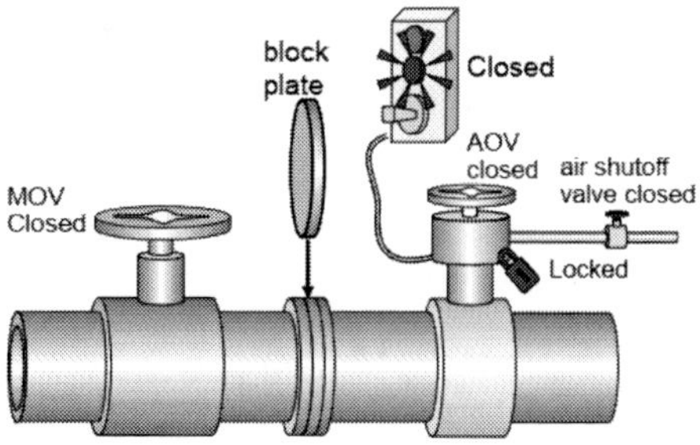

Fig. 15. Quenching oil control valves during plate/spacer exchange

3.2 The Accident

Equation (3) shows the design equation for the elements in Fig. 15 upstream of the block plate. Note that the equation looks like a clean uncoupled design without inclusion of human factors.

$$\begin{Bmatrix} \text{show AOV closed} \\ \text{lock AOV} \\ \text{shutoff AOV air} \\ \text{block oil flow} \\ \text{disable oil flow} \end{Bmatrix} = \begin{bmatrix} X & 0 & 0 & 0 & 0 \\ 0 & X & 0 & 0 & 0 \\ 0 & 0 & X & 0 & 0 \\ 0 & 0 & 0 & X & 0 \\ 0 & 0 & 0 & 0 & X \end{bmatrix} \begin{Bmatrix} \text{AOV switch box} \\ \text{physical lock} \\ \text{air shutoff valve} \\ \text{AOV closed} \\ \text{block plate} \end{Bmatrix} \quad (3)$$

On the day of the accident, preparing the quenching oil line for the decoking process went without trouble, however, there is no record of whether the procedures were properly followed. The accident broke out after the decoking was complete and when the operators were preparing the quenching oil line for the next thermal decomposition process.

The double protection for preventing quenching oil leakage were broken; the air shutoff valve was open and the physical lock on the AOV was not in place. If the situation was just so, the accident could have been avoided, however, an unfortunate event took place.

The heavy block plate had to be lifted out of place using a chain hoist. Figure 16 shows a chain hoist with an operator hoisting up the block plate.

Fig. 16. Imaginary sketch of operator hoisting the block plate

Anyone who has operated one or seen one in operation knows that the hand chain that the operator keeps pulling can swing and swish around like a whip. The swinging hand chain swished toward the AOV switch box and happened to hit the switch in the direction to open the AOV. Without its physical lock and the air shutoff valve open, the AOV started to open and the quenching oil gushed out of the pipe where the block plate used to be.

Then for an unknown reason, the oil caught fire and put the two operators lifting the block plate in flame. There were two other workers downstairs for a different job and they were suddenly covered with flaming oil.

3.3 The Cause

The cause of the accident were the following three points:

(1) Air shutoff valve was not closed and air line was not purged

(2) Physical lock on the AOV was not in place

(3) The hand chain of the chain hoist happened to hit the AOV switch box to open the AOV

An investigation by the company revealed that the field knew that the air shutoff valve had to be closed, the line purged, and the physical lock had to be installed on the AOV. The information, however, were not well documented and not relayed to the contractors in the field. Relying on memory for following important procedures should be avoided by any means in the field.

4 Human Factors in AD

4.1 Adding Human Factors in DP

Accidents should be avoided, however, without simple ideal ways of doing so, accidents keep repeating. In Section 3, we discussed how relying on memory can be a serious cause of accidents. Section 2 also explained how simple operations of machines rely on eyes, ears, and hands of human operators.

This paper proposes to include typical human factors in AD analysis so people can identify reliance on human of their processes and systems. The factors to add are: eyes, ears, hands, and for the brain, reasoning and memory. The worst of all to rely on is the brain memory. Even a sound person with good reasoning can happen to forget important steps in work. Steps in operation better be procedural, i.e., specified in procedure documents or checklists than relying on memory. So, we also added "procedural" as a DP to the design equation and revised Eq. (3) as follows:

$$\begin{Bmatrix} \text{show AOV closed} \\ \text{lock AOV} \\ \text{shutoff AOV air} \\ \text{block oil flow} \\ \text{disable oil flow} \end{Bmatrix} = \begin{bmatrix} X&0&0&0&0&X&0&0&0&0&0 \\ 0&X&0&0&0&0&0&X&0&X&0 \\ 0&0&X&0&0&0&0&X&0&X&0 \\ 0&0&0&X&0&0&0&X&0&0&X \\ 0&0&0&0&X&0&0&X&0&0&X \end{bmatrix} \begin{Bmatrix} \text{AOV switch box} \\ \text{physical lock} \\ \text{air shutoff valve} \\ \text{AOV closed} \\ \text{block plate} \\ \underline{\text{eyes}} \\ \underline{\text{ears}} \\ \underline{\text{hands}} \\ \underline{\text{reasoning}} \\ \underline{\text{memory}} \\ \underline{\text{procedural}} \end{Bmatrix} \quad (4)$$

4.2 How the Procedure Could Change

Blocking the oil flow by closing the AOV and disabling the flow with the block plate are steps for the process itself so they are procedural. The problem was relying on memory for the AOV air shutoff and the physical lock. We will discuss here the types of possible solutions and their effects in the remainder of this section.

4.2.1 Covering the AOV Switch Box

One of the solutions the plant implemented was to cover the switch box in a case [4]. This solution is quite effective because it blocks reason (3) in Section 3.3.

4.2.2 Documenting the procedures

In dealing with the other two reasons, the plant included the processes in their documents and further raised awareness in the field [5].

The efforts shifted the memory reliance to procedural thus the two Xs in the second last column of Eq. (4) are now moved to the right as Eq. (5) shows.

$$\begin{Bmatrix} \text{show AOV closed} \\ \text{lock AOV} \\ \text{shutoff AOV air} \\ \text{block oil flow} \\ \text{disable oil flow} \end{Bmatrix} = \begin{bmatrix} X & 0 & 0 & 0 & 0 & X & 0 & 0 & 0 & 0 & 0 \\ 0 & X & 0 & 0 & 0 & 0 & 0 & X & 0 & 0 & X \\ 0 & 0 & X & 0 & 0 & 0 & 0 & X & 0 & 0 & X \\ 0 & 0 & 0 & X & 0 & 0 & 0 & X & 0 & 0 & X \\ 0 & 0 & 0 & 0 & X & 0 & 0 & X & 0 & 0 & X \end{bmatrix} \begin{Bmatrix} \text{AOV switch box} \\ \text{physical lock} \\ \text{air shutoff valve} \\ \text{AOV closed} \\ \text{block plate} \\ \underline{\text{eyes}} \\ \underline{\text{ears}} \\ \underline{\text{hands}} \\ \underline{\text{reasoning}} \\ \underline{\text{memory}} \\ \underline{\text{procedural}} \end{Bmatrix} \quad (5)$$

We, however, still see problems in this solution when we think of the work environment of today. Work procedures and manuals are typically shelved in offices and work scheduled for the day are possibly reviewed at the start of the day. Careful workers may take copies of relevant pages to the field. Although the solution is much better than relying on memory alone, there are some limitations.

4.2.3 Interlocking

Large scale plants, like the chemical plant in this paper, or nuclear plants typically have interlocks to prevent disastrous operations by operators that are novices or were absent minded. They are quite effective because they disable unwanted movements. The problem is, however, they require cost and man-power to implement, and sometimes are not really feasible.

For example, let's say the plant decided to put an interlock so the bolts on the block plate flange cannot be loosened without closing the AOV shutoff valve and purging the line. Monitoring the status of a mechanical part is easy, however, blocking mechanical operation on physical parts is different from disabling an electrical pushbutton on the control panel. If possible, however, it is an ideal solution.

4.2.4 Solution with (Internet of Things) IoT

As we stated in the previous Section 4.2.3, monitoring status of mechanical parts is relatively easy. Thus, checking whether the air shutoff valve is open or not and whether the air line is purged or not are accomplished with a position or touch sensor and a pressure sensor. We can send these signals to an online system.

Another trend that we are starting to see and probably will be a major practice in the future is to readily have the manual on-site at the field, on the spot of operation. Carrying a PC to the spot is probably difficult, however, a tablet or a smartphone is easy to carry around. Operators can check the manual for procedures of their task while they are working.

Adding this technology to signals from statuses of crucial parts, we can notify operators if the system is ready for the next step or they have other tasks to clear before it.

Mechanically interlocking loosening of the bolts that hold the block plate in place is difficult, however, sending a confirmation if the system is ready for loosening the bolts or not is feasible.

5 Conclusions

We showed that human factors are usually left out from conceptual designs. We showed how we can incorporate them into DRG and design equations with AD.

Human factors left out from conceptual design tend not to pose serious threats to product safety during normal operation. Maintenance work, on the other hand, has serious reliance on human factors and not recognizing the burden on workers could lead to accidents. In such cases, it is easy to blame the operator, however, we need to identify excessive reliance on human before such accidents take place.

We showed how we can identify how systems rely on human by including, "eyes," "ears," "hands," "reasoning," and "memory" into the DP vector of AD.

Relying on human memory is a bad practice in operation and we added a DP element "procedural" so that when reliance on human memory are found, managers can make efforts to shift them to procedural reliance.

We believe that manuals and procedural documents will be readily carried around in the field in the future, and when critical parts can send their statuses to online systems, the electronic documents can notify operators if steps they are about to make are appropriate or not.

References

1. N.P. Suh, *Axiomatic Design, Advances and Applications* (2001)
2. K. Iino, and M. Nakao, Design Record Graph and Axiomatic Design for Creative Design Education, *ICAD 2016* (2016)
3. Mitsubishi Chemical Corporation, I. Summary and Causes of the fire accident, from Fire at the Kashima Plant No. 2 Ethylene Plant, https://www.m-chemical.co.jp/en/csr/kashima.html (accessed May 13, 2018)
4. Mitsubishi Chemical Corporation, III. Status Report of Measures for preventing a recurrence, from Fire at the Kashima Plant # 2 Ethylene Plant, Oct., 2008, https://www.m-chemical.co.jp/csr/pdf/kashima_j03.pdf (accessed May 13, 2018)
5. Mitsubishi Chemical Corporation, II. Measures for preventing a recurrence, from Fire at the Kashima Plant No. 2 Ethylene Plant, Mar., 2018, https://www.m-chemical.co.jp/en/csr/kashima.html (accessed May 14, 2018)

Application of Axiomatic Design for the Design of a Safe Collaborative Human-Robot Assembly Workplace

Luca Gualtieri*, *Erwin* Rauch, *Rafael* Rojas, *Renato* Vidoni and *Dominik T.* Matt

Faculty of Science and Technology, Free University of Bozen-Bolzano, Bolzano, 39100 Italy

Abstract. In the context of the Industry 4.0 wave, which is currently making its way into production engineering research, human robot collaboration is also a very important topic. With new technologies and ever more intelligent control systems for machines and robots, the cooperation between human and machine has become easier. In the smart factory of the future, robots are working hand in hand with people and support them, when their assistance is needed. However, the implementation of such collaborative human-robot workplaces is not so easy in practice. The design of collaborative workplaces also presents completely new challenges in terms of safety of the worker. Such a complex problem requires a systematic and structured approach for concept design, in order to avoid loops in the design stage or even worse during implementation. The research team therefore uses a laboratory case study to show how Axiomatic Design can be used as a method to design collaborative human-robot workstations. First, functional requirements for such workplaces are defined. Based on the functional requirements, the design parameters are derived by using the Axiomatic Design mapping and decomposition process. The result is a concept study for a collaborative workplace in the laboratory environment based on Axiomatic Design.

1 Introduction

With the introduction of Industry 4.0 into production, the cooperation between man and machine is becoming increasingly important. Especially in the field of human-robot collaboration, an increase in flexibility and an option for automation even with smaller batch sizes is expected. Despite new developments in collaborative robotics, the safety of robot cells plays a major role in the design of production systems.

Commercial collaborative robots are safe as such, but as soon as they are used in a specific application situation, this often changes. For example, the robot can enter or stop in a safety mode when in contact with the operator. However, if the robot is equipped with a dangerous gripper (sharp, pointed), the potential danger can change or increase. This means that the use of collaborative robotics no longer makes sense or that the robots can in turn be used with a safe enclosure. Therefore, possible sources of danger must be identified and eliminated or minimized by appropriate design solutions. A number of norms and standards have been developed for this purpose.

The various standards regulate different cases and situations and are often difficult for the user to understand due to their complexity and scope. In particular, there is a lack of an overview of which standards can be applied and for which situations. Users therefore often have difficulties in applying these standards.

This work uses Axiomatic Design to examine how functional requirements can describe sources of danger and classify them according to the applicable standards. This provides practitioners with a tool for making collaborative workplaces safer in the future. The work is based on a case study in the laboratory and will be extended to practice in a next step with the help of industrial case studies.

2 Theoretical background - Safety in Human-Robot Collaboration

Up to now, in order to improve production efficiency, the role of traditional industrial robots was to substitute human operators in repetitive, heavy and unsafe processes [1]. Due to safety requirements, high performance automated machines entail a total insulation by avoiding every kind of contact between humans and the operating parts of the robot. The main solutions are physical and/or optical barriers.

Collaborative industrial robotics introduces new forms of free physical interaction between operators and robots, creating a new paradigm from a human-machine interaction point of view. These machines are re-defining the concept of workplace design, by introducing hybrid and shared workspaces. According to ISO TS 15066 [2], it is possible to define a collaborative workspace as a "space within the operating space where the robot system (including the workpiece) and a human can perform tasks concurrently during production operation".

* Corresponding author: lgualtieri@natec.unibz.it

This means a common production environment where operators and robots can work hand-by-hand in a safe and efficient way. According to this definition, conventional protective systems designed for traditional industrial robotics no longer apply [3]. For this reason, it is necessary to develop new methods to design and manage the human robot (HR) collaboration and the sharing of workspace, by considering the human operator the main element of the production system [4].

Of course, this is a particular application of the so called anthropocentric or 'human centered design' approach applied to modern industrial human-machine interaction [5]. In addition, new Occupational Health and Safety (OHS) considerations should be properly introduced to ensure a safe collaborative workplace implementation [6]. The actual industrial problem is to define new approaches for the hybrid workspace design, considering OHS issues but also production efficiency requirements. In practice, the main challenge is to ensure operators safety when they are collaborating hand-by-hand with high performance robots, in a reconfigurable and therefore dynamic workspace.

In general, a HR collaborative workstation could be defined as a particular kind of robotic cell where the robot has to adapt its behavior according to the presence of the operator, in order to guarantee the safety requirements. Of course, from a production efficiency point of view, it is useful to define some spaces and tasks where the robot can operate in a more performing way, that means in a not-collaborative modality (such as a traditional industrial robot). For this reason, it is necessary to design the workstation safety systems by considering the OHS requirements for collaborative and non-collaborative applications and relative workspaces.

3 Current design of the manual assembly workplace in the laboratory

Prior to the Axiomatic design study, the current assembly situation in the laboratory and the product to be assembled are presented.

3.1. Manual pneumatic cylinder assembly workplace

This work refers to the study of a safe collaborative workstation using an Axiomatic Design methodology, according to main OHS standards.

In order to perform this work, an existing manual assembly workstation is used as a starting point for the concept development of the collaborative one, even if the proposed design approach could be implemented booth for new as for existing situations (re-design). The abovementioned assembly workstation is a flexible working area for the study of manual assembly of light industrial products (see Fig. 1), located in the Smart Mini Factory laboratory (SMF lab) of the Free University of Bolzano. In particular, it is a manual assembly training workstation where a single operator can completely assemble a pneumatic cylinder. The aim of this workplace is to simulate different assembly conditions and applications in order to analyze the production system performances through task and workplace organization and ergonomics [7].
The workstation is equipped with a mobile workbench, a block-and-tackle for lightweight applications, an integrated Kanban rack, a working procedures panel, a double lighting system, an industrial screwer and a knee lever press.

Main laboratory application are the development of case studies for manual lean assembly, workplace organization, human-centered design and ergonomics. Other analysis refer to safe HR collaboration in hybrid assembly of light products.

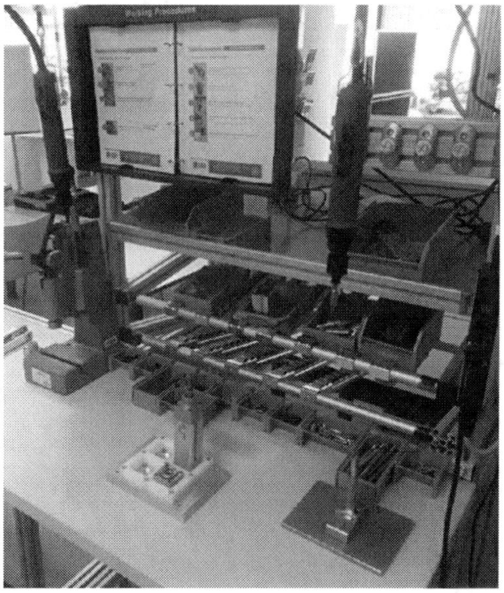

Fig. 1. Manual assembly workstation in the Smart Mini Factory lab.

3.2. Research objectives

The aim of this work is to provide useful guidelines for the design of an industrial HR collaborative workstation using an Axiomatic Design approach, mainly focusing on safety perspective.

Since hybrid workstations are a novel topic in modern manufacturing systems, it is necessary to provide new methodologies to design safe shared workspaces and physical HR interactions, also considering the indications provided by major safety of machinery standards.

4 Design of a Collaborative Human-Robot Assembly Workplace

This section begins with a brief overview of Axiomatic Design as research and design methodology, followed by the Axiomatic Design approach for designing a safe and collaborative assembly station in our Smart Mini Factory laboratory.

 https://doi.org/10.1051/matecconf/201822301003

4.1. Brief overview of Axiomatic Design

Axiomatic Design (AD) was developed by Nam P. Suh in the mid-1970s in the pursuit of developing a scientific, generalized, codified, and systematic procedure for design. The methodology gains its name from two axioms in AD that have to be respected. The first is the Independence Axiom: Maintain the independence of the functional elements, i.e., avoid coupling in the system (e.g., avoiding dependencies between the Design Parameters (DPs) and other Functional Requirements (FRs)). The second is the Information Axiom: Minimize the information content by selecting the solution with the least information content, i.e., the one with the highest probability of success [8]. In order to apply these axioms, parallel functional and physical hierarchies are constructed, the latter containing the physical design solutions. The impact of AD is that the designer learns how to construct large design hierarchies quickly that are more structured, thus freeing more time for mastering applications [9].

4.2. Workshop to define Customer Needs (CNs)

In the workshop, the research team collected the requirements and needs and categorized them in the following groups [10]:

- Constraints (Cs) are usually hard limits or values (minimum, maximum, between).
- Functional Requirements help the designer in the determination of the sub-levels requirements and related design solutions. They should be independent from each other to comply with axiom one, reduce complexity of the system design and are characterizing the functional needs of the artifact.

The following CNs could be identified (see table 1):

Table 1. Customer Needs (CNs).

Nr.	Customer Needs	C, FR,
CN_1	Guarantee the safety of the operator when is operating in collaboration with the robot into the workstation	FR_1
CN_2	Prevent unexpected dangerous contact into free-access zone of the workstation	FR_2
CN_3	Isolate the hazard zone of the workstation	FR_3
CN_4	Use the existing workstation for further improvements	C_1
CN_5	Maintain the same layout space (approximately)	C_2
CN_6	Re-use the single workstation components for other applications	C_3

It is important to underline that, according to the CNs, some FRs will be related to the design of the collaborative (shared) workspace and other to the not-collaborative workspace.

4.3. Definition of high-level Functional Requirements (FRs) and Design Parameters (DPs)

The highest level of FRs and DPs are:

FR_0 Achieve an acceptable level of safety for mechanical risks that could arise from unintentional HR physical interaction.

DP_0 Technical guidelines for a safe collaborative workstation design through the maximum reduction of risks probability and gravity (using, in the first instance, the major standards ISO 12100:2010 [11] and ISO 10218-2:2011 [12]).

Based on the outcome of the initial workshop, the following Cs for the design were defined:

C_1 Existing workstation as starting point.
C_2 Maximum space of 4 square meters.
C_3 Modular system with standard components.

Furthermore, the remaining CNs were associated to high-level FRs and relative DPs:

FR_1 Define the intrinsic safety parameters that can be set into the robot control system in order to reduce the intensity of unexpected HR contacts in the collaborative workspace.

FR_2 Define the safety functions that depend on a control system in order to prevent unexpected HR contacts.

FR_3 Define the safety functions that do not depend on a control system in order to physically block the access to dangerous zone.

DP_1 Operator protection during unexpected (but allowed) HR contacts through the energy exchange reduction according to "Power and Force Limiting" approach. Use, in the first instance, the guidelines explained in ISO 10218-1:2011 [13] and ISO TS 15066:2016 section 5.5.5 [2].

DP_2 Operator protection through an active prevention of HR contacts. Use, in the first instance, the guidelines explained in ISO 13849-1:2015 [14].

DP_3 Operator protection through the avoidance of HR contacts using physical limitations. Use, in the first instance, the guidelines explained in ISO 14120:2015 [15].

In order to clearly identify the link between the different DPs and FRs, the following "Relational Matrix" (see Fig.3) has been developed. The role of that matrix is to identify the different connections between the standards that can be directly addressed to the DPs. The links are obtained from the list of normative references contained in the first introductory part of every mentioned standard. This matrix shows that

https://doi.org/10.1051/matecconf/201822301003

standards for safety used for the design of a collaborative robotic cell are often very coupled, making them hard to implement appropriately.

Table 2. Collaborative robotic cell: main standards for the safety systems design.

Title	Standard type	Code
Robots and robotic devices -- Safety requirements for industrial robots -- Part 1: Robots	C	ISO 10218-1 : 2011
Safety requirements for industrial robot -- Part 2: Robot systems and integration	C	ISO 10218-2 : 2011
Safety of machinery -- General principles for design -- Risk assessment and risk reduction	A	ISO 12100 : 2010
Safety of machinery — Safety-related parts of control systems — Part 1: General principles for design	B	ISO 13849-1 : 2015
Safety of machinery -- Minimum gaps to avoid crushing of parts of the human body	B	ISO 13854 : 2017
Safety of machinery -- Positioning of safeguards with respect to the approach speeds of parts of the human body	B	ISO 13855 : 2010
Safety of machinery -- Safety distances to prevent hazard zones being reached by upper and lower limbs	B	ISO 13857 : 2008
Safety of machinery -- Prevention of unexpected start-up	B	ISO 14118 : 2017
Safety of machinery -- Guards -- General requirements for the design and construction of fixed and movable guards	B	ISO 14120 : 2015
Robots and robotic devices -- Collaborative robots	C	ISO TS 15066 : 2016
Safety of machinery - Application of protective equipment to detect the presence of persons	B	IEC 62046 : 2018

Table 2 shows the list of main standards used for the design of a collaborative robotic cell.

Relational Matrix											
Code	ISO 10218-1	ISO 10218-2	ISO 12100	ISO 13849-1	ISO 13854	ISO 13855	ISO 13857	ISO 14118	ISO 14120	ISO TS 15066	IEC 62046
ISO 10218-1		x	x	x							
ISO 10218-2			x	x	x	x	x		x		x
ISO 12100											
ISO 13849-1			x								
ISO 13854			x				x				
ISO 13855			x				x				
ISO 13857			x								
ISO 14118			x	x							
ISO 14120			x			x	x				
ISO TS 15066	x	x	x			x					x
IEC 62046			x	x		x					

Fig. 3. Relational Matrix about main safety of machinery standards for robotic-cell applications.

The design matrix on the first level is decoupled and shows the dependencies between the solutions (DPs) and the functional requirements (FRs):

$$\begin{Bmatrix} FR_1 \\ FR_2 \\ FR_3 \end{Bmatrix} = \begin{bmatrix} X & X & 0 \\ 0 & X & 0 \\ 0 & 0 & X \end{bmatrix} \begin{Bmatrix} DP_1 \\ DP_2 \\ DP_3 \end{Bmatrix} \quad (1)$$

According to the Relational Matrix, ISO 13849-1 is recalled in ISO 10218-1. For this reason, DP2 has also influence on FR1 and FR2. This off-diagonal interaction shows a coupling of DPs and other FRs. Fig. 4 shows the FR-DP tree of the highest hierarchical levels.

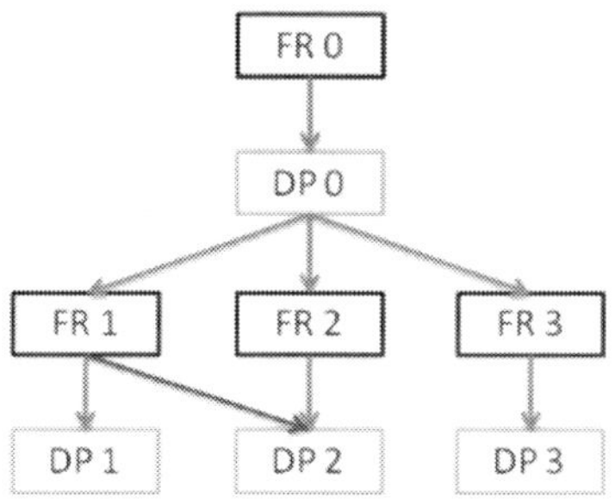

Fig. 4. Design decomposition at highest-level.

4.4. Decomposition and mapping process

The decomposition process of top-level FRs and DPs aims to transform the abstract requirements into more tangible parameters that are close to practical design guidelines and therefore relevant for the collaborative workstation implementation. The FR-DP pairs on the highest hierarchical level are the starting point for the top-down decomposition and mapping process. The decomposition is performed separately for each of the FR-DP pairs shown in Fig. 4 to obtain a better understanding of the process.

4.4.1 FR_1-DP_1 – Reduction of energy exchange during unexpected (but allowed) HR contacts

The design of the safety systems that safeguard the operator during unexpected (but allowed) HR contacts can be designed by reducing the energy exchange according to "Power and Force Limiting" approach. For the implementation of this DP the guidelines explained in ISO 10218-1:2011 [13] and ISO TS 15066:2016 section 5.5.5 [2] can be applied.

4.4.2 FR_2-DP_2 – Actively prevention of HR contact

The design of the safety systems that aims to actively prevent HR unexpected contacts can be satisfied using different complementary approaches. Depending on the final application, it is possible to apply one or more combined solutions.

Starting from FR2., further FRs and DPs of the successive hierarchical level can be defined as follows:

$FR_{2.1}$ Monitor HR speed and separation.

$FR_{2.2}$ Achive safety from rated monitored stop devices.

$FR_{2.3}$ Achive safety from protective equipment to detect presence of persons.

$FR_{2.4}$ Position the safeguards with respect to the human body part speed.

$FR_{2.5}$ Prevent an unexpected machine start-up.

$DP_{2.1}$ Guidelines explained in ISO TS 15066:2016 section 5.5.4 [2].

$DP_{2.2}$ Guidelines explained in ISO TS 15066:2016 section 5.5.2 [2].

$DP_{2.3}$ Guidelines explained in IEC 62046:2018 [16].

$DP_{2.4}$ Guidelines explained in ISO 13855:2010 [17].

$DP_{2.5}$ Guidelines explained in ISO 14118:2017 [18].

The design matrix shows a decoupled design:

$$\begin{Bmatrix} FR_{2.1} \\ FR_{2.2} \\ FR_{2.3} \\ FR_{2.4} \\ FR_{2.5} \end{Bmatrix} = \begin{bmatrix} X & 0 & X & X & 0 \\ 0 & X & 0 & X & 0 \\ 0 & 0 & X & X & 0 \\ 0 & 0 & 0 & X & 0 \\ 0 & 0 & 0 & 0 & X \end{bmatrix} \begin{Bmatrix} DP_{2.1} \\ DP_{2.2} \\ DP_{2.3} \\ DP_{2.4} \\ DP_{2.5} \end{Bmatrix} \quad (2)$$

According to the Relational Matrix, ISO 13855 and IEC 62046 are recalled in ISO TS 15066 (only for section 5.5.4). Furthermore, ISO 13855 is also recalled in IEC 62046. Finally, ISO TS 15066 is addressed to two DPs ($DP_{2.1}$ with section 5.5.4 and $DP_{2.2}$ whit section 5.5.2). For these reasons, $DP_{2.3}$ has influence on $FR_{2.1}$ and $FR_{2.3}$ and $DP_{2.4}$ has influence on $FR_{2.1}$, $FR_{2.2}$, $FR_{2.3}$ and $FR_{2.4}$. Also in this case, the off-diagonal interaction shows a coupling of DPs and other FRs.

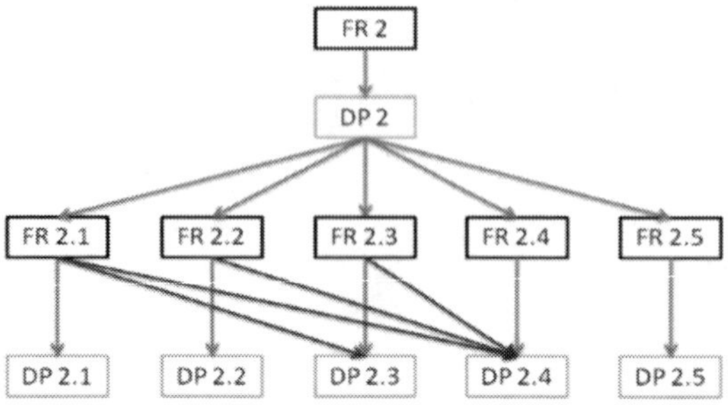

Fig. 5. Design decomposition $FR_{2.n}$-$DP_{2.n}$.

4.4.3 FR_3-DP_3 – Avoidance of HR contacts through physical limitations

The design of the safety systems that aims safeguard the operator by avoiding HR contacts using physical limitations can be satisfied through the preventive design of the components of the robotic cell as well as the design of safeguards.

Starting from FR3, further FRs and DPs of the successive hierarchical level can be defined as follows:

$FR_{3.1}$ Avoid forcing of parts of the human body.

$FR_{3.2}$ Prevent hazard zones being reached by operator during manual work activities.

$DP_{3.1}$ Guidelines explained in ISO 13854:2017 [19].

$DP_{3.2}$ Guidelines explained in ISO 13857:2008 [20].

The design matrix shows a decoupled design:

$$\begin{Bmatrix} FR_{3.1} \\ FR_{3.2} \end{Bmatrix} = \begin{bmatrix} X & X \\ 0 & X \end{bmatrix} \begin{Bmatrix} DP_{3.1} \\ DP_{3.2} \end{Bmatrix} \quad (3)$$

According to the Relational Matrix, ISO 13857 is recalled in ISO 13854. For this reason, DP3.2 has also influence on FR3.1 and FR3.2. This off-diagonal interaction shows a coupling of DPs and other FRs. Fig. 6 shows the FR-DP tree:

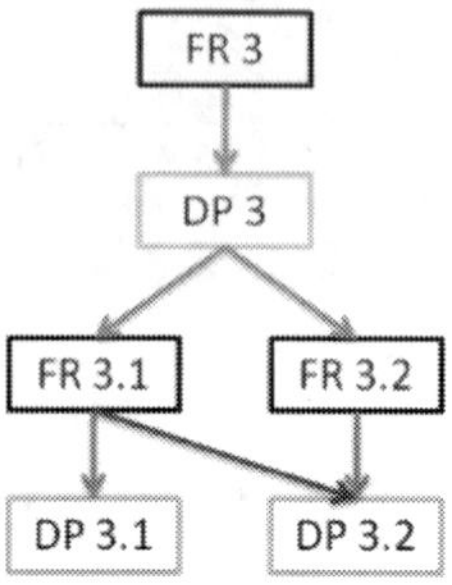

Fig. 6. Design decomposition $FR_{3.n}$-$DP_{3.n}$.

4.4.4 Overall relationships

Following, Fig. 7 shows the overall relationships between FRs and DPs of first, second and third level.

As showed, there is also a link between section 2 and section 3. In particular, FR2.4 and DP3.2 since the Relational Matrix shows a connection between ISO 13855 and ISO 13857.

4.4.5 Design matrix and summary

The complexity of the safety systems design for the implementation of the collaborative workstation was reduced trough the Axiomatic Design approach, in particular using the decomposition and mapping process. This approach helps the research team to better structure the safety requirements and to systematically obtain the design solutions (DPs), also respecting the constraints identified in section 4.2. The final design matrix was implemented using "Acclaro DFSS" software and is shown in Fig. 8:

	DP 0	DP 1	DP 2	DP 2.1	DP 2.2	DO 2.3	DP 2.4	DP 2.5	DP 3	DP 3.1	DP 3.2
FR 0	X										
FR 1		X	X	0	0	0	0	0	0	0	0
FR 2		0	X						0	0	0
FR 2.1		0		X	0	X	X	0	0	0	0
FR 2.2		0		0	X	0	X	0	0	0	0
FR 2.3		0		0	0	X	X	0	0	0	0
FR 2.4		0		0	0	0	X	0	0	0	X
FR 2.5		0		0	0	0	0	X	0	0	0
FR 3		0	0	0	0	0	0	0	X		
FR 3.1		0	0	0	0	0	0	0		X	X
FR 3.2		0	0	0	0	0	0	0		0	X

Fig. 8. Summarizing first, second and third level design matrix.

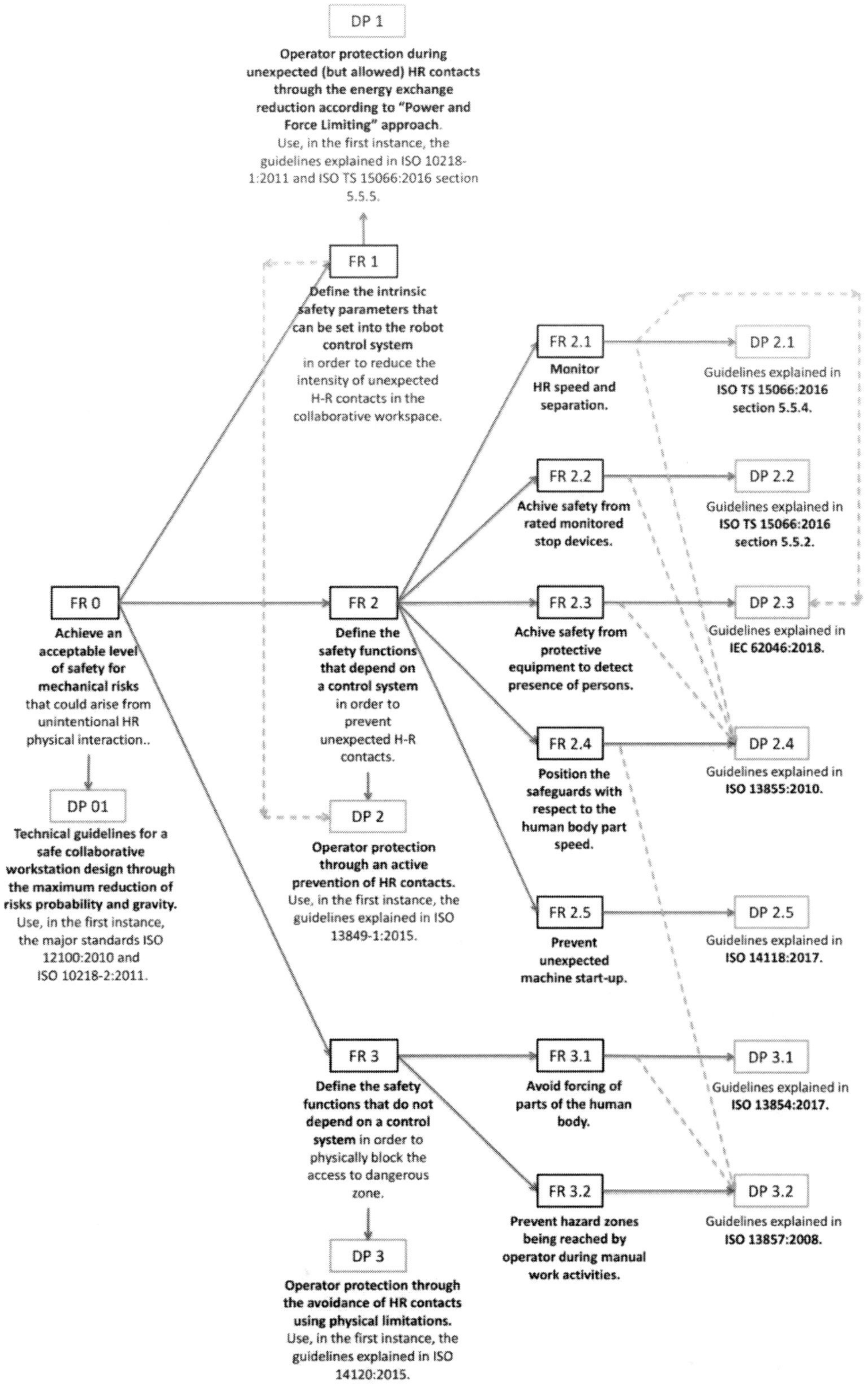

Fig. 7. First, second and third level overall relationships between FRs and DPs.

The design matrix is triangular and shows a decoupled design, which means that the Independence Axiom can be satisfied if the safety systems design sequence is correct. According to the proposed solution, DP2 has also influence on FR1 because, in general, the safety performance levels indicated in ISO 13849-1:2015 are requirements for the design of the safety-related control system of an industrial robot. In addition, DP2.3 has also influence on FR2.1 since the design of "Speed and Separation Monitoring Systems" needs the monitoring of the operators speed as indicated in IEC 62046:2018. DP2.4 has influence on FR2.1 , FR2.2 and FR2.3 since the design of "Speed and Separation Systems", "Safety Rated Monitored Stop" and electro-sensitive safety devices requires the indications discussed in ISO 13855:2010 in terms of position of safeguards in relationships to human motion.

In addition, DP3.2 has also influence on FR3.1 because the design of the parts of the workstation which has to avoid the forcing of human body parts is linked to ISO 13857:2008 which is related to the prevention of the achievement of hazard zones during manual work activities. Finally, DP3.2 has also influence on FR2.4 since the design of safety systems related to the operators speed requires the indications contained in ISO 13857:2008.

5 Concept of the Collaborative Human-Robot Assembly Workplace based on the results from the AD approach

Fig. 9 explains a preliminary concept layout of the new collaborative workstation, including the main safety systems and their related standards. As shown, there will be a collaborative space, where human and robot will share the workspace in order to perform a common production task, and a not-collaborative space, where operators are not allowed and the robot can work more performing.

Of course, different limited spaces involves different safety requirements and systems, which are regulated by different standards.

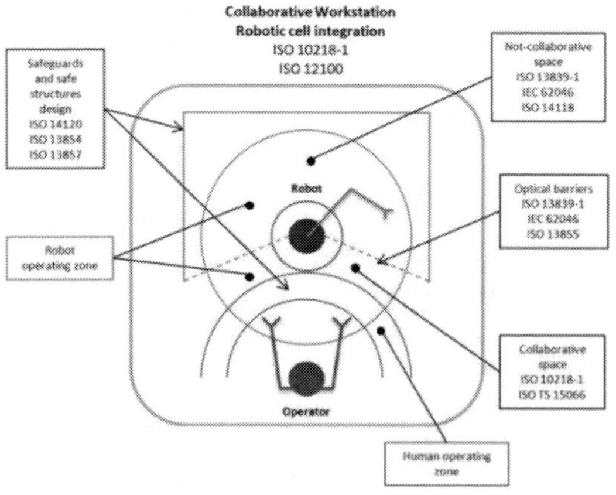

Fig. 9. New design of the collaborative assembly workplace.

6 Conclusion and outlook for further research

The present research work has shown the potential applicability of Axiomatic Design to the study and development of a complex situation such as the design of safety systems for a collaborative HR workstation, also considering OHS requirements. The output of that design is a list of standard-related guidelines, which can helps technicians and designer in implementing safety systems for industrial collaborative robot applications. These guidelines can simplify the complexity of the safety systems design stage, which can be very substantial due to the presence of a person into a robotic cell.

Future improvements can be:

- The further development of the proposed guidelines in order to define more precise safety parameters using an Axiomatic Design approach;
- The application of an Axiomatic Design approach to the design of the ergonomics solutions for HR collaborative workstations related to main international OHS standards;
- The introduction of production efficiency considerations as Non-Functional Requirements (non-FRs), in combination to safety and ergonomics requirements (FRs).

This research was conducted in the research project "SME 4.0". As the working title already reveals, research focuses on the development of new concepts of Industry 4.0 that are especially suitable for SME.

This project has received funding from the European Union's Horizon 2020 research and innovation program under the Marie Skłodowska-Curie grant agreement No 734713.

References

1. M. Huber, M. Rickert, A. Knoll, T. Brandt, S. Glasauer, Human-robot interaction in handing-over tasks, , the 17th International Symposium on Robot and Human Interactive Communication, 1-3 August 2008, Munich, Germany, 107-112, IEEE, (2008).
2. ISO, Ts 15066: 2011, Robots and robotic devices—collaborative robots, Geneva, Switzerland: International Organization for Standardization, (2011).
3. B. Matthias, T. Reisinger, Example application of ISO/TS 15066 to a collaborative assembly scenario, the 47th International Symposium on Robotics (ISR), 21-22 June 2016, Munich, Germany, 1-5, VDE (2016).
4. P. Fantini, M. Pinzone, M. Taisch, Placing the operator at the centre of Industry 4.0 design: Modelling and assessing human activities within cyber-physical systems, Computers & Industrial Engineering, (2018, in press).

5. B.C. Pirvu, C.B. Zamfirescu, D. Gorecky, Engineering insights from an anthropocentric cyber-physical system: A case study for an assembly station. Mechatronics, **34**, 147-159, (2016).

6. J. Fryman, B. Matthias, Safety of industrial robots: From conventional to collaborative applications, 7th German Conference on Robotics, 21-22 May 2012, Munich, Germany, 1-5, VDE, (2012).

7. D.T. Matt, E. Rauch, P. Dallasega, Mini-factory – a learning factory concept for students and small and medium sized enterprises, Procedia CIRP, **17**, 178-183 (2014).

8. N.P. Suh, *Axiomatic Design - Advances and Applications*. New York, Oxford University Press, (2009).

9. C.A. Brown, Teaching axiomatic design to engineers - Theory, applications, and software, Journal of Manufacturing Systems, **24**, 3, 186-195, (2005).

10. M.K. Thompson, A Classification of Procedural Errors in the Definition of Functional Requirements, in Axiomatic Design Theory, Proceedings of the 7thInternational Conference on Axiomatic Design, Worcester, MA, 107-112, (2013).

11. ISO, 12100: 2010, Safety of machinery—General principles for design–Risk assessment and risk reduction, Geneva, Switzerland: International Organization for Standardization, (2010).

12. ISO, 10218-1: 2011, Robots and robotic devices—Safety requirements for industrial robots–Part 1: Robots, Geneva, Switzerland: International Organization for Standardization, (2011).

13. ISO, 10218-2: 2011, Robots and robotic devices—Safety requirements for industrial robots–Part 2: Robot systems and integration, Geneva, Switzerland: International Organization for Standardization, (2011).

14. ISO, 13849-1 : 2015, Safety of machinery—Safety-related parts of control systems, Part 1: General principles for design, Geneva, Switzerland: International Organization for Standardization, (2015).

15. ISO, 14120: 2015, Safety of machinery—Guards—General requirements for the design and construction of fixed and movable guards, Geneva, Switzerland: International Organization for Standardization, (2015).

16. IEC 62046:2018, Safety of machinery—Application of protective equipment to detect the presence of persons, Geneva, Switzerland: International Electrotechnical Commission, (2018).

17. ISO, 13855: 2010, Safety of machinery—Positioning of safeguards with respect to the approach speeds of parts of the human body, Geneva, Switzerland: International Organization for Standardization, (2010).

18. ISO, 14118:2015, Safety of machinery—Prevention of unexpected start-up, Geneva, Switzerland: International Organization for Standardization, (2015).

19. ISO, 13854:2017, Safety of machinery—Minimum gaps to avoid crushing of parts of the human body, Geneva, Switzerland: International Organization for Standardization, (2017).

20. ISO, 13857:2017, Safety of machinery—Safety distances to prevent hazard zones being reached by upper and lower limbs, Geneva, Switzerland: International Organization for Standardization, (2017).

Application of Axiomatic Design for Agile Product Development

Erik Puik[1,*], and *Darek* Ceglarek[2]

[1]HU University of Applied Sciences Utrecht, Padualaan 99, 3584 CH Utrecht, the Netherlands
[2]International Digital Laboratory, WMG, University of Warwick, Coventry, CV4 7AL, UK

Abstract. Agile, and iterative, development methods for new product development are gaining in popularity under product engineers; where it initially was just applied for software development, now larger adoption takes place for product development in general. The design rules of agile development are somewhat conflicting with the guidelines of Axiomatic Design. In this paper, it is investigated why this is the case, what can be done about it, and how can the strengths of agile development be combined with Axiomatic Design to optimise methods for product design. It is shown that the methods are indeed advising on different and conflicting strategies, however, by attenuating the agile design rules in the early stage of design, and doing the same for AD in the later stage of design, best of both worlds can be combined.

1 Introduction

New product development (NPD) is getting more complex by the year due to the increased means for global communication, mainly supported by the internet. More development groups are globally active, which increases competition in research and development. Speed is an essence when executing NPD due to this competition. Products that are introduced to the market too late will miss substantial turnover [1]. Developers apply methods for 'Systems Engineering' in the development process, being able to oversee elements of the design process in the context of the whole system [2] (the term 'Engineering Design' is also applied in the US). Traditional system engineering models are applied in NPD to describe the process in a linear way, such as the 'Waterfall-Model', 'PRINCE2', or the 'V-Model'. Since the change of the century, the shortcomings of these models have grown to serious obstacles due to the increasing NPD-dynamics of modern days [3]. Agile and iterative methods, 'Scrum' being the most valued of many variants, have proven the ability to handle the dynamics, however, this tends to come at the cost of rigidity in NPD [4]-[6]. E. g. for the scum methodology, this lack of rigidity is mainly caused by client involvement and lack of visibility over the project outside the iterative 'sprints'. To address rigidity in NPD, there are basically two ways to be applied [7]:

(i) Organise the design, and all its elements, by the application of knowledge (as detailed understanding of the design is enabled by knowledge);
(ii) Test preliminary designs as soon as possible to enforce appearance of errors and address them accordingly (letting physics speak).

Since testing is a central theme in the application of agile product development methods, topic (ii) is well-embedded in virtually all agile methodologies. It is typically topic (i) that is causing the problems when agile development methods are used. As such, Scrum-sprints focus more on detailed issues than the 'design of the whole'. Agile development methods have a tendency to move attention from 'the whole' to smaller, more specific problems that stand between the now and the next demonstrable prototype. This is where Axiomatic Design (AD) is expected to contribute. With its Independence and Information Axioms, it focuses on respectively 'Doing the right things' and 'Doing these things right' [8]. Mainly the first proposition may be considered a valuable addition to most agile development methods, maintaining focus on the 'big picture'. Questions that arise are:

- Can typical errors in the agile development process be described in the context of AD;
- What are the consequences on the Axioms if these errors occur;
- How can AD be applied to prevent these errors from happening.

The paper is organised as follows. Section 2 explains the background of linear and agile methods. Section 3 explains the methodology of investigation, and Section 4 inventories possible errors in the (agile) development process. Finally, Section 5 discusses the findings and draws conclusions.

2 Background

In this background section, traditional linear models are inventoried. These linear models have been preceding the agile models that recently gained in popularity. The most-applied agile method being the Scrum-methodology.

* Corresponding author: erik.puik@hu.nl

2.1 The Waterfall Model

Widely applied models in industry are the 'Waterfall-Model' and the 'V-Model'. Royce, who was the first to report the Waterfall-Model [9] criticised the model in the same article blaming the lack of (old school) process iterations and testing. The Waterfall-Model also forms the basis for the process-model of the 'PRINCE' method that was introduced in 1989 (PRojects IN Controlled Environments). PRINCE'2', was a continued development to enable broader application than PRINCE that was mainly intended for ICT developments.

2.2 The V-Model

The V-Model, also based on the Waterfall-Model, was originally introduced by Boehm [10] and simultaneously developed further in Germany and the US in the second half of the eighties [11], [12]. In the 1991 proceedings for the National Council on Systems Engineering (NCOSE); now INCOSE as of 1995, the V-Model was adopted in the US for modelling of mainly software systems. Like all basic Waterfall-Models and PRINCE2, the V-Model suffers from the problem of 'missing iterations' [3], [9]. This is not as much a problem to accountants and project managers as it is for developers and testers. The most damaging aspect might be the effect that the V-Model effectively discourages user involvement in evaluating the design before arriving at the formal testing stages. By then it is too late to make significant changes to the design. It must be mentioned that the need for sufficient iterations was emphasised when Rook introduced the V-Model, but since the model does not specifically visualise it, unilateral application of the model has become the standard for most industrial applicants. Nevertheless, the V-Model, and in somewhat lesser extent the Waterfall-Model, today are popular systems engineering methods in industry since they meet needs for management. Though the V-model was presented over 30 years ago, discussion is still active and many variations of the model are still being developed [13]-[16].

2.3 Agile Methods for Product Development

Shewhart described in 1939 the 'Plan-Do-Check-Act cycle of continuous improvement' based on the principles of empiricism as induced by Bacon in his 17th century work 'Novum Organum' [17], [18]. The initial Plan-Do-Check-Act was advertised more broadly by Deming who replaced the stage 'Check' by 'Study' to emphasise that the analysis in this stage was to prevail over inspection [19]. The method was optimised in the sixties by respectively Asimow and Mesarovic as the 'Iconic model of the Design Process' [20], [21]. The Iconic model introduces the cycle of Analysis, Synthesis, Evaluation, and Communication. This foundation forms the basis for modern iterative models for iterative project control up to date.

The need for a combination of structure and dynamics in the ICT world has led to further development methods for iterative development. Agile software development methodologies focus upon incremental design and hence a cyclic approach. The aim with these methods is to: (i) make the development process more responsive in changing environments, (ii) pursue functioning software over extensive documentation, (iii) centre individuals and their interactions rather than tools and processes, and (iv) value customer collaboration over customer contract negotiation.

Of great influence are the 'Spiral Model of Software Development' by Boehm [22], the 'Engineering Design Process' by Ertas & Jones [23], HP's 'Product Development Process', the 'Scrum development method' [24], and IBM's 'Rational Unified Process' [25]. All these methods were initially developed to streamline software developments but later-on found their ways for broader application.

Scrum may be considered the most valued form within the family of agile development methodologies. Scrum uses incremental development procedures with an objective to get working software into the hands of the stakeholders as quickly as possible. As such, Scrum puts business value functions into stakeholder possession early on in the software development life cycle. The more traditional process-oriented development methods cannot provide this agile capability; stakeholders typically would not have access to any software produced until far later in the process. This agile performance is provided in a straightforward procedure that enhances focus and communication in an iterative process. Scrum starts with the business case just as one would do with process-oriented development. From this point, it diverges from linear development methods. The customer requirements are inventoried and refined in close cooperation with stakeholders and the project group. The remaining requirements or 'User Stories' are kept in a list known as the 'Backlog'. Cycles or 'Sprints' are initiated from the backlog to address the customer requirements with the objective to produce operating solutions. The solutions should be fully functional, tested, and documented with the ability to be shipped as a finished product, though with limited functionality. Sprints may last from one week to a month and their progression is kept in a 'Burn Down Chart' to feed its status back to the team. A structure of usually brief meetings takes care of extra information exchange within the project team and leads to joint decisions that are supported by the customer as he regularly participates meetings.

Scrum and related agile methods also suffer from drawbacks compared to the traditional methods. It may fail at the following aspects: (i) a drawback according to Highsmith & Cockburn is the fact that an external client has to be actively involved in the project [4]. The client has to be able and available to test the typical monthly releases and to suggest new or modified functionalities, (ii) by applying Scrum, the vision of the client highly influences development. Highsmith & Cockburn also show that if the client does not have a clear sense of the product's direction, the members of the development team will tend to behave in the same way, and the final product can be significantly different to what is expected. This makes the main strength of Scrum also one of the main weaknesses: client involvement in the development process, and (iii) another potential weakness is the relatively low visibility over the project outside sprints. This makes it difficult to estimate how long a project will take or how much it will cost. In projects with external clients, where bidding is used to determine the contractor for projects, this can be a major drawback.

3 Methodology

The methodology that is applied to investigate the success of agile methods is to compare agile development to good practice in AD.

3.1 Dubakov's model for the analysis of agile development

Dubakov describes the essence of agile software development and presents an interesting view on his weblog that matches particularly well with AD [26]. Though the analysis is born from a perspective of agile software development, they seem to work for general product development too.

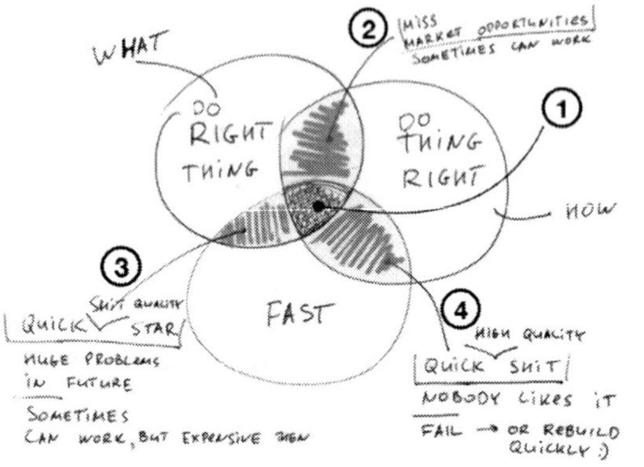

Fig. 1. Three goals of agile development processes as proposed by Dubakov (numbers 1-4 added)

In figure 1, the upper left-hand sphere states 'Do right things' (note that picture states 'thing' but referred text states 'things'). Dubakov explains that these are 'workable things that solve specific problems and solve them well'. This is analogue to satisfaction of the Independence Axiom that forces the definition of: (a) well-chosen Functional Requirements (FRs), (b) matching Design Parameters (DPs) and, (c) an uncoupled or decoupled design. It is only possible to 'Do right things' if the Independence Axiom is satisfied. The right-hand sphere states 'Do things right'. This addresses excellence in execution. From the perspective of AD, it means that the DPs are capable of satisfying the FRs under all circumstances. Doing things right is a process with strong stochastic elements, needing quality in execution, to guarantee that satisfaction of the FRs takes place in all imaginable situations. This means that axiomatic information of the relations between DPs and FRs are eliminated, thus satisfying the Information Axiom. The third element, and here it adds an element that is rather neglected in AD, is the element of development speed, indicated in the lowest sphere of Figure 1. The right things should be executed well, preferably in a small amount of time. It is clear that all three spheres exist in a field of tension.

There are four overlapping areas that have distinctive and characteristic project approaches (shaded areas as indicated and numbered in Figure 1):

(1) Ideal situation, the right things are done well in a short amount of time;
(2) The right things are done in the right way, however, not at the fastest pace;
(3) The right things are done fast, however, they are not done well;
(4) Things are done well and fast, however, they might be the wrong things.

Next, these overlapping areas, further referred to as Project Execution Practices (PEPs) will be evaluated from the perspective of AD.

3.2 Modelling good practice in Axiomatic Design

For the evaluation of the PEPs, a model called the Axiomatic Maturity Diagram (AMD) will be applied. AD prescribes a clear order in which the axioms should be satisfied; start with the Independence Axiom, after that, satisfy the Information Axiom. This design rule was analysed before using the AMD.

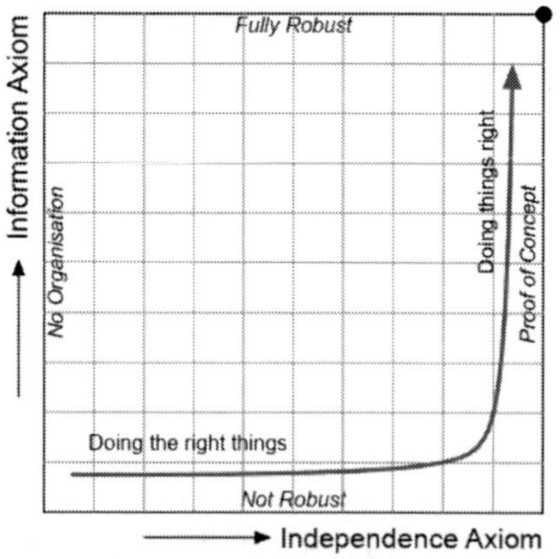

Fig. 2. Preferred development path through the Axiomatic Maturity Diagram, as indicated in literature, first moves to the right to satisfy the Independence Axiom. After this, the Information Axiom is satisfied in an upward direction

The AMD is a two-dimensional representation of the Axioms [8], [27]. On the horizontal axis, it shows the progression of the Independence Axiom, from 'No Organisation' to 'Proof of Concept'. On the vertical axis, it shows the progression of the Information Axiom going from 'Not Robust' to 'Fully Robust'. Product development, in the AMD, will start somewhere at the lower left-hand side and will move diagonally upwards. The design-path, according to 'Good Practice' in AD meets the following demands in that specific order [28]:

- Define FRs and find all relevant DPs to address unrecognised information. Next, if the design matrix is not uncoupled yet, decouple the design matrix to address recognised information (satisfy Axiom 1);
- Match the design ranges and system ranges to guarantee an adequate common range to address axiomatic information (satisfy Axiom 2).

This leads to a preferred path that first moves to the right and then angles upwards, as plotted in Figure 2.

In case of the rather conservative and slow but safe path of the Waterfall-Model, the procedure of following Independence and Information Axioms in that order would be persistent (Figure 3). A slightly riskier path that in practice enhances the development speed of projects is the path of 'Simultaneous Engineering' [8], [29]. This gives the designer more room to start early work on robustness, process technology, and other life cycle elements. It merges the work on Independence and Information Axioms and possibly shortens project lead time.

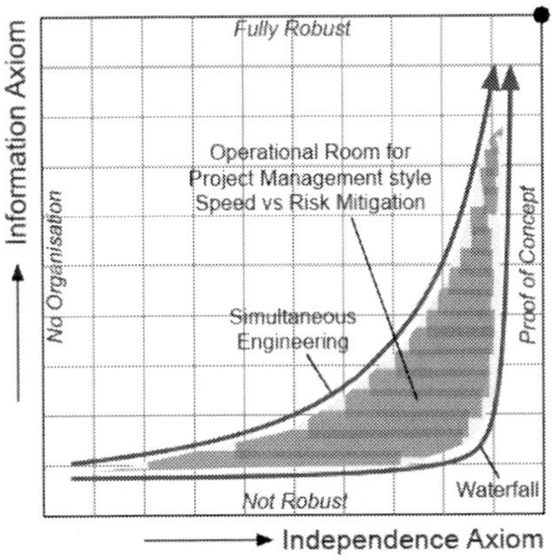

Fig. 3. Depending on the nature of the project, a different strategy may be followed. The right lower curve would represent a waterfall management approach, while the upper would represent the path in case of a simultaneous engineering strategy

Obviously, the safer path is the path proposed by the Waterfall Model, that is also the preferred path in AD. In this situation, the satisfaction of the Independence Axiom will at forehand assure conceptual rigidity of the system design. When this is completed, and the robustness of the system is increased, there is no risk that optimised relations between FRs and DPs need reconsideration. Simultaneous Engineering introduces risks; the fact that the conceptual design is not crystallised may cause conceptual design changes. This means that the FR-DP relations change. If the FR-DP relations were yet optimised, it means that the work for optimisations may indeed have been spent in vain (and work done is lost).

4 Evaluating the PEPs from the perspective of Axiomatic Design

The Project Execution Practices of Figure 1 (overlapping areas 1-4 of paragraph 3.1), will now be investigated using the Axiomatic Maturity Diagram.

(1) The right things are done well in a short amount of time

In this case, little criticism is possible. The product is conceptually strong, robust-engineered, and all that was accomplished in a short amount of time. This case more or less follows the path of simultaneous engineering; conceptual choices happened to be made in a correct manner (path 1 of Figure 4);

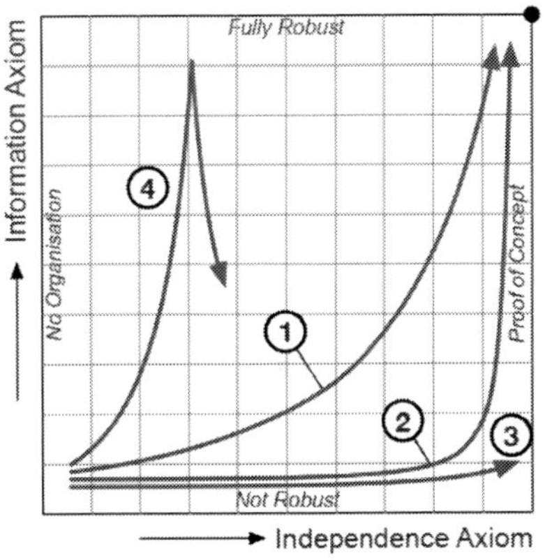

Fig. 4. The four Project Execution Practices and their path though the AMD

(2) The right things are done in the right way, however not at the fastest pace

In the second case, the standard development ways of AD or one of the derivatives of the Waterfall-Model were followed. This development may not be considered to be agile. Market introduction could be late, or later than ideal. In this case, total turnover over the lifecycle of the product may be lower than possible when an agile strategy would have been applied (path 2 of Figure 4);

(3) The right things are done fast, however, they are not done well

This third PEP is recognised because the product, though its concept is smart and well-defined, still does not perform well because the FRs cannot be maintained within their operational areas by the DPs. Customers may be irritated because the product fails. If launched in this state, the service cost may go high, as corrective actions for customers are needed without interruptions. This PEP can be upgraded to PEP2 by further optimising the design. By doing this, time will slip but the product may still become a 'Good Design' (path 3 of Figure 4);

(4) Things are done well and fast, however, they might be the wrong things

This is the most devastating of all four options. The product has the appearance of a well-engineered product; however, the product is not able to perform well under required circumstances because the underlying concept is structurally inadequate. Problems with the product cannot be fixed easily because it needs a total redesign to correct the bad genes of the design. A lot of work may be spent in vain as the total redesign renounces the conceptual choices of the old design and introduces new DPs to satisfy the FRs. FR-DP relations have to be composed from the ground up (path 4 of Figure 4);.

4.3 Further investigation of PEP 4 and its relation to agile design methodologies

The objective to get working software into the hands of the stakeholders as quickly as possible is an important feature of agile product development methods. This feature comes with strengths and drawbacks:

- The conceptual development of the product is part of multiple sprints. Sprints are initiated from the backlog to address the customer requirements with the objective to produce operating solutions. The solutions should be 'fully functional, tested, and documented with the ability to be shipped as a finished product, though with limited functionality' [30]. This means that relations between FRs and DPs are made robust, while the complete set of FRs is not known yet. As a result, the Information Axiom is addressed before complete satisfaction of the Independence Axiom. As such, product development follows a risky path straight through the middle of the AMD. This is shown in Figure 5, 'End of first sprint';

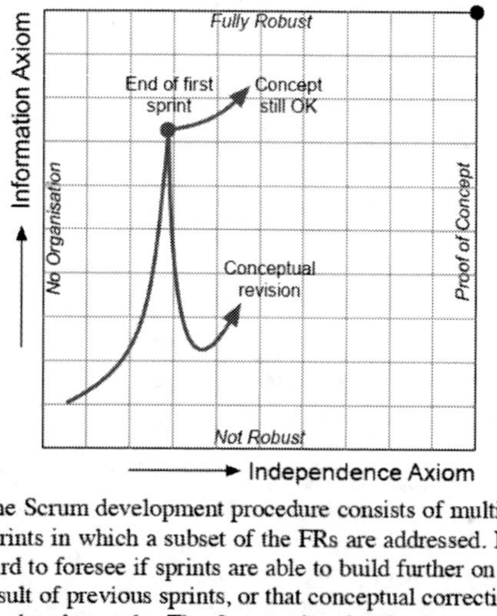

Fig. 5. The Scrum development procedure consists of multiple sprints in which a subset of the FRs are addressed. It is hard to foresee if sprints are able to build further on the result of previous sprints, or that conceptual corrections need to be made. The former situation leads to quick progression of the project. The latter slows the project down and work is spent in vain

- Depending on the conceptual choices made, further FRs may be satisfied in the next sprint without conceptual revision. If this is the case, the next sprint builds further on the previous (Figure 5, 'Concept still OK'). If the concept needs changes in order to satisfy the new FRs, the project status drops in the AMD. In this case, the development gets less efficient; new DPs are needed to satisfy the FRs and earlier optimisations are lost. This is shown in Figure 5, 'Conceptual Revision';
- The efficiency of these agile ways of product design could deliver dramatic results. In an unfortunate situation, the design could need many conceptual revisions. For every single revision, many optimisations of the design would need to be redone causing a lot of work is spent in vain (Figure 6). However, chances of this actually occurring seem moderate from a statistical perspective.

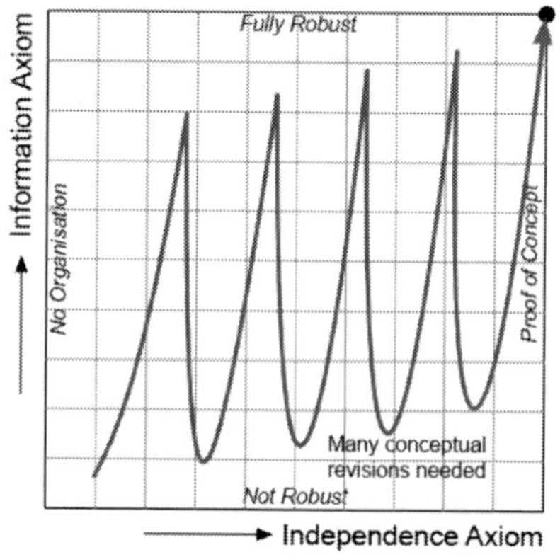

Fig. 6. In a worst-case scenario, many conceptual fixes of the product design would be needed

- A general advantage of agile development methods is that they pull testing towards the present. Earlier investigations have shown that testing and organisation are the most effective way to find hidden complexity ('unknown unknowns') in the design process [1], [8], [27], [31]. This hidden complexity is the main cause for surprises during the design process. Testing is an essential element for agile development, as it substantially increases the chances that these hidden artefacts are found in an early stage of the design process. The sooner hidden problems are found, the sooner they can be addressed, which reduces corrective actions in the conceptual design process. Agile development has great opportunities in this sense;
- Unsuccessful iterations in the design process do not automatically lead to an inefficient development process. As long as iterative cycles are organised as 'safe-fail' experiments, the test will provide positive results; (i) if the test succeeds, it provides for a solution, but (ii) if the test does not succeed, it may provide essential knowledge of the design process. A solid knowledge base of the design and the chosen solutions is essential as the result of the design process never exceeds the state of knowledge of its designers [7].

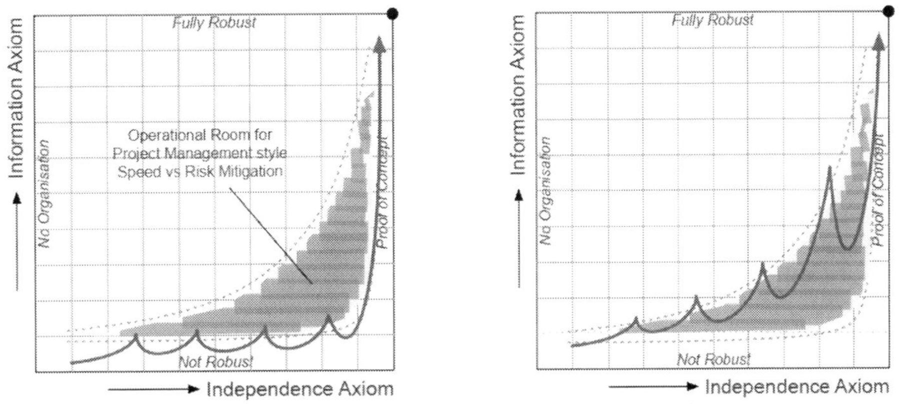

Fig. 7. Alternative development paths that are safer in execution. These paths are not completely conforming the Scrum methodology but approach the safer development order of AD to satisfy the Independence and Information Axioms in that order

5 Discussion

Strengths

Agile development methods, in this case mainly focussing on Scrum and AD appear rather complementary. The rigidity of AD seems superior compared to Scum, however, the power to apply large series of safe-fail tests seems a particular strength of Scrum. The rigidity of AD
and the agile properties of Scrum may also collide; during the development cycles, or sprints, time is limited, and there may be not enough time to spend extensive investigation to decouple the design.

Weaknesses

Scrum uses incremental development procedures 'with an objective to get working software into the hands of the stakeholders as quickly as possible' [30]. This means that every iteration cycle aims to end at the upper side of the AMD (fully robust). Mainly in the beginning of the project, there are substantial uncertainties which may lead to changes in the conceptual design of the product to be developed. This means that many FR-DP-PV relations that have been optimized to become robust are changed and may even be rejected from the final design. In these cases, work for optimisations is spent in vain and work done is lost.

Another problem is the plannability when Scrum is applied. Sprints may be planned as safe-fail processes and as such they can be successful even when the outcome of investigations are negative. Though knowledge development may be considerable, project progression is minimal. It is noted that this could occur in AD as well when the process of zigzagging is not successful and needs to be reconsidered and executed again.

Limitations

Dubakov's 'essence of agile software development' (Figure 1) is not particularly intended for application of traditional linear development methods. The concept however is basically so generic that it should not be a problem to apply it in a broader context. Secondly, the examples in this paper are mainly based on experience and literature. Other agile development methods, as mentioned in the introduction, may have other advantages and limitations. The focus on iterative development cycles though, is generic for most agile development methods and so are the strengths and the drawbacks. Thirdly, this analysis is an analytical approach based on the scientific characterisation of both Scum and AD; practice could work out differently. Therefore, this analysis would benefit from thorough experimental verification. This is not an easy task as such a verification would need many subsequent projects to be executed and monitored under a controlled or at least known environment.

Other considerations

Another finding is based on the analysis of Figure 3 [8]. It shows that it is unwise to spend energy to increase robustness when the system is far from decoupled yet. The chances that FR-DP relations have to be revised are quite large in this stage of development. As the development proceeds, and FR-DP relations start to crystallise, at this point the Independence Axiom is satisfied up to some extent, the chances become significantly smaller. As such, it is wise to stay in the shaded zone of Figure 3, eventually on the upper side. Acting outside this zone increase the chances on harming the FR-DP relations. Unfortunately, this is not what Agile development methods exhort. Using the insights of AD, it would be better to not divert completely from the development path of AD. Which path this should be is difficult to determine based on this study, mainly because the exact location of the higher curve was not investigated yet. Two possible boundaries for such a development path are shown in Figure 7.

6 Acknowledgements

This research was supported by the HU University of Applied Sciences Utrecht, and the project '(G)een Moer An', funded by Stichting Innovatie Alliantie (SIA) in the Netherlands.

References

[1] E. C. N. Puik, "Risk Adjusted Concurrent Development of Microsystems and Reconfigurable Manufacturing Systems," Coventry, 2017.
[2] R. C. Booton and S. Ramo, "The Development of Systems Engineering," *IEEE Transactions on Aerospace and Electronic Systems*, vol. 20, no. 4, pp. 306–310, Jul. 1984.
[3] J. Christie, "The Seductive and Dangerous V-Model," *Testing Experience*, no. 4, pp. 73–77, Dec-2008.
[4] J. Highsmith and A. Cockburn, "Agile software development: the business of innovation," *Computer*, vol. 34, no. 9, pp. 120–127, 2001.
[5] N. F. N. il Ionel, "Critical analysys of the Scrum Project Management Methodology," 2008.
[6] V. Vinekar, C. W. Slinkman, and S. Nerur, "Can Agile and Traditional Systems Development Approaches Coexist? An Ambidextrous View," *Information Systems Management*, vol. 23, no. 3, pp. 31–42, Dec. 2006.
[7] E. C. N. Puik and D. Ceglarek, "The Quality of a Design Will Not Exceed the Knowledge of its Designer; an Analysis Based on Axiomatic Information and the Cynefin Framework," *ICAD2015*, vol. 34, pp. 19–24, 2015.
[8] E. C. N. Puik and D. Ceglarek, "A Different Consideration on Information and Complexity in Axiomatic Design," 1st ed., no. 4, N. P. Suh and A. M. Farid, Eds. 2016, pp. 105–129.
[9] W. W. Royce, "Managing the development of large software systems," *proceedings of IEEE WESCON*, pp. 328–338, Sep. 1970.
[10] B. W. Boehm, "Guidelines for Verifying and Validating Software Requirements and Design Specifications," *IEEE Softw.*, pp. 1–20, 1979.
[11] P. Rook, "Controlling software projects," *Software Engineering Journal*, vol. 1986, no. 1, pp. 7–16, 1986.
[12] J. Friedrich, U. Hammerschall, M. Kuhrmann, and M. Sihling, *Das V-Modell XT*. Berlin/Heidelberg, Germany: Springer, 2009.
[13] P. C. Anitha, D. Savio, and V. S. Mani, "Managing requirements volatility while 'Scrumming' within the V-Model," *2013 IEEE Third International Workshop onEmpirical Requirements Engineering (EmpiRE)*, pp. 17–23, 2013.
[14] M. McHugh, O. Cawley, F. McCaffcry, I. Richardson, and X. Wang, "An agile V-Model for medical device software development to overcome the challenges with plan-driven software development lifecycles," *Software Engineering in Health Care (SEHC), 2013 5th International Workshop on*, pp. 12–19, 2013.
[15] R. Höhn, S. Höppner, M. Broy, A. Rausch, R. Petrasch, S. Biffl, R. Wagner, W. Hesse, and K. Bergner, *Das V-Modell XT*, 1st ed. Berlin/Heidelberg: Springer, 2008.
[16] S. Mathur and S. Malik, "Advancements in the V-Model," *International Journal of Computer Applications*, vol. 1, no. 12, pp. 29–34, 2010.
[17] W. A. Shewhart, *Statistical Method from the Viewpoint of Quality Control*. Mineola, New York: Dover Publications, 1939.
[18] F. Bacon, *Novum organum*. London: Forgotten Books, 1620.
[19] W. E. Deming, *Out of the Crisis*. Cambridge, Massachusetts: MIT Press, 2000.
[20] M. Asimow, *Introduction to design*. Upper Saddle River, New Jersey: Prentice Hall, 1962.
[21] M. D. Mesarovic, *Foundations for a general systems theory*. Cleveland, Ohio, U.S.: Systems Research Center, Case Institute of Technology, 1964.
[22] B. W. Boehm, "A spiral model of software development and enhancement," *Computer*, vol. 21, no. 5, pp. 61–72, 1988.
[23] A. Ertas and J. C. Jones, *The engineering design process*, 1st ed. Hoboken, N.J.: Wiley, 1996.
[24] K. Schwaber, "SCRUM Development Process," no. 11, pp. 117–134, 1997.
[25] P. Kroll and P. Kruchten, *The Rational Unified Process Made Easy: A Practitioner's Guide to the RUP*. Reading, MA: Addison Wesley, 2003.
[26] M. Dubakov, "The Future of Agile Software Development," *https://www.targetprocess.com/articles/the-future-of-agile-software-development/*.
[27] E. C. N. Puik and D. Ceglarek, "A Theory of Maturity," presented at the 10th International Conference on Axiomatic Design ICAD2014, Lisbon, 2014, 1st ed., pp. 115–120.
[28] N. P. Suh, "Axiomatic Design - Advances and Applications," no. 5, Cambridge, MA: Oxford University Press, New York.Oxford, 2001, Chapter 5, pp. 239-298., 2001.
[29] H. J. Bullinger and J. Warschat, *Concurrent Simultaneous Engineering Systems*. Berlin/Heidelberg, Germany: Springer Science & Business Media, 2012.
[30] K. Schwaber and M. Beedle, *Agile Software Development with Scrum*. 2002.
[31] E. C. N. Puik and D. Ceglarek, "A Review on Information in Design," presented at the 10th International Conference on Axiomatic Design ICAD2014, Lisbon, 2014, 1st ed., pp. 59–64.

Axiomatic decomposition of a zero-sum game: the penalty shoot-out case

Fernando Rolli[1,*], *João* Fradinho[2], *Alessandro* Giorgetti[1], *Paolo* Citti[1] and *Gabriele* Arcidiacono[1]

[1]Department of Innovation and Information Engineering, Guglielmo Marconi University, Via Plinio 44 - 00193 Rome, Italy
[2]UNIDEMI & DEMI, Faculdade de Ciências e Tecnologia, Universidade Nova de Lisboa, Campus de Caparica, Caparica 2829-516, Portugal

Abstract. The game of soccer has offered matter of wide scientific analysis about the effective application of the game theory in real-life. The field observations have often detected divergent behaviors from theoretical predictions. The basic problem comes from the fact that it is difficult to build scientific models reflecting reality as closely as possible. Axiomatic Design offers us a powerful tool of rational decomposition of a real and complex issue into elementary components. Independence Axiom guarantees that game decomposition will define a set of elementary actions logically consistent and free of redundancies. At the same time, Information Axiom can allow to select among alternative strategies, those that they predict the actions with a higher probability rate of success. In this paper, it is suggested the use of the Axiomatic Design methodology in the Collectively Exhaustive and Mutually Exclusive (CEME) mode, as a tool of analysis of the penalty shoot-out in extra time. This methodology allows to define the game strategies for goalkeepers and penalty takers. It will be analyzed both, the case when the opponents' behavior is well known and the situation when the statistics about the opponents are unknown. Axiomatic Design allows the process of decomposition to be simplified, enabling the selection of optimal game strategies. These strategies correspond to Nash's equilibrium solutions when you already know about your opponents' game behavior. On the contrary, when penalty takers whose behavior is unknown, then it is always possible to define a strategy corresponding to the Bayesian equilibrium game solutions.

1 Introduction

The game of soccer is the most popular sport in the world. It feeds an economic business of considerable proportions. In Italy, it represents an important economic sector in terms of business compared to the PIL [1]. The only lack of participation of the Italian national soccer team to the 2018 World Cup Russia, has been estimated as a direct loss of the state system amounting to EUR 100 million, without considering the income it would have been generated. At the same time, the game of soccer represents a useful workshop to ascertain the extent of the game theory. It has a very wide application in both finance and social science. In this paper, it is presented a case of functional decomposition application of the Collectively Exhaustive and Mutually Exclusive (CEME) methodology, already studied by authors in different areas [2, 3] so to define a process of drawing up of robust strategies for penalty shootouts. The penalty shootouts are used in play-offs, in case after extra time the two opposing teams are still in draw. They are constituted by five penalty shootouts the two teams kick alternately to decide the winning team of the match. Unfortunately, this kind of game cannot be formulated as a repeated one. The couple goalkeeper-kicker changes at every turn. Thus, the game agents are the two goalkeepers and at least ten kickers. The complexity of the game rises the necessity to identify a very affordable methodology of decomposition. Such a tool must allow to decompose a complex system in a sum of elementary games, preserving at the same time the intrinsic features of the primary game. For this reason, we propose the approach of the so-called Collectively Exhaustive and Mutually Exclusive (CEME) methodology [4, 5]. It allows to decompose in an affordable way this set of penalty shootouts alternately per team. They are elementary penalty shootouts, separately assessed. A complex situation can be organically modelled as a sum of elementary games in this way. AD also allows to selectively identify the critical situations diverting the real case from the theoretical model.

1.1 Big data and soccer

The building of a forecast model is the provision of accurate information about kickers, matches and tournaments. Compared to other American sports having a long history in the use of statistics, soccer has only shown an interest in this respect in the last few years [1]. There are several consulting firms providing accurate information on the market. Professional sport clubs widely rely on these consultancies. Big data analyses are used in the transfer market not only for the aim of recruiting soccer players to pick, but also to set valid game strategies, when you face up to specific opponents.

* Corresponding author: f.rolli@unimarconi.it

1.1.1 Axiomatic decomposition of the game actions

In the era of digital communication, the information is readily available. Unfortunately, this information is to be interpreted and duly tied up by each single team. Every technical staff has his own way to use such information. They range from conventional approaches based on coach's personal experience, to more structured ones, such as in American sports. In these latter cases, the building of a strategy is defined by rational rules of game actions decomposition. In this paper, we will focus on the CEME axiomatic methodology so to decompose a set of extra time penalty shootouts into elementary actions, by which you can define winning strategies.

1.1.2 Building of a structured DataBase

AD decomposition methodology of game actions defines winning strategies on elementary basis actions. Such decomposition is aimed at the matches already played and the upcoming matches against the next opponents. Thus, building a structured DataBase is equivalent to digitize the activities of the technical area of a soccer team. Such a tool can be implemented as a multilevel database on HNCR (Holistic non-Conformity Reduction) based approach [6-10]. These types of DataBase make it possible to record soccer players' individual actions through the allocation of structured and unique elementary data. This can proactively identify the strengths or weaknesses of the opposing teams, by making analytical insights having an impact on the soccer player in the game dynamics. It is to exploit the experiences gained over the years with a lesson learned that can help us to define the game plans and the specific interpretations made by the examined soccer players. Such an abstraction allows us to put in place preventive game plans, specific for each opponent. One can set up in a more rational way, avoiding being caught from a tactical perspective. Moreover, the system must allow the cataloguing and registration of soccer players' technical data including their mental and physical condition.

2 The penalty shoot-out in the game theory

The penalty shoot-out is a classic example of non-cooperative game between two zero-sum agents [11]. This means that kicker and goalkeeper do not cooperate with each other, but each of the two players pursues divergent objectives. Kicker's gain represents goalkeeper's loss and vice versa.

2.1 Premise

The rules of the game are very clear. The kicker places the ball on a stationary point in the penalty area which is 11 feet from the goal line. The goal door is 2,44 feet high and 7,32 feet wide. The goalkeeper stands still in the centre of the goal door. The kicker can in a simplified manner kick right, left or centre (R, L, C). Similarly, as for the kicker there is only three strategies a goalkeeper has, diving to the left, right or stand in the centre (R, L, C) [12]. For the sake of simplicity, we always mention the goalkeeper as a reference. Therefore, kicking left-side always means kicking to the goalkeeper left-side. The ball takes about 0.3 seconds to hit the back of the net. That means the goalkeeper cannot decide which strategy adopting after the player has kicked, because afterwards it will be too late. For this reason, both goalkeeper and kicker's strategies are independent. In this paper, the outline of a penalty kick, as defined by Chiappori *et alii* [13], acts as a model. Based on this model the penalty shoot-out can be represented by the matrix of Table 1. It is assumed that the kicker always hit the target.

Table 1. Payoff matrix

	Goalkeeper		
Kicker	**L**	**C**	**R**
L	P_L	π_L	π_L
C	π	0	π
R	π_R	π_R	P_R

P_L is the probability that the kicker might score, by kicking left, while the goalkeeper is diving in the same direction;
π_L is the probability that the kicker might score, by kicking left, while the goalkeeper stands still in the centre or dives to the right;
π is the probability that the kicker might score, by kicking centre, while the goalkeeper dives to the kicker's left or right;
π_R is the probability that the kicker might score, by kicking right, while the goalkeeper dives in the opposite direction or stands in the centre;
P_R is the probability that the kicker might score, by kicking right, while the goalkeeper dives in the same direction.
Mixed strategy is the game where at each single action of the kicker (L, C, R), does not correspond a certain (deterministic) action of the goalkeeper. This depends on the perfect coincidence in time of both goalkeeper and kicker's actions. Therefore, mixed strategies shall consist of a probability distribution among several possible strategies (P_L, π_L, π, 0, π_R, P_R) [12, 13].

2.2 Equilibrium conditions

The game is in equilibrium when all players have adopted a well combination of those strategies that none of them could be able to gain by changing their own strategy. The minimax (or maximin) theorem states that every game ended up in a constant sum between two agents, holds at least a minimax equilibrium point in pure or mixed strategies [13]. This means that each game ended up constant sum, admits a winning strategy. The existence of an equilibrium condition of this type would be true also for a generic game with *n* players. This result derives from Nash's theorem [14]. We can consider this last theorem as the generalisation of a *n* player in the minimax theorem [13]. In the specific case of the penalty shoot-out, the consequences of the minimax theorem (this is equivalent to the 2-players Nash's theorem) are the following [12]:

1. Each player has the same probability of success in case he has chosen one of the three possible strategies (L, C, R);
2. Each single player's choices must be independent. There cannot be any relationship with other choices made earlier.

This means that the minimax equilibrium condition (Nash's equivalent) consists of carrying out a completely random strategy [11-13].

2.3 Typologies of equilibrium

The game model proposed by Chiappori *et alii* [13] considers that soccer players may choose two different shooting techniques.

2.3.1 Restricted randomization equilibrium

Some kickers have a strong preference to kick penalty shootouts exclusively to the right or to the left of the opposing goalkeeper, avoiding shooting to the centre of the goal door. This case is about restricted randomization equilibrium (RR). It is characterized by very small values of π, meaning that the probability of the player shooting to the centre is zero or negligibly small. In this case, Nash's equilibrium condition reflects the fact that the player has the same probability of success kicking right or left.

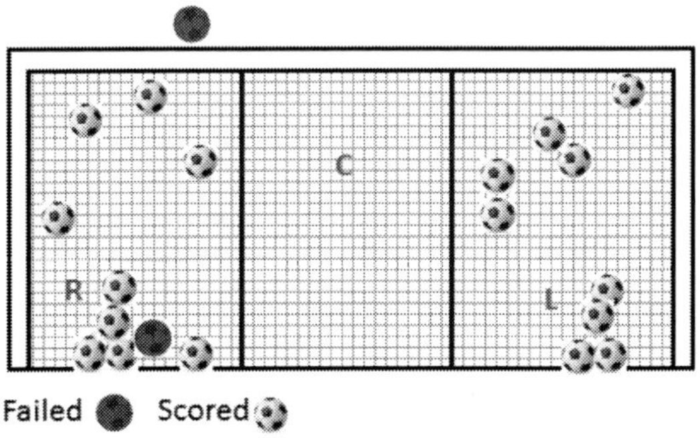

Fig. 1. Arturo Vidal's penalty shoot-out behavior. Source: The Wall Street Journal (2014)

2.3.2 General randomization equilibrium

Other players kick penalty shootouts in the three directions interchangeably. In this case is about randomization equilibrium (GR) and Nash's equilibrium condition corresponds to the fact that the player has the same probability of success to kick to the goalkeeper's right, centre or left.

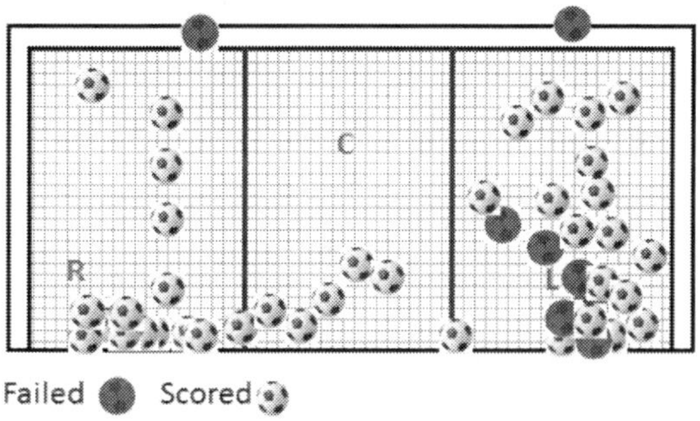

Fig. 2. Lionel Messi's penalty shoot-out behavior. Source: The Wall Street Journal (2014)

3 Interpretation of the penalty shoot-out in terms of AD

Penalty shoot-out decomposition into elementary strategies can occur in terms of Axiomatic Design according to two different but complementary points of view. We can consider kicker's perspective who wants to maximize his gain by scoring a goal. We can also side with the goalkeeper in the same way to minimise kicker's actions. Both players strategies are independent. They may be represented as two autonomous and complementary decompositions. Naturally, both decompositions are self-consistent, while representing two different perspectives. In the interests of simplification we consider only those players having a GR-type shooting behavior so far.

3.1 Penalty taker strategies in general randomization equilibrium (GR)

First up the application of the CEME methodology from the more general situation of the penalty shootouts (GR). The penalty taker kicks indifferently left, right or centre of the goal door. His only aim in front of the goalkeeper is to score the goal. In this case the functional requirement of more abstract level (FRa0) is: Maximize penalty shoot-out. Such a functional requirement can be met through kicker's strategy (DPa0). At this point, we can decompose FRa0 into three functional requirements of inferior level:

- Score goal on goalkeeper's left-side (FRa1);
- Score goal in the centre (FRa2);
- Score goal on the right (FRa3).

These three functional requirements can be met in an exclusive manner from the following three strategies:

- Kick on goalkeeper's left (DPa1);
- Kick in the centre of the goal door (DPa2);
- Kick on the left (DPa3).

Based on this model the penalty taker strategies can be represented by the matrix of Table 2.

Table 2. Penalty taker strategies in general randomization equilibrium

General randomization equilibrium				
	Possible strategies	**Penalty taker kicks left**	**Penalty taker kicks centre**	**Penalty taker kicks right**
Maximize the penalty shoot-out	**Score a goal on the left**	a_{11}		
	Score a goal in the centre		a_{22}	
	Score a goal on the right			a_{33}

We will be able to carry on our analysis to a more elementary level by introducing a successive decomposition. We could split the three detected shooting areas into three next sub-areas: low, medium and high. Such sectors would correspond to the level, medium and high-shots. By the way, for our essay this is not relevant.

3.2 Predicting goal-scoring in Nash's equilibrium

The three strategies referred to in the previous paragraph are *Collectively Exhaustive and Mutually Exclusive* (CEME). This guarantees the Independence Axiom is met. Furthermore, through Table 1 it is possible to measure each single scoring modality. Let us indicate with a_{11} the probability to score a goal left. Similarly, a_{22} is the probability to score a goal in the centre, while a_{33} is the probability to score a goal right. Let us consider g_L as the goalkeeper's probability to dive to the left, and g_C as the goalkeeper's probability to stand still in the centre. This way, goalkeeper's probability to dive himself to his right will be 1- g_L - g_C. Considering values in Table 1 there will be [12, 13]:

$a_{11}= g_L P_L + g_C \pi_L+\pi_L (1- g_L - g_C) = g_L P_L+\pi_L (1- g_L)$ (1);
$a_{22}= g_L \pi+g_C 0+\pi (1- g_L - g_C) = \pi (1 - g_C)$ (2);
$a_{33}= g_L \pi_L+g_C \pi_R+P_R (1- g_L - g_C)$ (3).

3.3 Goalkeeper strategies in general randomization equilibrium (GR)

Goalkeeper's duty is neutralizing the penalty shoot-out. In this case the functional requirement of more abstract level (FR_{b0}) is: Minimize the penalty shoot-out. Such functional requirement can be met through goalkeeper's strategy (DP_{b0}). At this point, we can decompose FR_{b0} into three lower level functional requirements: Catch left (FR_{b1}), Catch centre (FR_{b2}) and Catch right (FR_{b3}). These three functional requirements may be exclusively met by the following three strategies: Goalkeeper dives to the left (DP_{b1}), Goalkeeper stands still in the centre (DP_{b2}), Goalkeeper dives to the right (DP_{b3}). Based on this model the goalkeeper strategies can be represented by the matrix of Table 3. However, similarly as described in paragraph 3.1, Table 1 allows each catching technique to be measured.

Table 3. Goalkeeper strategies in general randomization equilibrium

General randomization equilibrium				
	Possible strategies	**Goalkeeper dives to the left**	**Goalkeeper stands still in the centre**	**Goalkeeper dives to the right**
Minimize the penalty shoot-out	**Catch left**	b_{11}		
	Catch centre		b_{22}	
	Catch right			b_{33}

3.4 Considerations around the Information Axiom

The application of Information Axiom leads us to a very active subject in game theory. In case of a pure and zero-sum game strategy, the Information Axiom would lead us selecting a robust solution. That solution would have corresponded to the equilibrium point of the minimax theorem for that game. Unfortunately, the penalty shoot-out is a zero-sum game but with a mixed strategy. The most valid game behavior is the random one for which all available strategies are valid [11-13]. So, this means that, a robust strategy does not exist, but an equilibrium situation that meets the Minimax theorem does. In other words, it has been shown that in volume and for professional soccer players, the averages of (P_L, π_L, π, 0, π_R, P_R) tend to converge towards fixed and steady values [12, 13, 15]. This means that in general randomization equilibrium conditions, the result is $a_{11}=a_{22}=a_{33}$. However, in conditions of restricted randomization the result is $a_{11}=a_{33}$ with $a_{22}=0$. On the contrary, goalkeepers have a constant behavior [13]. For this reason, in Nash's equilibrium conditions the result is $b_{11}=b_{22}=b_{33}$. On the contrary, in situations of relevant physical and mental stress each single player can have significant deviations from the medium values foreseen by the minimax theorem [12, 16]. Palacios Huerta [12] stated that, on a sample of 1417 penalty shootout kicked in the period September 1995 – June 2000 in the most important European championships, the scoring probability decreases as the game time increases. This means that kicker's behavior has the tendency to diverge from the standard model foreseen by the minimax theorem when some stress prevails.

	LL	LC	LR	CL	CC	CR	RL	RC	RR	All penalties
Scored penalties	16	2	17	10	0	9	12	6	7	79
Failed penalties	13	0	0	1	0	0	1	0	8	23
All penalties	29	2	17	11	0	9	13	6	15	102
Scoring rate Lionel Messi	55,17%	100%	100%	90,91%	0%	100%	92,31%	100%	46,67%	77,45%

Table 4. Lionel Messi's penalty shoot-out distribution

In these conditions, soccer players are lead to kick badly or being much more predictable by goalkeeper. During penalty shootouts in extra time such deviation is often even more marked. Thus, it often occurs that top players, used to kick penalty shootouts, fail them in these very particular situations. So, physical and mental stress induces soccer players to leave the standard random model towards specific behavior preferences [12, 16]. In other words, such that $a_{11} \neq a_{22} \neq a_{33}$ (similarly for the goalkeeper such that $b_{11} \neq b_{22} \neq b_{33}$). Later, in our essay, we will see what, despite everything, even with these deviations, we can build a useful forecasting model so to define a winning strategy in case of penalty shootouts in extra time.

3.5 How Hannes Halldorsson succeeded in catching Lionel Messi's penalty shoot-out

The recent 2018 World Cup Russia can be used as a lab for penalty shootouts. As such, it is a basis for studying mathematical models of real situations. Let us take as a case study the Argentinian champion Lionel Messi's shoot-out which has been so ably caught by the Icelandic goalkeeper Halldorsson. Lionel Messi has been the greatest soccer player, together with Cristiano Ronaldo for a decade. Messi has all the qualities to be considered as an ideal penalty kicker from a mathematical point of view. He is a very precise and strong left-footed player.
He has a fierce concentration and when kicking a shoot-out, he does not pay any attention both to the stadium crowd and to the opponent goalkeeper smirks. He looks deep in thought. We will notice, however that he does not have a high scoring average. In situations of relevant physical and mental stress he tends to have a scoring behavior in favour of Nash non-equilibrium solutions.

3.5.1 Lionel Messi's real shooting behavior in penalty shootouts

The website *https://www.transfermarkt.com* quotes 102 penalty shootouts kicked by Messi in official matches. The observation period goes from 2005 to the recent 2018 FIFA World Cup in Russia. Such a statistic basically includes almost the whole period where the Argentine soccer champion played like a pro. Every single shootout has been re-analyzed thanks to the videos available on the net. Observations were used as means of data collection. Data have been reported in Table 4 according to the approach followed by Palacios-Huerta [12]. Instead, referring to the already mentioned model by Chiappori *et alii* [13], we could make out 9 shooting strategies, as illustrated in Table 1. For example, by the abbreviation LL (Left-Left) we represent the shooting situation to goalkeeper's left who jumps in turn to his left. On the contrary, the abbreviation RL (Right-Left) indicates the shooting situation to goalkeeper's right who jumps in turn to the opposite side. Thus, the first letter means the shooting side of the penalty taker and the second one means the goalkeeper diving direction (L-Left, C-Center, R-Right). As for Lionel Messi there is a distribution of shootouts in official matches as stated in Table 4. Apart from the shooting strategy the table also shows if the shootout has been successful.

3.5.2 Empirical analysis of Lionel Messi's shooting strategies

Table 4 data suggests us that Messi tends to fail shootouts when kicking to the opponent goalkeeper 's right instead of the opposite direction. If, in addition, we use Figure 2, we can observe that the distribution shootouts kicked by Messi until 2014 is not completely standard on the whole door surface. Thus, we can glimpse some shooting strategies:

• S1. First shooting choice is represented by the opponent goalkeeper's left-side. This behavior is normal, since for a left-footed kicker comes easier kicking to the goalkeeper 's left side.
• S2. If you still observe Figure 2 you might notice that, when Messi kicks to the goalkeeper's right, he prefers kicking towards a very narrow door zone, halfway between the door center and the right goalpost. It is a door area where the goalkeeper can catch easier.

In these two areas is concentrated the almost total failed shootouts by Messi (Fig. 3).

3.5.3 Axiomatic interpretation of a failed shoot-out

From a theoretical point of view, Messi kicks his shootouts using the GR model. Thus, in Nash equilibrium conditions, in other words, in normal physical and mental conditions he can kick right, left or centre confounding the goalkeeper. However, the peculiar distribution of failed shootouts in the two above mentioned favorite areas will suggest us something else. Probably, Messi's shooting behavior goes from a General Randomization Equilibrium (GR)-type to a Restricted Randomization (RR without equilibrium) in conditions of physical and mental stress. Thus, in this new configuration the result is that $a_{11} > a_{33}$, on the contrary a_{22}=0. This means that the probability to score a goal on the goalkeeper's left side is higher than scoring a goal on the opposite side. Indeed, the fact that the second preference area (S2) is pretty narrow and easily reachable by the goalkeeper increases Messi's probability to fail a shootout kicked to his right side. Such behavior is more visible in Messi's shootouts kicked after 2014. Hannes Halldorsson has chosen the best strategy with the higher rate of success after all, by diving to his right side towards S2 area. Fortune gave him a great reward. Halldorsson has adopted a pure strategy. He is a professional filmmaker. Probably, before the game he will have seen many movies on the penalties taken by Messi. Instead, Lionel Messi disregarded the characteristics of the Icelandic goalkeeper. He adopted a mixed strategy, deciding the side of the shot at the time of the penalty kick. Perhaps, the psychological tension of the moment led him to adopt a solution that conforms to a RR without equilibrium behavior. Most likely, also the chaos in the Argentine team at the recent 2018 FIFA World Cup Russia charged Lionel Messi of excessive responsibilities. Such a situation might have had a heavy psychic burden and have contributed to redirect Messi's shooting behavior from a General Randomization Equilibrium-type (GR) to a Restricted Randomization without equilibrium one (RR without equilibrium).

3.5.4 Numerical verification of hypothesis of deviation from Messi's shooting behavior to Restricted Randomization without equilibrium

Starting from the premises of the previous paragraph, we can verify if the hypothesis of deviation from Messi's shooting behavior from GR to RR without equilibrium is also supported by numerical data. Such verification is possible by using equations 1, 2 and 3 described in § 3.2 and by data gathered in table 4 RR without equilibrium condition means the same as:

• Messi can kick to goalkeeper's right or left-side only. In other words, this means that: g_C= 0 and π=0;

• Probability to score goalkeeper's left-side differs from the one to score to his right. This means that the result is: $a_{11} \neq a_{33}$.

Furthermore, using test data produced by Palacios Huerta [12] we can put g_L = 0,4231 where g_L represents goalkeeper's probability to dive to the left. Instead, from Table 4 data we can set:

• P_R =RR(Scoring rate Messi)= 0,4667;

• P_L =LL(Scoring rate Messi)= 0,5517;

• π_L=LR(Scoring rate Messi)=1.

Under these conditions equations 1, 2 and 3 at § 3.2 become:

1. a_{11} =(0,4231*0,5517)+(0,5769*1)= 0,81032;
2. a_{22}= 0;
3. a_{33}= 0,4231*1+(0,4667*0,5769)= 0,69234.

That would mean that $a_{11} > a_{33}$

Thus, numerical data coming from the 102 shootouts' observation kicked by Lionel Messi (Fig.3) confirm the hypothesis of deviation from Messi's shooting behavior from GR to RR without equilibrium due to physical and mental stress. However, this hypothesis is a simple abstraction based primarily on a visual observation of the areas of Messi's shooting preferences (Fig.2). In this paragraph we have only verified that the proposed model is logically consistent with the numerical data of Table 4. This does not mean that it can completely and definitively define the player's behavior. Messi could also change shooting behavior. Therefore, this model can be understood only as an attempt to simplify the representation of a very complex behavior.

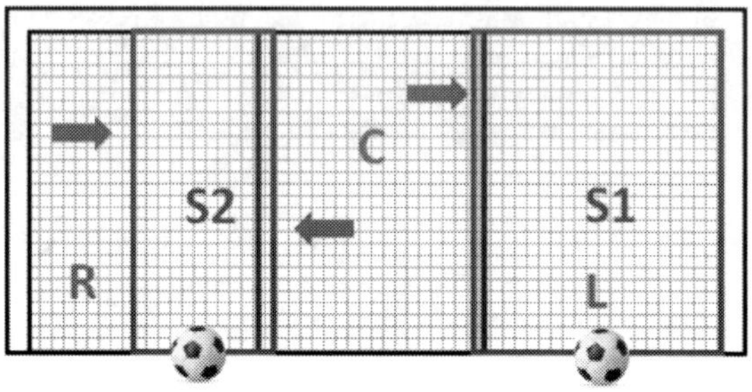

Fig. 3. Graphical representation of Lionel Messi's shooting areas under stress conditions (S1, P2)

4 AD CEME methodology application to the penalty shootouts in ideal conditions

The aim of each soccer team is scoring at least one additional goal than his opposing team. This objective is the first level functional requirement (FR0). Thus, each team seeks to maximize his own gain. This would mean scoring as many goals as possible. Equivalently, the same team tries to minimize his own loss. This would mean to adopt a strategy which allows his own goalkeeper to catch as many opposing kicker's shootouts as possible. This work uses the CEME methodology based on the functional metrics (FMs) and the parent-child equations for guiding the decomposition of a design for winning games [4, 5]. The hypothesis is that controlling appropriate FMs can increase the likelihood that a team can outscore their opponent [4].

4.1 Decomposition methodology

The penalty shootouts sequence in extra time consists of a series of simple and linear actions. In theoretical and ideal conditions there is no correlation among subsequent actions. In such conditions, every event is independent from the previous ones. These features allow to schematize the entire process through the building of a theoretical model, for which each single action is axiomatically independent from the previous one. Such hypothesis let us easily decompose the entire process into elementary actions in accordance with the AD methodology CEME-type. Every elementary action can be easily traced back to the penalty shoot-out case already dealt with in §3.

4.1.1 First level decomposition

At this point, first level functional requirement (FR_0) can be likely decomposed into two second level functional requirements, in accordance with the AD methodology with CEME approach [2, 3].

- FM_0: - Score = Σ (Scored shootouts) – Σ (Scored shootouts by opponents) -;
- FR_0: - Maximize score -;
- DP0: - Game strategy -;
- FM_1: - Σ (Scored shootouts) = Σ (Kicked shootouts) – Σ (Failed shootouts) -;
- FR_1: - Maximize Σ (Scored shootouts) = Minimize Σ (Failed shootouts) -;
- DP_1: - Kickers strategy -;
- FM_2: - Σ (Scored shootouts by opponents) = Σ (Shootouts kicked by opponents) - Σ (Failed shootouts by opponents) -;
- FR_2: - Minimize Σ (Scored shootouts by opponents) = Maximize Σ (Failed shootouts by opponents) -;
- DP_2: - Goalkeeper strategy -.

4.1.2 Methodological considerations

The two derived functional requirements (FR_1) e (FR_2) are collectively exhaustive because they include all FR_0 specifications. Furthermore, the same requirements are also mutually foreclosing as they do not have any element in common. Table 5 also shows that the Independent Axiom is met. However, the the greatest theoretical contribution of the proposed approach is representing a MiniMax problem through a smooth CEME decomposition. This is possible due to the axiomatic nature of both methodologies. For this reason, it was decided to proceed to the game actions decomposition resorting to their own use terminologies in game theory, so to underline the equivalence at every level of the two approaches.

Table 5. First level decomposition of penalty shootouts

		Game strategy (DP0)	
		Penalty takers strategy (DP1)	Goalkeeper strategy (DP2)
Maximize score (FR0)	Minimize Σ (Failed shootouts) (FR1)	X	
	Maximize Σ (Failed shootouts by opponents) (FR2)		X

4.2 Second level decomposition

FR1 can be decomposed into 5 penalty shootouts at the disposal of X team. To each penalty shoot-out we must associate an Xi kicker and the GY opposing goalkeeper. A specified shooting strategy will be linked to a penalty shoot-out. Every strategy depends on both Xi and GY features. Similarly, FR2 can be decomposed into 5 penalty shootouts kicked by the opposing team (Y). In this case i-th functional requirement consists of maximizing GX goalkeeper's action. He must try to let the opposing kickers (Yi) fail the penalty shoot-out. Both teams rotate in the penalty shootouts until both have kicked 5 each. However, if a team scored more shootouts than the other one and the latter is a tough act to follow, even scoring the remaining penalty shootouts, the match will end earlier. If, at the end of the ten penalty shootouts both teams have scored an equal number of goals, the match will go into sudden-death. It takes place then a shoot-out on each side until, after having kicked the same number of shootouts, a team will have an advantage over the other.

- FM_{1i}: - Pr (Fail i-th shoot-out by X_i kicker) -;
- FR_{1i}: - Score a goal by X_i kicker and GY goalkeeper -;
- DP_{1i}: - i-th shooting strategy by X_i kicker -;
- FM_{2i}: - Pr (Catch i-th shoot-out to Y_i kicker) -;
- FR_{21}: - Catch i-th penalty shoot-out to Y_i kicker -;
- DP_{21}: - Catch i-th penalty shoot-out strategy to the Y_i kicker -.

Considering the only sequence of 5 shootouts per team we get the decomposition of Table 6.

Table 6. Second level decomposition of penalty shootouts

			Game strategy (DP0)									
			Xi penalty takers strategy					GX goalkeeper strategy				
			DP11	DP12	DP13	DP14	DP15	DP21	DP22	DP23	DP24	DP25
Maximize score (FR0)	Minimize Σ (Failed shootouts) (FR1)	FR11	X									
		FR12		X								
		FR13			X							
		FR14				X						
		FR15					X					
	Maximize Σ (Failed shootouts by opponents) (FR2))	FR21						X				
		FR22							X			
		FR23								X		
		FR24									X	
		FR25										X

This decomposition meets the Axiom of Independence. The strategies adopted by the two teams are axiomatically independent. Players carry out independent choices, not affected by the influence of the previous actions.

4.3 Third level decomposition

It is possible to proceed to a successive axiomatic decomposition. The semplification referred to in paragraph 3 will let us state that a kicker has three shooting possibilities in general randomization equilibrium conditions instead of 2 as in restricted randomization. On the other hand, the goalkeeper can dive to his right, stand still in the centre or dive to his left. Furthermore, it is proved that kicker and goalkeeper's actions are statistically independent. [12, 13]. This scenario allows us to decompose each second level functional requirement into further lower level ones. For simplicity reasons, in the next paragraphs only players with a GR-type shooting behaviour will be considered.

4.3.1 Third level decomposition from kickers side

About X_i kicker's actions there are three possible shooting choices (L, C, R). Each single choice is associated a specific probability to score a goal. The associated probability triad (a_{11}, a_{22}, a_{33}) has already been estimated in paragraph 3.1. In valid conditions of Nash's equilibrium, the three probabilities are equal. However, in situations where physical and mental stress increases, after 120 minutes of game, some deviations from the standard behavior may arise. However, in ideal conditions or in case of low level of stress, CEME decomposition can be developed as follows for the X_i player:

• $FM1_{iL}$: - X_i kicker's probability to score a goal to GY goalkeeper's left: a_{11L} -;
• FR_{1iL}: - Score a goal to the left -;
• DP_{1iL}: - Choice kicking to the left -;
• FM_{1iC}: - X_i kicker's probability to score a goal in the centre of the goal door: a_{11C} -;
• FR_{1iC}: - Score a goal in the centre -;
• DP_{1iC}: - Choice kicking to the centre -;
• FM_{1iC}: - Probability for kicker X_i to score a goal with a shot to GY goalkeeper's right: a_{11R} -;
• FR_{1iC}: - Score a goal in the right -;
• DP_{1iC}: - Choice kicking to the right -.

4.3.2 Third level decomposition from goalkeeper side

GX goalkeeper strategy is also made up of three possible choices (L, C, R). The decomposition that has been introduced considers the overall probabilities to catch or make the opposing kicker fail. This triad of probabilities (b_{11}, b_{22}, b_{33}) has already been defined mathematically in paragraph 3.2. Ultimately, for each Y_i opposing player, with i=1…5 we can have an estimation of the triad (b_{2iL}, b_{2iC}, b_{2iR}). This estimation represents the probability distribution for GX goalkeeper to catch a penalty shoot-out to the Y_i kicker. Furthermore, for each couple of professional soccer players (GX and Y_i), the specific triads aim to standard values which are representative of Nash's conditions equilibrium theorem. However, in conditions of strong physical and mental stress one can have deviations from the standard behavior. Therefore, shooting or goalkeeper's dive preferences may be observed. The statistics analysis of these preferences allows us to estimate the triad values (b_{2iL}, b_{2iC}, b_{2iR}) by the end of extra time. Usually, deviations from standard behavior are more common in the penalty takers.

Such considerations lead us to the following decomposition.

• FM_{2iL}: - GX goalkeeper's probability to catch Y_i kicker's shot, by diving to his left: b_{2iL} -;
• FR_{2iL}: - Catch a shot to his own left -;
• DP_{2iL}: - Choice to dive left -;
• FM_{2iC}: - GX goalkeeper's probability to catch a goal by Yi kicker, standing still in the centre: b_{2iC} -;
• FR_{2iC}: - Catch in the centre -;
• DP_{2iC}: - Choice to stand still in the centre of the goal door -;
• $FM2_{iC}$: - GX goalkeeper's probability to catch a goal by Yi kicker, diving to his own right: b_{2iR} -;
• FR_{2iC}: - Catch a goal at his own right -;
• DP_{2iC}: - Choice to dive to the right -.

It is clear that the Independence Axiom is met. The overall matrix is diagonal.

5 AD CEME methodology application to the penalty shootouts in real cases

In real cases penalty shootouts are influenced by different variables. Not only physical and mental stress can make diverge kickers' behavior from the standard model previously described. However, the same shooting order can give an advantge to the team scoring first [12, 17]. Also, when you know the shooting behavior of those kickers often take penalty shootouts, we could not have any information about the other opposing kicker's behavior. In this case, the model previously defined might be insufficient for a reliable prediction. Thus, the definition of an overall shooting strategy could be inadequate.

5.1 The penalty shoot-out game under incomplete information

The necessary information is not always available to define the shooting behavior of a designated penalty taker. Some players rarely kick the penalty shootouts. For example, by quoting Chiappori's model, this means that there are situations where the goalkeeper ignores if the opposing kicker will adopt GR-type or RR-type strategies. It also means that Nash's equilibrium conditions are not met. The goalkeeper does not know the payoff matrix values associated to the game. Thus, it is not possibile to define solutions in Nash's equilibrium conditions. However, we can turn an incomplete information game into a game of imperfect information [18, 19]. At the same time, we can find an equilibrium state of the derived game. It is the so-called Bayes's equilibrium. This new equilibrium situation allows us to arise strategies both for kickers and goalkeeper as already done with Nash's equilibrium.

5.2 Axiomatic decomposition of a penalty shoot-out in Bayesian equilibrium

If reapplying the criteria of CEME-type AD methodology the decomposition can be represented by Table 7. A_{iiRR} and a_{iiGR} rules of derivation are the same stated in the previous paragraphs. However, equilibrium solutions have completely changed because they are functions of ϑ, which represents goalkeeper's probability to face a RR-type kicker [18].

Table 7. Decomposition in Bayesian equilibrium

		Penalty takers strategies				
	Possible strategies	RR penalty taker kicks left	RR penalty taker kicksl right	GR penalty taker kicks left	GR penalty taker kicks centre	GR penalty taker kicks right
Maximize penalty shoot-out in RR ϑ	Score a goal left	a_{11RR}				
	Score a goal right		a_{22RR}			
Maximize penalty shoot-out in GR (1-ϑ)	Score a goal left			a_{11GR}		
	Score a goal centre				a_{22GR}	
	Score a goal right					a_{33GR}

Differently from previous situations in Nash's equilibrium, Coloma [18] has already shown that in Bayesian equilibrium:

• Players of both game typologies have a higher probability of success than in Nash's equilibrium conditions;

• Goalkeeper, instead, has a much lower probability of intercepting the goal.

This theoretical result is in line with the empirical evidence that, during penalty shootouts, many penalty takers have failed. For them, goalkeepers are perfectly aware of their shooting behavior. Furthermore, before play-offs, coaches make kickers try shooting tests to simulate the opponents' behavior.

5.3 The impact of physical and mental stress in the penalty shootouts

Game theory suggests that both kicker and goalkeeper 's strategical choice they prefer is leave it to probability, putting the opponent in utter uncertainty regarding his own real intentions. A study conducted by Palacios Huerta [17] has demonstrated that professional soccer players adopt random strategies. The result is quite surprising because the idea has already been that psychological mechanisms anticipating his opponent's moves could play a greater role. It should be noted in this respect that soccer players' behavior is true in long-term observations and in normal physical and mental stress conditions. About the penalty shootouts in extra time the situation is much more complicated. In this case, you may observe clear deviations from the standard behavior [20-23].

5.4 Pursuit effect

Physical and mental stress may impair the strategy to be adopted. It was verified that who first starts kicking the penalty shootouts has a rate close to 60% to prevail over the opposing team [12, 17]. Kicking a penalty shoot-out first, entails a significant psychological advantage. The opposing penalty taker is obliged to "*pursuit*" [17]. For this reason, UEFA has been considering the reform on the penalty shootouts. The penalty shootouts sequence should change from alternate according to ABABABABAB sequence into the following ABBAABBAAB sequence shortly. This new rule should limit the pursuit phenomenon.

5.4.1 Axiomatic representation of the pursuit effect

Pursuit phenomena in the penalty shootouts can be modelled by means of Markov chains. In this case, the result of i-th kicker's penalty shoot-out will depend on j-th kicker opposing team's result, which immediately preceded it. However, it can also be formalized in terms of axiomatic decomposition. If we restrict our analysis to the second level decomposition it is easiest to see that, in the series of ABABABAB-type penalty shootouts, the team kicking first has an advantage over the opponents (Fig. 4). At least the first shoot-out is free from any influence. At this point, we are considering the following assumptions:

• There may be influences among successive penalty takers not belonging to the same team;

• There are no influences among successive penalty shootouts for kickers of the same team;

• The influences are limited at the very most to the immediately following shoot-out.

In this scenario, shootouts ABBAABBAA-type will have the same features of Figure 4, such as:

• No matter the team kicking first, the number of influences, detectable at most, is identical for both teams. In this specific case they are two;

• In terms of axiomatic decomposition the number of potential functional coupled requirements is reduced from four to two.

Both representations are not acceptable in terms of AD. This is obvious because such representations do not take account the variables leading to the deviation from the standard model. In real life, pursuit phenomenon could be considered in statistics methods on the basis of data acquired in DataBase HNCR-type. These methods would take into consideration the main physical and mental stress variables of each single kicker under stress conditions. There would be a new functional decomposition also including these new variables, in this way. So, the decomposition would return to be decoupled.

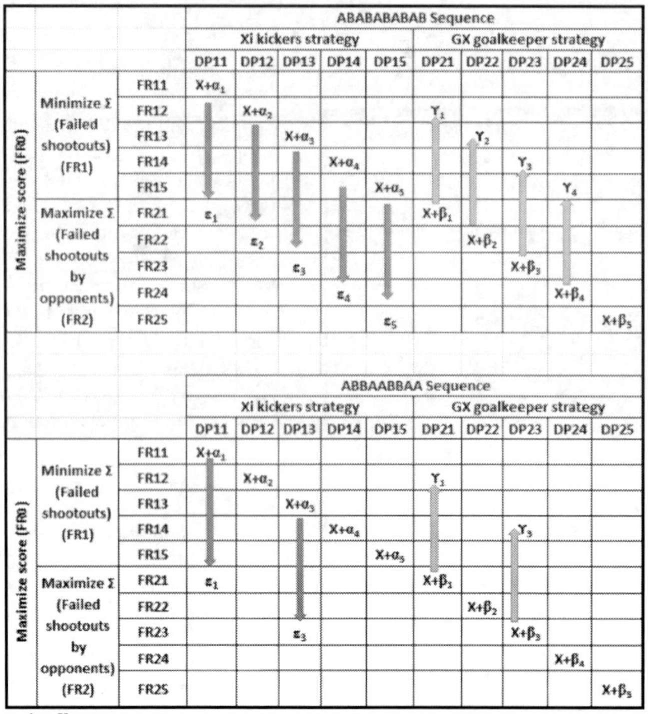

Fig. 4. Pursuit effect

5.4.2 Functional decoupling

Previous paragraph has pointed out that in real game conditions several factors need to be taken into account. The main effect of these factors is to diverge the shooting behavior from the standard model. The design matrix is coupled. So that the game representation could not meet the Independence Axiom. In order to overcome this obstacle one has two possibilities:

• Make sure constraints on shooting strategies among opposing kickers are null;
• Estimate the deviations from the standard behavior of soccer players through detailed observations, tests and finally report the statistics in a HCRN-type DataBase.

Situation 1 would be worthy, but in conditions of real game is difficult to guarantee it. Situation 2, instead, may be simulated during the match preparation phase. Necessary data can be acquired by specific consultancies and during trainings by monitoring soccer players' physical and mental condition. At this stage, regression functions, allow us to start an estimation of the parameters of our interest. On the basis of these estimates is possible to build accurate models simulating soccer players' behavior during particular physical and mental stress conditions. At § 3.5 we have defined Lionel Messi's behavior model under physical and mental constraint in this regard. Such deduction has been made possible due to a great volume of easily accessible data about the Argentinian top player. This way, we may decouple the model variables, by asserting the Independence Axiom. Figure 5 in the attached page shows this kind of decomposition for a series of 2 ABAB-type alternate penalty shootouts.

5.4.3 Typing

The conducted functional decoupling, as stated in the previous paragraphs, is reflected in the definition of a finite series of predefined behavior types for penalty takers. This means that in a worst-case scenario the goalkeeper could ignore which shooting behavior the opposing kicker will have. Therefore, also in this case, we turn a complex game with incomplete information into a set of simpler games with imperfect information. So, it is possible to identify some game strategies in Bayesian equilibrium. In fact, this situation is the generalization of a specific case concerning the comparison between a goalkeeper and a kicker, whom kicker's shooting behavior is not clear if it is a RR-type or a GR-type.

5.4.4 Definition of an axiomatic model by Lionel Messi's shootouts in penalties

Theoretical definitions of the previous paragraphs allow us to define a mathematical model simulating the real shooting behavior by Lionel Messi during penalties shootouts. Let us premise, however, that for simplicity we have neglected the functional decoupling of the pursuit effect. The purpose of this discussion is to try to build a realistic model of Lionel Messi's shooting behavior simulation. This will happen by putting together his two main behaviors. As already described in § 3.5, Messi behaves a GR-type shooting way in normal physical and mental conditions. However, during situations of particular stress, he tends to divert his

* Corresponding author: f.rolli@unimarconi.it

behavior into a Nash's non-equilibrium RR-type shooting model. Thus, shooting preferences of the last model show different success rate. Starting from these two divergent behaviors we can set a mathematical model which includes both cases. The overall model can be built up by using once again the Bayesian equilibrium theory. In this case, at the moment of penalty shootouts in extra time, we can assign a probability β when Messi is under stressed conditions. This will lead us to state that by probability β his shooting behavior will be Nash's non-equilibrium RR-type. On the contrary, by probability $(1- \beta)$ when his mental and physical conditions seem to be normal. Watching some videos, you might state that in normal conditions Messi is not influenced by any external events. He is blessed by an amazing concentration. In this case the pursuit effect of penalty shootouts is practically nil for him. On the contrary, we might suppose that under particular stress conditions, besides the deviation from the standard behavior, the player may be leant on by the consequences of the pursuit phenomenon. Regarding Messi, this phenomenon can be defined with the introduction of the disruption ε into Nash's non-equilibrium RR model. ε disruption may accentuate the distortion of such model, by restricting Messi's preferred shooting S1 or S2 areas (§ 3.5.3). This means that the pursuit effect can increase the asymmetry between S1 and S2. Such situation could make the opponent goalkeeper's intervention easier. Table 8 illustrates the overall model by Lionel Messi' penalty shootouts in extra time.

Table 8. Lionel Messi strategies in penalty shoot-outs

		Lionel Messi strategies				
	Possible strategies	Messi kicks left	Messi kicks right	Messi kicks left	Messi kicks centre	Messi kicks right
Maximize penalty shoot-out in RR β	Score a goal left	$a_{11MRR}-\varepsilon$				
	Score a goal right		$a_{22MRR}+\varepsilon$			
Maximize penalty shoot-out in GR $(1-\beta)$	Score a goal left			a_{11MGR}		
	Score a goal centre				a_{22MGR}	
	Score a goal right					a_{33MGR}

5.5 Utility

Kickers shooting modalities's typing in conditions of physical and mental stress allow us to define a powerful mechanism of penalty shootouts simulation. This mechanism is dynamic. It can be used to prepare for an identification algorithm of the penalty shootouts takers. It can also make it possible to determine the order by which the penalty takers must show by the opposing goalkeeper. It is then possible to simulate the probable opponents' shooting order with the axiomatic decomposition mechanism. Therefore, a series of soccer players minimizing the pursuit effect could be drawn. As regards goalkeeper, his thorough knowledge of the opponents behaviors, gives him a considerable advantage. Indeed, for a few years now, professional clubs have access to data, statistics and simulations made available by specific consultancies. In this respect, during the 2016 European Championship the German national team made use of shootouts simulations created by a famous IT company. Such simulations were developed by means of an accurate Big Data analysis in soccer. As a result, the German national team finally beated the Italian national team in shootouts. An extraordinary event given that the Italian team always historically predominated in the official matches between the two teams. However, the final victory of the match will get to the Portuguese national team.

6 Conclusions

Game theory is difficult to apply in particularly complex contexts. CEME methodology provides a powerful modeling tool. This derives from the common axiomatic basis of the two analytical approaches. For this reason, we can say that the main benefit that CEME can provide to Game Theory is to facilitate the decomposition of a complex zero-sum game into further elementary games, by preserving at the same time the intrinsic features of the primary one. This contributes to represent a minimax problem into a simple axiomatic decomposition of elementary actions. Thus, Independence Axiom allows to decrease the elementary actions into a minimum set exhaustively representing the whole game. Each single elementary action so decomposed is mutually independent from the others. Therefore, it is possible to act on every one of them, by modifying the related strategy. However, the Information Axiom application leads us to identify the strategies in Nash's equilibrium, if the game is with incomplete information or with solutions in Bayesian equilibrium. Both equilibrium typologies allow us to associate to each specific elementary action a measure which represents the probability of success for whom shall put it in place. This way, we can predefine a management of penalty shootouts in extra time during play-offs which allows us to:

• Define an overall strategy of penalty takers selection;
• Put the same players in order, along a predefined sequence minimizing the pursuit effect. This way, players with deviations from minor standard behavior will be chosen to kick the penalty shoot-out after the first one kicked by the opposing team and for the last, big shot;
• Arrange for a goalkeeper's strategy based on well known features of opposing kickers' shootouts.

References

1. S. Kuper, S. Szymanski, *Soccernomics: Why England Loses, Why Spain, Germany, and*

Brazil Win, and Why the US, Japan, Australia - and Even Iraq - Are Destined to Become the Kings of the World's Most Popular Sport, Nation Books, (2014);

2. G. Arcidiacono, K. Yang, J. Trewn, L. Bucciarelli, *Application of Axiomatic Design for Project-Based Learning Methodology*, Procedia CIRP, Vol. 53, pp. 166-172, (2016) ;
3. G. Arcidiacono, D.T. Matt, E. Rauch, *Axiomatic Design of a Framework for the Comprehensive Optimization of Patient Flows in Hospitals*, Journal of Healthcare Engineering, Article number 2309265, (2017);
4. R. Henley, C.A. Brown, *Axiomatic Design Applied to Play Calling in American Soccer*, Proc. CIRP **53**, 206-212 (2016);
5. C.A. Brown, *Decomposition and Prioritization in Engineering Design,* Proceedings ICAD2011 (2011);
6. C. Cavallini, A. Giorgetti, P. Citti, A. Meneghin, *Sviluppo di un approccio olistico per l'analisi e la risoluzione delle non conformità,* AISS, **3**, 1 (2012);
7. F. Rolli, A. Giorgetti, P. Citti, *Integration of Holistic Non-Conformities Management and Axiomatic Design: a case study in Italian Income Tax Returns Management,* Proc. CIRP **34**, 256-262 (2015);
8. F. Rolli, A. Giorgetti, P. Citti, M. Rinaldi, *Improvement of the compilation process of the Italian income certifications: a methodology based on the evaluation of the information content (Part 1)*, Proc. CIRP **53**, 56-62 (2016);
9. A. Giorgetti, C. Cavallini, A. Ciappi, G. Arcidiacono and P. Citti, *A holistic model for the proactive reduction of non-conformities within new industrial technologies*, IJMERR, **6**, 4 (2017);
10. A. Giorgetti, G. Arcidiacono, A. Ciappi, R. Barbieri, and P. Citti, *HNCR model following robust approach*, QREI (2018);
11. J. Von Neumann, O. Morgenstern, *Theory of Games and Economic Behavior*, Princeton University Press, (1944);
12. I. Palacios-Huerta, *Professionals Play Minimax*, Review of Economic Studies **70**, 395-415 (2003);
13. PA. Chiappori, S. Levitt, Steven and T. Groseclose, *Testing Mixed-Strategy Equilibria when Players are Heterogeneous: The Case of Penalty Kicks in Soccer*, American Economic Review, **92**,1138-1151 (2002);
14. J. Nash, *Non-Cooperative Games*, Annals of Mathematics, **54**, pp 286-295 (1951);
15. G. Coloma, *Penalty Kicks in Soccer: An Alternative Methodology for Testing Mixed-Strategy Equilibria*, Journal of Sports Economics, **8**, 530-545, (2007);
16. G. Jordet, E. Hartman, C. Visscher & K. A. P. M. Lemmink, *Kicks from the penalty mark in soccer: The roles of stress, skill, and fatigue for kick outcomes*, Centre for Human Movement Sciences, University of Groningen, University Medical Centre, Groningen, The Netherlands Published online (2007);
17. I. Palacios-Huerta, *Beautiful Game Theory. How Soccer Can Help Economics*, Princeton University Press, (2016);
18. G. Coloma, *The Penalty-Kick Game under Incomplete Information*, Serie Documentos de Trabajo, Universidad del CEMA: Área: economía, **487**, (2012);
19. J. Harsanyi, *Games with Incomplete Information Played by Bayesian Players*, Management Science, **14**, 159-182, (1967);
20. W. Schwarz, *Compensating tendencies in penalty kick decisions of referees in professional football: Evidence from the German Bundesliga 1963–2006*, Journal of Sports Sciences, **29(5)**, 441–447, (2011);
21. N. Anbarci, S. Ching-Jen, M. Utku Unver, *Fair Tiebreak Mechanisms: The Case of FIFA Penalty Shootouts*, SSRN Electronic Journal, **1**, (2015);
22. T. P. Vandebroek, B.T. McCann, G. Vroom, *Modeling the Effects of Psychological Pressure on First-Mover Advantage in Competitive Interactions: The Case of Penalty Shoot-Outs*, Journal of Sports Economics, **19(5)**, 725-754, (2016);
23. M. Bar-Eli, O. Azar, I. Ritov, Y. Keidar-Levin, G. Schein, *Action Bias Among Elite Soccer Goalkeepers: The Case of Penalty Kicks*, Journal of Economic Psychology, **28**, 606-621, (2007).

				ABABABABAB Sequence										
				Xi penalty takers strategy					GX goalkeeper strategy					
				DP11	DP11β	DP12	DP12β	DP12Y	DP21X	DP21α	DP21ε	DP22X	DP21α	DP21ε
Maximize score (FR0)	Minimize Σ (Failed shootouts) (FR1)	FR11	FR11X	X										
			FR11β		β_1									
		FR12	FR11X			X								
			FR11β				β_2							
			FR11Y					Υ_2						
	Maximize Σ (Failed shootouts by opponents) (FR2)	FR21	FR21X						X					
			FR11α							α_1				
			FR11ε								ε_1			
		FR22	FR21X									X		
			FR11α										α_2	
			FR11ε											ε_2

Fig. 5. Functional decoupling for a series of 2 ABAB-type alternate shootouts

Exploring and *Adapt!* – Extending the *Adapt!* Method to Develop Reconfigurable Manufacturing Systems

Kate Kujawa[1,*], *Jakob* Weber[1], *Erik* Puik[2], and *Kristin* Paetzold[3]

[1] Daimler AG, Process Development and Materials Department, 71059, Sindelfingen, Germany
[2] HU University of Applied Science, Research Centre for Technology and Innovation, Utrecht, 3500AD, the Netherlands
[3] Universität der Bundeswehr München, Institute for Technical Product Development, 85577, Neubiberg, Germany

Abstract. Automotive production is faced with the challenge of bringing new products to market faster, with decreasing turn-around times, meaning production must be continually changing to accommodate new products. This paper proposes an approach to decrease a product's time-to-market, by increasing the efficiency of automotive assembly unit design. Providing designers with conceptual information about future vehicle models early in the product design process, could shift the design start forward and enable a more efficient transition process. Large automotive companies work on vehicle design and development for years before a product is ready for production. If during these earlier stages of product design, significant changes are identified and communicated to production designers, the manufacturing system design can get a jump start with an early exploration phase. A method exists, which uses the Axiomatic Design theory to develop Reconfigurable Manufacturing Systems through a modular breakdown. A similar method *Adapt!* employs Axiomatic Design and Scrum to develop changeable or adaptable production systems. This paper proposes to extend the *Adapt!* method to include an exploration phase, which through early communication, provides an overview of the required design process, and enables faster identification of the critical design challenges. A case study is performed by analysing a currently produced vehicle and its future electric version.

1 Introduction

The automotive industry is facing increases in product variation, competition, customization, and market volatility. The pace of technological advancements is also accelerating, further challenging the industry [1]. Figure 1, shows six different trends all having a huge impact on the automotive industry [2]. Being first to market and decreasing the time-to-market of a product provides significant benefits and profits [3]. Automotive manufacturing is therefore being pushed to accommodate the continual product changes faster and more efficiently. Through the implementation of engineering design methods, changeable and Reconfigurable Manufacturing Systems (RMS) can be strategically developed.

Reconfigurable systems change the physical or soft characteristics of a system to create a new configuration. According to Zhang et al. [4], RMS provide the highest level of adaptability for a manufacturing system. To enable practical reconfiguration, systems are broken down into modules.

Fig. 1. Potentially disruptive trends [2].

Many methods have been proposed to facilitate modular manufacturing design. The Constituent Roadmap of Product Design proposed by Puik and Ceglarek [5] defines three chronological phases in project design: 1) exploration, 2) conceptualization, and 3) realization. For a truly holistic approach, all three phases should be considered. The exploration phase occurs before a particular project begins. This phase is relatively undefined in literature, however, many methods exist covering the phases of conceptualization and realization.

Puik et al. [6], propose a helpful method for implementing redesign for RMS once a product change has been initiated. This is founded on Axiomatic Design

* Corresponding author: kate.kujawa@daimler.com

(AD) and offers clarity on project progression during design conception.

The method *Adapt!* has been proposed by Stäbler et al. [7] to capture the process of methodically designing and developing a changeable production unit based on. *Adapt!* combines a holistic evaluation process, with AD and the agile project management method Scrum to create a modern technology design process [8].

This paper proposes a novel expansion of the *Adapt!* method to include an exploration phase using an indexing method to bridge the gap. The aim is to provide a holistic approach to improve final assembly design and development through product-assembly pairing, communication, indexing and *Adapt!*. The proposed method is an amalgamation and extension of existing methods to cover the three phases of exploration, conceptualization and realization.

2 Previous Work

2.1 Product, Assembly, and Modularity, - in theory

Both the product, in this case a passenger car, and its assembly process have their own architecture. Two typical architectural structures are integral and modular [9, 10]. Integral architecture refers to a product or process whose subsystems have multiple functions, are dependent on one another, and whose direct interaction is not clearly defined. If one subsystem is changed, the entire product may be affected.

Modular architecture on the other hand, is defined by the product being separated into defined subsystems each with one or a few functional elements whose interfaces are defined. In a modular system, an element can be changed, while the rest of the subsystems maintain their functionality [9-11]. Modularity is not constrained to physical products. Processes, activities and components may also have a modular form [12]. Automotive assembly may therefore, also be modular.

Process modularity, refers to the different production processes being independent of each other. If individual production modules can be changed independently of each other, without impacting the assembly system, it can be considered a RMS.

RMSs are defined by Koren [13] as systems designed for changes in both software and hardware components to enable adjustments in production. It is therefore technologically essential that these systems are composed of a modular architecture. RMS offer scalability, an adjustable machine structure, and customized flexibility. Much research exists on the topic of RMS and it is considered by many to be the future of manufacturing systems [14].

Alone a modular product or modular production are useful, however an ideal system would have a modular product and corresponding modular assembly. Figure 2 shows an ideal product and assembly set up where all product and process modules are independent [15]. In a completely modular system, when the product design changes, the design and development necessary to adopt the change into production is narrowed to the affected module. Once this change is set in place, the design and development of the new process commences. Everything is independent and the entire system does not need to be considered.

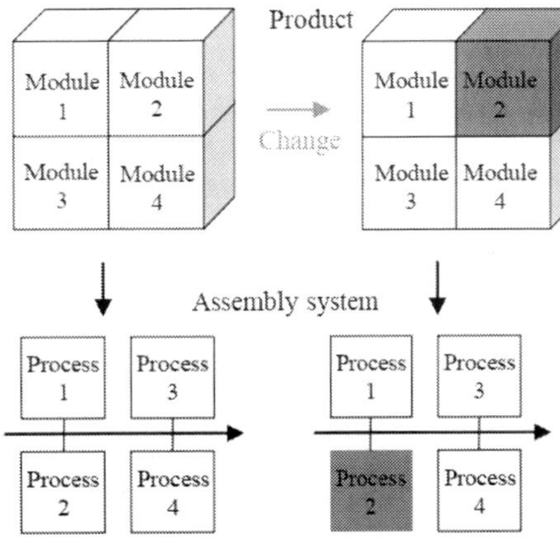

Fig. 2. Ideal modular product and assembly, after [15]

2.2 Product, Assembly, and Modularity, - in practice

In reality, nothing is ideal. As Ulrich [9] explains, nothing is one hundred percent modular or integral, but somewhere in between. The literature on passenger car architecture is mixed, some argue that the existing architecture is integral, however, others see it as modular. However, according to Ulrich, it is only a matter of the degree of modularity. Much research exists on dividing passenger cars into modules and different degrees of modularisation are found in industry [10, 12].

Most literature on process modularity for automotive manufacturing subdivides modules based on supplier-manufacturer relations. Most large automotive manufacturers have a wide array of suppliers providing smaller modules for the vehicles. An example would be a passenger seat; the seats are built from many smaller parts assembled together at a supplier's factory, the completed seat is brought to the large automotive plant where it is assembled in the vehicle. Some use the supplier parts as a way to identify modules, which are incorporated in the final assembly [4, 11, 16, 17]. This paper focuses only on assembly processes completed during assembly at the final vehicle-manufacturing plant. Modular assembly processes exist, however not on the scale of a full-vehicle [12, 15].

2.3 *Adapt!*

Adapt! is a design and development method tested and developed in the automotive industry in Germany [7, 8]. The approach enables a user-friendly design of changeable production units. The method combines a life-cycle with integrated change or re-design phases with AD.

2.3.1 Axiomatic Design

AD, a design theory proposed by Suh, provides a scientific basis for the design process using rational and logical processes. The design process uses four domains and two axioms to map out the requirements and solutions of a design [18, 19].

The four domains are customer, functional, physical and process. Customer requirements or attributes (CA) are gathered into the first domain, then converted into functional requirements (FR) in the functional domain. The mapping process commences through the answering of the questions "What do we want to achieve?" and "How do we achieve it?".

The second question leads to the design parameter (DP) in the physical domain. Through the repetition of these questions, the FRs are continually broken down until fully decomposed. The next step involves identifying process variables (PV) in the process domain.

The two axioms are the *Independence Axiom*, and *Information Axiom*. The *Independence Axiom*, as the name suggests, states that an optimal design guarantees the independence of all FR. The *Information Axiom*, focuses on reducing the information content of a design. In this context, the information context is related to the complexity of the proposed solution. [18, 19]

The *Adapt!* method uses a modification of AD and does not consider the second axiom. Further, *Adapt!* uses a color-coding system to link the FRs, DPs and CAs, with the department responsible for the requirement [20]. This colour coding helps clarify discussion and communication between the responsible departments, something often complicated in large companies with potentially complex organizational structures. Once the design task has been decomposed using AD, the development takes place using the framework scrum.

2.3.2 Scrum

Scrum is a framework for managing the development of complex products [21]. The framework outlines the project team, organisation, planning, communication, and breaks down the project time-line into fixed one month Sprints. Each sprint has specific goals and tasks to be carried out during the time period. The consistency and agility of the framework helps monitor progress and enables early response to unforeseen challenges. Scrum uses a product backlog, a list consisting of all product requirements which are divided throughout the sprints. *Adapt!* takes the results of AD as work tasks to fill the product backlog.

In summary, *Adapt!* uses AD to decompose the customer requirements into a detailed hierarchical tree of DP, and FR. These detailed elements are then used as tasks, allowing an agile Scrum team to continue the product development in a complex environment.

2.4 Indexing

When change is needed in a modular assembly process, the question arises, "Which modules need to be changed, and by how much?". Some modules may be able to remain the same, while others may need to be completely redesigned. Puik et al. [6] have proposed a method to index the modules based on axiomatic independence. Figure 3 shows the stages of the design progress. By indexing, or sorting, the modules into these phases, the design effort can be estimated.

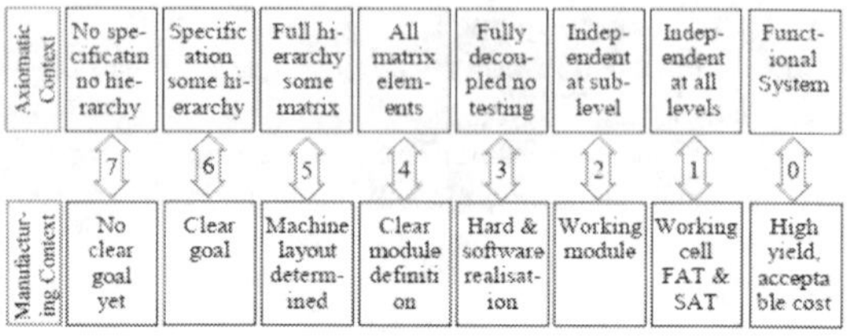

Fig. 3. Steps of RMS development [9]

In Figure 3 the phases are described in the context of AD and their mirrored position in a manufacturing context. By aligning these phases, the manufacturing development progression and AD progress can be easily understood and applied.

The seven stages have been recently simplified by Puik et al. [14], and consolidated into only three phases of reconfiguration. The three phases are described in Table 1.

Table 1. Simple classification of reconfiguration schemes [9].

Phase	Description
Repeat	Modules have been previously applied and documented, and the use case lies within a specified operating window. Module must only be tested to be at production level.
Adapt	Modules have been previously applied and documented, however the use case is outside the specified operating window. Module development is required to ensure the design.
Expand	Module does not exist und must be fully developed.

The simplification to three phases reduces the laborious effort needed to make accurate judgements for a large number of modules. This method ensures an effective assessment of the reconfiguration work needed. Having the design progress organised aids in planning, and enables an indication of the required resources and development ahead.

2.5 Design Process

Puik and Ceglarek propose three phases of the design process, exploration, conceptualisation and realisation. The exploration phase is where the project is defined. In this phase, the status of the project, parts and systems are unknown. The second phase, conceptualise, is where AD takes place. This phase poses to verify the concept and decouple the design matrices. At the end of this phase, the Independence Axiom is satisfied. The third and final phase is realisation, or robustness. This phase is completed with a satisfied Information Axiom [5- 7].

The main contributions to this paper are the *Adapt!* method and indexing approach. The *Adapt!* method fulfills the final two phases of the design process. The conceptual phase is represented by AD, and Scrum represents the realisation phase. The indexing method is used in between the first two phases, to help clarify the remaining redesign process and clarify what is yet to be done.

This paper proposes to extend *Adapt!* to include an exploration phase at the front end of the design process, and uses the indexing process as the link tying the exploration and conceptual phases together.

3 Proposed Approach

This paper proposes a holistic approach to improve automotive final assembly design and development through product-assembly module pairing, indexing, and *Adapt* with a focus on product-assembly module interaction in automotive manufacturing. The entire method is shown in Figure 4.

Part 1. Modular Communication:

The method begins with part 1. Modular communication. This is in the exploration phase of the design process. The top two rows of the hierarchy tree breaking down into modules in Part 1 of the figure, represents the automobile product breakdown. The following two rows, similar but upside-down, are a breakdown of the final vehicle assembly line. The modules of the vehicle, and its assembly are paired together, for example, the windshield is paired with the windshield assembly unit.

In the product row, research and development (R&D) departments designing new vehicles identify changes between the model currently in production, and the future vehicle model in development. Production can rely on the R&D department to provide early information about incoming changes to the product. The turquoise highlighted modules represent "changed" modules. The corresponding assembly modules are also highlighted. These changes are communicated with the company's production unit designers. The relevant experts from both sides of the affected modules, product and assembly, can now discuss implementation of the changes.

The modular breakdown of both sides enables easy communication between product development and manufacturing assembly teams at a module-specific level. Once focused discussions have occurred between the responsible groups, constructive collaboration can be initiated, long before the final design is finished. This enables early indications of change to be communicated within assembly before any detailed new product information is available. During these early communications, production unit designers can start an exploration phase and get a head-start in preparing for the design process ahead.

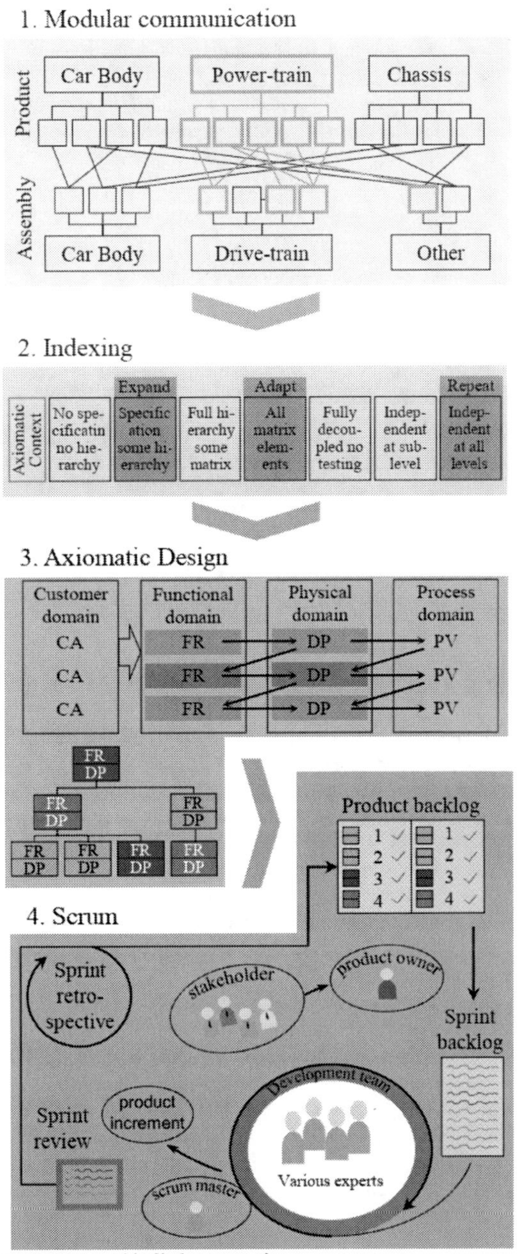

Fig. 4. Proposed holistic approach

Part 2. Indexing:

The second part of the method, is based on the indexing method proposed by Puik et al.. Once the affected modules have been identified, analysis is done to assess whether the current assembly process is suitable to produce the new model, or whether new assembly units must be designed. Experts rank the assembly modules based on the three phases (Repeat, Adapt, Expand) outlined in Table 1. If it is determined that some design is necessary, the production unit designer can orient the phase into the axiomatic context. The three phases are highlighted in axiomatic context in blue in Part 2 of Figure 4. When the indexing process is complete, this information is used to evaluate the required design and development effort, and time-to-market for the new model. Now that the axiomatic context is outlined, the remaining AD can be completed.

Part 3. Axiomatic Design:

The *Adapt!* method is then implemented to complete the assembly unit design and development. The Independence Axiom of AD is used to further decompose the remainder of the design task. Again, a colour code is used to link the FRs and DPs based on the responsible department. This color coding is demonstrated using the different shades of turquoise in Figure 4. Once the Independence Axiom is satisfied and the final design matrix is complete, a design concept is ready to enter the development phase.

Part 4. Scrum:

At this point, the production unit development is a more dynamic and practical effort. In Part 4, the transition to the scrum framework begins. The designer is joined by a team consisting of experts in different fields. The scrum framework supports an agile and self-directed working group. In *Adapt!*, the transition from AD to scrum takes place using the product backlog. The design parameters are put into the product backlog and once fully defined, enter the sprint backlog. The scrum team uses these defined tasks to complete the development of the production unit.

4 Modularity and product-assembly pairing in Industry

To enable the application of the proposed method for current products and assembly in industry, an analysis of the existing modular situation is necessary. The appropriate pairing of modules is also needed. Once the product and assembly are organised into appropriate subsystems, verification of the method can be accomplished.

A verification case study examines the switch from production of a conventionally powered vehicle to the production of an electric model. This is an example of a maturing power-train technology, identified as a potential disruptor in Figure 1. This disrupting technology is applicable to all automobile makers. To transform the assembly line for the production of the electric models, several modules would be affected, enabling a platform to verify this method using a practical industry case.

To apply the proposed method, the final assembly must first be arranged in a modular fashion and paired with product models. However, in the automotive industry today, existing vehicle assembly methods are typically non-ideally-modular. Based on current industry information and evaluation of existing assembly plants, final assembly is separated based on assembly order, vehicle assembly area, and assembly lines.

A case study at Daimler AG found that the entire final assembly is not organized into modules, however, some modules exist within the current assembly structure. In Figure 5, the assembly modules currently being used today and their appropriately paired product modules are shown. The modules affected by the change from a conventional drive train to electric are highlighted in turquoise. The next step is to commence communication between the groups responsible for the now turquoise modules. Now, based on the existing modules, the indexing can be performed. Each module shown in Figure 5 must now be assessed for whether it is in design phase is in a state of Expand, Adapt, or Repeat. According to ranking, the by the remaining design and development is to be completed using axiomatic design and scrum.

An added complexity to the modular form is the assembly lines. Assembly lines use fixed conveyor belt technology, and are therefore limited in their flexibility and location. Each module in the assembly must center itself around the conveyor belt. If the conveyor technology is not modular, the entire assembly has limited modularity. Further, the modules presented in Figure 5 do not include the entire vehicle, all its parts, and assembly.

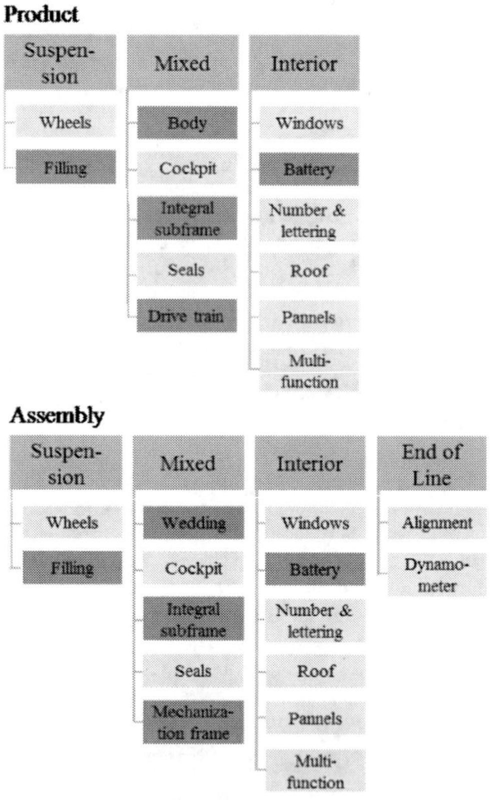

Fig. 5. Product and assembly modules

5 Discussion

During the pairing process, it is quickly evident that process in the end of line, typically testing procedures, are doubly paired with the product modules. The product module is connected to its assembly module as well as its testing and/or calibration process module. For the affected modules, all three parties are should to take part in the discussion.

Some concerns arise when considering the selected modules. A proper modular structure should limit dependencies, therefore the module interrelationships used here must be studied and multiple function integration should be evaluated. For an industry applicable method, it must be considered that existing modules do not necessarily have independent requirements. Following, during the continued design process using AD, further dependencies could arise which have not been originally considered. The method is lacking formality.

6 Conclusion

This paper proposed an extension of the *Adapt!* method, to improve automotive final assembly design and development. A modular architecture is used to enable early communication between product research and development, and production design and development. The modular architecture enables indexing and estimation of remaining design effort. Following which, design and development is carried out with the agile and user friendly *Adapt!* method. A case study for the modularisation of the assembly line is completed and the changing modules identified.

To further the validation of the application of this method in automotive assembly, future work is required in completing the modular decomposition of current assembly lines to attain independent modules. Once the remaining modules are identified, they can be paired with product modules. Additionally, an examination of the interdependencies of the current modules could increase the efficacy of the method. The case study on a realistic industry example, of the assembly transformation from conventional to electric vehicles, can then be completed.

References

1. O. Kuzgunkaya, H. ElMaraghy, "Economic and Strategic Justification of Changeable, Reconfigurable and Flexible Manufacturing", Changeable and Reconfigurable Manufacturing Systems, Springer, pp 303-320, (2009)
2. N. Ganguli, C. Burns, R. Goldsberry, Supplying the future of mobility. Deloitte, (2018). Accessed April 1, 2018 https://www2.deloitte.com
3. G. Stalk Jr., T.M. Hout, *Competing Against Time: How Time-Based Competition is Reshaping Global Markets,* Simon and Schuster (1990)
4. G. Zhang, R. Liu, L. Gong, and Q. Huang, "An Analytical Comparison on Cost and Performance among DMS, AMS, FMS and RMS", Reconfigurable manufacturing systems and transformable factories, pp. 659-673 (2006)
5. E. Puik, D. Ceglarek, "Axiomatic Product Design in three Stages; A constituent roadmap that visualises the status of the design process by tracking the knowledge of the designer", IMECE **15** (2015)
6. E. Puik, D. Telgen, L.V. Moergestel, and D. Ceglarek, "Assessment of Reconfiguration Schemes for Reconfigurable Manufacturing Systems Based on Resources and Lead Time", RCIM **43**, pp. 30-38, (2017)
7. M. Stäbler, J. Weber, K. Paetzold, „Adapt!Evaluation – Evaluation for Design and Re-Design of Production Systems based on Axiomatic Design, ICAD (2017)
8. J. Weber, D. Förster, M. Stäbler, K. Paetzold, „Adapt!-Agile Project Management Supported by Axiomatic Design", ICAD (2017)
9. K.T. Ulrich, "The role of product architecture in the manufacturing firm", Research Policy **24**(3), pp.419-440 (1995)
10. M. Jacobs, C. Droge, S.K. Vickery, R. Calantone, R. "Product and process modularity's effects on manufacturing agility and firm growth performance", Prod. Innov. Manag. **28**(1), pp.123-137. (2011)
11. F.E. Henriques, P.A. Cauchick Miguel, "Use of product and production modularity in the automotive industry: a comparative analysis of vehicles developed with the involvement of Brazilian engineering centers", Gest. Prod. **24** pp.161-177 (2017)
12. C.Y. Baldwin, K.B. Clark, *Design rules The Power of Modularity* **1,** MIT Press (2000)
13. Y. Koren *et al.* "Reconfigurable Manufacturing Systems", CIRP **48** pp. 527-540 (1999)
14. E. Puik, D. Ceglarek, "Guidelines for Application of the Constituent Roadmap of Product Design Based on Axiomatic Design", ICAD (2017)
15. G. Erixon, Modular Function Deployment – A Method for Product Modularisation, Ph.D. Thesis, The Royal Institute of Technology, Stockholm (1998)
16. W. Herlyn, *PP im Automobilbau,* Hanser Fachbuchverlag (2012)
17. J. Ihme, *Logistik im Automobilbau,* Carl Hanser Verlag GmbH & Co. KG (2006)
18. N.P. Suh, *The principles of design,* Oxford University Press (1990)
19. N.P. Suh, *Axiomatic design: Advances and applications,* Oxford University Press (2001)
20. Weber, J. Förster, D., Kößler, J., Paetzold, K., „Design of changeable production units within the automotive sector with Axiomatic Design", ICAD (2015)
21. K. Schwaber, J. Sutherland, *The Scrum Guide* (2016)

Recovery of waste heat from engines: an AD view

Miguel Cavique[1,*], *João* Fradinho[2], *António* Gabriel-Santos[2], *António* Mourão[2] and *António* Gonçalves-Coelho[2]

[1]UNIDEMI, CINAV & Escola Naval, Base Naval de Lisboa – Alfeite, 2810-001 Almada, Portugal
[2]UNIDEMI & DEMI, Faculdade de Ciências e Tecnologia, Universidade Nova de Lisboa, Campus de Caparica, 2829-516 Caparica, Portugal

Abstract. The Newcomen engine (1705) and the Watt engine (1769) are good examples of coupled and uncoupled designs. The Watt engine had an efficiency of about 3%, a shallow value when compared to engines of nowadays while resulting in a significant increase at those times. According to Axiomatic Design, Watt engine had a better performance than the Newcomen design due to its uncoupled nature. This work aims at applying the same reasoning to choose between new inventions designed for recovering waste heat from engines as to produce work. The most popular of those inventions are the organic Rankine cycle (ORC) and the Kalina cycle. Marine applications use those inventions to improve the efficiency of Diesel engines because the increase of weight of the recovery system does not affect power propulsion. A controversial regarding what system to develop occurred in scientific community as well as in the industry. The application of AD to those cycles classifies ORC as an uncoupled design and the Kalina cycle as a coupled design. Therefore, the ORC might be pondered for future development regarding energy efficiency.

1 Introduction

The conference of Paris (2015) organized by the United Nations ended with a settlement between the vast majority of the World countries regarding the reduction of the emissions of greenhouse gases (GHG). The World States were in accordance to reduce their carbon emissions "as soon as possible" and to do their best to keep global warming "well below 2 °C" of the pre-industrial level.

With this in mind, the EU goals for 2030 include achieving at least 27% energy savings when compared with the business-as-usual scenario. The most effective way of fulfilling this target is to increase the efficiency of energy production. The energy sector of the EU28 reports the production of electricity and transportation as responsible for 82% of the GHG emissions [1]. The transport sector accounts for 33% of the final energy use in the EU28, making this sector a target for the increase in energy efficiency. The EU policy on energy aims to develop new technologies to "ensure secure, affordable and climate-friendly energy" [2]. Therefore, a new market of new technologies for waste heat recovery (WHR) appeared in the EU, formerly for large industrial plants and recently for plants with shaft power in the order of magnitude of 1 MW.

The WHR technology for marine diesel applications can increase the efficiency of the engines with a tonnage surplus of 0.5%, which is insignificant regarding the required propeller power.

The most common WHR technologies for Diesel engines are the conventional steam Rankine cycle (SRC), the organic Rankine cycle (ORC) and the Kalina cycle (KC) [3]. All of these technologies can recover energy of waste heat of medium quality, ranging from 230 °C to 650 °C. SRC is a well-known and proven technology that can be adapted to work with medium quality waste heat. The ORC, developed in the sixties, performs a Rankine cycle similar to the SRC using a refrigerant as working fluid and can be seen as a reverse refrigeration cycle. Finally, the KC, named after its inventor, Alexander Kalina, in 1983, is the reverse of the absorption ammonia-water cycle.

At nominal load conditions, the temperature of the exhaust gas of the Diesel engines lies in the range of 300 °C to 500 °C. Large Diesel engines have shaft efficiency near 50% and an energy waste of about 25% to 30% in the exhaust gas. The WHR technologies, with efficiencies of about 20%, can increase the overall efficiency by about 10-15%. Dig Vijay Singh, *et al.* [3] discussed the overall increase in efficiency of Diesel engines, concluding that SRC allows increasing the efficiency in the range of 2-7%, ORC by 8-15% and KC in a similar range of ORC. SRC has the advantage of using a well-known technology, but the efficiency is moderate when compared to ORC or KC. Therefore, a controversy aroused in the industry regarding the best system, ORC or KC, for recovering medium range waste heat from Diesel engines.

Ulrik Larsene *et al.* [4] modeled the recovery of energy from a marine two-stroke low speed engine with ideal SRC, as well as ORC using R245ca as working fluid, and KC. They found likely to achieve 5% additional power using SRC, a similar value for KC, and 7% additional power with ORC. However, at similar conditions, the maximum pressure of KC exceeds the

* Corresponding author: cavique.santos@marinha.pt

high pressure of an ORC system. Paola Bombarda *et al.* [5] studied both systems applied to a truck Diesel engine that exhausts gas at 346 °C. The KC needs a maximum pressure of 100 bar while ORC using hexamethyldisiloxane needs 9.7 bar to achieve a similar efficiency. In cogeneration plants, the exhaust gas temperature is about 150 °C making the efficiency and pressure lower than on the previous examples [6]. Diedie Lin *et al.* [7] compared ORC with R245fa to KC with different concentrations of ammonia, as well as with a SRC-ammonia. They modelled the systems and varied the hot water temperature of the heat source from 100 °C to 200 °C, as to evaluate the sensibility of the efficiency concerning hot temperature. Regarding efficiency, ORC is better than any KC from 100 °C to 140 °C, slightly worst than KC with high ammonia concentration for higher values of temperature. In the range 140 °C to 200 °C, SRC-ammonia has the best efficiency of all systems under comparison [7].

This paper aims at using Axiomatic Design (AD) to choose between ORC and KC in what concerns to the recovery of energy from the exhaust gas of Diesel engines. Section 2 presents the simplest systems, ORC and KC, and section 3 evaluates these cycles using AD. On section 4 and 5 the paper concludes that KC is a coupled design while ORC is an uncoupled design.

2 Organic Rankine and Kalina Cycles

ORC and KC are reverse cycles of the vapor-compression refrigeration and the ammonia-water absorption refrigeration. Ammonia is a toxic substance that is easy to identify in case of leakage, and that needs special handling care. Ammonia belongs to the safety group B1 *i.e.*, a toxic non-flammable gas. It is a natural substance with no harmful effect to the ozone layer of the atmosphere and with zero global warming potential (GWP).

The used working fluids for ORC are non-toxic refrigerants, but the high values of their GWP make these products of environment concern. The EU F-Gas regulation imposes a decrease until 2030 on the average GWP of the refrigerants. From 2015 to 2030 the average GWP should drop from 2000 to 420, while it is 1260 in 2018. The most common working fluids for ORC are R245fa, a hydrofluorocarbon (HFC) with a GWP of 1030, and R245ca, which is also a HFC, with a GWP of 693. R245fa belongs to safety group B1, as well as ammonia, both causing some concern regarding the use in marine applications.

2.1. Organic Rankine Cycle

Organic Rankine cycle follows a Rankine cycle using a refrigerant as working fluid. Fig. 1 depicts a single stage ORC showing a pump (P) to maintain a high pressure in the lines 1 and 4, an evaporator (EVP) that receives heat from the exhaust gas, a turbine (ORCT), and a condenser (COND) that reject heat to a water stream. The ORCT expands the gas from the high-pressure line (1) to the low-pressure one (2), producing electricity in the generator G.

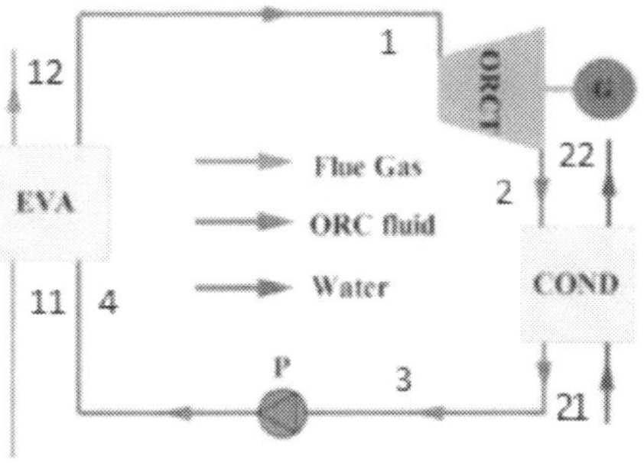

Fig. 1. ORC scheme (adapted from [6])

A variation of the single stage ORC uses a regenerator between the exit of the turbine and the entrance of the evaporator, reducing the heat released in the condenser. The temperature of the exhaust gases (11 to 12) determines the pressure on the evaporator, and the temperature of the condensing water at (21) determines the pressure on the condenser. Therefore, external conditions determine the behaviour of the system.

The coolant needs to be at the superheated vapour state at (1), in order to preserve the blades of the turbine from erosion. For R245fa, the pressure ratio in the turbine is about 20, and the evaporator pressure is about 1 bar. The mass flow and the temperature of the exhaust gas are the key factors to define the power of the ORC equipment.

2.2 Kalina Cycle

Kalina cycle may have many schemes, the most common one is the KC11 as depicted in Fig. 2. A common variation of the flow diagram of KC11 puts the separator (SEP) before the evaporator (EVA). Most of the current industrial applications of KC use a mixture of ammonia and water. There are experimental works that use zeotropic mixtures of HFC to low the evaporating pressure.

In KC, the turbine (AWT) needs a high concentration of ammonia because it produces more work per fluid flow unit than a lower concentration. The turbine has a pressure ratio of about 15 and drives the generator (G). In the condenser (COND), it is desirable a higher temperature than in the turbine exit, as to simplify rejecting the heat. The absorber (AB) makes the water to absorb the ammonia, therefore, increasing the temperature of the mixture. Due to the zeotropic behaviour of the ammonia-water, the boiling and condensing temperatures varies following the non-isothermal evolution of the fluids in the evaporator and the condenser.

Lines 1 and 2 have rich ammonia molar concentration (typically 95%), lines 3, 4, 5, 6 and 7 have a lean concentration (60%) and lines 8, 9 and 10 a very poor concentration of ammonia (30%). Pump (P) imposes a differential pressure between the low-pressure lines (2, 3, 4 and 10) and all the other high-pressure lines.

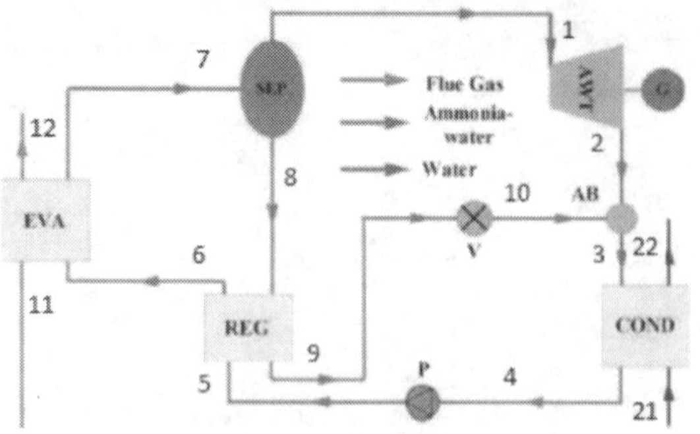

Fig. 2. KC11 scheme (adapted from [6])

The AWT and the valve (V) reduce the pressure from high to low. The regenerator (REG) allows recovering heat from the very poor concentration stream (8) to the evaporator stream.

The efficiency of the system is highly dependent on the concentration of ammonia in the AWT, therefore depending on the SEP and on the working mode of V. The valve V allows adjusting the amount of water rich solution that is required to correct the concentration of the ammonia rich solution. Thus, the efficiency of the KC mostly depends on the SEP and on the control of V, as they determine the ammonia concentration entering the turbine and the condenser. The optimization of the different concentrations is a key factor regarding the efficiency of the system.

As in any other thermal machine, the efficiency of KC depends on temperature of the heat source and the temperature of the cold source.

3 The AD evaluation

The highest-level functional requirement (FR) of the designs under evaluation is:

FR_0 - Produce work from waste heat,

and the corresponding DP is:

DP_0- Thermal engine.

For a thermal engine, the second law of Thermodynamics states that a cycled device needs to receive heat from a high temperature sink and reject heat to a low temperature sink in order to produce work. Moreover, the engine needs a working fluid to work, making the first level FRs of a thermal engine to be:

FR_1- Receive heat;
FR_2- Reject heat;
FR_3- Produce work;
FR_4- Transport thermal energy in cycle.

The next subsection reveals the DPs of each system, ORC, and KC, at the first and the second levels of decomposition.

AD classifies the designs as uncoupled, decoupled and coupled. The former are the best, and the latter are the poorest [8]. The FRs are actions that are formally defined in an independent way [9]. Moreover, FRs need to be cumulative exhaustive and mutually exclusive [10], which is a condition to attain during the decomposition process. At each level of decomposition, one may start by defining the nominal working conditions that allow defining the design matrix [11].

3.1 AD application to ORC

The ORC into consideration has R245fa as working fluid to transport thermal energy, uses the EVA to receive heat, COND to reject the heat, and the set of turbomachinery, P and ORCT, to produce work. Therefore the DPs are:

DP_1- EVA
DP_2- COND
DP_3- Turbomachinery
DP_4- R245fa

Equation 1 depicts the design equation of the ORC at the first level of decomposition showing that it is a decoupled design. Selecting a specific working fluid, DP_4, makes it an 3-FR, 3-DP uncoupled design.

$$\begin{bmatrix} FR_1 \\ FR_2 \\ FR_3 \\ FR_4 \end{bmatrix} = \begin{bmatrix} X & & & X \\ & X & & X \\ & & X & X \\ & & & X \end{bmatrix} \cdot \begin{bmatrix} DP_1 \\ DP_2 \\ DP_3 \\ DP_4 \end{bmatrix} \quad (1)$$

Therefore, FR_4 turns to be a leaf and the decomposition proceeds with the other FRs.

Table 1 shows the second level of decomposition.

Table 1. The second level of decomposition for ORC.

FR	DP
FR_{11}: Recover wasted heat	DP_{11}: Exhaust gas
FR_{12}: Transfer high temperature heat	DP_{12}: Heat exchanger of EVA
FR_{21}: Choose low temperature storage sink	DP_{21}: Sea water supply system
FR_{22}: Transfer low temperature heat	DP_{22}: Heat exchanger of COND
FR_{31}: Maintain a pressure differential	DP_{31}: Pump
FR_{32}: Perform fluid expansion	DP_{32}: ORCT

On the second level of decomposition, new relationships appear, expressed on a new design matrix.

The ORC engine works in cycle so that making any change in any component would affect all the others. The design of the system will be considered in nominal conditions, although one should notice the impact of the external conditions in the design matrix.

Transferring heat at high temperature depends on the temperature and mass of the exhaust gas, in the same way, that the sea water system influences the transfer of heat at low temperature. Moreover, defining the temperatures of source and sink reservoirs fix the working pressures of the refrigerant. Therefore, maintaining the pressure differential in P and ORCT is a function of the exhaust gas and the seawater temperatures.

Equation 2 shows the design matrix on the second level of decomposition. In order to compare systems, external conditions are set, fixing the temperature of exhaust gases and the sea water at nominal conditions. On Equation 2, the influence of external condition are set with a lowercase "*x*" standing for a minor influence. Setting values for the external conditions, then the design is an uncoupled design.

$$\begin{bmatrix} FR_{11} \\ FR_{12} \\ FR_{21} \\ FR_{22} \\ FR_{31} \\ FR_{32} \end{bmatrix} = \begin{bmatrix} X & & & & & \\ x & X & & & & \\ & & X & & & \\ & & x & X & & \\ x & & x & & X & \\ x & & x & & & X \end{bmatrix} \cdot \begin{bmatrix} DP_{11} \\ DP_{12} \\ DP_{21} \\ DP_{22} \\ DP_{31} \\ DP_{32} \end{bmatrix} \quad (2)$$

3.2 AD application to KC

The first level of decomposition for the KC is similar to the ORC. The difference is just the working fluid. Therefore, the DPs are the following:

DP_1- EVA
DP_2- COND
DP_3- Turbomachinery
DP_4- Ammonia-water

Equation 1 also applies to KC, as well as the considerations regarding the working fluid. FR_4 turns a leave, and the decomposition of the KC design proceeds with the other three FRs. According to the aforesaid on section 2.2, new internal relationships are expected for this system on the second level of decomposition.

Again, the exhaust gas impacts the heat transfer at high temperature. In addition, the seawater system affects the heat transfer at low temperature. At last, the temperatures of the exhaust gas and the seawater define the temperatures of the ammonia-water at the evaporator and condenser. Furthermore, Fig. 2 introduces a regenerator that has a positive impact on the needs of heat at high temperature.

The equations of state of ammonia-water make enthalpy and pressure to change according to the concentration of ammonia for a given temperature.

Table 2 shows the FRs and DPs for KC system on the second level of decomposition. It is worth to notice the introduction of new FRs regarding the changing of ammonia concentration along the thermodynamic cycle.

Table 2. The second level of decomposition of KC.

FR	DP
FR_{11}: Recover wasted heat	DP_{11}: Exhaust gas
FR_{12}: Transfer high temperature heat	DP_{12}: Heat exchanger of EVA
FR_{13}: Recover internal heat	DP_{22}: REG
FR_{21}: Choose low temperature storage sink	DP_{21}: Sea water supply system
FR_{22}: Transfer low temperature heat	DP_{22}:Heat exchanger of COND
FR_{23}: Reduce ammonia concentration	DP_{23}: Set V+AB
FR_{31}: Maintain a pressure differential	DP_{31}: Pump
FR_{32}: Perform fluid expansion	DP_{32}: AWT
FR_{33}: Increase ammonia concentration	DP_{33}: SEP

Therefore, the role of the valve control and the absorber to reduce the ammonia concentration in the condenser; as well as the role of the separator to increase the ammonia fraction in the turbine, strongly influence the behavior of the system. A trade-off must be made between the performance regarding the fluid expansion vs. the transfer of heat at low temperature, which affects each other. Moreover, the lean concentration of ammonia in line 7 (Fig. 2) affects the behavior of the evaporator.

The set, valve and absorber, plays a special role by influencing the transfer at low temperature in the condenser, and by changing the performance of fluid expansion in the turbine.

Equation 3 shows that KC is a coupled design, despite fixing the external temperatures at the nominal conditions.

$$\begin{bmatrix} FR_{11} \\ FR_{12} \\ FR_{13} \\ FR_{21} \\ FR_{22} \\ FR_{23} \\ FR_{31} \\ FR_{32} \\ FR_{33} \end{bmatrix} = \begin{bmatrix} X & & & & & & & & \\ x & X & x & & & x & & & x \\ & & X & & & & & & \\ & & & X & & & & & \\ & & & x & X & X & & & X \\ & & & & & X & & & \\ x & & & x & & & X & & \\ x & & & x & & X & & X & X \\ & & & & & & & & X \end{bmatrix} \cdot \begin{bmatrix} DP_{11} \\ DP_{12} \\ DP_{13} \\ DP_{21} \\ DP_{22} \\ DP_{23} \\ DP_{31} \\ DP_{32} \\ DP_{33} \end{bmatrix} \quad (3)$$

The most important relationships are set at Equation 3 by a "X", meaning they have a larger absolute value than all other off-diagonals. This decomposition is in accordance with a corollary of Theorem 8 of AD that allows neglecting low order $\partial FR/\partial DP$. Therefore, it is possible a design to be an uncoupled design at the first level of decomposition and coupled at the second level of decomposition.

4 Discussion

The efficiency of the ORC and the KC are similar in what concerns to the recovery of heat from the exhaust gas of a Diesel engine. Common installations of ORC use R245fa, which is a hazardous, toxic and non-flammable fluid of B1security class, which belongs to the same group of the ammonia fluid that is used in the KC systems. Anyway, ammonia KC systems need about 100 bar pressure to work, thus requiring special components. Moreover, the AWT turbine should be multistage or should rotate at high speed to have a reasonable isentropic efficiency, due to the head loss. Some concerns may arise regarding the corrosion caused by the ammonia-water mixture, but the market has already a strong experience on choosing steels to work with the ammonia fluid.

In what regards to this paper, we found that fixing the external conditions, then KC is a coupled design and ORC is uncoupled.

Considering the external conditions, at nominal conditions, ORC is a decoupled design, and KC is a coupled design.

According to AD, a good design needs to be uncoupled or decoupled. A coupled design is a poor design, having a lower probability of success. If it is possible to achieve two uncoupled, or two decoupled designs, then the design team must apply the information axiom and choose the design with lower information. The classification of the design may change during decomposition, being necessary to compare designs at the same level of decomposition.

Based on the application of the AD theory, the ORC is the design to choose, because it is a better design than the KC design.

5 Conclusions

This paper applies Axiomatic Design (AD) to compare the use of organic Rankine cycle (ORC) and Kalina cycle (KC) for recovering heat from the exhaust gas of a marine Diesel engine.

ORC and KC use hazardous working fluids that require special caution regarding the installation on marine vessels. Both cycles can achieve similar efficiencies, although the KC needs higher evaporating pressure and more technical concerns than for the ORC systems.

AD classifies KC as a coupled design and ORC as an uncoupled design. As a result, KC needs optimization in order to achieve the efficiency of the ORC, thus needing a special control of the valve V.

As a conclusion, according to the AD theory, the ORC system is a better design than the KC system. This result is in accordance to many technical opinions regarding this subject.

The authors gratefully thank the sponsorship of Fundação para a Ciência e Tecnologia through the Strategic Project UID/EMS/00667/2013 – UNIDEMI.

References

1. World Resources Institute, CAIT Climate Data Explorer, www.wri.org/blog/2017/04/interactive-chart-explains-worlds-top-10-emitters-and-how-theyve-changed , accessed May 20, 2018
2. https://europa.eu/european-union/topics/energy-en, accessed June 4, 2018
3. D. V. Singh, E. Pedersen, A review of waste heat recovery technologies for maritime applications, *Energy Conversion and Management*, **111**, 315–328 (2016)
4. U. Larsen, O. Sigthorsson, F. Haglind, A comparison of advanced heat recovery power cycles in a combined cycle for large ships, *Energy*, **74**, 260-268 (2014)
5. P. Bombarda, C. M. Invernizzi, C. Pietra, Heat recovery from Diesel engines: A thermodynamic comparison between Kalina and ORC cycles, *Applied Thermal Engineering*, **30**, 212–219 (2010)
6. A. Nemati, H. Nami, F. Ranjbar, M. Yari, A comparative thermodynamic analysis of ORC and Kalina cycles for waste heat recovery: A case study for CGAM cogeneration system, *Case Studies in Thermal Engineering*, **9**, 1–13 (2017)
7. D. Lin, Q. Zhu, X. Li, Thermodynamic comparative analyses between (organic) Rankine cycle and Kalina cycle, The 7th Int. Conf. on Applied Energy ICAE2015, *Energy Procedia*, **75**, 1618-1623 (2015)
8. N.P. Suh, *The principles of design*, Oxford Univ. Press, N.Y., (1990)
9. M. K. Thompson, A Classification of Procedural errors in the definition of functional requirements in axiomatic design in Axiomatic Design Theory, *Proc. 7th Int. Conf. on Axiomatic Design (ICAD 2013)*, Worcester, USA, (2013)
10. C. A. Brown, R. Henley, Metrics for Developing Functional Requirements and Selecting Design Parameters in Axiomatic Design, *Procedia CIRP*, **53**, 113–118, (2016)
11. M. Cavique, J. Fradinho, A. Gabriel-Santos, A. Gonçalves-Coelho and A. Mourão, The Iterative Nature of the "Zig" and How to Define the "Hows", 11th Int. Conf. on Axiomatic Design (ICAD 2017), *MATEC Web of Conferences,* **127**, 01007 (2017)

Application of Axiomatic Design principles in conceptual design

Josipa Delaš[1], *Stanko* Škec[1,*], and *Mario* Štorga[1]

[1]Faculty of Mechanical Engineering and Naval Architecture, University of Zagreb, 10000 Zagreb, Croatia

Abstract. The main objective of this paper is to propose a modified methodology for concept evaluation by applying Axiomatic Design principles. Several drawbacks were recognised during the literature review and application of established Axiomatic Design principles that limit its use for concept evaluation. These drawbacks include the lack of analysis of concepts that violate the Independence Axiom, the application to concepts that are not generated with Axiomatic Design and inclusion of constraints and requirements in the evaluation process. The proposed methodology consists of four steps of which the first one is to analyse the compliance of concepts with a set of functional requirements. Afterwards, to determine the possible violation of the Independence Axiom, non-diagonal elements need to be examined and reangularity and semiangularity values calculated for each concept. Finally, concepts are evaluated in terms of Information Axiom to include requirements, criteria and constraints other than functional requirements. Applying Information Axiom to all concepts regardless of Independence Axiom violation provides insight into the complexity of concepts. The proposed methodology was applied to mobility scooter conceptual design conducted in cooperation with an industrial partner. The partner company provided input and system constraints at the beginning of the project and guidelines for concept development. Constraints were taken into consideration by applying the Information Axiom in which constraints are compared with values measured on prototypes.

1 Introduction

A concept is an approximate description of the technology, working principles, and form of the product [1]. In a sufficiently developed concept, its aspects (e.g. ease of use, aesthetic, functionality etc.) can be evaluated. Concept evaluation is used to determine which concepts have the highest potential of becoming a quality product [2]. The evaluation usually occurs at the end of the conceptual design phase when developing a new product or when selecting the best concept variant among existing ones [3]. The evaluation includes a comparison of concept variants or a comparison of a concept variant with the defined ideal solution [3]. Along with several existing methods and tools, Axiomatic Design (AD) theory can also be applied for concept evaluation [4]. Application of Axiomatic Design principles usually defines how close the alternative is to the ideal one as opposed to directly comparing alternatives to each other. According to [5], ideal concepts in Axiomatic Design can satisfy the identified customer needs and are scarcely affected by sensitivity to possible alterations in later phases. Concepts' ideality is achieved by proper implementation of the Independence Axiom and, subsequently, the Information Axiom. Along with other AD principles (e.g. domains, mapping process, decomposition, hierarchy, and zigzagging [6]), axioms provide the systematic basis for solving design problems in various design areas.

One of the main advantages of Axiomatic Design, in terms of concept evaluation, is the timely detection of internal technical conflicts in generated concepts through the Independence Axiom [7]. Other advantages include the ability to evaluate complete and incomplete information criteria together [8] and visualise dependencies between design parameters [9]. Further on, the application of the Information Axiom can be used to calculate the designs' complexity [6].

When developing new concepts using AD principles, evaluation is an integral part of the design process. Axiomatic Design principles enable continuous evaluation of concepts that are being generated and improved since the conformance to axioms can be checked at every step. However, evaluation is often applied at the end of the conceptual design phase to concepts that were not solely generated using AD principles. Defining the best concept among them is time-consuming compared to other concept evaluation methods, such as concept scoring and Pugh's method [7]. This is due to the process of finding an independent set of functional requirements (FRs) and design parameters (DPs), which is iterative especially for complex designs.

This paper provides an analysis of existing principles for concept evaluation with Axiomatic Design and suggests certain improvements to evaluation methodology. These improvements are a part of the proposed modified concept evaluation methodology which aims to resolve drawbacks observed in literature as well as in the implementation of AD principles in concept evaluation. A case study serves as the validation of the proposed methodology which, combined with the conducted literature review, provided the basis for the discussion and the conclusion.

* Corresponding author: stanko.skec@fsb.hr

2 Theoretical background

Design using AD principles begins with defining functional requirements by reformulating customer needs (CNs) in a way that completely characterises the functional needs of a product. This first step enables comparison of different concepts designed to satisfy the same customer needs. The process of defining or selecting a DP that satisfies a certain FR is called the physical mapping [10]. Definition of DPs on higher decomposition level as specific solutions should be avoided, due to the risk of constraining the definitions of lower-level FRs and DPs. Instead, they can represent conceptual entities whose definition is extracted from the corresponding FR to prevent making early choices. Designs are detailed by decomposing FRs and DPs from a high level of abstraction to lower levels which contain detailed modularity elements [9]. The decomposition is achieved by zigzagging from FRs and DPs on different levels. From DPs on the higher-level, we define FRs on the lower level that completely satisfy the highest-level FR. DPs are then defined for lower-level FRs accordingly. These relationships between FRs and DPs are recorded in the design matrix.

The design matrices present the basis for the concept evaluation in terms of Axiomatic Design principles. The relationship between a specific FR and a corresponding DP found in the design matrix is called coupling. The Independence Axiom says that in an acceptable design, FRs and DPs are related in such a way that a specific DP can be adjusted to satisfy its corresponding FR without affecting other FRs [11]. Designs defined as uncoupled have coupling only in the main matrix diagonal and completely fulfil the Independence Axiom. The decoupled design has couplings on one side of the main matrix diagonal as well and therefore partially satisfies the Independence Axiom. Coupled design violates the Independence Axiom as it has couplings on both sides of the main matrix diagonal.

Concept evaluation using AD principles is based on a claim that a good concept completely satisfies the Independence Axiom. Depending on the number of couplings and design matrix size, in certain cases, it can be easy to distinguish which concept satisfies the Independence Axiom the most (by only looking at the design matrices). In other cases, independence is measured by calculating reangularity (R) and semiangularity (S). Reangularity relates the angles between the axes of the design parameters, while semiangularity measures the magnitude of the diagonal elements [12]:

$$R = \prod_{\substack{i=1,n-1 \\ j=1+i,n}} \sqrt{1 - \frac{\left(\sum_{k=1}^{n} A_{ki}A_{kj}\right)^2}{\left(\sum_{k=1}^{n} A_{ki}^2\right)\left(\sum_{k=1}^{n} A_{kj}^2\right)}} \quad (1)$$

$$S = \prod_{j=1}^{n} \frac{|A_{jj}|}{\sqrt{\sum_{k=1}^{n} A_{kj}^2}} \quad (2)$$

In these equations, A refers to the value inside the design matrix in the row defined with the first index and the column defined with the second index.

R value decreases as the degree of coupling increases. For $R=S=1$, the design is completely uncoupled, and for $R=S<1$ the design is decoupled. This calculation presents the basis for the coupling analysis which determines whether the Independence Axiom has been satisfied, and is implemented as the first part of the evaluation using AD principles. Procedure found in [11] is the most common for conceptualisation and analysis of the generated concepts with Axiomatic Design. It states that if multiple designs satisfy the Independence Axiom, the best among them is chosen by utilising the Information Axiom [Fig. 1]. The Information Axiom states that the information content in a design should be minimised. In other words, the design that results in the highest probability of meeting design specifications is the best one [11]. The highest probability of success indicates the lowest amount of information needed to manufacture (produce) the design [10]. However, the Independence Axiom is often satisfied, and thereby the Information Axiom is not utilised as a part of the evaluation procedure [8].

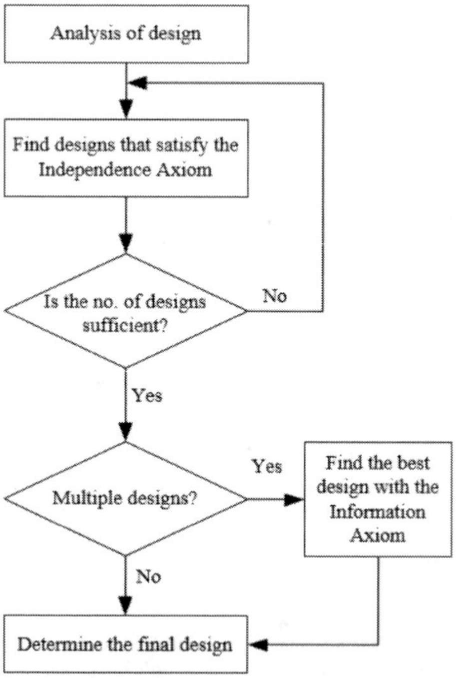

Fig. 1. Flowchart of the application of Axiomatic Design [11]

Several studies of evaluation with Axiomatic Design principles have been conducted ([13]–[15]) based on the aforementioned procedure. For example, AD principles were used to analyse and improve designs of emergency core cooling systems by complying to the Independence Axiom and, afterwards, the best among them was chosen with the Information Axiom [13]. Further, evaluation of the suspension systems was conducted by applying the axioms and analysing coupling to improve ride comfort [14]. In a case study that evaluated existing friction devices [15], the Information Axiom is applied even though none of the designs satisfies the Independence Axiom. In some studies, the evaluation was conducted as part of the application of Axiomatic Design principles for product development [16][17].

Based on these and other formerly conducted studies three drawbacks of concept evaluation with Axiomatic Design were recognised. To start with, problems occur when concepts that weren't generated with AD principles are being evaluated since the evaluation procedure itself doesn't alternate the relationships between defined FRs and DPs. To be more precise, procedure for evaluation is not defined if concepts that weren't generated using AD principles violate the Independence Axiom. However, concepts that are chosen for detailing can be subsequently modified by taking into consideration recognised couplings.

Secondly, there is a lack of guidelines for incorporating different types of requirements and criteria in concept evaluation. For instance, non-technical requirements are defined as constraints and, as such, are not part of the design matrix (and, consequently, not part of the evaluation) [7]. This exclusion of non-technical requirements can result in unaesthetic and costly products that fail to satisfy customer needs [11].

Thirdly, decomposition can include non-essential functions, which aim to increase attractive qualities of a product [18]. For instance, primary functions of a mobile phone are to send and receive phone calls, provide access to the Internet, take photos etc., but adding additional features to the camera can make the mobile phone more desirable. This approach leads to concepts that have a different set of FRs, even though they satisfy the same customer needs (CNs). When using AD principles for evaluation often certain concepts don't fulfil all identified FRs. As such, concepts have design matrices of various sizes what makes a comparison of concepts difficult. In other words, it is hard to achieve the ranking of alternatives since AD principles usually compare concepts to the ideal one.

Building on these premises, the following research methodology was used to structure and conduct this study.

3 Research methodology

The literature review was conducted during the preliminary research phase to analyse existing evaluation procedures based on Axiomatic Design principles.

Initial concept evaluation was done based on [11], which, along with the analysis of existing case studies, revealed its drawbacks. This procedure suggests applying Axiomatic Design in the same way for different purposes - concept development, analysis of existing designs and design improvement [11]. As such, it seems to be too generic and does not provide sufficient guidelines for the concept evaluation itself. For instance, in a case study of evaluating in-pipe robot design [16], dependencies of FRs and DPs were observed only at their own level of decomposition. This type of dependency analysis could lead to unrecognised couplings that, consequently, cause design issues in later stages of the design process. Other examples found in literature usually define a different design matrix for each concept. In such cases, concepts aren't compared to one another but only tested to see if and to what extent do they satisfy the Independence Axiom.

To address issues identified during the initial concept evaluation, the proposed methodology suggests creating a single design matrix equal for all developed concepts that includes their FRs and corresponding DPs. Mutual comparison of concepts can provide further insights into their strengths and weaknesses. Decomposition of a single concept rarely shows which FRs are missing, whereas having multiple concepts defined with the same FRs can indicate which FRs haven't been fulfilled by different concepts. Therefore, the analysis of fulfilment of FRs is set as a first step of the concept evaluation with the modified procedure. The second step, the analysis of non-diagonal elements, is added for similar reasons. An indication of mutual couplings can also help the designer to recognise reoccurrence of specific design problems, and imply potential solutions through comparison with other matrices. Examples found in the literature mostly aim at an analysis of concepts that are being generated by considering the Independence Axiom. Concepts that were not generated with AD principles often cannot be altered in such way, and therefore this methodology proposes an additional application of the Information Axiom to better inform a designer before deciding on a potential concept that should be further developed.

In order to illustrate the application of the modified methodology for concept evaluation, it was applied to mobility scooter conceptual design conducted in cooperation with an industrial partner.

4 Proposed modified methodology for concept evaluation

To tackle the previously mentioned problems in Sections 2 and 3, this paper proposes the modified concept evaluation methodology [Fig. 2]. The proposed procedure is primarily intended for evaluation of concepts that weren't generated with AD principles. In such cases, FRs are set after working principles of a product have already been defined. Such concepts cannot be changed to satisfy the Independence Axiom since alterations aren't a part of the evaluation process.

Unlike the procedure provided in [Fig. 1] where evaluation begins with the Independence Axiom, in modified methodology presented in this paper evaluation starts with an analysis of the number of fulfilled FRs. Therefore, evaluation applying Independence Axiom is conducted when there isn't a single concept that satisfies the set of FRs. This second part of the evaluation starts with an analysis of non-diagonal elements in the design matrix. Non-diagonal elements, i.e. couplings, found in one concept can perhaps be resolved by taking a partial solution from another concept which lacks that non-diagonal element.

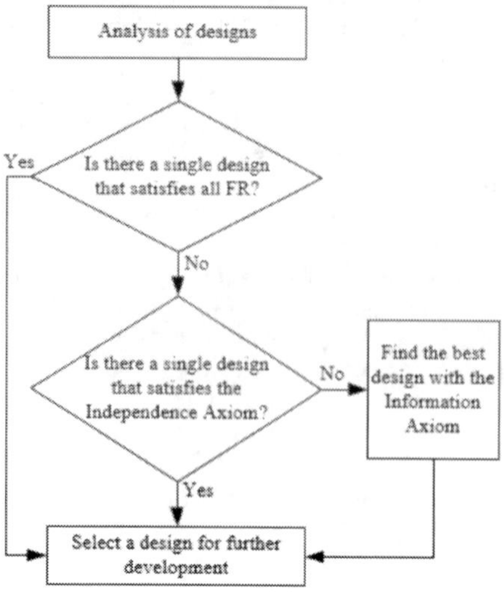

Fig. 2. Modified flowchart of the application of Axiomatic Design

This step is followed by the coupling analysis of the created design matrices. Design matrices of the highest level cannot be solely used for evaluation because they aren't related to concepts, but present general decomposition of the design problem. Therefore, lower-level design matrices are integrated into upper-level matrices until the single final matrix for all developed concepts is defined. If a concept does not fulfil a certain FR or lacks a specific DP, corresponding row or column needs to be removed from the design matrix creating a smaller matrix for that concept. Due to possible design complexity, obtained design matrices can be large, which is why reangularity and semiangularity should be calculated to determine the coupling measure for specific concepts. This calculation enables direct comparison of concepts based on satisfaction of the Independence Axiom. However, calculation of semiangularity and reangularity metrics often requires a substantial amount of data and is, therefore, more appropriate for later stages of the design process. This data could be obtained from computer simulations (e.g. FEM and kinematic analysis) or analysis of produced prototypes.

If a final decision cannot be made based on these steps, the Information Axiom is applied, because, unlike the Independence Axiom, it can take into consideration other requirements that have been set on the product. Various constraints can be used to calculate the information content and help choose the best concept. Values of these constraints can be used as the design range (DR), and the ability of the system to fulfil these values is called the system range (SR). The probability of success or, in other words, the information content, is the intersection between the design range and system range. The concept with the smallest information content is the best one according to the Information Axiom.

5 Application of proposed methodology

Within the scope of a student product development project course, new mobility scooter concepts were developed. Mobility scooters are electrically powered vehicles designed specifically for the people with limited mobility. The aim of the student development project was to develop a mobility scooter which can be folded and adjusted according to the user needs while considering its aesthetics and ergonomics constraints. At the end of the project, prototypes of developed concepts were produced. This enabled measurement of the fulfilment of the desired requirements set at the beginning of the project. Proposed evaluation methodology was afterwards applied to developed concepts in order to illustrate its application on the student project.

5.1 Defining requirements

Evaluation criteria for the case study were derived from customer needs, constraints and non-functional requirements. Customer needs were defined from information gathered through market research and interviews with customers. Most important CNs include the need for a mobility scooter to be lightweight enough for a single person to lift and carry, the possibility of transporting in a car trunk and airport luggage, and the ability to adjust the vehicle so that it suits various people, regardless of their height and mobility. In addition to this, non-functional requirements were defined, because they contain features essential to the customer which couldn't be incorporated into functional requirements (e.g. easy to clean). Industrial partner provided input constraints which present target values for parameters measured on produced prototypes (e.g. mass needs to be under 10kg). Legal obligations are translated into system constraints which must be met (e.g. max speed of 6 km/h).

Functional requirements on the highest level are defined from customer needs regardless of the partial solutions provided in concepts. Satisfying the FRs set on the highest level is a priority because otherwise the basic product functions aren't fulfilled. The defined set of FRs on the highest level is then decomposed to determine FRs on lower levels.

5.2 Generating design matrices

Design parameters of each level are obtained through the standard process of zigzagging as explained in Section 2. This zigzagging procedure results in initial design matrices that define relationships between FRs and DPs of each level separately and cannot be used for concept evaluation. The process of determining initial design matrices is iterative to ensure that FRs defined by decomposition are mutually exclusive and collectively exhaustive (MECE) [19]. In a collectively exhaustive decomposition, higher-level FR is completely defined with corresponding lower-level FRs. Mutually exclusive decomposition results in lower-levels FRs that do not overlap. As such, this process describes the minimum set of FRs that entirely characterises the design objective [4]. However, developed concepts can contain additional functional requirements that can result in deviations from the ideal design. Without introducing additional FRs, it wouldn't be possible to conduct the detailed evaluation.

Design matrices are filled with symbols *X* in case of an existing relationship between specific FR and a corresponding DP, and *0*, when there is no relationship between FR and DP. In other words, the designer determines which FRs and DPs are coupled. The relationship can be defined with a design equation to determine the exact value, but it usually assumes the value of 1 if an FR and a DP are completely coupled.

Design matrix of the highest level is upper triangular (decoupled) [Table 1]. Design matrices on lower levels need to be uncoupled or also upper triangular to satisfy the Independence Axiom. In other words, coupling that appeared on the highest level of decomposition must be reflected on lower levels as well. Subsequently, the coupling is affected by changing the order of fulfilling functional requirements. The order of rows in the design matrices indicates the order of fulfilling FRs.

Mobility scooter design was decomposed on 3 levels, and the total of 30 FRs and DPs was defined. For conciseness, only 3 out of 9 initial design matrices will be shown and explained.

Table 1. Decomposition on the highest level

INDEX	FR	DP
1	Ensure load capacity	Rigidity of basic structure
2	Allow movement of parts	Movable subsystem
3	Ensure the flow of energy required for movement	System for movement
4	Enable operating of the vehicle	Operating components

$$\begin{bmatrix} FR_1 \\ FR_2 \\ FR_3 \\ FR_4 \end{bmatrix} = \begin{bmatrix} X & X & X & 0 \\ 0 & X & 0 & X \\ 0 & 0 & X & 0 \\ 0 & 0 & 0 & X \end{bmatrix} \begin{bmatrix} DP_1 \\ DP_2 \\ DP_3 \\ DP_4 \end{bmatrix} \quad (3)$$

By further decomposition of the FR_1 *Ensure load capacity,* another upper triangular matrix was generated [Table 2]. This design matrix for FR_1 includes, in addition to others, the symbol *x*, which means that the FR and DP aren't coupled at the moment, but could become in later stages of the design process. We can define that $X>>x$, and the relationship containing *x* as currently uncoupled, but there is no guarantee of satisfying the Independence Axiom in case the concept is changed. For instance, DP_{12} *Dampening front fork* can affect the FR_{11} *Ensure construction rigidity* depending on the design.

Table 2. Decomposition of FR_1 Ensure load capacity

INDEX	FR	DP
11	Ensure construction rigidity	Shock-absorbent frame
12	Reduce the shock impact on the front part of the construction	Dampening front fork
13	User positioning	Adjustable seat
14	Secure user against fallout	Safety supports
15	Enable transportation of additional cargo	Removable storage space

$$\begin{bmatrix} FR_{11} \\ FR_{12} \\ FR_{13} \\ FR_{14} \\ FR_{15} \end{bmatrix} = \begin{bmatrix} X & x & 0 & 0 & 0 \\ 0 & X & 0 & 0 & 0 \\ 0 & 0 & X & X & 0 \\ 0 & 0 & 0 & X & 0 \\ 0 & 0 & 0 & 0 & X \end{bmatrix} \begin{bmatrix} DP_{11} \\ DP_{12} \\ DP_{13} \\ DP_{14} \\ DP_{15} \end{bmatrix} \quad (4)$$

Decomposition of the FR_{14} *Secure user against fallout* resulted in decoupled matrix [Table 3]. The DPs on this level are parts of the DP_{13} *Adjustable seat* what leads to couplings that potentially have to be resolved. Yet, FRs on the observed level are independent, and the couplings can be shown in the final matrix.

Table 3. Decomposition of FR_{14} Secure user against fallout

INDEX	FR	DP
141	Support legs	Stable leg support
142	Support arms	Firm seat armrests
143	Support back	Firm seat backrest

$$\begin{bmatrix} FR_{141} \\ FR_{142} \\ FR_{143} \end{bmatrix} = \begin{bmatrix} X & 0 & 0 \\ 0 & X & 0 \\ 0 & 0 & X \end{bmatrix} \begin{bmatrix} DP_{141} \\ DP_{142} \\ DP_{143} \end{bmatrix} \quad (5)$$

The FR_1 *Ensure load capacity* was decomposed with two matrices shown above. Decomposition is the same for each scooter which makes them comparable.

5.3 Evaluation based on achieved matrices

According to the first evaluation step, none of the mobility scooter concepts entirely fulfils the defined set of FRs. Moreover, 3 out of 4 concepts do not allow the transportation of additional cargo (FR_{15}). Other than this FR, concepts only partially fulfil the FR_{21} *Enable folding,* meaning that the mobility scooter concepts can be folded but not by satisfying the entire set of FRs on the lower level. This is due to the implementation of FRs that are specific to certain concepts. This problem can occur when evaluating concepts which were not generated using AD principles since the same higher-level FR can be achieved through a different set of lower-level FRs. In such cases, not fulfilling every FR defined on a lower level doesn't imply that a higher-level FR hasn't been satisfied. Fulfilment of FRs for each concept is shown in a tabular view, to make analysis easier [Table 4]. If a particular concept fulfils an FR, the table contains an *X*, otherwise it contains *0*.

Concept 4 fulfils more FRs in comparison to others and, therefore, its final design matrix contains the highest number of FRs and DPs. However, matrix size doesn't necessarily imply that concept represents a better solution. For instance, every scooter can fulfil FR_{21} *Enable folding* and, multiple FRs on its lower decomposition level present a complicated folding procedure for the user. In other words, additional FRs can be perceived as redundant. Since Concept 2 can fulfil all the higher-level FRs (*Enable transportation of additional cargo*, *Enable folding* and *Adjust vehicle to the user*), it is considered as a better concept, even though concept 4 fulfils all lower-level FRs for adjusting the vehicle to the user. Concepts 1 and 3 were identified as weaker solutions based on this first step of evaluation.

Table 4. Evaluation based on fulfilment of FRs that haven't been satisfied in all concepts

Functional requirements (FR)		Concept 1	Concept 2	Concept 3	Concept 4
Enable transportation of additional cargo (FR_{15})		0	X	0	0
Enable folding (FR_{21})	Alter frame length (FR_{211})	X	0	0	0
	Rotate seat carrier (FR_{212})	X	0	X	X
	Enable tiller folding (FR_{213})	X	0	0	X
	Enable frame folding (FR_{214})	0	X	X	X
Adjust vehicle to the user (FR_{23})	Adjust tiller height (FR_{231})	0	X	0	X
	Adjust tiller angle (FR_{232})	0	0	0	X
	Adjust seat height (FR_{233})	0	X	0	X
	Enable seat rotation (FR_{234})	0	X	0	X

The next step in evaluation is the analysis of non-diagonal elements in the final matrices of each concept. Table 5 shows how many non-diagonal elements are shared between different concept solutions. This comparison may indicate which independencies designers most often fail to satisfy. In addition, it can support designers in their search for partial solutions in other concepts that managed to satisfy Independence Axiom.

Table 5. Number of common and total number of non-diagonal elements in concepts

	Concept 1	Concept 2	Concept 3	Concept 4
Concept 1		20	21	22
Concept 2	20		21	29
Concept 3	21	21		22
Concept 4	22	29	22	
Total no. of non-diagonal elements	**24**	**36**	**22**	**40**

The total number of non-diagonal elements represents how many couplings appear in the final design matrix of each concept. Concept 4 has the highest total number of non-diagonal elements. This is partially due to the many FRs defined for folding of the scooter and adjusting it to the user. Concept 3 has the lowest number of FRs for folding and adjusting the vehicle, and the smallest number of non-diagonal elements. Comparison of the total number of non-diagonal elements and the common number of elements can sometimes indicate a common issue among different designs. In this case study, there are 19 non-diagonal elements common to all four concepts. Due to such a high number of non-diagonal elements, it can be concluded that maintaining the independence of FR_{21} *Enable folding* and FR_{23} *Adjust vehicle to the user* was a difficult task for designers. Beside these two FRs, by analysing the location of non-diagonal elements, partial solutions for couplings can be found and applied to other concepts. For instance, DP_{311} *Li-ion battery* is dependent on the FR_{46} *Usable in darkness*. This coupling can be resolved by providing an independent power source for the light that every scooter must have due to legal obligations.

Afterwards, concept comparison was done by calculating reangularity and semiangularity with equations given in Section 2 of this paper. At this stage of the design process, there was not enough information to determine the exact coupling values. Therefore, design matrices were populated with values based on designers' perception of coupling severity in the following way: *X* equals 1, *x* equals 0,1 due to the condition *X>>x*, and *0* remained 0. Calculated values are shown in [Table 6].

Table 6. Concept comparison by reangularity and semiangularity values

	Reangularity	Semiangularity

Concept 1	0,3266	0,001889
Concept 2	0,3952	0,000564
Concept 3	0,3462	0,003646
Concept 4	0,2933	0,000344

These values imply that none of the concepts satisfies the Independence Axiom. To our knowledge, literature doesn't provide guidelines whether the concept for further development should be the one with the highest value of reangularity (R=1 for uncoupled designs) or the one with the smallest difference between reangularity and semiangularity (R=S for a decoupled design). Concept 2 and Concept 4 are closer to satisfying the desired design matrix than concepts 1 and 3, but are still far away from fulfilling the Independence Axiom. Therefore, a final decision wasn't made and, the Information Axiom had to be applied for further evaluation.

In this final step, input constraints provided by the industrial partner were compared to the values measured on the prototypes [Table 7]. In addition to this, folding time was added as an important aspect for the users. The information content is calculated with equations provided in [10] where the SR is achieved value on a concept, and the CR is input constraint value. Information content is defined as zero if the achieved value is smaller or the same as required.

Table 7. Concept comparison based on Information Axiom

Criteria	Constraint value	Concept 1	Concept 2	Concept 3	Concept 4
Mass [kg]	≤10	26,1	23,1	26,3	24,5
Folding time [s]	min= 13	20	13	27	40
Length [mm]	≤900	950	810	950	780
Height [mm]	≤700	770	598	700	650
Width [mm]	≤400	620	670	550	870
Total information content	-	2,853	1,952	2,987	4,035

Since the ideal information content is 0, it can be concluded that Concept 2 is the best solution according to the Information Axiom. It has the smallest mass and the least folding time which are two aspects of the utmost importance for the user. On the other hand, Concept 4 which fulfils more FRs has proven to be more complicated compared to other scooters and particularly, Concept 2.

This application represents four steps explained in the proposed modified methodology for the concept evaluation with AD principles. Each step provided different insights into the strengths and weaknesses of the analysed concepts. The application also showed that results are inconsistent by using different AD evaluation criteria. Using the Independence Axiom, Concept 4 is perceived as the best solution due to the least amount of changes that are required for satisfaction and fulfilment of FRs. However, other steps in the evaluation, like calculation of reangularity and semiangularity values, non-diagonal elements and the Information Axiom, raised serious concerns about Concept 4 due to additional FRs. These results may be a consequence of working with concepts that weren't generated using AD principles since it can be hard to retroactively achieve the minimum set of FRs like AD principles demand. If the evaluation was based solely on the Independence Axiom, as is usually the case, Concept 4 could've been chosen as the best one. This application shows that a more extensive validation of various concept evaluation steps should be taken in further studies to embrace different criteria and aspects of the proposed solutions.

6 Discussion

Application of AD principles to concept evaluation relies more on technical knowledge, compared to other methods used for evaluation, since the designer reformulates the needs perceived by the customer into the functional requirements [12]. Therefore, this results in an evaluation process based on the fulfilment and independence of functional requirements and may reduce biased personal judgments [7]. However, Axiomatic Design doesn't provide a way to check whether the CNs have been adequately reformulated to FRs. In addition, there is still no detailed procedure for defining FRs. Other than defining FRs, it is crucial to specify non-technical requirements and constraints properly. Until now, these other types of information usually haven't been incorporated into the evaluation process.

In addition, literature doesn't acknowledge the difference of evaluating concepts generated with or without AD principles. Concepts that weren't generated with AD principles aren't improved to satisfy the Independence Axiom within the scope of the evaluation. However, conducted evaluation suggests improvements which can be applied in the later stages of the design process.

The proposed methodology suggests an implementation of constraints for the design range as a part of the Information Axiom. The implementation can be hard to conduct if there is not enough information about target values for concepts. However, implemented constraints can show to what extent the customer needs are satisfied. Examples found in literature mostly compared a single concept to its ideal solution [10]-[15]. Previously, concepts were often not compared to one another due to their different decompositions on lower levels. The proposed methodology aims to avoid this problem by generating a general common matrix for each concept that includes FRs found in all of them. If the concepts aren't comparable in such way, evaluation cannot be done based on fulfilment of FRs and number of total and shared non-diagonal elements. On the other hand, if the evaluation based on fulfilment of FRs isn't conducted, an incomplete solution could be chosen.

One of the advantages of applying the proposed methodology is the ability to combine different solutions from various concepts to solve certain couplings. Analysis of non-diagonal elements provides insight about couplings that are the most difficult for the designer to resolve. It also enables easy comparison of different solutions which can be beneficial when combining different concepts. These first two steps, the fulfilment of FRs and analysis of non-diagonal elements, are suitable for application in the earlier phases of conceptualisation. In addition, they are easy to implement.

In this case study, application of Independence Axiom in terms of calculating coupling measures (reangularity and semiangularity) hasn't provided sufficient information for concept selection. This may be due to the small differences between the obtained concept values and inadequate definition of the coupling values. Therefore, the Information Axiom was applied to the concepts that didn't satisfy the Independence Axiom, even though Axiomatic Design theory advises against it. Unlike the first two steps, calculating the coupling measures and the Information Axiom usually requires more data and is often more appropriate to implement in later stages of the design process. More case studies will be conducted to provide additional validation and testing of the proposed methodology.

7 Conclusion

The modified methodology proposed in this paper aims to solve reoccurring issues found in the literature about various aspects of concept evaluation using AD principles. The underlying logic of the proposed methodology suggests a definition of the common matrices for developed concepts and includes four subsequent steps to enable proper concept evaluation. Each of the evaluation steps showed its advantages and potential issues as pointed out in the previous section.

The validation of the proposed methodology was carried out by analysing concepts generated during mobile scooter development. After initial matrices were defined, couplings were affected by reformulating FRs and DPs and changing their order in the design matrix. The proposed evaluation methodology showed that none of the concepts fulfils the whole set of FRs and the Independence Axiom. Therefore, the evaluation at this stage was inconclusive, indicating the need for the Information Axiom.

Further research should examine the problem of carrying out different FRs throughout the different phases of the product lifecycle. For instance, the user either adjusts the mobility scooter or unfolds/folds it, but never simultaneously. Currently, such cases are usually presented as coupling even though it is preferable to have the same product fulfil different functions at different times. Coupling measures, R and S, should be also further studied to ensure the proper analysis and interpretation of obtained values. Although there are many ways to apply the Information Axiom, further research should be conducted to enable implementation of different types of requirements and criteria.

The case project was a part of the Erasmus+ Strategic Partnership programme and funded with support from the European Commission. This communication reflects the views of the authors, and the Commission cannot be held responsible for any use which may be made of the information contained therein.

References

[1] K. T. Ulrich and S. D. Eppinger, *Product Design and Development*, 5th ed. 2012.

[2] D. G. Ullman, *The Mechanical Design Process*. New York: McGraw-Hill, 2010.

[3] G. Pahl, W. Beitz, J. Feldhusen, and K.-H. Grote, *Engineering Design*, 3rd ed. Springer-Verlag, 2007.

[4] N. P. Suh, *The Principles of Design*. Oxford University Press, 1990.

[5] Y. Borgianni and D. T. Matt, "Ideality in Axiomatic Design and beyond," in *Procedia CIRP*, 2016, vol. 53, pp. 95–100.

[6] N. P. Suh, *Complexity: Theory and Application*. Oxford University Press, 2005.

[7] A. Xiao, S. S. Park, and T. Freiheit, "A Comparison of Concept Selection in Concept Scoring and Axiomatic Design Methods," *Proc. Can. Eng. Educ. Assoc.*, 2011.

[8] O. Kulak, S. Cebi, and C. Kahraman, "Applications of axiomatic design principles: A literature review," *Expert Syst. Appl.*, vol. 37, no. 9, pp. 6705–6717, 2010.

[9] A. Kreuzer, B. Nitsche, and J. Kantola, "Application of Axiomatic Design to Electric Bicycles," *Proc. ICAD2014, Eight Int. Conf. Axiomat. Des.*, pp. 35–42, 2014.

[10] B. El-Haik, *Axiomatic Quality: Integrating Axiomatic Design with Six-Sigma, Reliability, and Quality Engineering*. John Wiley & Sons, 2005.

[11] G.-J. Park, *Analytic Methods for Design Practice*. Springer Science & Business Media, 2007.

[12] D. Silverstein, P. Samuel, and N. Decarlo, *Axiomatic Design*, vol. 1. 2011.

[13] G. Heo and S. K. Lee, "Design evaluation of emergency core cooling systems using Axiomatic Design," *Nucl. Eng. Des.*, vol. 237, no. 1, pp. 38–46, 2007.

[14] J. H. Kim, K. S. Kim, and Y. J. Kang, "Ride comfort evaluation and suspension design using axiomatic design," *J. Mech. Sci. Technol.*, vol. 21, no. 7, pp. 1066–1076, 2007.

[15] A. Girgenti, A. Giorgetti, C. Monti, and P. Citti, "Conceptual Design Evaluation of Different Friction Devices Through the Use of Axiomatic Design," *Proc. ICAD2014, Eighth Int. Conf. Axiomat. Des.*, 2014.

[16] J. Qiao and J. Shang, "Application of axiomatic design method in in-pipe robot design," *Robot. Comput. Integr. Manuf.*, vol. 29, no. 4, pp. 49–57, 2013.

[17] G. Bragason, S. Porsteinsson, R. I. Karlsson, N. Grosse, and J. T. Foley, "Heat-activated Parachute Release System," *Proc. 9th Int. Conf. Axiomat. Des.*, vol. 34, pp. 131–136, 2015.

[18] M. K. Thompson, "Where Is the 'Why' in Axiomatic Design?," *Proc. ICAD2014 Eighth Int. Conf. Axiomat. Des.*, pp. 7–12, 2014.

[19] C. A. Brown, "Decomposition and prioritization in engineering design," *Proc. 6th Int. Conf. Axiomat. Des.*, pp. 41–47, 2011.

Design of a tablet holder with the help of Axiomatic Design

International Conference of Axiomatic Design 2017

Auðunn Herjólfsson[1], *Haraldur* Helgason[1], *Sindri S.* Ingvason[1], *Þráinn* Þórarinsson[1], and *Joseph Timothy* Foley[1,*]

[1] *Reykjavik University, Menntavegur 1, Reykjavik 101, Iceland*

Abstract. With the explosion of smart devices, tablets can currently be found everywhere. From schools to kiosks to watching movies in bed, these devices are prevalent everywhere in modern life. The problem with watching movies in bed using tablets is the necessity of hand usage. The market currently holds a few products that attempt to solve this, but none truly frees the user, allowing them hands-free usage with an easy exit of the bed. In this paper, we will describe a design which, utilizing axiomatic design, will out-perform anything currently existing in the same field, by giving a stable viewing experience while fitting to nearly any bed or sofa. Axiomatic Design ensured a comprehensive design process by ensuring customer needs were transformed into carefully thought out functional requirements and design parameters while maintaining modularity.

1 Introduction

Media has over the years become one of most popular recreational activity in the modern home. Not too long ago it was common to have a 2nd TV set in the bedroom but with increased usage in smart devices such as phones or tablets, they are becoming fewer. Watching a movie in bed or net-surfing is something most people can relate to in one way or another. The problem with the tablet is to gain a good viewing angle. This problem even existed with the TV sets as people tried to attach them near the ceiling. With the tablet, being a smaller object, people often hold it above their head, leading to bloodless arms or lay it on their knees leading to great neck pain. The Recreational Entertainment and Comfort-Enhancer, or TREC-E for short, aims to solve this 1st world problem with a unit resulting in a hands-free viewing experience ideal for anyone to catch up on his favorite series before sleep.

1.1 Customer Needs

For a design to happen, the first step is to accurately define the needs of the customer. And the first step of defining the needs of the customer is to realize who the customer is, so the product can be designed for the right person. The goals of identifying customer needs are, according to Ulrich and Eppinger [1], as follows:

- Ensure that the product is focused on customer needs.
- Identify latent or hidden needs as well as explicit needs.
- Provide a fact base for justifying the product specifications.
- Create an archival record of the needs activity of the development process
- Ensure that no critical customer need is missed or forgotten.
- Develop a common understanding of customer needs among members of the development team.

The customer of this product is a person who likes to watch movies or other media while lying down on a bed or a sofa. To assess the customer needs, the team had a brainstorming session to try and figure out the necessities of the product, considering the base idea and said customer.

- CN_1 Fit on as many different beds and couches as possible
- CN_2 Hold tablets/other smart devices of various size and weight
- CN_3 Push easily out of the way when the user is in need of getting up
- CN_4 Adjust easily while remaining stable

2 Prior Art

There are many types of tablet holders on the market. Even after narrowing them down into those who are suitable for the bedroom there are a only a few major concepts.

2.1 Similar Patents

A search of patents involving the fixturing and positioning of tablets to a surface results in a large variety of approaches.

- The "Tablet Holder", a device which seems to be designed for the purpose of holding tablets, but not mounting them to anything [2]

*e-mail: foley@ru.is

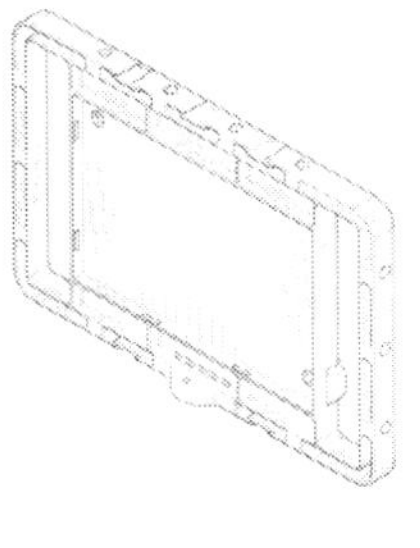

Fig. 1. The patented "Tablet Holder", as pictured in the patent. Image taken from Google patents.

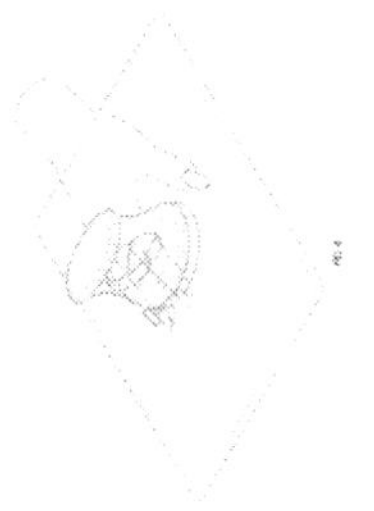

Fig. 2. The patented "Computer Tablet Holder", as pictured in the patent. Image taken from Google patents.

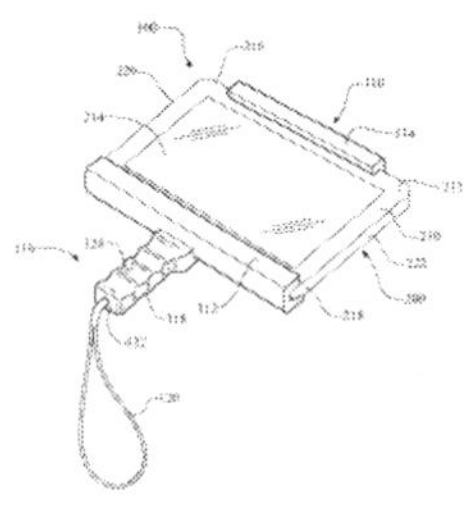

Fig. 3. The patented "Multi Media Tablet Holder", as pictured in the patent. Image taken from Google patents.

- The "Computer Tablet Holder", a device for gripping the tablet in a comfortable way, but requires a manual holding [3]
- The "Multi-Media Tablet Holder", similar to the "Tablet Holder", but with a piece of string, presumably to hang the device for hands-free usage [4]
- The oddly-named "Sqweezel", which is mentioned in this list despite only having a patent pending, is a custom-order product, for hands-free usage. It is available in several colors and a few different shapes, all utilizing a rubber clamp to fit a multitude of devices, and either a table mount or permanent wall mount. [5]
- The "Tabbi" is yet another concept and boasts the ability to attach to nearly any surface, through the utilization of a patented gel suction cup.

Fig. 4. The Tabbi, with the patented gel suction cup, as pictured on the official Kickstarter page. Image taken from Kickstarter.

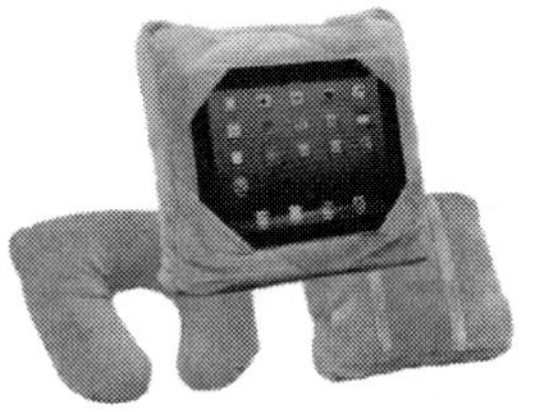

Fig. 5. GOGO Pillow [6]

2.2 Commercially available tablet fixtures

All of the market-available concepts do free the hands for other activities but do so in quite different ways. From resting on the mattress along with the user to merging into a pillow or clamping to tables, the goal always seems to be stability along with hands-free usage.

2.2.1 GOGO Pillow

One example is the GOGO Pillow shown in Fig. 5, with retail value from amazon.co.uk at 43.14£. Some of its notable features and limitations include:

1. Can only be placed at a relatively low viewing angle
2. A pillow resting on a bed is highly stable

The GOGO pillow is highly limited when it comes to the CN_4, as possible viewing positions are very few.

2.2.2 Tablift

Another concept is based on the idea of crouching over its user and therefore does not leave much room for moving around. For the same reason, it might be a tiring process to move it out of the way in a need of getting up. The four-legged design does not provide a variety of viewing positions and is limited to quite a low viewing angle. An example of this is the Tablift shown in Fig. 6 which sells at $39.95 on www.tablift.com.

Some of its notable features and limitations include:

Fig. 6. The Tablift [7]

Fig. 7. The Stanaway Gooseneck [8]

1. Provides limited space for users to move around
2. Does not provide adequate space to allow optimal comfort in viewing for two people simultaneously
3. Cumbersome to move out of the way in need of getting up
4. Provides some variety of viewing angles, but the number could be increased

The Tablift does not move out of the way as effortlessly as CN_3 indicates, and viewing angles are also limited in number, failing CN_4.

2.2.3 Flexible arm

One concept, which is a close cousin to the TREC-E, is an adjustable arm system made out of thin tubes which can be bent into various shapes, often attached to a desktop with a screw clamp. The adjustable arm allows multiple viewing angles. However, the thin tube does not provide a great stability. When extended to its limits it becomes quite flimsy and difficult to maneuver.

The Stanaway Gooseneck, shown in Fig. 7 is a example of this design an goes for $15,99 on amazon.com

Some of its notable features and limitations include:

1. Provides acceptable stability, except at great extension.
2. Does require mounting to a sturdy nearby object.

The Gooseneck most likely has room for improvement when it comes to stability, and also is not overly compatible with furniture, failing CN_1.

3 Design

Axiomatic Design teaches us that simple and independent features can make for an excellent design. [9]

> With a clear focus on functional requirements and their respective design parameters, a products geometry and features can be designed quickly, accurately, and effectively. The coupling between these FRs and DPs is another matter of high importance. This can be mathematically demonstrated, as is shown in 1 where a non-zero entity represents a connection between the two. If this Cartesian product shows zeros, the corresponding FR and DP are not connected. Should a diagonal line of non-zero values appear, with all other values in the matrix displayed as zeros, then the design can be called un-coupled. This is an ideal design, as changes in one DP do not alter more than the only designated FR. This is called a diagonal matrix, and it satisfies the Independence Axiom: "to maintain the independence of the functional requirements (FRs)" [10].

From the Customer Needs, we built a list of Functional Requirements.

- FR_1 Attaches securely between any hard surface and a cushion
- FR_2 Holds tablets/smart devices up to 14 inches and 1 kg. One of the largest and heaviest tablets on the market today is the Toshiba Excite 13 [11]
- FR_3 Pushes out of the way with minimal force, when the users are in need of getting up
- FR_4 Adjusts with minimal force while remaining stable

3.1 FR-DP Mapping

The next stage of the design process is to develop lists of design parameters, keeping in mind the Independence Axiom[1] and the Information Axiom[2]

- DP_1 Large mounting plate.

  > The bracket is designed with a relatively large plate at the bottom end of its first arm which allows it to be attached to any bed or sofa by simply putting the plate under the mattress or sofa cushion.

- DP_2 An adjustable clamp grips edge with rubber.

[1]Use modularity and avoid coupling

[2]Use robust components or techniques that meet their specifications in a reliable manner.

Table 1. First level FR-DP mapping.

ID	Functional Requirement	Design Parameter
1	Fit on furniture	Large baseplate
2	Hold tablet/smart phone	Adjustable grip
3	Push out of way	Bearing on baseplate
4	Adjust height, remain stable	Button to adjust joints

The clamp is meant to be equipped with small, adjustable arms so it can grab onto different sizes. The arms need to have high friction surface on the inside to avoid slipping and minimizing clamping force. Analysis in Section 3.2.3 resulted in minimum clamping force of 16,3 N with friction coefficient of $\mu = 0,6$.

- DP_3 Bearing on a swing arm.

  The 1st arm of the system is going to be vertical and rotate to swing the bracket out of the way.

- DP_4 Sturdy yet flexible joints

  The joints between arms are going to be very sturdy and rigid to make sure the bracket does not move while in use but they are also going to have the ability to release and become flexible to adjust the viewing angle.

We continue a "zig-zag" procedure to decompose and map the FRs to the DPs as shown in Table 1.

From this mapping we develop the uncoupled design matrix shown in Equation 1

$$\begin{Bmatrix} FR_1 \\ FR_2 \\ FR_3 \\ FR_4 \end{Bmatrix} = \begin{bmatrix} X & 0 & 0 & 0 \\ 0 & X & 0 & 0 \\ 0 & 0 & X & 0 \\ 0 & 0 & 0 & X \end{bmatrix} \begin{Bmatrix} DP_1 \\ DP_2 \\ DP_3 \\ DP_4 \end{Bmatrix} \quad (1)$$

3.2 Analysis

Online research yielded the results that one of the heaviest tablet available on the consumer market is the Toshiba Excite 13, according to gsmnation.com [11] The Toshiba Excite 13, according to specification from gsmarena.com [12], weighs 998 g. This weight will be used for further analysis.

3.2.1 Arms

When choosing material for the arms, it was decided to use aluminum for its low weight and high strength. After searching for vendors, it was found that aluminum tubes were also widely available in many different sizes and for low cost, which confirmed our choice. Other alternatives that were considered were iron tubing, which would have been heavier and carbon fiber tubing which would have been more expensive and more brittle.

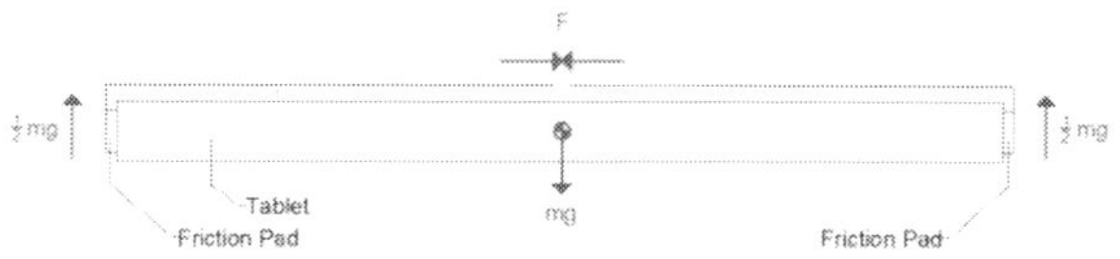

Fig. 8. Forces action on clamp.

The surface finish of the arms would be anodizing the aluminum tubes for a pleasant look and increase toughness. At first, the stand would be available in black, white and silver.

3.2.2 Joints

The joints need to survive a bending moment which equals the weight of a tablet at maximum extension. The torque can be calculated as a simple moment arm (Eq 2)

$$T = mgl \quad (2)$$

where T is the torque, m is the mass of the tablet and l is the total length of the arm system.

Considering the load from the tablet referenced in Section 3.2 and the arm lengths demonstrated in Section 3.3 results in $T = 9.79$ N m.

3.2.3 Clamp

The grip force of the clamp needs to be high enough so that the friction force of the friction pads can hold on to the tablet as illustrated in Fig. 8.

This leads to a simple normal-force friction calculation (Eq. 3):

$$F = \frac{2 \times \frac{1}{2}mg}{\mu} = \frac{mg}{\mu} \quad (3)$$

where F is the clamping force, m is the mass of the tablet and μ is the friction coefficient of the friction pads.

Using a friction factor of 0.6 [13] for rubber and the tablet hanging vertically from the clamp, Eq. 3 results in a 16.3 N clamping force.

3.3 CAD

At the bottom of the unit, there is a large plate that can be slid under a mattress or sofa cushion, see Fig. 9, and connected to that plate is a bearing block with two bearings and two threaded holes which you can use to lock it from rotating. Both parts are made out of plastic because it is light and easy to work with.

As illustrated in Fig. 10 the bearing block is a separate component from the bottom plate and has to be assembled to the bottom plate after a bearing has been inserted. For the threaded holes, there are flanged nuts because plastic threads aren't durable.

The joint, seen in Fig. 11, is 3D printed out of polypropylene. It has a 210° working angle and 13 possible positions.

Fig. 9. The bottom plate with the bearing block.

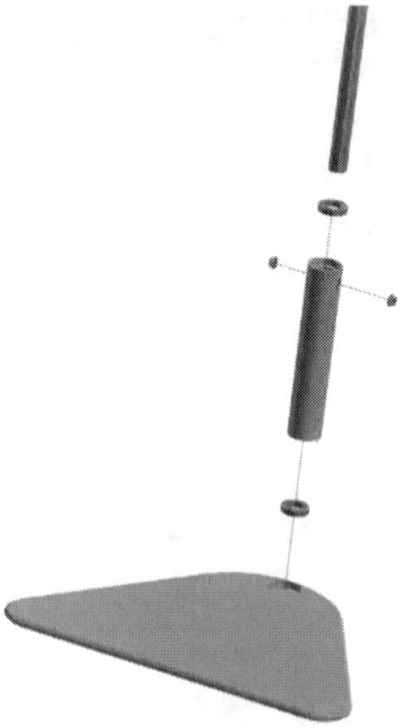

Fig. 10. Assembly presentation of the bearing block.

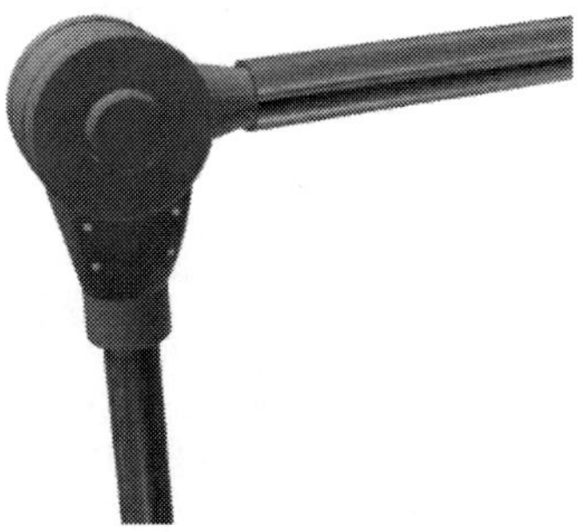

Fig. 11. The joint.

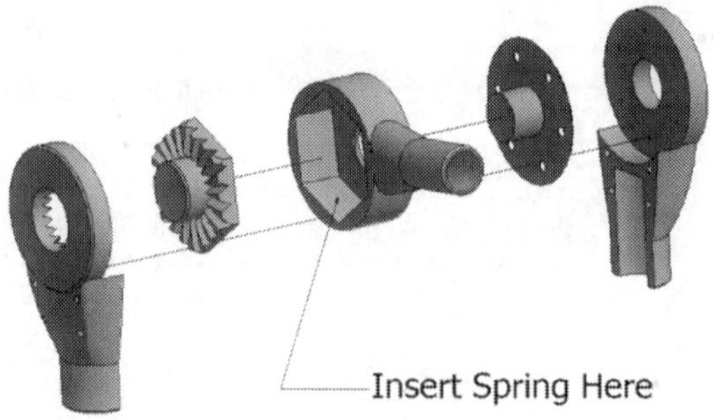

Fig. 12. Explosive view of the joint.

Fig. 13. Clamp and ball joint.

Fig. 12 shows 5 of 6 components of the joint and where a spring (the 6th component) should be installed. The spring makes sure the joint locks in place and by pushing a button on the joints side the spring compresses leaving the joint free to rotate.

Fig. 13 shows the back of the clamp and how it connects to the aluminum tubes with a plastic ball joint.

These components leave us with the final product shown in Fig 14.

The telescopic arm (B+C in Fig. 14) will be around 35 cm above the face of the user when in horizontal position, with the hight of a mattress of 25 cm and a head + pillow of 30 cm, the total length of the vertical arm (A in Fig.14) will be 90 cm. The length of the telescopic arm will be adjustable from 50 cm to 100 cm for different viewing distances. Finally, the second adjustable arm (D in Fig.14) will be 20 cm to allow for free adjustments of the ball joint holding the device clamp.

4 Experiments

From the start, the team realized that one of the weaker points was the joint between arms A and B. This joint holds a lot of torque, due to the weight of the tablet and

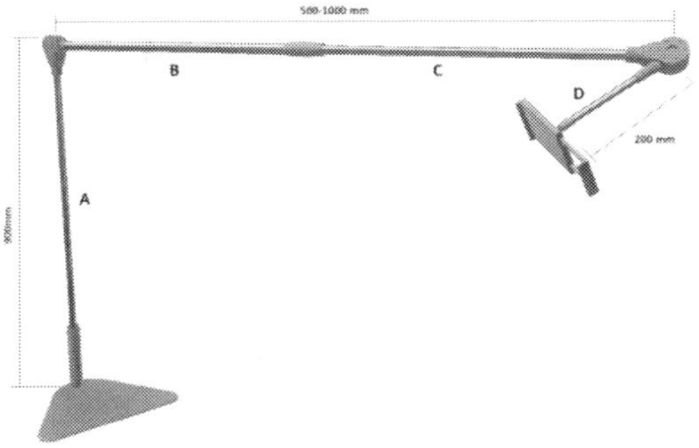

Fig. 14. Assembly of all components with dimensions and labels.

the length of the arm, and a decision was made to test the strength of the joint as soon as a prototype was available.

4.1 Joint strength test

The purpose of this test is to evaluate if the 3d-printed adjustment joint prototype is strong enough to hold a tablet safely as analyzed in Section 3.2.2.

For a safety factor of $n = 1$, the prototype joint is to be tested by attaching it to a pole and hanging a 1 kg mass from the pole at a distance of 1 m.

4.2 Aluminum tube strength/bending test

The purpose of this test is to evaluate what size of aluminum tubing would be sufficient to: (a) hold the tablet without failing, (b) holding the tablet without bending more than 2 cm for a 50 cm long tube and a 1 kg mass. a

The tubing is to be tested by fixing one end of a 50 cm tube securely and hanging a 1 kg mass from the end. The deflection will then be measured. The tube will be fixed to the bottom of a table with a clamp and the bottom of the table used as a reference point. Then the deflection of the tube will be measured before and after a 1 kg load is applied to the end of the tube. The tubes used will be 20×1 mm aluminum tubes. These tubes were chosen since they are the tubes in the construction that will be under the most bending moment.

5 Results and Discussion

5.1 Joint strength test

The joint withstood this experiment, even when the distance was altered to roughly 1.5 m, and excluding the weight of the pole holding the 1 kg mass.

The conclusion from the test is that the clamp has a safety factor of more than 1 for a 1000 g tablet at a horizontal distance of 1 m.

Fig. 15. Deflection of a 50 cm long, 20 × 1 mm aluminum tube. 1 kg mass at end.

5.2 Aluminum tube strength/bending test

A difference in deflection was observed to be 5 mm as shown in Fig. 15. This deflection is acceptable and will not lead to too much deflection of the stand while in use.

6 Conclusion

The TREC-E is a very capable tablet holder. It is powerfully built and can hold up to the heaviest of tablets on the market. It is highly adjustable and can be fitted to most beds and sofas. The FR's that were set at the beginning of the project were met using the DP's.

- FR_1 Attaches securely between any hard surface and a cushion

  This was solved by using a big baseplate that slides between the cushion of the bed/sofa and the base of the bed/sofa. Even without the mattress on top of the baseplate, stabilizing the holder, it was capable standing upright while holding a device.

- FR_2 Holds tablets/smart devices up to 14 inches and 1 kg.

  A powerful construction and tests to assure the strength of the design were used to fulfill this FR.

- FR_3 Pushes out of the way with minimal force, when the users are in need of getting up

  Using a swivel base design with bearings makes sure the TREC-E swivels easily out of the way. A force of 1 N, applied at the middle of the horizontal arm, was enough to swivel the device

- FR_4 Adjusts with minimal force while remaining stable

  To fulfill this FR, a joint and a ball joint were designed and 3d-printed. This would be made of cast plastic for a mass production which is stronger and has better detail.

6.1 Future work

The next project will be ambitious. The goal is to make a fully autonomous stand that reads what angle the viewers face is and auto adjusts to the perfect viewing angle and distance for a particular device.

6.2 Summary

In conclusion, we think that the design was successful. It achieves all of the goals set out at the beginning of the project. The TREC-E is capable of greatly increasing the comfort of viewing media on a smart device in bed or on a sofa.

References

[1] K.T. Ulrich, S.D. Eppinger, *Product Design and Development* (McGraw-Hill, 2012)

[2] J. Apter, *'tablet holder" patent*, US Patent D732,545, Issued June 23, 2015. Assignee Padcaster LLC.

[3] M. Stevens, B. Augood, *"computer tablet holder" patent*, US Patent D733147, Issued June 30, 2015. Assignee Kaylor Global, Inc.

[4] D. Girault, *"multi media tablet holder" patent*, US Patent application 20150009672A1, Applied January 8, 2015.

[5] Sqweezel, patent pending, *Sqweezel website*, website has been taken down for unspecified reasons as of 2017-08-07., http://www.sqweezel.com/

[6] *Gogo pillow (as seen on tv)*, https://www.amazon.co.uk/dp/B00D0DDR7C/ref=as_at?slotNum=4&ie=UTF8&linkCode=g12&imprToken=WtATkd1-ZYlo74DFEWRr6g&creativeASIN=B00D0DDR7C&tag=r0dfb1-21&creative=390957&camp=1789

[7] Tablift, *Tablift website*, https://www.tablift.com/collections/tablift-universal-tablet-stand-all-colors/products/buy-1-tablift-for-39-95

[8] *Stanaway gooseneck*, https://www.amazon.com/gp/product/B01KC15V1E/ref=s9_acsd_hps_bw_c_x_1_w

[9] N.P. Suh, *Complexity* (Oxford University Press, 2005)

[10] N.P. Suh, *Axiomatic Design - Advances and Applications* (Oxford University Press, 2001)

[11] M. Butler, *The Excite 13: The Biggest, Heaviest Tablet in the World*, GSMNation Blog (2013)

[12] *Toshiba excite 13 at335 (specifications)*, https://www.gsmarena.com/toshiba_excite_13_at335-4691.php

[13] *Friction coefficients table*, https://www.engineeringtoolbox.com/friction-coefficients-d_778.html

Complex Adaptive Blockchain Governance

Thomas John[1*], *Mantri* Pam[1]

[1]Cognitive Tools Ltd. LLC, P.O. Box 695; 255 North Ave; New Rochelle, NY 10801, USA

Abstract. The blockchain revolution upholds the decentralizing ideal of "control nothing." It is natural that such a pursuit would face issues of governance that demand reasonable control; control that is both operational as well as adaptive in nature. Eliminating middlemen and handing over controls to a trusted system of trustless agents does not thereby bestow trust across time. This is especially true when relentless change is the order of the day. Issues of governance rise up when blockchain systems (especially those that have embedded smart contracts) are forced to operate increasingly away from their original intent. Smart contracts need governance when beset with the problem of the unknown-unknowns. Guided by the axiomatic approach, this paper looks at the paradoxical issue of blockchain governance from a Complex Adaptive Systems (CAS) perspective that helps frame the fundamental problem of decentralization. The objective is to solve the Blockchain Governance Kernel Design. Real-life examples are used to illustrate the findings.

Keywords: Blockchain; Stigmergy; Governance; Complex Adaptive System; Heterarchical Hierarchy; Unknown-Unknowns; Smart Contract

1 Introduction

Consider C.P. Snow's proposition of the growing chasm between "The Two Cultures" [1]; i.e., between the sciences (which includes the social sciences) and the humanities, but now from a design perspective. Design as a discipline that deals with human artifacts (be they social, technical or socio-technical), has to bridge Snow's chasm in every single instance of design. This is because meaning and purpose, i.e., the root Functional Requirements (FR's) that mandate any given design, ultimately reside in the human-centric humanities which includes disciplines such as languages, history, philosophy, arts and the law [2-4]. Thus, for example, the design of an equitable governance system is ultimately rooted in the realm of law and justice. The research reported herein integrates across both the above cultures in order to make explicit the kernel (or germline, as opposed to somatic or operational) governance design in the context of the ongoing blockchain revolution.

There is a fundamental difference in the requisite bridging-over that is necessary when considering technical versus social systems. Technical system designers have well-developed disciplines such as cognitive engineering, business-analysis, ergonomics, and others to help establish the preamble and move the design activity into the technical realm. In contrast, social system design is barely a discipline. There is no similar preamble body of knowledge that helps translate the social system FR's and DP's (Design Parameters) into the language of the social sciences. There are no rich traditions, no well-accepted bodies-of-knowledge as to how design operates in the social realm. For example, it is only recently that the nascent concept of stigmergy is helping disambiguate Adam Smith's economy-wide, organizing principle of the "*invisible hand*" [5]. A disciplined approach to design, therefore, is more evident in the technical as compared to the social/organizational realms. The design of technological artifacts is more amenable to principled structuring as compared to the design of social artifacts. As Prof. Suh has noted, the ad-hoc approach is the accepted norm in the case of social artifacts [2]:

> *"In many organizations well-defined FRs are often lacking or not completely understood by everyone in the organization, and the organizational structure does not have specific DPs to satisfy FRs. The job of the management is to define FRs and establish DPs, but this has been done ad hoc, very much as in other fields of design."*

While technical system designs have come a long way since the 1990s when the above critique was first made, social system designs remain as is. Heretofore, the social and the technical have existed side-by-side, content to drift apart in their separately evolving cultures. However, now we are entering the realm of massively fine-grained socio-technical systems such as the world of IoT (Internet of Things). The above divide across these two cultures is therefore not sustainable. The odd marriage between the two cultures does not scale; instead, it has the potential to result in large-scale, out-of-balance socio-technical system failures. Every system has a certain capacity for change beyond which it starts to show pathologies. Current social systems are ill-prepared to receive dramatic

* Corresponding author: johntom@cogtools.com

influxes of technology such as the promise of IoT [6].

Design of the governance kernel of socio-technical systems is a challenge of the first order. This challenge is two-fold. Governance has to operate both at the agent as well as at the institutional level. Firstly, the design of social systems is more nuanced than the design of a purely technical system. This is because natural laws are easier to discern compared to the social. For example, the ideal of justice enshrined in the rule of law that governs a given social order is not as apparent as, the force of gravity enshrined in the Newtons law of gravity. Natural laws govern the physical sciences; there is, therefore, no other governance needed. In contrast, design (be it technical, social, or socio-technical) requires governance--since it needs to account for the human element. The bounded rationality problem conditions human decision-making. While natural laws are universal in scope, human decision making is constrained to operate within the limited knowledge scope of individuals and groups. Humans have different knowledge bases and perceptions. These differences inevitably lead to misunderstandings and conflicts that then needs governance at the agent level.

A second issue that social system designers face is that of institutionalized injustice. Human agents are endowed with free-will. As we just discussed, when bounded rationality meets free-will, human agents may commit erroneous decisions. However, free-will is also a significant reservoir for corrective governance forces that unleash when agents face institutional-level injustices. Indeed, the exercise of free will (both individually as well as collectively) has the power to change the course of nations and organizations. In other words, organizational units do not have the power to dictate commands that violate the moral code unilaterally. Given the painful history of how humans have socially engineered their way into political/criminal dominance over others, and then institutionalized this dominance, it is crucial to safeguard against such abuses via proper governance. Moreover, with the advent of massive socio-technical systems, the prospective danger of such institutionalized dominance via the exploit of cognitive biases is abundantly clear and present. Cultures may exhibit differences regarding their respective tolerance for injustice; but eventually, social elements rebel and overthrow nodes of injustice. This, of course, is a costly process of redress that a proper governance model can help address upfront. Thus, if properly designed, elements of governance can help safeguard against acts of injustice at the institutional level.

Governance operates at two levels: the agent and the institutional. Governance at the agent level primarily needs to safeguard against bounded rationality; governance at the institutional level needs to safeguard against institutionalized injustice. As discussed in Section 7 on CAS, these two levels of governance bifurcate into the α and β levels of governance respectively. Given the apparent differences in size and operational scale, making course-corrections at the institutional level is far more demanding than the same at the agent level. It is akin to maneuvering and changing course of a massive oil tanker versus an agile sports-car. Even so, and as we shall see, the kernel design for both of these governance systems may be obtained via a surprisingly similar lower-triangle arrangement of heterarchical hierarchies. This is because in both cases, governance ultimately does reduce to the problem of *unknown-unknowns* in the context of knowledge architectures that operate either at the agent or the institutional level. In either case, the addition of heterarchic controls may, therefore, help solve the governance issue.

In essence, this is the promise of the blockchain revolution (i.e., the addition of decentralized heterarchic controls). The blockchain technology initially was created as a support system for bitcoin transactions. However, it is now turning out to have far-reaching economy-wide implications for conducting peer-to-peer transactions absent any gatekeeper middlemen. Governance in a knowledge-economy implies the establishment of appropriate regulatory nodes that help keep open the flow of information and knowledge with proper regard for privacy and property-right concerns.

Note however that the design of a CAS system (that is emergent, self-organizing and adaptive) is a step removed from the traditional design of systems that are predominantly non-self-organizing. Here the design is left incomplete at a meta-level; the final stages are orchestrated in a self-actualizing boot-strap from its inchoate embryonic state to its fully actualized adult form. The closest exemplars of self-organization may be found in the realm of biological entities that have brought forth their ever adaptive, ever-evolving designs via genetic trial and errors spanning immense temporal expanses. Trapped within the sparse coils of the DNA (which consists of about 1.5 GB of DVD-sized data), one may witness the essence of the Information Axiom operating in a self-organizing context. Herein, the genetic code orchestrates the embryonic self-articulation and development of a complex living entity (consisting of about 150 zettabytes of data and requiring about 30 Manhattan-size datacenters to merely store) that can struggle, adapt and thrive in heretofore novel and unknown environments with ever-changing risks and opportunities. Biological as well as blockchain-based socio-technical systems may be studied under the rubric of CAS (Section 7) to help elicit issues of decentralization, self-organization, emergence, etc.

Section 2 surveys the relevant literature on governance as it relates to the blockchain technology. Section 3 highlights the issue of trust amongst trustless agents--which fundamentally undergirds the blockchain way. Section 4 studies the rise of complexity as a driving force for creating new organizational structures. Section 5 summarizes research on organizational design. Section 6 presents the phenomenon of stigmergy and stigmergic gearings that help structure a CAS. Section 7 describes the CAS system; i.e., the basic as well as iterative. Section 8 establishes the concept of decentralization (that underpins much of the blockchain technology) in terms of CAS. Section 9 defines the role of governance. Section 10 looks at the phenomenon of Emergence and Self-Organization in the context of governance. Section 11 explores heterarchies and hierarchies in the context of governance. Section 12 helps reduce the problem of governance (both agent level as well as institutional) to the heterarchical-hierarchy of knowledge architectures. Section 13 examines governance regarding the unknown-unknowns. Section 14 frames the Axiomatic Design framework for CAS. Section 15 structures the basic blockchain design from an axiomatic perspective. Section 16 extends this design to include smart contracts. Section 17 discusses the kernel blockchain governance design. Section 18 concludes and wraps up the current work.

2 Literature Review

Governance of digital assets takes on a whole new meaning when almost anything and everything can be tokenized and traded by quasi-anonymous agents which include machines and IoT's.

In [7], Campbell-Verduyn provides a broad-brush introduction to the issue of global governance in the context of the blockchain. Blockchain-based trading platforms started showing the cracks in the operative governance framework (or the lack of it) when enterprises such as Mt. Gox and SilkRoad started surfacing the underlying "*deep and dark-web*" side of the new technology. The key issue raised is whether the blockchain technology "*gives rise to new governance problems and pathologies? [7]*" Every shift in the technological front leaves many who are vulnerable to new information asymmetries. If so, what is the role of governance in mitigating these asymmetries while allowing innovation to proceed forward? Hastily drawn governance rules could very well kill the golden goose that may just turn out to be immensely transformative and liberating. Also, as the governance researchers clearly understand, blindly subscribing to the Lawrence Lessig formulation of "*Code is the Law [8]*" is an invitation to enter a Hobbesian Leviathan monolith. It is therefore critical to understand the foundational basis of human trust; and how much of it could be replicated via a trusted system of trustless agents?

The fundamental problem of interdisciplinary complexity inherent in the blockchain ecosystem is echoed in [9] wherein Lopp asserts that: *"One challenge to understanding bitcoin is that it is a multifaceted cross-disciplinary system that is constantly evolving."*

In [10], Ehrsam (co-founder of Coinbase) asserts the strategic significance of blockchain governance in that it could be "*the largest determinant of our future trajectory as a species*" when it potentially gets used to bootstrap powerful AI across the distributed landscape. Crossing over to the humanities end, Ehrsam highlights that it is governance that "*keeps communities together and, in turn, gives a token value.*" He further argues for on-chain governance (i.e., code is law) in terms of its consistency, fairness and speed of decision making. He does, however, caution that the Leviathan metasystem could easily get exploited if flaws were to be discovered; also, that it becomes "*harder to change once instituted.*"

As a direct rebuttal to Ehrsam's stand on the costs and benefits of on-chain governance, Zamfir (lead developer at Ethereum's Casper protocol) asserts in [11] that blockchain governance (as well as governance in general) cannot "*be understood as a design problem.*" The reason suggested as to why governance falls outside the purview of design is because governance is a process, and processes presumably fall outside the scope of design on account of the dynamics involved. This, of course, is an untenable position in favor of adhocracy; processes can and should be subject to design. Nevertheless, Zamfir's highlighting of the need for adaptiveness when designing governance structures is on target. Furthermore, it dovetails well with the adaptiveness embedded in a CAS architecture. Zamfir also takes issue with Ehrsam's stand on on-chain governance as being "*incredibly risky*" in inviting automatic upgrades of the governance processes without adequate human due-process and oversight. Again, a proper design of the governance kernel ought to make clear the appropriate contexts where one may resort to on-chain versus off-chain governance.

In [12], DuPont forensically analyses the governance failure in the Ethereum based DAO (Decentralized Autonomous Organization). The DAO promised transparency, efficiency, fairness and a democratic decision-making process. In just a month, it managed to raise USD 250 Million; yet within days of its launch, it suffered a massive "attack" (draining it off USD 35 million) from which it never recovered. The study exposed the "*inherent complexity of bringing to life an algorithmic and experimental organizational model.*" After the attack there were three post-attack options presented:

- Code is Law (on-chain): Let the attack stand. Attacker gains USD 35 million
- Soft Fork (off-chain): Let USD 35 million vanish.
- Hard Fork (off-chain): Return the funds to the "investors" who willingly participated in the trading platform but felt taken advantage of. The attacker lost USD 35 million.

Ultimately the DAO that was supposed to be hands-off and accepting of the "Code is Law" dictum, violated its own governance and did a hard-fork by reverting to human governance.

Based on the DAO failure, Voshmgir highlights the problem of the Unknown-Unknowns in [13]: *While machine consensus can radically reduce bureaucracy, the question of how to deal with unknown unknowns that manifest over time has not yet been resolved.*

3. Trust: Sed Quis Custodiet Ipsos Custodes?

At its root, all socio-technical systems either rely on trust or make costly allowances for a potential breach of trust. With social trust in place, one can tentatively foresee, plan and design our socio-technical engagements. Trust is the underlying basis for designing socio-technical artifacts. Society pays an enormous overhead for securing trust. Traditionally, trust-systems (both internally as well as externally) are hierarchically orchestrated. Internal hierarchies preside over breaches of trust within an organization. External hierarchies preside over breaches that cross organizational boundaries. Hierarchic governance structures are inherently flawed in the sense that the top nodes can be compromised over time. Hence Lord Acton's dictum in [14] that "*power tends to corrupt, and absolute power corrupts absolutely*." This same sentiment was expressed two millenniums ago by the Roman poet Juvenal when he coined the phrase [15]: *Sed quis custodiet ipsos custodes?* (i.e., but who will guard the guardians?). Going further back into antiquity, similar suggestions may be discerned in Plato's *The Republic*. Having established an authoritarian top-down hierarchical social order, Socrates is here first shown to raise the problem of corruption at the top nodes; he then appeals to self-governance in order to help resolve this conflict; i.e., the self-indulgent notion that the "*best man has within himself the divine governing principle*" [16]. However, within *The Republic* itself, there are passages [17] that indicate that Plato looked down upon such a self-deceptive, self-referential design construct as a contemptable "*noble lie,*" (γενναῖον ψεῦδος: i.e., a lie or wrong opinion about the true origins).

Fundamentally, there is no escaping the fact that all hierarchical systems lack sufficient design parameters to help resolve the problem of the top-nodes going rogue. It was founding father, James Madison who first recognized in [18] the fatal flaw in a purely hierarchical design (symbolized as |H henceforth and as in [19]). Instead he proposed the now institutionalized heterarchic governance (symbolized as |h henceforth and as in [19]) within the US federal government; i.e., a model of *checks and balances* along with a clear *separation of powers* across three co-equal hierarchies in order to help make sure that the top nodes always have external oversight. It, therefore, may be argued that the ongoing US experiment in self-governance is indeed a lower-triangle decoupled design as the coupling via self-referentiality so evident in the Platonic logic has now been eliminated.

The blockchain model is likewise potentially revolutionary in scope in that it has within it, the ability to democratize and make ubiquitously available such heterarchic controls across all levels of any given socio-technical system; not just at the highest echelons of the US Federal government.

4. Rising Socio-Technical Complexity

In [20], Prof. Bar-Yam suggests that society at large is shifting away from deeply hierarchic models, and in favor of more and more decentralized, heterarchic or mixed-mode |h-|H control. This is because distributed governance/control has a larger capacity for dealing with increasing socio-technical complexity. One may witness this in the academic realm, where interdisciplinarity is on the rise; and (traditionally) hierarchical disciplinary group boundaries are becoming porous.

Heterarchic linkages add extra burden in the realm of governance for the simple reason that heterarchies do not play nice; they instead jostle for dominance. Here, governance involves sense-making across domains and disciplines. And in order to be coherent and make sense, one of the erstwhile co-equals eventually starts to dominate the heterarchic complex. For example, in the case of the US Federal government, historically we do have three co-equal branches. However, over time, the judiciary (given its ability to explicate the governance narrative and create consistency across the total political span) has carved out a dominant long-term role; the executive (given its protagonist role in the near term) similarly dominates the contemporary stage; and much of the legislative branch stands reduced in stature The executive and judiciary have usurped much of the law-making ability of the legislative at both the consequential coarse as well as the fine-grain. The judiciary is not per se at fault; instead the default is in the purview of the other two as they lack explicit grasp of a missing FR, namely the need for historical consistency similar to judicial review. This is indeed a flaw in the founding design; for there is a hidden sense-making functional requirement that has been left unaddressed. Each of the co-equal branches ought to have had an ongoing sense-making role. Contrary to Emerson [21], consistency is not "*the hobgoblin of little minds*"; it in fact is what provides the directive stigmergic thrust (Section 6). Court precedents are not easily overturned; established case law sets the stage for what follows. Such binding sense-making is missing in the other two co-equal branches.

Sense-making is intimately related to the nature and shape of human knowledge. As discussed in Section 12, human knowledge is heterarchically hierarchical. Human knowledge dynamics, therefore, have a key role in the evolution of governance. Governance ultimately refers to the over-arching body of knowledge that provides guidance wherever conflicts arise. While heterarchical contributions enrich the growing corpus, it is the hierarchical aspect of human knowledge that is responsible for sense-making. Sense-making is fundamentally hierarchical in nature. Absent the distilling of such knowledge hierarchies, information fails to make sense. Larger the number of agents engaged in abstract, high-order sense-making, greater the chance that the engagement will devolve into heterarchic nonsense. Such is the fundamental weakness that the legislative faces. While it is heterarchically able to bring multiple points of views to the governance table, it is unable to integrate this into coherent hierarchically-sound agreements. Here, for example, is a report [22] on the attempt to merely determine the number of federal criminal laws at hand:

> *"In 1982, while at the Justice Department, Mr. Gainer oversaw what still stands as the most comprehensive attempt to tote up a number. The effort came as part of a long and ultimately failed campaign to persuade Congress to revise the criminal code, which by the 1980s was scattered among 50 titles and 23,000 pages of federal law.*

Justice Department lawyers undertook "the laborious counting" of the scattered statutes "for the express purpose of exposing the idiocy" of the system, said Mr. Gainer."

Consequences of such accountability failures in the governance corpus are dire. For example, the above report summarizes the legislative failure on sense-making with the following comment [22] by law professor Prof. John Baker: "*There is no one in the United States over the age of 18 who cannot be indicted for some federal crime. That is not an exaggeration.*"

Sense-making is especially relevant in the modern context of vastly expanded and heterarchically-rich, socio-technical systems such as the coming world of IoT's where machines directly transact with other machines at an unprecedented scale. The speed and scale of modern socio-technical operations make it abundantly clear that humans are increasingly left out of the decision loop as it is beyond our human comprehension. Fundamentally, humans are conceptual entities. The new era of human/machine symbiotics [23] we are now entering, ultimately has to make sense. Governance is fundamentally rooted in sense-making. It is this that is at stake when dealing with technologies of trust across the human/machine divide. And unless we are careful, just as the case was with the judiciary dominating the sense-making role and by default, taking up the "*first amongst equals*" position, machines may likewise be deliberately or accidentally programmed to serenade us with convincing but deceptive "*noble lies*" that exploit our individual and collective cognitive biases & weaknesses. When cast in this sense, the design of an equitable governance structure for the coming blockchain way of organizing our socio-technical systems may prove to be of existential import.

It is worth noting here that Cynefin [24-25] is also about sense-making in an interdisciplinary setting. Indeed, as the Welsh word Cynefin suggests, the emphasis is on multiple-belongings, i.e., multiple domains that mash-up to create the unwieldiness of modern complexity.

5. Complex Socio-Technical Organizational Design

Prof. Banathy was a pioneer in advocating for a disciplined design of social systems. He was of the opinion that we are now squarely in the "*postindustrial information/knowledge era [3].*" Consequently, organizational designs that arose in the industrial machine age does not scale given the exponential rise in the "*speed, intensity, and complexity of change.*" Compared to design initiatives in other disciplines, he was painfully aware of the lack of attention regarding social-systems design. Prof. Banathy held that when considering social systems design, there is a tangible "*shift from product thinking to process thinking* [3]." In direct contrast to this view was Ethereum's lead developer, Mr. Zamfir who dismissed processes as being outside the purview of design.

Social-systems have an overarching "*concern for justice* [3]." Ethics, therefore, plays a pre-eminent role when designing social systems. The system ought to be equitable and just to all parties concerned, be they central or peripheral in the activities subsumed. In other words, governance plays a central role in all social system designs. The proper design of the governance unit for a blockchain-based social system ought to help establish clear boundaries that when breached may trigger appropriate smart contracts and/or legal recourse. Blockchain governance is therefore not independent and free-floating outside the appropriate societal moral code. What is, however, a departure from the norm is the fact that the blockchain based governance structures can adjudicate many of the conflict scenarios with machine-like precision and efficiency. It is as if vast parts of the social order may now be governed by benevolent arbitration judges that reside in the form of smart contracts coded up within the machine.

Social system designers are often faced with problems that are "*anything but well defined* [3]." Such problems may have inconsistent FR's, inconsistent constraint-sets, upstream designs that are coupled, problem-space that is dynamic across time, etc. This is to be expected since we are dealing with inconsistent ontologies across far-flung inter-disciplinary fronts. While keeping the holistic view, design may, therefore, have to proceed in small iterative steps across the FR-DP divide. When inconsistencies are detected, this may lead to repeat back-tracks up the design hierarchy.

Social systems are primarily designed towards the benevolent nurture, growth, and development of the human potential. A properly designed governance unit helps adjudicate equity throughout the system--both in its homeostatic phase as well when the system adapts and evolves beyond its stable stage; i.e., "*self-organization incorporates self-transcendence, the creative reaching out of a system beyond its boundaries* [3]." CAS is capable of modeling such shape-shifting behaviors. Díaz and Olaya highlight the role of emergence in [4]:

> *"Human beings co-design the social systems that they form, this is why those designs might be intentional up to some point but they are also emergent, dynamic, incomplete, unpredictable, self-organizing, evolutionary and always 'in the making'."*

In 2014, Prof. Norman and others put forth the DesignX framework [26] for tackling the design of complex socio-technical systems. It had nine problem categories within its scope. These categories include some of the problem areas mentioned above such as cognitive-biases, bounded-rationality, interdisciplinarity, requirements & constraints that do not always cohere (but can periodically or chaotically change), precedent designs that are inherently coupled, non-linearity in the element-to-element interactions, causality that operates across multiple scales and long/unpredictable latencies. Armed with these complexities, Prof. Norman critiqued the Axiomatic Framework along the following lines [26]:

"With sociotechnical systems, it is seldom possible to follow the Independence Axiom: two-way or even n-way interdependencies are common. Moreover, these interdependencies are often unknown, discovered only after the fact."

In other words, the design-matrix (that tracks FR-DP couplings two-by-two), is inadequate when dealing with FR-DP clusters that may not compose between them into a static, well-integrated, 2-dimensional matrix. The example referred to in [26] that illustrates this phenomenon pertains to the design of the treatment schedule in an elderly healthcare service where patients often present multiple ailment complexes and severe side-effects from earlier treatments. What usually starts out as a single-organ failure quickly devolves into a chaotic complex of treatment and care that spans multiple specialties [26]:

"When patients have multiple chronic conditions, a common occurrence in the elderly, there are numerous different professionals involved in the treatment, with complex interconnections among them (including, in some cases, a lack of communication). These problems defy easy analysis."

The above set of nine problem categories are some of the fundamental design challenges of the modern world--and there are no easy answers. However, easy answers include the "*muddling through*" approach advocated in the DesignX framework. This approach advocates small, incremental steps that in principle, refuses to consider the problem as a whole [26]:

"This approach requires a different design philosophy than might be used when considering the project as a whole. Now, the design must be modular, with multiple small, relatively independent parts, incremental changes that can be implemented, and linkages that are designed for flexibility."

Indeed, if such a "*muddling through*" approach were to be institutionalized in medical-care, it would be cause for alarm. Furthermore, such an approach fails to take advantage of some of the modern tools at our disposal, such as stigmergy (Section 6), Axiomatic Design [27], Cynefin [24,28], Agent Base Modeling (ABM) [29], Data-Sciences [30] and others. Each of these approaches attempts to learn workable heuristics that are holistic in scope while also attempting to meet the current expediency. These are a more responsible approach than merely "*muddling through*." Indeed, the muddling-through approach may be considered as being unnecessarily defeatist in embracing of the adhocracy philosophy of yesteryears--even as complexities abound.

Even so, Prof. Norman's critique about the inadequacy of the design-matrix in tracking complex coupling clusters is well taken and needs to be addressed. Indeed, biological systems are highly coupled. In fact, an uncoupled biological system may legitimately be considered to be dead. Thus, while the design axioms continue to inspire (i.e., the FR-DP mapping could be considered as "*form follows function*" in the biological realm), the tools used to implement the axiomatic design framework may need to be extended.

For example, the AD/CT extension [31] recognizes the time-dependence of a given design. In other words, the design matrix (along with its couplings) are not static and unchanging across all the operational phases that a given design is faced with. It is in fact, time-dependent. In this expanded sense, the overall design is an ensemble of appropriately governed designs that are either pre-set or just-in-time improvisations composed of known elements. The underlying time-dependence may be periodic or aperiodic. AD/CT can help streamline and resolve many of the objections raised by Prof. Norman.

6. Governance

Governance has taken center-stage on account of at least two major global trends, and often working at cross purposes [32]:

1. Globalization
2. Democratization

Globalization as the top-down legacy framework is being challenged by the bottom-up democratic fervor that has swept across the world stage ever since ubiquitous smart-phones and blogs brought about an overthrow of the highly scripted and staged "*noble lie.*" Now added into the mix is the promise of the blockchain technology that threatens to flatten and shorten the existing value-chains, end-to-end. Consequently, a traditional firm now faces competitive and regulatory challenges from multiple dimensions. A governance misstep in any of the exposed fronts may have serious consequences.

Governance is about collective decision-making, and may be defined as in [32] as follows:

"Governance is about the rules of collective decision-making in settings where there are a plurality of actors or organisations and where no formal control system can dictate the terms of the relationship between these actors and organisations."

Note the emphasis on:

1. Rules
2. The collective scope
3. The decision-making process, and the
4. Lack of formal control systems

While formal rules may easily get coded in smart contracts, informal, on-the-fly, negotiated rules are much harder to codify. Also, the collective scope squarely places modern-day governance in the unwieldy heterarchic side of the ledger as opposed to the well-behaved hierarchic side that may be safely encoded in smart contracts. Also, the decision-making process itself has to have its own slowly-changing meta-rules as to "*who can decide what, and how decision-makers are to be made accountable [32].*" But the most challenging aspect of modern-day governance is the realization that really "*no one is in charge*"; i.e., "*no formal control system can dictate the relationships and outcomes*". And as we shall see (in sections 7-8), this aspect of "*no formal control*" is what makes modern governance a CAS problem. The provenance of decentralized control may be traced at least as far back as the writing of the Old Testament [33]:

"Go to the ant, you sluggard; consider its ways and be wise! It has no commander, no overseer or ruler, yet it stores its provisions in summer and gathers its food at harvest."

The lack of formal control mechanisms is a distinct departure from traditional models of top-down governance.

7. Stigmergy

So how is it that non-conceptual entities like ants, that even though lacking a central controlling agent, are still able to coordinate and collaborate in vast numbers (i.e., in billions [34])? The answer to this is *stigmergy*. Etymologically it is of Greek origin (*stigm-oi* meaning pricking, signing, marking; and *erg-on* meaning work), while entomologically it is from a study in 1959 by P.P Grasse on termites [35]:

"The stimulation of the workers by the very performances they have achieved is a significant one inducing accurate and adaptable response, and has been named stigmergy."

Stigmergy denotes call to work based on local signs or markings left by self or other agents at some time in the past and during the course of their work (either as a side-effect of the said work or as something in addition to the work). These markings aggregate to provide organizational directives available at various levels, both within the environment as well as within and between agents, thus leading to the visual of stigmergic gearings (Fig. 1). Thus, even though there is no one controlling, there is nevertheless system-wide control. These gear-trains may or may not all engage simultaneously; instead, they may be asynchronously meshed in different groupings as per some meta-level (α_i-β_j) logic.

Examples of stigmergy abound in nature. For example, the pheromone markings that an agent ant (α_i) leaves behind as it navigates an unknown terrain helps it to navigate back home instead of being lost. Moreover, if perchance, it does chance upon a choice food item, these same trails then help recruit other ant compatriots in jointly squirreling away the find back to the nest (Fig. 2).

The pheromone trails that aggregate across the environment is the emergent pattern (β_j). Gearing upwards, the pattern-making potential (i.e., the chance ability to create, sense and communicate asynchronously via pheromones), must have had to be evolutionarily written into the genetic constitution of the ant or its predecessors (at some remote point in the past).

Stigmergy is thus a two-way street; it is not just that the agent is leaving tell-tale markings in the environment; the environment is also signing back but at a much more glacial gearing pace. This captures the A and the Ω, but there could be many more engagements across the span that could veer off laterally.

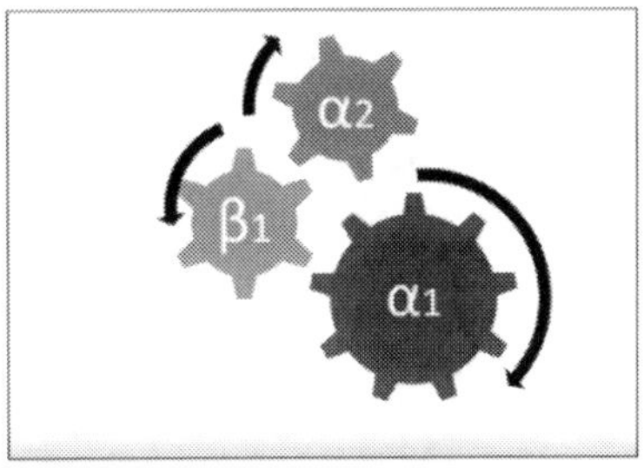

Fig. 1. Stigmergic gearings

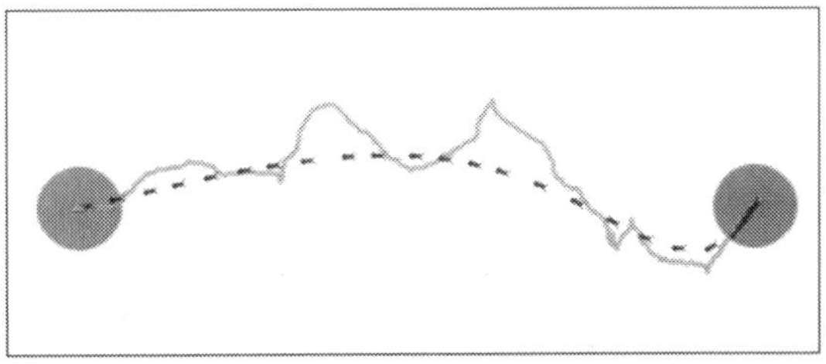

Fig. 2. Stigmergic trails (using NetLogo [36])

Thus, these gear-trains are not just linearly laid-out; instead, they constitute fractal-networks, and networks-of-networks that branch off and engage other such gearings. Governance is the two-way aggregate effect of the multi-faceted β-level gear-train network on the evolving α-level agent body, and vice-versa.

Stigmergic gear trains may work to enhance or inhibit a given agent/group-level activity, thus leading to non-linear effects [37]:

"In more complex self-organising systems, there will be several interlocking positive and negative feedback loops, so that changes in some directions are amplified while changes in other directions are suppressed."

Also, these stigmergic gear-trains are a direct analog to the modern blockchain; except that nature displays abundant varieties of these offerings, each of which has painstakingly been forged in its exacting survival-of-the-fittest workshop. One such example is the immune system which we discuss in Section 15. Blockchain designers would be wise to study similar nature-inspired chains.

The two-way nature of stigmergic-governance (as mentioned above) does not thereby imply any additional agency embedded in the environment; but that the environment is also signing back (in an "*action/reaction*" Newtonian sense) and thus shaping the evolution of the protagonist agent. Longer the stigmergic chain, greater the need to unitize and embed the ricochet as second nature within the agent. Emergence is the global precipitation of these stigmergic patterns into the environment; while submergence is the local embedding of the unitized write-back (i.e., the ricochet) into the constitution of the agent for facilitating future emergence.

As illustrated above, stigmergy helps in the social organization of lower level life forms such as ants and termites. However, stigmergic ordering is not just limited to the lower forms; indeed, much of human organization (or the lack of it) may be attributed to stigmergic successes and failures. For example, the organizing market power captured in Adam Smith's "invisible hand" metaphor may be attributed to stigmergy [5]:

> *"Adam Smith's ''invisible hand'' metaphor used to denote the unintended emergent consequences of a multiplicity of individuals' actions, is stigmergic in all but name..."*

Indeed, the price of goods are the pheromone markings that helps organize the vast reaches of our global economy without explicit direction (i.e., the invisible in the "invisible hand" metaphor). Stigmergy operates as a problem-solving coordination mechanism wherever living entities are faced with problems that are beyond their limited individual ken. Billions of ant's and other insects wouldn't be able to coordinate and thrive but for their stigmergic know-how. It is therefore not surprising that we humans have also been engaging in stigmergic rituals without explicitly knowing it. Parunak analyses a whole slew of such human-level stigmergic processes in [38], including forest trail-formation, highway traffic-flows, democratic elections, document editing, social-media groupings, viral-marketing, Google page-ranks, peer-to-peer computing, Amazon-style recommender-systems, etc. The blockchain is yet another stigmergic innovation to help coordinate human (as well as human-machine) activities. In each of these systems, the patterns that emerge have significant potential to help organize and scale the human potential.

The study of emergence spans many domains including economics [39], biology [40], sociology [41], mechatronics [42], nanotechnology [43], spatial computing [44], philosophy [45] etc.

From a designer's viewpoint, stigmergy is critical in learning to read nature without stumbling on "*intelligent design [46].*" It is crucial for understanding and deciphering designs in nature towards creating and validating an integrated perspective that spans across the natural as well as the artificial. It is the causal thread that connects function and form; i.e., the Functional Requirement (FR) to its Design Parameter (DP) in the natural world. Given the scale, scope, immense time frames as well as the vast combinatorial sweep across which nature operates, it behooves us as keen students of design, to perk up and listen. Deciphering the submerged building blocks would render much of the biological order transparent and seamless across the artificial/natural divide. This is of significance given that while throughout 20th century, physics was the dominant science, the 21st century is the century of biology. And stigmergy can help bridge the conceptual bridge across these vastly different sciences. But that requires carefully mapping the underlying gear-train. Or in the words of Francis Bacon: "*nature, to be commanded, must be obeyed [47].*" In this context, the axiomatic framework could be fruitfully employed in tracking the myriad gear-trains that nature employs to keep its machinery fine-tuned and humming. For example, from a design-matrix perspective, the aforementioned +/- feedback effects across the gear-train complex could be qualitatively captured in a matrix as shown in Fig. 3 below. Here the design matrix captures the delivery of the FR along the diagonal (denoted X), as well as its off diagonal +/- control-set gearings to help keep the main FR-DP (along the diagonal) on its track. And moving across the A-Ω gear-train spectrum, the aforementioned unitization would result in the familiar design hierarchy that helps drill down from the macro-view and into the micro.

X	**0**	**0**
+	**X**	**0**
—	**+**	**X**

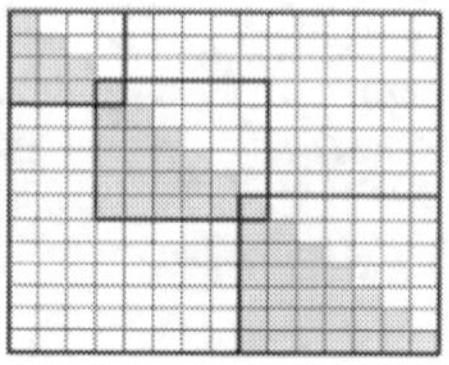

Fig. 3. Design Matrix of Stigmergic Gearings/Hierarchy

Unlike direct and imperial command and control in the human realm, stigmergic command is far subtler, indirect, distributed and democratic. This is because there is no master gear; no single point of control; instead there are very many stigmergic gears distributed across the unwieldly control landscape. Indirection implies asynchrony as well as a lack of specificity as to who the recipient of the message is. Needless to say, stigmergy is thus intimately connected with governance as it is via stigmergic gearings that the individuals in a group as well as the group as a whole is able to orchestrate a global order despite having "*no commander, no overseer or ruler [33].*"

Note that the stigmergic signal is not a clear explicit imperative command for the next agent to do something or the other. Instead it is like a mark left on a shared common blackboard for the next agent that comes by, to use it as it pleases. For example, the openly displayed stigmergic signal may very well be read by an adversary and then put to nefarious uses against the original agent and/or its group. Stigmergic signals are therefore not an imperative command of what should be done next; instead it is a recording of what has transpired up to the point when the mark was made. The imperative element instead resides in the collective emergences as well as in the agent that picks up the baton. Thus, from an agent modeling perspective, the "*what next*" is probabilistic.

In an abstract sense, markets are primarily an expression of the human quest for freedom (via division of labor); i.e., freedom to make better use of our scant resources, especially time. The blockchain technology helps escalate this timeless quest as it unblocks and frees up the agents towards engaging in many more degrees of freedom and ad-hoc mashups than previously imaginable. If prior to the advent of the blockchain, the markets were operating along highly choreographed pathways; after the advent of the blockchain, the markets have now entered a world of jazz-like improvisations that have the potential to topple many of the strait-jacketed middle-men controlled pathways. With the elimination of superfluous middlemen, not just organizations; whole industries may be flattened.

 https://doi.org/10.1051/matecconf/201822301010

Note that lock-in is a problem that stigmergic systems (such as cryptocurrencies) face. As suggested in [48]:

> *"...path-based idiosyncrasies may become locked in as material artifacts, institutions, notations, measuring tools, and cultural practices."*

Under lock-in, stigmergic systems are unable to fork away from the dominant strand on account of lack of followership. The first movers therefore have a strategic advantage which is not easily overcome. In the natural world diseases, viruses and bacteria are the heterarchical pathways that nature exploits in order to constantly stress-test the resilience/viability of the total evolving biomass away from stagnant lock-in. Likewise, in the blockchain context one may expect similar heterarchic thrusts and parries across the unguarded/evolving attack surfaces.

While stigmergic-coordination is remarkable in its scale and scope, it is not the same as cognitive thought and reasoning. Attempts to anthropomorphize stigmergy and posit the existence of an "*extended mind*" is in error. There is no "*extended mind*" agency, no stigmergic cognition, and therefore no basis for stigmergic epistemology as in [5]. Hypothetically speaking, if the extended mind exists in a distributed, asynchronous sense, it must incarnate whenever an agent partakes or contributes to the growing stigmergic corpus. It is then like the luminance of the lightning bug--it comes and goes out of existence. Even so, the fundamental problem is that of will. No executive center animates the extended mind figment. All will, action, and responsibility remain vested in the underlying agents. This restriction has jurisprudential implications for the blockchain enterprise. Legally speaking, one cannot litigate against the emergent β_j-pattern; one may only sue the α_i-agents either individually or collectively [49]. The extended-mind concept is a flawed concept; it serves no rational purpose. Thinking along this line could place the blockchain founders in legal jeopardy.

Similar restrictions also apply to humans operating stigmergically as a group. There is no organ that can be posited as a repository of group cognition. Stigmergic epistemology [5] is, therefore, an oxymoron. Anthropomorphically positing otherwise is an error. Same is true for the rest of the philosophical train (i.e., there is no validity to stigmergic metaphysics, ethics, politics, aesthetics, etc.). However, what can be studied is the validation of stigmergically arrived conclusions via cognitive means resident in independent individual entities. Thus, the philosophic underpinnings of stigmergically arrived truths revert to normal philosophy. There can, therefore, be no stigmergic validation of design or governance. Thus, no matter how good a stigmergically arrived design may be, it still needs independent analysis and validation using the normal tools of human reasoning. Conceptual knowledge therefore has dominance.

8. Complex Adaptive Systems (CAS)

Professor John H. Holland (1929-2015) is rightly considered the father of genetic algorithms. He also laid the foundational work in the study of CAS. As he has described it [50], CAS's *"are systems that have a large number of components, often called agents that interact and adapt or learn."* Holland proposed a two-tiered system as shown in Fig. 4a below. The lower α-tier follows a fast-dynamic and is engaged in the flow of resources between diverse agents (α_i grouped in level *i*) that are also leaving behind stigmergic markings; while the upper β-tier follows a slower-dynamic that captures and aggregates the stigmergic markings into emergent patterns (β_j grouped in level *j*), which is then emitted system-wide as stigmergic signals that help the governed agents to self-organize and scale.

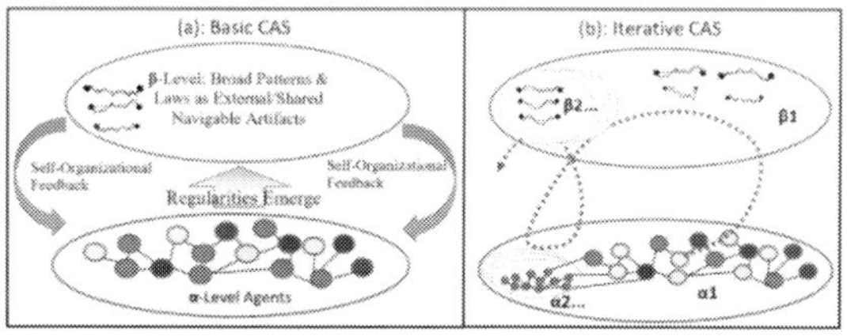

Fig. 4. Complex Adaptive System: Basic vs. Iterative

Note that for the sake of simplicity, all the agents in Fig. 4(a) have been placed homogeneously in the lower tier, while all the emergent artifacts have been placed homogenously in the upper tier. Such a simplification does not quite capture the aforementioned gear-train logic. Instead, what may be happening is that each follow-on feedback-loop/iteration is bifurcating the target population into higher levels of organizational complexity. In each subsequent iteration, the population is now composed of bifurcated ensembles of agent-nodes and artifacts (as indicated by the dotted-ovals in Fig. 4(b)). Gearing, therefore, iteratively creates self-organization and structure in both of these interacting entity spaces. In each follow-on iteration, the respective number of nodes in each of these dotted-ovals is asymptotically decreasing (with allowance for population dynamics) while the dotted-ovals proliferate. Agents may, of course, migrate across these boundaries.

While it is true that the β-tier is entrusted with the governance mandate (i.e., the role of control and governance) of a vast network of unwieldy, decentralized agents that populate the α-tier, it is likewise, not immune from further restructuring (i.e., higher order gearings).

In his post "*Notes on Blockchain Governance* [51]," Buterin (who founded Ethereum) gives partial evidence of the α-β CAS structuring in the blockchain architecture when he writes:

> *"Generally speaking, there are two informal models of governance, that I will call the "decision function" view of governance and the "coordination" view of governance."*

The coordination view is the β-tier view, while the decision-function view pertains to the α-tier agents that act on the coordination signals. Also, as mentioned earlier in Section 7, it is the decision-function view that has legal liability.

Buterin also gives evidence about the layering (at least in the β-tier) when he writes that "*the coordination model of governance…exists in layers* [51]."

9. Centralization/Decentralization & CAS

Here we explore centralization vs. decentralization in the context of CAS. In [52], Paul Baran was the first to outline the distinction (see Fig. 5) between the two:

> *"Although one can draw a wide variety of networks, they all factor into two components: centralized (or star) and distributed (or grid or mesh). The centralized network is obviously vulnerable as destruction of a single central node destroys communication between the end stations. In practice, a mixture of star and mesh components is used to form communication networks."*

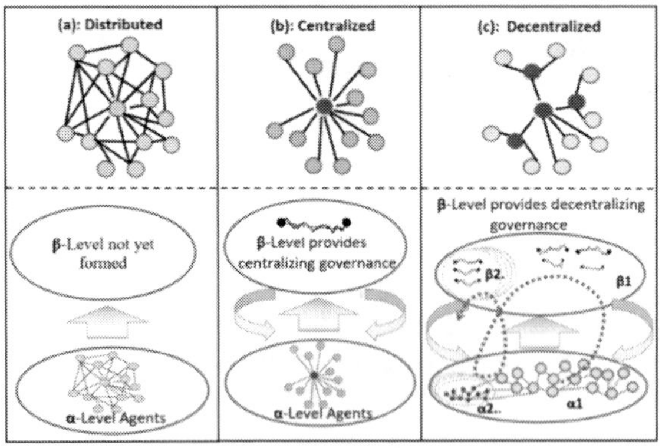

Fig. 5. Distributed vs. Decentralized from a CAS Perspective

When cast in the CAS-framework, it is clear that centralized vs. decentralized is relative. Absent the β-tier, α-tier agents are distributed (Fig. 5a). It is only in the governance context of the β-tier that the α-agents may be considered as centralized (Fig. 5b) or decentralized (Fig. 5c). Also, there is a natural progression across these three self-organizing architectures. Extending this natural progression, one could easily see that there are far more architectures beyond the above mentioned three. Indeed, the full rigor of network sciences may be put to use in extending the categories. For example, the mammalian nervous system is a hybrid architecture that incorporates both centralized as well as distributed control. The vocabulary, therefore, needs to be enriched with mathematical rigor. Also, note the loss-factor approach being used in defining these critical concepts; i.e., the "*centralized network is obviously vulnerable as destruction of a single central node destroys communication between the end stations.*" While such vulnerability duly needs to be noted, it, unfortunately, fails to capture the positive functions that the β-tier provides. It is akin to saying that the stoppage of the heart muscle will result in death which doesn't quite describe the positive function the heart muscle performs. This same loss-function approach may be witnessed in the works of other researchers who followed Baran's approach. Nevertheless, the above four preliminary concepts may be summarized as follows:

- **Distributed/Non-Distributed**: Pertains to the agent-spread in the α-tier, and across its various bifurcations/groupings.
- **Centralized/De-Centralized**: Pertains to the governance/control-logic in the β-tier (as arranged across its various bifurcations/groupings).

With the β-tier providing the controlling logic, all of the α-agents would appear as centralized to the β-tier if indeed there was agency embedded in β. But there is no agency in the β-tier; hence usage of "*control*" as it pertains to the β-tier is purely anthropomorphic.

Buterin categorizes centralization vs. decentralization along the following three axes [53]:

- *"**Architectural (de)centralization**: how many agents is a system made up of? How many of these agents may be lost, without loss of function?*
- ***Political (de)centralization**: how many agents ultimately control all other agents/infrastructure the system is made up of?*
- ***Logical (de)centralization**: how monolithic or dispersed are the underlying data structures/interfaces? How much of this infrastructure may be lost, without loss of function?"*

In parsing the above classification, there is a level of ambiguity that is clarified using the CAS-framework:

- **Architectural (de)centralization**:
  - *"How many agents is a system made up of?"* Agent population size pertains to the α-tier; this does not directly pertain to the issue of centralization vs. decentralization.
  - *"How many of these agents may be lost, without loss of function?"* This refers to system resiliency and therefore does pertain to the governing β-tier. However, Buterin does not explicate how merely the counting of α-level agent's, as well as the fraction that may be lost, is thereby sufficient in helping establish the system as being centralized vs. decentralized. Indeed, until we look at the controlling patterns that have been established in the β-tier, it is impractical to say whether a given system is architecturally centralized or decentralized. The example that Buterin provides is equally ambiguous: "*traditional corporations are architecturally centralized as it has just one head office.*" While this may sound plausible, note that this has nothing to do with the number of agents as well as the loss function. It is, therefore, a non-sequitur.
- **Political (de)centralization**:
  - *"How many agents ultimately control all other agents/infrastructure the system is made up of?"* While the element of control is salient in the context of centralization/decentralization, it is an error to think that the controlling logic of a system

(that often outlives the agent life-expectancy) is to be found in such short-lived agent entities. Consider the suggested example: "*traditional corporations are politically centralized (one CEO).*" This again is erroneous; the political power is indeed being exercised by the transient CEO agent; but the pattern of power assimilates in the office of the CEO, which is a β-tier artifact that outlives any given CEO. So, the question is not regarding how many agents control the rest of the organization; instead, it is whether the rules and protocols vested in the office of the CEO help establish a centralized or a decentralized organization (which in the case of the traditional corporation, is indeed centralized—but it doesn't have to be).

- **Logical (de)centralization**:
  - "*How monolithic or dispersed are the underlying data structures/interfaces? How much of this infrastructure may be lost without loss of function?*" Now, this is indeed part of the β-tier, as it pertains to information flows and the patterns around it. However, consider the example suggested: "*traditional corporations are logically centralized (can't really split them in half).*" A centralized corporate database, in and of itself does not guarantee centralized control; indeed, a decentralized organization could very well harness a centralized corporate database. Instead, the focus ought to be on the β-tier rules and protocols that help establish centralized vs. decentralized control.

Using the above ambiguous framework, Buterin classifies the blockchain technology along the three axes [53]:

> "*Blockchains are politically decentralized (no one controls them) and architecturally decentralized (no infrastructural central point of failure) but they are logically centralized (there is one commonly agreed state and the system behaves like a single computer).*"

The problem with Buterin's classification scheme is that it doesn't address the heart of the decentralization issue. Also, the three suggested axes are ad-hoc and could be easily augmented; for example, they could very well include economic (e.g., microfinance), aesthetic (e.g., decentralized control among jazz musicians), scientific (e.g., the citizen science movement), etc.

Consider the legal implications of the above misclassifications. If (as Buterin asserts) no one controls the blockchain, then no one may be litigated against. However, that is not what is happening in the real world. For example, SilkRoad had six of its decentralized servers tracked down, and its founder Ross Ulbricht, arrested for money-laundering [54]. Ripple is currently facing multiple class-action lawsuits (with CEO Bradley Garlinghouse named as a defendant) claiming securities law violation [55]. Similarly, Tezos and its founders face multiple class-action lawsuits [56] for securities law violation. The case against Tezos is significant as it was designed as a meta-level operator that would smoothen all future governance issues. However, because of poor corporate governance structuring and the resultant fallout between the founders, their ICO (Initial Coin Offering) got stalled, resulting in the lawsuits [56]:

> "*One thing is clear though: there is a certain irony in how Tezos, the cryptocurrency aiming to solve governance issues on the blockchain, crashed due to governance issues.*"

From a legal as well as business point of view, it is critical to understand the relative nature of centralization versus decentralization. What appears decentralized for agents at the α_i-level (and below) is indeed centralized for agents operating at the level of α_{i+1} (and above) and under the direction of β_i. That being the case, agents at the α_{i+1} (and above) are legally liable. Buterin is therefore in error when he claims that "*blockchains are politically decentralized (no one controls them) [53].*" In fact, wherever two or more human agents engage, legal disputes are certainly possible. Furthermore, litigation is more than likely when necessary boundaries are left unstated. In the blockchain context, disputes can occur between agents at the same level, or across levels. It serves no one any favors when the leadership tries to hide the agency issue behind the decentralization veil whenever disputes cross levels. True blockchain leadership would be in setting up timely and appropriate responsibilities, limitations and boundaries as the system scales. Or as Robert Frost would wisely but reluctantly suggest, "*good fences make good neighbors* [57]."

Srinivasan and Lee [58] have proposed a Lorenz Curve/Gini Coefficient based framework to help quantify the degree of decentralization in a given system. The Gini coefficient spans the range of 0.0-1.0. The closer the coefficient is to 1.0, more centralized the system. A related concept, the Nakamoto Coefficient is also reported in [58] that tracks the agent level thresholds that tip the cumulative area under the Lorentz curve into 51% control. From the CAS-perspective, the key insight is in the fact that this framework suggests studying the blockchain system as being composed of 6 essential subsystems, namely:

1. Mining: by reward
2. Client: by codebase
3. Developers: by commits
4. Exchanges: by volume
5. Nodes: by country
6. Ownership: by addresses

This approach comes closer to the CAS-ideal as it acknowledges the existence of a variety of controlling gear-trains that need to be independently & jointly tracked. Also, note that the metrics are focused on stigmergic outputs (such as measuring the developer-focused commit distribution). But lacking an integrated framework, this approach is unable to combine the Gini/Nakamoto subsystem measurements into a coherent system-level measure; it is therefore forced to treat the subsystems as stand-alone. Furthermore, the concept of

 https://doi.org/10.1051/matecconf/201822301010

decentralization is far more generic than just the blockchain context; for example, the above six subsystems play no role when considering the degree of decentralization in a corporate organization. Here, the underlying bipartite α-β CAS machinery is what is missing. By highlighting and referring to the generic CAS machinery, we may be able to liberate the decentralization concept to its rightful stature. Also, from a principled design perspective, it is important to articulate the driving functional requirements in the above endeavor; i.e., the "why" we are looking for decentralization here vs. centralization there. For example, taking a page from the biological realm, there is a reason why parts of our nervous system are under central control; while other parts are under decentralized control. Blindly optimizing along the decentralization ideal would miss out on these hybrid architectures.

10. Emergence, Self-Organization and Governance

In [37], Wolf and Holvoet differentiate between emergence and self-organization. Referring to Fig. 4, emergence is the upward moving arrow from α to β; while self-organization is the downward pointing feedback loop from β to α. These two flows can and often do occur asynchronously. Long-winded asynchronous loops easily confound the tracing of the causal structures. Governance is predominantly associated with the downward β→α command orchestrations, but it is equally important to underscore the formative α→β pattern-captures. In this sense, emergence ought to precede self-organization. However, it is possible to graft foreign patterns and artifacts onto an immature blockchain offering, resulting in lack of coherence. All the key elements (including the governance units) selected from the overall blockchain ecosystem [59] needs to cohere within the evolving context of a given blockchain community setting to make a unique blockchain offering. Once the base structures have materialized, every new emergence and its corresponding self-organizational restructurings ought to be appropriately governed. Given the speed, anonymity, and heterarchically-hierarchical reach of the blockchain based markets, traditional governance structures do not seamlessly carry over. Governance artifacts ought to have the same level of speed, anonymity-piercing and heterarchically-hierarchical reach (on an as-needed basis) that closely parallels any of the breaches across these dimensions. Or to quote Callimachus of Cyrene, we have got to "*set a thief to catch a thief [60],*" but now in real-time.

11. Hierarchy, Heterarchy & Governance

Closely related to the conceptual pair of centralization-decentralization is the conceptual pair of hierarchy-heterarchy. We briefly considered this earlier when discussing the issue of trust (Section 3) as well as the rise of complexity (Section 4). For example, in Section 3 we asserted that "*it, therefore, may be argued that the ongoing US experiment in self-governance is indeed a lower-triangle decoupled design.*" Such a design may be depicted as shown in Fig. 6 below:

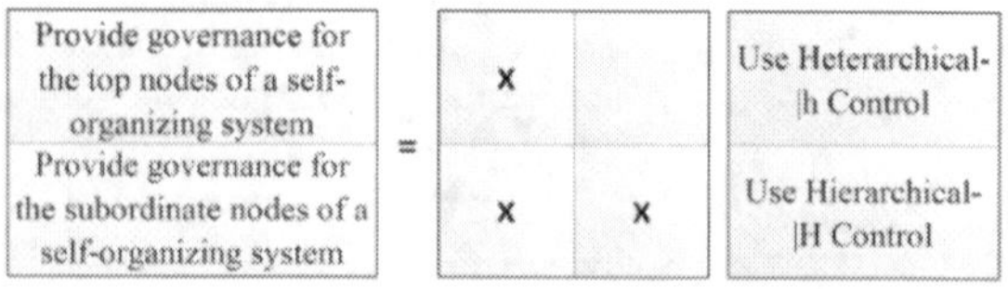

Fig. 6. Heterarchically Hierarchical (|h-|H) Governance

Heterarchic control of hierarchical systems (i.e., |h-|H as depicted above) is an expensive proposition as it demands a delicate balancing act of power-sharing between competing hierarchies. It is therefore rarely used, except in providing governance of the very top-most nodes; and in the cases of national import. However, the problem of "*who will guard the guards themselves [15]*" occurs throughout the system; not just at the top nodes. Indeed, Lord Acton's insight that "*power tends to corrupt, and absolute power corrupts absolutely [14],*" is applicable across all nodes, (except maybe the lower-most) in every socio-technical hierarchy. This is because as a hierarchical system scales, it provides sufficient latency for information flow, sufficient nooks and crannies to bury the proverbial skeletons of misconduct. It is similar to the distinction between local vs. global maximum in the field of mathematical programming (Fig. 7). Thus, while there may be just one global optimum, there may indeed be many local optima based on the local settings. Likewise, in hierarchic (as well as in heterarchic) organizations, there may be local as well as global top nodes that may be compromised. Indeed, it may even be asserted that it is the local top nodes that jostle to take on the mantle of the global top node (Shakespeare's Othello vs. Iago being a case in point [61]). Hence it may be crucial to nip the bud of corrosive power at the early local stages before it scales and migrates over to the global slot.

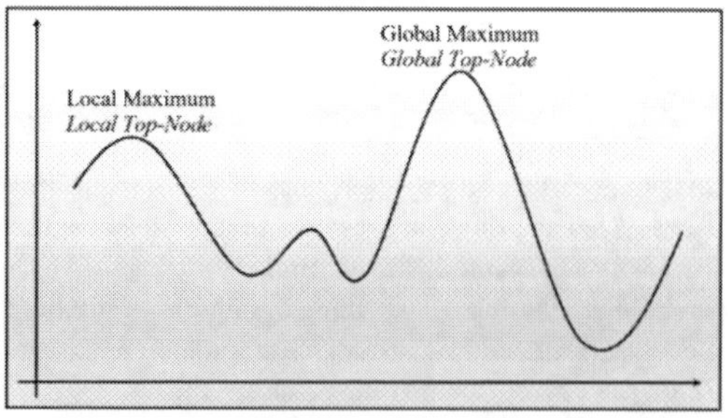

Fig. 7. Problem of the Local vs. Global Top-Node

If properly designed, the blockchain approach could effectively democratize and make available the above |h-|H governance architecture across the board. This is why establishing a proper governance model for the blockchain approach has significant beneficial implications society-wide. As discussed in Section 2, the fundamental problem in democratizing and scaling up the governance kernel is in clearly understanding when to use the machine vs. when to apply human intervention; in other words, when is it appropriate to use on-chain vs. off-chain governance vs. a mixed setup?

How should one go about adding heterarchic controls (via the blockchain technology) into traditional hierarchic governance models, and across the board? Here, an analogy may help in grasping the auxiliary evidence scheme that the blockchain technology offers. Consider the task that a particular lawyer is faced with, i.e., of ascertaining the veracity of a given client or witness. The task is to check if the client is telling the truth. One way is to painstakingly check each statement, to check for internal consistency and to independently validate it against other bodies of evidence. However, there is yet another way to check if the client is lying; and that is to bring in a micro-expressions expert. Micro-expressions [62] are fleeting (i.e., lasting less than half a second) betrayals of inner conflict that the subject is incapable of hiding or suppressing. The act of concealment is being orchestrated by the pre-frontal cortex, which the amygdala effectively short-circuits by leaking the subterfuge in an involuntary micro-expression. In this sense, micro-expressions are auxiliary evidence streams that may help catch a lie. Using the blockchain technology is akin to using micro-expressions to help adjudicate a conflicted situation; it provides easily verifiable auxiliary streams of evidence that may be available to anyone in public. However, note that on its own merit, micro-expressions do not reveal the factual basis of the conflicted case; only that whatever the client is asserting has an element of concealment in it. In this sense, it is preserving the client-attorney privilege as far as the micro-expressions expert is concerned. Likewise, the blockchain technology cryptologically conceals the factual basis of a given transaction; but it has the potential to reveal if that transaction is conflicted with something prior that happened and as recorded within the ledger the blockchain controls. Such self-on-self is what makes current blockchain governance hierarchical in nature. It, however, does not have to be so. Similar to the US Federal Government (Fig. 6), co-equal blockchain governance structures may be designed to mesh heterarchically (at both local as well as global top-nodes).

The problem of hierarchic governance was painfully evident on June 17th, 2016, when the Ethereum based DAO (Decentralized Autonomous Organization) suffered the infamous DAO attack that legally exploited weaknesses in its code-base [3]. Section 6 briefly described Ethereum. It is a programmable, Turing-complete blockchain infrastructure that can authenticate and run code (in the form of smart contracts), not just keep track of the underlying transactions. The DAO was built on top of Ethereum as a decentralized, cryptocurrency-based, crowd-funded platform where investors could directly fund and manage new enterprises that would, in turn, run on Ethereum. In a period of just one month, the DAO was able to raise the equivalent of 250 million USD, the largest crowdfunding success as of May 2016.

However, the DAO attack fundamentally crippled the visionary zeal. Faced with dire losses (in the order of 35 million USD), the principals banded together in an ad-hoc manner to perform a hard-fork; i.e., to violate their own pre-established rules of conduct, to revert back to the genesis state while simultaneously changing the rules of operation to make it favorable to the majority. This is indeed the ancient problem of governance at the top nodes of an organizational hierarchy, be it human or technology-based at the top-nodes. Merely handing the administration of agreements between willing agents over to smart contracts (i.e., a rule-based digital logic used to verify and enforce an agreed upon contract between two or more agents) does not obviate the top-node problem. Hierarchically governed socio-technical designs are fundamentally coupled on account of too few DP's. To understand how one may go about introducing elements of heterarchic gear-train governors into a predominantly (smart contract based) hierarchic mix, one has to delve into the architecture of human knowledge alongside the issue of the unknown-unknowns.

12. Heterarchically-Hierarchical Knowledge and Governance

Earlier, in Section 4 we had asserted that governance is intimately related to sense-making, which in turn is related to the nature, shape, and dynamics of human knowledge. It is by understanding the epistemological roots of human knowledge that one may formulate the proper division of labor between the human and the machine (i.e., between off-chain and on-chain governance). In other words, what is it that the human is good at; likewise, what is it that the machine is good at? Smart contracts are smart only to the extent that the human ingenuity has embedded the smarts within them, including the necessary smarts for knowledge dynamics originating both within as well as outside one's ken.

Given the abstract nature and spread of human knowledge, it may be observed that knowledge has a dynamical and heterarchically-hierarchical (|h-|H) structure as shown in Figs 8.a-f below. This figure is adapted from [19]. Concretes are far more numerous than abstractions; this implies that domain-specific human knowledge (Fig. 8b) has a conical/hierarchical shape.

Induction flows along an upward arch, while deduction flows along a downward arch. Abductive cascades utilize both inductive as well as deductive streams in problem-solving (including designerly) situations [63]. These distinctions ought to inform the on-going debate as to the proper division-of-labour between humans and machines: induction (that favours human faculties) versus deduction (that favours the machine) ought to be the proper role demarcation between the two sets of entities in any socio-technical system. Call this demarcation the *Inducto-Deductive Front (IDF)* shown as the dotted line in Fig. 8.a-d. For abductive cascades (with the IDF at cascade apex), both human and machine agents would need to work in close symbiotic coordination [23,64].

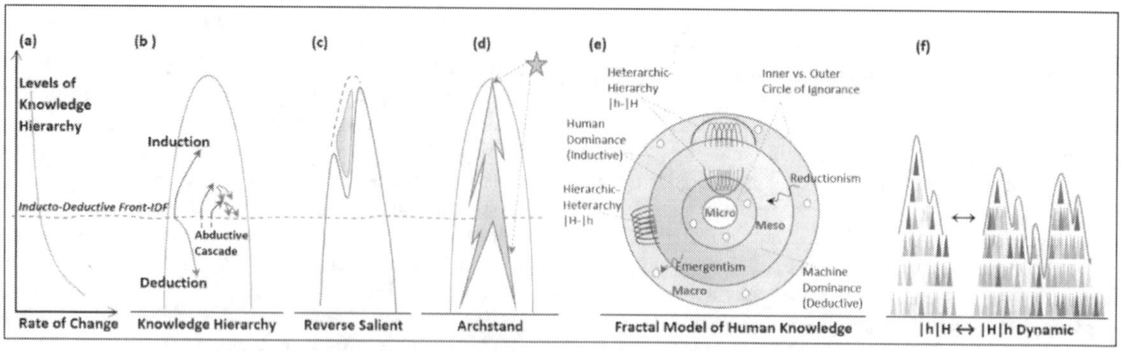

Fig. 8. Human knowledge as heterarchically hierarchical (|h-|H)

The rate of change in the knowledge corpus is more pronounced along the lower rungs as compared to the higher, abstract levels (Fig. 8a). Reverse-salients (Fig. 8c) are lagging knowledge fronts (the *known-unknowns*) that occur because of differentials in growth spurts across domains that are close enough to make sense if conceptual barriers didn't exist. When they do gap-close, it ripples across the knowledge fabric radially (i.e., hierarchically-|H) as well as tangentially (i.e., heterarchically-|h). Another source of knowledge dynamic is the archstand [63]—an integrated external perspective such as the Non-Euclidean framework that led to the Theory of Relativity.

When stand-alone domains are organized using domain kinship metrics, one may expect these conics to exhibit a self-similar fish-scale (hierarchically-heterarchic) fractal structure (Fig. 8e). Humans are at the mesoscale. Unknowns from the macro-world dominate the outer realms; unknowns from the micro dominate the inner regions. Knowledge is sandwiched between these two outer and inner circles-of-ignorance that are expanding and contracting respectively. Regions beyond are the ultimate terra incognita; the vast unknown-unknowns.

Between hierarchies and heterarchies, hierarchies exhibit relatively stable vertical linkages; whereas heterarchies exhibit dynamic ties that are conceptual mashups in the making. At finer grains, hierarchies may contain heterarchies and vice-versa, and switch dominance across time (Fig. 8f). Knowledge flux involves the constant jostling between heterarchies and hierarchies. Without hierarchies, higher-level heterarchies do not form nor engage; without heterarchies, hierarchies tend to become stale, iconoclastic and insular. The emergence/flourishing of a discipline arises from heterarchic assaults and hierarchic defenses; both forces are necessary. Heterarchies encourage falsifiability while hierarchies encourage verifiability; both are essential. Therefore, in the context of governance, both of these forces ought to be judiciously engaged. When heterarchical assaults reach above the IDF, inductive human ingenuity ought to be marshaled; in contrast, when heterarchic assaults land below the IDF, the machines may well be capable of handling the issue. Likewise, when issues of verifiability range above the IDF, it would again demand human ingenuity to overcome the default. But if it occurs below the IDF line, the smart contract infrastructure may be sufficient to handle it.

In Section 4 (on rising complexity) we had indicated that there is an on-going phase shift away from deep-hierarchies and into hybrid |h-|H systems with many ad-hoc laterals. Interdisciplinarity is on the rise; and traditional disciplines are heterarchically being cross-pollinated. This has been discussed at length in [19]. One of the progressive schemes (i.e., the Jantschian) is as shown in Fig. 9 below. In CAS-terms, such a progression is to be expected, given the upward gearing across $\alpha \leftrightarrow \beta$.

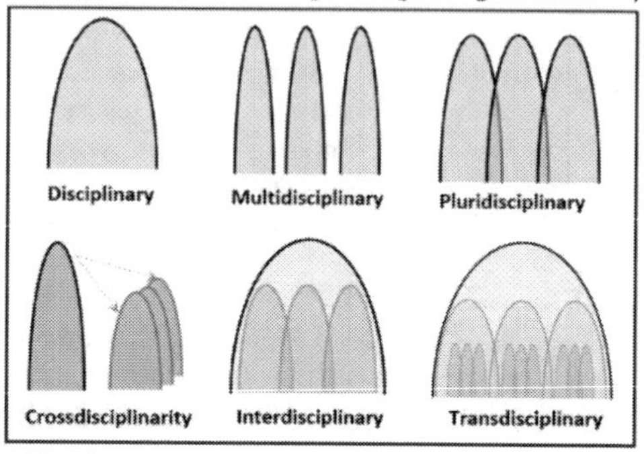

Fig. 9. Terms of Interdisciplinarity (Jantschian) [19]

While the overall envelope of the unknown-unknowns is as shown in the knowledge sandwich of Fig.8.e, there are many nuances (such as the case of reverse-salients, i.e., known-unknowns) that need to be addressed. We turn to the issue of unknown-unknowns next.

13. The Unknown-Unknowns and Governance

Defense Secretary, Donald Rumsfeld popularized the issue of the unknown unknowns [65]:

> *"Subject. What you know. There are known knowns. There are known unknowns. There are unknown unknowns. But there are also unknown knowns. That is to say, things that you think you know that turns out you did not."*

The problem is how to parse this with logical consistency in mind.

You/Team→			c	c	c	c	s	s	s	s
			h	h	l	l	h	h	l	l
Society/Adversary↓			t	f	t	f	t	f	t	f
C	H	T	CHTcht (KK)	CHTchf (KU)	CHTclt (KK)	CHTclf (KU)	CHTsht (Kk)	CHTshf (Ku)	CHTslt (Kk)	CHTslf (Ku)
C	H	F	CHFcht (UK)	CHFchf (UU)	CHFclt (UK)	CHFclf (UU)	CHFsht (Uk)	CHFshf (Uu)	CHFslt (Uk)	CHFslf (Uu)
C	L	T	CLTcht (KK)	CLTchf (KU)	CLTclt (KK)	CLTclf (KU)	CLTsht (Kk)	CLTshf (Ku)	CLTslt (Kk)	CLTslf (Ku)
C	L	F	CLFcht (UK)	CLFchf (UU)	CLFclt (UK)	CLFclf (UU)	CLFsht (Uk)	CLFshf (Uu)	CLFslt (Uk)	CLFslf (Uu)
S	H	T	SHTcht (kK)	SHTchf (kU)	SHTclt (kK)	SHTclf (kU)	SHTsht (kk)	SHTshf (ku)	SHTslt (kk)	SHTslf (ku)
S	H	F	SHFcht (uK)	SHFchf (uU)	SHFclt (uK)	SHFclf (uU)	SHFsht (uk)	SHFshf (uu)	SHFslt (uk)	SHFslf (uu)
S	L	T	SLTcht (kK)	SLTchf (kU)	SLTclt (kK)	SLTclf (kU)	SLTsht (kk)	SLTshf (ku)	SLTslt (kk)	SLTslf (ku)
S	L	F	SLFcht (uK)	SLFchf (uU)	SLFclt (uK)	SLFclf (uU)	SLFsht (uk)	SLFshf (uu)	SLFslt (uk)	SLFslf (uu)

Legend:
Process by which knowledge gained: C/S (Conceptual/Stigmergic) for {Society,Adversary} vs c/s (conceptual/stigmergic) for {you, team}
Confidence in knowledge possessed: H/L (High/Low) for {Society,Adversary} vs h/l (high/low) for {you, team}
True status of knowledge possessed: T/F (True/False) for {Society,Adversary} vs t/f (true, false) for {you,team}

Fig. 10. The Unknown-Unknown Knowledge Asymmetry Exploit

For the sake of brevity, let us notate these options as KK (Known-Known), KU (Known-Unknown), UU (Unknown-Unknown) and UK (Unknown-Known). Elsewhere [66] Rumsfeld also opined that:

> *"There are known knowns. These are things we know that we know. There are known unknowns. That is to say, there are things that we know we don't know. But there are also unknown unknowns. These are things we don't know we don't know."*

This quote considers just three of the options: KK, KU, and UU, with UK missing. The way Rumsfeld has parsed the second option KU (i.e., things that we know we don't know) suggests that the first lettering is about our state of confidence in our state of knowledge; and the second lettering is about the base state of our knowledge. Thus, the missing variant UK in the above formulation indicates poor confidence in a given assertion that we accept.

Once we parse this base structure, it then becomes clear that there are many more shades of the Unknown-Unknowns that lurk in the shadows, especially when we start considering issues of stigmergic knowledge as well as what our adversaries likewise know. Understanding the problem of the Unknown-Unknowns is central to understanding how blockchain governance is likely to evolve. For example, in analyzing the DAO debacle, Voshmgir highlights the problem of the unknown-unknowns faced by on-chain "*codified governance rulesets*" (CGR's) [13]:

> *"In reality, formalised and codified governance rulesets can only depict known knowns and known unknowns, but have very limited capabilities to properly deal with unknown unknowns."*

The earliest formulation of one of the combinations may have been by the poet John Keats in Endymion wherein love-struck demi-god Endymion ponders the mysteries that wrap the object of his affections, the moon: "*O known Unknown! from whom my being sips [67].*" The realm of the unknown-unknowns can inspire as well as frustrate inquiry. Here Keats puts forth the idea that things of beauty have both familiar as well as unknown facets; and that we come to grasp the unknown by systematically working our way to the edge of the known realms.

Indeed, there are many pathways into the realm of the unknowns, not just the four that Rumsfeld put forth. One's true state of knowledge about some pertinent issue may be cross-mapped against what the society-at-large (or your adversary in a game-theoretic sense) is aware of. Also relevant to the problem is how the knowledge being claimed was arrived at; i.e., whether conceptually or stigmergically? In the human context, stigmergic knowledge gets coded in mores, heuristics and, habits of individual thought and action (both at the individual as well as at the societal level).

If it was conceptually arrived at, then it has a greater chance of error; but if true, it has far-reaching potential to scale. In contrast, if it was stigmergically arrived at, then its basis may be stronger (provided it avoids the problem of the aforementioned stigmergic lock-in); but being pre-conceptual, it does not scale easily. It is therefore of strategic value to convert stigmergic knowledge into the conceptual realm.

So, what are the combinatorial possibilities that populate the realm of the unknown-unknowns? Denote you (or your teams) state of knowledge in small-caps. Denote the state of knowledge of society-at-large (or perhaps your adversary) in large-caps. The resultant combinatorics may then be bifurcated along the following dimensions:

- Process by which knowledge is gained: C/S (Conceptual/Stigmergic) for {Society, Adversary} vs. c/s (conceptual/stigmergic) for {you, team}
- Confidence in knowledge possessed: H/L (High/Low) for {Society, Adversary} vs. h/l (high/low) for {you, team}
- True status of knowledge possessed: T/F (True/False) for {Society, Adversary} vs. t/f (true, false) for {you, team}

Mapping the resultant combinations into the known/unknown characterization is fairly straightforward with stigmergically derived true and false states in small-caps {k, u}; and conceptually derived true and false states in large-caps {K, U}. Thus CHTcht(KK) would denote both you as well as your adversary possessing conceptually-derived knowledge that is of high-confidence and happens to be true, leading to a situation of conceptually derived known-knowns. When the adversary's knowledge is mapped against one's own, there are 64 combinations as shown in Fig. 10 above. Note that the matrix assumes a two-player game structure, though one or both players could represent coordinated groups. Also note that the UK style coding (in parenthesis) is different from the Rumsfeldian coding as it denotes two opposing agents. Each new such player expands the combinations by a multiple of 8. These combinations create knowledge asymmetries (with comparative advantage to the {K, k} team, if paired against a {U, u} adversary) that are ripe for exploitation, thus triggering governance. These asymmetries are, therefore, at the foundation of the governance conundrum, that in its essence, checks to see if agreed-upon knowledge flows have been thwarted to result in the given asymmetry. Consider for example the cell *CHTshf (Ku)* highlighted in green in the top-right quadrant of Fig.10. Here the adversary's knowledge about some matter (say the true worth of a smart contract) is conceptual, of high confidence and true; in contrast, your knowledge about that same matter is mere stigmergic hearsay, but of high confidence and happens to be wrong. Diagonally across from *CHTshf (Ku)* is the diametrically opposite case of *SHFcht (uK)* (highlighted in red) where the asymmetry now favors the individual actor as opposed to society at large. Here the socially networked group is operating stigmergically, has fatally high confidence in its findings which in fact is wrong; in contrast, the lone operator is operating conceptually, has high confidence in its findings and is in fact right. In the world of finance, hedge-funds try to exploit *SHFcht (uK)* types of knowledge asymmetries. And when a smart contract is executed based upon such asymmetries, there are bound to be outcries of failures in governance. This indeed is what transpired in the case of the DAO-attack.

Playing the role of the adversary, if indeed one wishes to widen the {K, k}- {U, u} gap even further strategically, it may be worth introducing Axiomatic Design/Complexity Theory based complexing red-herrings as suggested in [68]. This may be even more potent when dealing with a {k}-{u} type knowledge gaps (which happenstance is much of the operative human knowledge); the reason being that it is challenging to debug stigmergic linkages that have been deliberately sabotaged for the explicit design purpose of throwing off one's adversaries.

14. Axiomatic Design for Complex Adaptive Systems

The creative mashup between two diametrically opposed design methodologies (i.e., the top-down Axiomatic approach vs. the bottom-up Design Patterns approach) was discussed in [69-70]. Thus, the top-down V-approach was juxtaposed with the bottom-up Λ-approach to create the N-model. As it turns out, the N-model comports well with the Complex Adaptive Systems framework. The design-patterns approach that leads with the upward-stroke of Λ is akin to the α→β emergent stroke in a CAS system; likewise, the axiomatic approach that leads with the downward stroke of V is akin to the β→α self-organization stroke in a CAS-system. Together they compose to make the N-model which indeed is the overall gearing dynamic behind the α↔β CAS system. However, as mentioned earlier (in Section 1), the design of a CAS System is a step removed from the traditional design of systems that are predominantly non-emergent/non-self-organizing. There is an inherent embryology of the CAS system that the designer has to yield to; i.e., the CAS designer needs to think more like a farmer rather than an engineer and adjust to the vagaries of emergence, such as that between pests and pollinators [71].

To come up with a design that is holistic and emergent requires the designer to be steeped in the practice of design; i.e., it is combinatorically challenging. Also, emergence requires beneficial interaction between the design elements, thus favoring lower-diagonal decoupled vs. uncoupled designs, which is not the usual norm. In the case of the diagonal design, the whole is equal to the sum of the parts. Emergence, however, requires beneficial interaction, which is feasible only if non-diagonal elements are present. Thus, in most cases, the uncoupled has dominance over the decoupled given the lower informational complexity. Emergence is the rare occurrence that could be flipping this dominance to combinatorically win the race with lower information content. This, however, is merely a hypothesis that needs to be validated. Many of the biological systems (given the enormous temporal-combinatorial space that they have been stigmergically operating over and finessing the information axiom) have strong elements of emergent qualities (such as life, consciousness, everything that pertains to the emotional faculties, etc.). Biological designs present rich opportunities to test this hypothesis.

By adopting the axiomatic approach, the β→α design is decomposed both

- laterally and non-hierarchically across the various realms such as customer, functional, physical, process (CR, FR, DP, PV, etc.) as shown in Fig. 11 below, and
- vertically and hierarchically within each of the above realms.

In a rapidly evolving design context, it is impractical to approach design in staged, linear waterfall fashion as in CR↔FR↔DP↔PV. Instead, it is better modeled (as shown in Fig. 11 below) as a fully linked network of information nodes. The linear structuring still dominates, but it is now augmented with auxiliary flows. Each of these realms has its own α↔β CAS structure that forms over time. Furthermore, since domain knowledge is hierarchical, the design trace that leverages this knowledge is likewise hierarchical.

By visualizing the design in the context of knowledge hierarchies, one may begin to appreciate the historical import of Prof. Suh's work [2]. In fact, something similar (see Fig. 12) happened in Renaissance Italy around 1420, with the invention of linear perspective [72] by the Italian architect/artist Filippo Brunelleschi. Ancient Rome indeed did have something close to linear perspective; however, the ancients used multiple vanishing points in its paintings, thus leaving a sense of lack of coherence in the presentation. Brunelleschi did study the ancients. He then came back to Florence to revolutionize the world of representational art as we now know it. With a single vanishing point, all the objects in the field of vision compose in a realistic, coherent, eye-pleasing fashion. Indeed, juxtaposing any of the art-works prior to Brunelleschi's approach, one immediately senses the flatness and lack of proportions in the former vs. the three-dimensionality and compositionality in the later.

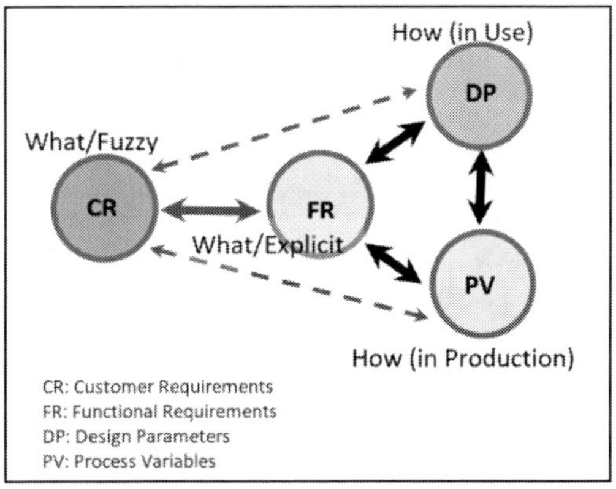

Fig. 11. Design Information Flow Network

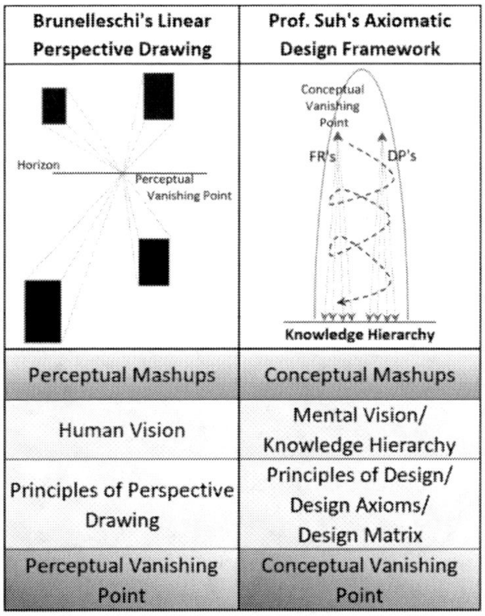

Fig. 12. Perceptual vs. Conceptual Mashups

Likewise, Prof. Suh's work on axiomatic design is at least of equal stature (if not more); for what Brunelleschi stipulated in the realm of perceptuals, Prof. Suh has stipulated in the realm of conceptuals. The ability to bring unity and coherence in the realm of the conceptual artifact space is monumental in scope, especially in the field of education in general; and not just design education. Here, the teaching of anatomy and physiology from a "*Form follows Function*" perspective [73] is worth noting as it offers significant insights into the potential scope. As was the case for paintings prior to Brunelleschi's perspective drawing, much of education today is a sprawl that lacks conceptual unity and coherence. This same sprawl is evident in the blockchain realm [9]. Again, there is untapped potential in modeling instructional sciences along the biological template.

15. Basic Blockchain Design

The web has evolved from a sprawling network of hyperlinks in the 1990s (Web1), to being programmable (Web2) in the 2000's--thus enabling social media, e-commerce, and other similar restructurings. These restructurings allowed a few to scale upwards and enjoy global reach.

So now we are on to the third phase; i.e., Web3. The problem with Web2 was that (as was the case with the Napster-model with its centralized set of index files), at the center of many of the Web2 business models, there exists a centralized database that amasses immense power to structure and shepherd the flow of thought and commerce. These models implicitly took advantage of power-laws that favor the highly connected central nodes. It is true that on the one hand, these Leviathans have enabled tremendous productivity gains compared to what existed prior; but on the other hand, they have de facto established governance-in-stealth for all the peripheral nodes. It is not to say that there is any malevolent element in these designs; it is merely that anything so centralized (as per Lord Acton's dictum) will perforce be restrictive towards the free-flow of thought and association.

Allow discreet agent stigmergy		X						Cryptographic Tokens
Verifiability of Transactions		X	X					Cryptographic Hash
Lightweight transaction-set		X	X	X				Merkle Tree, Patricia Tree, etc
Trustless Trust	=	X	X	X	X			Consensus Model (POW, POS, etc)
Immutable Transactions		X	X	X	X	X		Blockchain Ledger
Distributed Resilience		X	X	X	X	X	X	Distributed P2P Ledger

Fig. 13. Basic Blockchain Design

To put things in perspective, every google page-rank discriminates against those who create and search for the road-less-traveled; for the average person rarely goes beyond the first five search results [74]. In contrast, Web3 portends to be genuinely democratic by eliminating all central nodes and associated intermediaries who currently enjoy a high degree of betweenness-centrality [75] by inserting themselves in between nodes that otherwise would be P2P. Human/machine agents now genuinely can engage P2P without the need for gatekeepers and connectors. To put this in context, the ongoing revolution portends the ability "*to build ridesharing without Uber, apartment sharing without Airbnb, and social media without Facebook and Twitter* [76]."

The top-level CR for the blockchain may be stated as follows:

*Need **consensually-trusted, immutable, distributed and decentrally-managed, verifiable, publicly and efficiently searchable** record of all transactions (since genesis) that are **private and discreet, but stigmergically-marked** for public-viewing, that pertains to a given economic activity and that may be made by adversarial/trust-less agents.*

When restated in the FR-DP framing, the above CR translates into the basic blockchain design as shown in Fig. 13 above. The design-matrix indicates a decoupled, lower-triangle design. The couplings systematically build-up across the FR list, top to bottom. For example, the FR: Trustless-Trust (highlighted in red) is being delivered using all the previous DP's, along with the Consensus Model DP.

In the BitCoin case, just as soon as consensus is achieved, new tokens are released as a reward for the successful miner who expended computational resources to help bring about consensus. Thus, in this phase of token creation, a small part of the overall design has one of the design matrices in a different form which leads off with the consensus model. This agrees with the extended AD/CT (i.e., TDPC: Time-Dependent Periodic Complexity). In the discussion below, we have chosen to focus on just the broad design (as shown in Fig. 13 above) and ignore all such finer variations.

The blockchain is a CAS system that fundamentally operates on stigmergy. Discreet stigmergy requires agents be allowed to mark their environment (here, the blockchain ledger) discretely (i.e., without having to reveal their respective true identities). This is similar to ants leaving pheromone droppings—except that in the blockchain context, the agents enjoy a certain degree of anonymity. Cryptographic tokens (bitcoin, ether, gas, etc.) are the cash-like pheromones that various stakeholders use to engage in economic activities. They are cash-like in the sense that they shield the privacy of the agents; but they are stigmergic in the sense that the transaction now has a permanent, publicly-viewable/traceable record. Thus, when spent, the tokens leave their stigmergic markings that if properly aggregated, could help evolve the system forward. Cryptographic stigmergy [77] looks at the stigmergic design of the overall system to help precipitate direction-providing emergences and the corresponding self-organization around it.

Transaction security is obtained via standard, cryptologic hash functions such as SHA-256.

The Merkle tree data-structure that encodes all the transactions in a given block is designed to help verify the existence and validity of the growing chain of transactions in a computationally efficient fashion (costing less than O(Log2(N)) in space and time).

The paradoxical property of trustless-trust is obtained via various consensus models (such as PoW: Proof-Of-Work; PoS: Proof-Of-Stake, etc.). Cryptoeconomics [78] studies the creation of economic incentives (such as tokens allocated to miners for performing computationally intensive work such as PoW) to bring about consensuses in a distributed and potentially adversarial setup. For example, the PoW model embedded in the BitCoin system allows decision-making via consensus (via the Byzantine Fault Tolerant algorithm [79]) despite approximately 1/3rd of all agents going rogue. Blockchain offerings may be differentiated using the consensus model differentiator that power their respective answers to the problem of securing Trustless Trust.

As a biological analog, the immune system [80] is a perfect example of the blockchain along with its own Proof-of-Work (called the fever) which is the computational struggle that various cells from the immune system go thru in order to recognize invading antigens as a friend or a foe. Once identified, the body never forgets. It keeps the evidence of all its successful struggles in its growing ledger, i.e., its collection of antibodies.

The blockchain ledger is a growing linked list of transaction records that have been bundled into timed blocks. The chained ledger has been accumulating these blocks ever since the genesis of the blockchain under study. Each such timed block of transactions is bundled in an efficient, easily verifiable data-structure such as the Merkle tree. Each new addition contains in its header the hash of the previous block. This makes both the nodes as well as the overall chain highly resistant to modification. Longer the chain grows, harder it is to break.

Finally, Network Resilience is obtained via the P2P distributed protocols.

Satoshi Nakamoto designed the PoW based blockchain for the P2P bitcoin cryptocurrency [81]. The contractual logic that is embedded in the BitCoin blockchain may be abstracted out and generalized to help secure trusted transactions across the whole gamut of global economic activity. The Ethereum project was the first to recognize the value of such decoupling's. While the Blockchain provides the underlying infrastructure, it is what gets built on top of it that defines the business offering. Each such offering provides unique affordances targeting specific business eco-systems. The rules and boundaries of these eco-systems (along with their governance protocols) are established via the logic of the smart contracts.

16. Smart Contract and Governance

Smart contracts are contracts written in code that will execute when matching conditions that make up the agreement are met. In other words, it is "*cocked, locked and ready to fire*"; there are no off-ramps. Smart contracts have been envisioned across multiple domains, including crowdfunding, financials (buying and selling of tangibles/intangibles, insurance, derivatives), legal, etc.

Smart contracts are point-to-point with all middlemen having been dis-intermediated. It, therefore, has substantial potential to inflict losses in the hands of the naïve, careless or uninitiated (i.e., the KU type asymmetry).

The blockchain-based smart contract technology has the potential to transform society as a whole for the better; better in the sense of faster, cheaper and fairer transactions. Thus, given the enormous potential to smoothen the flow of commerce while bringing down costs, it is incumbent on the designers of blockchain based smart contracts to get the governance aspect done right. If it is designed for scaling, it ought to cover for the variety of knowledge asymmetries that exist across the spectrum of participants as well as the dynamics along a fast-moving front. Voshmgir emphasizes the pace with which the context for a smart contract design could rapidly move away from its original intent [82]:

> *"First use cases show that as circumstances change, protocols can become inappropriate for the new environment and require modification."*

In other words, it is not just that the design space is rapidly evolving; here the FR's themselves are rapidly evolving; i.e., the half-life of any given FR is also rapidly being cut short. This in itself is highly unprecedented in the world of design. In other words, there is a high premium for designing systems based on first principles as compared to short-sighted pragmatics.

Since the smart contract offering sits on top of the blockchain infrastructure, the CR for the design may be stated as follows:

> *Need the ability to **structure** and **verify** auto-executing contracts that incorporate arbitrarily complex business rules and trade on a given blockchain offering.*

Structure Auto-exec Contracts		X								Smart Contract
Contract Verification		X	X							Oracle
Allow discreet agent stigmergy		X	X	X						Cryptographic Tokens
Verifiability of Transactions		X	X	X	X					Cryptographic Hash
Lightweight transaction-set	=	X	X	X	X	X				Merkle Tree, Patricia Tree, etc
Trustless Trust		X	X	X	X	X	X			Consensus Model (POW, POS, etc)
Immutable Transactions		X	X	X	X	X	X	X		Blockchain Ledger
Distributed Resilence		X	X	X	X	X	X	X	X	Distributed P2P Ledger

Fig. 14. Blockchain-Based Smart Contract Design

When restated in the FR-DP framing, the above CR translates into the blockchain-based, smart contracting infrastructure as shown in Fig. 14 above. The smart contract is the structured, auto-executing contract. It is neither a legal contract nor necessarily smart. Just as any other trading instrument, the legality of the contract needs to be ironed out in the appropriate legal setting. The smart in the smart contract depends on how well the coding reflects the underlying economic incentives. For example, the DAO as a smart contract [12] was anything but smart.

The blockchain infrastructure wouldn't necessarily have the necessary data/logic to verify if and when all the preconditions specified in a given smart contract have been sufficiently met. An oracle is a 3rd party service that exists outside the blockchain to heterarchically reach out and help verify the preconditions encoded within the smart contract. These artifacts provide ways and means to interface with the real world. Being outside the underlying blockchain setting, they may have unique governance issues that need to be addressed independently. Also, they could provide heterarchic governance monitoring services.

17. Blockchain Governance Kernel Design

As was discussed in Section 13, knowledge asymmetries create governance issues. However, knowledge asymmetries are the basis for initiating any successful trade; and is therefore not wrong per se. Indeed, wealth creation requires such knowledge asymmetries. Also, the half-life of knowledge is short and getting shorter. In other words, there are no guarantees that a given vantage point will remain forever. However, at any given time, if the asymmetries are severe or resulted from a prior information-agreement breach, it then opens up problems of poor governance. Good governance, therefore, involves creating adequate channels of information flow for timely decision-making for all parties to participate in sufficient amount of openness while also allowing specific strategic/proprietary information to remain hidden and off the grid (either permanently, or at least for a while). Insights from Cryptographic Stigmergy [77] as well as Cryptoeconomics [78] would be needed to design the appropriate information signaling mechanisms and economic incentives that help streamline the required information flows. Here we delimit the context to the kernel governance design to help decide between the off-chain/on-chain approaches.

When we place the matrix of the Unknown-Unknown asymmetries (Fig. 10) alongside the *Inducto-Deductive Front (IDF),* it raises the issue of how the design-matrix gets transformed when one of the parties on either side is a machine working off a highly specified Codified Governance Ruleset (CGR) as opposed to a human working off a more abstract Principled Governance Ruleset (PGR)? While the CGR could be codified into the on-chain governance modules, the PGR would be administered in pre-agreed, human-centered, arbitration-like off-chain governance setups. Either may cross hierarchical boundaries; i.e., PGR/CGR may be either |h or |H in scope. Fig. 15 shows the kernel governance design indicating when one or the other ought to be used.

When knowledge context is conceptual and below the IDF, CGR-coded machines can adjudicate governance modules coded as on-chain, smart contracts (i.e., via X_2 CGR, Fig. 15a). In contrast, when the knowledge context is conceptual but above the IDF, governance remains off-chain and human adjudicated (i.e., via X_1 PGR, Fig. 15a).

When the knowledge context is stigmergic and above the IDF, governance remains firmly off-chain and human adjudicated (i.e., via X_3 PGR in Fig. 15b). The case where the knowledge context is stigmergic and below the IDF is a bit more nuanced. For even though the knowledge context is safely below the IDF (and therefore could use CGR), given the stigmergic uncertainties, it always needs human oversight. It is a case of the decoupled design (as shown in the lower half of Fig. 15b). It is, therefore, a mixed case that uses both off-chain as well as on-chain logic. This is the fundamental answer to the on-chain vs. off-chain governance debate between Ehrsam [10] and Zamfir [11] that we discussed in Section 2.

a: Uncoupled Design

Governance for Conceptual Context Above IDF	=	X1			PGR (Off-Chain)
Governance for Conceptual Context Below IDF			X2		CGR (On-Chain)

b: Decoupled Design

Governance for Stigmergic Context Above IDF	=	X3			PGR (Off-Chain)
Governance for Stigmergic Context Below IDF		X4	X5		CGR (On-Chain)

c: Governance Problem Context

Choices ↓	Conceptual		Stigmergic	
	Below IDF	Above IDF	Below IDF	Above IDF
PGR (Off-Chain)		X1	X4	X3
CGR (On-Chain)	X2		X5	

Fig. 15. Governance Kernel Design

From a CAS-perspective, the various configurations (in Fig.15 a-b) are in dynamic flux; protagonists are continually re-positioning for strategic advantage. However, each of these configurations has β-level patterns that frame the governance issue. Most dynamic (and therefore requiring the highest amount of governance effort) are those patterns that have intrinsic knowledge asymmetries (i.e., the UK type); and the ones that need the least amount of governance have fundamental knowledge symmetries (i.e., UU, KK type). However, here too, if the β-level patterns indicate that one or both parties suffer from high-confidence coupled with poor-grasp (or alternatively, good grasp, but low confidence), then problems of governance may surface. This adds greater onus to the "*Know Your Customer*" (KYC) type guidelines.

Fig. 16 shows the overall composition of the Blockchain design along with the governance sub-modules (as discussed above) factored in. DAO was missing these governance sub-modules. Dominance of the governance sub-modules is evident given its top-row position. Within the governance sub-modules (and in agreement with Section 7), the conceptual dominates the stigmergic on account of its logical consistency. However, the conceptual does need to factor in the broader inductive base that the stigmergic provides.

Controlling knowledge-architectures dictate the requisite governance logic. |H-structures demand |H-governance; likewise, |h-structures demand heterarchic, Madisonian-like governance (Fig. 6). In either case, PGR will need to be invoked whenever dealing with pre-conceptual, stigmergic facts as well as concepts that reach beyond the IDF. Consider the |h-case. The blockchain architecture allows for |h-controls both in the somatic/operational (i.e., via the consensus model) as well as germline/kernel (i.e., via stigmergic/conceptual PGR's & CGR's) cases (Fig. 16). Same is true for the less demanding |H-case. Furthermore, there is no fundamental difference between the governance of agents at the α_1 level versus those engaged at a more evolved $\alpha_{n,\, n>1}$ level. Either the agent conforms to the governing β-level; or, alternatively, the β-level itself needs to evolve towards greater consistency. The former is the case of operational governance; the latter is the more demanding, shape-shifting, kernel/germline governance that in dealing with the various shades of unknown-unknowns, helps evolve the CAS system towards greater consistency and reach.

Gov-Conceptual above IDF	=	x												Conceptual PGR (Off Chain)
Gov-Conceptual below IDF			x											Conceptual CGR (On Chain)
Gov-Stigmergic above IDF		x	x	x										Stigmergic PGR (Off Chain)
Gov-Stigmergic below IDF		x	x	x	x									Stigmergic CGR (On Chain)
Structure Auto-exec Contracts		x	x	x	x	x								Smart Contract
Contract Verification		x	x	x	x	x	x							Oracle
Allow discreet agent stigmergy		x	x	x	x	x	x	x						Cryptographic Tokens
Verifiability of Transactions		x	x	x	x	x	x	x	x					Cryptographic Hash
Lightweight transaction-set		x	x	x	x	x	x	x	x	x				Merkle Tree, Patricia Tree, etc
Trustless Trust		x	x	x	x	x	x	x	x	x	x			Consensus Model (POW, POS, etc)
Immutable Transactions		x	x	x	x	x	x	x	x	x	x	x		Blockchain Ledger
Distributed Resilence		x	x	x	x	x	x	x	x	x	x	x	x	Distributed P2P Ledger

Fig. 16. Governance Kernel for the Blockchain Design

19. Conclusions

Given the leveling of the playing field, the dis-intermediation of the middle-men, and the transparency of blockchain-based transactions, it is highly likely that the information flows are on the verge of scaling exponentially. Stigmergy steps in when information flows scale beyond aided/unaided human cognitive limits. In other words, the α↔β gearing (as discussed in Section 7) will most likely ramp up as the technology gains mainstream support. This paper has provided CAS based governance guideposts as to what may be expected. Salient points include:

- Review of blockchain governance to highlight novel pathologies and the problem of unknown-unknowns.
- Issue of trust as it relates to the top nodes in a hierarchical organization going rogue; and its solution via heterarchical control (courtesy James Madison) that conforms to a decoupled lower-diagonal design.
- How organizational structures as well as sense-

making changes with rising complexity.

- The unique challenges faced in the context of large scale socio-technological organizational designs.
- The challenge of governance where "*formal controls*" are missing.
- The role of stigmergic gearing in both biological as well as human decision-making context.
- The original formulation of an iterative CAS.
- The original formulation of how the iterative CAS framework may be utilized to help understand the crux of the centralization/decentralization issue.
- The framing of governance from a heterarchically-hierarchic human knowledge architecture perspective. Then using this approach to fundamentally frame the issue of human vs. machine dominance in decision making (i.e., induction vs. deduction).
- The framing of the Unknown-Unknown nuances and the way these show up in the context of governance.
- The distinction between emergence vs. self-organization; and how the disruption of the natural flow between these two processes can lead to governance pathologies.
- Highlighting the historical significance of Axiomatic Design as providing a unifying conceptual vanishing point (similar to the perceptual vanishing point in the case of perspective drawings); except being in the realm of conceptuals, it has far greater import, especially in education.
- The blockchain technology when viewed from an axiomatic perspective is seen to be a lower-triangle decoupled design.
- The promise as well as the governance problem of smart contracts.
- The design of the blockchain governance kernel as helping decide between on-chain vs. off-chain governance.

References

1. C. P. Snow. The Two Cultures: And a second Look Hardcover. Cambridge University Press; First Thus edition (1965)
2. N. P. Suh. The Principles of Design. 1st ed. New York: Oxford University Press; 1990
3. B. H. Banathy. Designing Social Systems in a Changing World. Springer. 1997.
4. C. Olaya, C. García-Díaz. Social Systems Engineering: The Design of Complexity. Wiley. December 2017
5. L. Marsh, C. Onof. Stigmergic epistemology, stigmergic cognition, Cognitive Systems Research (2007), doi:10.1016/j.cogsys.2007.06.009
6. J. Compton. How Blockchain Could Revolutionize The Internet Of Things. Forbes. Jun 27, 2017. https://www.forbes.com/sites/delltechnologies/2017 06/27/how-blockchain-could-revolutionize-the-internet-of-things/#a969acf6eab4
7. M. Campbell-Verduyn. Introduction: What are blockchains and how are they relevant to governance in the contemporary global political economy? In Bitcoin and Beyond. Cryptocurrencies, Blockchains, and Global Governance. Edited by Campbell-Verduyn M. Routledge Press. 2018
8. L. Lessig. Code: And Other Laws of Cyberspace, Version 2.0 2nd Edition. Basic Books. 2006
9. J. Lopp. Nobody Understands Bitcoin (And That's OK). Mar 11, 2017. https://www.coindesk.com/nobody-understands-bitcoin-thats-ok/
10. F. Ehrsam. Blockchain Governance: Programming Our Future. Nov 27, 2017. https://medium.com/@FEhrsam/blockchain-governance-programming-our-future-c3bfe30f2d74
11. V. Zamfir. Against on-chain governance. Dec 1, 2017. https://medium.com/@Vlad_Zamfir/against-on-chain-governance-a4ceacd040ca
12. Q. DuPont. Experiments in Algorithmic Governance: A history and ethnography of "The DAO," a failed Decentralized Autonomous Organization. In Bitcoin and Beyond. Cryptocurrencies, Blockchains, and Global Governance. Edited by Campbell-Verduyn M. Routledge Press. 2018
13. S. Voshmgir. Blockchain's Problem with Unknown Unknowns.2017. https://medium.com/blockchain-hub/blockchains-problem-with-unknown-unknowns-6837e09ec495
14. Lord Acton (John Emerich Edward Dalberg). Letter to Archbishop Mandell Creighton. Apr. 5, 1887. https://history.hanover.edu/courses/excerpts/165acton.html
15. Juvenal (Decimus Iunius Iuvenalis). Satire VI, lines 347–348. http://www.thelatinlibrary.com/juvenal/6.shtml
16. Plato, Republic. http://www.perseus.tufts.edu/hopper/text?doc=Perseus%3Atext%3A1999.01.0168%3Abook%3D9%3Apage%3D590
17. Plato, Republic. http://www.perseus.tufts.edu/hopper/text?doc=Perseus%3Atext%3A1999.01.0168%3Abook%3D3%3Asection%3D414c
18. J Madison, A. Hamilton. The Federalist Papers : No. 51. Friday, February 8, 1788. http://avalon.law.yale.edu/18th_century/fed51.asp
19. J. Thomas, A. Zaytseva. Mapping Complexity/Human Knowledge as a Complex Adaptive System. 2016 Wiley Periodicals, Inc., Vol. 21 No. S2. DOI 10.1002/cplx.21799. 24 June 2016. https://onlinelibrary.wiley.com/doi/abs/10.1002/cplx.21799
20. Y. Bar-Yam, Complexity rising: From human beings to human civilization, a complexity profile, Encyclopedia of Life Support Systems (EOLSS UNESCO Publishers, Oxford, UK, 2002)

21. R. W. Emerson. Self-Reliance. 1841. https://emersoncentral.com/texts/essays-first-series/self-reliance/
22. G. Fields, J. R. Emshwiller. Many Failed Efforts to Count Nation's Federal Criminal Laws. New York Times. July 23, 2011
23. J. R. Licklider. Man-Computer Symbiosis. IRE Transactions on Human. Factors in Electronics, HFE-1. 4-11. 1960.
24. D. E. Snowden, M. E. Boone. A Leaders Framework for Decision Making. Harvard Business Review. Nov 2007
25. E. Puika. D. Ceglarek. The quality of a design will not exceed the knowledge of its designer; an analysis based on Axiomatic Information and the Cynefin Framework. Procedia CIRP 34 (2015)
26. D. A. Norman, P. J. Stappers. DesignX: Complex Sociotechnical Systems. She Ji. The Journal of Design, Economics, and Innovation Vol. 1, No. 2, Winter 2015
27. A. Scott-Wright A, A. A. Boxwala, Y. Denekamp, R. A. Greenes, D. Tate. Applying Axiomatic Design Methodology for Guideline Revision. AMIA Annual Symposium Proceedings. 2003;2003:1000.
28. T. Shannon. Cynefin and Healthcare. https://frectal.com/book/chaos-complex-complicated-simple-and-cynefin/cynefin-and%C2%A0healthcare/
29. S. S. Jones, R. S. Evans. An Agent Based Simulation Tool for Scheduling Emergency Department Physicians. AMIA Annual Symposium Proceedings. 2008;2008:338-342.
30. E. Schadt. The role of big data in medicine. November 2015 https://www.mckinsey.com/industries/pharmaceuticals-and-medical-products/our-insights/the-role-of-big-data-in-medicine
31. N. P. Suh. Complexity: Theory and Applications. 1st ed. New York: Oxford University Press; 2005
32. V. Chhotray, G. Stoker. Governance Theory and Practice A Cross-Disciplinary Approach. Palgrave Macmillan. 2009
33. Bible. New International Version. Proverbs 6:6-8. https://www.biblegateway.com/passage/?search=Proverbs+6%3A6-8&version=NIV
34. M. Walker. Ant mega-colony takes over world. BBC. July 1, 2009. http://news.bbc.co.uk/earth/hi/earth_news/newsid_8127000/8127519.stm
35. P. P. Grassé. Insectes Sociaux VI. 79. 1959
36. Ants. NetLogo Models Library http://ccl.northwestern.edu/netlogo/models/Ants
37. T.D. Tom De Wolf, T. Holvoet. Emergence Versus Self-Organisation: Different Concepts but Promising When Combined. In Engineering Self-Organising Systems: Methodologies and Applications (Lecture Notes in Computer Science). Edited by Brueckner S. A, Serugendo, G. D. M, Karageorgos A. Springer. 2005
38. H. V. D. Parunak. A survey of environments and mechanisms for human-human stigmergy. 2006. Environments for Multi-Agent Systems II: 163-186.
39. J. F. Padgett, W. W. Powell. The Emergence of Organizations and Markets. Princeton University Press (October 14, 2012)
40. S. A. Kauffman. The Origins of Order: Self-Organization and Selection in Evolution. Oxford University Press; 1 edition (June 10, 1993)
41. R. K. Sawyer. Social Emergence: Societies As Complex Systems. Cambridge University Press (October 27, 2005)
42. F. Klein, H. Giese. Separation of Concerns for Mechatronic Multi-agent Systems Through Dynamic Communities. In: R. Choren, A. Garcia, C. Lucena, A. Romanovsky (eds) Software Engineering for Multi-Agent Systems III. SELMAS 2004. Lecture Notes in Computer Science, vol 3390. Springer, Berlin, Heidelberg
43. S. E. H. Murph, E. Simona. Nanoscale Materials Fundamentals and Emergent Properties in Anisotropic and Shape-Selective Nanomaterials: Structure-Property Relationships. In: S. E. H. Murph, Dr. G. K. Larsen, K. J. Coopersmith (eds) Anisotropic and Shape-Selective Nanomaterials - 2017 Structure-Property Relationships. Springer; 1st ed. 2017 edition (July 15, 2017)
44. M. Viroli, J. Beal, K. Usbeck. Operational Semantics of Proto. Science of Computer Programming. October 22, 2012
45. M. A. Bedau, P. Humphreys. Emergence: Contemporary Readings in Philosophy and Science. A Bradford Book; 1 edition (March 21, 2008)
46. F. Heylighen. Stigmergy as a generic mechanism for coordination: definition, varieties and aspects. ECCO Working paper 2011-12 http://pespmc1.vub.ac.be/Papers/Stigmergy-Springer.pdf
47. F. Bacon. Novum Organum (1620) https://en.wikisource.org/wiki/Novum_Organum/Book_I_(Spedding)
48. M. J. Doyle., L. Marsh. Stigmergy 3.0: From Ants to Economies, Cognitive Systems Research (2012),
49. S. D Palley. How to Sue A Decentralized Autonomous Organization. Mar 21, 2016. https://www.coindesk.com/how-to-sue-a-decentralized-autonomous-organization/
50. J. H. Holland. Studying complex adaptive systems. Journal of Systems Science and Complexity 2006, 19(1), 1-8.
51. V. Buterin. Notes on Blockchain Governance. Dec 17, 2017. https://vitalik.ca/general/2017/12/17/voting.html
52. P. Baran. On Distributed Communication Networks. IEEE Transactions of the Professional Technical

Group on Communications Systems. Volume CS-12, Number 1, March 1964.

53. V. Buterin. The Meaning of Decentralization. Feb 6, 2017. https://medium.com/@VitalikButerin/the-meaning-of-decentralization-a0c92b76a274
54. D. L. Leger. How FBI brought down cyber underworld site Silk Road. USA TODAY. May 15, 2014 https://www.usatoday.com/story/news/nation/2013/10/21/fbi-cracks-silk-road/2984921/
55. C. Harper. Another Class Action Filed Against Ripple, Claims XRP Has "Hallmarks of a Security". Jul 5, 2018 https://bitcoinmagazine.com/articles/another-class-action-filed-against-ripple-claims-xrp-has-hallmarks-security/
56. T. Maas. The Curious Tale of Tezos —from a $232 MILLION ICO to 4 class action lawsuits. Apr 6. 2018 https://hackernoon.com/the-curious-tale-of-tezos-from-a-232-million-ico-to-4-class-action-lawsuits-6f411b7aad7e
57. R. Frost. Mending Wall. 1914 https://www.bartleby.com/104/64.html
58. B. S. Srinivasan, L. Lee. Quantifying Decentralization: We must be able to measure blockchain decentralization before we can improve it. July 27, 2017. https://news.earn.com/quantifying-decentralization-e39db233c28e
59. S. Ivanov. Op Ed: What Do We Mean When We Talk About the "Blockchain Ecosystem"? Feb 26, 2018. https://bitcoinmagazine.com/articles/op-ed-what-do-we-mean-when-we-talk-about-blockchain-ecosystem/
60. M. Yeroulanos, O. Taplin. A Dictionary of Classical Greek Quotations. I.B. Tauris & Co Ltd. 2017
61. W. Shakespeare. Othello. Arden Shakespeare; 3rd edition. http://shakespeare.mit.edu/othello/full.html
62. Paul Ekman Group. Micro Expressions. https://www.paulekman.com/micro-expressions-2/
63. J. Thomas. Archstand Theory of Design for Innovation. PhD Thesis, 1995. MIT. Available at: http://dspace.mit.edu/handle/1721.1/11722
64. G. Kasparov, M. Greengard. Deep Thinking: Where Machine Intelligence Ends and Human Creativity Begins. PublicAffairs; 1 edition (May 2, 2017)
65. D. Rumsfeld. The Unknown Knowns https://www.youtube.com/watch?v=nAnKdq5Yty8
66. E. Morris. The Certainty of Donald Rumsfeld (Part 1). New York Times. March 25, 2014. https://opinionator.blogs.nytimes.com/2014/03/25/the-certainty-of-donald-rumsfeld-part-1
67. J. Keats. Endymion. Book-1. The Poetical Works of John Keats. (1795–1821). http://www.bartleby.com/126/32.html
68. J.T. Foley, E. Puik, D. S. Cochran. Desirable complexity. The 10th International Conference on Axiomatic Design, ICAD 2016. Procedia CIRP 53.
69. J. Thomas, P. Mantri. Axiomatic Design/Design Patterns Mashup: Part 1. In: 9th International Conference on Axiomatic Design (ICAD), Procedia CIRP, 2015, 34, 269-275. Available at: http://www.sciencedirect.com/science/article/pii/S2212827115008501
70. J. Thomas, P. Mantri. Axiomatic Design/Design Patterns Mashup: Part 2. In: 9th International Conference on Axiomatic Design (ICAD), Procedia CIRP, 2015, 34, 276-283. Available at: https://www.sciencedirect.com/science/article/pii/S2212827115008513
71. M.E. Saunders, R.K. Peisley, R. Rader, G.W. Luck. Pollinators, pests, and predators: Recognizing ecological trade-offs in agroecosystems. Ambio. A Journal of the Human Environment. February 2016, Volume 45, Issue 1, pp 4–14.
72. S. Y. Edgerton. The Mirror, the Window, and the Telescope: How Renaissance Linear Perspective Changed Our Vision of the Universe. Cornell University Press (January 29, 2009)
73. T. H. McConnell, K. L. Hull. Human Form, Human Function: Essentials of Anatomy & Physiology. Lippincott Williams & Wilkins. 2010
74. M. Jacobson. How Far Down the Search Engine Results Page Will Most People Go? SEO. 2017. https://www.theleverageway.com/blog/tag/seo/
75. D. Prountzos, K. Pingali. Betweenness Centrality: Algorithms and Implementations. PPoPP '13 Proceedings of the 18th ACM SIGPLAN symposium on Principles and practice of parallel programming. Volume 48 Issue 8, August 2013.
76. S. Voshmgir, V. Kalinov. Blockchain-A Beginners Guide. blockchainhub. https://blockchainhub.net/blockchain-technology
77. P. Goorha. The Return of 'The Nature of the Firm': The Role of the Blockchain . The JBBA. The Journal of The British Blockchain Association. 2018 Vol 1, Issue 1.
78. Awesome Cryptoeconomics. An awesome curated list of Cryptoeconomic research and learning materials. https://github.com/jpantunes/awesome-cryptoeconomics
79. M. Castro, B. Liskov. Practical Byzantine fault tolerance. OSDI '99 Proceedings of the third symposium on Operating systems design and implementation. Pages 173-186
80. A. K. Abbas, A. H. H. Lichtman, S. Pillai. Cellular and Molecular Immunology, Elsevier; 9 edition (May 25, 2017)
81. S. Nakamoto. Bitcoin: A Peer-to-Peer Electronic Cash System. https://bitcoin.org/bitcoin.pdf
82. S. Voshmgir. Disrupting governance with blockchains and smart contracts. In Strategic Change: Briefings in Entrepreneurial Finance. The Future of Money and Further Applications of the Blockchain. Volume 26, Issue 5. September 2017.

Students List FRs Chronologically and DPs Spatially, and Need to Integrate FRs Functionally and DPs Physically

Masayuki Nakao[1,*], and *Kenji* Iino[1]

[1]School of Engineering, The University of Tokyo, Japan

Abstract. The authors have students draw Functional Requirement (FR) – Design Parameter (DP) charts for their free subject design assignments before teaching them Axiomatic Design (AD) in detail. The students cannot list all important FRs and DPs even with Zigzag thinking between FR and DP from higher level to lower; then, they tend to list FRs chronologically like flowcharts and DPs spatially like bill of material. The strategy, however, often results in different counts of FRs and DPs and a number of interferences among them. When this happens, we lead the students to carry out the thinking processes of functional integration of FRs and physical integration of DPs so they can reach a regular matrix for the design equation. Once regularization is reached, the students can apply independence axiom to improve their designs.

1 Introduction: Problems in defining FRs for design projects

Engineers start design thinking about some new solutions to meet social needs (design for creation) or, upon recognizing problems in conventional physical products or organizational systems, to improve them (design for improvement). In either case, taking on the design in a rush by gathering what is available on hand to put together a quick and imperfect solution is not recommended. The key to success is to put down the prototyping tools, organize the variety of concepts that construct the design, and define the design that is about to be built.

In our department, we assign design projects to undergraduate and graduate students for which they are free to select their own project goals. [1] The instructors hope that the students will come up with designs for creation that can lead to patents, however, their deep search into the Internet often leads to imitate something good and carry out design for improvements at the end. Our instructions have the students start on their designs by first defining their functional goals before they start physical prototyping. We, however, keep the definitions at the minimum, so the students do not lose the desire that they want to start prototyping immediately. The minimum definition is a set of functional requirement (FR) without planning on any design parameter (DP), that is, "FR first." In fact, FR is the very indicator that evaluates the new DP constructed by the designer, and at the same time it is the index for the customer to evaluate the design itself.

In defining a design, we must first extract and select phrases that express elements literately to use in the conceptual design definition. We then analyse those concepts as they are, organize them and redefine them. In this difficult analysis phase, the instructors need to help the students in defining these phrases and concepts; thus, all that are left for the students to work on are only to realize the concepts. At these tasks, Japanese engineering students can notice that they are not good at handling such abstract concepts. They are particularly weak in dealing with FRs without physical substance.

Fig. 1 shows the phased methodology of defining a design we teach. The authors translated the Suh's textbook on Axiomatic Design (AD) [2] into Japanese in 2004; we started to teach the undergraduate students to define their designs as the textbook instructed. The class, however, didn't work well because our Japanese design curriculum imported from England in 1888 was too classic, and the students had firstly learned artifacts; for example, screws, gears, engines, wings and so on, namely, "DP first." The students were already imprinted that design thinking was only a physical implementation of DPs. So we added some pre-processes like mind mapping or work breakdown structuring to think about customer need (CN) and FR before teaching AD. The students have no experience to use words, not CAD/CAM/CAE, in a design class. So we let the student take on a project only with words. They want to define the design literally, but don't have enough volume of words. They are like a chef who wants to cook the dinner, but doesn't have enough materials such as meats, fishes, salt, etc.

* Corresponding author: nakao@hnl.t.u-tokyo.ac.jp

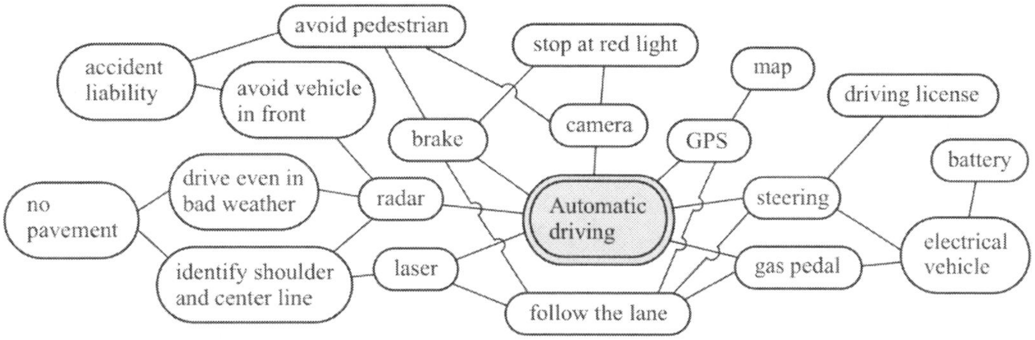

(a) Mind map: List out elements of design concepts as they come to mind

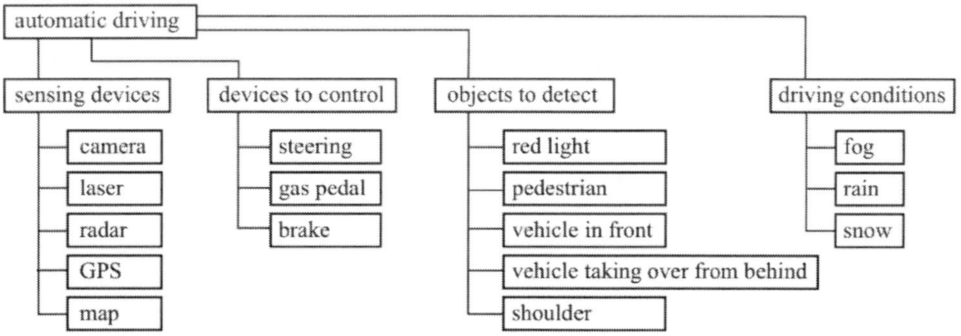

(b) Work breakdown structure: Collect similar concepts and bring them all out

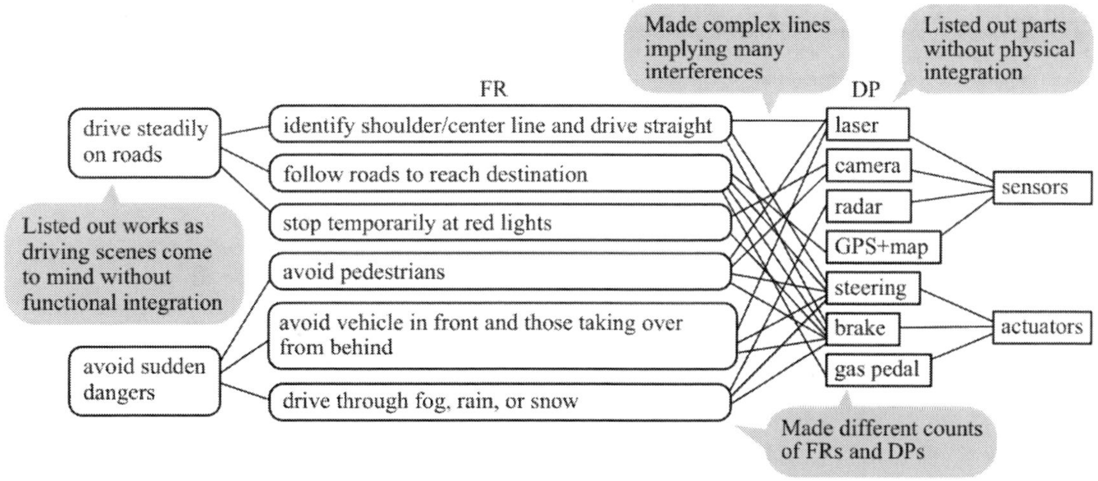

(c) FR-DP chart: Group FRs and DPs and make connections for relations

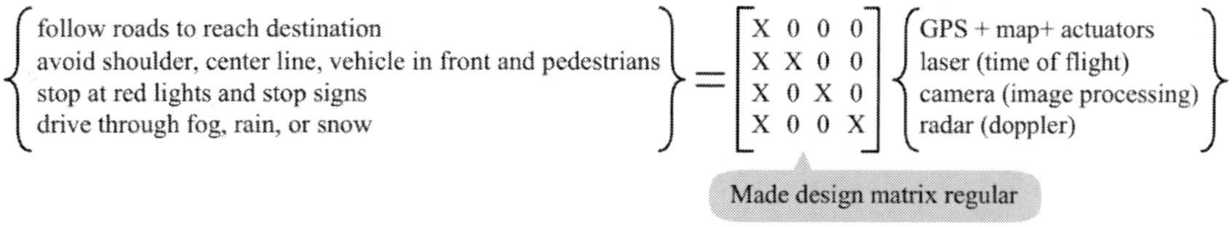

(d) Design equation: Integrate FRs functionally and DPs physically

Fig. 1. Methods for manipulating design concepts.

For example, the project is to design automate driving of a car as shown in Fig. 1(a). When told to list elements for conceptual design, they would start thinking about mechanisms (DPs) for automatic control like "camera," "laser," "radar," "GPS," "steering wheel," and "brake." Students today rely on their searches on the Internet and the searched information easily their work.

Following the next instruction to identify functions (FRs) related with each DP, they list, for example, "follow roads," "stop at red lights," "avoid vehicle in front," "avoid pedestrians," and "drive through poor weather." Listing out all these elements, however, is difficult. Nobody knows if these are all or not. Students always miss some intrinsic FRs.

Fig. 1(a) shows a mind map, often used for hitting all the needed elements. The method pulls out all the elements instinctively in a manner like pulling objects attached to a string one after another, and sets the concepts in nodes and draws lines for relations among them. At least, the number of nodes should be 20 or more.

The next step is to group the concepts and to avoid anything from slipping the mind. The systematic approach of work breakdown structure is effective (Fig. 1(b)). The elements here are still not categorized into design concepts; namely, FRs, DPs, constraints, effects, risks and so on are mixed together. Thompson introduced kinds of functional information [3] and procedural errors in the definition of FR [4]. According to her classification, the authors could often find the errors of "mixing FRs with other types of requirement information" in the design class as mentioned at 3.4 later; FRs were mixed, for example, with non-functional requirements (durable, easy to use, etc.), or with input constraints (cost, weight, operating temperature range, etc.). Thompson pointed out that even Suh [2] or Brown [5] had made the errors of mixing FRs with input constraints.

Our design education has emphasis on recognizing FRs and we have the students pull out verbs for FRs and nouns for DPs and have them draw FR-DP charts like Fig. 1(c) shows. The instructors tell the students to list out all the FRs and DPs, and the students tend to list FRs chronologically like flowcharts and DPs spatially like bills of material. Consequently, each FR has some DPs which correspond or relate to the FR, but not the only one DP which satisfies the FR.

Of course, the students should draw the FR-DP chart in a manner following Suh's Zigzag thinking [2] by traversing the chart. At first, they should set a higher FR, then set the higher corresponding DP, then go down a lower FR, and set the lower DP. That is to alternate between FR and DP in setting the concepts in the order of abstraction, then both sides will have the same number of FRs and DPs with a symmetric tree structure, and the design matrix will be regular (regular: square with an inverse matrix; determinant is non-zero). We teach the students this Zigzag methods; the students, however, still miss some important FRs, or want to recover the shortage of FRs from the DPs reversely. In results, Fig. 1(c) shows complex lines between FRs and DPs. The lines implied many interferences of FRs.

The last phase is to derive design equation shown in Fig. 1(d) for AD. In the previous phase, the students draw the complex lines in Fig 1(c). As the numbers of FRs and DPs do not match, the design matrix should not be regular. As lines that connect FRs with DPs make a number of intersections, the design should not be uncoupled. We need an exact one-to-one relation between FRs and DPs.

Generally, the students make their efforts in listing up all the design elements, and identify FRs chronologically and DPs spatially. The trend is not special to students who are novices in design, but even experienced engineers at corporations, without any experience of defining the products, have the same tendency. Their recoverable method, nevertheless, meets their purposes of identifying all the FRs and DPs. Then, they start to try the Zigzag method with the collected FRs and DPs, and make a regular and uncoupled design matrix. Fig. 1(d) shows the regular and lower triangular design matrix. All four FRs were the higher FRs; this design didn't need the Zigzag method to find lower FRs. To make the square matrix, the instructors tell the students to integrate FRs functionally and DPs physically to condense into enough small numbers of FRs and DPs.

In applying AD, it is ideal to match the counts of FRs and DPs and arrange them in the same tree structure with the Zigzag method. To cope with the situation, the thinking processes of functional integration for FRs and physical integration for DPs is also effective. This paper introduces this functional integration and physical integration with actual design cases.

2 Actual cases of design definition

Defining the FR is clearly more difficult with "design for creations" compared to "design for improvement." The former does not yet realize the new DPs, in the conceptional design process. Thus, FRs cannot be inferred from DPs and the students have to express invisible FRs with words alone.

We give the undergraduate students free subject design assignments for Stirling engines or Internet of Things (IoT), we hope to see "designs for creations" that are worth patenting, but we know that the results may end up in "design for improvement" because about 30 hours of its project term is too short to invent something and define the right set of FRs and DPs.

The problem with these assignments for undergraduate students are the process where they tend to deploy FRs chronologically and DPs spatially. Thus, the design equation for AD turns out non-regular. This is the time when the instructors have to support the students in their analyses to carry out functional integration for FRs and physical integration for DPs. This chapter discusses our work with three actual cases.

Throughout the academic years, we constantly see students' researches for degrees of bachelor, master's, and doctoral. Even such a novel creative academic thesis reveals that most of the work are dependent on past researches, it has only a few DPs that are worth insisting priority and creativity when we have the students draw FR-DP charts. In 2018, 42 graduate students (51%) out of 83 could draw the right FR-DP charts and indicate the prior and creative DPs; 24 students (29%), however, made the errors of "mixing the FRs of the designer" (the project budget, the project dead line, etc.) which should be constraints according to Thompson [3]. These 51% students had already published their own academic papers; they could pick up FRs functionally from the purpose of the research in the papers.

2.1 Case 1: Fan design

Fan is a simple mechanical design without any control computers, probably ideal to have the students identify FRs. The authors asked junior students in the design class to make an FR-DP chart and a design equation of the fan. Fig. 2(a) shows an example of the FR-DP chart which most of them made. We can see complex lines between FRs and DPs.

This student chronologically extracted the FRs thinking about a customer that just made a purchase. The student first thought about the operations of "connecting to AC power" and "pressing the airflow switch." The student also came up with the operations of "pressing the oscillation switch" and "turning the shutoff timer" when

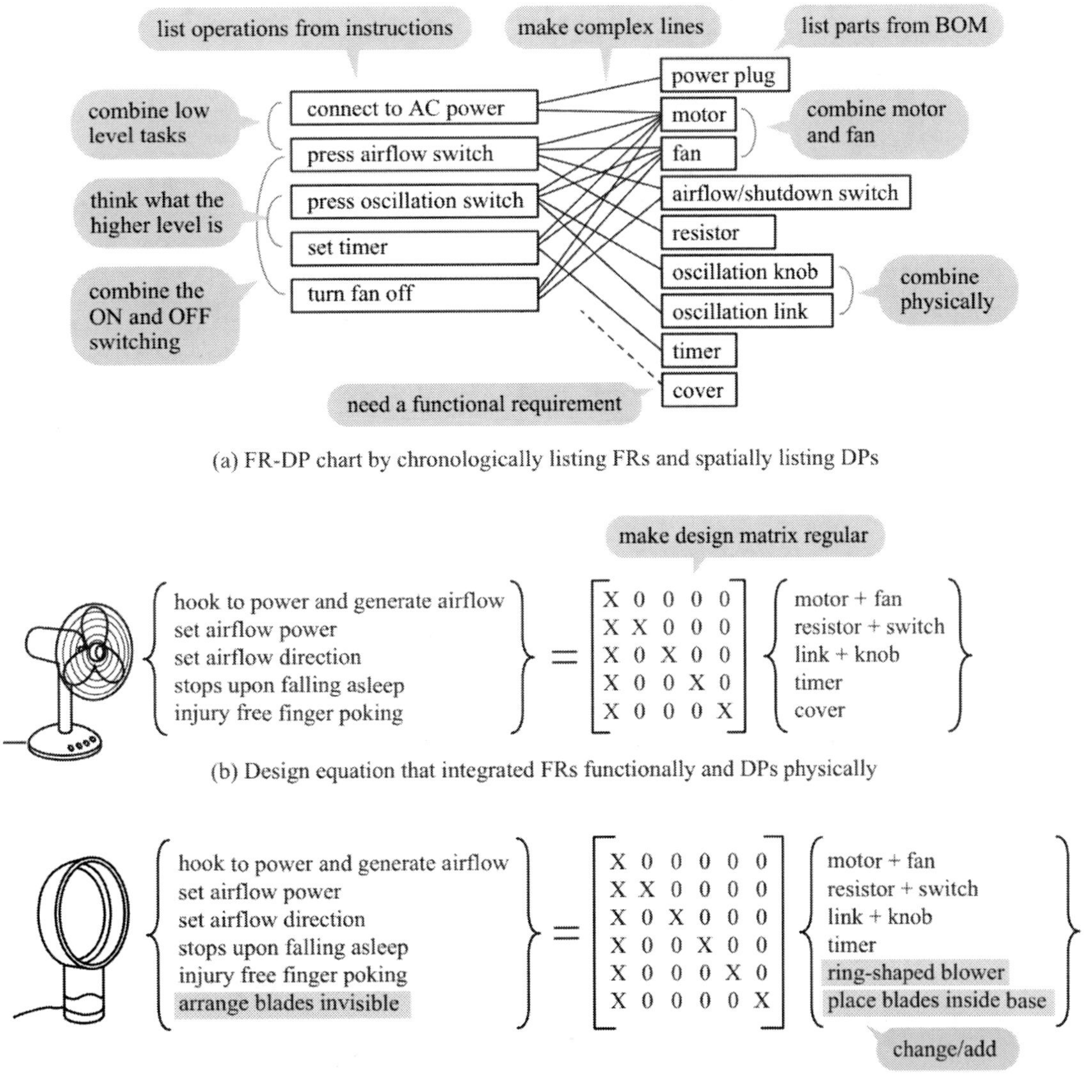

(a) FR-DP chart by chronologically listing FRs and spatially listing DPs

(b) Design equation that integrated FRs functionally and DPs physically

(c) Design equation of a bladeless fan

Fig. 2. Fan design.

going to bed.

On the other hand, the bill of material led to spatial decomposition of "power plug," "motor," "fan," "airflow/shutdown switch," "resistor," "oscillation knob," "oscillation link," "timer," and "cover." They can not represent a DP as something to satisfy an FR.

The student then connected related FRs on the left and DPs on the right with lines. The first FR of "connect to AC power" related to DPs of "power plug" and "motor." The lines had many branches and crossings, however, they were inerasable. On the other hand, the student recognized that the last DP of "cover" did not have a line to an FR and added the FR of "prevent finger poking by children."

Following our instruction, the students then started functional integration of FRs and physical integration of DPs. "Motor" and "fan" connected to the same FR, thus, the student physically integrated them. Similarly, "oscillation knob" and "oscillation link" combined as well.

The FR of "turn fan off" related to DPs of "motor," "fan," and "airflow/shutdown switch" and so did the another FR of "press airflow switch." The student then integrated these two FRs into a single FR of "set airflow power." The FR of "connect to AC power" was a lower FR to the FR of "press airflow switch," thus, the two FRs could integrate to the one FR of "hook to power and generate airflow."

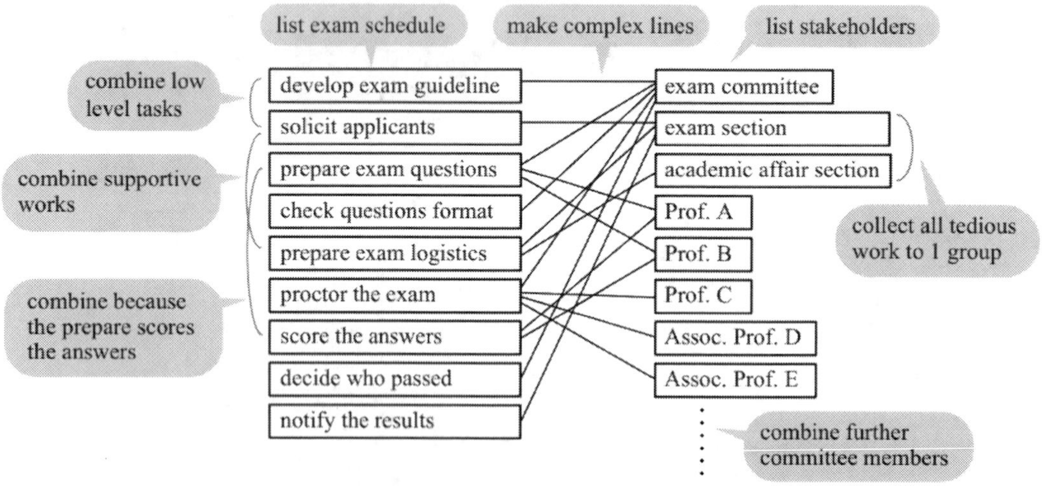

(a) FR-DP chart by chronologically listing FRs and spatially listing DPs

make design matrix regular

$$\begin{Bmatrix} \text{combine exam administration} \\ \text{prepare questions and score answers} \\ \text{proctor the exam} \\ \text{support exam administration} \end{Bmatrix} = \begin{bmatrix} X & 0 & 0 & 0 \\ X & X & 0 & 0 \\ X & 0 & X & 0 \\ X & 0 & 0 & X \end{bmatrix} \begin{Bmatrix} \text{exam committee} \\ \text{exam preparer} \\ \text{exam proctor} \\ \text{exam related staff} \end{Bmatrix}$$

(b) Design equation that combined FRs functionally and DPs physically

$$\begin{Bmatrix} \text{combine exam administration} \\ \text{prepare questions and score answers} \\ \text{proctor the exam} \\ \text{support exam administration} \\ \text{eliminate errors in questions} \end{Bmatrix} = \begin{bmatrix} X & 0 & 0 & 0 & 0 \\ X & X & 0 & 0 & 0 \\ X & 0 & X & 0 & 0 \\ X & 0 & 0 & X & 0 \\ 0 & 0 & 0 & 0 & X \end{bmatrix} \begin{Bmatrix} \text{exam committee} \\ \text{exam preparer} \\ \text{exam proctor} \\ \text{exam related staff} \\ \text{exam review committee} \end{Bmatrix}$$

should be independent   change/add

(c) Design equation for eliminating errors in questions

Fig. 3. Planning administration of admission exam.

Figure 2(b) is the design equation after these changes. It means a decoupled design, and the DP of "motor + fan" needs to be decided at first. FRs were functionally organized and each corresponded to a physically integrated DP. The design matrix shows that all FRs related to the first DP of "motor + fan" with all first column elements being X; "motor + fan" was the key component of the fan.

Once the design equation is polished up, we could see how design for improvements affect the product. For example, the "bladeless fan" in Fig. 2(c) only changed the "cover" to a "ring-shaped blower." This change in how the FR of "prevent finger poking" was realized, however, does not explain the explosive sale by order of magnitude. We can then add the new FR of "arrange blades invisible." We inferred that this FR surprized the consumers and generated the next generation value of a fan.

One of the authors, Nakao has a bladeless fan in his office, however, the shortcoming is that the noise of the airflow is large and annoying. We should set quietness as a constraint in a way similar to cost or durability.

2.2 Case 2: Entrance exam administration

Administration for an entrance exam is a good simple task for designing an organization. Figure 3(a) shows an FR-DP chart made by a junior student who wore a professor's hat.

The student listed the FRs following the time sequence of reaching the day of the exam. The FRs were chronologically set to "develop exam guideline," "solicit applicants," "prepare exam question," "check questions format," and so on. DPs, on the other hand, started by listing up the stakeholders spatially. They were "exam committee," "exam section," "academic affair section," "Prof. A," and so on.

Connecting related elements with lines produced a complex chart similar to the previous fan example, thus, the student needed some integration work. The FRs, for example, of "prepare exam questions" and "score the answers" were carried out by the same person, thus, they could be functionally integrated to "prepare questions and score answers." DPs of "exam section" and "academic affair section," together, were in charge of the FR of supportive administration, thus, they could physically integrate to "exam related stuff."

Figure 3(b) shows the design equation after integrating FRs into 4 categories. The four FRs were "combine exam administration," "prepare questions and score answers," "proctor the exam" and "support exam administration." Elements in the first row of the design matrix are all X meaning all FRs were affected by the leader "exam committee."

Once the design equation was organized to this level, the effect of "design for improvement" was foreseeable, like in the case of bladeless fan. For example, a newspaper recently made large noise about mistakes in entrance exam questions and the University of Tokyo set a new FR of "eliminating errors in questions." The School of Engineering assigned a young faculty member with a flexible thinking as "exam review committee" and had this member challenge the questions. Some errors in questions were identified every year before the exam. During this checking, it is important that the exam review committee looks at the questions independently without knowing "who made the questions." If the member starts to worry like "If I find an error in the work by that big professor, that may influence my future," errors in the questions may not surface.

2.3 Case 3: Umbrella that follows the owner

Next, we will introduce a case from free subject design assignment. A student group designed an umbrella that followed movement of the owner as the sketch in Fig. 4(a) shows in the next page. They first used a drone but the noise from the four nearby rotors was too big to the ears. They then generated lifting force with a helium balloon to counter the dead weight of the machine. The design also used two small motored propellers powered by small batteries to linearly move the balloon to follow the owner and make yawing motions to the left and right.

Fig. 4(b) shows the FR-DP chart. The students forced a one-to-one correspondence among the FRs and DPs, however, the tree shows the left half FR and right half DP trees had different structures. This mismatch was caused by defining a DP for each part. Fig. 4(c) shows the prototype in motion. The instructors lead the students to integrate FRs and DPs. The number of FRs after the integration might to be 5 or less.

The umbrella followed the owner with a camera finding his head and Raspberry Pi reasoning the propeller activation. The owner wore a red cowboy hat for better recognition, however if the head moved too far away from the camera, the camera was lost, and the next step under discussion is to use a fisheye lens. Also, the double propeller design caused the balloon to roll and pitch, and the stable floating would last for only a short time. A tail wing is also under evaluation to prevent rolling and pitching.

Fig. 4(d) is the design equation we constructed after the results and discussion. In addition to the FR of "control umbrella to follow owner," we added the FR of "prevent pitching and rolling" and the corresponding DP of "tail wing."

3 Discussions: Teaching methods to make design equation right for design projects

The above three case studies clarified the processes of identifying all FRs and DPs and then applying integration to regularize the design matrix. We can collect so many FRs, but for the analysis using AD, the FRs might be condensed into about 5. Whatever the design is, the same process can lead to a good uncoupled or decoupled design matrix, however, this work is still challenging for students. We introduce our teaching methods for design projects.

 https://doi.org/10.1051/matecconf/201822301011

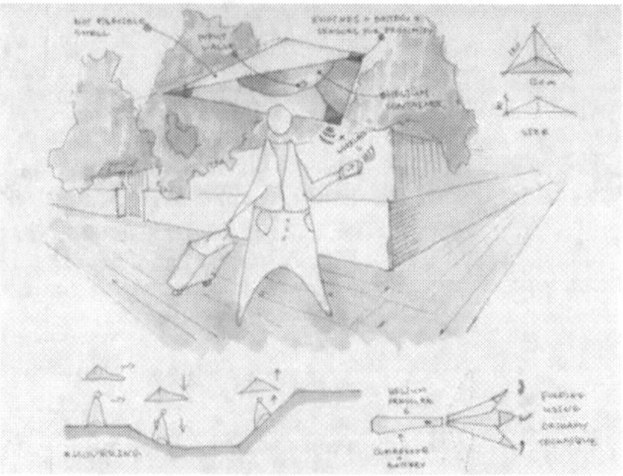

(a) Conceptual sketch of the design

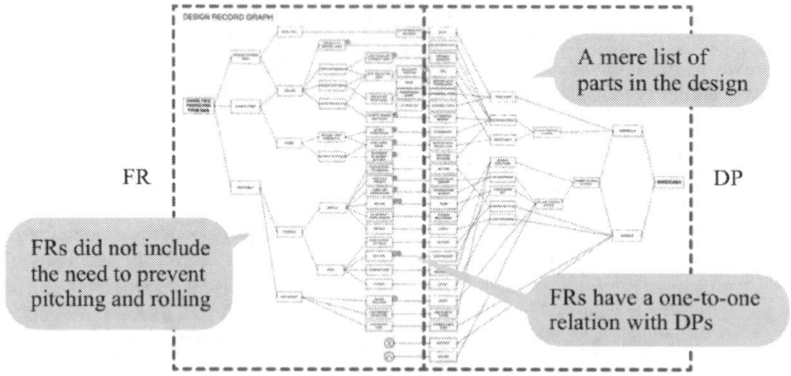

(b) FR-DP chart

(c) Actual prototype (camera finds the red hat and follows it by controlling the left and right propellers)

$$\left\{\begin{array}{l}\text{find owner location}\\ \text{lift umbrella}\\ \text{control umbrella to follow owner}\\ \text{prevent pitching and rolling}\end{array}\right\} = \begin{bmatrix} X & 0 & 0 & 0\\ 0 & X & 0 & 0\\ 0 & 0 & X & X\\ 0 & 0 & 0 & X\end{bmatrix} \left\{\begin{array}{l}\text{Raspberry Pi with camera and fisheye lens}\\ \text{balloon}\\ \text{left and right propellers}\\ \text{tail wing}\end{array}\right\}$$

add (prevent pitching and rolling) add (tail wing) add (fisheye lens)

(d) Design equation after functional integration for FRs and physical integration for DPs

Fig. 4. Design of umbrella that follows the owner.

3.1 Coordinate transformation of FRs

Students often ask us "which is a right set of FRs?" The right set of FRs is not only one. In most cases, any sets of uncoupled or decoupled designs are right because a right set of FRs can change to another right set of FRs with a thinking process of a kind of "coordinate transformation." Figure 5 shows design equations of Stirling engine. We have a design project for juniors to design and prototype a free-style Stirling engine [1], and also have them define their own design. Figure 5(b) lists FRs chronologically such as FRs of Newcomen's steam engine in Suh's textbook [2]. Figure 5(c) lists FRs functionally because the juniors have already learned the common law of heat engines. The both are correct and can improve the yellow-marked interference that a burner also heats an air cooler and the engine finally stops. This coordinate transformation will change a set of FRs and DPs, but will keep a type of design matrix like a triangular matrix in Figure 5(b) (c).

3.2 MECE is similar to independence axiom

The students in the School of Engineering also take the course of Methods in Business Administration for those who want to look for consultant type jobs when they graduate. The instructor of this course emphasizes that consultant has to identify a customer's problems in a mutually exclusive and collectively exhaustive (MECE) way and propose actions against problems for the customer in a one-to-one manner. This class has a higher impact and when we teach the students in the Axiomatic Design class to map one DP that satisfies a specific FR and set all FRs independently, they say they understand the concept because it is the same with MECE. Our strategy was to have the students list out all the FRs and DPs to meet the CE part of MECE using the FR-DP chart and then to make the first ME part with the design equation with AD. When the students actually took on their projects, we found that they needed additional thinking operations of functional integration of FRs and physical integration of DPs.

3.3 Physical integration in Suh's textbook

Studies in Axiomatic Design has already shown the

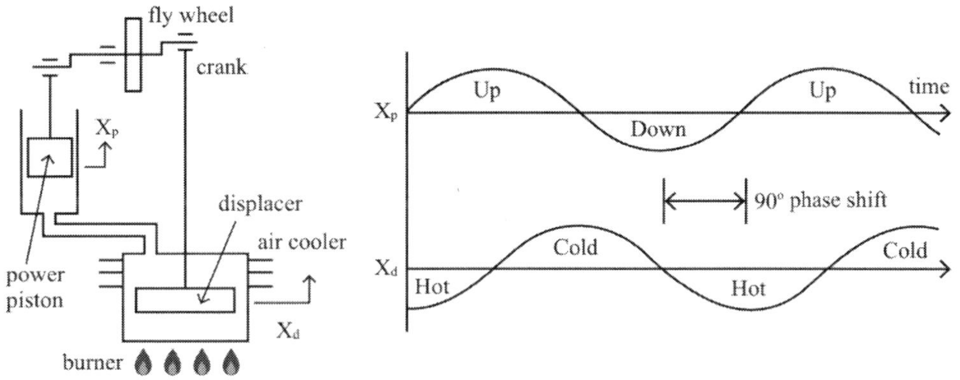

(a) Illustration of Stirling engine

$$\begin{Bmatrix} \text{generate hot air} \\ \text{push up power piston} \\ \text{generate cold air} \\ \text{pull down power piston} \end{Bmatrix} = \begin{bmatrix} X & 0 & 0 & 0 \\ X & X & 0 & 0 \\ X & 0 & X & 0 \\ 0 & 0 & X & X \end{bmatrix} \begin{Bmatrix} \text{lower position of displacer at burner} \\ \text{power piston with } 90^\circ \text{ phase shift} \\ \text{upper position of displacer at air cooler} \\ \text{inertia of fly wheel + replacement to cold air} \end{Bmatrix}$$

(b) Design equation that list FRs chronologically

$$\begin{Bmatrix} \text{input heat} \\ \text{output heat} \\ \text{do work} \\ \text{operate cyclically} \end{Bmatrix} = \begin{bmatrix} X & 0 & 0 & 0 \\ X & X & 0 & 0 \\ 0 & 0 & X & 0 \\ 0 & 0 & X & X \end{bmatrix} \begin{Bmatrix} \text{burner} \\ \text{air cooler} \\ \text{power piston with } 90^\circ \text{ phase shift} \\ \text{displacer + crank + fly wheel} \end{Bmatrix}$$

(c) Design equation that list FRs functionally

Fig. 5. FRs of Stirling engine that are listed chronologically or functionally.

concept of physical integration. In our design engineering course, we first have the students list up FRs of PET bottles and beverage cans, as introduced in Suh's textbook [2]. The students are first surprized that the two have different physical structures, however, the 12 plus FRs are almost identical. Only the PET bottle has two additional FRs of "keep leftover drink for later" and "show contents." Also, both the beverage can and PET bottle have 12 plus FRs but they only have three physical parts of container, tab (cap), and sticker. The students then understand that each part is a result of a number of DP integrations.

3.4 Common DP or general FR should be changed to a constraint

When we have students construct design matrices in their design classes, the designs tend to be decoupled, and not uncoupled, because the DPs of key components or leaders related to multiple FRs. In many cases, such a long line of interferences in the design matrix cannot be improved by Axiomatic Design.

A common DP that relates to multiple FRs in a similar manner is for example, "electrical power," "control computer," "activity funds," or "related regulation." They are not key DPs for each design, however, once they are set to a DP, the corresponding column in the design matrix is filled with Xs. Similarly, a general FR like "keep low production cost," "last long," or "keep total weight light" relates to multiple DPs and the corresponding row in the design matrix will be filled with Xs. When the design has a number of such columns or rows, it is coupled and there is no room for the independence axiom. When the students come across cases with rows or columns of Xs, they tend to underestimate the power of Axiomatic Design.

When we face such cases, we can change the constraint conditions. By setting the limits with inequalities, the relations turn into constraints and they are removed from the FR-DP relations and we can decouple the design matrix. For example, "related regulations" and "legal liabilities" for automatic driving in Fig. 1, "cost" and "quietness" for the fan in Fig. 2 or the umbrella in Fig. 4, "activity funds" for entrance exam administration in Fig. 3 can be handled as constraints. We had the errors of mixing FRs with input constraints in the Thompson's classification. [3]

4 Conclusions

In defining a design, we have to exhaustively list up all the FRs and DPs. Students, who are novices in design, think about FRs chronologically and about DPs spatially. If we follow the listings with design thinking of functional integration of FRs and physical integration of DPs, we can match the FR and DP counts to regularize the design matrix and it is then easier to apply Axiomatic Design. This paper introduced the listing and integration processes with simple design cases. For free subject design assignments during the courses that we taught, we found the integration to be challenging tasks for the students. Our future task is to enhance our teaching methods so all students can start design thinking of integration.

References

1. K. Iino, and M. Nakao, Design Record Graph and Axiomatic Design for Creative Design Education, PROCIR-D-16-00377, ICAD 2016 (2016)
2. N.P. Suh, *Axiomatic Design, Advances and Applications* (Oxford Press, 2001)
3. M.K. Thompson, Improving the requirements process in Axiomatic Design Theory, Annals of the CIRP 62(1): 115-118 (2013)
4. M.K. Thompson, A classification of Procedural Errors in the Definition of Functional Requirements in Axiomatic Design Theory, Proc. of the 7th ICAD (2013)
5. C.A. Brown, Axiomatic Design of Manufacturing Processes Considering Coupling, Proc. of the 8th ICAD: 149-153 (2014)

Axiomatic Design based Design of a Software Prototype for Smart Shopfloor Management

Erwin Rauch[1,*], *Andrew* Vickery[2], *Manuel* Garcia[1], *Rafael* Rojas[1] and *Dominik T.* Matt[1,3]

[1] Faculty of Science and Technology, Free University of Bozen-Bolzano, Bolzano, 39100 Italy
[2] Dept. of Mechanical Engineering, Worcester Polytechnic Institute, Worcester, 01609, MA, USA
[3] Innovation Engineering Center, Fraunhofer Italia Research scarl, Bolzano, 39100, Italy

Abstract. Shopfloor management systems are currently undergoing a change. With the era of Industry 4.0, traditional shop floor management concepts are changing to new and digitally supported approaches for the coordination and management of production at the shop floor level. In order to investigate this change, the research project "Smart Shopfloor" is aiming to develop a software prototype for production management in the era of Industry 4.0. Requirements of industry are collected through literature review and workshops with industry and are translated into software functionalities. These functionalities lead, via an Axiomatic Design (AD) decomposition to design solutions for Smart Shop Floor Management systems. The results of the AD study form the basis for the software architecture and the definition of core and add-on functionalities of the software prototype. The focus of this paper lies on the AD decomposition of the design concept and further gives an overview of potential functionalities. In future, the developed concept will then be implemented in a lab environment before implementing and testing it in industrial case studies.

1 Introduction

In recent years, the industrial environment is changing radically with the introduction of industry 4.0. In order to use and to implement new and emerging technologies for digitization and connectivity efficiently, fundamental changes and adaptations in the production of products are necessary [1]. Through the introduction of so called cyber-physical systems (CPS) and the internet of things (IoT) data models work in real time and the production becomes transparent [2]. Production data are provided in a completely new quality supporting production to manufacture individual products [3] and to make complex decisions faster and thus to be more reactive [2].

Shopfloor management (SFM) is a widely used instrument for operative production control and management in manufacturing companies, which primarily includes detecting deviations and problems in the operational environment and systematically solving these problems [4, 5]. Over the past decades, SFM has been strongly influenced by methods and tools from lean production and quality management [6, 7]. The era of industry 4.0 and the trend towards digitization in production will significantly change the current image of SFM.

In this work, the development of SFM is analysed over time based on a literature review. Afterwards a modern approach of smart shop floor management (SSFM) and related software applications will be presented and explained. These are further underpinned and explained by a practical example.

2 Theoretical background - Smart Shopfloor Management in the industry 4.0 era

The theory section presents a brief overview and the state of the art regarding Shopfloor Management in the past and how it will change with the introduction of Industry 4.0.

In the future, production data will be provided in a completely new quality and with real-time information about production processes. This is made possible by the comprehensive equipping of production with sensors for data acquisition and the consistent integration of intelligent objects [2, 3]. The future representation of the data models in real time makes production transparent and thus easier to control. In the future, such a production control system can also cope with short-term changes in demand and capacity utilization and make complex decisions decentralized in a human-centred production environment [2]. The digitisation and collection of production data promises better use of the data in the use of shopfloor management to increase efficiency and sustainability [4].

Due to increasingly adaptable production systems and the introduction of Industry 4.0 in companies, the pursuit of economies of scale as a means of reducing costs is losing importance, as many process steps can be combined much more flexibly. This means that customer-specific production at low costs is possible with connected production technologies. In classic production systems,

* Corresponding author: erwin.rauch@unibz.it

https://doi.org/10.1051/matecconf/201822301012

this is only possible through frequent variant changes or execution of individual production steps, which usually means higher costs [8].

A critical success factor in global competition is and remains the ability to make the right decisions in a short time. The comprehensive real-time transparency in industry 4.0 enables early decision making and flexible reactions to turbulence in production as well as global optimization across locations. The overall goals, such as the highest possible output (resource productivity) and the lowest possible use of resources for a given product quantity (resource efficiency), are also maintained in industry 4.0. Production processes can be optimized by CPS and throughout the entire value chain [9]. In addition, it is becoming increasingly important to continuously monitor and optimize the system during production with regard to resource and energy consumption as well as emissions [10, 11].

The "smart factory" can control complex and geographically distributed industrial processes. It describes a production environment consisting of intelligent, self-controlling objects. Self-controlled objects can be containers, products, devices or materials. Smart Products are an example of such self-directed objects and can be clearly identified and localized at any time. They already have the knowledge of their manufacturing process. Smart products will therefore be able to independently control the various stages of their production in the future [10].

The introduction of CPS in production also leads to a change in working conditions for employees in the production environment. Employees benefit from more flexible, age-appropriate and, through the use of assistance systems, simpler workstations with greater responsibility and independence in work design. In addition to positive influencing factors, however, employees also face a higher work density and higher demands on competences and skills in dealing with CPS [12].

3 Current functionalities of the Smart Shopfloor Management software Visual Shopfloor®

In traditional lean management, SFM has often taken place in the so-called lean war room (Japanese obeya) with the support of analogue visualization and communication tools. The digitization of SFM requires the introduction of SSFM systems and applications. As described in [5], such mobile and web based software applications are a suitable instruments for connecting employees, methods and technologies in SFM.

Based on existing expertise in industrial companies the research partner Solunio GmbH developed a commercial software for smart shopfloor management with three layers (see Figure 1).

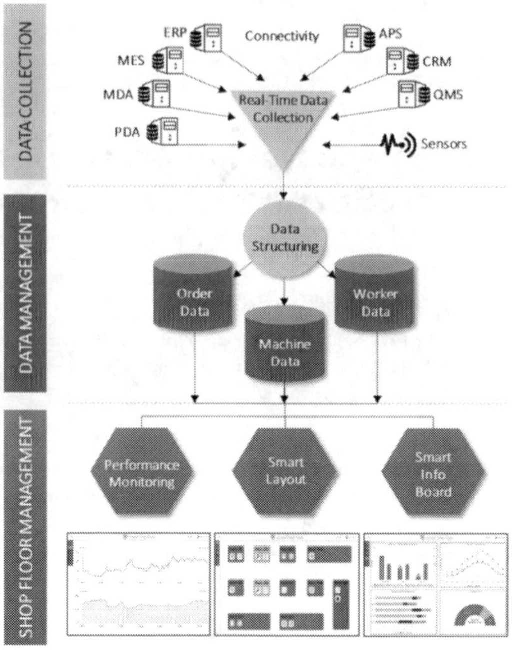

Fig. 1. Existing functionalities of the commercial software Visual Shopfloor® from Solunio GmbH.

3.1. Data collection

At layer 1 (*Data Collection*), data are collected by connecting the SSFM application with various systems and equipment in the company. Such systems can be the internal ERP (enterprise resource planning), a MES (manufacturing execution system) or MDA/PDA (machine or production data acquisition), as well as specific systems such as CRM (customer relationship management), APS (advanced planning system), QMS (quality management system) or intelligent sensors installed on machines.

3.2. Data structuring and management

At layer 2 (*Data Management*), all data collected is then aggregated and structured by filtering relevant data and transferring it into structured data models. The initially large data flood ('big data') is thus transformed into smart and relevant data ('smart data'). The data are then grouped into (i) order data, (ii) machine data and (iii) worker data.

3.3. Current shopfloor management functions

Layer 3 (*Shopfloor Management*) uses the data for shopfloor management by means of various functions. The "Performance Monitoring" function makes it possible to display Key Performance Indicators (KPIs) or statistics in real time avoiding complex updating of reports. The "Smart Info Board" function enables general information to be displayed to all or specific monitors in production at the touch of a button, eliminating the need for time-consuming manual update of paper. The "Smart Layout" function enables the user to visualize the current situation in production by means of a dynamic graphical layout representation. If the user zooms in or out, more details such as machine status or job data appear.

4 Design of a software prototype for Smart Shopfloor Management with AD

In this section, a short overview of the use of Axiomatic Design for software design is presented. Afterwards, the research team analyses the input of potential industrial users and applies AD to deduce a design concept for a new and extended version of Visual Shopfloor in sense of a Smart Shopfloor Management software prototype.

4.1. Design of software systems based on Axiomatic Design

Axiomatic Design theory is applicable to many different kinds of systems, including machines, large systems, organizations as well as software systems [13]. According to [13] software development can be done efficiently in the shortest possible time, reliably with full confidence when it is done based on axiomatic design.

In Axiomatic Design [14] requirements (CNs – customer needs or attributes) are translated into functional requirements (FRs) and constraints (Cs). Hereafter starts a mapping process selecting design parameters (DPs) for individually fulfilling each FR. The following four domains form the base of the Axiomatic Design methodology [14]:

- *Customer domain*: the customer domain defines the desires and needs of customer, usually defined as customer needs (CNs).
- *Functional domain*: the functional domain focuses on the functional (FRs) and non-functional requirements (n-FR) of the system, which derive from customer needs. System constraints (Cs) are also considered.
- *Physical domain*: the physical domain contains the design parameters (DPs) that help to satisfy the functional requirements.
- *Process domain*: the process domain transforms the design parameters into real process variables (PVs).

The mapping process in AD then enables the application of the Independence Axiom and the Information Axiom. The Independence Axiom means that Axiomatic Design favors DPs that do not influence FRs other than the one they were selected to fulfil (means a diagonal design matrix and therefore an uncoupled design). In case of a triangular design matrix the design is a decoupled design satisfying the Independence Axiom if the design sequence is correct. If the design matrix is neither diagonal nor triangular (coupled design) a redesign of the system is required. Furthermore, the Information Axiom assures that in case of alternative satisfactory DPs, the best DP has the lowest information content required for success, i.e., least complexity, or greatest probability of success. Through a top-down decomposition approach FR-DP pairs are decomposed from an abstract level to a detailed one. In the following both Axioms are described more in detail [14]:

- *Axiom 1 – Independence Axiom*: the design of a system is considered ideal if all functional requirements are independent of the others in order to avoid any kind of interaction among them. Each defined design parameter is only related to one functional requirement and has no influence on other functional requirements.
- *Axiom 2 – Information Axiom:* the Information Axiom helps the designer to choose among multiple possible solutions. The design parameter should have the smallest information content, to ensure a higher probability to satisfy a requirement. The aim is to minimize the information content of the design.

In case of software design there are some small differences to other system designs. In the case of products, DPs may be physical parameters or parts or assemblies, whereas in the case of software, DPs may be software modules or program code segments. The software modules build a software architecture which provides a good guideline for software development [13]. In AD a 'module' is defined as the row of design matrix that yields the FR of the row when it is multiplied by the corresponding DP [15].

4.2. Customer needs (CNs) for shopfloor management in the era of industry 4.0

Based on the determination of customer needs and system requirements in workshops with industrial companies and a subsequent discussion with experts the following summary of CNs was elaborated (see Figure 2).

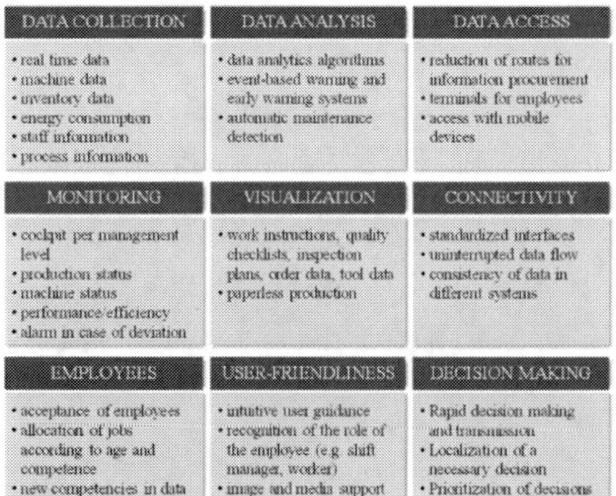

Fig. 2. Collected and clustered customer needs in the industry workshop.

The research team used the collected customer needs to define the functional requirements for the software development. In an additional internal workshop of the research team the results in Fig. 2 were analyzed in order to define which inputs are constraints (Cs) and which ones are functional requirements.

4.3. Definition of high-level functional requirements (FRs) and design parameters (DPs)

The highest level of FRs and DPs can be expressed as follows:

FR_0 Manage the production shopfloor in a smart way.

DP_0 Smart Shopfloor Management software.

Based on the outcome of the initial workshop the following high-level Functional Requirements and related Design Parameters were defined:

FR_1 Collect real time data of machines, processes, resources and energy
FR_2 Avoid inconsistency of data
FR_3 Visualize needed and related data everywhere for individual roles in production without using paper
FR_4 Monitoring of performance (input-output) in production
FR_5 Allow individual and production related data analysis
FR_6 Avoid problems and increase reactivity in decision-making if problems arise
FR_7 Facilitate acceptance of employees.

DP_1 Data Collection module with interfaces and smart sensors
DP_2 Data structuring module
DP_3 Digital visualization technologies
DP_4 Monitoring tools
DP_5 Tools for production data analysis
DP_6 Problem Prevention and problem solving tools
DP_7 Dedicated training of employees and tutorials.

The design matrix on the first level is decoupled and shows the dependencies between the solutions (DPs) and the functional requirements (FRs):

$$\begin{Bmatrix} FR_1 \\ FR_2 \\ FR_3 \\ FR_4 \\ FR_5 \\ FR_6 \\ FR_7 \end{Bmatrix} = \begin{bmatrix} X & 0 & 0 & 0 & 0 & 0 & 0 \\ 0 & X & 0 & 0 & 0 & 0 & 0 \\ 0 & 0 & X & 0 & 0 & 0 & 0 \\ 0 & 0 & 0 & X & 0 & 0 & 0 \\ 0 & 0 & 0 & 0 & X & 0 & 0 \\ 0 & 0 & 0 & X & X & X & 0 \\ 0 & 0 & X & X & X & X & X \end{bmatrix} \begin{Bmatrix} DP_1 \\ DP_2 \\ DP_3 \\ DP_4 \\ DP_5 \\ DP_6 \\ DP_7 \end{Bmatrix} \quad (1)$$

Fig. 3 shows the FR-DP tree of the highest hierarchical levels.

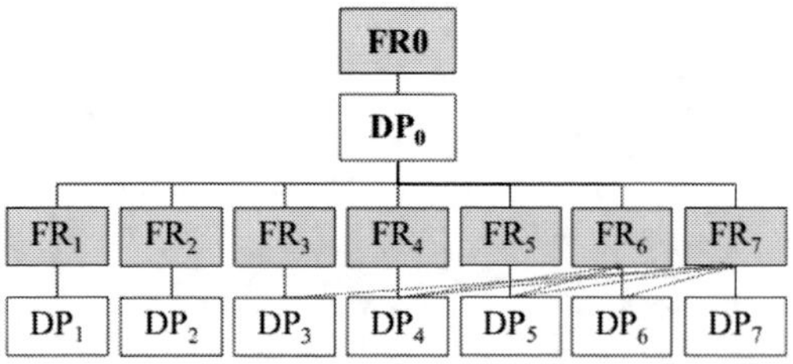

Fig. 3. Highest-level FR-DP tree.

4.4. Decomposition and mapping process

The decomposition process of top-level FRs and DPs aims to transform the abstract requirements into more tangible parameters that are close to the daily practice and therefore relevant for implementation. The FR-DP pairs on the highest hierarchical level represented in Fig. 3 are a starting point for the top-down decomposition and mapping process in AD. The decomposition is performed separately for each of the FR-DP pairs shown in Fig. 3 to obtain a better understanding of the process.

4.4.1 FR_1-DP_1 – Data Collection

The DP_1 Data Collection does not need a further decomposition as this module is already realized in the existing commercial software and works well for the planned software redesign.

4.4.2 FR_2-DP_2 – Data Structuring

Same as above occurs also for DP_2 Data Structuring. The data structuring method has already been realized and is not part of the redesign.

4.4.3 FR_3-DP_3 – Digital visualization

Digital visualization technologies are supporting to visualize specific contents to operators or other users in production. Mobile apps help to visualize data everywhere, while an own function is visualizing only data relevant for the own position (shift-leader, operator, etc.) while an Info Board contains general information. Problems are visualized graphically in the layout as problem map.

$FR_{3.1}$ Visualize data everywhere.
$FR_{3.2}$ Visualize relevant data for the own role.
$FR_{3.3}$ Visualize general information.
$FR_{3.4}$ Visualize problems transparently.

$DP_{3.1}$ Mobile App module.
$DP_{3.2}$ MyRole View module.
$DP_{3.3}$ Info Board module.
$DP_{3.4}$ Problem Map module.

The design matrix shows a decoupled design:

$$\begin{Bmatrix} FR_{3.1} \\ FR_{3.2} \\ FR_{3.3} \\ FR_{3.4} \end{Bmatrix} = \begin{bmatrix} X & 0 & 0 & 0 \\ X & X & 0 & 0 \\ X & 0 & X & 0 \\ X & 0 & X & X \end{bmatrix} \begin{Bmatrix} DP_{3.1} \\ DP_{3.2} \\ DP_{3.3} \\ DP_{3.4} \end{Bmatrix} \quad (2)$$

The Mobile App module consists of an app containing a mobile version of the software. Thus it has a dependency to other FRs. The Info Board module is also able to visualize problems transparently.

4.4.4 FR_4-DP_4 – Monitoring

Production performance indicators are monitored in a performance monitoring function while energy consumption is monitored in an energy cockpit. The smart layout function shows changes in the layout.

$FR_{4.1}$ Monitoring of production performance.
$FR_{4.1}$ Monitoring of energy performance.
$FR_{4.1}$ Monitoring of changes in the layout.

$DP_{4.1}$ Performance Monitoring.
$DP_{4.2}$ Energy Cockpit.
$DP_{4.3}$ Smart Layout.

The design matrix shows an uncoupled design:

$$\begin{Bmatrix} FR_{4.1} \\ FR_{4.2} \\ FR_{4.3} \end{Bmatrix} = \begin{bmatrix} X & O & O \\ O & X & O \\ O & O & X \end{bmatrix} \begin{Bmatrix} DP_{4.1} \\ DP_{4.2} \\ DP_{4.3} \end{Bmatrix} \quad (3)$$

4.4.5 FR_5-DP_5 – Data Analysis

The software should not only allow to see general monitoring dashboards but also to do more detailed data analysis using the data stored in the software. Thus the SSFM software provides a digital value stream mapping function in order to compare different situations and to identify potentials for optimization. Further individual data analytics should also be possible.

$FR_{5.1}$ Allow lean production data analysis.
$FR_{5.2}$ Enable individual data analysis.

$DP_{5.1}$ Digital Value Stream Map.
$DP_{5.2}$ Data Analytics.

The design matrix shows an uncoupled design:

$$\begin{Bmatrix} FR_{5.1} \\ FR_{5.2} \end{Bmatrix} = \begin{bmatrix} X & O \\ O & X \end{bmatrix} \begin{Bmatrix} DP_{5.1} \\ DP_{5.2} \end{Bmatrix} \quad (4)$$

4.4.6 FR_6-DP_6 – Problem Management

Problems due to machine stops should be avoided in future through early warning systems or predictive maintenance. A digital problem issue tracking function should also reduce the duration of the procedure to solve a problem. The introduction of a location based decision making can further improve also the reactivity for problem solving. This means that e.g. the nearest shift leader will be informed if the production system identifies a problem where a certain decision is needed.

$FR_{6.1}$ Prevent stops of production machines.
$FR_{6.2}$ Reduce duration of problem solving.
$FR_{6.3}$ Increase reactivity in problem solving.

$DP_{6.1}$ Predictive maintenance module.
$DP_{6.2}$ Issue tracking.
$DP_{6.3}$ Location based decision.

The design matrix shows a decoupled design:

$$\begin{Bmatrix} FR_{6.1} \\ FR_{6.2} \\ FR_{6.3} \end{Bmatrix} = \begin{bmatrix} X & O & O \\ O & X & O \\ X & X & X \end{bmatrix} \begin{Bmatrix} DP_{6.1} \\ DP_{6.2} \\ DP_{6.3} \end{Bmatrix} \quad (5)$$

Predictive maintenance as well as issue tracking increases the reactivity for problem solving showed in the matrix by the dependencies of the DPs with the last FR.

4.4.7 FR_7-DP_7 – Acceptance of users

It is crucial for the implementation of such a Shopfloor management system that all user are accepting the software. Thus the AD design foresees two further lower level FR-DP pairs.

$FR_{7.1}$ Support users if problems arise.
$FR_{7.2}$ Increase skills of users in data management.

$DP_{7.1}$ Online Tutorial.
$DP_{7.2}$ Dedicated trainings in the SSFM software.

The design matrix shows a decoupled design:

$$\begin{Bmatrix} FR_{7.1} \\ FR_{7.2} \end{Bmatrix} = \begin{bmatrix} X & O \\ X & X \end{bmatrix} \begin{Bmatrix} DP_{7.1} \\ DP_{7.2} \end{Bmatrix} \quad (6)$$

There is a dependency as the regular use of online tutorials is also helping to train people working with the software.

4.4.1 Design matrix and summary

The following design matrix illustrated in Fig. 4 summarizes all higher and lower level FR and DP. Acclaro DFSS (Design for Six Sigma software tool by Functional Specs Inc.) was used to elaborate and check the overall design matrix.
The design matrix is decoupled, which means that the design sequence must be followed in the development work in order to minimize complexity and iterations in the software development process. The AD approach provides software developers with an instrument for sequencing the development of the single software modules in an appropriate manner.

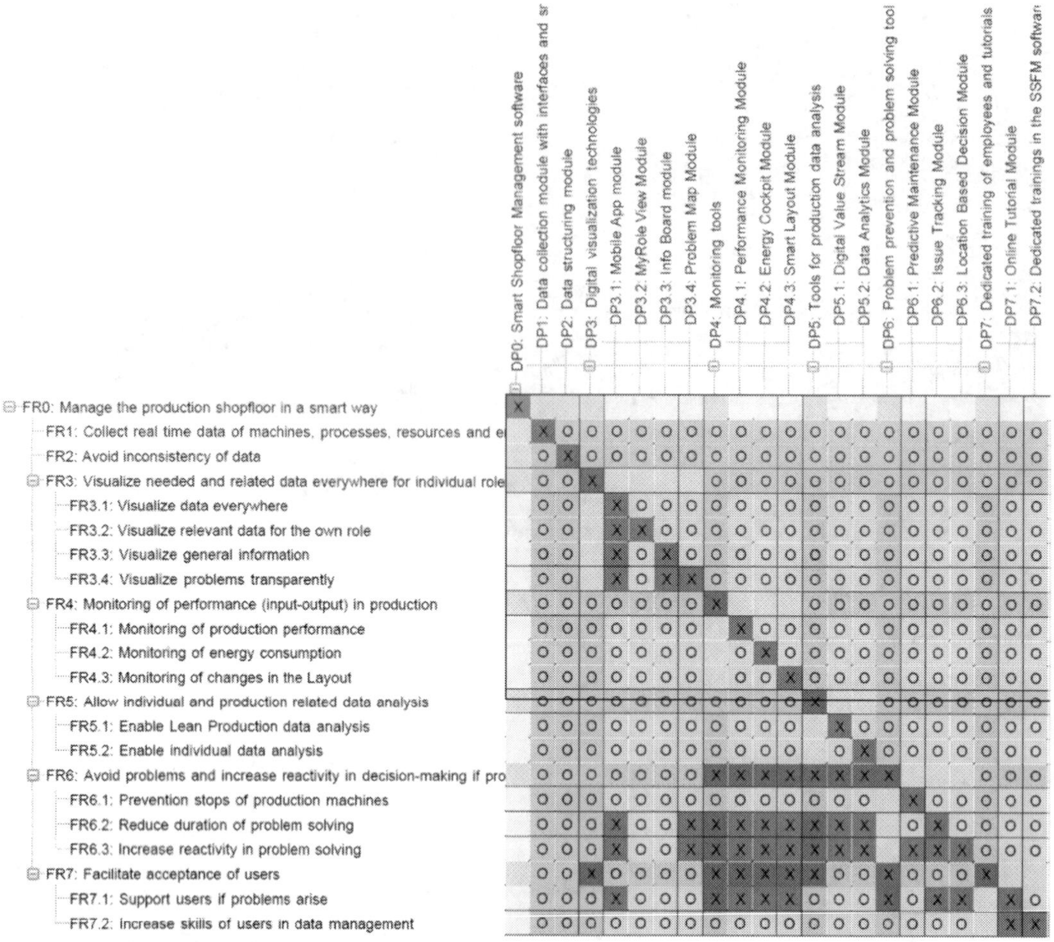

Fig. 4. Summarizing first and second level design matrix.

5 Architecture and concept of a Smart Shopfloor Management software prototype

Fig. 5 shows the final concept and structure of modules or functionalities of the software prototype. The module "Data Analytics" enables the user to create individual data analyses in an intuitive way without any specific knowledge, thus using existing data effectively and efficiently. The "Mobile App" module enables the user to access the SSFM system from mobile devices. In order to keep distances short and reaction speed fast, the module "Location-based Decision" supports calling the closest decision authority to the place of the immediate decision. The "myRole View" module enables the user to switch between a standard view and a role-specific view in order to display only that information that is important and useful for their role (e.g. worker, shift-leader). The "Smart Layout" module enables the user to visualize the current situation in production by means of a dynamic graphical layout representation. If the user zooms in or out, more details such as machine status or job data appear. The "Performance Monitoring" module makes it possible to display KPIs or statistics in real time avoiding complex updating of reports. The "Smart Info Board" module enables general information to be displayed to all or specific monitors in production at the touch of a button, eliminating the need for time-consuming manual update of paper. Based on internal data algorithms the "Predictive Maintenance" module determines automatically, when the next maintenance intervals are to be carried out. The "Problem Map" module graphically shows where quality problems arise in the company and therefore enables intuitive and quick detection of problem areas or machines. The "Issue Tracking" module digitally tracks the systematic processing of occurring problems in production by allowing the status of open problems to be continuously and in real time updated by the parties involved. The "Energy Cockpit" module shows the current energy consumption in the company and warns the user as soon as the consumption exceeds a defined warning limit or follows a negative or positive trend. The "Digital Value Stream Map" module is the digital image

* Corresponding author: erwin.rauch@unibz.it

of a traditional value stream map, which is updated continuously and in real time and thus avoids time-consuming manual data collection. The "Dedicated Trainings" module offers access to training documents or video material directly at the workplace in order to facilitate the training phase of new employees at the workplace or during the start-up of new products. The last module "Online Tutorial" enables decentralized access to tutorials for problem solving and for frequently asked questions.

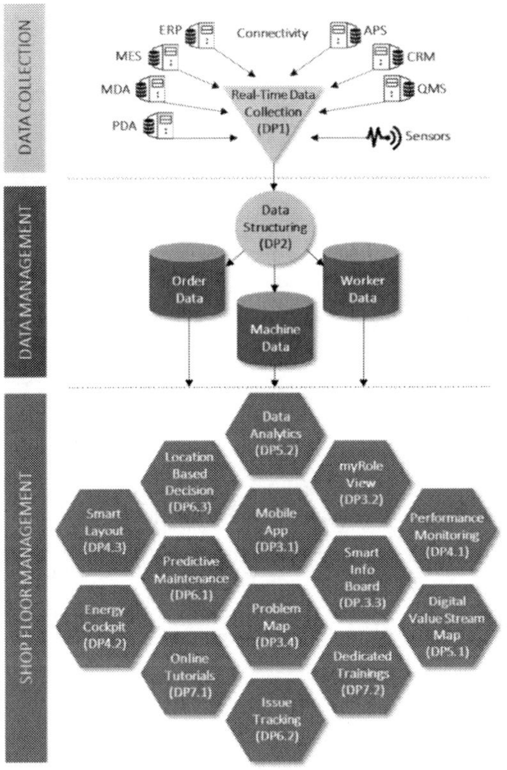

Fig. 5. Future modules of the SSFM software prototype.

6 Conclusion and outlook for further research

This work summarizes current results of an ongoing research on SSFM. Previous studies have shown that small and medium-sized companies in particular require simplified and modular solutions for digitization in the shop floor management [16, 17]. Taking this need into account, this work tries to define a basic concept for bringing shopfloor management to a new digital level. Through a higher connectivity of production systems, existing data can be used for a more intelligent SFM. Thus, a framework based on three layers has been developed to design and realize a prototype application of a SSFM in the lab. Aim of this SSFM system is to support indirect and direct people in production and to change from a paper-based SFM system to a digital one. The currently commercialized SSFM application visual shop floor® from the research partner Solunio will be used in a next step to develop, realize and test the newly identified modules shown in the AD decomposition and in Fig. 5. The AD approach supports the developers to define the right sequence for software development as the design matrix shows a decoupled design. An important task in the context of software development will be to make the user aware of which functional requirements have been implemented via the various software modules (DPs), so that the user can make full use of the developed SSFM. The testing of the new software prototype will take place in the Smart Mini Factory Laboratory of the Free University of Bolzano which focuses innovative applications of Industry 4.0. Further tests in an industrial environment should help to evaluate the suitability of this software prototype in industrial companies and especially in small and medium sized companies.

This project has received funding from the Free University of Bolzano under the grant agreement TN2079 (project title: Smart Shopfloor - Development of a software prototype for intelligent Shopfloor Management through Industry 4.0 technologies).

References

1. U. Sendler. Industrie 4.0 – Beherrschung der industriellen Komplexität mit SysLM (in German: Industry 4.0 - mastering industrial complexity with SysLM). Munich: Springer, 2013.
2. D. Spath, O. Ganschar, S. Gerlach, T. K. Hämmerle and S. Schlund. Manufacturing work of the future – Industry 4.0. Stuttgart: Fraunhofer Verlag; 2013.
3. M. Gneuss. Als die Werkstücke laufen lernten. Industrie 4.0: Die vierte industrielle Revolution (in German: When the workpieces learned to walk. Industry 4.0: the fourth industrial revolution). Berlin: Reflex; 2014.
4. C. Hertle, J. Hambach, A. Meißner, S. Rossmann, J. Metternich, J. Rieger. Digital shopfloor management – New ideas for improvements in production. *Productivity Management*, vol. 22, no. 1, pp.59-61, 2017.
5. L. M. Liao, C. J. Huang and G. H. Lin. A case study of production scheduling and shop floor control for hybrid flexible flowshop. In: Proceedings of the 6th International Conference on Industrial Engineering and Operations Management, Kuala Lumpur, Malaysia, 2016.
6. U. Dombrowski, T. Belz and F. Jäger F. Shopfloor management in the loop control of the implementation of Lean Production Systems (LPS): Supporting lean leadership with corporate-wide and standardized performance measurement systems. *Zeitschrift für wirtschaftlichen Fabrikbetrieb*, vol. 109, no. 1-2, pp. 20-25, 2014.
7. U. Dombrowski, T. Belz and F. Jäger. The use of shop floor management for support of quality management systems - operational implementation of the requirements of ISO 9001: 2015 in manufacturing

companies. *Zeitschrift für wirtschaftlichen Fabrikbetrieb*, vol. 111, no. 4, pp. 169-173, 2016.

8. Bundesministerium für Bildung und Forschung. Zukunftsbild „Industrie 4.0“. Berlin: Bundesministerium für Bildung und Forschung, 2012.
9. E. Rauch, S. Seidenstricker, P. Dallasega and R. Hämmerl. Collaborative Cloud Manufacturing: Design of Business Model Innovations Enabled by Cyberphysical Systems in Distributed Manufacturing Systems. *Journal of Engineering*, Article ID 1308639, 2016.
10. H. Kagermann, W. Wahlster and J. Helbig. Umsetzungsempfehlungen für das Zukunftsprojekt Industrie 4.0. Abschlussbericht des Arbeitskreises Industrie 4.0, Promotorengruppe Kommunikation der Forschungsunion Wirtschaft – Wissenschaft. Frankfurt: acatech – Deutsche Akademie der Technikwissenschaften e.V., 2013.
11. F. Shrouf and G. Miragliotta. Energy management based on Internet of Things: practices and framework for adoption in production management. *Journal of Cleaner Production*, vol. 100, pp. 235-246, 2015.
12. A. Sanders and J. Wulfsberg, J. Industrie 4.0: Shopfloor Management im Wandel: Konzeptionelle Handlungsempfehlungen. *Zeitschrift für wirtschaftlichen Fabrikbetrieb*, vol. 110, no. 10, pp. 653-656, 2015.
13. N. P. Suh. Axiomatic design theory for systems. *Research in engineering design*, vol. 10, no. 4, pp. 189-209, 1998.
14. N. P. Suh. Axiomatic design: Advances and applications. New York: Oxford University Press, 2001.
15. N. P. Suh and S. H. Do. Axiomatic design of software systems. *CIRP Annals-Manufacturing Technology*, vol. 49, no. 1, pp. 95-100, 2000.
16. P. R. Spena, P. Holzner, E. Rauch, R. Vidoni and D. T. Matt. Requirements for the Design of flexible and changeable Manufacturing and Assembly Systems: a SME-survey. *Procedia CIRP*, vol. 41, pp. 207-212, 2016.
17. D. T. Matt and E. Rauch. Design of a scalable modular production system for a two-stage food service franchise system. *International Journal of Engineering Business Management*, vol. 4, no. 1, pp. 4-32, 2012.

MATEC Web of Conferences 223, 01013 (2018) https://doi.org/10.1051/matecconf/201822301013
ICAD 2018

Axiomatic Selection of Health and Social Care Web Services on the Basis of Use Cases

Chiara Parretti[1,*], *Fernando* Rolli[1], *Elaheh* Pourabbas[2], *Paolo* Citti[1]

[1]Department of Innovation and Information Engineering, Guglielmo Marconi University, Via Plinio 44 - 00193 Rome, Italy
[2]Institute for System Analysis and Computer Science "A. Ruberti", National Research Council, Via dei Taurini, 19 - 00185 Rome, Italy

Abstract, in recent years remote patient monitoring systems, which are conceived to monitor patient and store the recorded data, employ Service Oriented Architectures (SOA). In health care systems, if on the one hand the SOA features allow enriching the offer of services to patients and their families, on the other hand the problem arises of selecting the most appropriate set of web services for homogeneous groups of users or for each individual clinical case. In this paper, we propose a methodology based on the Axiomatic Design for the composition and selection of web services, which are based on the case stories studied, built using semi-structured interviews to different stakeholders involved in the care process. The proposed methodology detects in a systematic way all functional requirements by taking into account the different stakeholders involved in the process and their interactions. Thus, it identifies the interested actors for a specific health protocol, and consider all information to be exchanged and the Web Services to be implemented. The development of this methodology opens interesting scenarios even in areas not currently affected by such systems, such as health and safety at work for monitoring patients with chronic illnesses or for their work reintegration following acute clinical events. A specific case study is considered in order to illustrate the proposed approach.

1 Introduction

1.1 Context

In health care domain, the progressive aging of the population and the recent migration flows, in particular in Italy, are leading to a substantial increase in the costs of health services. Paradoxically, also, the progress in medical and scientific fields has increased the cost of individual health care services [1], which increasingly require the contribution of more specialists and advanced technologies [2]. It should also be noted that the increase in chronic illnesses and the lengthening of working life open important scenarios in the field of health and safety at work with regard to the monitoring and management of the worker suffering from chronic diseases. [3, 4]. For this reason, numerous approaches and strategies capable of optimizing the provision of health care services are proposed, see for instance [5-7]. Their main objectives are, in essence, to reduce waste, guarantee optimal levels of service for users, and to effectively prevent the emergency. In this context, the reduction of patient hospitalization length is an evident factor. In fact, this reduction involves saving resources in terms of more available beds, less care in hospital and personnel costs, abatement of social costs related to the management of a professional illness. Furthermore, the possibility of providing satisfactory home-based services allows the patient and his family to be assured of a better quality of life. This objective can be achieved by involving in a coordinated way all the operators and health and non-medical specialists involved in the treatment of the patient.

1.2 Service-oriented architecture

In recent years remote patient monitoring systems, which are conceived to monitor patient and store the recorded data, employ Service-Oriented Architecture (SOA). They create federated, distributed and scalable architectures, and are mainly based on web services [8]. SOA is a design approach based on the service concept. Service is component of distinctive functional meaning that typically encapsulate a high-level business concept. In this architecture, an application consists of software services and software service consumers (also known as clients or service requesters). This approach allows interoperability between different systems and technologies. Web services (WS) are self-contained, modular, distributed, dynamic applications that can be published or invoked over the network to create products and processes. These applications can be local, distributed, or web-based. This interoperability is due to the use of open standards.

1.3 Identification of web services

One of the challenging tasks in the SOA design is the identification of web services to be implemented. Accordingly, in health care systems if on the one hand the SOA features allow enriching the offer of services to patients and their families, on the other hand the problem arises of selecting the most appropriate set of web services for homogeneous groups of users or for each individual clinical case. Based on the description of the medical practices to be provided, it is possible to define the actors involved, the activities to be performed and the tools to be

* Corresponding author: c.parretti@unimarconi.it

used [9, 10]. Since the different actors involved can belong to different organizations, institutions and professional categories, the adoption of a SOA makes interoperability its strength, and enable patients and the different actors involved to access available web services. These requirements lead to the formalization of the conceptual design of the system, which allows the identification of web services candidates for implementation.

1.4 Design optimization

In this context, Axiomatic Design (AD) [11] can be used as a powerful tool to optimize the selective process [12-16]. An interesting application of AD in health care is the optimization of the patient flow in hospitals [17]. Essentially, this approach consists of decomposing the web services and their identified functional requirements to a more detailed level in order to highlight logical inconsistencies and suggest improvements to the initial design. In particular, the axioms of independence and information allow, at each level of decomposition, to identify the minimum set of web services to be implemented in compliance with the criteria of completeness, consistency and plausibility of the information to be processed. In this paper, we propose a methodology based on the AD for the composition and selection of web services, which are based on the case stories studied in the context of the Health@Home project [9]. In the mentioned paper, the case stories are built using semi-structured interviews to different stakeholders involved in the care process, and Web services are defined based on the business process modelling approach. Whereas, our methodology that is based on the AD paradigm detects in a systematic way all functional requirements by taking into account the different stakeholders involved in the care process and their interactions. The purpose of this work is two folds, i.e., firstly, to identify the interested actors for a specific health protocol, and secondly, to consider all those information to be exchanged and the web services to be implemented. Finally, a specific case study is considered in order to illustrate the proposed approach.

2 Methodology

2.1 Premise

In this paper we will refer to terms *case study*, *case story* and *use case*. A case study is a factual representation of what happened along with some analysis that provides insights and learning for the future. In the social and life sciences, a case study is a research method involving in-depth and detailed examination of a subject of study (the *case*), as well as its related contextual conditions [18, 19]. Whereas, a case story depicts what happened through people, place, and plot and brings emotional context into the portrayal of what happened. Finally, a use case is a list of actions or event steps typically defining the interactions between a role (known in the Unified Modelling Language-UML as an actor) and a system to achieve a goal [20].

2.2 Methodological approach

An earlier work published by F. Pecoraro et alii [9] proposes to identify, through the use of case stories and Unified Modelling Language (UML) modelling, the web services to be implemented in relation to a specific clinical case. In this article, we propose an approach based on AD. The proposed methodology is based on the use of UML contextual modelling techniques and an axiomatic decomposition process of the functional requirements (FR) of the system. The main goal of methods of system analysis, which are based on use cases, is to capture from the real world the set of requirements needed for the system implementation. As a first step, it is necessary to generate the case stories, i.e. semi-structured interviews with the actors involved in the use of the system. The goal of the case stories is describing the functions of the system from the point of view of a particular user-actor involved. Subsequently they are grouped, analyzed and translated as use cases in Unified Modeling Language (UML) [7]. This level of formalization allows us to identify the interactions between the parts and to define an accurate diagram of the sequences. Already at this stage, we could identify the web service candidates for implementation, but the result would be strongly linked to the experience of software designers [9, 21]. Instead, we want to introduce a process to optimize the whole selection process based on quantitative evaluations [21, 22]. In this sense, AD approach provides us with a powerful evaluation tool, based on a solid theoretical basis, made up of axioms and corollaries, easily applicable also in this context [23, 24]. In fact, by reporting the relationships between the different components of the system in terms of project matrices, it is possible to keep track of the decomposition operations and assign a measurement to different decompositions, but always referable to the same level of detail. The integration of the two methodological approaches derives from the correspondence between the concept of FR of the AD approach and that of use case [22]. Therefore, initiating an axiomatic decomposition process, starting from the level of maximum abstraction, it is possible to obtain a logical process to the construction of the interaction diagram and the activities [22]. The decomposition can be pushed to the logical design of the system [22-27]. In fact, all levels of decomposition have a double representation, in terms of diagrams and in terms of matrices [26, 27]. While diagrammatic forms provide the tools to design and implement the system, representations of the matrix guide the identification of the most solid engineering solutions. Figure 1 schematically illustrates the whole process of design solution selection [28].

2.3 Modalities of application of axiomatic selection

The application of the axiomatic decomposition expected a mapping process between four conceptual domains

(Figure 2). In this context, the case stories represent the description in semi-structured language of the behavior of the system with respect to the various actors. To start the axiomatic selection we can place the case stories as the Customer Attributes (CA) of the process and the use cases identified as high level FR. Design Parameters (DP) are instead created by the designers and correspond to the interactions between the various uses case. In this way, the first level decomposition describes the network of interactions between use cases.

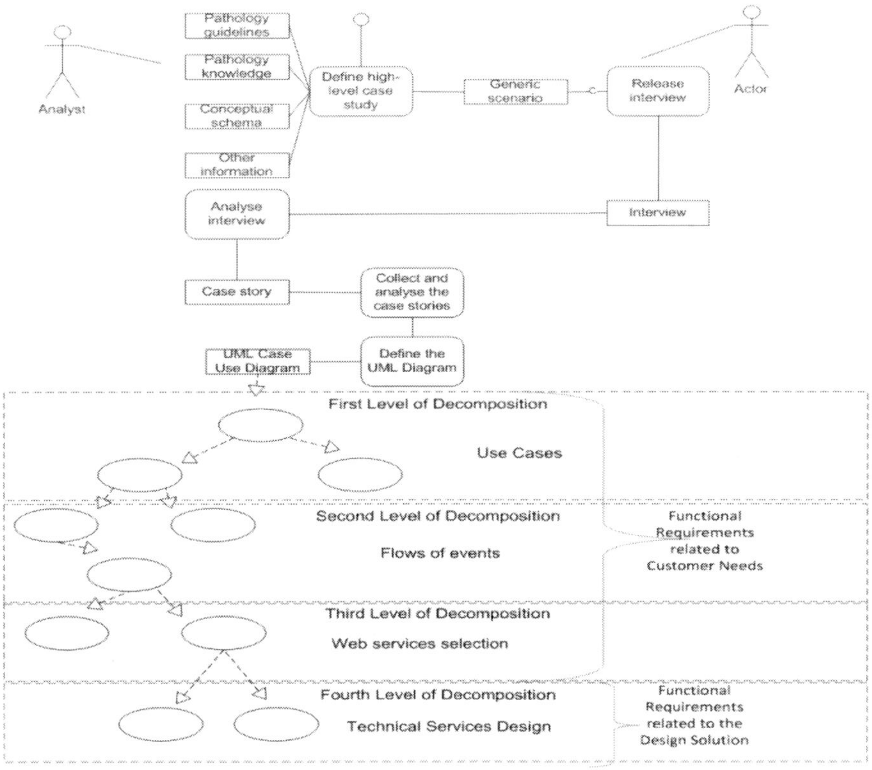

Fig.1. Axiomatic Selection Health and Social Care Web Services on the Basis of Case Stories.

Finally, we can define the process variables (PV) that, in this specific case coincide with the applications WS that implement the services to select. Therefore, in this paper web services (WS) are the design process variables (PV). They represent the tools for the implementation of the data communication system, described in a formal way using UML diagrams. The axiomatic design continues with successive decompositions, up to a level of detail that allows the implementation by the developers. In the last phase of decomposition, the decomposed FR are basic functions, while the design variables (DP) are data sets, corresponding to the objects of the upper classes [26, 27]. This decomposition can be extended to the process domain. This allows us to perform a mirror decomposition between design parameters (DP) and Process Variables (PV), i.e., a mirror decomposition between parameters of the construction of the two project matrices through a zigzagging process between three domains, as illustrated in Figure 2. The Process Domain allows us to identify the most appropriate technical solutions to meet customer needs. This zigzagging process has the advantage of focusing the designer's attention on FR [28]. The choice of solutions to be implemented takes place later, when the framework of functional requirements is clearer. The zigzagging process can initiate an iterative cycle if the identified solution has an impact on functional decomposition. Therefore, this process of cross-domain zigzagging is iterative.

2.4 Project constraints

During the axiomatic decomposition phase of the FR it is necessary to consider the constraints of the project. Constraints (Cs) are bounds on acceptable solutions. Such [23] has introduced two kinds of constraints: input constraints and system constraints. Input constraints are imposed as part of the design specifications. System constraints are imposed by the system in which the design solution must function. We can distinguish two classes of limitations in the implementation of web services in a health care setting (Figure 2). The first limitation concerns the regulatory restrictions related to the processing of health data (input constraints). In fact, these data are classified as highly sensitive. Therefore, the legislature has established a set of strict rules to protect patient privacy, where non-compliance is a criminal offense. The second limitation concerns non-functional constraints or system constraints [23]. For example, medical equipment must be as compatible as possible with the SOA, as to limit the manual intervention of communication of health parameters to the management platform. Figure 2 schematically illustrates the modalities of application of AD. The first limitation concerns the regulatory restrictions related to the processing of health data. In fact, these data are classified as highly sensitive. Therefore, the legislature has established a set of strict rules to protect patient privacy, where non-compliance is a criminal offense.

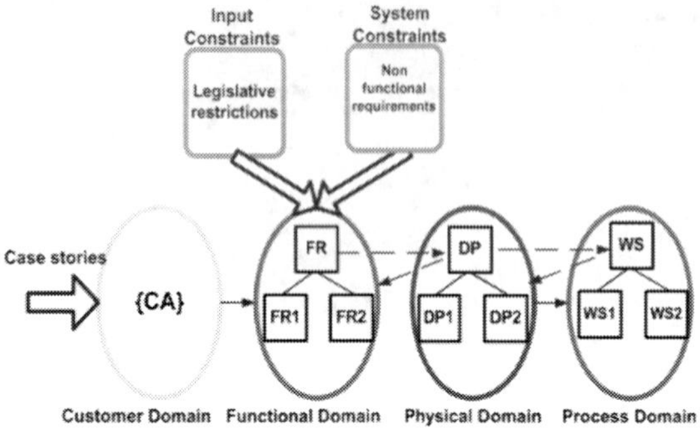

Fig. 2. Functional decomposition process.

The second limitation concerns non-functional constraints. For example, medical equipment must be as compatible as possible with the SOA, as to limit the manual intervention of communication of health parameters to the management platform. Figure 2 schematically illustrates the modalities of application of AD.

2.5 Considerations about the axiom of independence

This paper proposes the design of a robust web services selection system. It uses the FR selection approach based on the verification of the axioms of independence and information [29, 30]. The axiom of independence consists in trying to keep the identified FRs independent. In terms of matrix representation, it means that the relationships between FR and project parameters (DP) are represented by a diagonal matrix (Eq. 1). When the matrix is triangular, the design is called decoupled (Eq. 2). In particular, a quantitative parameter R (Eq. 3), called Reangularity [22, 31] was introduced, capable of measuring the level of orthogonality of the matrix. In the presence of different design solutions of decoupled type, you need to select the solutions with a higher R [22, 31]. The sparse or rectangular matrices, on the other hand, present sub-optimal engineering solutions and are defined as coupled (Eq. 4). The validity of the independence axiom ensures compliance with the criteria of completeness, consistency and plausibility of the information to be processed.

$$\begin{bmatrix} a11 & \\ & a22 \end{bmatrix} \tag{1}$$

$$\begin{bmatrix} a11 & \\ a12 & a22 \end{bmatrix} \tag{2}$$

$$R = \prod_{\substack{i=1,n-1 \\ j=1+i,n}} \left(1 - \frac{\left(\sum_{k=1}^{n} a_{ki}\ a_{kj}\right)^2}{\left(\sum_{k=1}^{n} a_{ki}^2\right)\ \left(\sum_{K=1}^{n} a_{kj}^2\right)}\right)^{\frac{1}{2}} \tag{3}$$

$$\begin{bmatrix} a11 & a21 \\ a12 & a22 \end{bmatrix} \tag{4}$$

2.6 Information axiom considerations

2.6.1 General aspects

The axiom of the information allows the selection of the most robust solution, in case of presence of more substantial decompositions the robustness of a software development project translates into the development of a software solution, consisting of logically consistent web services that must meet the requirements, with the minimum value of information content. Often in the field of software engineering, recourse to the information axiom is neglected, because it is problematic to quantify the information content of the systems. In this context, the axiomatic planning is limited to the verification of the consistency of the decompositions. The choice of the most suitable solution remains instead linked to the designer's experience and creativity. This can be technically dangerous, because it risks causing developmental delays due to subsequent iterations or the need to release procedures with anomalies that have not yet been resolved, which may have important consequences in the operation of the system. With the approach proposed in this paper, the designer will be able to evaluate among several functional decompositions, the solution that requires the least effort in terms of resources and development time [26, 27]. This is equivalent to choosing functional decomposition with the least information content. For this reason, it is proposed to measure the information content of the system by means of the Function Point (FP) counting technique, in [32, 33].

2.6.2 Function Point Analysis

WS are software objects made up of data and methods. In terms of Function Point Analysis (FPA), the data sets correspond to the data files i.e., Internal Logical Files (ILF) and External Interface Files (EIF). . Instead, the methods are the transactional functions [32, 33]. These findings can provide a measure in terms of function points for each FRi functional requirement. The ILF correspond to the data structures maintained (modified) by the system. The EIF correspond to data structures that are only read by the system. Transactional functions can result in the following operations:

- Including \ modifying \ deleting data in the chart (External Input - EI);
- Visualization of the information contained in the chart (External Inquiry - EQ);
- Data production through the information process contained in charts (External Output - EO).

The function point analysis method is performed as follows:

- Determine all functions of all function types (ILF, EIF, EI, EO, EQ);
- Rate the complexity of every function (Low, Average, High);
- Calculate the total unadjusted function point count, as seen in Table1.

The complexity is determined according to the following parameters [32, 33]:
DET (Data Element Type): the field is not repeated, it is recognizable by the user. For the transactional functions, these are the fields where EI / EO / EQ have access in read / modify mode. For data files, it is the number of fields making up the structure.
FTR (File Type Referenced): For the FTR transactional functions, it is the number of data files or their subgroups to which EI / EO / EQ have access in read / modify mode.
RET (Record Element Type): recognizable (by the user) data subgroup within an ILF / EIF. A data structure may be composed of homogeneous subsets of data.
Table 1 summarizes the values in function points in the various cases.

Table 1. Count FP matrix.

	Low	Average	Large
ILF (Internal Logical File)	7	10	15
EIF (External Interface File)	5	7	10
EI (External Input)	3	4	6
EO (External Output)	4	5	7
EQ (External inQuiry)	3	4	6

2.6.3 Productivity and robustness of the software design

In fact, the measurement of the information level in terms of FP of the selected decomposition allows us to define the productivity of the software implementation. Moreover, the use of algorithms such as Constructive Cost Model II (COCOMO II) allow to estimate the time and resources needed for the project compared to the FP measurement of the selected decomposition [34-36]. Indeed, COCOMO II allow determining an estimate of the time required to complete the project. Then, the knowledge of a particular type of project allows categorizing the estimated man/resources by their professional profile, and matching them to the various phases of the software's life cycle. Therefore, the concept of robustness in AD terms translates into selecting the minimum set of web services, which requires less human resources for equal functional requirements. Figure 3 illustrates the process of applying the axiom of independence and information for a specific level of functional decomposition. This process is iterative. It could be prolonged for a long time. This would mean increasing the costs of the project and endangering its realization. This leads to a trade-off instance, as to whether to release the application first -implying a high risk of non-conformities for the final customer- or to continue with the analysis activities. For this purpose, Benavides [37] have introduced in AD a new concept of quality, which is based on the following formula: Quality = FR satisfied / resources spent.

Fig. 3. Application of axioms of independence and information.

3 Case study

3.1 Clinical case

To illustrate the application of the proposed methodology we refer to the clinical case represented by a patient suffering from hypertension, which is studied in [7]. It follows the general scheme of Figure 1.

3.1.1 Definition of a general scenario

In the level of maximum abstraction of functional requirements, the general scenario of Figure 4 can represent the prescribed medical treatment. A scenario describes the software at a high level and give a rationale for each feature of the system existing. Instead, the use cases give a detailed account of what each feature does. A use case is a set of actions or event steps to achieve a specific goal. The use case actor can be a human or other external system [38, 39]. In Figure 5 each use case of the scenario is related to the actors involved in its execution. In this Figure, on the top-right side, we insert the web services coordination platform. For practical reasons, from now on, we will call this infrastructure simply Platform.

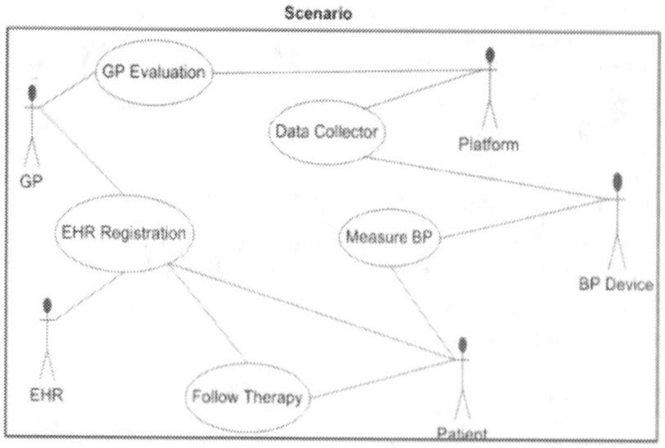

Fig. 4. Use case describing the general treatment of hypertension.

3.1.2 Health protocol analysis

The general scenario of the case study can be inferred, as suggested by F. Pecoraro et alii [9], through the analysis of the health protocol for the pathology under examination. This allows us to identify the actors involved in the treatment. With the same identified actors, the case stories are defined by using semi-structured interviews. This allows us to draw the information flows between the different parts. In designing an information system, we must start from defining the application limits, that is, the boundaries that specify the scope of the services to be implemented. If we consider the clinical case of hypertension control we can, at least in a first phase, consider only two actors: the patient and the general practitioner. We can collect the stories of both actors in the form of semi-structured interviews.

3.1.3 Collaboration diagram

By putting together the two interviews, we can schematize the execution of the process that involves them both. This allows us to define the general scenario of the system (Figure 4). The collaboration diagram of use cases (Figure 5) [38, 39] describe general scenario of the system. In summary, we can say that this two-actor process is activated by the periodic measurement of pressure by the patient in the home environment. Every 10 days a report is sent to the Platform, which is responsible for sending it to the general practitioner. In Figure 5 the red arrows represent this data flow. These arrows are interactions (also called collaborations) among the following use cases: "Measure BP", "Data Collector" and "GP Evaluation". The general practitioner (GP) analyzes the report. If he/she considers abnormal the values of pressure, he/she can change the dosage of the drug, can prescribe another drug, or can prescribe a visit with the specialist doctor. These prescriptions are recorded in the patient's health record (EHR). This event generates the sending of a message (via email and text message) to the patient. The patient signs in to his EHR account and picks up the prescription. In Figure 5 the green arrows represent this data flow. These arrows are interactions (also called collaborations) among the following use cases: "GP Evaluation", "EHR Registration" and "Follow Therapy".

Fig. 5. Collaboration diagram describing the general treatment of hypertension.

3.1.4 Extensionality of the general scenario

Figure 4 shows the clinical case of pressure control as the only interaction between patient and general practitioner. We can define this scenario as a "restricted scenario". In reality, other actors can also participate in the process. The inclusion of new actors involves the execution of new activities (new use cases) and the intensification of communications between the parties. For simplicity in this paper, we focus on the analysis of the "restricted scenario" (only two actors).

3.2 Functional decomposition

The classical techniques of modelling processes to be automated aim to capture functional requirements from reality. The process usually started by identifying the main actors and activities. Later we proceeded to define the communications between the parts and the elementary actions. Formalization can take place through structured languages, such as UML diagrams. Therefore, we pass from scenarios of representation of the general processes to schemes that are more detailed. In practice, traditional user analysis techniques perform functional decomposition. It proceeds from use cases up to the elementary functions to be implemented in terms of classes and objects [22]. The AD allows a further step forward. It allows you to translate the diagrammatic representations of the traditional approaches into matrices [23, 24]. In a context characterized by a strong intangibility, this step allows to apply quantitative measuring instruments derived from the algebra of matrices [22, 27] that otherwise would not be possible to apply. The whole process has an iterative nature. In the case of identifying critical issues, it is necessary to go back to the previous step to eliminate them, and then continue. For the clinical case introduced in the previous paragraph, we will limit, for reasons of simplicity, the process of decomposition at only two steps. In the first stage of decomposition to the collaboration diagram of the use cases of Figure 5, a specific project matrix will be constructed. The matrix representation of the collaboration diagram will be a quantitative assessment tool, which follows the completeness, consistency and plausibility criteria of the information flow. In the second phase of decomposition, the collaboration diagram is decomposed into a sequence diagram It describes the activities and the relationships between them. The dual representation in terms of the second level project matrix will allow to select the web services to be implemented. Respecting the axioms of independence and information will ensure that the collaboration diagram in Figure 5 can be represented in terms of the project matrix as in Table 1. In this case, the rows represent the various use cases; the columns constitute the collaborations between use cases (interactions) [22]. An "X" at the cell relating a given use case and a collaboration indicates that this collaboration realizes this use case. Similarly, an "X" at the cell relating a given use case and a collaboration of another use case indicates that the realization of this use case requires a method of a software object (class) used in this interaction identified design solution is robust. They are described below.

3.3 First level decomposition

This means that these use cases are dependent one another [22]. For example, the use case "FR_2 Data Collector" depends on the realization of the use case "FR_1 Measure BP". We will see that the use case "FR_2 Data Collector" can be activated by the "Send (Set_BP)" method of the "DP1 Collaboration Measure" (Figure 7). This indicates that this use case can be activated, only when the "Send (Set BP)" method records the patient's periodic data in the Platform. This means each of these methods constitutes the transactional functions of web services to be implemented.

3.3.1 Application axiom of independence

The project matrix of Table 1 is diagonal lower (decoupled). For this reason, we can say that the first level decomposition respects the axiom of independence. However, the process allows of the iterations. In fact, in the presence of decoupled matrix representations we should have revised the general scenario of use cases. This would have meant reviewing the definition and processing of customer needs.

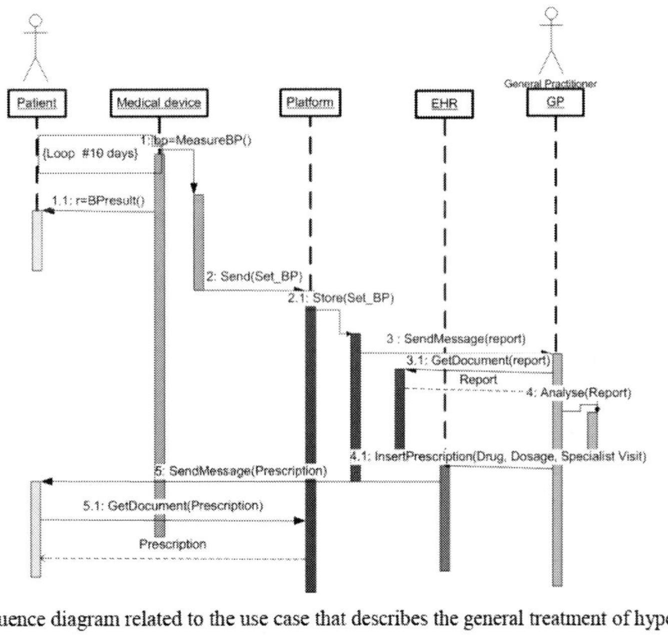

Fig. 6. Sequence diagram related to the use case that describes the general treatment of hypertension.

The iteration process continues until the design solution is satisfying. From engineering point of view, the validity of the axiom of independence guarantees us the respect of the criteria of completeness, consistency and plausibility of the information flow based on quantitative elements. In fact, the axiom of independence provide us not only with a visual tool to evaluate the quality of a decomposition (based on the structure of the project matrix), but also a tool to measure the independence of the functional requirements, based on the degree of regularity of the project matrix. In this case, using algebra of matrices, we have that an identity matrix has reangularity = 1. The decoupled matrices have a reangularity between 0 and 1. Therefore, in the presence of multiple scenarios of alternative use cases we can favor the one with a reangularity closer to 1. In this case, the matrix of Table 2 has reangularity R = 0,215166 (Eq. 3). In general, the level of functional independence can be increased by

 https://doi.org/10.1051/matecconf/201822301013

inserting a new use case. It leads to a decoupling of functional dependencies, increasing the degree of reangularity.

Table 2. Project matrix related to the case that describes the general treatment of hypertension.

	DP1 Collaboration Measure BP	DP2 Collaboration Data Collector	DP3 Collaboration GP Evaluation	DP4 Collaboration EHR Registration	DP5 Collaboration Follow Therapy
FR1 Measure BP	X				
FR2 Data Collector	X	X			
FR3 GP Evaluation	X	X	X		
FR4 EHR Registration			X	X	
FR5 Follow Therapy			X	X	X

However, the introduction of a new use case could increase the level of complexity of the system. This consideration introduces us to the next verification.

3.3.2 Axiom application of information

The axiom of information suggests us to select low complexity design solutions. The FP technique allows us to estimate the size of the software. This measurement represents the end user's point of view and is all the more accurate as the project details are evident. For high abstraction levels, we can consider derived estimation techniques such as the Early and Quick Function Point [35]. Therefore, the application of axiom results in the selection of design solutions with a lower value in terms of information with the same functional requirements [25, 26]. Moreover, always with the same defined functional requirements, the designer could find himself in the condition of having to evaluate if in the presence of alternative decompositions favor the design solution with greater functional independence (greater reangularity) or the one with less complexity. Naturally, the answer depends on the particular context.

3.3.3 The web services matrix

The mapping process between Physical Domain and Process Domain leads us to the definition of the so-called web services matrix. This matrix is mirrored to the matrix of project of Table 2, by effect to the process of zigging interdomain. It illustrates the dependencies between the interactions with the previously defined use cases and web services to be implemented. The interactions are the rows of the matrix, while the web services are the columns. The Process Domain allows the designer to assign to the functional requirements a mode of realization. The zigzagging process is an iterative process. For this reason, the choice of an implementation may require the reformulation of functional requirements. This means that functional decomposition takes place simultaneously on two domains. Therefore, if we wanted to report the web services in terms of functional requirements, it would be enough to make product between the matrix of project and the WS matrix

3.4 Second level decomposition

The use case diagram of Figure 4 and the collaboration diagram of Figure 6 can be used to implement the sequence diagram of Figure 6 [9]. This last diagram represents the sequence of activities related to the relationship between patient and general practitioner (GP) as regards pressure control [38, 39]. This diagram presents a series of more details in terms of flow and activities to be performed. In addition, the diagram of sequence has a representation in terms of the project matrix (Table 3). The previous use cases have been decomposed into activities and the activities inserted on the rows of the matrix. On the columns, instead, we insert the collaborations (interactions between activities) for specific activities. This new representation provides us with the tool to verify if the modelling performed is optimal or presents critical points in terms of completeness, consistency and plausibility of the information flow. For this reason, we can apply the axioms of independence and information.

3.4.2 Application axiom of independence

The structure of the project matrix in Table 3 respects the axiom of independence. For the sake of brevity, we will not elaborate on the measurement of the matrix reangularity. The same considerations as in the previous paragraph apply. So it is possible not only to verify that the identified activities are independent, but also, the degree of independence. The process structure is always iterative, so it is possible to improve the modelling of the activities.

3.4.3 Axiom application of information

The activities that have been identified in this phase can be calculated in terms of the function point. At this level, we have the information to proceed with the calculation. The size of the system provides us with a tool to evaluate its complexity. Furthermore, this measure allows us to plan the effort needed to implement the system.

3.4.4 The web services matrix

The mapping process between Physical Domain and Process Domain leads us to the definition of the matrix of second level web services (Table 4). This matrix is mirrored with respect to that of Table 3. It is obtained through a zigzagging interdomain process and schematizes the dependencies between the interactions and the web services to be implemented. The interactions are the rows of the matrix, while the web services are the columns. This allows us to report the activities decomposed here in terms of web services. This new mapping can be obtained as a product between the project matrix and the web service level matrix.

Table 3. Project matrix related to the sequence diagram that describes the general treatment of hypertension.

		DP1 Collaboration Measure BP			DP2 Collaboration Data Collector		DP3 Collaboration GP Evaluation			DP4 Collaboration EHR Registration		DP5 Collaboration Follow Therapy
		DP1.1 Collaboration Read BP	DP1.2 Collaboration Periodic Data Pressure Report	DP1.3 Collaboration Send BP Report to Plataform	DP2.1 Collaboration Register BP Report	DP2.2 Collaboration Send message to GP	DP3.1 Collaboration Get Report	DP3.2 Collaboration Analyse Report	DP3.3 Collaboration Prescription	DP4.1 Collaboration Register Prescription	DP4.2 Collaboration Send Message(Prescription)	DP5.1 Collaboration Get Prescription
FR1 Measure BP	FR1.1 Read BP	X										
	FR1.2 Periodic Data Pressure Report		X									
	FR1.3 Send BP Report to Plataform		X	X								
FR2 Data Collector	FR2.1 Register BP Report		X	X	X							
	FR2.2 Send message to GP		X		X	X						
FR3 GP Evaluation	FR3.1 Get Report		X		X	X	X					
	FR3.2 Analyse Report		X		X	X	X	X				
	FR3.3 Prescription					X	X	X	X			
FR4 EHR Registration	FR4.1 Register Prescription								X	X		
	FR4.2 SendMessage(Prescription)								X	X	X	
FR5 Follow Therapy	FR5.1 Get Prescription								X	X	X	X

Table 4. WS matrix related to the sequence diagram that describes the general treatment of hypertension.

		WS1			WS2		WS3			WS4		WS5
		WS11	WS12	WS13	WS21	WS22	WS31	WS32	WS33	WS41	WS42	WS51
DP1	DP1.1 Collaboration Read BP	X										
	DP1.2 Collaboration Periodic Data Pressure Report		X									
	DP1.3 Collaboration Send BP Report to Plataform		X	X								
DP2	DP2.1 CollaborationRegister BP Report		X	X	X							
	DP2.2 Collaboration Send message to GP		X		X	X						
DP3	DP3.1 Collaboration Get Report		X		X	X	X					
	DP3.2 Collaboration Analyse Report		X		X	X	X	X				
	DP3.3 Collaboration Prescription					X	X	X	X			
DP4	DP4.1 Collaboration Register Prescription								X	X		
	DP4.2 Collaboration Send Message(Prescription)								X	X	X	
DP5	DP5.1 Collaboration Get Prescription								X	X	X	X

3.5 Selection of web services

The web services defined in Table 4 represent the minimum set of services necessary to implement the system of management of communications between patient and general practitioner for the control of hypertension. The axiomatic decomposition process allows to directly associating each of them with specific functional requirements. Depending on the level of decomposition, the decomposed functional requirements are the use cases or specific activities or parts of them. This means that functional decomposition ensures that the case stories prepared in the analysis of user requirements are effectively translated into web services. Furthermore, the selection obtained must be considered optimized because the axioms of independence and information make it possible to provide quantitative measurements of the degree of independence of web services and their informative complexity. Table 5 shows the identified web services. They are broken down by system of competence according to information, communication direction (Interaction), and type of operation. The operations that the web service can perform are writing on archives (I), or reading (O).This information allows us to measure the effort in functional points of the system, but also to plan the other activities of the software life cycle, from the implementation to the testing and testing activities [36, 27]. It should also be noted that the development of a system of this type involves the allocation of implementation activities among the management teams of different systems. This means that the project documentation must be understandable and up-to-date at every stage of the software life cycle, to avoid delays or malfunctions in the services. In this sense, AD allows the preparation of very detailed and easily understandable documentation, even at the logical design level of the system.

4 Conclusions

The SOA allows the implementation of web services on interoperable platforms and systems, and create a virtual network of services to support patients in home therapy and health monitoring. For each specific clinical case, it is possible to define a series of services to be implemented, able to monitor the patient, manage the therapy, monitor his health according to the work activities and coordinate the activities of all the operators involved in the treatment and management of his healthHowever, the design of such networks poses important questions. For example, how can we capture user requirements for each specific case in a health context that may be evolving?

To answer questions of this kind it is necessary to focus on the quality of the services offered. In this paper, we proposed an approach based on the AD for the composition and selection of web services, which are based on the case stories studied, built using semi-structured interviews to different stakeholders involved in the care process.

Table 5. Table of web services selected for the general treatment of hypertension in the home system.

Functional requirements	System	Interaction	Data	Type	WS to implement
FR1.1 Read BP	Medical Devise	Medical Devise →Patient	Daily Data Pressure	O	WS11
FR1.2 Data Pressure Report	Medical Devise	Medical Devise Loop	Data Pressure Report, Fiscal Code, Health Card	O	WS12
FR1.3 Send BP Report to Platform	Medical Devise	Medical Devise →Platform	Data Pressure Report, Fiscal Code, Health Card	O	WS13
FR2.1 Register BP Report	Platform	Medical Devise →Platform	Data Pressure Report, Fiscal Code, Health Card	I	WS21
FR2.2 Send message to GP	Platform	Platform →GP	Fiscal Code, Health Card ID, Other Personal Data , Request for Get Periodic Report	O	WS22
FR3.1 Get Report	Platform	GP →Platform	Data Pressure Report, Fiscal Code, Health Card ID, Other Personal Data	I	WS31
FR3.2 Analyse Report	GP	GP loop	Data Pressure Report, Pressure Report Trend	O	WS32
FR3.3 Prescription	GP	GP loop	Medical Data	O	WS33
FR4.1 Register Prescription	EHR	GP →EHR	Request for specialist visits, Drug Prescription, Dosage, Fiscal Code,	I	WS41
FR4.2 SendMessage(Prescription)	EHR	EHR →Patient	Fiscal Code, Health Card ID, Other Personal Data , Request for Get	O	WS42
FR5.1 Get Prescription	EHR	Patient →EHR	Request for specialist visits, Drug Prescription, Dosage, Fiscal Code, Health Card ID	I	WS51

The purpose of the approach is to detect in a systematic way all functional requirements by taking into account the different stakeholders involved in the care process and their interactions. In this paper, we focused on the case of hypertension treatment, to which we applied our AD approach. The AD allows guiding the design based on quantitative measuring instruments, and define a dynamic and robust design mechanism, based on the dual representation of the system, in terms of UML diagrams and project matrices with multiple benefits. First, AD allows direct tracking between patient needs (CA), functional system requirements (FR), design parameters (DP) and implementation solutions (WS). This means that, by changing the needs of the patient, it is possible in a short time to start a readjustment of the system. Furthermore, the application of the axioms of independence and information is linked to the algebraic structure of the project matrix. Therefore, it is possible to derive parameters based on quantitative criteria to be attributed to the design solutions identified through the use stories technique, which the use of an iterative and incremental design improvement process. It facilitates the production of updated documentation at each stage of the software life cycle. This means facilitating the exchange of information, both between the members of the same team and between different teams of developers, with a view to interoperability between multiple technological and organizational systems.
As a future work, we plan to measure the effort needed to implement the composition and selection of web services, which are modelled according to the AD approach.

Acknowledgment

This study is part of the H@H (Health @ Home) – Smart Communities for the wellbeing of the citizens – project granted within the National Operational Programme for Research and Competitiveness 2007-2013. Identification code: SCN_00558.

References

1. G. Arcidiacono, J. Wang, K. Yang, (2015) *Operating room adjusted utilization study*, International Journal of Lean Six Sigma, Vol. 6, Issue 2; pp.111 – 137.
2. G. Arcidiacono, A. Pieroni, (2018) *The Revolution Lean Six Sigma 4.0*, International Journal on Advanced Science, Engineering and Information Technology, Vol. 8, Issue 1, pp. 141-149.
3. F. O'Hagan (2017). *Work, organizational practices, and margin of manoeuver during work reintegration. Disability and rehabilitation*, pp. 1-10.
4. I. Giorgi, G. Calsamiglia,, M. Negri, F. Scafa, R. Colombi, S. M. Candura, & O. Bettinardi. (2007). *Management of occupational stress among patients with cardiac diseases*. Giornale italiano di medicina del lavoro ed ergonomia, 29(3 Suppl), pp. 695-696.
5. G. Du , X. Liang, C. Sun, (2017) *Scheduling Optimization of Home Health Care Service Considering Patients' Priorities and Time Windows*, Sustainability 9, 253.

6. S. Landers, et al., (2016) *The Future of Home Health Care-A Strategic Framework for Optimizing Value*, Home Health Care Management & Practice, 28(4) 262 –278.

7. F. Wang (2012) *Measurement, Optimization, and Impact of Health Care Accessibility: A Methodological Review*, Annals of the Association of American Geographers, 102(5): 1104–1112.

8. K. Avila, P. Sanmartin, D. Jabba, M. Jimeno, (2017) *Applications Based on Service-Oriented Architecture (SOA) in the Field of Home Healthcare*, Sensors, 17(8): 1703.

9. F. Pecoraro, D. Luzi, E. Pourabbas, F.L. Ricci, 2017 *A methodology to identify health and social care web services on the basis of case stories*. Proceedings of E-Health and Bioengineering Conference (EHB).

10. S. Crowe, K. Cresswell, A.Robertson, G. Huby, A. Avery, A. Shikh, (2011) *The case study approach*, Medical Research Methodology, 1.

11. A.M. Farid, (2016) *An engineering systems introduction to axiomatic design*. In Farid AM, Suh NP (eds) Axiomatic design in large systems: complex products, buildings and manufacturing systems, Chap. 1, Springer, Berlin, Heidelberg, 1–47.

12. C. Monti, A. Giorgetti, A. Girgenti (2015) *An Axiomatic Design Approach for a Motorcycle Steering Damper*, Procedia CIRP, vol. 34, pp. 150–155.

13. F. Rolli, A. Giorgetti, P. Citti, (2015) *Integration of Holistic Non-Conformities Management and Axiomatic Design: a case study in Italian Income Tax Returns Management*, Proc. CIRP 34, 256-262 (2015);

14. A. Giorgetti, A. Girgenti, P. Citti, M. Delogu (2016) *A Novel Approach for Axiomatic-Based Design for the Environment*. In Axiomatic Design in Large Systems: Complex Products, Buildings and Manufacturing Systems, ed. Springer. doi:10.1007/978-3-319-32388-6_5.

15. G. Arcidiacono, K. Yang, J. Trewn, L. Bucciarelli, (2016) *Application of Axiomatic Design for Project-Based Learning Methodology*, Procedia CIRP, Vol. 53, pp. 166-172.

16. G. Arcidiacono, C. Brown, L. Bucciarelli, F. Melosi, (2016) *Axiomatic Design of Production Systems for Performance Improvement: A Project Identification and Prioritization Model*. In Axiomatic Design in Large Systems: Complex Products, Buildings and Manufacturing Systems, ed. Springer.

17. G. Arcidiacono, D.T. Matt, E. Rauch, (2017) *Axiomatic Design of a Framework for the Comprehensive Optimization of Patient Flows in Hospitals*, Journal of Healthcare Engineering, Volume 2017, 19 June 2017, Article number 2309265.

18. Z. Zainal, (2007) *Case study as a research method*, Jurnal Kemanusiaan bil.9.

19. B. Flyvbjerg, *Case Study* (2011). Norman K. Denzin and Yvonna S. Lincoln, eds., *The Sage Handbook of Qualitative Research*, 4th edition, (Thousand Oaks, CA: Sage, 2011), chapter17, pp. 301-316.

20. I. Jacobson, M. Christerson, JP. Onsson, G. Övergaard. (1992), *Object-Oriented Software Engineering* - A Use Case Driven Approach, Addison-Wesley.

21. D.Tarenskeen, R.Bakker, S.Joosten, (2015) *Applying the V Model and Axiomatic Design in the Domain of IT Architecture Practice*; Procedia CIRP 34, 263-268.

22. P. Pimentel, C. Stadzisz, (2006) *A Use Case based Object-Oriented Software Design Approach using The Axiomatic Design Theory*. Proceedings of ICAD2006 Fourth International Conference on Axiomatic Design, 4:1-8.

23. N.P. Suh, Axiomatic Design - *Advances and Applications*, (Oxford University Press, 2001);

24. S.H. Do, N.P. Suh, (2000) *Object-oriented software design with axiomatic design*, Proc. CIRP 49, 278-84.

25. F. Rolli, A. Giorgetti, P. Citti, M. Rinaldi, (2016) *Information content evaluation to obtain robustness of the management in Italian fiscal process (Part 2): optimization of Italian income certification process of the year 2016*, Proc. CIRP 53, 63-69.

26. F. Rolli, A. Giorgetti, P. Citti, M. Rinaldi, (2016) *Improvement of the compilation process of the Italian income certifications: a methodology based on the evaluation of the information content (Part 1)*, Proc. CIRP 53, 56-62.

27. F. Rolli, C. Parretti, P. Citti, M. Rinaldi, (2017) *Functional case test design to optimize the software development in Italian tax processes (Part II): the F23 tax payment form*, MATEC Web Conf. Volume 127, 2017.

28. D.S. Cochran, W. Eversheim, G. Kubin, & M.L. Sesterhenn, (2000). *The application of axiomatic design and lean management principles in the scope of production system segmentation*, International Journal of Production Research, 38(6),pp. 1377-1396.

29. B. Pacifici, C. Parretti, A. Girgenti, and P. Citti, (2017) *Axiomatic Design for an Efficient Development of Optimized RPM Systems*, MATEC Web Conf. Volume 127, 2017.

30. L.E.S. Oliveira, A.J.Alvares , (2016) *Axiomatic Design Applied to the Development of a System for Monitoring and Teleoperation of a CNC Machine through the Internet*, Procedia CIRP 53, pp.198-205;

31. N.P. Suh, (1990) *The Principles of Design*, Oxford Series on Advanced Manufacturing.

32. A. J. Albrecht, (1979) *Measuring Application Development Productivity*, Proceedings SHARE/GUIDE IBM Applications Development Symposium, October 1979;

33. IFPUG - *Function Point Counting Practices Manual*, Release 4.1 - Westerville - Ohio, 1999;

34. T. Rollo, (2006) *Functional Size measurement and COCOMO–A synergistic Approach*. In: Proc. of Software Measurement European Forum. pp. 259-267.
35. R. Meli, L. Santillo, (1997) *Function point estimation methods: a comparative overview*, Data Processing Organization srl, IFPUG - Fall Conference - September 15-19,- Scottsdale, Arizona USA.
36. F. Rolli, C. Parretti, P. Citti, M. Rinaldi, (2017) *Functional case test design to optimize the software development in Italian tax processes (Part I): Methodology definition*, The 11th International Conference on Axiomatic Design (ICAD 2017).
37. E. Benavides, (2011) *Advanced Engineering Design*, Woodhead Publishing in Mechanical Engineering.
38. G. Booch, J. Rumbaugh, I. Jacobson, (1999) *UML User Guide*, Addison-Wesley.
39. M. Fowler, (2010) *UML Distilled*, Addison-Wesley.

Managing Functional Coupling Sequence to Decrease Complexity and Increase Modularity in Conceptual Design

Chu-Yi Wang[1,*], and *Stephen C.-Y.* Lu[1]

[1]Viterbi School of Engineering, University of Southern California, Los Angeles, CA 90089-1453, USA

Abstract. Conceptual design is the stage where the upstream objectives and downstream constraints meet, so both the ideality and practicality are important in conceptual design. Modularity supports designing complex system while the design can take advantages from the downstream resources. According to Axiomatic Design Theory (ADT), the design with the least complexity is the ideal design, and managing functional coupling sequence can lead to the minimal complexity of design concepts. In this paper, Design Coupling Sequence (DCS) was introduced to bridge the ADT and the modular design. The 'precedence' and 'functional sets' were defined in DCS to manage the coupled design concepts in order to support the modularity of the design concepts. The 'precedence' identified by the level of functional coupling helps realize the sequencing order. The two 'functional sets' were defined as the independent U-set: the collection of functionally dependent concepts, and the coupled C-set: the collection of the strongly coupled concepts. The faucet design case study shows how the DCS method and its strategy to decrease relative complexity and increase modularity, and the results between design by extra coupling elimination and design by the existing modules are compared. The DCS method bridges the design theory to design practice.

1 Introduction

Conceptual design is an early design stage that is commonly regarded as the transformation stage from Functional Requirement (FR) to Design Parameter (DP) [1-5]. Since the conceptual design is where upstream objectives (i.e., Customer Needs, CNs) and downstream constraints (i.e., Process Variables, PVs) are "balanced" through creative mappings (i.e., ideations) from FRs to DPs, it is important for innovators to ideate design concepts that are as ideal and practical as possible. The "ideality" of a product refers to its ability to use the most superlative manner to satisfy upstream market demands during product development, and in this paper it follows the definition in Axiomatic Design Theory (ADT) [6], that the ideal design is the simplest design (i.e. the design with minimal complexity). The "practicality" of a product refers to its ability to take advantage of existing resources at downstream of product development. To approach ideal design, functional independence is essential to minimize the relative complexity; to approach practical design, physical integration is favoured to take advantages of the downstream resources or database, which often are modules and existing components (i.e. to increase modularity).

Some case studies [7-9] have shown the usefulness of using ADT to reduce the complexity in conceptual design. However, Chen et al. [10] discussed the difficulties of directly using ADT to modularize the design concepts. The gap between design theories and design practicality needs to be bridged. Wang et al. proposed Design Coupling Sequence (DCS) method to decrease the complexity [11]. In this paper, the DCS method is further modified and explained for not only complexity reduction but also modularity enhancement.

1.1 Complexity Reduction by Axiomatic Design

1.1.1 Real Complexity and Imaginary Complexity

Logically, the concept generation process from FR to DP follows synthetic proposition [12] so that the relationship between FRs and DPs is built. In the ideal case, each of the FRs "is satisfied by" only one DP. However, in the most design cases, one FR is satisfied by two or more DPs because it is difficult to follow the Independence Axiom all the way, so that the functional coupling exists in the design. According to ADT, the functional coupling relationship between FR and DP can be depicted by design matrix (DM) where X denotes the non-negligible relationship and O denotes the negligible relationship. Since there is no specific value for each parameter in such early stage, X presents a placeholder for the non-negligible relationship. For example, the DM in Fig. 1 shows that FR_1 is satisfied by DP_1, DP_2, and DP_4; in other words, there is a functional coupling of FR_1 between DP_1, DP_2, and DP_4 in the case. In Suh's Complexity Theory [6], relative complexity includes real and imaginary complexities. The real complexity is caused by the functional couplings between DPs, which are captured as the 'X's at the off-diagonal locations in

* Corresponding author: chuyiwan@usc.edu

the DM. When it is the ideal case, the DM is a diagonal matrix, which has no complexity (i.e. uncoupled design). Oppositely, if every FR is satisfied by all the DPs, then the design is a full design matrix, which has 100% complexity (i.e. fully coupled design). In the halfway, the design with a solid triangular matrix is a decoupled design. These three typical design types were introduced in Suh's Axiomatic Design Theory [13]. The rest design types are a triangular but not solid DM and a non-diagonal non-triangular DM, which are named partially decoupled design and partially coupled design respectively in this paper (Fig. 2).

$$\begin{bmatrix} FR_1 \\ FR_2 \\ FR_3 \\ FR_4 \end{bmatrix} = \begin{bmatrix} X & X & O & X \\ O & X & O & O \\ X & X & X & X \\ O & X & O & X \end{bmatrix} \begin{bmatrix} DP_1 \\ DP_2 \\ DP_3 \\ DP_4 \end{bmatrix}$$

Fig. 1. An example of the design matrix.

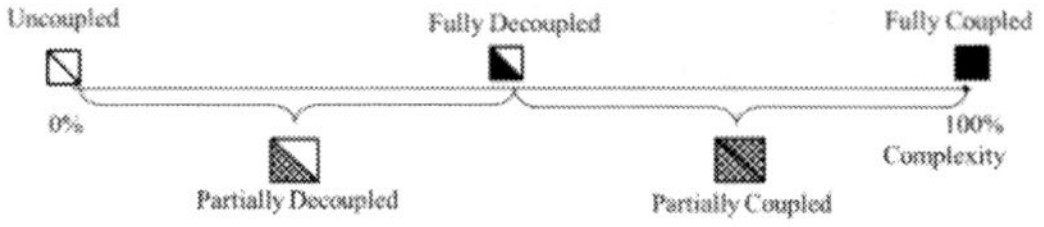

Fig. 2. The relationship between the complexity and design matrix

Imaginary complexity arises when the designer lacks understanding of the system. For the example in Fig. 1, the complexity of the design would be higher than fully decoupled design's because the DM is partially coupled, but if one understands the system, the DM could be rearranged into a fully decoupled design as shown in Fig. 3, then the complexity could be reduced. That extra complexity is imaginary complexity.

$$\begin{bmatrix} FR_2 \\ FR_4 \\ FR_1 \\ FR_3 \end{bmatrix} = \begin{bmatrix} X & O & O & O \\ X & X & O & O \\ X & X & X & O \\ X & X & X & X \end{bmatrix} \begin{bmatrix} DP_2 \\ DP_4 \\ DP_1 \\ DP_3 \end{bmatrix}$$

Fig. 3. The rearranged DM from Fig. 1.

The order of DP in Fig. 3 leads the design to the minimal real complexity, and the order is called "execution sequence" because the designer can have the minimal real complexity when he/she uses the sequence of DP to execute the concept decision-making during concept improvement. Therefore, in ADT, the imaginary complexity can be quantified by the equation 1, where z is number of the execution sequences, and m! is the total number of sequences for the design with a m-by-m design matrix. According to the equation 1, the imaginary complexity can be reduced if one can know more execution sequence.

$$C_I = -log_2\left(\frac{z}{m!}\right) \quad (1)$$

1.1.2 Complexity Reduction with Design Coupling Sequence

Based on above, both real complexity and imaginary complexity can be reduced by extra coupling elimination, design matrix rearrangement, and/or execution sequence. As shown in Fig. 4, except uncoupled design and fully coupled design cases in which the execution sequence is trivial, execution sequence is the essential step during the concept improvement. Design Coupling Sequence (DCS) was proposed by Wang et al. [11] to obtain the execution sequence for partially coupled and partially decoupled designs. DCS uses set, branch, and arrow to reconstruct the functional coupling relationship into sequence, and proposed a concept of "precedence" to help the determination of the order of DP.

The steps of DCS in the paper include count Xs, list DPs, manage underlined DPs, and arrange into sequences. To count Xs aims to obtain the precedence. However, the precedence is not as simple as the non-zero term of the DP, the number of the non-zero term of the FR affects the precedence. Therefore, a revised algorithm is proposed in this paper to help obtain the execution sequence for complexity reduction.

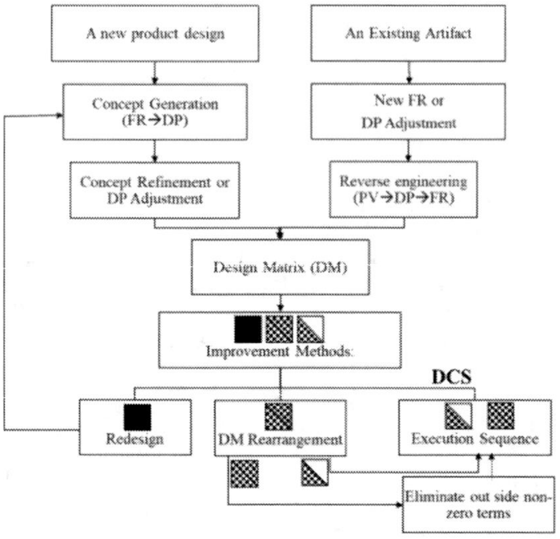

Fig. 4. The concept improvement roadmap.

1.2 Design Modularity

1.2.1 Modularity and Functional Coupling

Modularity is a bottom-up process that arises from the decomposition of a product into subassemblies and components [14]. In other words, it is some isolated collections/sets of the components in the system. During the modularity process, some metrics or methods are used to cluster the components. In conceptual design, the components are the DPs, and the metrics or the methods could be developed from the information of DM or Design Structure Matrix (DSM), where there depicts the relationship among the DPs.

Most modular designs more focus on the interaction of the DPs [15-18], so the DSM is usually used. However, clustering the DPs with DSM may result in additional coupling or unwanted imaginary complexity. For example, FR_1 is satisfied by DP_1 only, and FR_2 is satisfied by DP_2 and DP_3, so DP_1 and DP_2 are functionally independent, and DP_2 and DP_3 are functionally coupled. If DP_1 and DP_2 are grouped as a module because of the physical integration, when improve DP_3 to better satisfy FR_2, the module of DP_1 and DP_2 needs to be improved correspondingly, then the DP_1 is coupled with DP_3 because of the grouping. Since conceptual design stage should consider both upstream side and downstream side, DM would be better than DSM for modularity during conceptual design as it carries the coupling information between FRs and DPs.

1.2.2 Using DCS to Support Modular Design

It is difficult to direct use DM to identify the modules because the design is usually either in the partially coupled type (such as the example in Fig.1) or with the different amount of FR and DP (i.e. rectangular DM) in most design cases. DCS is a functional coupling sequence management method which can apply to rectangular design matrix and prescribe execution sequence for partially coupled design. In this paper, two types of functional sets to cluster DPs with the DCS results to increase the modularity is proposed. The research goal is to develop a theoretically sound practical approach that can reduce relative complexity on one hand and to increase modularity on the other hand during the conceptual design stage.

2 The Redefined Precedence and The Functional Sets

For obtaining execution sequence, the precedence in DCS includes higher, lower, and equal precedence. Previously, it was defined by the number of non-zero terms of the DP in DM. Since the number of the non-zero term of the FR impacts the functional coupling as well, the precedence is redefined as the elaboration in Section 2.1.

For increasing modularity, the two functional sets are defined to use DCS results to support modular design. They are the independent U-set: the collection of functionally dependent concepts, and the coupled C-set: the collection of the strongly coupled concepts. Because U-sets are mutually independent and C-sets find the DPs that need to be improved together, the designer can select concepts or get ideas from the existing modules according to the sets. The details are presented in Section 2.2.

2.1 Precedence

The precedence indicates the priority of the DP in order for less complexity. In other words, it determines which DP should execute first during concept improvement. The rules were developed based on Linear Algebra and Suh's design matrix rearrangement method [19]. It has two rules:

• The DPs that relate to the FR which has the less sum of the correlation numbers in its row are in the higher level of precedence, and

• The more functionally coupled DPs (i.e. the larger sum of the numbers in its column) has the higher precedence.

Using Fig. 5 as an example, the related FRs to DP_1 and DP_3 have one non-zero term (for FR_1) and two non-zero terms (for FR_3) respectively, so DP_1 has higher precedence than DP_3. The DP2 has higher precedence than the DP3 because the DP2 has more non-zero terms than the DP3 does.

$$\begin{bmatrix} FR_1 \\ FR_2 \\ FR_3 \\ FR_4 \\ FR_5 \\ FR_6 \\ FR_7 \\ FR_8 \\ FR_9 \end{bmatrix} = \begin{bmatrix} X & 0 & 0 & 0 & 0 & 0 & 0 & 0 & 0 \\ 0 & X & 0 & 0 & 0 & 0 & 0 & 0 & 0 \\ 0 & X & X & 0 & 0 & 0 & 0 & 0 & 0 \\ 0 & 0 & 0 & X & 0 & 0 & 0 & 0 & 0 \\ 0 & 0 & 0 & X & X & 0 & 0 & 0 & 0 \\ 0 & 0 & 0 & X & 0 & X & 0 & 0 & 0 \\ 0 & 0 & 0 & 0 & 0 & 0 & X & X & 0 \\ 0 & 0 & 0 & 0 & 0 & 0 & X & X & 0 \\ 0 & 0 & 0 & 0 & 0 & 0 & 0 & 0 & X \end{bmatrix} \begin{bmatrix} DP_1 \\ DP_2 \\ DP_3 \\ DP_4 \\ DP_5 \\ DP_6 \\ DP_7 \\ DP_8 \\ DP_9 \end{bmatrix}$$

Fig. 5. A sample design matrix to explain precedence.

When the above metrics are equal, these DPs have equal precedence. There are two types of equal precedence:

1) If these DPs are functionally independent, the order of these DPs doesn't matter (i.e. any of them can execute first).
2) If there are functional couplings between these DPs, they would be the unsolvable DPs (strongly coupled) and should be consider together.

For example, the DP_1 and DP_9 in Fig. 5 are with the type 1 of equal precedence. Also, the DP_5 and DP_6 in Fig. 5 are with the type 1. The DP_7 and DP_8 in Fig. 5 are with the type 2 of equal precedence.

2.2 Functional Sets

In this paper, two types of functional sets are defined based on the functional coupling and the equal precedence.

1) The completely independent set **U**: U-set is the collection of all functionally dependent DPs in the system, so that the set is independent to any other U-sets in the system. U stands for "uncoupled".
2) The insolvably coupled set **C**: C-set is the collection of these coupled concepts that can't be decoupled by sequencing, so these groups of DPs must be considered together as a module. C stands for coupled, and it is the type 2 of equal precedence.

In Fig. 6, there are five U-sets in this DM, and they are U_1: DP_1, U_2: DP_2 and DP_3, U_3: DP_4, DP_5, and DP_6, U_4: DP_7 and DP_8, and U_5: DP_9. There is only one C-set in the DM, which is the set of DP_7 and DP_8. The set of DP_7 and

DP_8 is fully coupled as a C-set, but it is independent from other DPs in the system, so it is also a U-set.

$$\begin{bmatrix} FR_1 \\ FR_2 \\ FR_3 \\ FR_4 \\ FR_5 \\ FR_6 \\ FR_7 \\ FR_8 \\ FR_9 \end{bmatrix} = \begin{bmatrix} X & 0 & 0 & 0 & 0 & 0 & 0 & 0 & 0 \\ 0 & X & 0 & 0 & 0 & 0 & 0 & 0 & 0 \\ 0 & X & X & 0 & 0 & 0 & 0 & 0 & 0 \\ 0 & 0 & 0 & X & 0 & 0 & 0 & 0 & 0 \\ 0 & 0 & 0 & X & X & 0 & 0 & 0 & 0 \\ 0 & 0 & 0 & X & 0 & X & 0 & 0 & 0 \\ 0 & 0 & 0 & 0 & 0 & 0 & X & X & 0 \\ 0 & 0 & 0 & 0 & 0 & 0 & X & X & 0 \\ 0 & 0 & 0 & 0 & 0 & 0 & 0 & 0 & X \end{bmatrix} \begin{bmatrix} DP_1 \\ DP_2 \\ DP_3 \\ DP_4 \\ DP_5 \\ DP_6 \\ DP_7 \\ DP_8 \\ DP_9 \end{bmatrix}$$

Fig. 6. A sample design matrix to explain functional sets.

3 The Modified Design Coupling Sequence Method

The modified DCS method uses the same representations and the same way to transform from DCS results to execution sequences. The differences from the original DCS are the algorithm to order the DPs and the view point and the use of the sets in DCS.

Following sections will give a short introduction of the representations and the execution sequence, the modified DCS algorithm, and the strategies of using DCS.

3.1. DCS Introduction

3.1.1 The Representation of DCS

Based on the section 2, a typical outcome of the DCS method is some U-sets of DPs containing some C-sets and/or arrows (Fig. 7). U-set in DCS refers to a functionally independent set that is completely uncoupled with other sets, and the arrow (→) in the U-set shows the direction of the sequence. C-set is represented by braces { , }, and it indicates the unsolvable couplings. Branch in the U-set is uncoupled with other branches, and it is a kind of the type 1 of the equal precedence.

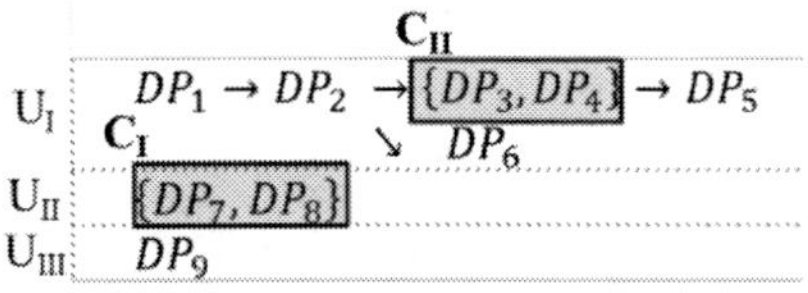

Fig. 7. An example of DCS outcome for representation explanation.

U-sets and C-sets function differently. An U-set is like a unit that can be an independent module, or can physically integrate with other U-sets. A C-set denotes the strongly coupled DPs, whose couplings can not be decoupled by sequence. The functional coupling between the DPs in a C-set is suggested to be eliminated, or the designer would consider all the DPs in the set as a module while determining the design concepts.

The DCS algorithm orders the DPs by their "precedence," and the arrow in the U-set indicates higher to lower precedence on one hand, and the sets and branches indicate equal precedence on the other hand.

3.1.2 The Execution Sequence

The execution sequences can be formed from DCS algorithm outcome by permutation and combination. Arrow indicates the order; besides, branch can be any order with other branches, and the order of the DPs in the branch follows above rules. The order in a C-set is meaningless because all the DPs in the set should be determined together. The number of all acceptable DCS sequences (that can minimize the complexity) is calculated by multiplying the factorial of the number of the U-sets and that of the branches for each node. The formula can be written as

$$u! \times \prod_{i=1}^{n} b_i! \qquad (2)$$

where u is the number of the U-sets, b is the branch number of the node, and n is the number of the node.

For the example in Fig. 7, there should be 12 acceptable sequences in that design (3!×2! = 12).

3.2 DCS Algorithm

3.2.1 The Algorithm Logic

The logic of the algorithm firstly is following the precedence to order each DPs. When assess the level of the precedence, the level of the functional coupling with FRs is examined first then the level of the functional coupling of DPs. Meanwhile, the equal precedence DPs are labelled as groups to further examine. Next, each member in the group will be examined the functional coupling with its group members. Those equal precedence with functional coupling DPs indicates the unsolvable coupling, which is represented by the braces of C-set. Finally, the functional coupling relationship of each DP ordered by precedence is examined to build the connection forming the U-set.

3.2.2 The Notions in the Algorithm

Some notations are needed to better explain the algorithm. The calculation in the algorithm uses zero for O and one for X with the binary design matrix. The element at row "m" and column "n" in the DM is denoted by DM_{mn}. The sets

$$S\_DP_n: \{m \mid DM_{mn} \neq 0\} \qquad (3)$$

$$S\_FR_m: \{n \mid DM_{mn} \neq 0\} \qquad (4)$$

express the position of those non-zero elements which indicate functional couplings between FRs and DPs. In addition, the parameters

$$Sum\_DPn = \Sigma|DMmn| \quad (5)$$

$$Sum\_FRm = \Sigma|DMmn| \quad (6)$$

represent the degree of coupling of a specific DP and FR.

3.2.3 The Steps of the Algorithm

There are three steps in the modified DCS algorithm: put DPs in a line by precedence, manage equal precedence DPs, arrange DPs into U-sets.

Step 1: put DPs in a line by precedence

Find the S_FR_i that its Sum_FR_i is the smallest, and obtain the n in S_FR_i. Add the DP_n in a line, and then remove the column of the DP from the DM. Repeat this step until all the DPs are in a line.

If there are more than one different n, add these DP_n in the line by Sum_DP_n from the most to the least, and mark the DPs with same values of Sum_DP as a group by underlining.

Step 2: Manage equal precedence DPs

Manage the grouped DP_j starting from the second DP in the first underlined group. Check whether exists an $x \in S\_DP_j$ of DP_j such that x equals any $y \in S\_DP_k$ of its preceding DP (DP_k).

- If yes, put DP_j in the set (i.e. { , }) with DP_k.
- If no, move DP_j to a new line under DP_k, and then repeat the following checking process with its current preceding DP (i.e. the preceding DP of DP_k) until it is put into a set or reach the first DP of the group.
- The checking process can be expressed by

$$\begin{cases} \{DP_j, DP_k\}, & \exists x \in S\_DP_j : x = y \\ \begin{matrix} DP_k \\ DP_j \end{matrix}, & \forall x \in S\_DP_j : x \neq y \end{cases} \quad (7)$$

where $y \in S\_DP_k$ and DP_k is the preceding DP of DP_j.

Step 3: Arrange DPs into U-sets

Arrange all the DPs (DP_p) into sequences starting from the second DP in the first line. Check whether exists a $u \in S\_DP_p$ of DP_p such that u equals to $v \in S\_DP_q$ of its preceding DP (DP_q) or one of the DPs in the preceding set (DP_q).

- If yes, put a rightward arrow (→) between DP_p and its preceding DP or set.
- If no, put DP_p to a new line under DP_q, and then repeat the following checking process until the DP_p is linked by an arrow or reach the first DP in the line.
- The checking process can be expressed by

$$\begin{cases} DP_q \text{ or } \{\ldots, DP_q, \ldots\} \rightarrow DP_p, & \exists u \in S\_DP_p : u = v \\ \begin{matrix} DP_q \text{ or } \{\ldots, DP_q, \ldots\} \\ DP_p \end{matrix}, & \forall u \in S\_DP_p : u \neq v \end{cases} \quad (8)$$

where $y \in S\_DP_q$ and DP_q is the preceding DP (or DP in the preceding set) of DP_p.

The flow chart of the steps is shown in Fig. 8.

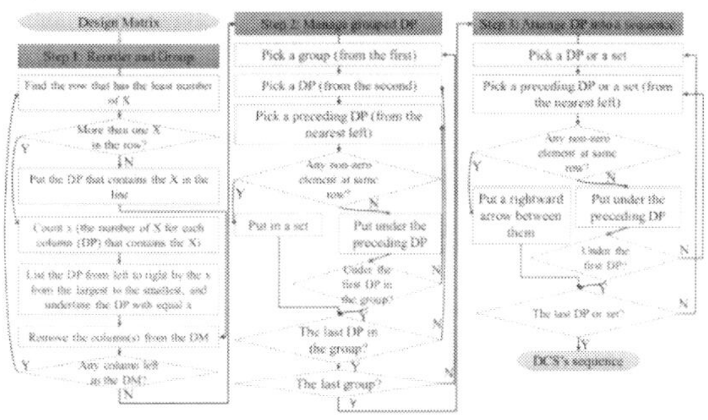

Fig. 8. The flowchart of DCS algorithm.

3.3 DCS Strategies

DCS prescribes some strategies to reduce complexity and increase modularity for three common concept improvement tasks.

3.3.1 For complete improvements of design concepts

After the concept generation process or re-engineering, to refine the concept with the execution sequence, one can follow one of execution sequences to determine DPs. When facing the C-set, one can look up the handbook or searching the existing modules with same functions to see if any similar modules can be retrieved as the best solution (i.e. modular design), or one can eliminate the extra coupling among the DPs in the C-set.

If more than one design are satisfied the FRs in design range, choosing the design with more acceptable execution sequences would result in less imaginary complexity.

3.3.2 For design improvements without DM changes

Sometimes the improvement task is to change a part of the design but the design matrix can remain the same. The scenario could be, for example, to adjust one of the DPs such as out of stock (where the concept is from re-engineering) or difficult to make it real (where the concept is from conceptual design).

For the task, one is suggested to find the changed DP in the U-set, and then follow the sequence in the U to determine the rest DPs. If the corresponding FR of the higher precedence DP in U can't be satisfied due to the change, the complete U-set is suggested to be determined from the first DP in the set.

3.3.3 For design improvements with DM changes

In some cases, the improvement task is resulted in the design matrix change. The scenario could be, for example, to modify the DPs when new FRs involved or some FRs change (where the concept is from re-engineering).

For this task, one is suggested to rebuild the DM with new FRs and new DPs (either expand the design matrix or re-identify the whole DM). Then, one is suggested to follow the strategy of whole design refinement in Section 3.3.1 or the partial design change in Section 3.3.2.

4 Case Study: A Kitchen Faucet Design

Kitchen faucet is a common equipment in a household. As it has been developed for a long time, there are many different designs on the market and are sold as modules. Also, in Suh's Axiomatic Design [4], the faucet problem was used as an example to explain uncoupled and coupled design. In this section, a case of the kitchen faucet design is studied to demonstrate how DCS helps with the functional sets to improve the existing product.

4.1. The Problem Statement

The focused design for the improvement is the kitchen faucet as shown in Fig. 9. By reverse engineering, the design has been transformed into four FRs and four DPs, which are

FR_1: to control the flow rate,
FR_2: to control the water temperature,
FR_3: to control the flow-out direction,
FR_4: to control the reach-out position,
and
DP_1: Cold valve,
DP_2: Hot valve,
DP_3: An outlet head,
DP_4: A hose.

The relationships between FRs and DPs have been identified as shown in Fig. 10. The design ranges for those FRs were assigned as shown in Table 1.

Fig. 9. The original kitchen faucet design. (Kingston Kitchen Faucet, Model # FB2121NDL, $23.99 at Amazon)

$$\begin{bmatrix} FR_1 \\ FR_2 \\ FR_3 \\ FR_4 \end{bmatrix} = \begin{bmatrix} X & X & 0 & 0 \\ X & X & 0 & 0 \\ 0 & 0 & X & X \\ 0 & 0 & 0 & X \end{bmatrix} \begin{bmatrix} DP_1 \\ DP_2 \\ DP_3 \\ DP_4 \end{bmatrix}$$

Fig. 10. The FRs, DPs, and DM of the original kitchen faucet.

Table 1. The design ranges for the kitchen faucet.

FR	Design range
FR_1	1.0-1.5 ±0.1 gallons per minutes (gpm)
FR_2	70˚F-105˚F ±5˚F
FR_3	The tilted angle from -80˚ to 80˚ ±5˚
FR_4	In a partial cylinder with a height of 0.30±0.01 m and a 160˚±5˚ sector with radius of 0.15±0.01 m

The design is a partially coupled design because the design matrix is neither triangular nor diagonal. The following section is applying DCS to improve the design.

4.1. The DCS Design Results

The improvement task matches the first improvement task, so the DCS algorithm was directly operated.

In the first step, DP4 was first picked because FR_4 has the least coupling (only one 'X'), and it is related to DP_4. Then DP_3 was picked because after removing DP_4, DP_3 was the one whose FR has the least coupling. Since the coupled DP numbers of the correlated FRs between DP_1 and DP_2 as well as the number of the correlated FRs between DP_1 and DP_2 are both equal, DP_1 and DP_2 were underlined to note the equal precedence:

DP_4 DP_3 $\underline{DP_1\ DP_2}$.

In the second step, there checked the grouped DPs, DP_1 and DP_2. Since the coupling was found at FR_1 and FR2, DP_1 and DP_2 were put in a set:

DP_4 DP_3 $\{DP_1, DP_2\}$.

In the third step, the checking process was starting from DP_3. One checked the DP_3 is functionally coupled with DP_4 at FR_3, so an arrow was put between them. So far, the line was like:

$DP_4 \rightarrow DP_3$ $\{DP_1, DP_2\}$.

Since $\{DP_1, DP_2\}$ was not found any couplings with DP_3, so they moved to a new line:

$DP_4 \rightarrow DP_3$
$\{DP_1, DP_2\}$.

Then, after checking the functional coupling between $\{DP_1, DP_2\}$ and DP_4, there was no coupling found, so it moved to the place below the DP_4. Since DP_4 is the first DP in the line, the DCS process was complete. The result was shown in Fig. 11.

Basing on the DCS result, one obtained the execution sequences as shown in the equation 9 and 10. The calculated execution sequence number is also two (2! = 2).

$$\begin{bmatrix} FR_1 \\ FR_2 \\ FR_3 \\ FR_4 \end{bmatrix} = \begin{bmatrix} X & X & 0 & 0 \\ X & X & 0 & 0 \\ 0 & 0 & X & X \\ 0 & 0 & 0 & X \end{bmatrix} \begin{bmatrix} DP_1 \\ DP_2 \\ DP_3 \\ DP_4 \end{bmatrix}$$

DCS:
$DP_4 \rightarrow DP_3$
$\{DP_1, DP2\}$

Fig. 11. The DCS outcome for the studied case.

$$\{DP_1, DP_2\} \rightarrow DP_4 \rightarrow DP_3 \tag{9}$$

$$DP_4 \rightarrow DP_3 \rightarrow \{DP_1, DP_2\} \tag{10}$$

In this case study, the equation 10 was selected as the execution sequence to work on.

With the execution sequence as Eq. 10, DP_4 was improved first to satisfy the FR4. Among the options DP_{4A} to DP_{4E} (Fig. 12), the DP_{4E} was determined by considering the cost and the design range (Option A and B don't match the design range, and Option E is cheaper than the other two). Based on the determined DP_4, the DP_3 was improved to satisfy the FR_3. Among the options DP_{3A} to DP_{3C} (Fig. 13), the DP_{3A} was determined by considering the DP_4, cost, and the design range (Option

A is the cheapest, and the design range can be satisfied because of the selection of DP_{4E}).

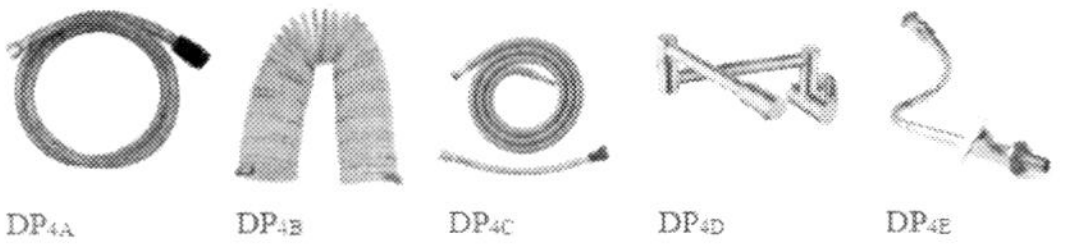

Fig. 12. The DP_4 options from the existing modules. (DP_{4A}: PartsmasterPro Faucet Hose, Model # 58583, $6.98 at Home Depot; DP_{4B}: Husky Recoil Hose, Model # 4-50E-RET-HOM, $12.98 at Home Depot; DP_{4C}: Hansgrohe Pull-down Kitchen Faucet Hose, $35.00 at Home Depot; DP_{4D}: KES Kitchen Faucet, Model # K9250, $39.99 at Amazon; DP4E: YOSIL Bendable Kitchen Sink Faucets, $19.99 at Amazon)

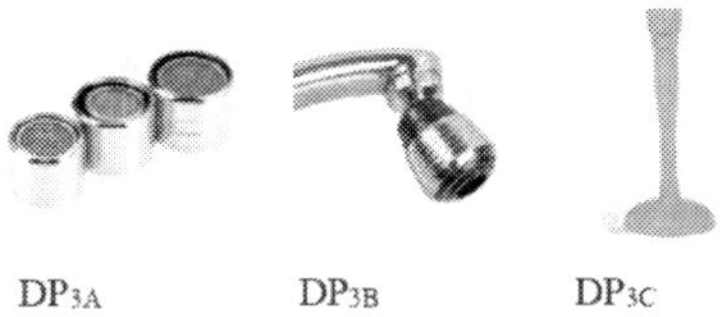

Fig. 13. The DP_3 options from the existing modules. (DP_{3A}: Sonline Faucet Aerator, Model # 017097, $2.18 at Amazon; DP_{3B}: Topbeu 360 Swivel Tap Aerator, Model # LB52, $3.29 at Amazon; DP_{3C}: WillsCase Faucet Extender, $8.99 at Amazon)

Then the improving faces a C-set, *{DP_1, DP_2}*. According to the first strategy of concept improvement task, the strong coupling could be improved by either eliminating the extra coupling terms or considering them as a module to improve together. The following sections demonstrate the improvement with extra coupling elimination via TRIZ method and with existing modules respectively.

4.1.1 Improved Design Results with TRIZ

Theory of inventive problem solving (TRIZ) by Altshuller [20] is widely used for generating innovative solutions and eliminating contradictions in the design. In this case study, the TRIZ approach is used to eliminate the extra coupling. The extra coupling was obtained to be the term between FR_1 and DP_2 after DM rearrangement according to the execution sequence from DCS method (Fig. 14).

$$\begin{bmatrix} FR_4 \\ FR_3 \\ FR_1 \\ FR_2 \end{bmatrix} = \begin{bmatrix} X & 0 & 0 & 0 \\ X & X & 0 & 0 \\ 0 & 0 & X & X \\ 0 & 0 & X & X \end{bmatrix} \begin{bmatrix} DP_4 \\ DP_3 \\ DP_1 \\ DP_2 \end{bmatrix}$$

Fig. 14. The eliminate term in the DM.

To eliminate that non-zero element by using TRIZ, one would have the improving FR_1, which is in terms of number 9, speed, in TRIZ matrix and have the conflict of DP_2, which is in terms of number 17, temperature, in TRIZ. Therefore, the possible principles are 28-Mechanics Substitution, 30- Flexible Shells and Thin Films, 36- Phase Transitions, and 2- Taking Out. By using the principle 2A of TRIZ, a water heater switch was generated as DP_2*. As a result, the improved DM is shown in Fig. 15.

$$\begin{bmatrix} FR_4 \\ FR_3 \\ FR_1 \\ FR_2 \end{bmatrix} = \begin{bmatrix} X & 0 & 0 & 0 \\ X & X & 0 & 0 \\ 0 & 0 & X & 0 \\ 0 & 0 & X & X \end{bmatrix} \begin{bmatrix} DP_4 \\ DP_3 \\ DP_1 \\ DP_2^* \end{bmatrix}$$

$$DP_4 \rightarrow DP_3 \rightarrow DP^1 \rightarrow DP_2^*$$

Fig. 15. The decoupled C-set and its execution sequence.

To further improve the design, DP_1 can remain the same as a simple cold valve per the design range, and then the DP_2* is determined as water heater switch (when on, the flow rate is 0.5gpm) in an adjustable temperature to satisfy the FR_1 and FR_2.

Therefore, the final design by the extra coupling elimination is
FR_1: to control the flow rate,
FR_2: to control the water temperature,
FR_3: to control the flow-out direction,
FR_4: to control the reach-out position,
and
DP_1: A cold valve,
DP_2^*: A water heater switch,
DP_{3A}: A simple faucet aerator,
DP_{4E}: A bendable hose.
The result is similar to the design in Fig. 16.

Fig. 16. The design result by extra coupling elimination. (A.B Crew Electric Hot Water Heater Kitchen Faucet, Model # COMIN18JU011922, $49.98 at Amazon)

4.1.2 Improved Design Results by Existing Modules

To improve the U module as well as the C module, {DP_1, DP_2}, one could consider those DPs as an indivisible module to function both “to control the flow rate” and “to control water temperature”. By looking up the existing modules, there are four options (Fig. 17), and the $\{DP_1, DP_2\}_C$ was selected because of the functional independence and physical integration. Although the design was pointed out that the actual values of flow rate and the temperature were somehow dependent [21], the control operation for the FR_1 and FR_2 are still independent from users’ perspective (because users don’t seriously calculate the temperature and flow rate as long as the temperature and the flow can be varied as the users’ wish during each operation). The final design consequently made the set {DP_1, DP_2} uncoupled (Fig. 18).

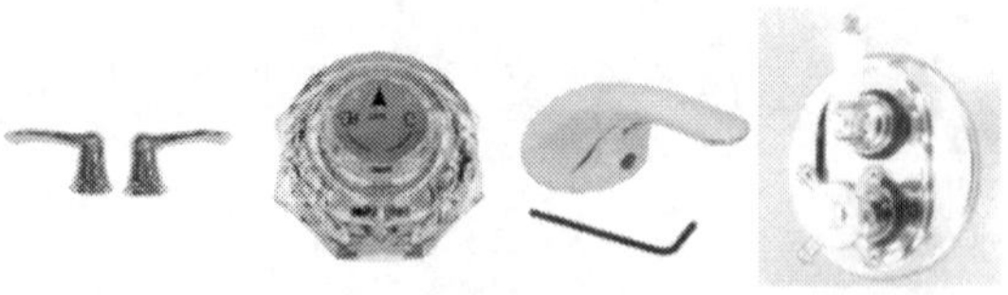

{DP₁, DP₂}A {DP₁, DP₂}B {DP₁, DP₂}C {DP₁, DP₂}D

Fig. 17. The $\{DP_1, DP_2\}$ options from the existing modules. ($\{DP_1, DP_2\}_A$: DANCO Replacement Lavatory Faucet Handles, Model # 10422, $10.12 at Home Depot; $\{DP_1, DP_2\}_B$: DANCO Lavatory Handle, Model # 80967, $9.97 at Home Depot ; $\{DP_1, DP_2\}_C$: American Standard Colony Soft Lavatory Faucet Handle, Model # M961627-0020A, $14.06 at Home Depot; $\{DP_1, DP_2\}_D$: CHINAURBANLAB Temperature Control Shower Faucet, Model # T21CP32B00-33, no price info.)

$$\begin{bmatrix} FR_1 \\ FR_2 \\ FR_3 \\ FR_4 \end{bmatrix} = \begin{bmatrix} X & X & 0 & 0 \\ X & X & 0 & 0 \\ 0 & 0 & X & X \\ 0 & 0 & 0 & X \end{bmatrix} \begin{bmatrix} DP_1 \\ DP_2 \\ DP_3 \\ DP_4 \end{bmatrix}$$

$$\Downarrow$$

$$\begin{bmatrix} FR_1, FR_2 \\ FR_3 \\ FR_4 \end{bmatrix} = \begin{bmatrix} X & 0 & 0 \\ 0 & X & X \\ 0 & 0 & X \end{bmatrix} \begin{bmatrix} \{DP_1, DP_2\} \\ DP_3 \\ DP_4 \end{bmatrix}$$

$$\Downarrow$$

$$\begin{bmatrix} FR_1 \\ FR_2 \\ FR_3 \\ FR_4 \end{bmatrix} = \begin{bmatrix} X & 0 & 0 & 0 \\ 0 & X & 0 & 0 \\ 0 & 0 & X & X \\ 0 & 0 & 0 & X \end{bmatrix} \begin{bmatrix} DP_1^* \\ DP_2^* \\ DP_3 \\ DP_4 \end{bmatrix}$$

Fig. 18. The process of $\{DP_1, DP_2\}$ improvement by existing modules.

The final design by the existing modules is
FR_1: to control the flow rate,
FR_2: to control the water temperature,
FR_3: to control the flow-out direction,
FR_4: to control the reach-out position,
and
$\{DP_1, DP_2\}_C$: An integration module of the up-down flow control valve and left-right temperature control valve,
DP_{3A}: A simple faucet aerator,
DP_{4E}: A bendable hose.
The result is similar to the design in Fig. 16.
The final result is similar to the design in Fig. 19.

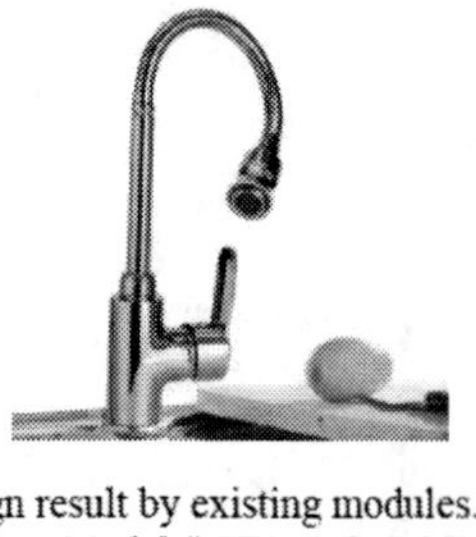

Fig. 19. The design result by existing modules. (Churun Kitchen Sink Faucet, Model # ZT100, $32.99 at Amazon)

4.2. Discussion

Both the design results enable the system range to match the design range, and the coupled design has been improved into at least a decoupled design.

In the case of using coupling elimination, the original design that using different proportions of the hot and cold water to achieve the function of "to control water temperature" was changed by using a heater because the hot water valve turned into a switch due to the elimination of the coupling non-zero element. The result shows that the elimination changes the fundamental design. In addition, during the improvement by elimination, the cost of the design couldn't be considered. As a result, the use of the heater would increase the cost. Therefore, when operating the elimination, the designer is suggested to check the cost and make sure whether the change of the fundamental design is allowed or not.

In the case of using existing modules, the fundamental design wasn't changed but improved. The function of "to control water temperature" is still satisfied by mixing the hot and cold water in different ratios. That is because the design took the advantages of the existing designs and resources. Taking the C module in DCS to improve the design not thinking the elimination makes the concept improvement of a coupled design in a simpler way with lower cost than the way of eliminating the coupling terms. While the modularity increase, the design was improved with minimal relative complexity.

5 Conclusion and Future Work

The precedence and functional sets were defined to reduce complexity and increase modularity, and the DCS algorithm was modified with functionally independent U-set and insolvably coupled C-set to better obtain the execution sequence and taking the advantage from existing modules. The results of this research have significant impacts on both design theory and design practice. Theoretically, the approach in this research 1) guides designers to improve concepts not only organizing design matrix but also extract additional coupling information to increase modularity and 2) is a more generalized approach than the previous methods that can be applied to any design cases with design matrix. Practically, the research 1) demonstrates the usability of the DCS algorithm and strategies to a kitchen faucet design case and 2) allows the principle of functional dependency and the practice of modular design to be considered simultaneously as much as possible during the conceptual design stage. It is a fundamental contribution that demonstrates how the ideal principles (or axioms) of design theories can be used together strategically with practical design methods (or considerations) in industry practices to generate real-world design results that are both most practical and creative.

For future research, a complete framework for conceptual design would be developed. Also, more design cases would be studied to examine the DCS method and strategies. Numerical design matrix case would be investigated to see the applicable of the DCS method.

References

1. K. Ulrich and W. Seering, Computation and conceptual design. Rob. & Comput.-Int. Manuf., **4**, 3, pp.309-315 (1988)
2. G. Pahl and W. Beitz, *Engineering design: a systematic approach*. 2nd Ed. Springer (1996)
3. T. McNeill, J.S. Gero, and J. Warren, Understanding conceptual electronic design using protocol analysis. Res. Eng. Des., 10, 3, pp.129-140 (1998)
4. N. P. Suh, *Axiomatic Design*, Oxford University Press, NY (2001)
5. C.-Y. Wang and S. C.-Y. Lu, The Comparison of Three Different Reasoning Approaches of Dual-Hierarchical Representation in Conceptual Design with Computer-Aided Product and Process Development. In: CIE Grad. Res. Poster Session, 34th ASME-CIE Conference, Buffalo, NY (2014)
6. N.P. Suh, A theory of complexity, periodicity and the design axioms. Res. Eng. Des., **11**, 2, pp.116-132 (1999)
7. D.E. Kim and N.P. Suh. Decoupled Design of Cylinder Liner for IC Engines. SAE Tech. Paper No. 911231 (1991)
8. D.A. Gebala and N.P. Suh. An Application of Axiomatic Design. Research in Engineering Design, **3**, 3, pp.149-162 (1992)
9. C.B. Park, D.F. Baldwin, and N.P. Suh. Axiomatic design of a microcellular filament extrusion system. Res. Eng. Des., **8**, 3, pp.166-177 (1996)
10. W. Chen, D. Rosen, J.K. Allen, and F. Mistree. Modularity and the independence of functional requirements in designing complex systems . Concur. Prod. Des., **74**, pp.31-38 (1994)
11. C.-Y. Wang, S. C.-Y. Lu, and A. Liu. Managing Functional Coupling Sequences to Reduce Design Complexity during Concept Improvements. In: ASME 2015 IDETC/CIE, pp. V004T05A034-V004T05A034 (2015)
12. S.C.Y. Lu and A. Liu. A logic-based foundation of axiomatic design. In Proceedings of the 6th ICAD (2011)
13. N.P. Suh. *Axiomatic Design*. Oxford Univ. Press, New York (2001)
14. J.K. Gershenson, G.J. Prasad, and Y. Zhang. Product modularity: definitions and benefits. J. Eng. Des., **14**, 3, pp.295-313 (2003)
15. M.E. Sosa, S.D. Eppinger, and C.M. Rowles. Identifying Modular and Integrative Systems and Their Impact on Design Team Interactions. J. Mech. Des., **125**, 2, pp.240-252 (2003)
16. J.K. Gershenson, G.J. Prasad, and Y. Zhang. Product modularity: measures and design methods. J. Eng. Des., **15**, 1, pp.33-51 (2004)
17. K. Hölttä-Otto, N.A. Chiriac, D. Lysy, and E.S. Suh. Comparative analysis of coupling modularity metrics. J. Eng. Des., **23**, 10-11, pp.790-806 (2012)
18. S. Jung and T.W. Simpson. New modularity indices for modularity assessment and clustering of product architecture. J. Eng. Des., **28**, 1, pp.1-22 (2017)
19. N.P. Suh. *Complexity: Theory and Applications*. Oxford Univ. Press, New York (2005)
20. G. Altshuller and L. Shulyak, TRIZ, 565 the theory of inventive problem solving, Technical Innovation Center, Inc. (1996)
21. J.T. Foley, E. Puik, and D.S. Cochran. The Faucet Reloaded: Improving Axiomatic Design by Example. ICAD 2017, MATEC Web of Conferences, **127**, 01009 (2017)

Guiding Manufacturing Enterprises to Achieve Long-Term Business Sustainability Using the Collective System Design Approach

Shahab A. Shah[1,*], *Joseph J.* Smith[1], and *David S.* Cochran[1]

[1]Purdue University Fort Wayne, Fort Wayne, IN 46835 United States

Abstract. This paper addresses several issues discovered by working with different industries attempting to sustain their business enterprise and to become "Lean." The three key points addressed by the paper are: 1) Designing a new system or re-designing an existing system should focus on collecting a complete set of customer needs and deriving functional requirements from those needs. 2) Illustrating the path-dependency or sequence of implementation of Physical Solutions (PSs) to achieve Functional Requirements (FRs) of partially coupled designs. 3) Lean is not what we *implement* as a system, rather lean is what we *become* as a result of meeting customer needs with the utilization of the least amount of resources possible in a sustained manner. When lean is viewed as a set of tools to implement, the people in an enterprise will face ever-increasing difficulty in long-term business sustainability. The primary problems arise early in the design/re-design phase due to the lack of a clear set of system functional requirements. Without clearly defined system FRs, driven by recognizing customer needs/concerns, an enterprise will implement point solutions in an attempt to improve part(s) of a system. The Manufacturing System Design Decomposition (MSDD), a product of Axiomatic Design (AD), illustrates the path-dependency among the solutions of the associated requirements of any manufacturing facility. The MSDD provides a system-wide view and a clear sequence for system design implementation. The Collective System Design approach is discussed to provide the steps for senior leadership to re-design an existing system or to design a new system that results in long-term sustainability and become "lean."

1 Introduction

The aim of this paper is to offer an approach to manufacturing system design and to "become lean" and provide the long-term business sustainability using the Collective System Design approach.

The term "lean" was first coined by J. Krafcik in 1988 [1], the reference was to a system conceived in the 1950s and is known as the Toyota Production System (TPS) [2]. The major contributors to TPS were Taichii Ohno, Eiji Toyoda, and Shigeo Shingo at the Toyota Motor Corporation, Japan [2]. Masaki Imai claimed in 1986 that Toyota came up with the idea of a system in which small quantity and a large variety of many different vehicles are manufactured using a tightrope of inventory, which eventually became the reason behind Toyota's success [3].

There are many different definitions of lean [4], but early on, lean was misunderstood to be the elimination of waste from the system [5]. Later on, lean meant "cutting heads" and positions, resulting in part shortages as lean meant zero inventory [6, 7]. Womack, Jones, and Roos introduced the term "lean production" to the Western world to describe the TPS which defines a lean system as a system that prioritizes the improvement of the flow of product/service to the customer without any non-value added activities by integrating the best aspects of craft production with those of mass production [2, 8].

*e-mail: shahab.alishah05@gmail.com

The lean ideology is growing popular in both the manufacturing and service sector. However, most industries suffer in getting the right understanding of the lean ideology of satisfying the customer needs. These industries consider lean to be a toolbox which can be implemented in an enterprise [9]. Some industries consider lean implementation to be a package of several tools such as 5S (Sort, Set in order, Shine, Standardize, and Sustain), Single Minute Exchange of Die (SMED) visual control, poka-yoke (i.e., mistake-proofing), Just in Time (JIT), Heijunka Box (production leveling), continuous improvement, etc. [10–12]. All these tools help improve parts of the system rather than enhancing the system-wide outcome.

A lean system is not a toolbox or an activity that can be implemented. Implementation of a tool without knowing the real purpose behind its selection results in unknown consequences and the lack of sustainability. Rather, lean can be defined as, "the result of a system design that is tailored to meet customer needs." Meeting customer needs involves eliminating non-value added activities by employing the right tone and by understanding the path-dependency of implementing solutions within the system design [13–15].

The CSD approach enables an enterprise team to develop a long-term enterprise design that is sustainable using AD. This paper illustrates the CSD approach and an application with a commercial vehicle manufacturer.

2 Literature Review

According to the literature, only less than 10% of the industries that implement lean are able to sustain the system design after three years [13, 14, 16]. The question arises that if all the tools that can help a system to become lean are available, what is missing to make the use of these tools sustainable [17]?

There are numerous studies and quotations regarding the importance of positive attitude in a system towards becoming lean. For example, a keynote speaker at the 2014 Oklohama conference stated that a system needs to have the presence of two factors (tools and culture) with the following proportion in order to become lean:

1. Implement the necessary tools which are about 40% of the total effect.
2. Develop the people in the system with positive attitude, which is about 60% of the total effect [18].

In addition, Dr. Deming said "94% of the problems in business are system driven and only 6% are people driven" which captures the importance of positive tone [19].

Numerous industries employ the various tools used by Toyota (i.e., 5S, producing to takt time), but often fail to achieve the desired outcomes. These tools represent the "how," but without knowing the "why," the tools will be misused. The problem with not understanding the why before implementing the how is a characteristic of many different industries including agriculture [20]. The culture of traditional management accounting is to jump for the tools and solutions followed by TPS rather than knowing the real intent for which the tool is used [21]. As such, an understanding of the motivation and the design intent behind using a tool plays a vital role in bringing the success of the function provided by the tool.

Once the intent behind the selection of a tool for a requirement is known, the enterprise needs to know the sequencing of operations. That is, which operations come first before the implementation of the chosen tool. In other words, understanding the system as a whole and not trying to improve parts of the system should be the central focus of interest. According to Taiichi Ohno, "The key to the Toyota Way and what makes Toyota stand out is not any of the individual elements. But what is important is having all the elements together as a system. It must be practiced every day in a very consistent manner, not in spurts [22]."

The lack of understanding in the manufacturing system design is analogous to the lack of understanding of medication interactions and the resulting adverse effects on the patients' health. For instance, a patient who is on four or more medications has an increased risk of suffering from adverse drug reactions, which results from a lack of understanding of the system as a whole [23].

According to Taiichi Ohno, "Where there is no Standard there can be no Kaizen (continuous improvement) [24]." Therefore, it is very important to develop a standard work for implementing the chosen solution and look for opportunities for improvement by changing either the FRs or the PSs or both [19, 25].

3 Approach

Collective System Design (CSD) is an enterprise system design approach that Dr. David S. Cochran began developing during the mid-2000's. CSD is the practice of the System Engineering Center that Dr. Cochran directs at Purdue University, Fort Wayne [26].

3.1 CSD Language

The CSD language employs the terminology of Functional Requirements (FRs) and Physical Solutions (PSs), that aims to segregate what the system must achieve (FRs) from how to achieve (PSs), adapted from AD [26, 27], as shown in Fig. 1.

The terminology used for the mean(s) of achieving a Functional Requirement (FR) in the traditional Axiomatic Design is "Design Parameter (DP)" [27], which has been re-named/updated to "Physical Solution (PS)" in the CSD approach for two reasons:

1. The physical domain in the design framework of axiomatic design expresses a physical thing/object that is proposed to achieve the functional requirements stated within the functional domain.
2. Many technical and most non-technical professionals may not be familiar with the term, "Design Parameters," and may lack the connection that to achieve an FR, it requires the selection of a PS as the "How" to achieve an FR. The PS acknowledges that we are choosing a physical thing (noun) to achieve an FR that starts with a verb.

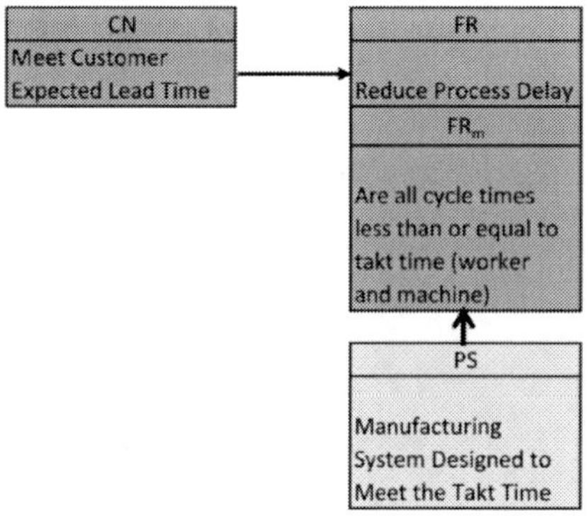

Figure 1. CSD Representation of FR

3.2 General Overview of CSD: The Flame Model

CSD is a 12-step design approach for designing new and improving the existing systems with a focus on sustainability of system designs to meet the customer needs. Step 1-3 covers the tone and culture of the senior leadership, step 4-7 covers the thinking part of the enterprise for meeting the customer needs which is based on Axiomatic Design principles, step 8 covers the structure, step 9 covers the plan for continuous improvement, and step 10-12 covers the feedback for sustainability and growth of the enterprise [28]. No improvement can be sustained in an enterprise if the feedback for sustainability steps are not part of the tone of the people in the enterprise. In this paper, the flame model provides a general overview of CSD approach, as shown in Fig. 2.

3.3 Elements of the Flame Model

The flame model represents a hierarchy of the different elements that make up systems namely, tone, thinking, structure, and work/actions. These elements are expressed as different layers cohesively connected like the different layers within a flame. All these elements are present within any system at any given time. The outcome of each layer is either formed intentionally or becomes unintentional due to the lack of attention given to that associated element. The work/actions and structure are the physical elements that can easily be seen, however, the thinking and tone are the hidden elements [30].

Diagnosis of a problem and design (or redesign) of a system are both expressed by the flame model.

3.4 Diagnosis Phase

The diagnosis phase looks at determining the root cause of the problem by first understanding the work and actions (this layer is often referred to as going to the Gemba) [31]. After determining the root cause, it is important to understand that whether the problem arises due to the operator's fault or due to the system's fault. That's why the structure of the system that drives the work and actions is understood next. The succeeding element is the thinking layer of the system and this is where FRs and associated PSs are defined. The thinking layer is where people may or may not know what the FRs are or people do or do not collectively agree on those FRs. And the last element is the tone, which represents the attitude of the people, or what many refer to as the culture of the system [32].

3.5 Design Phase

3.5.1 Tone

Once the problem is diagnosed and a conscious choice to change is made by the senior leadership, the system design can be realized by moving outward through the layers of the flame. A proper leadership tone is required for meeting the needs of the internal customer (people working inside the enterprise) resulting in a high working morale of the internal customers which would indirectly help achieve the needs of the external customers (end customers). A proper tone basically facilitates a respectful environment that allows both the direct and indirect people to be engaged [5], and the understanding that a system should not let the people fail but rather keeps them from failing [19]. Recognizing the failure of a system is an opportunity for continuous improvement in the system that leads to the sustainability of the system design.

3.5.2 Thinking

This tone of conscious decision making by the leadership leads to the Manufacturing System Design Decomposition (MSDD)' focus on meeting all the customer needs, as shown in Fig. 3, illustrates the thinking layer of the CSD Flame Model [32]. The MSDD is developed with the first axiom of axiomatic design theory [26].

This decomposition is a translation of all the external and internal customer needs of a manufacturing system to become lean and to achieve the long-term sustainability of the system design using the language of CSD. Whereas, external needs refer to the needs of the end customer and internal needs refer to the needs of the people working inside the enterprise.

Overall, the requirements in the MSDD can be grouped into six key areas: Quality, Identifying and Resolving Problems, Predictable Output, Delay Reduction, Operation (direct and indirect labor) Costs, and Investment [34]. These six key areas consist of a total of seventy FR-PS pairs, typically used in manufacturing.

The MSDD represents an adaption of Axiomatic Design theory. By maintaining the independence of the FRs (derived from customer needs), the path-dependency from left to right of the design relationships within a manufacturing facility can be realized as shown in Fig. 3 [27]. For example, Quality branch impacts all the branches to the right in a manufacturing system, based on the proposed MSDD.

The design relationship matrix for level III of MSDD, showing the partially dependent design, is shown in Eq. 1.

$$\begin{pmatrix} FR111 \\ FR112 \\ FR113 \\ FR121 \\ FR122 \\ FR123 \end{pmatrix} = \begin{bmatrix} X & 0 & 0 & 0 & 0 & 0 \\ X & X & 0 & 0 & 0 & 0 \\ X & X & X & 0 & 0 & 0 \\ X & X & X & X & 0 & 0 \\ X & X & X & X & X & 0 \\ X & X & X & X & X & X \end{bmatrix} \times \begin{pmatrix} PS111 \\ PS112 \\ PS113 \\ PS121 \\ PS122 \\ PS123 \end{pmatrix} \quad (1)$$

To simplify the communication of the MSDD to the people within a manufacturing enterprise, the seven teaching FRs were developed:

FR1: "Provide a safe, healthy environment,"

FR2: "Produce the customer consumed quantity every shift,"

FR3: "Produce the customer consumed mix every shift,"

FR4: "Do not advance a defect to the next customer of your work,"

FR5: "Achieve FR1 through FR4 in spite of variation,"

FR6: "Rapidly identify problems and resolve them for the long-term," and

FR7: "Achieve FR1 through FR6 with the least time in system,"

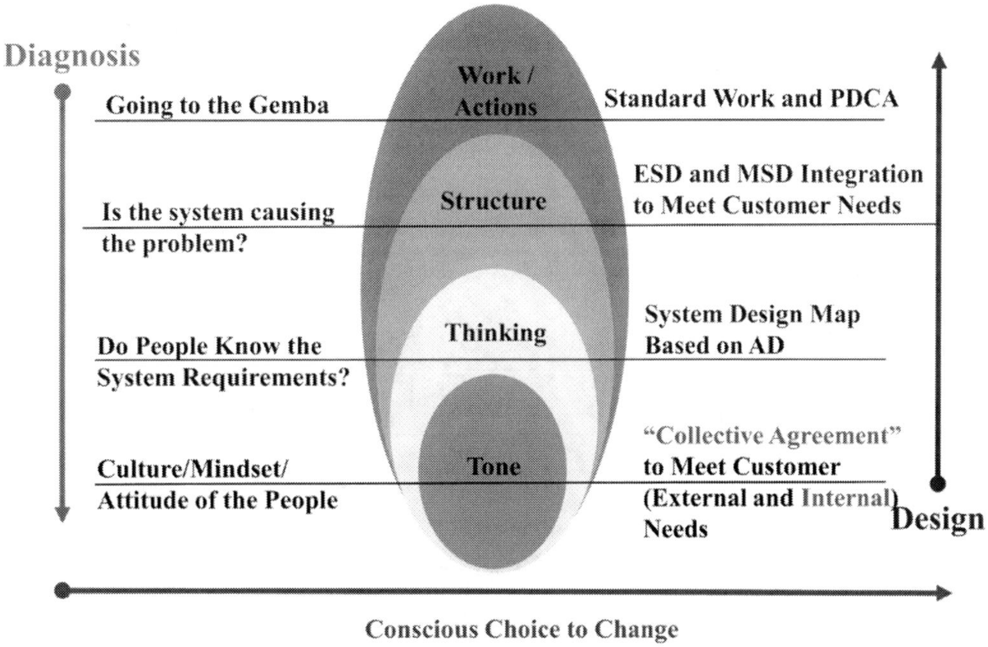

Figure 2. Flame Model of CSD. Updated from [29]

Within the seven teaching FRs (see Fig. 3), FR1: "Provide a safe, healthy environment," is depicted to be at the very left, indicating its criticality and that it impacts all the rest of the FRs. However, due to the liability associated with plant safety, the safety branch was not included on the MSDD. Also, the PSs are intentionally left blank in the teaching FRs of MSDD to be filled up by the users with collective agreement among the team members. Since the path-dependency of FR-PS pairs is based on the PS selection, no dependencies are yet drawn for the teaching FRs.

3.5.3 Structure

The structure of an enterprise determines how the stations are laid out in the workplace and who reports to who. According to CSD, the Manufacturing System Design (MSD) and Enterprise System Design (ESD) need to work together to sustain the system design that helps achieve customer needs, as shown in Fig. 4. Whereas, ESD contains Engineering Director (ED), Quality Director (QD), Finance and Accounting (F & A), Management (M), Human Resource (HR), Sales (S), and Controller (C) etc. And the MSD consists of value stream mapping, process mapping, machines, and operators etc. to produce to the customer needs. For instance, a product design team may develop a design for a product with a very good quality (low tolerance) but if the resources (machines, operators, or layout etc.) are unable to produce a product to the design specifications so all the efforts of the design team will go in vain and vice versa.

3.5.4 Work/Actions

Work/Actions refers to defining and implementing the standard work methods. The standard work may include the Process Variables (PVs) but normally devise the procedure to implement a PS. For instance, if a chef is backing the cake so the whole procedure is devised through work/actions but setting the parameters like the temperature of the cake etc. can be the PVs.

Standard work methods should be defined based on the current best-known methods to be improved in the future as new methods are known, as opposed to planning for perfection. These different layers of the CSD flame model are utilized in the next sections to sustain the long-term business system design and to become lean.

4 Becoming Lean using CSD Approach

4.1 Leadership Behavior

The CSD approach begins by framing the problem that needs to be overcome, in order to understand the stakeholders of the system. This approach fosters an environment where the stakeholders work together as a team

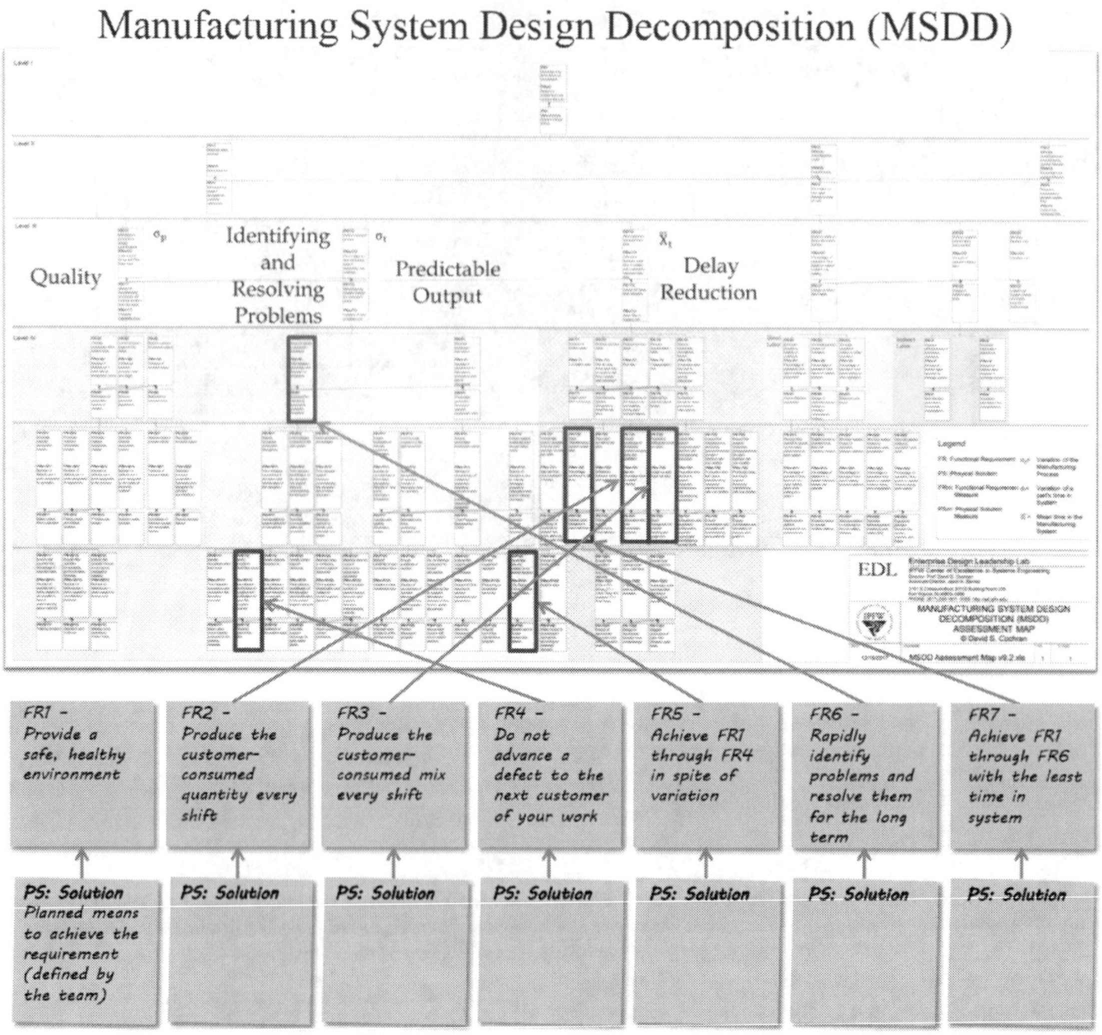

Figure 3. Manufacturing System Design Decomposition. Updated from [33]. For detailed observation of the individual FR-PS pair, Zoom-in on the figure in the digital copy.

and make a conscious choice to change in the system. These days, most of the manufacturing industries either run into overproduction waste or lack of enough production to meet the customer needs leading to sub-contracting. Besides, the industries also usually suffer from being flexible enough to offer product customization based on varying customer needs [35]. Therefore, in this paper, change in the system is indicating the redesign of the system to become lean. i.e., to meet the customer consumed quantity and mix of good quality parts every shift with the consumption of the least amount of resources possible.

4.2 Collective Agreement on FRs, driven by Customer Needs

Once the leadership team makes a conscious decision to become lean, the enterprise must collectively agree on determining the FRs of the system before choosing the PSs. Rather than just replicating an idea/tool employed by TPS without understanding the intent (FR) of the tool (PS). For instance, TPS has chosen the PS: "Manufacturing System Designed to Takt Time" to achieve the FR: "Reduce Process Delay" to help assist in meeting the customer expected lead time with the least amount of non-value added activities [36].

Takt time synchronizes the production flow of each shift to the average customer demand desired per shift. Mathematically, takt time is defined in Eq. 2 [30]. Takt time sets the pace for production by limiting the maximum cycle time of the line. Takt time represents the time available for the system to produce a single part, measured in mins/part.

$$Takt\ Time = \frac{Available\ Time\ per\ Shift}{Average\ Customer\ Demand\ per\ Shift} \qquad (2)$$

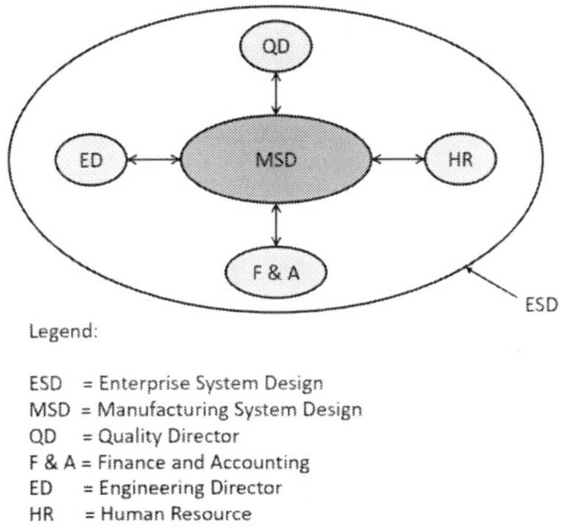

Figure 4. Integral Structure of MSD and ESD

However, one of the industry clients has replicated the PS: "Manufacturing System Design to Meet the Takt Time" from TPS with a lack of understanding of the design intent. Choosing the PS without a conscious understanding of the FR: "Reduce Process Delay" leads to certain undesirable behaviors such as producing to the minimum cycle time (produce as fast as possible). That's why the tool is just simply used for checking the monthly numbers rather than producing to the customer expected lead time (intent).

CSD, the proposed approach, addresses this issue of lack of understanding of the customer need or intent behind implementing a tool by understanding the customer need (CN) first, followed by FR-PS pair derivation as shown in Fig. 1. This approach of implementing a tool in manufacturing system would compel the management to have a clear and an accurate understanding of the customer need.

4.3 Precedence Order of Implementation of PSs

After understanding the purpose/intent of a tool, the precedence/sequential order of implementation of the PSs to achieve the associated FRs plays a crucial role in providing a strong foundation for lean.

For instance, an industry could set the precedence order of tools by asking a question, "Does the PS1 affect the achievement of FR2?" If the PS1 does affect the achievement of FR2, so the indication is to proceed to PS2 (used for achieving FR2) after PS1 implementation. However, if the PS1 does not affect the achievement of FR2, then there is no precedence order between the FR1-PS1 pair and FR2-PS2 pair.

In the current example of choosing the PS: "Manufacturing System Designed to Takt Time," the industry has to improve the quality first to ensure production of good parts to takt time. If the cell is designed to takt time and there are repetitive quality failures so the system may produce parts to the customer consumed quantity but after removing the rejected parts, the production to takt time will not be ensured. Next, the industry has to have a procedure for detection and response to production disruptions by employing many different tools. e.g., an alarm system would sound in the management offices or any other alert system for identifying disruptions when the actual quantity produced is not meeting the schedule etc. Next, the manufacturing system designed to have a standard work defined for achieving predictable production resources (people, equipment, information) leading to minimizing the production disruptions. Next, the cells/stations should be designed to single-piece flow for achieving the FR: "Reduce lot (batch) delay."

Once all these tools/solutions are implemented following a precedence order, that's when the manufacturing system can be designed to takt time to help produce to customer expected lead time. In the similar fashion, if all the FR-PS pairs of MSDD, as shown in Fig. 3, that apply to a manufacturing enterprise is being implemented knowing the effect on the customer needs, the enterprise will result in becoming lean.

5 Sustaining the Long-Term Business Sustainability

A system can attempt to employ two different approaches to sustain itself while meeting the customer needs in the long run: (1) Implement a single-step, point solutions approach and (2) CSD approach, i.e., decompose the highest-level PS into the lowest (leaf)-level FR-PS pairs that can be implemented easily as shown in Fig. 5 and Fig. 6.

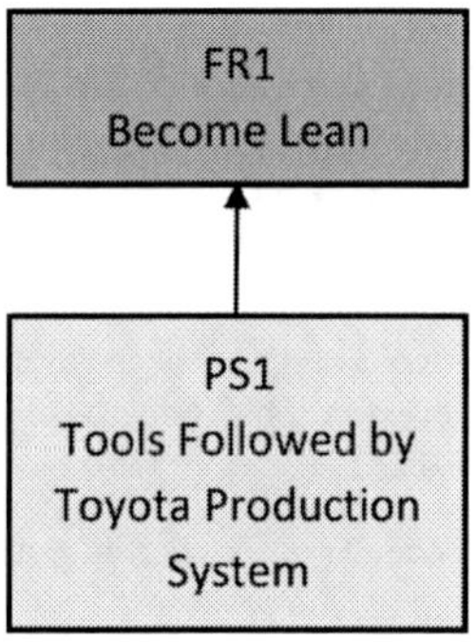

Figure 5. Single-Step, Point Solution Approach, Failing to Sustain the System Design

5.1 Single-Step Approach vs. CSD Approach to Sustain the System Design

In the single-step approach, the system attempts to achieve only a single FR by implementing a point solution. For instance, the system may or may not be able to achieve the FR, derived from the CN: "Meet customer consumed

 https://doi.org/10.1051/matecconf/201822301015

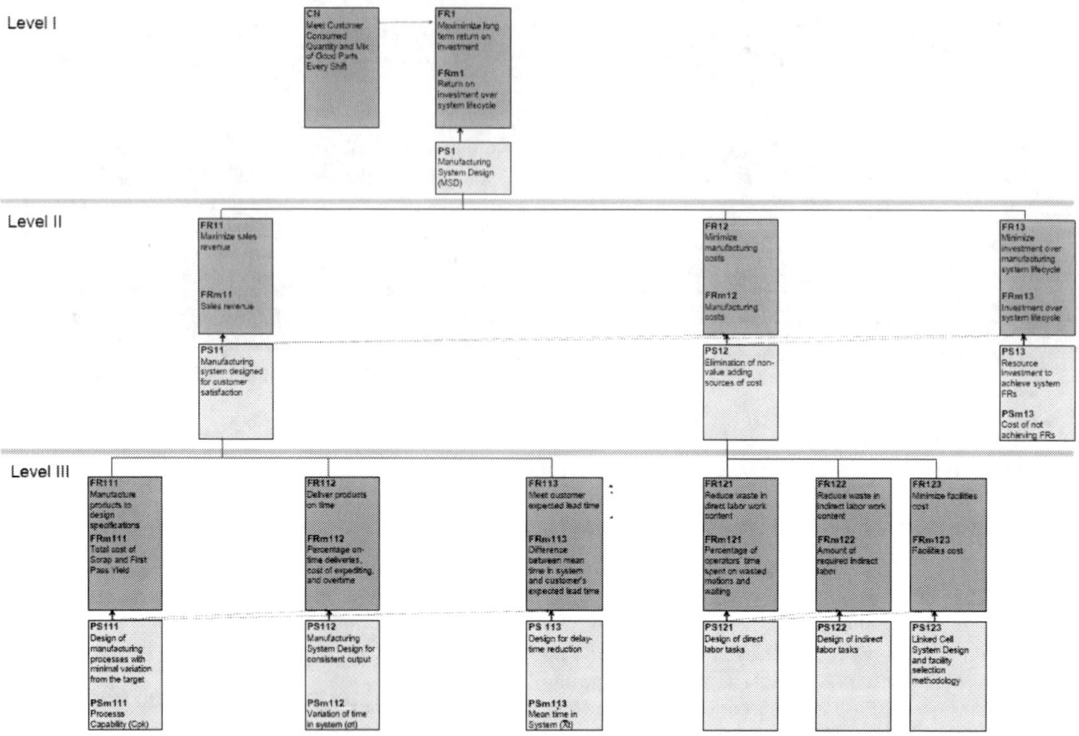

Figure 6. CSD Approach to Sustain the System Design

quantity and mix of good parts every shift" with the implementation of the chosen PS.

The trap that an industry usually falls into is that to become lean and sustain the system design, requires achieving all of the FRs of the system design simultaneously. This point illustrates that choosing only one solution does not ensure that an industry will become lean.

The CSD approach is to:

1. The design intent of the tool.
2. All the FR-PS pairs of the system design decomposition needed to achieve the top-level FR to achieve customer need.
3. The precedence order (partial-coupling) of the FR-PS pairs.

Each FR-PS pair has associated measures, called FRm and PSm which indicates the success or failure. Examples of FRm are shown in Fig. 1 and Fig. 6 . A good measure for the PS should be in the form of "Yes" or "No" questions. i.e., the system either achieve what it was supposed to achieve or not with the implemented solution, rather than in the form of complicated mathematical algorithms and calculations. The decomposition clarifies the achievement of individual FRs in a sequential order using the implementation of associated PSs. If the system is showing a consistent increase in the system-wide outcome with the implementation of each leaf PS then the system is always approaching towards the highest-level FR. A system that becomes lean using this decomposition approach would be able to sustain the system design in a long-run due to both the readiness of process replication for developing standard work and the ease of continuous improvement.

5.2 Standard Work

Standard work is a key aspect of sustaining the system design to provide long-term business sustainability at any enterprise. Usually, industries end up with having a large buffer of inventory to meet the customer needs (quantity and mix) because the operations are not predictable. Standard work is a list of instructions that all the operators of each shift are trained to follow to provide a very repeatable, consistent, and predictable output. This predictable output would lead to tightening of the rope of inventory and a single-piece flow resulting in the reduction of the 5 different transportation delays (batch delay, process delay, run size delay, reduce transportation delay, and systematic operational delays) thereby reducing the associated cost measures as well, as shown in Fig. 3 [36]. Two types of standard work documents are important in a lean enterprise:

1. White sheet standard work details the day-in and day-out practices that need to be followed in a workplace and

2. Green sheet standard work details the response plan for abnormal condition(s). i.e., visual management for identifying problems at their source (source inspection), and then resolving the problems immediately (control poka-yoke) etc. [37].

Consider the importance of standard work in the case of baking a cake. If a chef makes a cake by adding all the required ingredients without documenting the ratios of the ingredients and the environmental factors like temperature, humidity, etc, how will the process be repeatable? Maybe the cake comes out to be either dry, moist or even the best cake the customer has ever eaten. Upon request for another cake of the same shape and taste, the chef may never be able to replicate the baking process to result in the same kind of cake.

In order to replicate the process in a similar fashion every time, the chef has to document the instructions, detailing the ratio of ingredients, the timing, the temperature of the oven, and the environmental factors. This list of instructions would be known as white sheet standard work. In the case of baking a cake, green sheet standard work may be necessary when the chef forgets to grease the pan or for any other abnormality that may occur when baking a cake.

5.3 Continuous Improvement

In the CSD approach, after standard work is defined, the Plan-Do-Check-Act (PDCA) cycle is employed for continuous improvement. The PDCA cycle is aligned with the design relationships expressed by the MSDD, as shown in Fig. 7, to ensure that the requirements of the system are being met.

In the PDCA cycle, "Plan" refers to the development of standard work by collectively agreeing on the FRs of the manufacturing system design. Standard work also incorporates the proposal of PSs for achieving the associated FRs, along with measures of success defined for both the FRs and PSs. The standard work document associated with each station/department should be disseminated throughout the entire system with visual cues for easy reference.

"Do" refers to the implementation of the planned standard work in the enterprise. All of the stakeholders and employees are trained on the standard work documents to ensure everyone, even across different shifts, perform the work in the same manner. "Check" means to compare the physical outcomes of the implemented standard work against the defined measures of FRs and PSs. If the system outcome is in accordance with the measures defined for the FRs and PSs, then the proposed plan is accepted. Otherwise, an action needs to be taken to either change the PSs or/and in some cases even the FRs which leads to another iteration of the cycle for continuous improvement. The PS is changed if the FR is not achieved. However, the FR is changed if it is not correctly derived from a customer need, or in an event where the customer need changes itself [25].

In either of the two action scenarios described in PDCA cycle, training has to be provided based on the "updated" standard work to sustain the path of improvement for further iterations.

The analogy of baking a cake used earlier showed the importance of standard work, which is the basis for continuous improvement. Now if the FR for the chef is to bake a light and fluffy cake, the chef can add an extra ingredient (an egg etc.) to the cake (Plan), expecting an even softer cake while aiming for continuous improvement to exceed the customer satisfaction level. Once the cake is baked (Do), the chef would assess the cake against the order details provided by the customer (Check). If the cake does not turn out to be light and fluffy, the type or amount of ingredient needs to be changed (Act-Change PS). However, if the cake does turn out to be light and fluffy and is presented to the customer but the customer describes a different need other than a light and fluffy cake, that means the FR derived from the customer need(s) was wrong, and the recipe needs to be changed to the updated FR (Act-Change FR).

6 Re-design of a Manufacturing System Based on the MSDD Evaluation and Simulation

The innovation that CSD brings is the integration of understanding FRs and the leadership that is necessary for a team to collectively agree on and implement PSs. Therefore, CSD serves as both an approach for change leadership and a system design using AD.

MSDD can be used to evaluate/compare many different manufacturing system designs [38]. The Heating-Ventilation-Air Conditioning (HVAC) small bus manufacturing system design at Mobile Climate Control (MCC), Goshen, IN. was chosen for evaluation on the basis of the MSDD, as shown in Fig. 8, highlights the opportunities for improvement in the system.

Based on the improvement opportunities dictated by the MSDD evaluation, MCC created a team which included the leadership, management, and the shop floor production operator. This versatile team led to different system viewpoints that collectively agreed on focusing to achieve the FR2: "Produce to customer-consumed quantity" and FR3: "Produce customer-consumed mix" out of the seven teaching FRs. Also, the company agreed on the importance of achieving FR5 that is about achieving FR1 through FR4 in spite of any variation (see Fig. 3). This collective understanding of the manufacturing system FRs led the team to develop a design decomposition focused on the pull system to support production to takt time, which would be effective for their company in order to meet the customer need of "on-time delivery of the demanded products." The analysis led to the top-level re-design FR-PS pair for the small bus: FR1: "Produce what is needed to ship today" PS1: "HVAC Small Bus Production System re-design". The re-design effort led to three major sub FR-PS pairs. The areas of re-design and the chosen high-level solution along with sub FR-PS pairs are highlighted in the system design map of the HVAC small bus manufacturing system shown in Fig. 9.

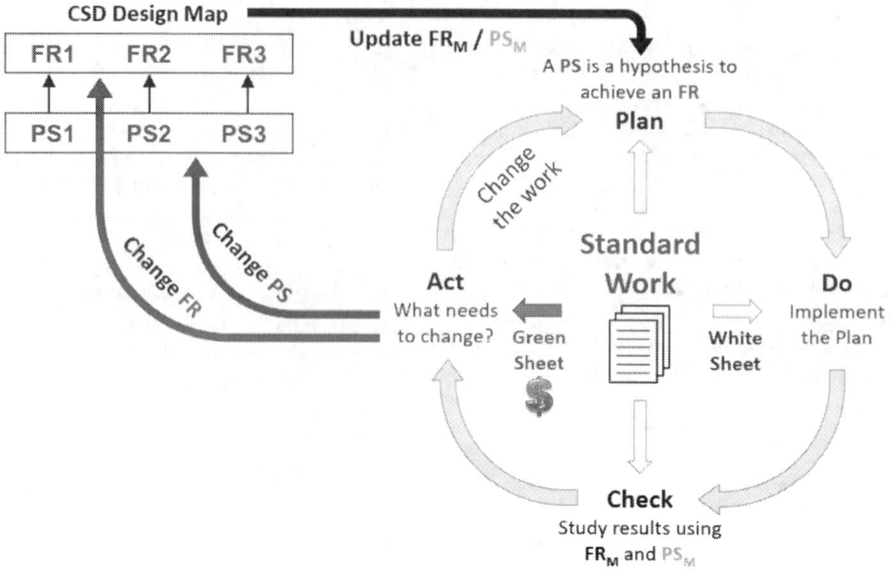

Figure 7. PDCA Cycle [19, 25]

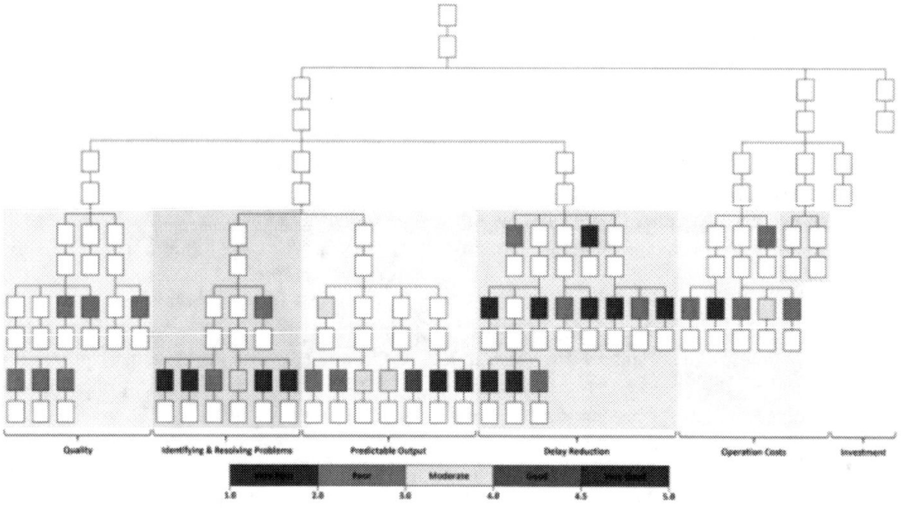

Figure 8. Analysis of Current System Design based on MSDD Evaluation

6.1 Single-Piece Flow

Collective agreement of team members upon deriving FRs from customer needs and choosing PSs for achieving those FRs was developed through physical simulation (Lego blocks) as shown in Fig. 10. The team collectively chose the PS: "Single-piece flow of production" for achieving the FR: "Reduce production delays" and simulated the production flow several times to balance the production lines to takt time of 6 mins 40 secs based on their average customer demand. The simulation also indicated that the single-piece flow of production was partially coupled with FR2 and FR3 of the decomposition in Fig. 9. The parameters chosen for the simulation are shown in Fig. 11

6.2 Lean-linked Cell System Design

In the past, there were several off-line stations called preparation units and still, the production lines could not produce to takt time because of system delays. The operators would work long hours to deal with increased production volume. Manufacturing cells were developed that integrated these off-line operations. Next, the lean linked cell system was designed by connecting the supplied parts,

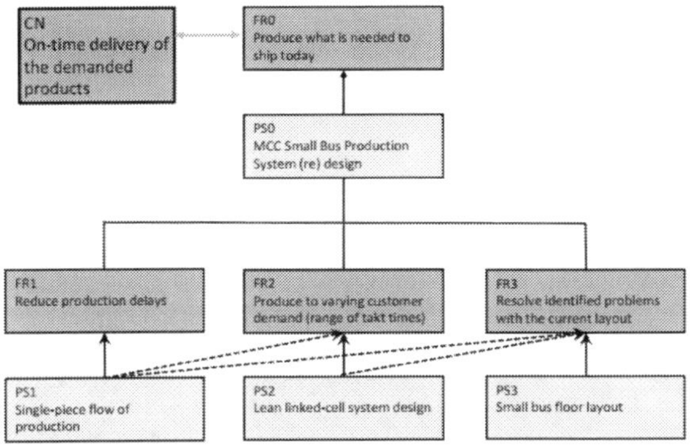

Figure 9. HVAC Manufacturing System Redesign on the Basis of MSDD Evaluation

Figure 10. Collective Agreement of the Desired FR-PS pairs Using Physical Simulation (Figure used with permission from Mobile Climate Control)

assembly, and shipping with pull production information to achieve the FRs mentioned in the decomposition in the Fig. 12.

Standard work was designed for all the stations by balancing the operations to address changes in takt time. An increase/decrease in takt time was dealt with by re-arranging work tasks among the stations and by adding/removing a station to sustain the line balancing to takt time. Time studies were performed to balance the cycle time of each station (CT_i) of the production lines to takt time as defined by Eq. 3 [38, 39].

$$CT_1 \approx CT_2 \approx \ldots \approx CT_n \leq Takt\ Time \quad (3)$$

Ergonomic station design was developed in order to reduce the cycle time of the stations by eliminating the unnecessary motions of turning back and forth for the parts at 180°. Besides, the potential for musculoskeletal disorders that used to result from picking the heavy parts off the floor were minimized.

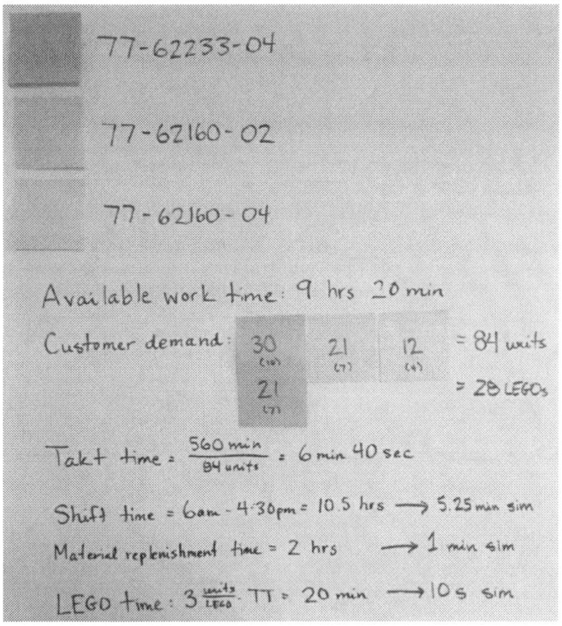

Figure 11. Simulation Parameters

For achieving the FR22: "Build any model at any time," the material inflow and outflow of smaller parts were located from the front to the station with an angle of inclination and declination of 15° respectively. This approach of station re-design also helped the replenishment personnel to easily identify which bin is empty and which one is needed to be replaced. The pallets (larger parts) availability was assured at the right side of the station, as shown in Fig. 13.

The number of racks designed was according to the number of containers needed to hold all the material types and the number of rows in the flow-rack was designed on the basis of SWIP quantity. The height (90") of the flow rack and the length (30") of the working table was designed ergonomically to provide an easy access for the operator to the flow racks. Besides, the working-table height (35") was also designed according to the comfort level of the operator.

Standard Work In Process (SWIP) quantity for each part type at each station was ensured so that the production runs smoothly and all the parts are available at all times as opposed to the "zero inventory system." The calculation for SWIP quantity shown in Eq.s 4, 5, and 6. Let suppose,

TT = Takt time

np = parts needed per assembled unit (number/unit)

nc = container size (number/container)

td = Time to detect (minutes)

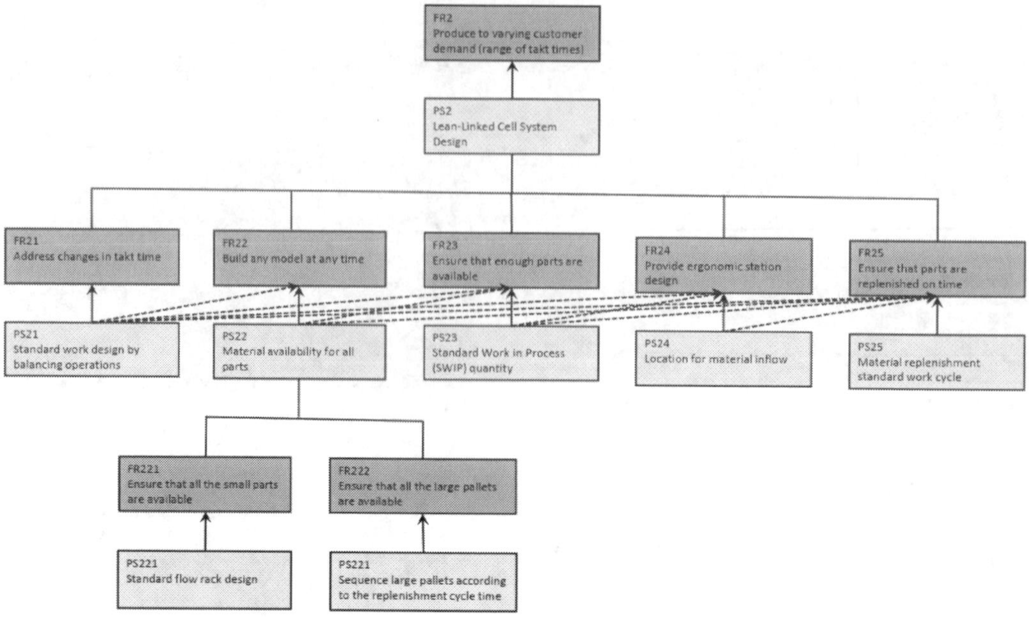

Figure 12. Lean-Linked Cell System Design Decomposition

tr = Time to replenish (minutes)

ORT = Operator Replenishment Time (minutes)

F = Float needed/Emergency Work in Process (EWIP) (or uplift) needed (15 percent).

Where,

$$td = tr \tag{4}$$

$$ORT = td + tr \tag{5}$$

Now, the formula developed for SWIP quantity is:

$$SWIP = np * (ORT)/TT * (1 + F) \tag{6}$$

The float percentage in the SWIP quantity is kept high in the beginning but is lowered down with improvement in the system predictability. This reduction of SWIP quantity is analogous to the reduction of medicine intake with health recovery.

A standard work cycle for the material replenishment was developed to ensure that parts are replenished on time to the operators, according to which the replenishment cycle time for smaller parts was set to two hours and for larger parts/pallets was set to one hour. The formula for the number of containers (nc) to be replenished after each standard work cycle is shown in Eq. 7:

$$\text{Number of containers} = ((SWIP + F)/nc) + 1 \tag{7}$$

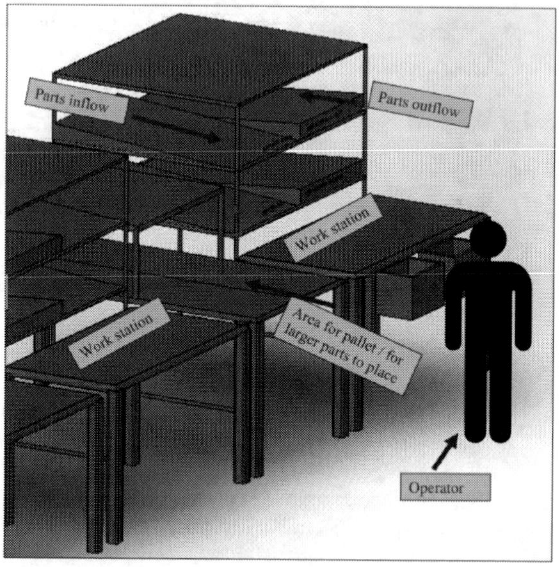

Figure 13. Ergonomic Station Design

6.3 Revised Floor Layout

The lean-linked cell system design led the team to agree on re-designing the line to ensure that enough space was available for production and assembly. The team came up with the idea of re-designing the lines in a way that operators would have to work inside the lines while the replenishment of the material would be done from backside/outside of the lines as shown in Fig. 14. The team had incorporated the replenishment personnel and the working operators for collective agreement on the line re-design so that the operators would help implement the change rather than resist the change. This idea was brought up specifically from the replenishment personnel for the replenishment personnel knew the types of interference problems with the working operators that both of them used to encounter in the current system. Re-designing the lines resulted in saving the space of **2100 square feet** as an additional benefit to meeting the customer needs of quantity and mix of products. This saved space resulted in developing the designated aisles for material supply and finished goods, thereby eliminating the earlier issue of blocking the racks in the raw material warehouse with finished products to be shipped. Only finished product inventory meant to be shipped today would be stored in the dedicated lanes.

The planned system helped the plant in meeting the customer needs. The evaluation result at the end of the project depicted significant improvement indicated by the highlighted areas, as shown in Fig. 15.

7 Conclusion

Becoming lean means the system is intending to enact a system-wide change. That's why the CSD approach begins with the collective agreement of senior leadership to make a conscious decision to change (become lean). To enact change, there are several TPS tools available that can help assist a system to become lean. However, in order to become lean and sustain the long-term business sustainability, the system must address these three concerns: (1) Why should a tool(s) be implemented/used? (2) What sequence of implementing the tools ought to be followed? and (3) How to ensure customer needs are satisfied in a sustainable manner? The proposed approach, CSD, addresses the first concern by clarifying the intent behind using a tool(s) through its well-defined language that begins by understanding the internal and external customer needs prior to implementing a tool. The thinking layer of CSD (expressed as MSDD in this paper) deals with the FR-PS pair(s) for achieving customer needs with an understanding of the implementation sequence. The MSDD covers the customer needs by maximizing the quality of the product followed by minimizing the non-value added activities (resulting in reducing the mean time of the product in the system) and minimizing the long-term investment, which provides an implementation sequence for a system to result in becoming lean. The concern of the sustainability of a system design resulting in achieving customer needs is addressed by the work/actions layer of the CSD flame model. i.e., the employment of the PDCA cycle for continuous improvement with a consistent modification of the defined standard work in response to each improvement in the system design.

MCC system design was developed through a collective agreement process of all the people in the industry (leadership, management, operators) rather than just the leadership/consultants making the choices for change. This approach led to an easy replication of the small bus production system design to the rest of the facility. The collective agreement process also led the operators to assist in applying the change rather than resisting the change for their views were respected and valued during the system re-design development, thus resulting in sustainable systems.

8 Acknowledgment

A sincere thank you to the Mobile Climate Control team for working with the Center of Excellence in Systems Engineering at Purdue Fort Wayne, to apply the Collective System Design approach to design their manufacturing system to meet the customer needs. Also, a thank you is owed to Jason Barnes who is the Associate Director of the Center of Excellence in Systems Engineering at Purdue Fort Wayne. He assisted with simulation and mathematical analysis.

References

[1] M. Graban, *The Term "Lean Production" is 25 Years Old - Some Thoughts on the Original John Krafcik Article* (2013), www.leanblog.org

[2] P.M. Gibbons, S.C. Burgess, International Journal of Lean Six Sigma **1**, 134 (2010)

[3] M. Imai, *Kaizen: The Key To Japan's Competitive Success*, 1st edn. (McGraw-Hill Education, New York, 1986), ISBN 978-0-07-554332-9

[4] J. Langstrand, The TQM Journal **21** (2009)

[5] T. Ohno, *Toyota Production System; Beyond Large Scale Production* (Productivity Press Portland, 1988)

[6] R.W. Hall, *Zero Inventories* (Dow Jones - Irwin, Homewood, IL, 1983), ISBN 978-0-87094-461-1

[7] D. Cochran, J. Swartz, *Collective System Design of St. Francis Hospital ER* (2015)

[8] J.P. Womack, D.T. Jones, D. Roos, *The Machine That Changed the World* (Free Press, 1990), ISBN 978-0-7432-9979-4

[9] S. Mostafa, J. Dumrak, H. Soltan, Production & Manufacturing Research **1**, 44 (2013)

[10] Sweta, IPEDR **75.26**, 127 (2014)

[11] G. Dulhai, Management & Marketing **3** (2008)

[12] P. Arunagiri, A. Gnanavelbabu, Procedia Engineering **97**, 2072 (2014)

[13] D. Cochran, M. Kawada, *Education Approach in Japan for Management and Engineering of Systems* (San Antonio, 2012)

[14] D.S. Cochran, S. Hendricks, J. Barnes, Z. Bi, Journal of Manufacturing Science and Engineering **138**, 101006 (2016)

[15] D.S. Cochran, in *Lean Accounting* (Wiley-Blackwell, 2015), pp. 263–297, ISBN 978-1-119-19680-8

[16] J. Womack, *"Keynote Presentation"* (2011)

[17] D.S. Cochran, *Systems Approach to Sustain Lean Organizations* (Cobo Hall, Detroit, MI, 2007)

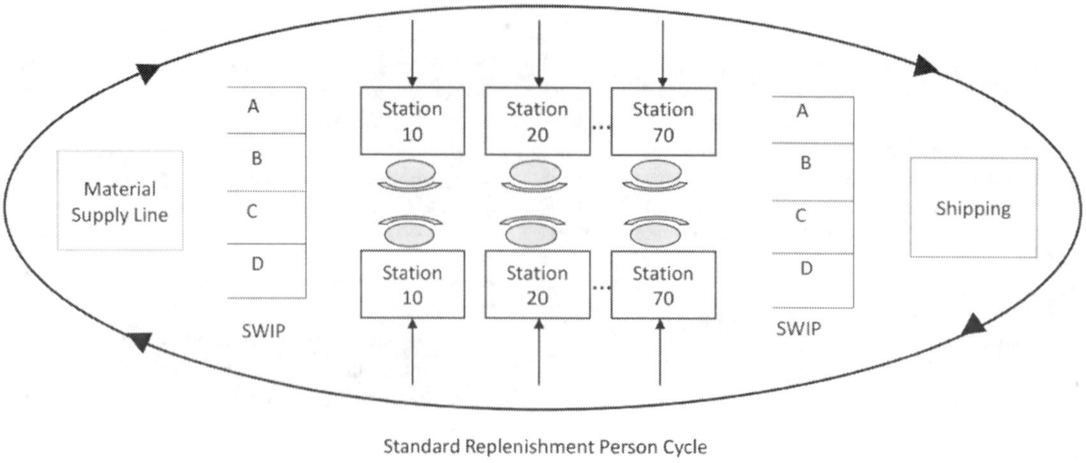

Figure 14. Re-designed Line Layout Achieved Through Collective Agreement

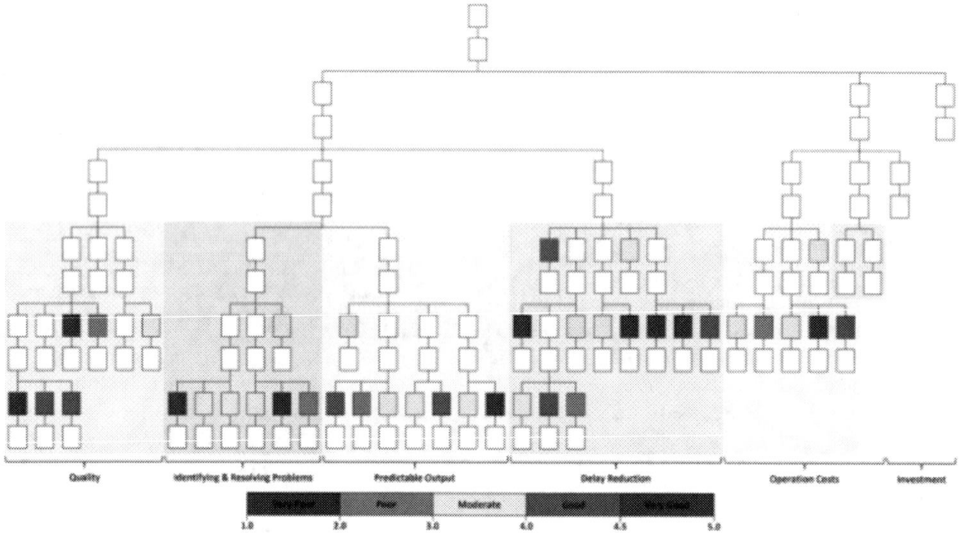

Figure 15. Analysis of Planned System Design based on MSDD Evaluation

[18] *Why lean doesn't work?* (Industrial Solution Inc., 2014), p. 62

[19] D.W. Deming, *Out of the Crises*, 1st edn. (The MIT Press, 2000), ISBN 0-262-54115-7

[20] J. Salatin, *You Can Farm*, 1st edn. (Polyface, 1998)

[21] D. Cochran, J. Barnes, *Collective System Design (CSD) in sustaining the lean enterprise* (2013)

[22] *Taiichi Ohno Quotes Help Drive Lean Culture and Acceptance* (2008), http://matthrivnak.com

[23] Commissioner, *Consumer Updates - Avoiding Drug Interactions*, https://www.fda.gov/ForConsumers/ConsumerUpdates/ucm096386.htm

[24] V.E. Emiel, P. Pollet, *Did Toyota fool the lean community for decades?* (2014), https://www.slideshare.net/EmielVanEst/did-toyota-fool-the-lean-community-for-decades/79-Emiel_van_EstWhere_there_is

[25] D.S. Cochran, R. Sereno, W. Aldrich, p. 12 (2014)

[26] D.S. Cochran, *System design; lean manufacturing; tps* (2007), http://systemdesignllc.com/about.html

[27] S. Nam-pyo, *Complexity: Theory and Applications* (Oxford University Press, 2005), ISBN Oxford University Press

[28] D.S. Cochran, J.J. Smith, Procedia Manufacturing **26**, 1369 (2018)

[29] A. Spencer, D. Cochran, Procedia CIRP **34**, 143 (2015)

[30] J. Linck, D. Cochran, *The Importance of Takt Time in Manufacturing System Design* (1999)

[31] J. Womack, J. Shook, *Gemba Walks*, expanded 2nd edition edn. (Lean Enterprises Inst Inc, 2013), ISBN 978-1-934109-38-0

[32] D. Cochran, Annual Conference & Exposition pp. 15.287.1–15.287.12 (2010)

[33] D.S. Cochran, Y.S. Kim, J. Kim, *The Impact of Performance Measurement on Manufacturing system design* (Cambridge, MA, 2000), pp. 1–8

[34] D.S. Cochran, J.F. Arinez, J.W. Duda, J. Linck, Journal of Manufacturing Systems **20**, 371 (2001)

[35] A. Simboli, R. Taddeo, A. Morgante (2014)

[36] W.J. Hopp, M.L. Spearman, *Factory Physics: Foundations of Manufacturing Management*, first edition edition edn. (Richard D Irwin, Chicago, 1995), ISBN 978-0-256-15464-1

[37] N.K. Shimbun, H. Hirano, *Poka-Yoke: Improving Product Quality by Preventing Defects* (Productivity Press Portland, 1988), ISBN 0-915299-31-3

[38] D. Cochran, J. Foley, B. Zhuming, pp. 870–890 (2016)

[39] D.S. Cochran, D.C. Dobbs, Journal of Manufacturing Systems **20**, 390 (2001)

Development of a Design Procedure for Class E Amplifiers

Mattison S. Siri[1,*] and *David S.* Cochran[1]

[1] *Center of Excellence in Systems Engineering, Purdue University Fort Wayne, Fort Wayne, IN, 46835, United States*

Abstract. Here, the step-by-step design procedure for a Class E amplifier is presented. An existing Class E amplifier system is described using a systems architecture approach. The design decomposition for the case study is written so that Physical Solutions (PSs; equivalent to Design Parameters) are in terms of component parameters (such as frequency or capacitance). Coupling issues are found to arise given constraints on transistor use. The design decomposition is altered to reflect the case where an amplifier is required to power a specific load. A discussion of transistor failure enables a design procedure to be developed by observing path-dependent coupling. The design procedure is tested through the design of a real amplifier. The designed amplifier is built and its performance measured.

1 Introduction

This paper presents the logic of the development of a step-by-step procedure for the design of Class E power amplifiers.

1.1 Motivation

When designing a radio frequency (RF) power amplifier, it is difficult to choose an appropriate transistor to meet the needs of a given application. However, once a transistor is chosen, one of many approaches to computing component values can be used [1–3].

1.2 Systems Design Use

A systems approach is used to clarify the role of the designer, to determine how to choose a transistor based on transistor failure modes, and to specify the requirements for a set of design equations to compute component values. Axiomatic Design (AD) is used identify the logical difficulties in transistor choice by discussing the mathematical consequences of design coupling and to determine an appropriate step-by-step procedure for designing Class E amplifiers.

In this paper, the AD conventions of [4, 5] are used. Conventions of note include:

- A statement of how a system, subsystem, or component is to function is a Functional Requirement (FR).
- A feature of a design which addresses an FR is a Physical Solution[1] (PS).
- Each PS satisfies an FR while observing the relevant design constraints.

*e-mail: mattisonsiri@gmail.com

[1] traditionally referred to as a "Design Parameter" [4].

2 Describe/Understand What Exists

To understand the design of Class E amplifiers, an existing case is described: the PRF-1150 RF generator module. The PRF-1150 is a 1 kW, 13.56 MHz RF source developed in 2002 by Directed Energy, Inc. (DEI) [6].

2.1 Describing the PRF-1150

2.1.1 Description Methodology

The understanding of a *System of Interest*[2] (SOI) can be built in several ways:

- by identifying and describing the systems which interact with the SOI (*the surroundings*)
- by describing the relationships among the systems in the surroundings
- by decomposing the SOI into subsystems and describing the relationships among the subsystems
- by describing any of the above from additional viewpoints

For the purposes of describing an existing system employing a Class E amplifier, the SOI is the PRF-1150 module.

2.1.2 Identifying Surroundings

In the PRF-1150 documentation, DEI states [6],

> "DEI has developed an RF module to demonstrate the capabilities of our DEIC420 RF MOSFET gate driver IC and DE275-102N06X2A 1000V 6A RF MOSFET [Metal Oxide Semiconductor Field Effect Transistor] at ISM [Industrial, Scientific, and Medical] frequencies."

[2] Adapted from IEEE 42010, a systems architecture standard [7].

Here, DEI is viewed as the client. The author of [1] served as the designer of the Class E amplifier used in the PRF-1150 module. The PRF-1150 documentation also includes test data taken by an operator or technician. The designer and operator may well have been the same person, but each is treated as a distinct system in the surroundings.

The client, the designer, and the operator not only interact with the SOI, but interact with each other as well. For example, the designer understands the needs of the client and how the operator is going to use the system. Figure 1 shows the relationships between personnel (surrounding systems) and the SOI.

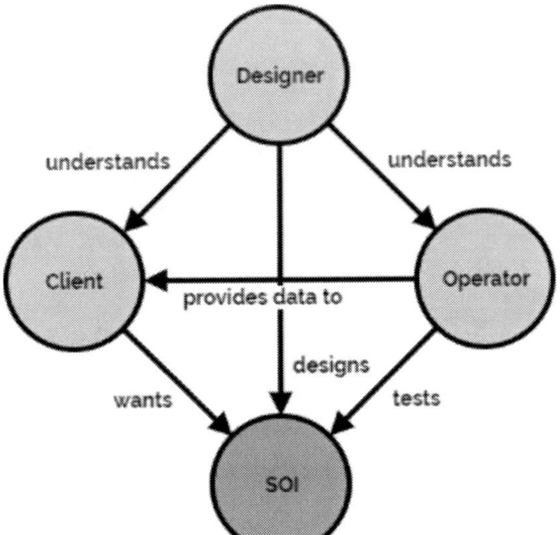

Figure 1. High level relationship diagram for the PRF-1150 and its surroundings. *Understanding relationships in the surroundings of the SOI improves the understanding of the SOI itself.*

2.1.3 Client and SOI

The quote in 2.1.2 describes the client's view of the SOI and can be translated into AD Language:
FR1: Demonstrate the capabilities of the chosen chipset.
PS1: PRF-1150 Module
Constraints:

- $C1a$: The application should be an RF application.
- $C1b$: The operating frequency (f) should be an ISM frequency.
- $C1c$: Use the chosen chipset (MOSFET: DE275-102N06X2A, Gate Driver: DEIC420).

2.1.4 Operator and SOI

A use case can clarify the relationship between the SOI and the operator. Figure 2 shows how the operator and SOI interact with many other systems when the PRF-1150 is being tested. The use case is developed from descriptions in [6].

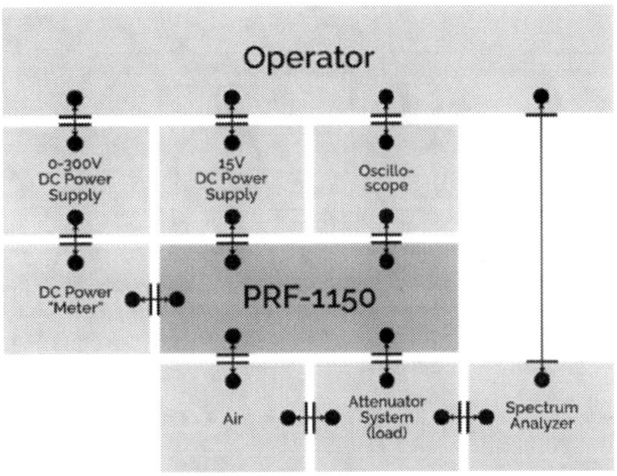

Figure 2. Relationship diagram for the use of the SOI by the Operator. *The operator operates power supplies and takes measurements of the PRF-1150. This is a more specific way to state the original relationship between the SOI and the Operator.*

The operator controls the SOI by turning on or off power supplies and by adjusting the output voltage of the 0-300 V DC source. The 0-300 V DC source provides electrical power to the SOI as measured by the DC power meter. Figure 3 depicts the use case from a physics viewpoint by detailing the energy transfer into and out of the SOI.

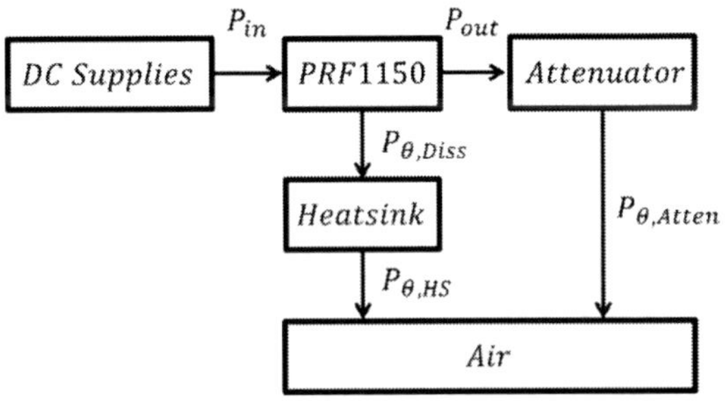

Figure 3. Power distribution diagram of the use case of Figure 5. *Note: these powers are average powers. Also note: the heat sink is included in the PRF-1150 system, but is intentionally called out here to introduce the thermal power dissipated by the SOI.*

Where

- P_{in} = DC power supplied to SOI
- P_{out} = RF output power of SOI
- $P_{\theta,Diss}$ = thermal power dissipated by SOI
- $P_{\theta,HS}$ = thermal power dissipated by the heat sink = $P_{\theta,Diss}$
- $P_{\theta,Atten}$ = thermal power dissipated by attenuator = P_{out}

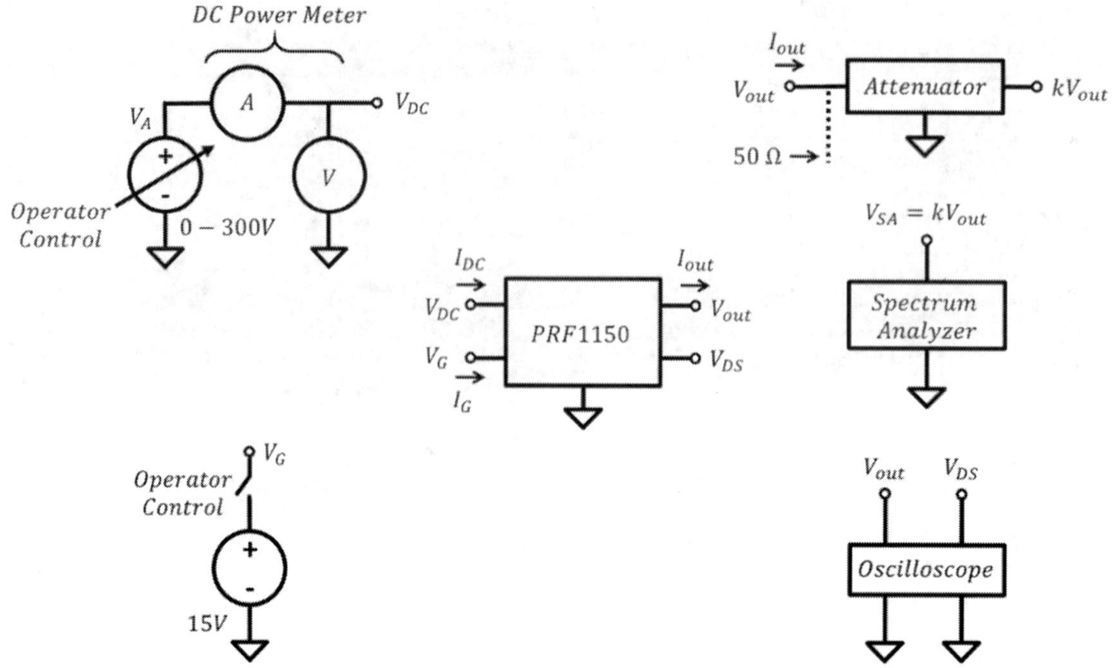

Figure 4. Electrical representation of relationships among surrounding subsystems and SOI.

Figure 4 furthers the energy transfer description of Figure 3 by calling out the voltages and currents among interactors.[3] The voltages and currents are:

- $V_A = V_{DC}$ = main DC supply voltage to the SOI (0 V to 300 V)
- I_{DC} = current supplied to the PRF-1150 via the main DC power supply
- $V_G = 15V$ = secondary DC supply voltage to the SOI
- I_G = current supplied to the PRF-1150 via the secondary DC power supply
- V_{out} = RF output voltage of SOI
- I_{out} = RF output current of the SOI
- $V_{SA} = kV_{out}$ = attenuated V_{out} as measured by the spectrum analyzer
- V_{DS} = an internal voltage of the SOI measured externally[4]

2.1.5 Designer, SOI, and SOI Subsystems

To effectively design the SOI, the designer needs to understand the inner workings of the SOI as well as its surroundings. The schematics and descriptions in [6] are used to construct Figure 5 - a view of the PRF-1150 subsystems.

The signal source output is amplified by the gate driver to provide a switching signal (V_{GS}) for the Class E amplifier. A heat sink aids in the dissipation of thermal power (as in Figure 3). The output impedance of the amplifier is matched to a load via the matching network.

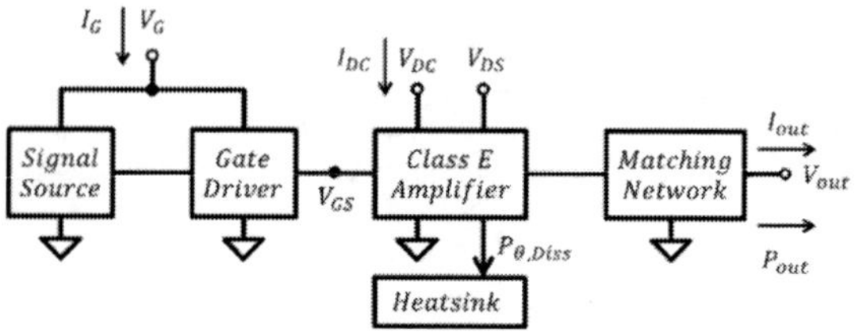

Figure 5. The main electrical subsystems internal to the PRF-1150

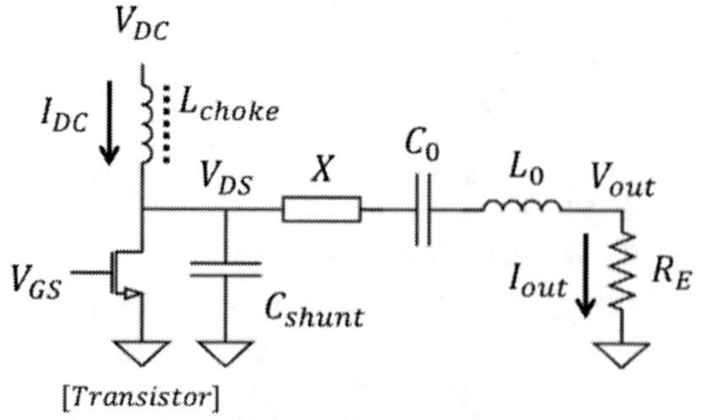

Figure 6. Conventional Class E Circuit

[3]The accuracy of the description is limited by assuming that the measurement currents are negligible from the view of the SOI.
[4]This voltage is described more specifically in 2.1.5

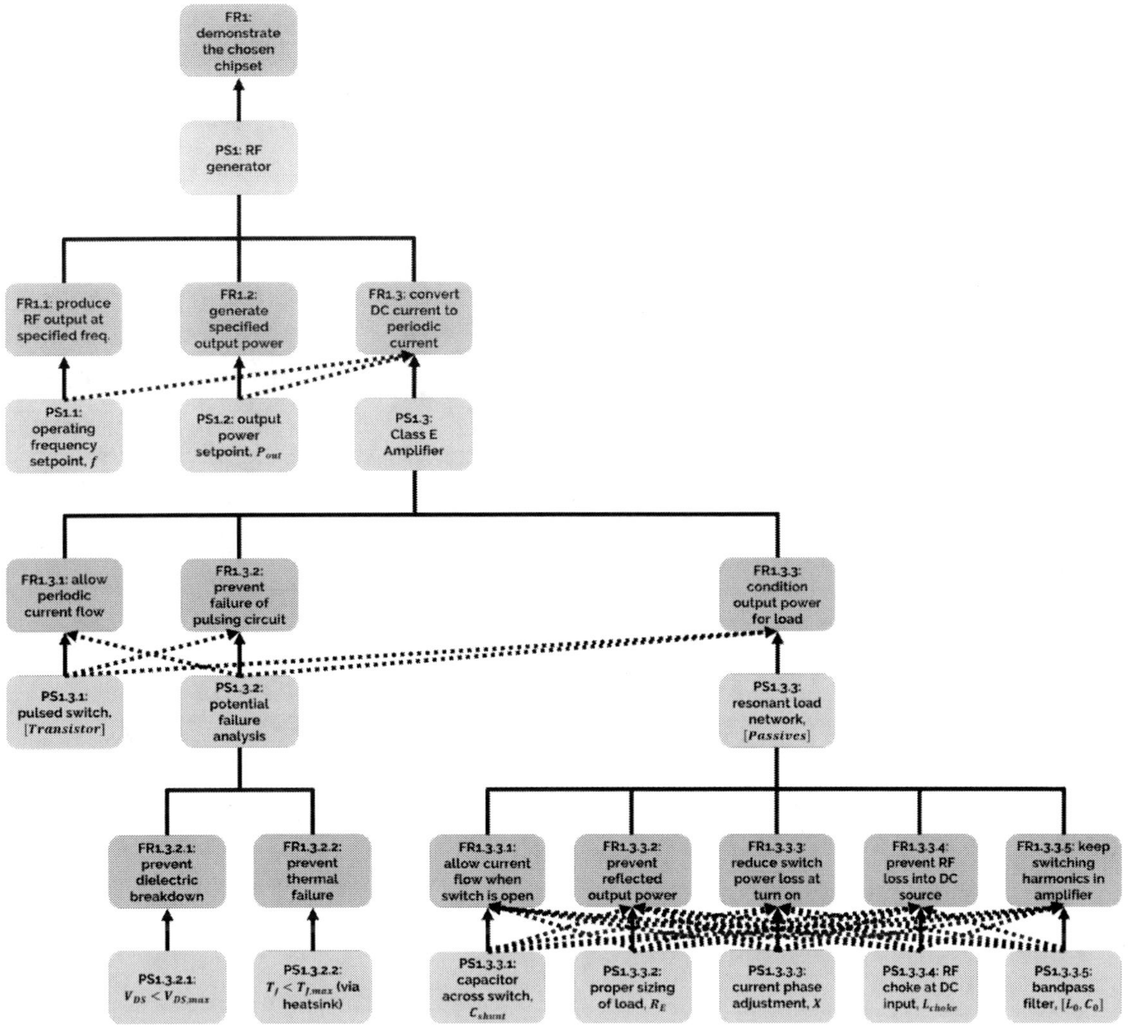

Figure 7. Design Decomposition of a Class E amplifier

Class E Amplifier Subsystem

The Class E arrangement used in the PRF-1150 is as the original arrangement presented by N. Sokal and A. Sokal in 1975 [8]. Figure 6 shows the general Class E amplifier schematic.
Here,

- V_{GS} = the RF input signal to the Class E amplifier
- $[Transistor]$ = a switch controlled by the input signal (typically a MOSFET)[5]
- V_{DS} = voltage across the switch
- L_{choke} = inductance of the RF choke (only allows DC current to flow)
- C_{shunt} = capacitance across switch to allow RF current to flow when switch is open

[5]A note about notation: $[item]$ = the set of constants and variables specific to *item*. For a car, $[car] = [make, model, year, color, ...]$.

- $[C_0, L_0]$ = bandpass filter
- R_E = load resistance required for Class E operation
- X = extra reactance in series with the Class E load network R_E, L_0, C_0

2.2 Design Decomposition

Using [1, 3, 9], the Class E portion of the SOI can be described with a design decomposition (Figure 7). The coupling[6] shown here is determined via the equation sets in [1, 3, 9, 10] and by consideration of potential failure modes (discussed in 3.0.1).

[6]AD, the unintentional relationships (coupling) between PSs and FRs is shown with dashed arrows [5]. Coupling means that the PS of one FR affects the accomplishment of another FR. In some cases, the coupling between two FR-PS sets is only path-dependent (partial). For example, if two FRs (FR_A and FR_B) are accomplished by two PSs (PS_A and PS_B respectively) and PS_A affects the accomplishment of FR_B, then by implementing PS_A before PS_B a recursion can be avoided.

2.2.1 Passive Component Coupling

In the field of electronics, the traditional Class E amplifier is well understood at a component level [1–3, 8, 9]. Since the introduction of the Class E amplifier, papers have been written which relate the operation of the Class E amplifier (output power, frequency, harmonic content) to the values of the passive circuit elements [1–3]. While the specific relationships vary from paper to paper, overall, the variables related are the same. It is possible that more sets of passive component equations will be developed in the future. Therefore, these equations are expressed in a general form (equation 1).

$$[Passives] = E_{passives}([Op], [Transistor], V_{DC}) \qquad (1)$$

Where,

- $[Passives] = [X, L_0, C_0, L_{choke}, C_{shunt}, R_E]$ = set of passive component values constituting the resonant load network
- $[Op] = [P_{out}, f]$ = set of operating parameters (output power and frequency)
- $[Transistor]$ = set of relevant characteristics of the chosen transistor
- $E_{passives}$ = set of Class E equations to compute $[Passives]$

As a given set of operating conditions, $[Op]$, results in a single point in the space of $[Passives]$ which will behave as a Class E amplifier [1–3, 8, 9], the complete coupling in the resonant load network branch of the design decomposition ($PS\,1.3.3$) will not be an optimization problem if the path-dependency of the design is followed. Instead, it is a single PS (a complete set of parameters) to a single FR ($FR1.3.3$).

2.2.2 Transistor-First Design

For the Class E amplifier in the PRF-1150, the designer was constrained to a particular choice of transistor ($C1c$). That is, $PS\,1.3.1$ was implemented first - despite path-dependent coupling suggesting otherwise ($PS\,1.1$ and $PS\,1.2$ before $PS\,1.3$). Figure 8 shows the optimization problem caused by the partial implementation of $PS\,1.3$ before $PS\,1.1$ and $PS\,1.2$. By choosing an operating frequency at this point (13.56 MHz in the case of the PRF-1150), the number of free variables is reduced to one, P_{out}. As $FR1$ is to demonstrate the capabilities of the chipset, maximizing P_{out} would serve this FR well. Maximizing is indeed an optimization problem.

Transistor-First Design Procedure

Currently, the design decomposition and the PRF-1150 description suggest the following procedure:

1. **Choose a transistor**
2. **Choose an operating frequency**
3. **Choose a set of passive equations, $E_{passives}$**

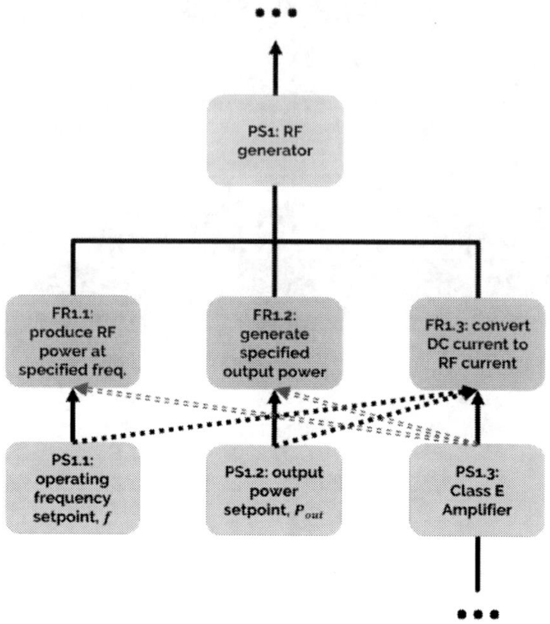

Figure 8. Optimization problem caused by choosing a transistor first. *The red lines show the forced direction of the relationship between PSs and FRs.*

4. **Maximize the output power by manipulating $[Passives]$.**[7]

3 Adapt/Improve What Exists

When an amplifier is needed to power a particular load, there is no constraint on transistor use. Instead, the given load requires a specific amount of RF power at a specific frequency - a specific set of operating parameters, [Op]. For example, the authors have determined that a particular plasma experiment requires at least 1 kW of RF power at a frequency of 13.56 MHz. There are no restrictions on transistor use other than keeping costs low. The authors have access to a heat sink with a thermal resistance of 0.1 $°C/W$.

3.0.1 Transistor Failure

To design a Class E amplifier for a given $[Op]$, the maximum power required by the load should coincide with the maximum power output power of the amplifier. To find the maximum output power of the amplifier, it is important to understand what is meant by "maximum"

[7]Choosing the transistor first no longer allows a single point in $[Passives]$ to be computed easily (as per Eq 1). Instead, $E_{passives}$ is used to maximize P_{out} with respect to $[Passives]$.

and what happens when the maximum output power is *exceeded*. Passive components such as inductors and capacitors are of low enough cost that these typically will not be what limit the output power. The transistor, often the most expensive component, is the bottleneck. At an output power just above the maximum, the transistor will fail. A transistor can fail in two ways (which are relevant): dielectric breakdown of the junction or excessive temperature [11].[8] Both of these result in irreparable physical and chemical change to junction itself.

Dielectric Failure

Avoiding dielectric breakdown ($FR1.3.2.1$) is straightforward. A transistor's datasheet [12, 13] provides a maximum voltage rating between the drain and source of the device ($V_{DS,max}$). As the voltage across the device is proportional to the electric field in the junction, exceeding $V_{DS,max}$ guarantees dielectric breakdown. In operation, maintaining $V_{DS} < V_{DS,max}$ at all times (PS 1.3.2.1) will prevent dielectric failure. As the operation of the amplifier is determined by component choice, $E_{passives}$ must consider the maximum drain-source voltage experienced by the transistor in terms of the rest of the Class E parameters.

Thermal Failure

Preventing thermal failure is not straightforward. The junction temperature is determined by how much thermal power the transistor is dissipating (P_{diss}), the ambient temperature, and the total thermal resistance between the junction and the ambient thermal mass (air, water, etc.). To facilitate thermal power dissipation (reduce the total thermal resistance), the transistor is mounted to a heat sink. The thermal resistance between the junction and the heat sink depends on the transistor, the heat sink, and the quality of the mounting. For a given heat sink and ambient temperature, the maximum allowable power dissipation is [11] (equation 4)

$$P_{diss,Max} = \frac{T_{J,Max} - T_{Ambient}}{(R_{\theta,J-HS} + R_{\theta,HS-Ambient})} \quad (4)$$

Where

- $P_{diss,Max}$ = maximum power dissipated by the transistor
- $T_{J,Max}$ = maximum junction temperature of the transistor
- $T_{Ambient}$ = ambient temperature
- $R_{\theta,J-HS}$ = total thermal resistance between the junction and the heat sink
- $R_{\theta,HS-Ambient}$ = thermal resistance between heat sink and the ambient thermal mass

[8]Note: *excessive current* is not a root cause of failure. A transistor's current rating is derived from its maximum junction temperature and by assuming that it is mounted to an ideal heat sink [12].

Maximum Output Power and Dissipated Power

Maximum output power occurs when the thermal power dissipated by the transistor is also at a maximum (as long as $V_{DS} < V_{DS,max}$). The maximum allowed dissipated power depends on transistor parameters, $[Transistor]$, and heat sink parameters, $[HS]$. A larger heat sink allows a smaller transistor to be used. A larger transistor allows a smaller heat sink to be used. These sets of parameters are coupled. Choosing a transistor first, as in [6], still leaves the output power and the heat sink undetermined. Choosing the output power first (by choosing $[Op]$) still leaves the transistor and heat sink undetermined - another optimization problem (with respect to cost).

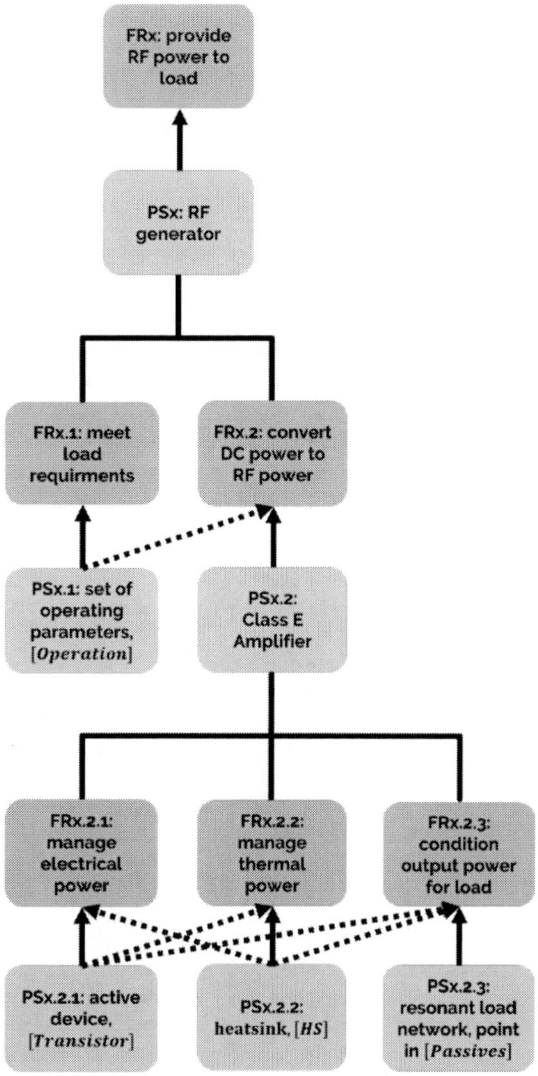

Figure 9. Simplified design decomposition for Application-First Design. *The number x is used to denote that FRx is part of a larger design decomposition*

3.1 Application-First Design

When the application is determined first, $PS\,1.1$ and $PS\,1.2$ can be implemented before $PS\,1.3$. This is consistent with the coupling shown in the design decomposition (Figure 7).

3.1.1 Rearranging the Design Decomposition

Manipulation of the design decomposition will allow further steps to be more obvious. As $FR1.3.1$ and $FR1.3.2$ depend on $[Transistor]$ and $[HS]$, the PSs related to $FR1.3.1$ and $FR1.3.2$ should be the physical components, transistor and heat sink. This requires the rewriting of $FR1.3.1$ and $FR1.3.2$. The rewritten FRs should contain the same information as the original FRs. The resulting design decomposition is shown in Figure 9.

3.1.2 Application-First Design Procedure

Coupling in the updated design decomposition prescribes the following procedure for designing Class E amplifiers.

1. **Identify the RF power and frequency for the application, $[Op]$.**
2. **Choose an appropriate set of design equations.**[9]
3. **Simultaneously choose a transistor and a heat sink.**
4. **Compute the passive component values.**

Step 3 is not practical as it requires an ideal relationship which describes the coupling in the lowest level of the updated design decomposition:

$$([Transistor], [HS]) = F([Op]) \quad (2)$$

Where F is a function which, given a set of operating parameters, outputs all of the needed PSs for the corresponding Class E amplifier. This is not possible, but a tool may be developed to allow it to be accomplished. By using the maximum output power optimization technique in section 3.0.1, the maximum output power, $P_{out,max}$, of a transistor-heat sink combination can be computed for any frequency. The region bounded by $P_{out,max}(f)$ (and the $P_{out,max}$ and f axes) forms the allowed region of $[Op]$ for the chosen transistor and heat sink. If the allowed operating region (Transistor Capability) is computed for every possible combination of transistor and heat sink in a library of transistors and heat sinks, then, given $[Op]$, the transistor-heat sink sets which are capable of meeting the operating setpoints can be found. From the remaining sets of transistors and heat sinks the lowest cost option can be chosen.

[9] As discussed in 3.0.1, the design equations must include considerations for P_{diss} and V_{DS}.

4 Proof of Concept

4.1 Library Development

The authors start with a library of 3 transistors and 1 heat sink to demonstrate the design process. The heatsink is part of an author-built amplifier prototyping kit and the 3 transistor candidates were identified via their application notes:

- Transistor 1: DE275X2-102N06A MOSFET [6]; \$69.26 (Newark, 7 May 2018)
- Transistor 2: IXZ631DF12N100 MOSFET and driver [12]; \$64.09 (Mouser, 7 May 2018)
- Transistor 3: DFR1200 MOSFET and driver [13]; \$145.62 (Mouser, 7 May 2018)

For each of the transistor-heat sink combinations, the operating region is computed (using the Class E equations in [1, 10]) (Figure 10).

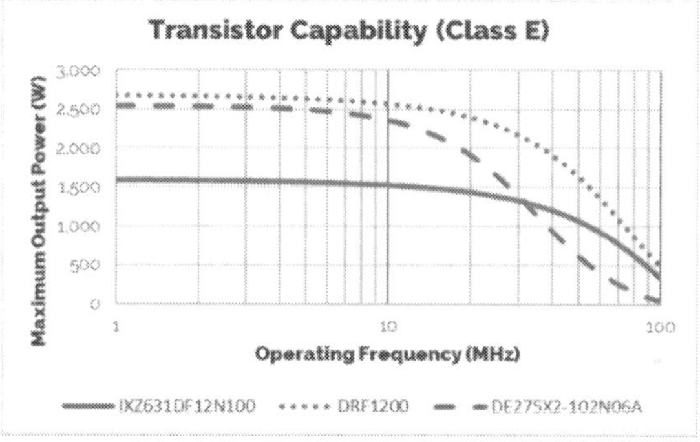

Figure 10. Operation Capability of Transistor-Heat Sink Combinations

4.2 Application-First Design of a Class E Amplifier

1. **Identify the RF power and frequency for the application.**

   $$[Op] = [P_{out}, f] = [1\ kW, 13.56\ MHz]$$

2. **Choose an appropriate set of design equations.**

   The chosen design equations are from [1, 10].

3. **Simultaneously choose a transistor and a heat sink.**

   As all three of the transistor-heat sink combinations in the library are capable of meeting the operating requirements, the combination with the lowest cost and fewest number of consequences (read as "lowest information content") is chosen, Transistor 2 and Heat Sink 1 (the only heat sink in the library).

4. **Compute the passive component values.** Using the chosen design equations, the passive values and supply voltage are computed to be:

- $X = 24.97\ \Omega$
- $L_0 = 57.45\ nH$
- $C_0 = 2.4\ nF$
- $L_{choke} = 20\ \mu H$
- $C_{shunt} = 177\ pF$
- $R_E = 14.93\ \Omega$
- $V_{DC} = 260\ V$

4.3 Implementation

The design was simulated using LTspice and found to meet the given operating requirements. A prototyping kit was used to quickly implement the design. As is standard [6, 14], an L-type matching network was added to the output of the Class E amplifier to match the output impedance (R_E) to 50 Ω. The resulting amplifier is shown in Figure 12.

The amplifier was tested as in the use case of Figure 2. An exception being that the attenuator was replaced by an author-built, 50 Ω test load (called out in Figure 11). The voltage across this load was measured via a 200 MHz, 100:1 oscilloscope probe (BK Precision PR200B) and a 200 MHz oscilloscope (Siglent SDS 1202CNL+). The time-resolved voltage and calibration data taken for the load-probe system (reflection coefficient measured via Rohde & Schwarz ZVA 24) were used to compute the output power of the amplifier with respect to frequency via Matlab. The measurement setup is shown in Figure 11.

Figure 12. The designed amplifier is implemented with the prototyping kit.

4.4 Measurement Data

The maximum output power measured was 866 W (input power: 1163 W). Higher powers than this would exceed the maximum output power of the DC power supply used (48 V to 280 V, 1200 W). Figure 13 shows the efficiency of the amplifier with respect to the output power.

At an output power of 866 W, the spectral content is as shown in Figure 14. The spectrum is normalized with respect to the output power at the fundamental frequency (13.56 MHz). The second harmonic (27.12 MHz) is 19.07 dB lower than the fundamental. In linear units, the ratio between output powers at the second and first harmonics is 0.012.

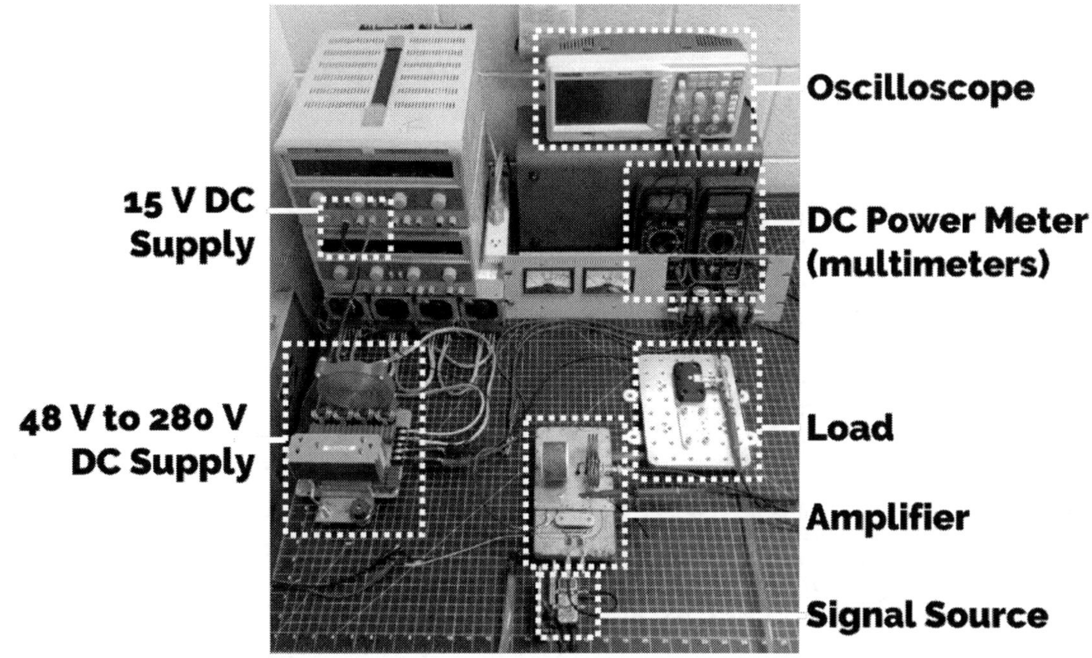

Figure 11. The prototyping kit and its surroundings for charactering the RF output power and DC input power

 https://doi.org/10.1051/matecconf/201822301016

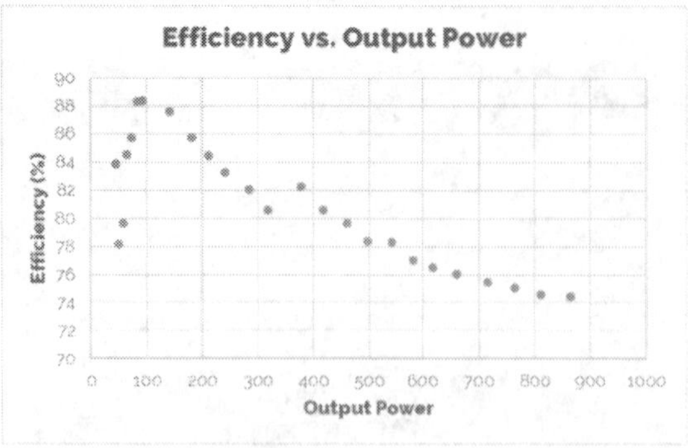

Figure 13. Amplifier Efficiency

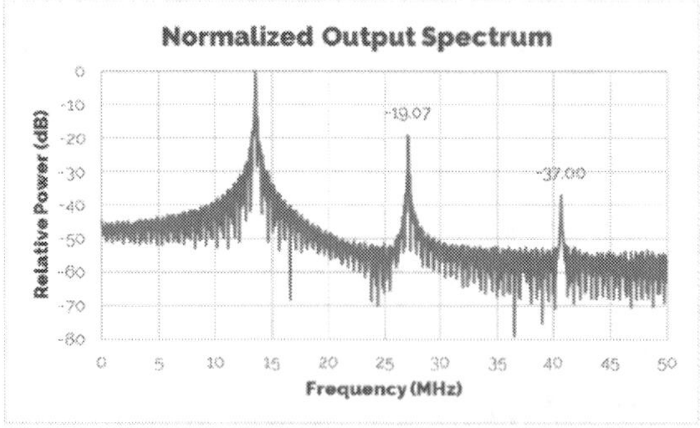

Figure 14. Output spectrum of amplifier up to 3rd harmonic (output power is 866 W)

5 Conclusion

An existing Class E amplifier system was described using a design decomposition. When the design was subjected to the constraint of a client-chosen transistor, coupling issues arose. The resulting optimization of output power was with respect to at least six other PSs. By shifting FR1 to reflect an the Application-First design of a new amplifier and by removing the transistor choice constraint, the remaining optimization problem became manageable by computing the operating range for sets of heat sinks and transistors. An Application-First design procedure was developed and tested using a library of transistor-heat sink pairs.

6 Future Work

6.1 Transistor and Heat Sink Library

The library used in the proof of concept was limited. Future amplifier designs would benefit from a choice among many more options.

6.2 Note about Choosing Specific Components

The design procedure presented here only discusses how to choose passive component values, not specific components. The actual parts can be chosen by way of the second design axiom [4]. The design procedure should be expanded to include the choice of real components.

References

[1] N.O. Sokal, QEX p. 9 (2001)

[2] F.H. Raab, IEEE Transactions Circuits and Sys. **24**, 527 (1977)

[3] M. Acar, A.J. Annema, B. Nauta, IEEE Int. Symp. on Circuits and Systems (2007)

[4] N.P. Suh, *The Priciples of Design* (Oxford University Press, 1990)

[5] D.S. Cochran, *A System Design Language Primer* (IPFW Center of Excellence in Systems Engineering, 2018)

[6] M.W. Vania, *PRF-1150 1KW 13.56 MHz Class E RF Generator Evaluation Module*, Directed Energy, Inc. (2002), Rev. 1, Technical Note

[7] *ISO/IEC/IEEE 42010 Systems and software engineering – Architecture description* (ISO/IEC/IEEE, 2011)

[8] N.O. Sokal, A.D. Sokal, IEEE J. of Solid-State Circuits **10**, 168 (1975)

[9] M. Ozalas, *Keysight EEs of EDA Mar. 2015. How to Design an RF Power Amplifier: Class E*, https://www.youtube.com/watch?v=mpbWQbkl8_g (2018)

[10] F.H. Raab, N.O. Sokal, IEEE J. of Solid-State Circuits **13** (1978)

[11] R.B. Frey, *Determining a Transistor's Maximum RF Output Power Rating* (APT, 2004)

[12] *IXZ631DF12N100 RF Power MOSFET and Driver* ((IXYSRF), 2004), Datasheet

[13] G. Choi, *13.56 MHz, Class E, 1 kW RF Generator using a Microsemi DRF1200 Driver/MOSFET Hybrid*, Microsemi PPG (2008), Application Note

[14] M. Jones, *Application Note IXZ631DF12N100 Class E 27.12 MHz* (IXYSRF, 2017)

MATEC Web of Conferences 223, 01017 (2018) https://doi.org/10.1051/matecconf/201822301017
ICAD 2018

A Student's Axiomatic Design Application Example of Battery Thermal Controller for High Altitude Balloon

Yuchen Wang[1,*], Ang Liu[1]

[1]University of New South Wales, School of Mechanical and Manufacturing Engineering, NSW Kensington 2052, Australia

Abstract. The axiomatic design plays a critical role in transferring FRs into DPs and organising scattered design information. Nowadays, the axiomatic design is commonly applied to student engineering design education. Although it assists design organisation, some procedures can be challenging for invoice students. This paper is written to reflect benefits, challenges and potential mistakes when the axiomatic design is applied by invoice students. The reflection is based on a case study, a student lead battery thermal controller (BTC) on a high-altitude balloon is used as the example. Relevant background about the high-altitude balloon was introduced at first. Previous essential information of customer domain and functional domain was clarified before the axiomatic design. Design parameters(DPs) were generated with Morphological Chart to compose candidate concepts. FR-DP matrix was used to evaluate the independence of functional requirements(FRs). Candidate concepts were then selected by probability density function graphs. The most proper concept then was out of Pugh's Matrix. Through this axiomatic design application, benefits, challenges and potential mistakes were reflected for invoice students. Benefits included convenient errors correction and competent concepts generation. Challenges contain the DPs performance value determination and physical integration of concept. Potential mistakes include generation of inconsistent performance value for bottom-level FRs and invalid DPs.

1 Introduction

As the bridge between functional domain and concept domain, the axiomatic design is commonly used to generate well-organised engineering design concepts and assist decision making. To date, the axiomatic design has been applied in engineering design education in a wide range. Compared to experienced engineers in academic and industrial work, invoice students are relatively lack of mature technical skills, problem-solving experience, and professional engineering habits. Although the axiomatic design has a general sequence, some procedures are still highly flexible, such as candidate DPs generation and concept evaluation preference. To satisfy customer demands, experience, technical skills and resources are essential to assist decision making when dealing with these flexible procedures. As a result, invoice students might find it challenging to apply several procedures properly. Considering this feature, for students' engineering design education of the axiomatic design, educators should think of possible challenges for invoice students. In correspondence to these challenges, special educational strategies should be applied to help students apply the axiomatic design properly.

This paper is written to explore benefits, challenges and potential mistakes of the axiomatic design when applied by primary students. These features are discussed based on a case study, a student lead BTC development project is used as the example. Section 2 will introduce relevant customer review and functional domain results at first. In section 4, independent axiom design is presented at first, including concepts generation and independence check. For information axiom design, DPs are compared via probability density graphs, and concepts are compared by Pugh's matrix. In addition, all concepts are visualised, and the chosen concept is displayed by CAD model. In each procedure, the student's reflection of benefits, challenges and mistakes are clarified, which will be summarised in final discussion. This paper majorly focuses on the axiomatic design application itself. The BTC is used as a case study only, and technical details are not specifically clarified. The applied axiomatic design procedures in this case study is presented in Figure 1.

This case study is representative for research purpose of the paper. For the BTC development project, the motivation of this student lead project is to improve students' design, research, manufacturing and test skills. The required objective does not require knowledge beyond the student's ability. Hence, central of this project is on design rather than technical problems. Meanwhile, the BTC involves coordination of various system, which can be a good platform to test design issues such as FRs management, constraints management and DPs independence. For the student, the developer of this BTC is an undergraduate aerospace engineering student, who finished the axiomatic design study in the previous semester, and this project is his first isolation of the design

* Yuchen Wang: yuchenwang2@student.unsw.edu.au

theory application. Therefore, the student can be a typical example of invoice engineering student.

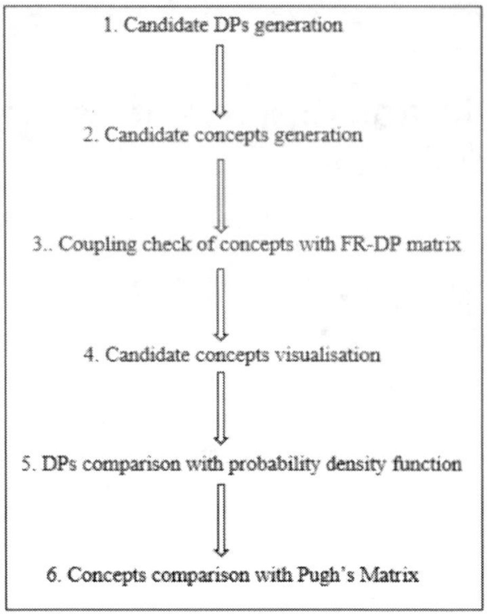

Fig. 1. Flow Chart of Axiomatic Design Procedures

2 Background of High Altitude Balloon

The high-altitude balloon refers to an objective-assigned carrier, which is usually launched 60,000-12,000ft altitude. Depending on filled gas, some high-altitude balloons will remain at a constant height to collect data. The others will be continuously lifted until the balloon explosion. The high-altitude balloon is capable of various objectives, weather balloon, telecommunication balloon, science research balloon and navigation balloon are some typical categories. Structure of high-altitude balloon is simple, and most of the components are available off-the-shelf. As a result, the manufacture is at low cost. Due to these features, some education institutes and students launch high-altitude balloons to execute science experiments and engineering tasks.

As the environments at balloon-launching altitude and low-earth-orbit are similar in some aspect, for low-earth-orbit satellite developers, the high-altitude balloon can be used to make an early test for satellite devices. However, there are some critical differences between low-earth orbit and high-altitude environments. The altitude of low-earth-orbit is 300km. When the elevation is over 160km, the impact of the atmosphere on air drag and radiation are weakened to a negligible-level. In result of this, heat conduction and convection between satellite and air do not exist anymore while the effect of heat radiation dramatically increases. Besides, orbit period of the low-earth-orbit satellite is approximately 84 to 127 minutes. Short period results in rapid temperature change on satellite surface. In result of this, both superheating and undercooling might occur due to fast heat transfer [1]. Compared to low-earth-orbit, the environment at high-altitude is simpler. The high-altitude balloon remains in the stratosphere (below 9km) during the whole lifting process. As shown in Figure 2, the temperature in stratosphere linearly decreases when altitude increases [2]. From temperature indication in the figure, the high-altitude balloon will only suffer the undercooling condition. Moreover, atmosphere effect is still significant at high altitude, which means heat radiation, convection and conduction are all critical.

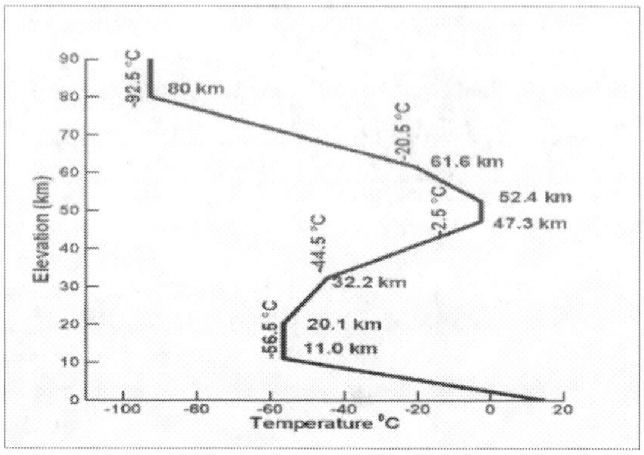

Fig. 2. Atmospheric Temperature at Different Altitudes

Electronic components require appropriate temperature ranges to guarantee high working efficiency and extended durability. The temperature ranges of different elements are specified. Compared to other electrical components, the battery is relatively the most impressible one, the required temperature range is between -5°C and 20°C. To secure the successful work and long durability of battery in the undercooling or overheating environment, BTC is essential to maintain a proper temperature.

3 Results Retrieved from Customer Domain and Functional Domain

Before the axiomatic design was applied, information concerning customer domain and the functional domain was gathered, which was essential to formulate the concept domain. To collect the customer reviews, interviews were done with power system leader, finance administrator and all significant members of the balloon team. The gathered customer needs(CNs) were summarised as:

- CN_1: The BTC should maintain the battery temperature no lower than 5°C before the altitude reaches 18,000m.
- CN_2: The BTC should have a heating region to simulate the overheating condition. A corresponding cooling system should be installed as an early test for the low-earth-orbit cubesat battery cooling system. This cooling system was constrained to be a passive system.
- CN_3: The cooling system should maintain the thermal carrier temperature of heat region no higher than 20°C.
- CN_4: The BTC should minimise power consumption. Meanwhile, it must automatically shut down when

the left battery power was less than 30% to guarantee the work of GPS system.

- CN_5: The BTC should work only during the lifting session.
- CN_6: The BTC electrical system should be compatible with the original PCB in balloon payload.
- CN_7: The BTC should be controlled by CPU on the original PCB in balloon payload.
- CN_8: The new PCB of BTC should be no larger than 10cm x 10cm.
- CN_9: The total dimensions of BTC and original PCB should be no larger than 12cm x 25cm x 10cm.
- CN_{10}: All components required to build the BTC should be available off-the-shelf.
- CN_{11}: The budget should be within an acceptable range.
- CN_{12}: Ease of the manufacturer should be maximised.

Correspondingly, the functional hierarchy was made as shown in Figure 3. The bottom-level FRs were:

- $FR_{1.1}$: Detect the temperature of battery surface with a range of 10-80°C and less than 2°C tolerance.
- $FR_{1.2}$: Detect the left battery volume under the temperature between -20-80°C and the tolerance should be less than 10%.
- $FR_{1.3}$: Detect the acceleration of battery under -20-80°C with 2g sensitivity.
- $FR_{1.4}$: Communicate with the central processor to transfer detected information every 0.1s.
- $FR_{2.1.1}$: Heat up the battery to maintain battery surface temperature at 30°C in -10°C environment.
- $FR_{2.1.2}$: Preserve the temperature with thermal insulation material of which the thermal conductivity is no more than 0.12 W/mK under room temperature.
- $FR_{2.2.1}$: Create a heat region which could remain at 50 °C in 10°C environment.
- $FR_{2.2.2}$: Cooling down the region to make it no higher than 30°C under 50°C.
- $FR_{2.3.1}$: Conduct heat via solid material of which the thermal conductivity is higher than 225W/mK.
- $FR_{2.3.2}$: Conduct the heat via the surface gap with the liquid conductor of which the thermal conductivity was higher than 6 W/mK.
- $FR_{3.1}$: Terminate heating system within 0.5s when the temperature is higher than 15°C.
- $FR_{3.2}$: Terminate heat region within 0.5s when the temperature is higher than 50°C.
- $FR_{3.3}$: Trigger and terminate the thermal controller within 0.5s. Trigger it after balloon starts to lift. Terminate it after the balloon explosion or battery has less than 30% power left.
- $FR_{4.1}$: Connect the electrical system to payload PCB within 10cm x 20cm PCB size in total.
- $FR_{4.2}$: Integral the mechanical system together and compress the dimensions within 12cm x 25cm x 10cm.

In addition to the FRs list, another discussion was made with mentioned stakeholders. With their opinions on the priority of FRs, a classification table was made based on Kano Customer model and House of Quality (HOQ). The result indicated that the following five FRs were relatively more important. Analysis of these five FRs will be highlighted in the following axiomatic design.

- $FR_{2.1.1}$: Heat up the battery to maintain battery surface temperature at 30°C in -10°C environment.
- $FR_{2.1.2}$: Preserve the temperature with thermal insulation material of which the thermal conductivity is no more than 0.12 W/mK under room temperature.

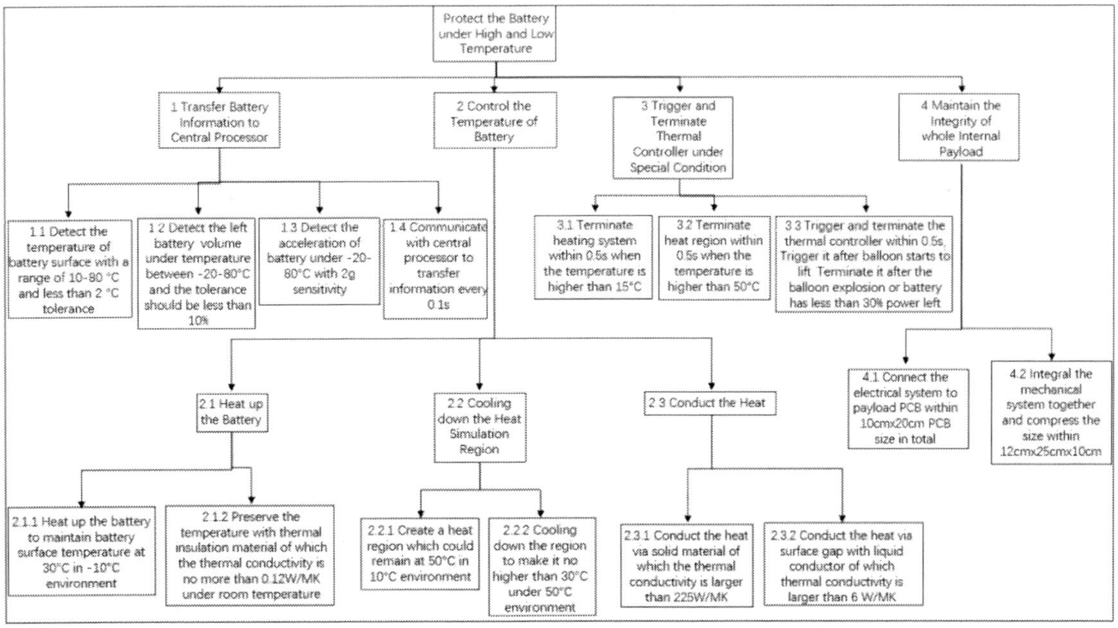

Fig. 3. Functional Hierarchy of BTC

- $FR_{2.2.2}$: Cooling down the region to make it no higher than 30°C under 50°C.
- $FR_{2.3.1}$: Conduct heat via solid material of which the thermal conductivity is higher than 225W/ mK.
- $FR_{2.3.2}$: Conduct the heat via the surface gap with the liquid conductor of which the thermal conductivity was higher than 6 W/ mK.

It should be noticed that those FRs were the modified results based on independence axiom design feedback. The initial FRs were checked to be dependent according to concept organisation procedures. Some typical changes would be emphasised in independence axiom design part.

4 The Axiomatic Design of BTC

4.1 DPs Generation and Composing

For each bottom-level FRs, three alternative DPs were generated to compose candidate BTC concepts. Although there would be a relatively most proper concept, all three DPs were supposed to satisfy CNs in special situations. The five significant FRs mentioned in forewords were specially analysed, while others were briefly summarised.

For battery heating($FR_{2.1.1}$), as the BTC was based on an electrical system, chips resistors matrix can be a proper solution, especially chip resistors were available in bulk. Moreover, chip resistor had long durability and high tolerance to temperature, which will increase the stability of the heater. Apart from chip resistors, nichrome wire had already been used to develop heater elements by some amateurs due to simple manufacture on PCB. Moreover, inspired by computer CPU and electromagnetic oven, a simplified high-frequency heater could be an alternative option. As the battery provides DC power, necessary DC/AC converting components are essential as assistance.

For temperature preservation($FR_{2.1.2}$), several categories of materials had been applied as thermal insulation in different industrial sectors. For instances, the polymer-ceramic composite was a common thermal insulation material for architecture exterior wall and fire belt [3]. Meanwhile, Special categories of phenolic resin and epoxy resin had been developed by oil companies to preserve heat for steel pipes [4]. Glass wool could be another option, which had been utilised to maintain temperature for hot water pipes [5].

For cooling system($FR_{2.2.2}$), as it was mentioned in customer domain part, the cooling system was constrained to be a passive system. There were some well-developed cooling system concepts available. Cooling fins were commonly used in the laptop. The heat sink was applied to Raspberry Pi 3 Model B. Special heat radiation coat has been applied on satellite.

For heat conduction via the solid material($FR_{2.3.1}$), CN_{10} and CN_{11} required that all materials should be available off-the-shelf at an acceptable price, in this case, some advanced materials like graphene film and carbide would not be considered. Among those familiar metals, aluminium, copper and silver had significantly higher thermal conduction coefficients which had been well-utilised on computers [6]. To save cost, silver would be replaced by silver plated copper.

For heat conduction via the surface gap($FR_{2.3.2}$), the DP is applied to battery-heating system contacting surface and heating region-cooling system contacting surface. Referring to CPU-heat pipe contacting surface and GPU-heat pipe contact surface in laptops, thermal metal compound, silicone thermal compound and metal oxide thermal grease were selected to satisfy this FR.

All candidate DPs of each FRs were shown as a Morphological Chart in Table 1. To generate candidate composed concepts, all candidate DPs were divided into three groups to form three candidate concepts. An assessment was made to evaluate feasibility and competence of compose. The candidate DPs and three concepts were indicated in different Rome number. Concept 1 was represented by I, concept 2 was represented by II, and concept 3 was represented by III.

In this procedure, one challenge for the student was coming up valid candidate DPs. In engineering design education, students might not be familiar with the chosen design project. In this condition, online search might be the common way to find enough candidate DPs. Random search is ineffective, educators should apply strategies, which help students with accurate information search.

Table 1. Morphological Chart of BTC

FRs	DP1	DP2	DP3
$FR_{1.1}$	A/D Output Thermal Sensor (I)	NTC Thermistor (II)	Resistance Temperature Detector (III)
$FR_{1.2}$	Battery Fuel Gauge (I)	Current Sense Resistor with OPA (II)	Capacitance Meter (III)
$FR_{1.3}$	Accelerometer with Analog Voltage Output (II)	Digital Accelerometer (I)	A/D Accelerometer (III)
$FR_{1.4}$	I2C (I)	SPI (II)	PCI (III)
$FR_{2.3.1}$	Aluminium (II)	Copper (I)	Silver Plated Copper (III)
$FR_{2.3.2}$	Metal Thermal Compound (III)	Silicone Thermal Compound (II)	Metal Oxide Thermal Grease (I)
$FR_{2.1.1}$	Heating Region Combined by Small-Value Resistors 1 (I)	Heating Elements Assembled by Nichrome Wire 1 (II)	High-Frequency Heater 1 (III)
$FR_{2.1.2}$	Polymer-Ceramic Composite Thermal Cover (I)	Phenolic Resin Cover (III)	Glass Wool (II)
$FR_{2.2.1}$	Heating Region Combined by Small-Value Resistors 2 (I)	Heating Elements Assembled by Nichrome Wire 2 (II)	High-Frequency Heater 2 (III)
$FR_{2.2.2}$	Cooling Fins (III)	Metal Heat Sink (I)	Dissipation Coating (II)
$FR_{3.1}$	Active or Sleeping Mode of I/O Expander Pin 1 (II)	Analog Switch 1 (III)	Low-Mode Power Input via I/O Expander 1 (I)

$FR_{3.2}$	Active or Working Mode of I/O Expander Pin 2 (II)	Analog Switch 2 (III)	Low-Mode Power Input via I/O Expander 2 (I)
$FR_{3.3}$	Pin-Mode on Central Processor Unit (I)	IC Signal Switch (III)	Resettable Fuse (II)
$FR_{4.1}$	One Single PCB Shared by BTC and Original PCB (II)	Double Layers Structure Fixed by Standoffs (I)	Two Independent PCB(Flexible Structure) (III)
$FR_{4.2}$	Internal wire connection (II)	Connection with Headers (I)	External wire connection (III)

4.2 Concept Organisation and Visualisation

To reduce complexity and increase feasibility, functional dependency should be minimised. Three FR-DP hierarchies were used to evaluate functional dependence for all three concepts. Each FR was assessed to check if other DPs were required to execute the function apart from their corresponding DPs. Once decouple design existed, the relevant current candidate DPs would be replaced by alternative concepts to achieve uncouple design. If this step was not applicable, corresponding FR would be checked whether it was broken down to bottom-level. If uncouple design still could not be generated, corresponding customer demand would be reviewed to modify the FR. After several adjustments, the final adjusted FR-DP matrixes of three concepts were indicated in Figure 4,5 and 6.

Some typical changes through this feedback process should be emphasised. Initially, heat conduction was not divided into $FR_{2.3.1}$ and $FR_{2.3.2}$, when Morphological Chart was firstly generated, it was found that heat conduction required both solid and liquid thermal conduction material to achieve. Considering this, 'conducting heat' was evaluated as 'not broken down to bottom-level', which led to $FR_{2.3.1}$ and $FR_{2.3.2}$. Another typical change was BTC triggering and termination. Initially, terminating and triggering system were classified based on execution conditions, for example, three FRs were generated at first as the heating system should be discontinued when the temperature was higher than 15°C, battery power was lower than 30% or after balloon explosion. In result of this FRs generation outcome, the three FRs could be executed by only one or two DPs, which caused a regional coupled design. Those FRs were combined into $FR_{3.1}$ and $FR_{3.2}$ eventually to formulate the current uncoupled design. The similar issue happened to information transferring as well, $FR_{1.4}$ was initially three FRs which corresponded to information transferring of $FR_{1.1}$, $FR_{1.2}$ and $FR_{1.3}$, noticed that those were executed by I2C/SCL/PCI this single DP, those FRs were combined into current $FR_{1.4}$.

Three corresponding concept visualisations were made according to the Morphological Chart, which were shown in Figure 7,8 and 9. These visualisations were illustrative, and the real product might differ. Some DPs were based on the original balloon PCB, which contained a Raspberry Pi Mini as CPU and detection sensors. DPs and corresponding FRs were annotated in visualisation figures as well.

4.3 Concept Selection

In this section, the information axiom design was applied to select the relatively most proper concept. At first, candidate DPs of each FRs were evaluated, analysis of the five most important FRs would be clarified, others would be briefly summarised. The final result would be out of the Pugh's Matrix. It should be pointed out that due to lack

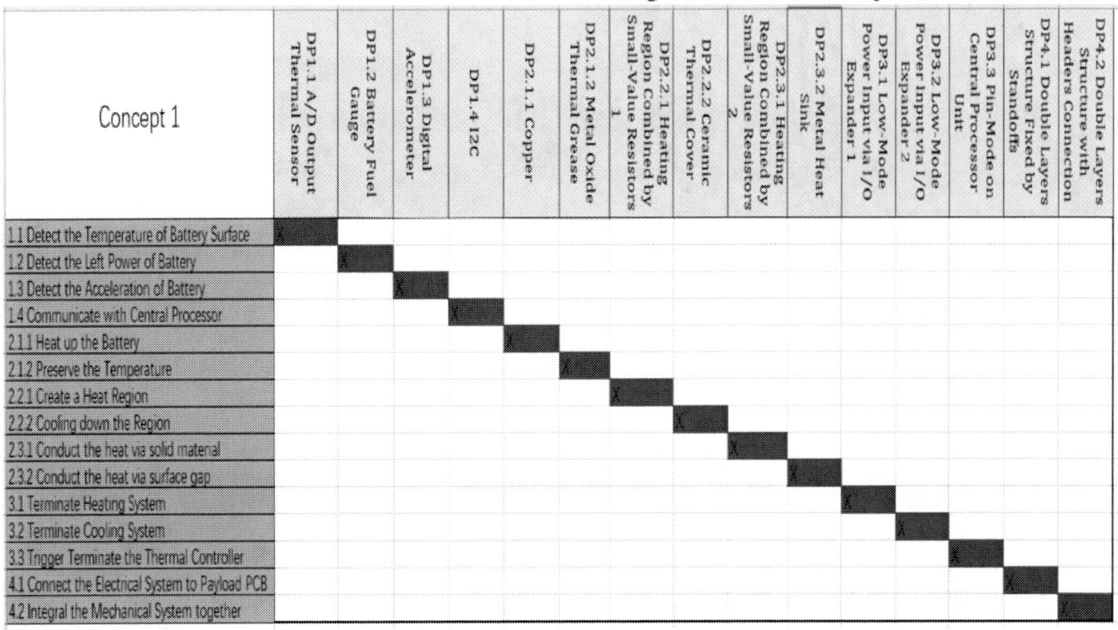

Fig. 4. FR-DP Matrix of Concept 1

https://doi.org/10.1051/matecconf/201822301017

Concept 2	DP1.1 NTC Thermistor	DP1.2 Current Sense Resistor with OPA	DP1.3 Accelerometer with Analog Voltage Output	DP1.4 SPI	DP2.1.1 Aluminum	DP2.1.2 Silicone Thermal Compound	DP2.2.1 Heater assembled by Wire Helix 1	DP2.2.2 Glass Wool	DP2.3.1 Heater assembled by Wire Helix 2	DP2.3.2 Heat Radiation Coat	DP3.1 Active Sleeping Mode of I/O Expander Pin 1	DP3.2 Active Working Mode of I/O Expander Pin 2	DP3.3 Resettable Fuse	DP4.1 Thermal Controller and Internal Payload PCB are on the Same PCB	DP4.2 Thermal Controller and Internal Payload PCB are on the Same PCB with internal wire
1.1 Detect the Temperature of Battery Surface	X														
1.2 Detect the Left Power of Battery		X													
1.3 Detect the Acceleration of Battery			X												
1.4 Communicate with Central Processor				X											
2.1.1 Heat up the Battery					X										
2.1.2 Preserve the Temperature						X									
2.2.1 Create a Heat Region							X								
2.2.2 Cooling down the Region								X							
2.3.1 Conduct the heat via solid material									X						
2.3.2 Conduct the heat via surface gap										X					
3.1 Terminate Heating System											X				
3.2 Terminate Cooling System												X			
3.3 Trigger Terminate the Thermal Controller													X		
4.1 Connect the Electrical System to Payload PCB														X	
4.2 Integral the Mechanical System together															X

Fig. 5. FR-DP Matrix of Concept 2

of test apparatus and relevant research information, all the concept evaluations were based on similar condition tests, past relevant research results, inspiration from similar FR-DP of other products and some essential environmental assumptions, which made the whole evaluation a rough result. This would be discussed later.

For the $FR_{2.1.1}$, Li-ion battery was applied to power the whole system. When the temperature was below -10°C, the charge-transfer resistance of battery would start to rapidly decrease while bulk resistance and layer resistance was still in an acceptable range [7]. According to the temperature recording from previous balloon test data, the whole lifting process lasted for 61 minutes, the period when the temperature was below -10°C just lasted for 12 minutes. As BTC was expected to be the most power-consuming system in balloon payload, while heat transferred more rapidly when temperature difference was higher [8], out of the consideration to save battery power, -10°C was determined as the threshold above which battery temperature should be maintained at a proper range. Meanwhile, 20°C should be the maximum proper temperature for battery working. In result of these, 'maintain the temperature at 20°C in -10°C environment' should be the ideal demand value for $FR_{2.1.1}$. However, the real environment might be much more complex than the theoretical hypothesis, to guarantee the competent

Concept 3	DP1.1 Resistance Temperature Detector	DP1.2 Capacitance Meter	DP1.3 A/D Accelerometer	DP1.4 PCI	DP2.1.1 Silver Plated Copper	DP2.1.2 Metal Thermal Compound	DP2.2.1 High-Frequency Heater 1	DP2.2.2 Phenolic Resin Cover	DP2.3.1 High-Frequency Heater 2	DP2.3.2 Cooling Fins	DP3.1 Analog Switch 1	DP3.2 Analog Switch 2	DP3.3 IC Signal Switch	DP4.1 Two Independent PCB(Flexible Structure)	DP4.2 Flexible Structure with wire connection
1.1 Detect the Temperature of Battery Surface	X														
1.2 Detect the Left Power of Battery		X													
1.3 Detect the Acceleration of Battery			X												
1.4 Communicate with Central Processor				X											
2.1.1 Heat up the Battery					X										
2.1.2 Preserve the Temperature						X									
2.2.1 Create a Heat Region							X								
2.2.2 Cooling down the Region								X							
2.3.1 Conduct the heat via solid material									X						
2.3.2 Conduct the heat via surface gap										X					
3.1 Terminate Heating System											X				
3.2 Terminate Cooling System												X			
3.3 Trigger Terminate the Thermal Controller													X		
4.1 Connect the Electrical System to Payload PCB														X	
4.2 Integral the Mechanical System together															X

Fig. 6. FR-DP Matrix of Concept 3

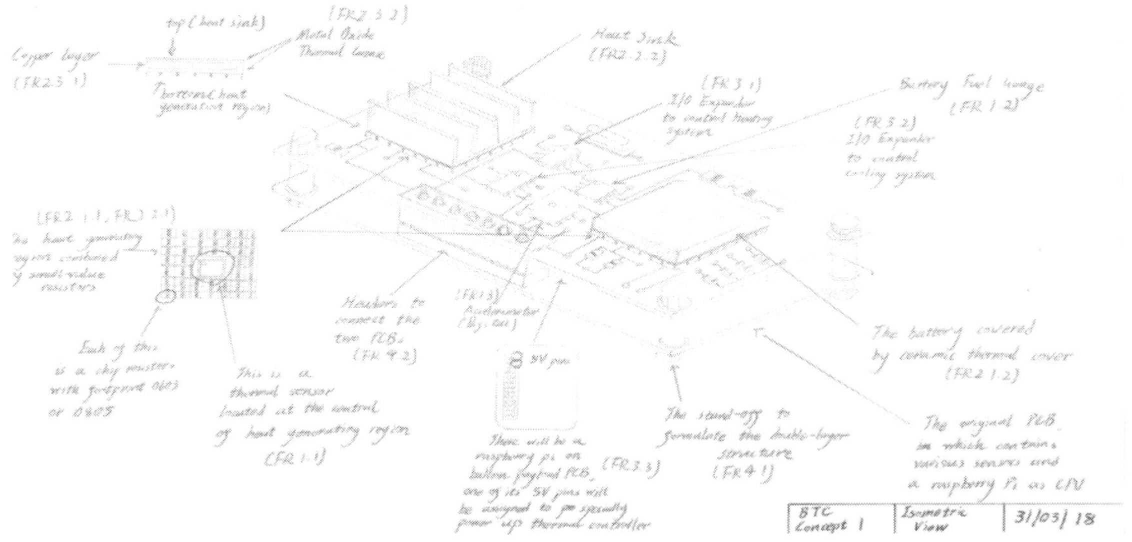

Fig. 7. Visualisation of Concept 1

performance, required maintained temperature was increased to 30°C. To make a rough estimation of concepts performance, two simple prototypes were made to test small-value resistors matrix and high-frequency heaters. The small-value resistors matrix was based on a previous obsolete PCB which contained a 3x3 0805 footprints matrix. A 10V DC power generator was used as power source. Meanwhile, 20 turns copper wire loops, and a short copper stick were used together to make a simple high-frequency heater, which was powered by 10V AC 5KHz. Detecting surface of a temperature sensor was attached to resistors surface and end of the copper stick to detect temperature. An Arduino Uno was used to receive the signal from the temperature sensor. A freezer was applied to achieved 5°c environment. The tests results indicated that temperature of small-value resistors matrix vibrated between 26°C to 30°C, while that of high-frequency heater vibrated between 29°C to 36°C. As for the nichrome wire heat element, a similar test had been made by a senior student in the club. The test was taken under 4°C, and the nichrome heat element maintained approximately between 43°C to 46°C, the thickness of nichrome wire was chosen as 1mm and gap between wires was 0.75mm. According to the heat transfer equation, when attachment area and thickness of conductor were the same, heat transfer speed was proportional to temperature difference [9]. Based on this, 'maintain between 43°C to 46°C under 4°C' was equivalent to 'maintain between 34°C to 37°C under -5°C'. The result of $FR_{2.1.1}$ concepts evaluation was shown in Figure 10. One critical problem was that many factors in the real environment and test conditions varied significantly such as pressure difference and power source efficiency, which made this a rough evaluation and might not be valid in actual application.

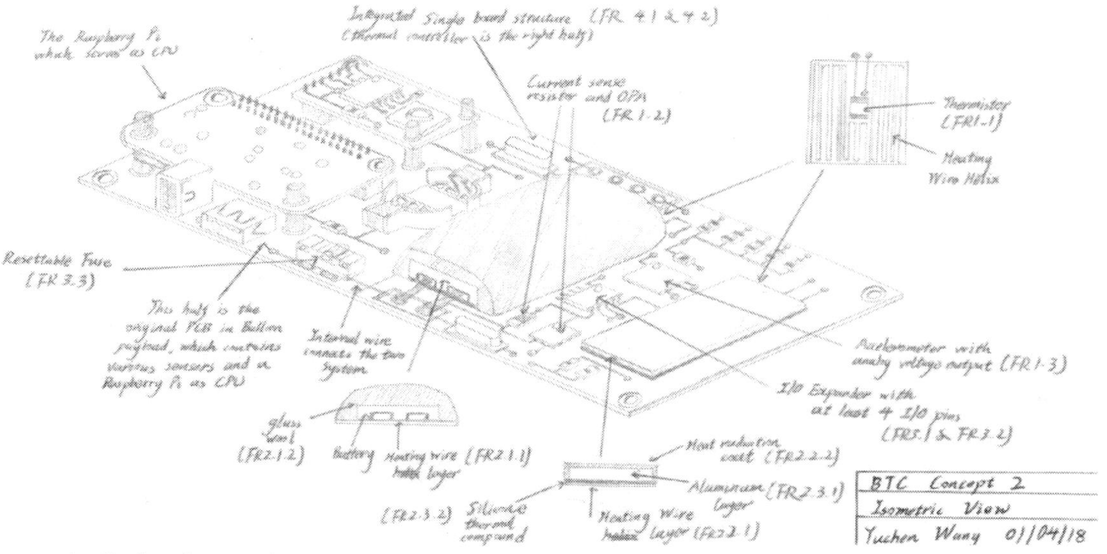

Fig.8. Visualisation of Concept 2

https://doi.org/10.1051/matecconf/201822301017

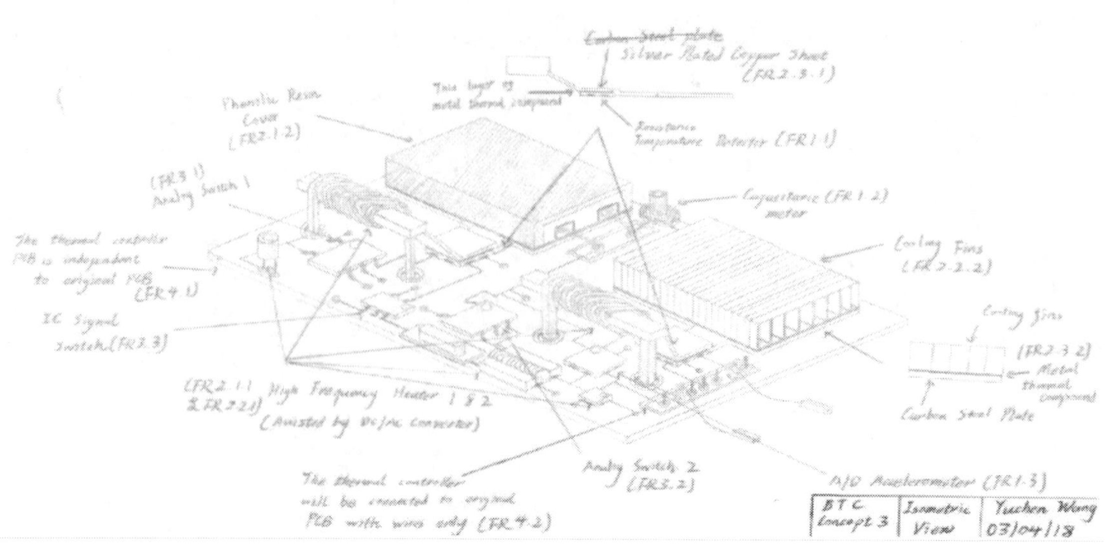

Fig. 9. Concept Visualisation of Concept 3

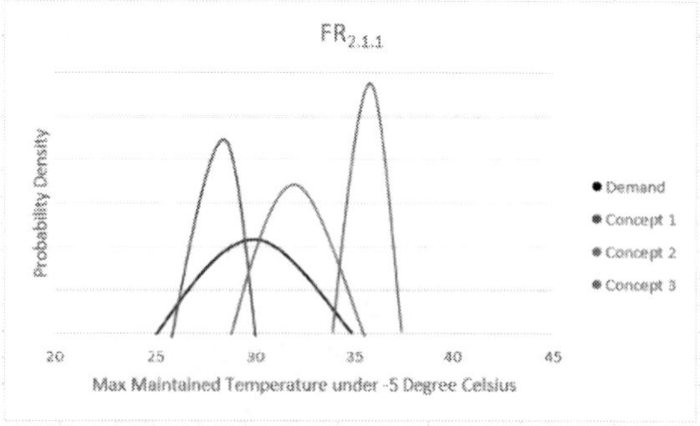

Fig. 10. PDF for $FR_{2.1.1}$ Candidate DPs

For $FR_{2.1.2}$, currently, the bottom threshold for thermal insulation material was roughly 0.12W/mK as thermal conduction coefficient under room temperature, which determined the fundamental demand of $FR_{2.1.2}$. Industrial thermal-insulation material frequently had that around 0.045W/mK [10]. When constraints could be maintained, the thermal conduction coefficient should be as low as possible. For polymer ceramic, the composition could contain ZrO_2, 3YSZ, CeO_2 and Al_2O_3. Some tests had been done under 1273K and result indicated that the thermal conduction coefficient was around 1.5-3.5W/mK [11]. Meanwhile, another research stated that thermal conduction coefficient might raise several times for solid and liquid materials [12]. As a result, compositions of solid polymer ceramic roughly had thermal conduction coefficient 0.3-0.7W/mK. By adjusting composition proportion, density and internal structure, composed polymer ceramic could be lowered to 0.1W/mK. As for glass wool, it accounted for 60% European market of thermal insulation material for building [5]. Depending on the composition of glass fibres, the thermal conductivity of solid glass wool varied between 0.15-0.26W/mK [13]. Similar to the polymer, industrial-utilised glass fibre had much lower thermal conductivity due to the unique structure and mineral composition, which was around 0.035W/mK. In the real application, its performance might be more competent by being stacked. As for phenolic resin, similar to glass wool and polymer-ceramic, the thermal conductivity was significantly affected by fibre structure and composite proportion. For instance, phenolic foam used for building walls had the thermal conductivity at around 0.02W/mK[14]. The evaluation of three materials was shown in Figure 11.

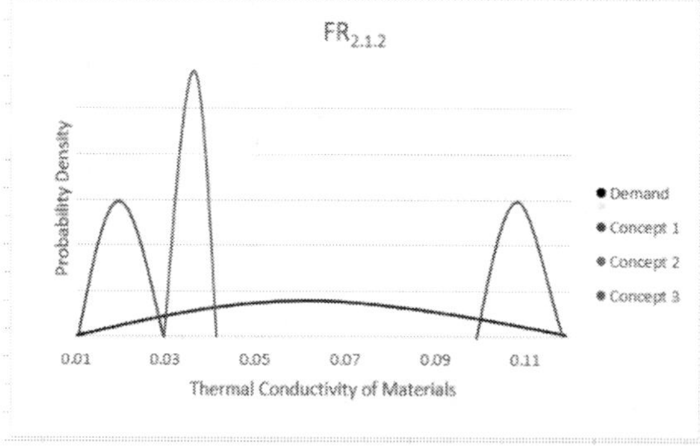

Fig. 11. PDF for $FR_{2.1.2}$ Candidate DPs

For $FR_{2.2.2}$, the demand value came from coordination to $FR_{2.2.1}$. Same DP was used to achieve both $FR_{2.2.1}$ and $FR_{2.1.1}$. As the low-temperature environment at high altitude would significantly affect the high-temperature maintenance of heat simulation region, the performance of $FR_{2.2.2}$ and $FR_{2.2.1}$ would be based on low altitude phase. The temperature maintenance requirement for $FR_{2.2.1}$ was 50°C, correspondingly, cooling effect was based on 50°C as well. As mentioned in the foreword, 20°C or below should be proper to maintain a longer Li-ion battery cycle life, when the temperature was increased to 30°C, life cycle reduced for approximately 20% [15], which was determined as the bottom-effect threshold. 4°C tolerance was allowed for concept effect. For the simple evaluation test, the 3x3 small-value resistors matrix mentioned in $FR_{2.1.1}$ was used to generate high temperature. The model remained between 48°C to 51°C under room temperature with 10V DC power, which roughly satisfied the 50°C test requirement. The same temperature sensor and Arduino UNO in $FR_{2.1.1}$ test were applied in this test. A copper metal heat sink of Raspberry 3 Model B was used to test concept 1. The result indicated that the temperature vibrated between 31°C to 33°C. As for cooling fins, a mini-size aluminium one made by milling machine was applied in the test, which remained between 35°C and 36°C. For the dissipation coating, graphene was chosen as the material. The temperature result was between 40°C to 42°C. The probability density function chart was shown in Figure 12. The test was based on hypothesis such as the temperature of cooling system surface and battery surface were the same. Similar to the $FR_{2.1.1}$ test, differences existed between analysis and real condition as well, which made the evaluation result might be significantly different compared to practical effect. Although concept 2 and 3 were out of demand range, however, concept 2 had relatively lower cost, and concept 3 was more stable, which made them still probably useful for future optimisation.

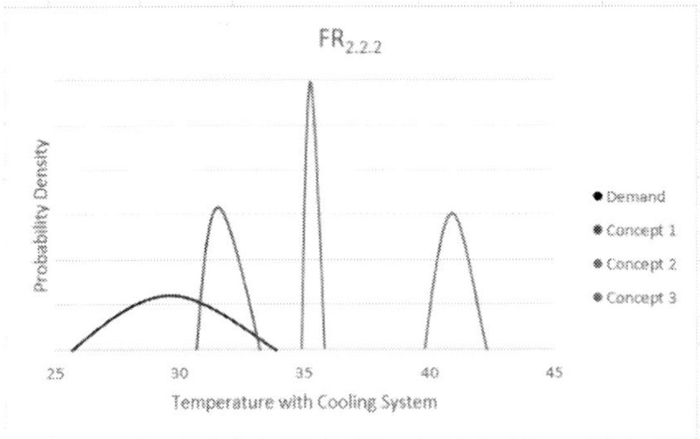

Fig. 12. PDF for $FR_{2.2.2}$ Candidate DPs

For $FR_{2.3.1}$, the evaluation criterion was inspired by laptop cooling fins and heat pipes. The heat conduction system in a laptop was commonly the combination of copper and aluminium. Relatively, copper had better thermal conduction while aluminium benefited heat transferring more. The aluminium applied in laptop cooling fins had thermal conduction coefficient at around 247W/mK while that of copper might reach 398W/mK [15]. Operating temperature and extent of oxidising could impact the thermal conduction. Considering that the internal temperature of laptop CPU could reach 80°C which was higher than test demand, the demand value of thermal conductivity could be slightly lower than that of aluminium used in the laptop. In this case, thermal conduction coefficient of ordinary high-purity aluminium was chosen as lowest evaluation threshold which was 225W/mK. Within an acceptable cost range, thermal conductivity should be the higher, the better. For concept 3, silver was one of the best heat conduction material. However, its price was much higher than pure copper while thermal conduction increasing was limited. Considering this, silver plated copper was selected to replace pure silver. According to the database, the probability density function evaluation was indicated in Figure 13.

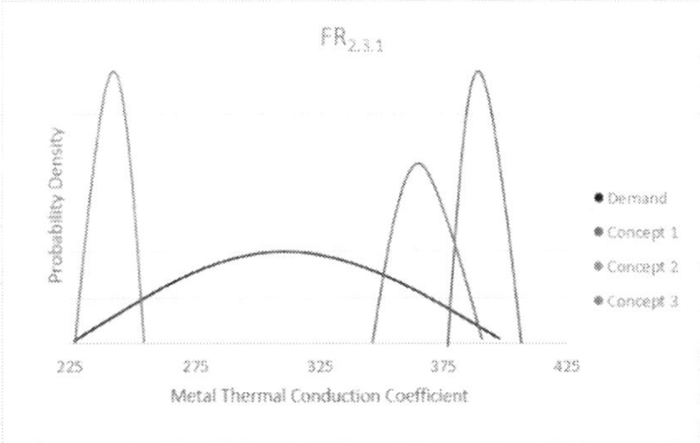

Fig. 13. PDF for $FR_{2.3.1}$ Candidate DPs

For $FR_{2.3.2}$, some extra information should be introduced at first. The thermal conduction coefficients of metals were commonly higher than 100 W/mK, while that of air was 0.029 W/mK under room temperature [15]. Theoretically, if the contact surfaces of metals were perfectly flat, thermal conductivity would reach maximum. However, metal surface was rough under the electronic magnifier, which left small gaps between contacting surfaces. As thermal conduction coefficient of air was much lower than metal, thermal conduction across these gaps was significantly negatively impacted. In this case, thermal compound was essential to weaken this effect. Similar to $FR_{2.3.1}$, the demand range of $FR_{2.3.2}$ was inspired by heat releasing of CPU and GPU in the laptop, silicone thermal compound was applied to solve this case. Depending on the brands of thermal compound and laptop, thermal conduction coefficient generally varied between 4-7 W/mK. CPU and GPU temperature was significantly higher than balloon battery so 6W/mK thermal conduction coefficient should be sufficient, especially considering that thermal compound layer was thin. However, the higher the thermal conduction coefficient was, the better the performance would be. As for metal oxide thermal grease, it was a kind of compound which contained a high proportion of metal dust. Relatively, due to the high percentage of metal inside, its thermal conduction coefficient was higher than usual silicon thermal compound, which was around 26W/mK for the silver injected category. For thermal metal compound, which could be regarded as liquid metal, its thermal conduction coefficient could reach more than 100W/mK. However, the thermal metal compound required strict electricity insulation treatment, and the price was relatively much higher either. The evaluation result was indicated in Figure 14.

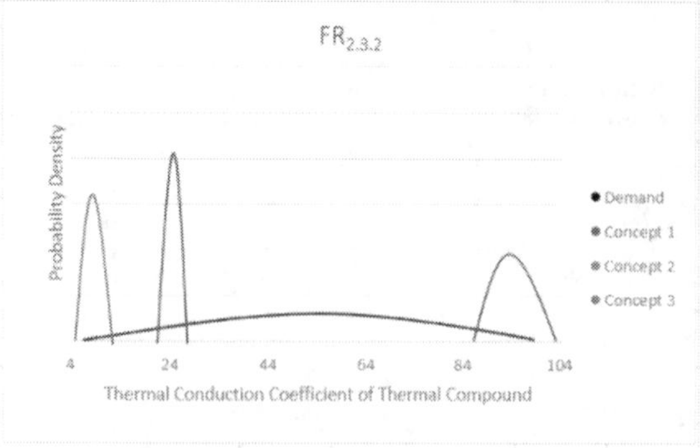

Fig. 14. PDF for $FR_{2.3.2}$ Candidate DPs

To select the final concept, a Pugh's Matrix was made to compare each concept based on CNs and corresponding engineering characteristics(ECs). The ECs were listed as:

- EC_1: A heater to heat up the battery to a proper temperature.
- EC_2: A heater to generate a high-temperature region.
- EC_3: A passive cooling system to cool down the region.
- EC_4: A battery fuel gauge and low-power-consuming subsystems.
- EC_5: An accelerometer.
- EC_6: The code of BTC would be in Python.
- EC_7: Interface bus and the electrical circuit.
- EC_8: 10cmx10cm or smaller PCB.
- EC_9: Dimensions of BTC and original PCB in total would be less than 12cm x 25cm x 10cm.
- EC_{10}: Off-the-shelf components and materials.
- EC_{11}: Low price components and materials.
- EC_{12}: The whole construction should be finished by hand, bench work tools, milling machine, 3D printer and soldering tools.

The Pugh's matrix was shown in Table 2. The score of each criterion as classified into '0', '1' and 2. '0' represents 'not competent', '1' represents 'competent' and '2' represents 'highly competent'. The weights and scores were out of the discussion with several stakeholders. The result indicated that concept 1 was comprehensively the most appropriate selection. However, concept 2 was relatively at low cost and concept 3 relatively achieved main FRs better. These two concepts might still be useful for future development.

Table.2. Pugh's Matrix of Three Candidate Concepts

CNs	ECs	Weight	Concept 1	Concept 2	Concept 3
CN_1	EC_1	5	2	1	2
CN_2	EC_2	4	1	1	2
CN_3	EC_3	5	2	1	1
CN_4	EC_4	3	2	1	0
CN_5	EC_5	3	1	1	2
CN_6	EC_6	4	1	1	1
CN_7	EC_7	2	1	1	1
CN_8	EC_8	1	1	1	1
CN_9	EC_9	1	1	1	1
CN_{10}	EC_{10}	2	2	2	1
CN_{11}	EC_{11}	3	1	2	0
CN_{12}	EC_{12}	1	1	1	0
Total			49	39	39

4.4 FR-DP Hierarchy and CAD Model

A final FR-DP hierarchy was made for concept 1 as shown in Figure 15. Bottom-level DPs were made corresponding to Morphological Chart, and assigned

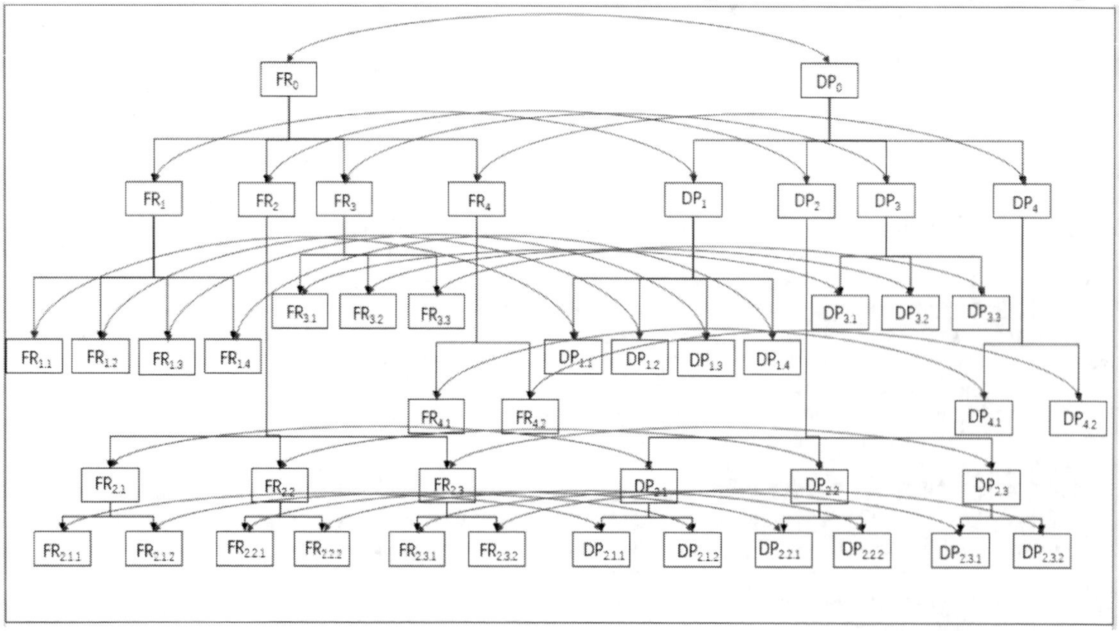

Fig. 15. FR-DP Hierarchy of Concept 1

numbers were referring to bottom-level FRs. Some additional high-level DPs were added including:

- DP_0: Battery thermal controller
- DP_1: Sensors with the I2C interface bus
- DP_2: Thermal control system
- DP_3: I/O expanders with the I2C interface bus
- DP_4: Standard PCB base with expansion pins
- $DP_{2.1}$: Heat generator and preservation system
- $DP_{2.2}$: Overheating simulation region with the cooling system
- $DP_{2.3}$: Thermal conduction materials

A CAD model draft was made of concept 1 as shown in Figure 16 and 17. Figure 16 was the isometric view of BTC, while Figure 17 displayed the schematic of original balloon PCB. This CAD model was just an illustrative example, component types, layout, specific dimensions and appearance were not determined yet.

Fig. 16. Isometric View of BTC

Fig. 17. Isometric View of Original PCB

5 Discussion and Reflection

5.1 Benefits

Design is primarily an information processing activity. A significant amount of scattered information is involved in customer domain, functional domain and concept domain. With the axiomatic design, scattered information becomes well-organised.

This significantly benefits two aspects. One is design mistake correction. Through the axiomatic design process, logical bonds are formulated among the three domains, customer domain determines FRs and constraints, FRs will determine candidate DPs, and DPs compose into concepts, which will be evaluated according to CNs. Except for this sequence, feedback process also exists within this design sequence. These characteristics make mistakes more accessible to be noticed, while correction can be made to target procedure accurately by reviewing the design sequence. For instance, in the information axiom design procedure, when candidate DPs are compared via probability density functions, if a candidate DP is entirely out of demand scope, and there is no sufficient reason to support its validation as an exception, this DP then can be regarded as inappropriately generated DP. A new competent DP would replace it. Like the dissipation coating of $FR_{2.2.2}$, the performance value is entirely out of demand range, which demonstrated that it should be replaced. However, dissipation coating is cheap and manufacture-friendly, if the practical test proves that demand range can be more liberal or budget need reducing, it will be competitive. Consequentially, it becomes an exception. Another example is the FR-DP matrix. From the matrix, it can be noticed if the concept is uncoupled design. If not, independence of FRs or DPs should be revised.

The other aspect is competent and convenient-use concepts generation. When design objectives are assigned, students might incline to two trends. One is applying redundant DPs to secure the achievement of FRs. The other is using insufficient DPs to minimise some constraints like size and cost. Essentially, both trends are due to lack of experience, which makes students unconfident in achieving FRs or securing constraints with a certain amount of DPs. Following these trends, redundant DPs leads to over-constraint characteristics, while insufficient DPs causes incompetence or inconvenient use. With the axiomatic design, FRs are kept independent, and DPs will be generated correspondingly under control of constraints and CNs, which make the final concept both competent and irredundant. For example, for $FR_{2.1.1}$ and $FR_{2.2.1}$, without the organisation of axiomatic design, students might use a large heater to heat up both regions at the same time, which will formulate a coupled design with FRs that are relevant to automatic control. Consequentially, BTC will not achieve independent control in heaters and heat region.

5.2 Challenges

Through this high-altitude balloon design process, two challenging parts were noticed. One is determining the performance value range for demand and DPs in information axiom design part. To make the demand value and DPs performance value accurate and valid, a rigorous process should generally include four steps. First one is an initial estimation based on previous experience. The second is searching for academic resources about similar design. Then it comes to data analysis from experiment under strict environmental control. Finally, practical application will give feedback to design quality. However, students usually are lack of industrial experience and professional experimental apparatus. Besides, data from similar design test is not readily accessible either. Due to these constraints, students might just evaluate based on simple prototype test like $FR_{2.1.1}$ or reference from similar DPs like $FR_{2.3.2}$. The only accurate data feedback might be the final application in this case.

The other challenging part is improving physical integrity of composed design concept while maintaining functionally independent. In customer domain, CNs relevant to size, price and convenience appear at a critically high frequency. Physical integrity extent of design significantly affects these three CNs. However, DPs are generated from FRs while FRs are secured to be independent of each other through independence axiom design. As a result, DPs are relatively independent of each other as well. In concept visualisation part, it could be seen that 15 DPs mostly correspond to 15 components. Integrating physical DPs on fewer elements requires qualified design principle education, design experience and students' creation, of which a large proportion of undergraduate students might not be capable. More importantly, if the inappropriate attempt of integrating is made, the design might not be uncoupled anymore.

5.3 Potential Mistakes

Through interviews with some students and the reflection of fore-procedures, two common mistakes were observed at a high probability. One is generating inconsistent demand value for bottom-level FRs. The functional hierarchy had been modified several times to formulate the current version. When the functional hierarchy was firstly done, some inconsistent demand value existed for some bottom-level FRs. For instance, initially, $FR_{3.1}$ was 'Terminate heating system when the temperature is higher than 15°C.' This FR should be achieved by a logical switch. However, the demand value was 'when the temperature is higher 15°C', which was a requirement for a temperature sensor. Another example is that in a student vehicle design project, a similar case was observed as 'Decelerate to 10cm/s when the load is heavier than 300g', deceleration should be achieved by power system and brake system, while 'when the load is heavier than 300g' is achieved by a pressure sensor. Primarily, this problem happens at higher probability when dealing with conditional FR, which means the FR will perform under a specific condition, just like the 15°C temperature and 300g load mentioned in the two examples.

The other potential mistake is generating invalid candidate DPs and concepts in concept domain. After obtaining customers' demands, students might already have a general design concept idea. This idea would be potentially inclined in rest design procedures. If the DPs and concepts generation is an isolation task, to filter out this preferred concept as the final result, students might deliberately generate invalid DPs which seem reasonable but incompetent to make a comparison. For instance, if copper is the preferred candidate DP to serve $FR_{2.3.1}$, to filter it out, carbon steel and artificial diamond could be used to replace aluminium and silver-plated copper. Carbon steel is utilised for many cookers, and artificial diamond has the thermal conduction coefficient at around 1000W/mK. These two DPs seem rational, but thermal conduction coefficient of carbon steel is just around 100W/mK, and artificial diamond is too expensive, which make them both not competent to meet customers' demands. Consequentially, information axiom design is meaningless in this case. The possible motivation behind this is saving time for students while the design logic still makes sense. This problem might occur when the axiomatic design assignment time is intense, which should be paid attention to student education.

6 Conclusion and Future Work

In conclusion, the axiomatic design effectively assists this student lead project. However, due to invoice students' inherent constraints, some procedures can be difficult to properly apply. For benefits, the axiomatic design made the information processing well-organised, which significantly assist mistakes correction, and generating competent and convenient-use concepts. As for challenges, students might find it hard to determine demand and performance value for DPs when evaluating the competence of DPs with probability density function graph due to lack of experience, resources and experiment apparatus. Increasing physical integration extent for composed concepts was the other challenge. For potential mistakes, generating unmatched performance demand value for bottom-level FRs could be a possible mistake, while generating incompetent DPs should be focused as well.

Regarding future work, firstly, based on mentioned challenges and potential mistakes in this design application, corresponding education strategies will be researched. These strategies will focus on guiding invoice students to make rational and objective decisions with available resources to offset their inherent constraints. Candidate strategies include making simple prototypes, academic resources cloud searching and peer reviews. Secondly, the BTC is currently under manufacturing, and it will be tested in spring. Based on practical test results, the second-round reflection will be made. The validation of this axiomatic design will be assessed according to practical test result. When the test data is retrieved, an analysis will be made to classify successful design parts and incompetent design parts. Corresponding to the analysis result, benefits, mistakes of axiomatic design application will be discussed at a further level. Meanwhile, for those incompetent DPs, the failure of theory application will be reflected, education strategies that assist students to utilise the axiomatic design more effectively will be researched in correspondence.

References

1. J. Wilson, F. Badavi, M. Kim, M. Clowdsley, J. Heinbockel, F. Cucinotta, G. Badhwar, W. Atwell, S. Huston, *Natural and Induced Environment in Low Earth Orbit*, NASA, Virginia, (2002)
2. E. Weast, *Handbook of Chemistry and Physics*, The Chemical Rubber Co, Ohio, (1964)

3. B. Kumar, L. Scanlon, MATER. RES. SOC. SYMP. P **124**, 239 (1999)
4. K. Hirano, M. Asami, REACT. FUNCT. POLYM **73**, 256 (2012)
5. A. Papadopoulos, ENERG BUILDINGS **37**, 77 (2005)
6. D. Chung, APPL THERM ENG **21**, 1593 (2001)
7. S. Zhang, K. Xu, T.Jow, J POWER SOURCES **115**, 137 (2003)
8. T. Bergman, A. Lavine, F. Incropera, D. DeWitt, *Introduction to Heat Transfer* (John Wiley & Sons, Inc, US, 2011)
9. J. Shim, R. Kostecki, T. Richardson, X. Song, K. Striebel, J POWER SOURCES **112**, 222 (2002)
10. A. Korjenic, V. Petranek, J. Zach, J. Hroudova, ENERG BUILDINGS **43**, 2518 (2011)
11. X. Cao, R. Vassen, D. Stover, J EUR CERAM SOC **24**, 1 (2004)
12. C. Andrade, E. Zaparoli, J BRAZ SOC MECH SCI **22**, (2000)
13. G. Kalaprasad, P. Pradeep, G. Mathew, C. Pavithran, S. Thomas, COMPOS SCI TECHNOL **60**, 2967 (2000)
14. A. Demharter, CRYOGENICS **38**, 113 (1998)
15. D. Chung, APPL THERM ENG **21**, 1593 (2001)

Prevention, Early Detection, and Reversal of Type-2 Diabetes using Collective System Design

Joseph J. Smith[1,*], Shahab A. Shah[1], and David S. Cochran[1]

[1] Purdue University Fort Wayne, Fort Wayne, IN 46835 United States

Abstract. Type-2 Diabetes remains a progressive chronic disease that takes more and more lives every year. Small studies are beginning to show that a lifestyle approach could reverse type-2 diabetes in most individuals. The key discoveries from these studies are captured and formulated into a System Design Map for Prevention, Early Detection, and Reversal of Type-2 Diabetes using Collective System Design. Collective System Design describes systems as four aspects that interrelate: tone, thinking, structure and work. The tone in Collective System Design fosters an environment that views human failure as a failure of the system design itself. The thinking in Collective System Design is communicated by Axiomatic Design (AD). With the Collective System Design Approach, a model for prevention, early detection, and reversal of chronic disease is developed. The motivation for this paper is the ability to save millions of lives through a sustainable lifestyle program by identifying the required diet and exercise.

1 Introduction

The approach for diabetes prevention and reversal presented in this paper is in reference to only type-2 diabetes. Type-2 diabetes is commonly referred to as non-insulin-dependent diabetes, whereas type-1 diabetes is characterized by the dependence on insulin [1]. However, to begin to understand how diabetes develops, an understanding of the role of insulin and the concept of resistance is essential. These concepts will be discussed in the literature review.

This paper explores the current hypothesis regarding the development of diabetes. The hypothesis, and the corresponding research, provides the foundation for the development of the Collective System Design (CSD) Map for Prevention, Early Detection, and Reversal of Type-2 Diabetes. An overview of CSD is provided in order to support the idea that the CSD Methodology is applicable to creating a model for early detection and reversal of chronic disease.

For the role of reversing existing cases of diabetes, a Very Low Carbohydrate Ketogenic Diet (VLCKD) is proposed to be the underlying treatment method[2, 3]. The System Design Map presented in this paper expands upon the VLCKD to provide a systems engineering view of disease prevention and reversal. Systems Engineering at its core provides a sound foundation for developing disease prevention and reversal protocols, and this claim will be explained further in the methodology section of this paper.

First, the effectiveness of the VLCKD will be discussed by analyzing the supporting research. This paper does not attempt to argue that this approach is the only approach, or the best approach, it only provides standard work for diabetes prevention, early detection, and reversal. This standard work provides a starting point for a continuous improvement process to further progress this approach by new research and discoveries.

*e-mail: smitjj09@students.ipfw.edu

2 Literature Review

The theory for the treatment of type-2 diabetes presented within this paper is becoming prevalent in the medical literature [2–5]. The approach is comprised of using carbohydrate restriction to control insulin secretion with the underlying theory that insulin resistance is a response to chronic hyperglycemia and hyperinsulinemia [1, 4, 6].

2.1 The Development of Type-2 Diabetes

Insulin, commonly referred to as the "fat storage hormone," is responsible for shuttling sugar out of the blood stream and into the cells [1, 4, 5]. When dietary carbohydrates from highly processed sources are ingested on a regular basis, large amounts of insulin must be circulated throughout the blood stream to keep glucose levels in a safe range. Over time, cells become resistant to the effects of insulin, thus, requiring more insulin to properly regulate glucose levels [4].

The pancreas, the organ responsible for the production of insulin, will continue to produce more and more insulin to overcome the resistance. After five to ten years, the pancreas will no longer be able to produce enough insulin to maintain blood sugar levels. This lack of insulin, or lack of effectiveness, occurs when an individual starts showing signs of high blood sugar, but the disease, and damage, have been progressing for many years [4].

2.2 Reversing Type-2 Diabetes

To reverse or eliminate insulin resistance, the stimulus must be removed. Being that insulin's role is to shuttle sugar out of the blood, removing that sugar in the first place, would reduce the need for insulin (i.e., remove the stimulus). All carbohydrates, including everything from unprocessed fruit to highly refined dessert items, are digested and broken broken down into sugar in the blood stream which stimulates the need for insulin [4].

Developing a resistance to insulin is synonymous with developing a resistance to alcohol. Over many years, as an individual consumes alcohol, he/she will become more resistant to its effects (i.e., requiring more alcohol to become intoxicated)[7]. To remove this resistance, one must abstain from alcohol. Similarly, with insulin resistance, one must abstain from the key drivers of insulin secretion, which are dietary carbohydrates, in order to reverse the resistance.

The result of restricting carbohydrates can be defined physiologically by recognizing the shift in the body's fuel source from one of glucose (sugar) to one of ketones (fat) [3]. This shift in homeostasis is commonly defined as nutritional ketosis and represents a range in blood ketone levels from 0.5 to 5 mM [3]. The human body responds well to the lack of dietary carbohydrates by switching to fat for its primary fuel. Since fat is efficiently used as the main energy source, blood sugar levels are kept stable and at a low level. The small amount of glucose, required by the brain and other areas, is produced by the body through gluconeogenesis [3]. In this process, blood glucose is produced from glycerol: the backbone of triglycerides(or fat molecules).

The relevant literature on the use of a VLCKD to reverse diabetes shows great promise [2, 8–11]. One study in particular guides the motivation and design set forth in this paper [2]. The study, conducted by many of the leading physicians and researchers in the field of nutritional ketosis, set out to examine the effect of nutritional ketosis on patients with type-2 diabetes. The study consisted of 262 participants. The program participants "were enrolled in an outpatient protocol providing intensive nutrition and behavioral counseling, digital coaching and education platform, and physician-guided medication management" [2]. At baseline, only 19.8% of the participants had a glycated hemoglobin percentage (HbA1c, a 3-month average of blood glucose levels) of less than 6.5% (the lower end of the diabetic range). After 10 weeks, 56.1% of participants had an A1c below 6.5%.

2.3 Early Detection of Type-2 Diabetes

In addition to the research that supports the reversal of diabetes, the literature also examines potential blood markers that could predict diabetes at an earlier stage. Fig. 1 shows a representation of when the onset of diabetes occurs in reference to when the actual diagnosis takes place. The graph was adapted to depict how a person might feel during this time frame. This addition helps show why diabetes

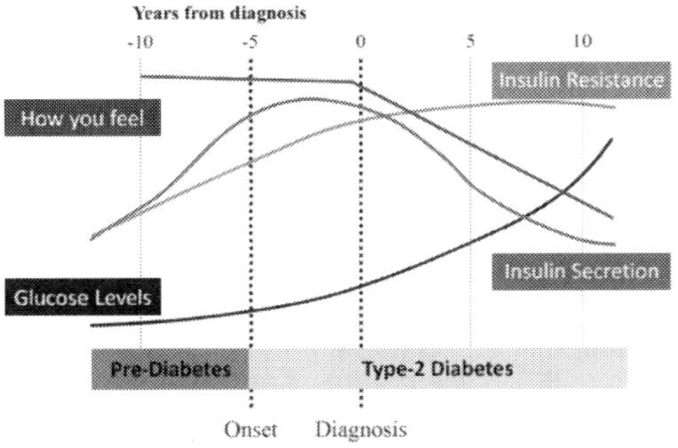

Figure 1. Time line depicting physiological changes 5 years before and after diagnosis. Adapted from [13].

is often detected around five years after the onset has taken place.

Recognizing that many physiological changes occur during the five year period prior to being diagnosed, provides insight into what tests could detect diabetes early on. Waiting for an individual to begin to feel worse allows for this five year period of physiological damage to go unnoticed, making further treatment and reversal even more difficult.

As ever increasing insulin levels are required to keep blood sugar within a normal range, an individual will not feel the biological effects that are taking place. Only after the pancreas can no longer produce enough insulin will a person begin to feel the effects of the resulting high blood sugar. Understanding this concept sheds light on what tests could predict diabetes earlier.

To further detail the possibility of early detection of diabetes, the Whitehall II study provides useful insight. In the Whitehall II study, 6,538 non-diabetic individuals were tested for fasting and two hour post-load glucose, and HOmeostasis Model Assessment (HOMA) for insulin sensitivity. After seven to nine years, 505 of these individuals were diagnosed diabetic. Retrospective trajectories of the above blood markers revealed that elevated fasting and two hour post-load glucose levels were present three years prior to diagnosis, and a steep decrease in HOMA insulin sensitivity began five years prior to diagnosis [12].

This research provides a foundation for which a system design map can be constructed. In the following section, the methodology and process behind constructing a system design map is discussed.

3 Methodology

The systems engineering methodology used for this research is known as Collective System Design (CSD). CSD is a product of Dr. David S. Cochran's work that began in the mid 2000's [14]. Systems Engineering is a discipline of engineering that focuses on the development and sustainment of systems to meet customer needs in a specific (path-dependent) manner throughout their life-cycle [15]. CSD is a methodical approach to product or system

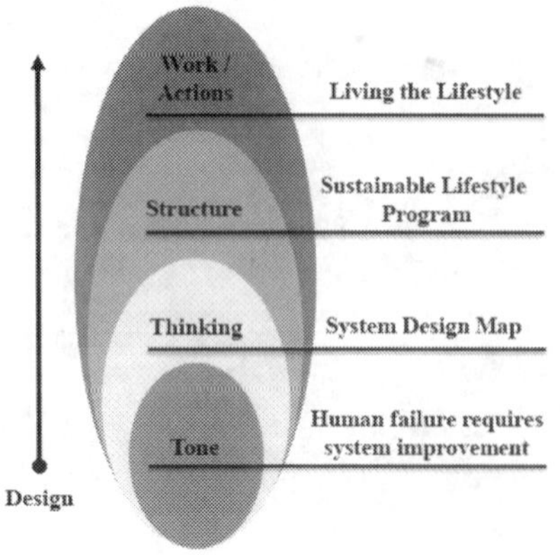

Figure 2. Flame Model of CSD for Prevention, Early Detection, and Reversal of Type-2 Diabetes. Adapted from [20].

design that facilitates a collective agreement regarding the requirements of the system or product [16–19].

The Flame Model of CSD in Fig. 2 represents the elements that exist within all systems, like the different layers within a flame. All elements are present within a system at any given time, and the outcome of each layer is either formed intentionally, or becomes unintentional due to the lack of attention given to that element. The work/actions and structure are the physical elements that we can see, and the thinking and tone are the hidden elements [20, 21].

The "tone" of a system, or organization, represents the attitude and mindset of the people [22]. A proper tone facilitates a respectful environment that allows everyone to be engaged, and the understanding that a system should not let someone fail. When, not if, a failure occurs, the system and the people within the system should view the failure as an opportunity for improvement.

The Collective System Design Methodology starts with the tone, and the thinking is biased by the tone that is defined. Axiomatic Design is then used to codify the thinking layer of the Flame Model that results from the tone [22]. The tone should recognize that understanding customer needs is important to the success of the project. This recognition of customer needs is fundamental to the Axiomatic Design Theory [23].

Functional Requirements (FRs), or what the system must achieve, are derived from the customer needs. Physical Solutions (PSs) are then collectively chosen by the leadership team to achieve those requirements. A physical solution is a prerogative of the system and is referred to as Design Parameters (DPs) in Axiomatic Design [22, 23].

The thinking layer of the CSD Flame model seeks to understand the "why" before choosing the "how." Understanding the "why" is fundamental to the success of a system and has been recognized as a reason for failure in various types of industries even agriculture [24].

To understand when an FR is achieved, a measure (denoted by FRm) is placed on the FR. Likewise, a measure can be placed on a PS to identify when the PS is implemented correctly. These measures play a crucial role in continuously improving the system design by recognizing when FRs are not achieved.

4 Collective System Design Map

The legend in Fig. 3 provides the nomenclature for understanding the System Design Map for Prevention, Early Detection, and Reversal of Type-2 Diabetes. The left to right precedence within the top level of the system design map (see Fig. 5) is realized by understanding that the design is partially-coupled, or said another way, the design is path-dependent, meaning that there is an implementation sequence of the Physical Solutions. Fig. 4 shows an overview of the Collective System Design Map for Prevention, Early Detection, and Reversal of Type-2 Diabetes. This research began as a project for a Systems Engineering Course (SE530) taught by Professor David S. Cochran at Purdue University Fort Wayne. Later this research was expanded upon for the 2018 Purdue University Fort Wayne Student Research and Creative Endeavor Symposium [15]. In addition, this paper expands the Creative Endeavor Symposium research to include a prevention branch.

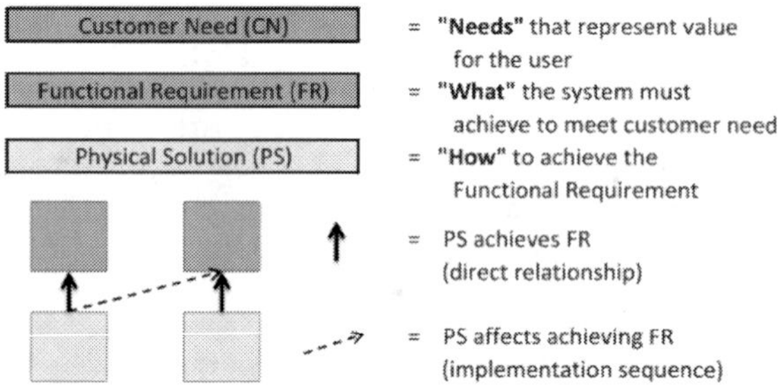

Figure 3. Legend regarding the Collective System Design Map

4.1 Application of Axiomatic Design

Axiomatic Design provides a scientific approach to design which can prevent designers from "tinkering" and ultimately reduce the amount of rework required. For the application of AD presented here, the prime focus was on the use of the Independence Axiom (Design Axiom 1). The Independence Axiom requires the designer to maintain the independence of the Functional Requirements [23]. Maintaining this independence will result in a specified implementation sequence of the Physical Solutions.

This implementation sequence is presented at a high level in Fig. 5. Thus, the design matrix for the second level (in Fig. 5) is decoupled and shows the dependencies among the PSs and FRs. Therefore, the implementation sequence of the different solutions is from left to right.

$$\begin{pmatrix} FR11 \\ FR12 \\ FR13 \\ FR14 \\ FR15 \end{pmatrix} = \begin{bmatrix} X & 0 & 0 & 0 & 0 \\ X & X & 0 & 0 & 0 \\ X & 0 & X & 0 & 0 \\ X & 0 & X & X & 0 \\ X & 0 & X & X & X \end{bmatrix} \times \begin{pmatrix} PS11 \\ PS12 \\ PS13 \\ PS14 \\ PS15 \end{pmatrix} \quad (1)$$

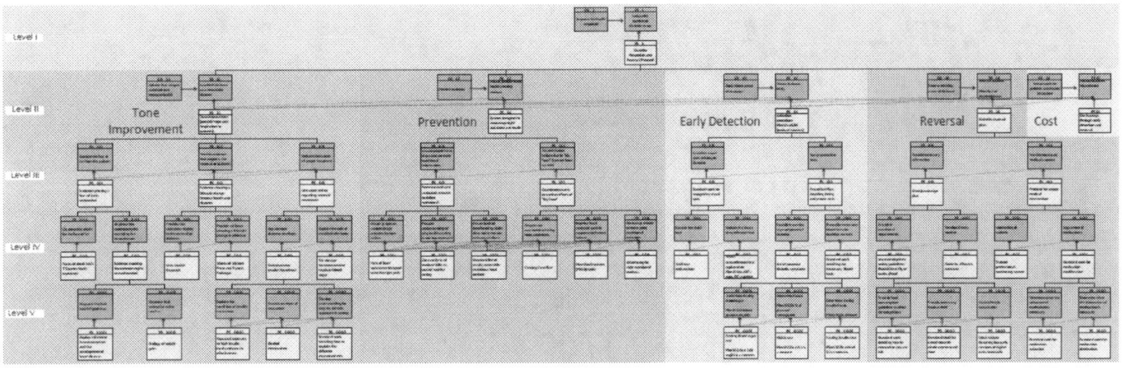

Figure 4. Overview of CSD Map for Prevention, Early Detection, and Reversal of Type-2 Diabetes (enlarge digital copy for full detail)

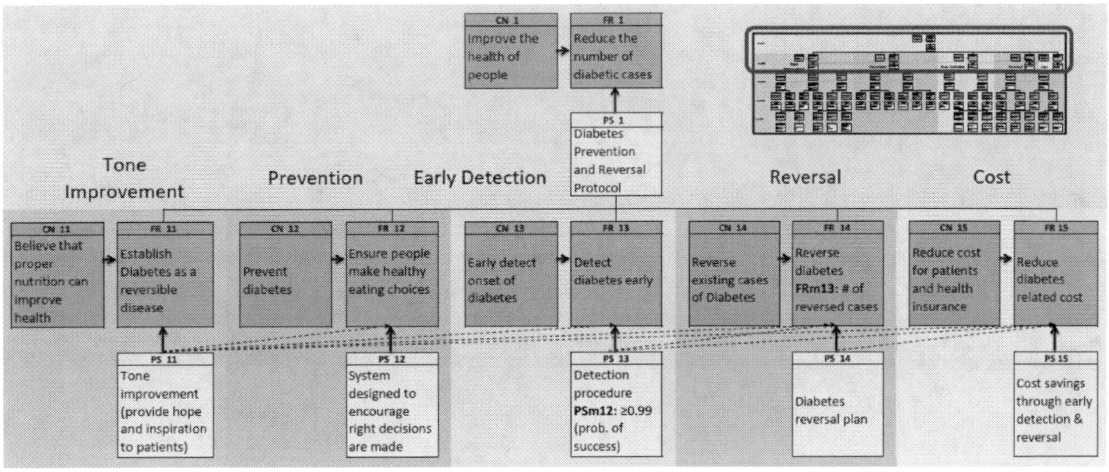

Figure 5. Top level of the Collective System Design Map for Diabetes Reversal

Top-Level

The top-level FR for the CSD map (FR1) is to "Reduce the number of diabetic cases," and the proposed PS to achieve this FR (PS1) is the "Diabetes Prevention and Reversal Protocol." This protocol represents an amalgamating PS that is further decomposed into additional FRs, which include tone improvement, prevention, early detection, reversal, and cost. The details of each branch are explained in the following sections.

4.2 Tone Improvement

Tone improvement, in the case of the CSD map for diabetes reversal (see Fig. 6), helps provide hope to everyone involved through education. This hope comes from understanding that being diabetic is not a death sentence or a predefined destiny [1]. The potential to reverse existing cases or prevent future ones, lies in the design of this CSD map for diabetes reversal and the openness of people to accept a paradigm shift in treatment.

A lifestyle program that removes carbohydrates from a person's diet must replace those calories with fat. For the last century, fat has been viewed as a key player in the development of heart related diseases and obesity, but there may be more to the story [3, 5, 27–29]. Asking patients to remove carbohydrates (i.e, potatoes, rice, whole grains, sugar, etc...) and to replace those calories with fat (i.e., butter, bacon, steak, cheese, avocados, etc...) will require educating them on why such a diet will provide wellness. In addition, explaining the biological mechanism behind the chosen treatment method (PS1131) will further provide confidence in accepting the VLCKD as a treatment method.

When the tone of people is that systems fail and people do not, and diabetes is not a death sentence, an environment for reversal is established. This proper tone of the people involved in the system represented by the CSD map for diabetes reversal is first and foremost to reducing the number of diabetic cases. Without the recognition that people have control over their health, patients will lack the courage to engage in the prevention, early detection, and reversal process. Providing the necessary information for the patients to understand why this treatment method is not only safe, but also effective, is paramount to the success of

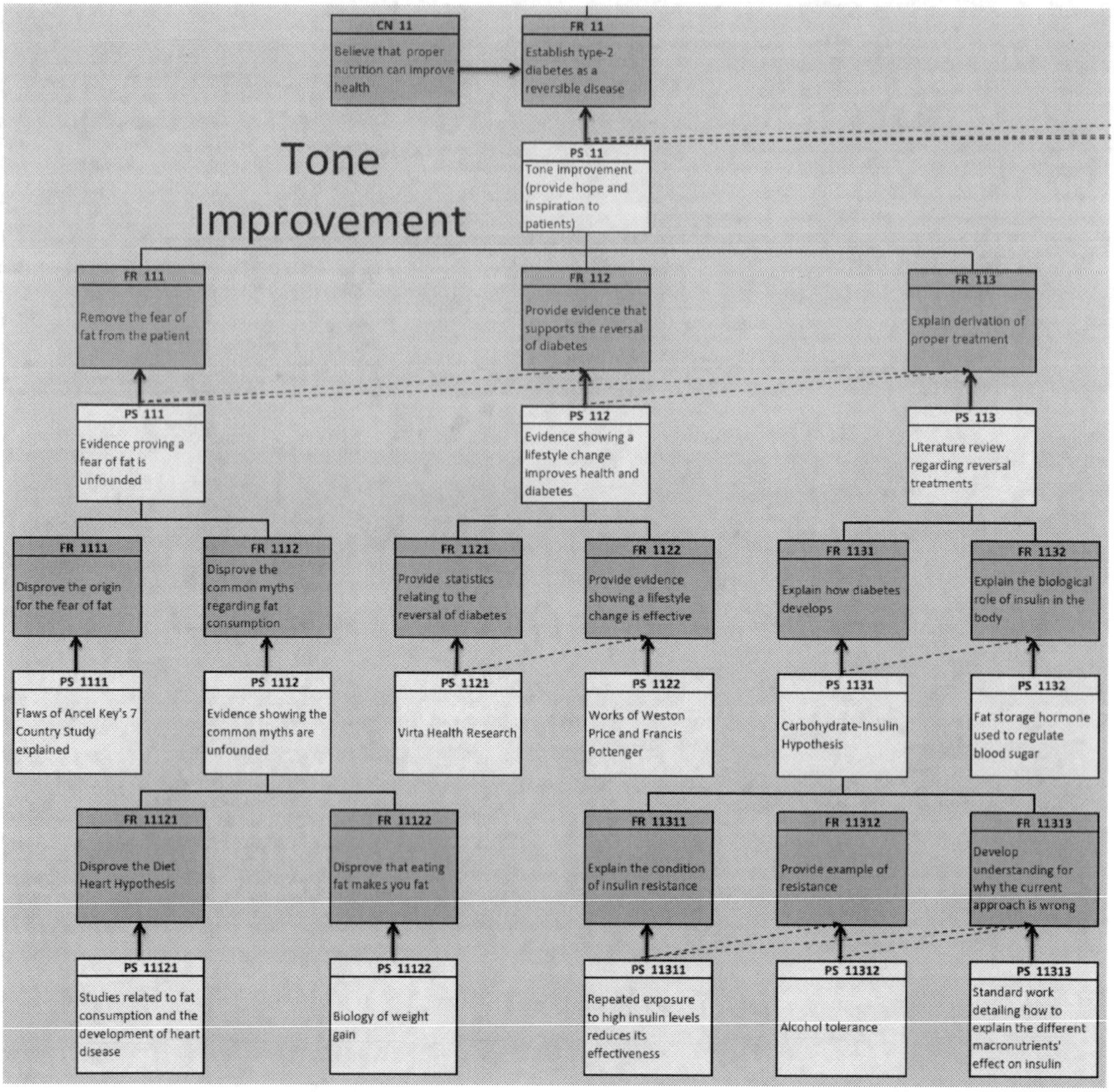

Figure 6. Tone Improvement Branch of the CSD Map for Diabetes Reversal; [2] supports PS1121, and [25, 26] supports PS1122.

reversing diabetes. Dr. Jason Fung presents much of this information to his patients to explain why the long standing treatment for type-2 diabetes, to inject insulin, should not be the standard for treating type-2 diabetes [4].

The path-dependency of the CSD map illustrates that the ability to educate and provide hope and encouragement (Tone Improvement) will affect a system's ability to prevent, early detect, and reverse diabetes. With this understanding, the Prevention branch is next in the implementation sequence.

4.3 Prevention

The FR to prevent future cases of diabetes is to "ensure people make healthy eating choices" (FR12), and this FR is achieved by a "system designed to encourage making the right nutritional decisions" (PS12) (see Fig. 7). For an individual to make the right decision, one has to know what the right decision is, but, in many cases, this information alone will not be enough to drive change. For example, food addictions and other habits will need to be overcome to ensure the right eating choices are made. In the Toyota Production System, defects were prevented by mistake-proofing operations (Poka-yoke) [31]. Viewing wrong lifestyle choices as a type of defect allows for mistake-proofing various situations that patients will encounter. For example, having easy access to healthy food will help prevent making wrong food choices in times of stress (PS12223).

The current food supply is one that has created a society of overfed but undernourished people [27, 29]. Both Gary Taubes and Nina Teicholz, investigative journalists, have presented the politics and unfortunate events that

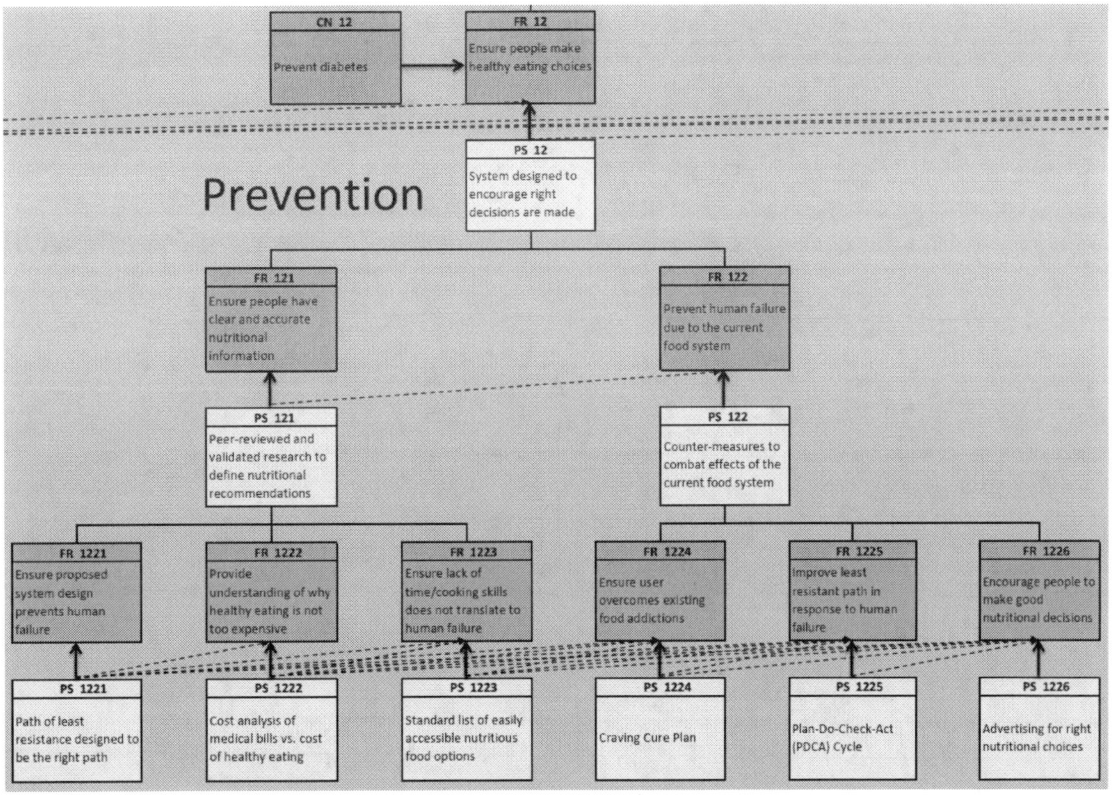

Figure 7. CSD Map for Diabetes Reversal; [30] supports PS1224.

have led to the dietary recommendations over the last century. Arguing whether the dietary recommendations where based on the best known science at the time, or on political or financial influence, is not the intent of this paper, but it is important to recognize that the current food system is failing to improve the health of society. Every indicator of health is moving in the wrong direction and people are not to blame.

Understanding that the current food supply is not designed for wellness allows for a new system to be designed to prevent failure in response to the current food supply. The Prevention branch of the CSD Map for Prevention, Early Detection, and Reversal of Type-2 Diabetes is built on this understanding. Understanding how to prevent diabetes, leads to the ability to early detect future cases.

4.4 Early Detection

The motivation for the Early Detection branch (see Fig. 8) is represented in Fig. 1. Recognizing that physiological changes begin to occur around five years prior to diagnosis provides a large window to begin or to improve prevention measures. Health markers involving blood glucose levels will not detect diabetes as early as those relating to insulin. Blood glucose measures, including fasting glucose and HbA1c are the standard for predicting and diagnosing diabetes [4].

Measuring blood glucose is analogous to measuring the water that spills out of a bucket once it is full, but measuring insulin would be like measuring the height of the water in the bucket. If the bucket spilling over represents the diagnosis of diabetes, it is clear that measuring the height of the water (insulin) would predict the overflow long before it occurs.

Understanding the difference in measuring insulin versus blood glucose leads to a detection procedure comprised of visual cues (PS131), fasting blood sugar (PS13221), HbA1c (PS13222), and fasting insulin (PS13223). With this detection procedure, future diabetic cases can be predicted early on, or currently undiagnosed diabetics can be properly diagnosed. The ability of the system represented by the CSD map for diabetes reversal to provide early detection and proper diagnosis affects the ability to reverse existing cases of diabetes.

4.5 Reversal

The Diabetes Reversal Plan (PS14) referred to in Fig. 9 is built on the theory presented in the literature review of this paper. The approach is comprised of using carbohydrate restriction to control insulin secretion with the underlying theory that insulin resistance is a response to chronic hyperglycemia and hyperinsulinemia [1, 4, 6].

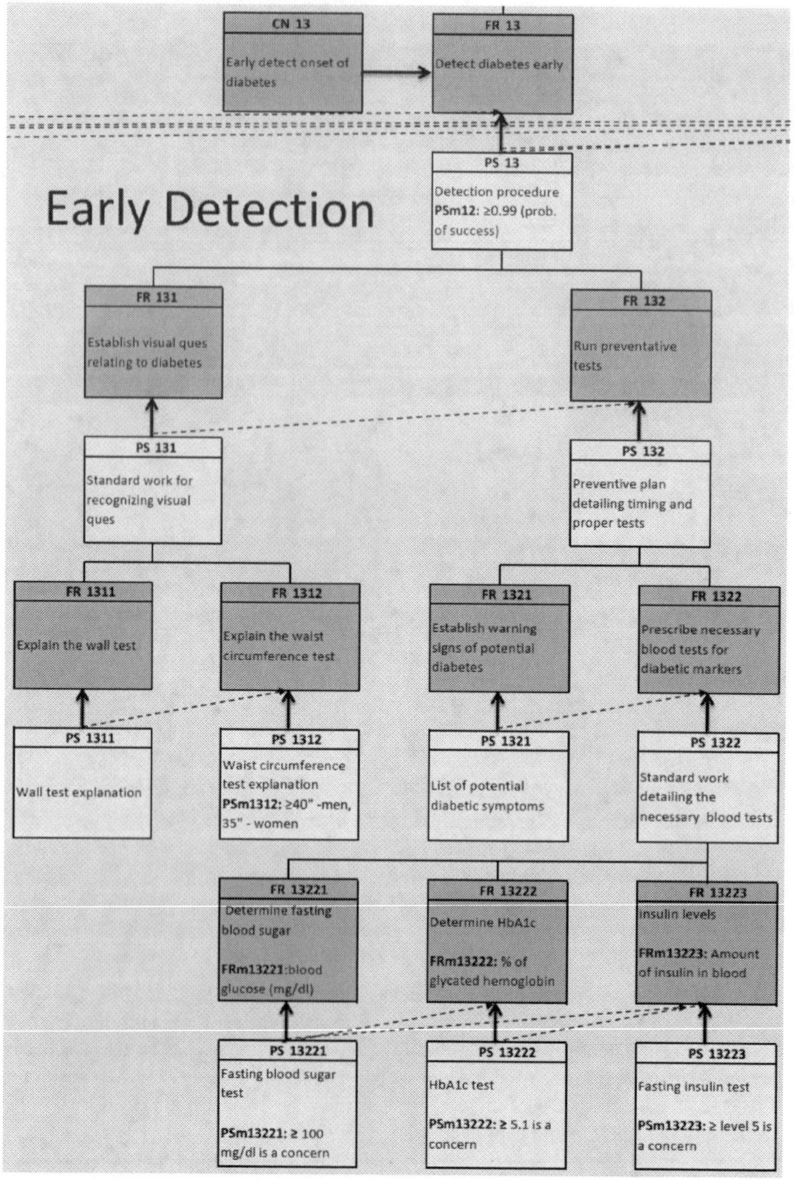

Figure 8. Early Detection Branch of the CSD Map for Diabetes Reversal

Continuing with the bucket analogy, if water represents blood sugar, then reversing and preventing diabetes is based on removing that sugar (i.e., reduce the amount of water in the bucket). Carbohydrates, even in naturally occurring fruits and vegetables, break down to blood glucose [3]. Thus, these food items represent adding water to the bucket.

Carbohydrate restriction was first documented in 1864 in William Banting's Letter on Corpulence as a diet for weight loss [32], but more recently it has been viewed as a "fad" diet because it restricts natural food products such as potatoes, rice, and fruit. Although the intent of this paper is not to argue which diet approach is most effective, the validity of the low carbohydrate diet is an important point to establish in order to understand why it was used as the basis for this system design.

Processed sugar and white flour are food products that are highly refined from their natural state. Refining these food items in order to incorporate them into many processed food products increases the absorption rate of glucose into the blood stream. Consuming these highly processed foodstuffs is unnatural and would not be possible without modern processing capabilities[25]. Recognizing that processed (unnatural) food can harm the body and put it into a diseased state provides an argument for an unnat-

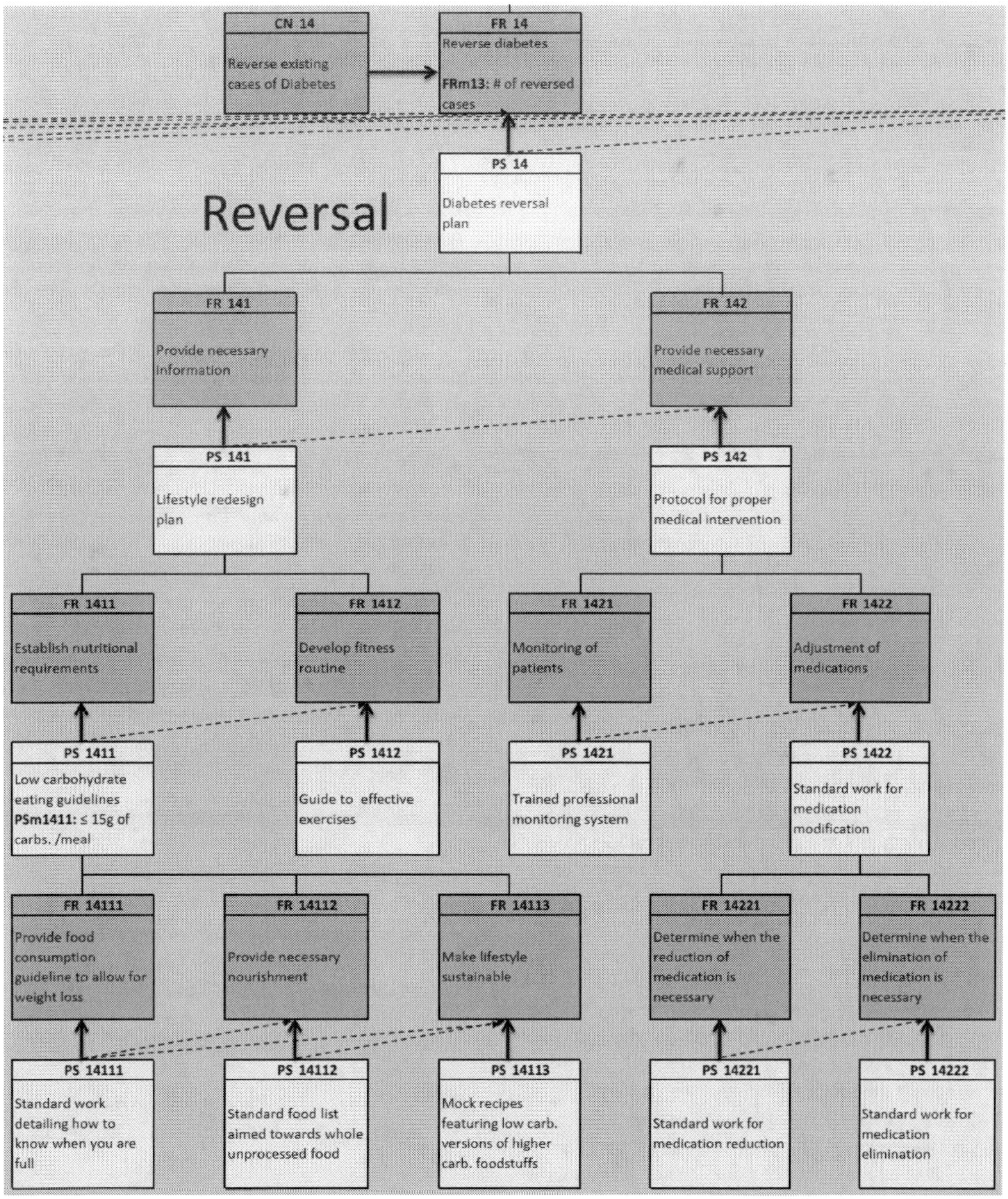

Figure 9. Reversal Branch of the System Design Map

ural treatment method (or what many people refer to as a fad diet.)

The Reversal branch of the CSD map depicts the use of a low carbohydrate diet to reverse diabetes in addition to reducing and eliminating any medication the patient may be taking. This support, in terms of medication reduction and elimination, is a key aspect to maintaining the safety and health of the patient. Standard work for medication management can provide a baseline for current practice, but it ultimately establishes a standard that can continuously be improved. The process for continuous improvement is explained in the following section.

5 Removing Blame by Continuous Improvement

To understand the applicability of applying a system design methodology to disease management, an example from a manufacturing setting may best set the stage for this argument. Within manufacturing, there is a never ending pursuit for perfect quality. One aspect of achieving this requirement is to ensure that operator human errors do not translate to defects (FR-Q113 from the Manufacturing System Design Decomposition (MSDD))[33]. To best achieve this requirement, the solution is to mistake proof the operations (Poka-Yoke)(PS-Q113). Therefore, an operator should not be able to install something backwards, or forget to install something. When a failure does occur due to an operator, a well designed system will look to improve the system and prevent further occurrences of this failure mode.

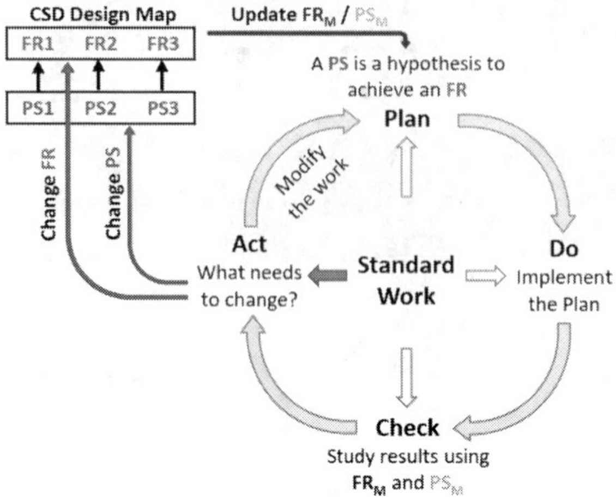

Figure 10. Plan-Do-Check-Act (PDCA) Cycle [34]

In the case of type-2 diabetes, the PSs of the Collective System Design Map are implemented through standard work. Thus, when a chosen PS does not achieve an FR, a continuous improvement process modifies the map to reduce and account for human failure. The Collective System Design Methodology provides a structured approach to the process of continually improving the system design map. This approach, known as the Plan-Do-Check-Act (PDCA) cycle, has been adapted from Dr. Deming's work to provide a process for adapting a system design map[35]. The PDCA cycle presented in Fig. 10 provides 4 ways to modify a system design map. The 4 possible ways to "act" include modifying the work, modifying the physical solutions, modifying the functional requirement, or modifying the measures on the FR or PS.

With this systems view of disease prevention and reversal, an individuals will power, or the lack of, can no longer be cited as the cause of poor results. When an individual is overcoming food addictions, which will often be the case, binging on carbohydrates does not represent a lack of character, it represents an opportunity to improve the system. **The systems engineer has the responsibility of improving a system in response to human failure** [36]. For this reason, a systems engineering view provides the core mindset required to help overcome food and lifestyle habits.

6 Conclusion

With the growing prevalence of type-2 diabetes around the world, a new approach needs to be taken for preventing and reversing this chronic disease. The current system "design," as it has evolved, rewards behaviors that are not aligned with the CSD Map presented here. For instance, if the lifestyle re-design plan from PS141 is implemented, the pharmaceutical treatments may not be required.

A new system, defined by a Collective System Design map for the Prevention, Early Detection, and Reversal of Type-2 Diabetes provides a way to document the best-known practices right now, in addition to providing a way to continually improve the map as more research is completed. This product of Axiomatic Design provides a road map to implement such a system. By understanding the path-dependency of the design prior to implementation, rework is minimized and the design can be clearly communicated to the individuals involved with implementation.

The understanding of the path-dependency of a system to reverse diabetes provided the realization that tone improvement would affect the rest of the system design. Patients' would require support and a practical understanding of the treatment in order to be successful. Thus, the outcome of implementing the PSs within the tone improvement branch will provide this support and practical understanding.

With the Axiomatic Design approach to disease management, the system design map proposed in this paper can not only be replicated across the world by different clinics, but this map can also be used as a model for the management of other chronic diseases. With this systems thinking view of disease management, failure is viewed as an opportunity to improve the system, which stands in stark contrast to blaming a patient for their lack of will power.

References

[1] R.K. Bernstein, *Dr. Bernstein's Diabetes Solution*, 4th edn. (Hachette Book Group, 2011)
[2] A.L. McKenzie, S.J. Hallberg, B.C. Creighton, B.M. Volk, T.M. Link, M.K. Abner, R.M. Glon, J.P. McCarter, J.S. Volek, S.D. Phinney, JMIR Diabetes **2**, e5 (2017)
[3] S.J. Volek, D.S. Phinney, *The Art and Science of Low Carbohydrate Living* (Beyond Obesity, LLC, 2011)
[4] J. Fung, *The Diabetes Code: Prevent and Reverse Type 2 Diabetes Naturally*, 1st edn. (Greystone Books, 2018)
[5] G. Taubes, *The Case Against Sugar*, 1st edn. (Alfred A. Knopf, 2016)
[6] R.D. Feinman, J.S. Volek, Scandinavian Cardiovascular Journal **42**, 256 (2008)
[7] *Alcohol and Tolerance - Alcohol Alert No. 28-1995* (1995), `https://pubs.niaaa.nih.gov/publications/aa28.htm`
[8] S.J. Hallberg, A.L. McKenzie, P.T. Williams, N.H. Bhanpuri, A.L. Peters, W.W. Campbell, T.L. Hazbun, B.M. Volk, J.P. McCarter, S.D. Phinney et al., Diabetes Therapy **9**, 583 (2018)
[9] R. Tate, *The Magic Pill* (2018)
[10] A. Accurso, R.K. Bernstein, A. Dahlqvist, B. Draznin, R.D. Feinman, E.J. Fine, A. Gleed,

D.B. Jacobs, G. Larson, R.H. Lustig et al., Nutrition & Metabolism **5**, 9 (2008)

[11] L.R. Saslow, A.E. Mason, S. Kim, V. Goldman, R. Ploutz-Snyder, H. Bayandorian, J. Daubenmier, F.M. Hecht, J.T. Moskowitz, Journal of Medical Internet Research **19**, e36 (2017)

[12] A.G. Tabák, M. Jokela, T.N. Akbaraly, E.J. Brunner, M. Kivimäki, D.R. Witte, The Lancet **373**, 2215 (2009)

[13] *American Diabetes Advocates (ADA) - National Diabetes Information Clearinghouse Home*, `http://www.diabetesadvocates.info/Complications.html`

[14] D.S. Cochran, Journal of Cost Management **20**, 20 (2006)

[15] J. Smith, S. Shah, *Disease Management Through Collective System Design (CSD) Approach* (2018), first place recipient, `https://opus.ipfw.edu/stu_symp2018/47`

[16] D.S. Cochran, J. Oxtoby, M. Hensley, J. Barnes, Journal of Enterprise Transformation **7** (2017)

[17] D.S. Cochran, The Journal of Reliability, Maintainability, Supportability in Systems Engineering **Winter Journal**, 6 (2009)

[18] D.S. Cochran, The Journal of Reliability, Maintainability, Supportability in Systems Engineering **Spring Journal**, 16 (2010)

[19] D.S. Cochran, in *Lean Accounting*, edited by J. Stenzel (John Wiley and Sons, New Jersey, 2007)

[20] D.S. Cochran, J. Swartz, *Sustaining Improvement through Tone in Collective System Design* (Anaheim, CA, 2016)

[21] D.S. Cochran, *Systems Approach to Sustain Lean Organizations*, in *SAE International World Congress* (Cobo Hall Detroit, MI, 2007), Vol. 2007-01-1377

[22] D.S. Cochran, *Collective System Design in Industrial and Systems Engineering Education* (Louisville, KY, 2010)

[23] N.P. Suh, *Complexity: Theory and Applications* (Oxford University Press, 2005)

[24] J. Salatin, *You Can Farm*, 1st edn. (Polyface, 1998)

[25] W. Price, *Nutrition and Physical Degeneration: A Comparison of Primitive and Modern Diets and Their Effects*, 8th edn. (Price Pottenger Nutrition, 1939)

[26] *Pottenger's Cats: A Study in Nutrition*, 2nd edn. (Price Pottenger Nutrition, 2012)

[27] N. Teicholz, *The Big Fat Surprise: Why Butter, Meat and Cheese Belong in a Healthy Diet*, 1st edn. (Simon & Schuster, 2014)

[28] M. Pollan, *The Omnivore's Dilemma*, 1st edn. (The Penguin Press, New York, 2006)

[29] G. Taubes, *Good Calories, Bad Calories*, 1st edn. (Alfred A. Knopf, 2007)

[30] J. Ross, *The Craving Cure*, 1st edn. (Flat Iron Books, 2017)

[31] S. Shingo, A. Dillon, *A Study of the Toyota Production System: From an Industrial Engineering Viewpoint (Produce What Is Needed, When It's Needed)*, 1st edn. (Productivity Press, 1989)

[32] W. Banting, *Letter on corpulence : addressed to the public* (New York, 1864)

[33] D.S. Cochran, J.T. Foley, B. Zhuming, International Journal of Production Research **55**, 870 (2017)

[34] D.S. Cochran, J. Barnes, *Sustainable Enterprise Design* (Fort Wayne, IN, 2015)

[35] W. Deming, *Out of the Crisis*, 1st edn. (The MIT Press, 2000)

[36] D. Long, *Reimagining Systems Engineering* (2017)

Axiomatic Design Based Complexity Measures to Assess Product and Process Structures

Vladimir Modrak[1,*], *Zuzana* Soltysova[1]

[1]Faculty of Manufacturing Technologies, Technical University of Kosice, 04200 Kosice, Slovakia

Abstract. Definitions of complexity often depend on several circumstances, such as the nature of investigated complex system, the kind of complexity, the conceptual framework used for a study, the theoretical approach taken, and the like. In this paper, two complexity measures that are based on Boltzmann's entropy concept and AD theory are proposed and described. The first measure quantifies product variety complexity and the second one focuses on process structure complexity. Such complexity techniques will be used to determine product platform complexity and related process complexity for early stage of design decision-making. The method focused on product platform complexity assumes that the distribution of FR-DP couplings offers a suitable complexity concept, which prescribes that coupled designs should be decoupled, if possible, since uncoupled design is ideal and a decoupled design is less good, while a coupled design is the least satisfactory. Analogically, the same principle is used for the purpose to quantify topological process complexity by transforming input components into process variables and product modules including final product into design parameters. Subsequently, relevant properties of these measures will be analysed by computational experiments. Finally, practical findings for mass customization practice will be presented.

1 Introduction

Definitions of complexity often depend on several circumstances, such as the nature of investigated complex system, the kind of complexity, the conceptual framework used for a study, the theoretical approach taken, and the like. Overviews of complexity approaches and theories were offered by number of studies, see, e.g., [1-4] which provide complementary information among them. According to Gao et al [5] Shannon information concept seems widely recognized as essential building block of complexity theory. Traditional complexity metrics are associated with an absolute measure of complexity in contrast to the axiomatic design complexity, where this system attribute is treated as relative quantity based on the information concept and axioms of Axiomatic Design (AD). The complexity is expressed as: "A measure of uncertainty in understanding what it is we want to know or in achieving a functional requirement (FR) [6]." A relative information quantity in this approach is determined by the overlap between the system range of FRs and the design range of FRs. By this complexity theory, four different types of complexities: time-independent real complexity, time independent imaginary complexity, time-dependent combinatorial complexity, and time dependent periodic complexity are identified. The key idea of the theory is reduction of a complexity of system design in order to increase system reliability at each level of the design hierarchy. The dependencies between the FRs and the design parameters (DPs) can be classified by three types of design matrix (DM): uncoupled, decoupled and coupled. Among them, coupled design where FRs are influenced by possible changes of individual FRs, is more complex than an uncoupled design. Guenov [7] extends AD complexity theory for computing the information content of all types of design matrices. For this purpose, he developed complexity measures of design representations by adopting Boltzmann's entropy concept. Existing research literature on AD (see, e.g. [8-11]) offers other challenging approaches and inspirational studies including complexity issues.

In this paper, two complexity measures are proposed. The first one, determines product variety complexity and the second one is dedicated to measure process structure complexity. Both of them adopt one of the complexity measures from the work by Guenov [7].

Such complexity measures will be used to define product platform complexity and related process complexity for early stage of design decision-making based on the assessment of topological structures of design matrices. The method focused on product platform complexity assumes that the distribution of FR-DP couplings offers a suitable complexity concept, which prescribes that coupled designs should be decoupled if possible, since uncoupled design is ideal and a decoupled design is less good, while a coupled design is the least satisfactory [6]. Analogically, the same principle is used for the purpose of quantifying static process complexity based by

* Corresponding author: vladimir.modrak@tuke.sk

transforming input components into process variables and product modules including final product into design parameters.

2 Theoretical background

Adapted complexity measures used in our approach are based on Boltzmann's formula [12] for statistical entropy introduced in 1872. This formula in case of an ideal gas exactly corresponds to the thermodynamic entropy. According to Anderson [13] Boltzmann's entropy is simply related to disorder in many field of science, even though this resemblance for the most part have nothing to do with the second law of thermodynamics. Guenov [7] substituted number of elements (molecules) in formula for degree of disorder (Ω) by total number of couplings (N) in design matrix in order to calculate design complexity based on the assessment of topological structure of the design matrix as follows:

$$\Omega = N!/(N1!...NK!), \quad (1)$$

where K is number of design parameters (number of columns in design matrix).
The same author recognized that formula:

$$SDC = \Sigma N_j \ln N_j, \quad (2)$$

which was derived from the statistical entropy seems to convey better the meaning of axiom 1 of AD, where N_j is the number of couplings per design parameter (i.e. per column), $j = 1, \ldots, K$.
Therefore, this complexity measure denoted by us as Systems Design Complexity (SDC), will be applied for the purpose to estimate *product variety complexity* and *process structure complexity*.
A simple example demonstrating the application of this measure can be shown by using random design matrix (DM) with its couplings distribution depicted in Figure 1.

	DP_1	DP_2	DP_3	DP_4	DP_5
FR_1	X	0	0	X	X
FR_2	0	X	0	0	0
FR_3	0	0	X	0	0
FR_4	0	0	0	X	0
FR_5	0	X	X	0	X

Fig. 1. An example of DM with couplings denoted by symbol "X".

Then, SDC= $\Sigma N_j \ln N_j = 1\ln1 + 2\ln2 + 2\ln2 + 2\ln2 + 2\ln2 = 5{,}55$ nats.

3 Adaptation of SDC to measurement of product variety complexity

3.1. Description of the product complexity measure

In order to adopt SDC measure for quantifying product variety complexity, the following steps are involved:

1) Classification of input components (ICs) entering an assembly process in terms of mass customization,

2) Description of graphical model interpreting relation between ICs and possible product (module) configurations (PPCs),

3) Conception of transformation mechanism of the relation between ICs and PPCs into a DM.

3.1.1. Classification of input components

Due to the fact the structure of variable product components determines total number of product combinations, it is reasonable to introduce working classification of input components. We consider three types of initial components entering an assembly process. They are as follows:

Stable components (S) are considered to be assembled for ensuring the functionality of the module or final product.

Optional components (O) are useful in some cases but they are not required. They can be selected according to the customer's requirements and are optional in any combination, including cases when only individual components are chosen. Selection by customer without this type of component is also an option.

Compulsory optional components (CO) are different from O by the number of components that may be chosen from all of them. They are limited in selection. Thus, restrictions are determined by three specific selection rules: minimum, maximum and exact requirements on selection. These selection rules can be specified in a simple way by combinatorial number $\binom{k}{l}$, where l defines ways of picking component combinations from a set of all k, while $1 \leq l < k$.

In mass customization environment, practically any number of stable, voluntary and compulsory optional components can be combined. However, the following specific selection rules of the selections for the set of CO components with number k may occur when identifying product configurations. They are:

Individual selectivity rule, where it is possible to define exact number of 'l' of components to be chosen from all 'k' of CO components;

Maximum selectivity rule where it is possible to define the maximum number 'l' of CO components to combine within an assembly choice of all 'k' of CO components (note that 'l' is max. k-1);

Minimum selectivity rule where it is possible to choose/combine at least '*l*' CO of components from available '*k*' of CO components (note that '*l*' is min. *1*).

Combinatorial formulas for determining numbers of product (module) configurations according to the above described components types and selection rules are presented by Modrak [14]. The example of customizable chair containing of three types of initial components is shown in Fig. 2.

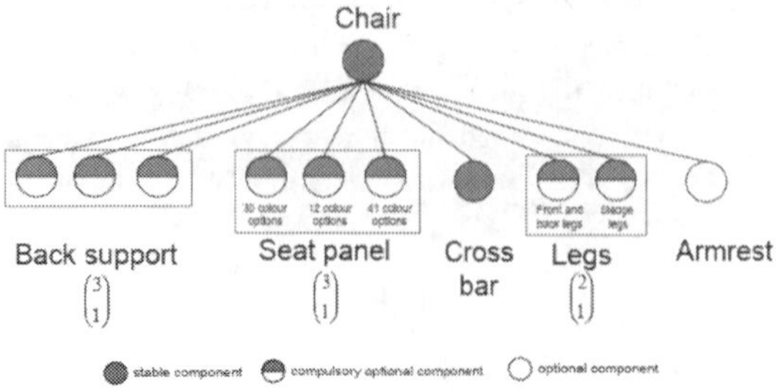

Fig. 2. Example with three types of initial components.

3.1.2. Graphical interpretation of relation between ICs and PPCs

Subsequently, it is useful to model the relation between ICs and PPCs by incomplete bipartite graphs (see an example in Figure 3a) with two independent sets of vertices U and V, where the set U consists of ICs and the set V contains from related PPCs. The set U in given case involves three stable components (*i=3*), one optional component (*j=1*), and three compulsory optional components with the individual selectivity rule $\binom{3}{1}$. Frequently, practitioners used to express product variety complexity by number of PPCs. However, the graphical models can be helpful to study product variety complexity in more detail way.

3.1.3. Transformation mechanism of scheme of relation between ICs and PPCs into a DM

The transit mechanism, which was partly outlined in our previous work [15], is based on substitution of set U consisting of ICs by DPs. Subsequently, elements of set V, i.e. PPCs will be replaced by FRs. Moreover, the transformation takes under consideration the fact that number of stable components does not impact on number of PPCs. Therefore, all stable components occurring as initial assembly inputs are represented only by one DP as shown in Figure 3b.

Finally, the bipartite graph represented by FR-DP relations can be easily transformed into a system design matrix shown in Figure 3c.

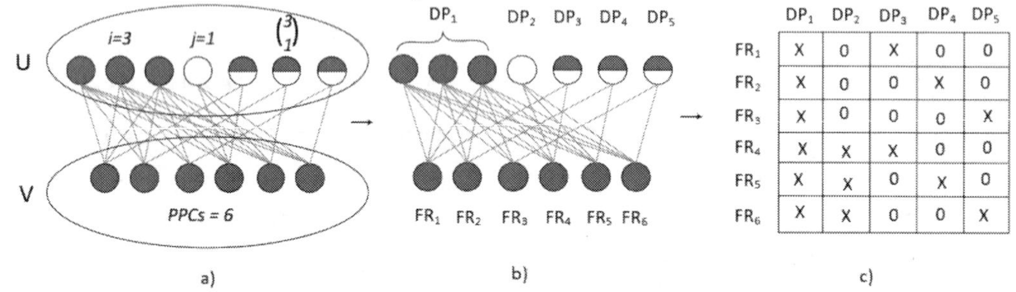

Fig. 3. a) Two independent sets of vertices U and V; b) Relation between DPs and FRs; c) Final transformation of the relation between ICs and PPCs into DM.

Then, product variety complexity can be enumerated by using formula (2) as follows:

$SDC = \Sigma N_j \ln N_j = 6\ln6 + 3\ln3 + 2\ln2 + 2\ln2 + 2\ln2 =$ 18,21 nats.

This transformation assumes that DPs considered as inputs components are determined by individual customer's specific needs through FRs of the product. Such defined FRs are directly included in selected product configuration. Then, the model of FR-DP relations depicted in Figure 3b is coherent with three of four domains of the design world [16] as shown in Figure 4.

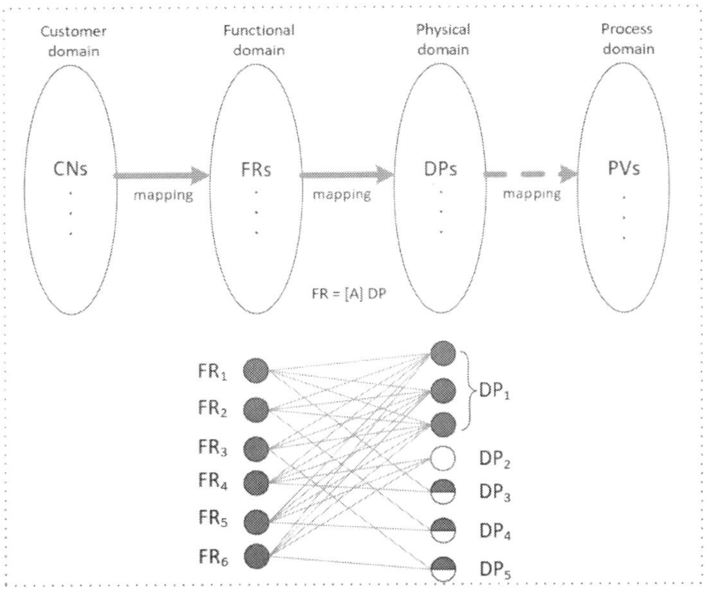

Fig. 4. The relation between ICs and PPCs in context of four domains of the design world.

3.2. Comparison of SDC against PPCs

In order to analyse possible differences between two possible product variety complexity measures, i.e., SDC and PPCs, two scenarios will be considered.

3.2.1. Scenario #1

In this scenario, structure of ICs is assumed as combination of two and more S components and one and more O components. Let's compare SDC and PPCs by using numbers of these ICs as described in Table 1.

Table 1. PPCs and SDC values for selected combinations of S and O components.

Number of S	Number of O	PPCs	SDC [nats]
2	1	2	1,39
	2	4	8,32
	3	8	33,27
3	1	2	1,39
	2	4	8,32
	3	8	33,27
4	1	2	1,39
	2	4	8,32
	3	8	33,27

As it can be seen from Table 1, number of *S* does not impact on PPCs and SDC values. This fact can be simply explained by transforming selected three combinations of ICs as shown in Figure 5.

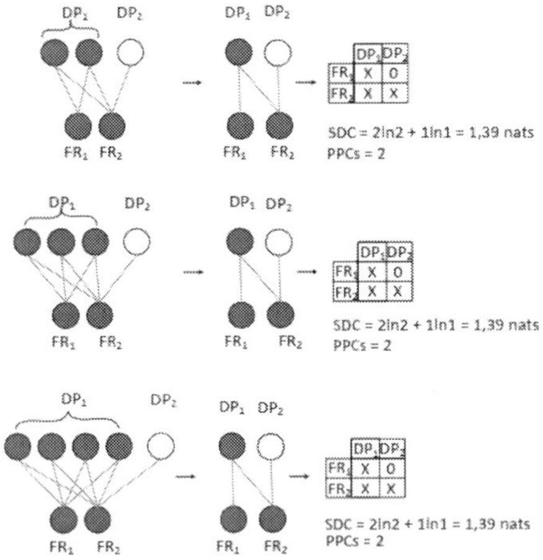

Fig. 5. Examples of combinations of ICs with different number of S.

In Figure 5, all stable components in original bipartite graphs are replaced only by one stable component. Then all three modified graphs are identical, which logically proves that SDC measure reflects this reality adequately.

3.2.2. Scenario #2

This scenario supposes several CO components with all possible individual selectivity rules. Let's use the example with five CO components and all possible individual selectivity rules, namely $\binom{5}{1}$, $\binom{5}{2}$, $\binom{5}{3}$ and $\binom{5}{4}$ as shown in Figure 6.

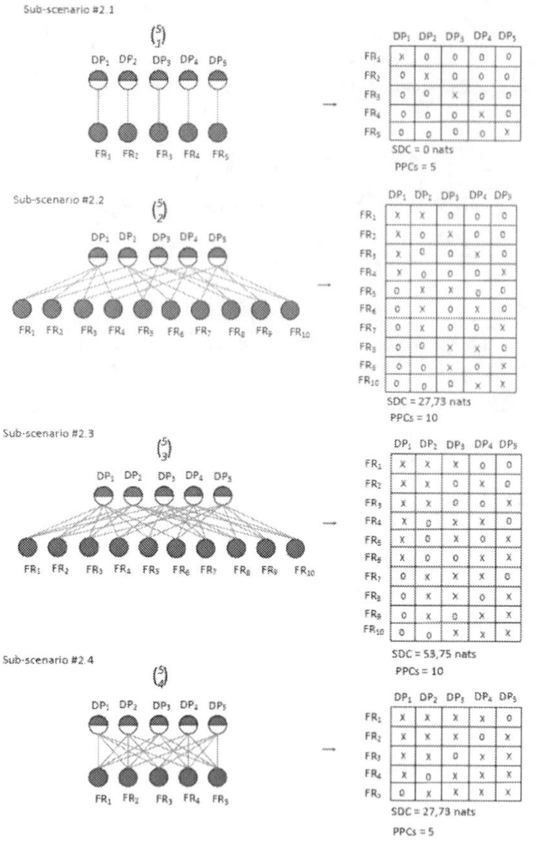

Fig. 6. An example of scenario with 5 CO components with all possible individual selectivity rules.

Then, it is easy to quantify SDC and PPCs values. Analogically, it could be possible to generate SDC and PPCs values for arbitrary number of CO components with all possible individual selectivity rules. SDC and PPCs values for such cases with five, six and seven CO components are graphically depicted in Figure 7.

As it can be seen from the Figure 7, PPCs and SDC values for a given number of CO components principally differ from each other. Especially, it can be pointed that number of PPCs for pairs of individual selectivity rules $\left[\binom{k}{1},\binom{k}{k-1}\right]$ are equal, while SDC values for the same individual selectivity rules are different. Then, there is a question about which of the two indicators reflect the complexity in more realistic way. To find the answer, the example from Figure 6 will be used. By comparing two bipartite graphs for the rules $\binom{5}{1}$ and $\binom{5}{4}$, it is empirically evident that product variety complexity for the rule $\binom{5}{4}$ is higher than for the rule $\binom{5}{1}$. However, this practical view can be proved by formal verification.

For this purpose, the following definition for structural complexity will be employed. The complexity of a system scales with the number of its elements, the number of interactions between them, the complexities of the elements, and the complexities of the interactions (Gershenson 2002) [17].

By applying the previous definition for the two sub-scenarios *#2.1 and #2.4* from the Figure 6, the following results can be obtained.

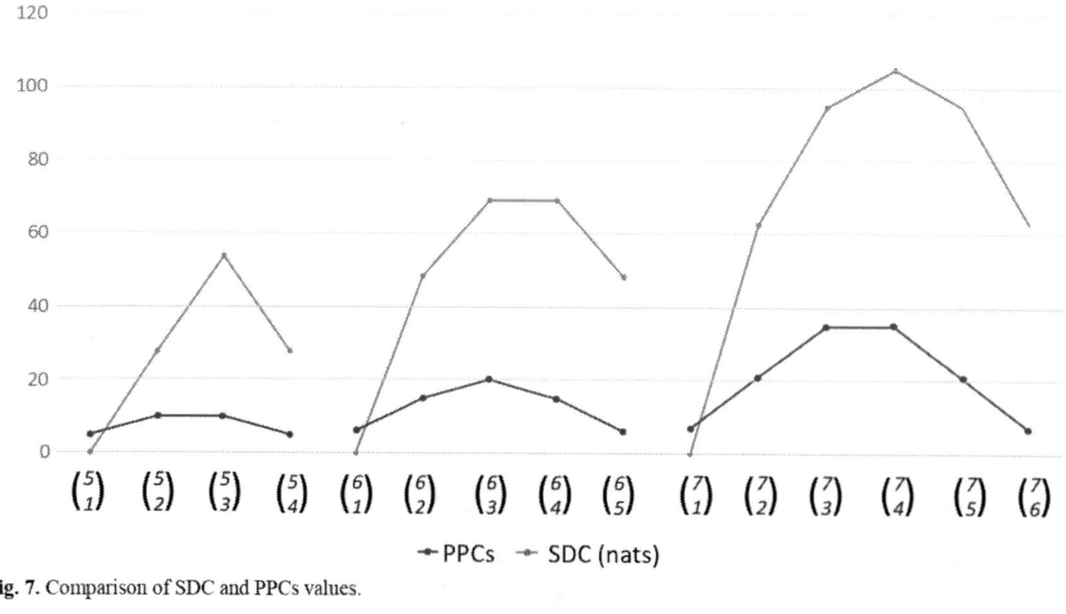

Fig. 7. Comparison of SDC and PPCs values.

Sub-scenario #2.1 with the rule $\binom{5}{1}$:

- number of nodes: 10,
- number of edges: 5,
- the complexity of the edges: one edge set
- the complexity of the nodes: one component set

Sub-scenario #2.4 with the rule $\binom{5}{4}$:

- number of nodes: 10,
- number of edges: 30,
- the complexity of the edges: one edge set
- the complexity of the nodes: four component set

Then, according to the previous complexity definition, it is proved that product variety complexity for the rule $\binom{5}{4}$ is higher than for the rule $\binom{5}{1}$.

By analogy it can be proved that product variety complexity for the rule $\binom{5}{3}$ is higher than for the rule $\binom{5}{2}$.

The same logic can be used to verify that SDC values better reflect product variety complexity than number of PPCs for different amount of compulsory optional components.

4 Adaptation of SDC to the process complexity measure

Similarly, as in the case of adaptation of SDC to measurement of product variety complexity, manufacturing process structure will be transformed into coupled design matrix. This transformation in subsequent subsection will be described.

4.1. Description of the process complexity measure

Prior to transformation of manufacturing process structure into DM, model of assembly process structure will be introduced.

4.1.1. Description of model of assembly process structure

Assembly type of operations are commonly interpreted using graph theory as convergent graphical models. Under convergent assembly structure we understand the chain where one process node has at most one successor, but has to have at least two predecessors. Our framework of assembly structures follows the work of Hu et al. [18], who outlined the way to model possible supply chain structures based on the number of original suppliers. An example of the model of assembly process structure is shown in Figure 8 a), where $i=1,2,\ldots,m$ is the number of stable input assembly components; $O=1,2,\ldots,p$ is the number of assembly operations, while O_0 represents final assembly operation.

4.1.2. Transformation mechanism of manufacturing process structures into a DM

In this transformation, equally as in Subsection 3.1.3, stable input components will be substituted by DPs and process nodes will be replaced by PVs (see Figure 8 b)). Subsequently, the convergent graph represented by DP-PV relations can be easily transformed into a system design matrix shown in Figure 8 c).

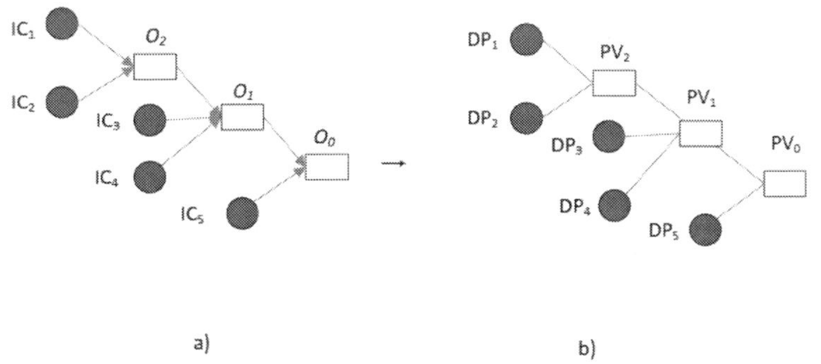

	DP_1	DP_2	DP_3	DP_4	DP_5
PV_2	X	X	0	0	0
PV_1	X	X	X	X	0
PV_0	X	X	X	X	X

Fig. 8. a) Initial model of assembly process structure; b) Converted model of assembly process structure; c) Transformation of the converted process structure into DM.

Then, process complexity can be enumerated by using formula (2) as follows:

$SDC = \Sigma N_j \ln N_j = 3\ln3 + 3\ln3 + 2\ln2 + 2\ln2 + 1\ln1 = 9{,}36$ nats.

In such graphs, input assembly components are mapped from physical domain to process domain as can be seen in Figure 9.

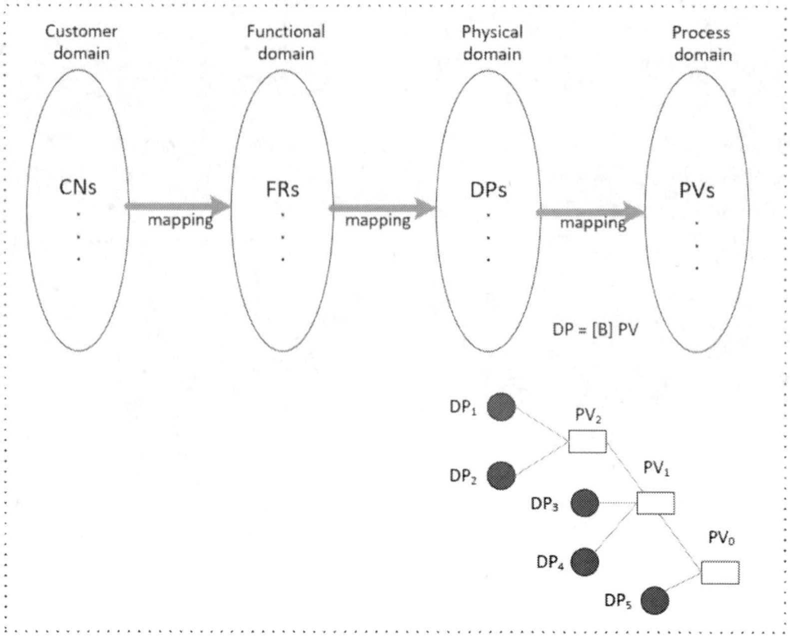

Fig. 9. The relation between input assembly components and process nodes in context of four domains of the design world.

4.2. Comparison of SDC against to concurrent measure

Competitive properties of the SDC measure can be found by its comparison with possible concurrent measures. Possible alternative complexity indicators were already mutually compared in previous studies [19, 20], where so called Index of vertex degree (Ivd) met optimality criteria for assessment of network complexity in the best way. Index of vertex degree has been introduced by Bonchev and Buck [21] and is expressed for Graph G consists of a set of V vertices, $\{V\} \equiv \{v1, v2, \ldots, vV\}$, by formula:

$$Ivd = -\sum_{i=1}^{V} deg(v)_i \log_2 deg(v)_i \quad (3)$$

where $deg(v)$ is the degree of vertex v in G.

Differences between these two process complexity measures, i.e., SDC and Ivd, will be analysed and evaluated through the following two computational experiments.

4.2.1. Description of computational experiment #1

The aim of the first experiment will be an investigation of complexity differences between assembly process structures resulting from product variants. For this purpose, real industrial case for assembly of chairs will be used. The chair contains of 7 assembly input components, namely, (1) back support, (2) cross bars, (3) front legs, (4) back legs, (5) sledge legs, (6) seat panel, and (7) arm rest. The feature product diagram describing the product structure is depicted in Figure 10.

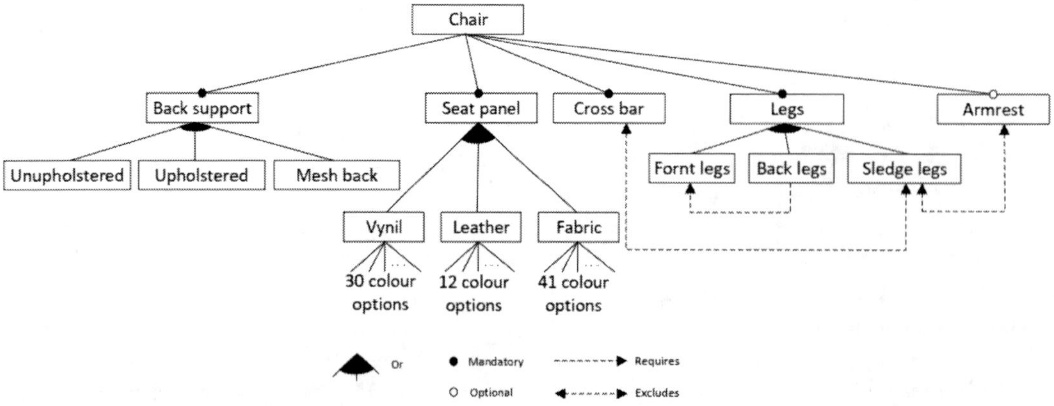

Fig. 10. Feature product diagram.

Customization of the chair includes colour and material variants of the seat panel, two modifications of the legs design, and three types of back support. Totally, there are 747 possible product variants. When material and colour varieties are omitted, there are three variants of product design and the same number of assembly process structures (see Figure 11).

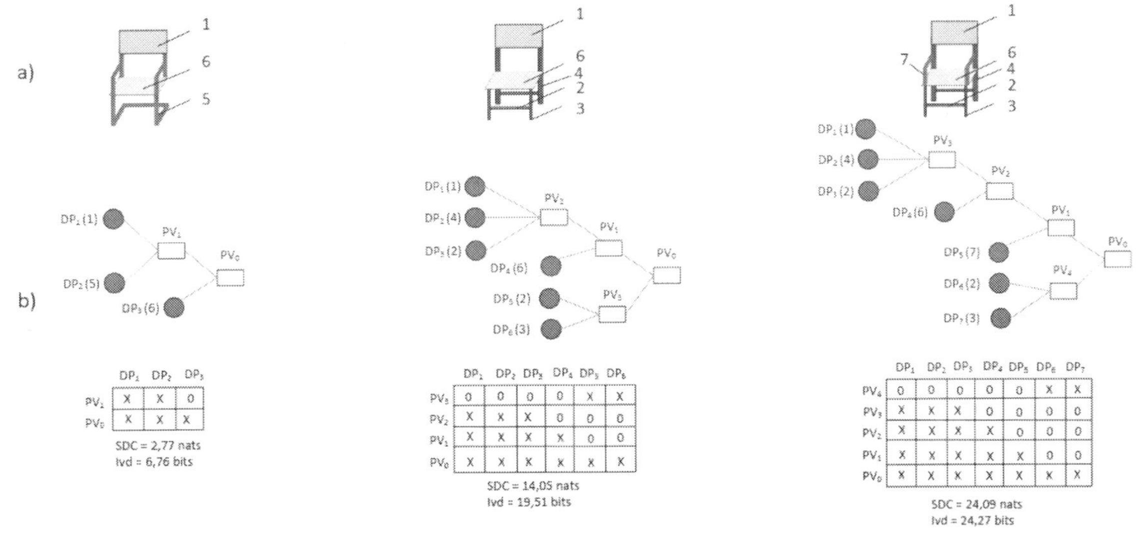

Fig. 11. a) Design variants of customized chair; b) Related process models of assembly operations with DMs.

For example, assembly process structure No. 1 consists of 2 operations. The first one includes assembly of back support with compact legs, and subsequently seat panel is added.

When applying two concurrent complexity measures, Ivd and SDC, for determination of topological complexity of the structures in Figure 11 b) one can see that complexity values of both indicators have the same tendency and provide similar results. It justified the applicability of the measurement method of SDC for intended purpose.

4.2.2. Description of computational experiment #2

The aim of the second experiment is to show differences in sensitivity between the two indicators. The experiment is based on the real assumption that each of the 3 assembly structures can be topologically modified by splitting or integrating process operations. For example, when number of initial assembly components is 6, then number of all possible process alternatives is 33. When we compared complexity of all possible theoretical process structures for 4, 5 and 6 initial input components we found that there are the same complexity values for different process structures by using Ivd indicator. For such process structure, we applied SDC indicator as shown in Figure 12.

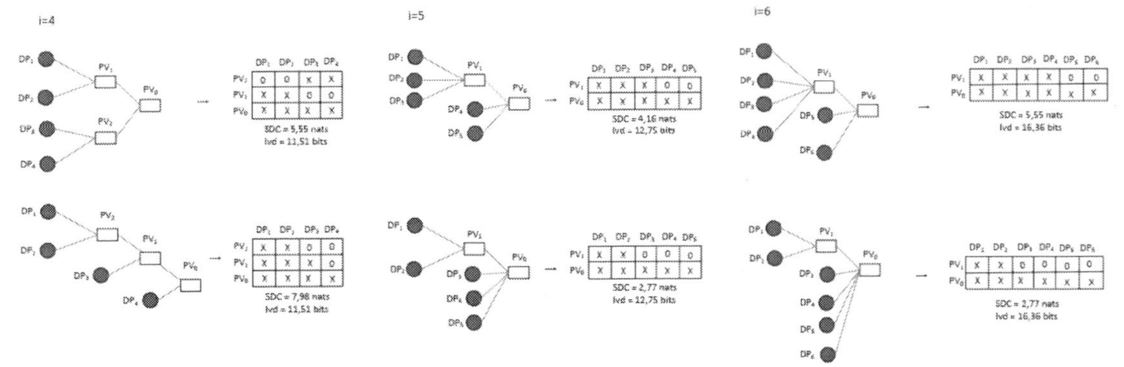

Fig. 12. An examples of process structures containing four, five and six assembly ICs with SDC and Ivd values.

As can be seen from obtained results in Figure 12, indicator SDC identifies different complexities between the pairs of the structures. It proves that SDC reflects the differences between these structures more sensitively.

5 Conclusion

The evaluations of the obtained results from computational experiments applied in the Section 3 and 4, indicate strong theoretical and promising practical potential of the two complexity techniques for the control and reduction of complexity in mass customization environment. The inherent properties of these two techniques for measuring observed complexity seem to be more suitable for given purpose than analysed concurrent indicators Ivd and PPCs.

Moreover, both indicators fit into the theoretical construct of axiomatic design not only from the viewpoint of partial dependencies between FRs-DPs and DPs-PVs, but there are clear mutual relations between all four domains of the design world as it is shown by Figures 4 and 9.

Finally, we would like to point out that our both proposed techniques for measuring observed product complexity and process complexity at the same time validated systems design complexity metric by Guenov [7] using fundamentals of Architectural Design and Axiomatic Design for comparison of alternatives. Even though this complexity metric does not include the information axiom of AD, it disposes of useful practical applications.

This paper has been supported by VEGA project Nr. 1/0419/16 granted by the Ministry of Education of the Slovak Republic and is part of actual research activities in the project SME 4.0 (Industry 4.0 for SMEs) with funding received from the European Union's Horizon 2020 research and innovation program under the Marie Skłodowska-Curie Grant Agreement No 734713.

References

1. K. Efthymiou, A. Pagoropoulos, N. Papakostas, D. Mourtzis, and G. Chryssolouris. *Manufacturing systems complexity review: challenges and outlook*. Procedia CIRP, 3, 644- 649. (2012)
2. N. P. Suh. *Complexity in engineering*. CIRP Annals-Manufacturing Technology, 54(2), 46-63. (2005).
3. J.P.M. Schmitz, D.A. Beek, J. E. van, Rooda. *Chaos in Discrete Production Systems?* Journal of Manufacturing Systems 21, p.236. (2002)
4. T. Tomiyama, V. D'Amelio, J. Urbanic and W. ElMaraghy. *Complexity of multi-disciplinary design*. CIRP Annals-Manufacturing Technology, 56(1), 185-188. (2007)
5. J. Gao, Y. Cao, W. W. Tung, and J. Hu. *Multiscale analysis of complex time series: integration of chaos and random fractal theory, and beyond*. John Wiley & Sons. (2007)
6. N. P. Suh, *Complexity: theory and applications*. Oxford University Press on Demand. (2005)
7. M. D. Guenov. *Complexity and cost effectiveness measures for systems design*. (2002)
8. M. Marchesi, S. G. Kim and D. T. Matt. *Application of the axiomatic design approach to the design of architectural systems: a literature review*. In Proceedings of ICAD (pp. 27-28) (2013)
9. C. A. Brown. *Axiomatic design for understanding manufacturing engineering as a science*. In Proceedings of the 21st CIRP Design Conference. (2011)
10. D. T. Matt and E. Rauch, E. *Design and implementation approach for distributed manufacturing networks using axiomatic design*. In Axiomatic Design in Large Systems (pp. 225-250). Springer, Cham. (2016)
11. A. M. Farid and N. P. Suh. *Axiomatic design in large systems: Complex products, buildings and manufacturing systems*. Switzerland: Springer. (2016)
12. E. T. Jaynes. *Gibbs vs Boltzmann entropies*. American Journal of Physics, 33, 391- 398. (1965)
13. G. M. Anderson. *Thermodynamics of natural systems*. Cambridge University Press. (2005)
14. V. Modrak (Ed.). *Mass Customized Manufacturing: Theoretical Concepts and Practical Approaches*. CRC Press. (2017)
15. V. Modrak, S. Bednar and Z. Soltysova. Application of Axiomatic design-based complexity measure in mass customization. *Procedia CIRP*. 50, 607-612 (2016).
16. N. P. Suh. *Axiomatic design: Advances and applications (the oxford series on advanced manufacturing)*. (2001)
17. C. Gershenson. *Complex Philosophy. Proc 1st Biennial Seminar on Philosophical, Methodological & Epistemological Implications of Complexity Theory*. La Habana, Cuba. (Unknown publisher.) (2002)
18. S. J. Hu, X. W. Zhu, H. Wang, Y. Koren. *Product Variety and Manufacturing Complexity in Assembly Systems And Supply Chains*. Annals of the CIRP 57, p. 45 48. (2008)
19. V. Modrak, D. Marton. *Complexity metrics for assembly supply chains: A comparative study*. Advanced Mathematical Research, 629, 757–762. (2013)
20. V. Modrak, D. Marton, W. Kulpa, R. Hricova. *Unraveling complexity in assembly supply chain networks*. In Proceedings of the LINDI 2012—4th IEEE International Symposium on Logistics and Industrial Informatics, Smolenice, Slovakia, 5–7 September 2012; pp. 151–156. (2012)
21. D. Bonchev, G. A. Buck. *Quantitative measures of network complexity*. In Complexity in Chemistry, Biology and Ecology; Bonchev, D., Rouvray, D.H., Eds.; Springer: New York, NY, USA, pp. 191–235. (2005)

An axiomatic approach to a cork granulation facility design

Diogo Martins[1], *João* Fradinho[2,*], *Miguel* Cavique[3], *António* Gabriel-Santos[2], *Alberto* Martinho[2] and *António* Mourão[2]

[1] DEMI, Faculdade de Ciências e Tecnologia, Universidade Nova de Lisboa, Campus de Caparica, 2829-516 Caparica, Portugal
[2] UNIDEMI & DEMI, Faculdade de Ciências e Tecnologia, Universidade Nova de Lisboa, Campus de Caparica, 2829-516 Caparica, Portugal
[3] UNIDEMI, CINAV & Escola Naval, Base Naval de Lisboa – Alfeite, 2810-001 Almada, Portugal

Abstract. In the conceptual step of any industrial design, there is a considerable amount of decisions that directly affect the quality of the final product. These decisions are often made with lack of knowledge about the subjects, limitative trains of thought and repetition of traditional solutions. The present paper is focused on the use of Axiomatic Design in the design of a cork granulation industrial plant, with a particular emphasis on the Independence Axiom. An innovative design solution was made, aiming to reduce or overcome the current issues and to reevaluate many of the decisions made in the past. In this study, some parts of the production process were analysed. The verified lack of independency gave rise to new design solutions and consequently to a better production process.

1 Introduction

From the design of machines [1], the optimization of medical surgery sessions [2], or the management of healthcare systems [3], many are the areas in which Axiomatic Design (AD) has proven its usefulness. This paper intends to be another good example of its versatility by exploring the application of AD in an engineering design, particularly in the design of a cork granulation industrial plant.

The present work starts with a small introduction to the cork granulation process in its current state, going through the used raw materials, its basic principles and a simplistic glance at the existing transformation operations.

Some specific parts of the whole process are explained on a basis of AD. Each case will be analyzed as it is currently done in the traditional cork industry and described through a design matrix. The main issues and faults in these systems will be stated, followed by an alternative design to respond to such problems. The new designs will then be shown in an equation regarding the changes in both functional requirements (FRs) and design parameters (DPs) [4].

2 The cork granulate process

The cork granulate process can be viewed as a relatively simple process. There are some differences between competing companies, but overall there are very few variations between each industrial plant.

The cork used to feed the process can have various origins, varying in quality and shape [5]. The three main sources of cork for granulation are cork planks, which is a type of cork that doesn't have the required thickness or quality to be used in the manufacturing of cork stoppers, cork trims, originated from the production of natural cork stoppers, and disc scraps, which are the leftovers from the production of cork discs.

These materials are usually fed into a buffer that will continuously supply the first mill. This machine will break the input material into an aggregate of smaller pieces of cork, which is called "Broken". The maximum dimension of these grains varies from 30 to 50 millimeters, depending on the manufacturer. The dust that's produced at this stage is removed from the process through pneumatic aspiration.

Instead of proceeding straight to the next milling phase, the "Broken" goes through a screening machine, generally, a vibrating screener, which will separate the granulates in two dimensions.

The cork is then guided into different milling machines, which are adjusted to their optimal working condition according to grain size, and thus creating less dust and improving efficiency. This second phase of the reduction of the cork size transforms the cork into its final granulate size. Much tighter screens are used, producing grain sizes ranging from 0.5 to 7 millimeters [6].

The number of used screening machines and mills, as well as grain size range, may vary amongst manufacturers. Some plants use parallel production lines to improve their capability.

Once the granulates satisfy the dimensions imposed by the mill screens, the cork proceeds to a drum dryer to achieve the right humidity content. Humidity is a very

* Corresponding author: jmf@fct.unl.pt

important topic as the right water content will determine the quality of the products that the granulates will produce. The drying operation can be executed in a single stage or along the process in multiple dryers. Some facilities dry their cork as "Broken" instead of in its final form.

Being a natural product that needs 9 years to be harvested, all sources of cork have a certain impurity content which is practically impossible to remove. Cleaner and lighter cork has more market value than lower quality and unclean cork. For that reason, after being dried to an approximate humidity content of 14%, there is a need to separate the cork granules according to their specific weight. To do so, the bulk of granulates goes through another set of screening machines and is divided into small granulometry intervals. The common intervals to be found are: [0.5; 1], [1; 2], [2; 3], [3; 5] and [5; 7] in millimeters. At this stage, grains smaller than 0.5 millimeters are considered dust and are removed from the process. Grains larger than 7 millimeters are reintroduced in the previous mills.

The density separation itself is made through densimetric tables. By using streams of air and vibration, alongside with a small inclination of the table plate, these machines separate heavier and dirt granules from the clean and lighter ones. Ideally, the output of this process will be granules rounding specific weights of about 50 to 70 kg/m3 as the best quality, and from 70 to 100 kg/m3 as medium quality products. Above those sizes, the granules are reintroduced in the previous mills, as to extract the maximum amount of clean cork possible.

The processed granulates are then guided to silos or stored in Big Bags.

In most facilities, the transportation of cork between the different stages is made through pneumatic or gravity conveyors. These plants are typically built in height rather than in length.

The dust produced along the process is collected into silos and can be sold as a product or used in furnaces to generate thermal energy for the plant.

A flowchart of the process can be seen in Figure 1.

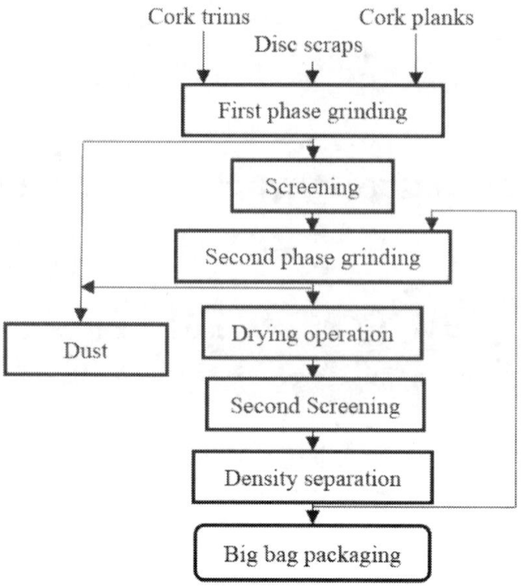

Fig. 1. Flowchart of the cork granulation process

This study is based on the relations between the functional and the physical domains. The functional requirements derive from the customer needs (CNs), which in this case is the owner of the industrial facility, who wants to achieve a good yield in the production of cork granules within certain dimension and density ranges, as to be used mainly in his cork stoppers plants. It is worth noting that the relations between CNs and FRs are "loosely structured", as noted by Harutunian *et al.* [7].

3 Improvements made through the use of Axiomatic Design

Being a process that has had few innovations in the past decades, few modern and innovative ideas were considered in the existing industrial layouts. In fact, many of these plants grew thanks to small improvements to the original ones. This lead to many coupled systems and therefore many opportunities for improvement.

Axiomatic Design is the tool that was used in this paper to explore some of the main issues that have been found in the lifetime of these processes. Using the AD's concept of independence, better designs were attained. In this section, the current condition, as well as the several issues of the cork granulation industries are analyzed. and new proposals are presented.

3.1 Raw material storage

Starting from the very beginning, there's a critical issue in the traditional cork granulating processes related to the control of the fraction of the three different raw materials that are referred in the previous section. The source of this problem can be traced to the shared storage area used for different raw materials.

The mixing of the various types of cork will result in an unstable proportion in the cork feed over time. This will lead to a fluctuation in the final blend that will affect in a negative way the efficiency of the process machinery and, thus, of the whole plant.

In the viewpoint of AD, it's easy to see beforehand that this problem will result in coupled designs in the following stages of the process.

Regarding this issue, and through the analysis of the cork feed operation, the following functional requirements are defined:

FR_1- Ensure the continuous feed of cork
FR_2- Minimize transportation times
FR_3- Minimize the variability of cork types in the process

The answers to these requirements are currently given by the following design parameters:

DP_1- Wheel loading shovel
DP_2- Distance between the piles of cork and the first mill

The following design equation is representative of the process in hand:

$$\begin{Bmatrix} FR_1 \\ FR_2 \\ FR_3 \end{Bmatrix} = \begin{bmatrix} \times & 0 \\ 0 & \times \\ \times & 0 \end{bmatrix} \begin{Bmatrix} DP_1 \\ DP_2 \end{Bmatrix} \quad (1)$$

AD's Theorem 1 states, "when the number of DPs is less than the number of FRs, either a coupled design results or the FRs cannot be satisfied" [8].

The current case represents a coupled design and consequently does not correspond to a good design.

A possible alternative to this system is to separate the different types of cork into distinct piles at arrival, using either different storage locations or using separate compartments in the same storage unit.

Due to the average production rate of a cork granulating process, storing all the cork in the same location would require a huge warehouse. On the other hand, having the cork scattered in different locations would jeopardize the fulfillment of FR_2.

In this scenario, the best solution is to aggregate both alternatives stated above, *i.e.* store the various types of cork in separate locations, and create an intermediate buffer with compartments for each type of cork near the first mill.

These changes will create an additional design parameter:

DP_3- Separation of input materials storage by type

The result is the following design equation:

$$\begin{Bmatrix} FR_1 \\ FR_2 \\ FR_3 \end{Bmatrix} = \begin{bmatrix} \times & 0 & 0 \\ 0 & \times & 0 \\ \times & 0 & \times \end{bmatrix} \begin{Bmatrix} DP_1 \\ DP_2 \\ DP_3 \end{Bmatrix} \quad (2)$$

This simple modification of the plant, allow achieving a decoupled design and therefore a better overall design.

3.2 Cork fraction control

Although the supply of the different types of cork was designed in the last section to be made independent through the addition of an extra design parameter, there is still an issue with controlling the fractions of the final cork blending used in the process.

As the cork is supplied to the mill by using a loader, the quantities that are fed each time the operator drops a cargo differ from the previous ones. Since the loader is hand-operated, then the fractions of the different types of cork will vary according to the operator's skills and experience.

Analyzing the feeding sequence through the AD viewpoint, the following functional requirements can be attained:

FR_1- Ensure the required feed of cork into the process
FR_2- Process the cork into smaller pieces
FR_3- Keep steady the fractions of the different cork types over time.
FR_4- Adjust the fractions of the three types of cork

The answers to these requirements in the traditional facilities are given by the following design parameters:

DP_1- Full-time loader operator
DP_2- Mill

therefore, following design equation holds.

$$\begin{Bmatrix} FR_1 \\ FR_2 \\ FR_3 \\ FR_4 \end{Bmatrix} = \begin{bmatrix} \times & 0 \\ 0 & \times \\ \times & 0 \\ \times & 0 \end{bmatrix} \begin{Bmatrix} DP_1 \\ DP_2 \end{Bmatrix} \quad (3)$$

Eq. (3) portrays a coupled design, as per AD's Theorem 1.

To control the fractions of cork types, it is necessary to completely rearrange the initial layout of the plant.

Cork planks are cheap but unclean, while trims and discs are high quality materials.

Two independent mills would be used to allow the independent milling of the two quality groups of cork, instead of the traditional milling of a multi typed cork blend. This change would significantly improve the control over the final mixture, as it creates two independent flows of material (DP_3').

Associated with each milling station, a mechanical conveying system would be installed. These two conveyors would converge the two cork flows into the dryer (the next phase of the process) in the required fractions.

Using a variable speed drive (DP_4') in each conveyor would allow adjusting the feed rate of each cork quality type and, thus, fulfilling FR_4.

Regarding these new components, a new functional requirement arises at this level:

FR_5- Ensure the continuous material feed to the conveyor

The use of silos located after the mills and above the conveyors (DP_5'), working as buffers, would ensure the continuous feed of the conveyors, fulfilling FR_5.

Therefore, the new design parameters are defined as follows:

DP_1' - Full-time loader operator
DP_2' - Two mills
DP_3' - Two separate and independent circuits (mill, silo and conveyor)
DP_4' - Variable speed drives
DP_5' - Silos over the conveyors

This results in the following design equation:

$$\begin{Bmatrix} FR_1 \\ FR_2 \\ FR_5 \\ FR_3 \\ FR_4 \end{Bmatrix} = \begin{bmatrix} \times & 0 & 0 & 0 & 0 \\ 0 & \times & 0 & 0 & 0 \\ \times & \times & \times & 0 & 0 \\ 0 & 0 & \times & \times & 0 \\ 0 & 0 & 0 & \times & \times \end{bmatrix} \begin{Bmatrix} DP_1' \\ DP_2' \\ DP_5' \\ DP_3' \\ DP_4' \end{Bmatrix} \quad (4)$$

As shown by Eq. (4), a decoupled design was attained. This represents a better design when compared to the previous coupled design. Nevertheless, some dependencies are important to notice.

First, as to ensure that the mechanical conveying system will actively maintain the fractions of the two cork quality types, a certain amount of cork should be always kept in both buffers. Although each buffer will allow the system to work for a limited period, this will happen only if the associated mill is working and the loader operator is performing accordingly to the plant's needs.

Second, the adjustments on the fractions of the cork types are only assured by the variable speed drive if the mechanical conveyors are operational.

Even though these inconvenient situations could occur, then there is a considerable improvement in the satisfaction of the various functional requirements.

Furthermore, the dependencies that can be found in the design matrix in Eq. (4) are relatively simple to manage.

Another interesting advantage of this system is that it would allow running with different fractions of the various cork types with the final goal of finding an optimal price/quality ratio.

The main causes of stopping the production are maintenance operations and failures of the first grinding stage. This leads to maintenance interventions that can last from a couple of hours to days at a time.

Since the design changes introduced the use of two separate mills, a very suitable approach to minimize the down times of the plant can be implemented.

It would be possible for the plant to work at full speed with one single mill for a limited period through the installation of a diverter connecting each mill to both the silos associated with the fraction control. This period would be mainly defined by the mill maximum speed and the volume of cork that can be stored in each silo.

This way, considering the possibility of processing both quality types of cork in both mills, the fraction control method used before would be assured, even during this temporary production method.

In addition, if the malfunction or intervention requires a much longer period to resolve, one could assure the full speed of the facility by using the same mill for the three types of raw material.

3.3 Drying efficiency

One of the most critical characteristics of cork is its humidity content.

If the cork goes into the mills with a high level of moisture, then the cutting tools will suffer more abrasion than in normal operation and will wear out in a much shorter period. On the other hand, if the humidity level is too low, then the separation of the cork grains will release a large amount of cork dust, thus reducing the quantity of grains that are produced. Regarding the final product, the right amount of moisture is crucial in many processes that use cork granulates.

The cork moisture is often higher than the required, so most industrial cork processes rely on drum dryers to lower its value.

Drum dryers use a combination of heat and airflow, as well as a tumbler movement that circulates the cork granulates around the drum's carcass. Heat, airflow and movement are responsible for removing water from the cork, as well as for the power consumption of the drum dryer. Having the dryer set to the minimum temperature and airflow required to reach the right level of humidity is a big step for having an energy efficient plant.

In the current industry, the humidity control is made through the measurements of samples that are regularly withdrawn from the production line. This slow process results in a considerable delay in the required adjustments of the dryer's operating parameters.

Looking for an alternative approach, the following functional requirements were defined:

FR_1- Dry the granules
FR_2- Inspect granule moisture

Considering the standard plant design, the following design parameters were considered:

DP_1- Drum dryer
DP_2- Airflow control
DP_3- Temperature control
DP_4- Quality control operator

resulting in the following design equation:

$$\begin{Bmatrix} FR_1 \\ FR_2 \end{Bmatrix} = \begin{bmatrix} \times & \times & \times & \times \\ 0 & 0 & 0 & \times \end{bmatrix} \begin{Bmatrix} DP_1 \\ DP_2 \\ DP_3 \\ DP_4 \end{Bmatrix} \quad (5)$$

This system represents a redundant decoupled design as it has a right-trapezoidal design matrix [9].

The adjustment of the airflow will impact the temperature of the air that goes into the drum dryer. A higher airflow will result in cooler air and a slower airflow will result in a temperature rise inside the dryer.

In what to drying concerns, the current design parameters were questioned as to achieve a better design.

Instead of having an operator to adjust the various settings of the drum dryer, according to some humidity readings, it would be interesting to use an automated system.

Fourier transform near-infrared (FT-NIR) spectroscopy was taken into consideration to automatically measure humidity fluctuations of the granules. This method is used in some specific applications with granulates such as sugar, green tea leaves, and some pharmaceutical products.

Ideally, there would be two humidity measuring devices, one at the entry and the other at the exit of the drum dryer. The difference between both levels, as well as the output humidity, would be controlled by a computer program that regulates the temperature and the flow of air that goes into the dryer.

Currently, automated systems to measure the humidity content of cork are not commercially available, but such a method seems to be suitable for this kind of application.

Studies would have to be made to better understand the limitations of such method, if there are any, and to understand its outputs in order to define appropriate parameters' values.

Under these circumstances, the design parameters would be:

DP_1 - Drum dryer

DP_2' - Continuous and automated control of the drying parameters through a system based on FTNIR spectroscopic sensors.

The resulting design equation is the following:

$$\begin{Bmatrix} FR_1 \\ FR_2 \end{Bmatrix} = \begin{bmatrix} \times & \times \\ 0 & \times \end{bmatrix} \begin{Bmatrix} DP_1 \\ DP_2' \end{Bmatrix} \quad (6)$$

The design matrix of Eq. (6) represents a decoupled design, since its design matrix is triangular.

There is no evidence of any work done to support the usage of the FTNIR spectroscopy in the cork industry.

3.4 Densimetric table optimization

Gravity tables are used to separate different density intervals of cork granulates into three different grades: light and clean cork, slightly dirty and medium weighted cork; and, at last, dirty and heavy cork.

The characteristics of each grade will determine the price range to which buyers are willing to pay for. For instance, the dirtier and heavier cork has such a low market value that it is often reintroduced in the mills to try removing any smaller pieces of clean cork that are embedded in the dirty grains. For this reason, the efficient separation of the three grades is an important subject as to ensure the maximum profit.

The current industry often presents fluctuations in each cork grade. This is due to the high sensitivity to small adjustments of the machines. Additionally, it is very difficult to fully understand how the design parameters will affect the efficiency of the cork separation.

Regarding the need for a more efficient process, the following functional requirements were defined:

FR_1- Separate the various cork grades
FR_2- Adjust working parameters

Considering the standard plant design, the following design parameters were considered:

DP_1- Densimetric table
DP_2- Control devices

The resulting design equation is the following:

$$\begin{Bmatrix} FR_1 \\ FR_2 \end{Bmatrix} = \begin{bmatrix} \times & \times \\ 0 & \times \end{bmatrix} \begin{Bmatrix} DP_1 \\ DP_2 \end{Bmatrix} \quad (7)$$

At a lower level of decomposition, the parameters that define the efficiency of the densimetric tables are the airflow and the flow rate of the granules, as well as the longitudinal and transverse inclination of the table. In a usual layout, the adjustable parameters (table inclination and air flow) are hand-controlled, at the mercy of human mistake or misusage. Therefore, their impact on the efficiency of the process depends on the operator.

Regarding the cork granulate feed rates, they are imposed by the amount of cork produced in the mills, which is directly conveyed to the tables. The variability of the input materials will lead to the inconsistency of the feed rates, resulting in a recurring excess or lack of material in the machines. Since the working principle of these machines is the sliding of lighter granules over the heavier ones, an unbalanced feed rate will lead to fluctuations in the cork grades previously defined. For this reason, the densimetric tables are very sensitive to the amount of granules that they are separating.

According to the previous statements, even though the current design is decoupled, there is a manner to achieve a better result, by adding two more FRs, as follows:

FR_3- Memorize working set-ups
FR_4- Control the cork feed rate

Switching the man-operated controls for an electronic system panel makes small adjustments easier. Furthermore, this system would allow creating a database of the various set-ups and standard combinations for each particular cork blend.

Other issues associated with adjusting the parameters in the traditional cork processes are the blend differences over time. The changes in the initial milling operation described in section 3.2 are bringing benefits to this operation as well, improving the overall process.

Another issue to resolve is the unsteady feed of the cork granulates into the tables. With the introduction of a buffer with a flow-restricting valve, a very common system in other industries, there would be a better-controlled feed to the tables.

This new ideas and systems will result in the addition of the following design parameters:

DP_3- Electronically controlled system
DP_4- Buffer over each table

Thus, the next design equation holds:

$$\begin{Bmatrix} FR_1 \\ FR_2 \\ FR_3 \\ FR_4 \end{Bmatrix} = \begin{bmatrix} \times & \times & 0 & 0 \\ 0 & \times & 0 & 0 \\ 0 & 0 & \times & 0 \\ 0 & 0 & 0 & \times \end{bmatrix} \begin{Bmatrix} DP_1 \\ DP_2 \\ DP_3 \\ DP_4 \end{Bmatrix} \quad (8)$$

As it can be seen in the design matrix of Eq. (8), a decoupled design is attained. The addition of two functional requirements with the matching design parameters will improve the separation efficiency. The present design represents a better design than the traditional.

4 Conclusions

The Axiomatic Design theory is a very powerful tool to achieve good designs for any kind of component or system. This paper presents another good example of its versatility.

In a direct application regarding the very particular industry of cork granulation, a considerable amount of issues were minimized or even resolved through the adaptation of the existing layouts to the axiomatic perspective.

It is visible that using this theory in the initial stages of a big scale industry project such as this one, will greatly improve its overall efficiency as well as many other important factors such as management operations and quality control.

In this work, four sub-processes of the cork grinding were analyzed. All of them showed lack of independency and were redesigned to fix this issue. The previous and the proposed design matrixes were presented.

The main changes that were considered in the various phases of the process are of relatively simple nature, since building the systems from scratch won't represent a major difficulty. On the other hand, changing the existing layouts to fit these new considerations would be costly and required a lot craftmanship and engineering. This is yet another indicator that design theories have a major role in the earlier stages of any design. Furthermore, the axiomatic approach may sometimes have positive impacts in the following stages, as shown in section 3.4.

The difference in the initial investment (machines, equipment and assembly) of the new design in comparison to the traditional vision is considerable, particularly in the cork fraction control system. However, given that the proposed modifications lead to a decoupled solution, then it is always a better solution than the traditional coupled one, as per Axiomatic Design viewpoint.

The authors gratefully thank the sponsorship of Fundação para a Ciência e Tecnologia through the Strategic Project UID/EMS/00667/2013 – UNIDEMI.

References

1. J. W. Melvin, *Axiomatic System Design: Chemical Mechanical Polishing Machine Case Study*. PhD Thesis, MIT, Dept. of Mechanical Engineering (2003).
2. D. Bottacci, P. Citti, A. Giorgetti, "Development of a tailored tool for the optimization of the surgery sessions", *Proc. 5th Conf. on Axiomatic Design (ICAD 2009)*, p. 85-91, Campus de Caparica, Portugal (2009).
3. H. L. Oh, "Scheduling pre-admission testing: A case study on reducing complexity in heralthcare delivery", *Proc. 6th Conf. on AxiomaticDesign (ICAD 2011)*, p. 170-176. Daejeon, Rep. of Korea (2011).
4. M. K. Tompson, "A classification of procedural errors in the defenition of functonal requirements in Axiomatic Design Theory", *Proc. 7th Conf. on Axiomatic Design (ICAD 2013)*, Worcester, USA (2013).
5. J. Ferreira, *Contributos para o aumento do rendimento de uma unidade de trituração de cortiça*, MSc Thesis FCT-UNL (in portuguese) (2017).
6. J. Apolinário, *Melhoria da Fiabilidade de uma Unidade de Trituração de Cortiça*, MSc Thesis FCT-UNL (in portuguese) (2017).
7. V. Haratunian, M. Nordlund, D. Tate, N. P. Suh, "Decision Making and Software Tools for Product Development on Axiomatic Design Theory", *CIRP Annals - Manuf. Tech.* **45**:1, pp. 135-139 (1996).
8. N. P. Suh, *The principles of design*. Oxford University Press (1990).
9. A. M. Gonçalves-Coelho, G. Neştian, M. Cavique, and A. Mourão, "Tackling with redundant design solutions through Axiomatic Design," *Int. J. Precis. Eng. Manuf.*, **13**, 10, pp. 1837–1843 (2012).

Axiomatic Design in Obtaining a Device for Ultrasonic Machining

Oana Dodun[1,*], *Ema* Panaite[2], *Petru* Duşa[1], *Gheorghe* Nagîţ[1], *Margareta* Coteaţă[1] and *Laurenţiu* Slătineanu[1]

[1]"Gheorghe Asachi" Technical University of Iaşi, Department of Machine Manufacturing Technology, Blvd. D. Mangeron, 59A, 700050 Iaşi, România
[2]"Gheorghe Asachi" Technical University of Iaşi, Department of Mechanical Engineering and Road Automotive Engineering, Blvd. D. Mangeron, 43, 700050 Iaşi, România

Abstract. Ultrasonic abrasive cavitational machining is a nonconventional machining method applied to remove surfaces in workpieces made of brittle, hard, or non-conductive materials that cannot be efficiently machined by other classical or nonconventional machining methods. Among the factors that can affect the values of the parameters of technological interest for the ultrasonic machining process, the relative pressure between the ultrasonic tool and the workpiece surface to be machined could be considered. The main objective of the research presented in this paper was to analyze the possibilities of selecting the most convenient solution among many such available solutions to ensure the tool feed motion, when designing a device for achieving an ultrasonic drilling process. At present, this selection could be achieved by means of an optimal selection method. Taking into consideration some functional requirements of the device, the method of analytic hierarchy process and the axiomatic design theory were used to solve some problems met in the design process.

1 Introduction

One of the manufacturing processes allowing the generation of the final part surfaces could be a process in which the material is removed from the workpiece in various ways. Over the years, distinct methods were identified and applied to remove the material from the workpiece. If the basic phenomena are considered, the machining methods applied in manufacturing processes could be grouped into two essential categories. Firstly there are machining methods based on the plastic deformation of the workpiece material by the tool up to the moment when a shearing phenomenon develops and a part of the workpiece material is removed as a chip; due to their first appearance and actual widespread use, these machining methods are called *classical* or *conventional*. Classical machining methods include cutting methods such as turning, milling, drilling, planing grinding, honing, etc.

On the other hand, there are situations when, due to the high hardness of the workpiece material or to the complex shapes of the part to be obtained, the conventional machining methods proved to be less convenient or really inapplicable. In order to remove or diminish the disadvantages specific to such situations, the researchers investigated the possibilities to bring more energy in the machining zone, so that either the classical machining methods could be applied in better conditions or new machining methods were proposed and afterward promoted. The technologies corresponding to this last group were called *nonconventional* or *non-traditional machining methods*. Nowadays, some relatively distinct methods are considered as belonging to the nonconventional machining methods; such methods are ultrasonic machining (*USM*), electrical discharge machining, electrochemical machining, chemical machining, plasma machining and ion machining, laser beam machining, electron beam machining, machining with moving liquid or gases, etc. The field of the nonconventional machining methods is not clearly delimited; in the last decades, other new machining methods were included in this field and, on

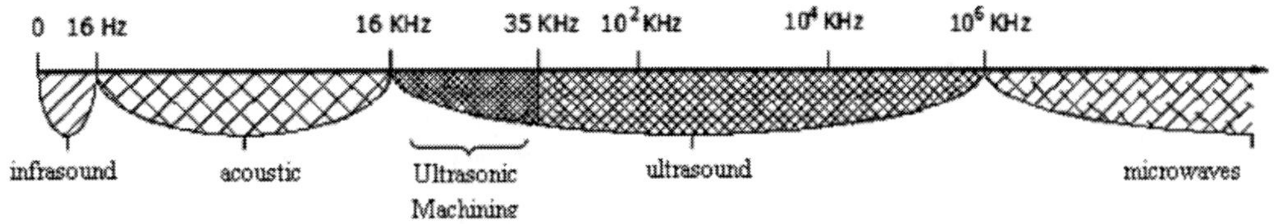

Fig. 1. Frequency domains of elastic mechanical oscillations.

[*] Corresponding author: oanad@tcm.tuiasi.ro

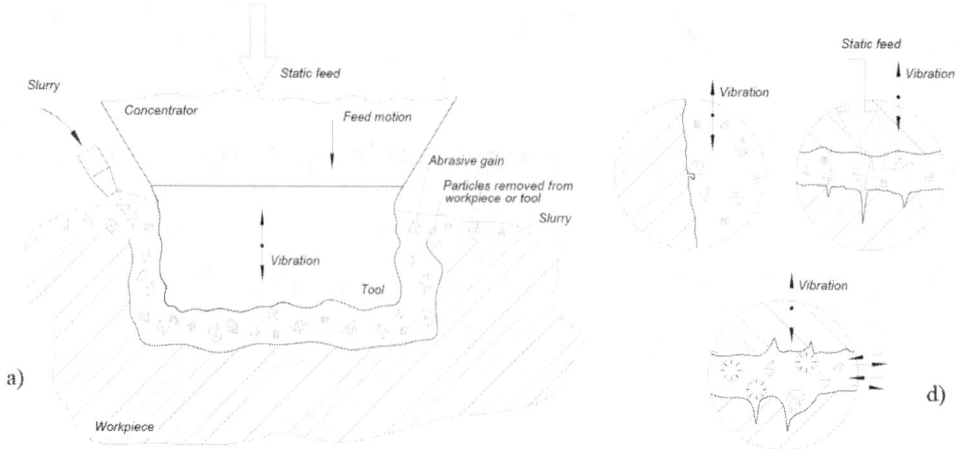

Fig. 2. Scheme of ultrasonic machining process (*a*) and material removal processes by microchipping (*b*), microcracking (*c*) and cavitational phenomena (*d*).

the other part, hybrid machining methods were proposed by combining either classical machining methods with nonconventional machining methods or just two or many nonconventional machining methods.

A group of nonconventional machining methods supposing the material removal from the workpiece are based on the use *of ultrasounds* called thus due to the use of vibration motions that have a frequency higher than the frequencies corresponding to the human audible field (Figure 1). The used vibration frequency is of about 19 - 25 kHz and the amplitude is of 10 - 50 μm.

One of the design methods initiated and developed in the last decades is the axiomatic design method. It is known that this design method essentially takes into consideration two axioms, namely the axiom needing the independence of the functional requirements and the axiom of minimum information, respectively [1]. Even the method was initially proposed as a method of designing mechanical equipment, manufacturing processes, and systems, at present the method was applied to solve a large variety of problems.

Over the years, the researchers tried to establish connections between the ultrasonic machining process or equipment and the axiomatic design method.

Thus, in a paper aiming to highlight the use of fuzzy axiomatic design principles in the selection of the non-traditional machining processes, Khandekar and Chakraborty took into consideration inclusively the ultrasonic machining as a machining technique applicable to materialize processes of micro-drilling in workpieces made of hardened tool steel [2]. They concluded that in such a case, the electrical discharge machining is an adequate machining process, followed by abrasive jet machining and ultrasonic machining.

In a book in which the problem of using axiomatic design in the fabrication of composite structure was approached, Lee and Suh referred inclusively to the ultrasonic machining [3]. They appreciated that within this machining method, the stress generated by a very short contact time between the tool and workpiece (10 to 100 μs) is able to produce microchipping and erosion effects, but the method is limited to workpieces of size below 100 mm, due to the difficulty of tool penetration in deeper cavities.

Mourão et al. developed an analysis of the way in which certain distinct non-conventional machining systems could be selected using the axiomatic design theory [4]. They analyzed inclusively the capability characteristics of the ultrasonic machining systems, when as selecting criteria the material removal rate, accuracy, surface roughness, damage depth, corner radii, capital cost, tooling and fixture cost, power requirement and tool consumption are considered.

The objective of the research presented in this paper was to identify and design constructive solutions for the investigation of the influence exerted by some factors corresponding to the ultrasonic abrasive cavitational machining on the values of the parameters of technological interests specific to such a nonconventional machining technique.

2 Work principle in the case of ultrasonic machining

Within the techniques able to materialize a process of material removal from the workpiece, there is a group which uses the vibration of a suspension of abrasive grains found in a liquid (frequently, water). Due to the phenomena developed in the work zone, this group constitutes the *abrasive cavitational machining techniques*.

There are distinct techniques able to exploit the abrasive cavitational processes; one may take into consideration the ultrasonic drilling, ultrasonic turning, ultrasonic cutting etc. Essentially, there is a tool which is pressed against the surface to be machined, in the presence of the abrasive slurry (Figure 2).

If the processes developed in the work zone are analyzed, one could notice:

- *a microchipping process*, due to the vibration of the sharp and hard abrasive grains found in contact with the workpiece surface; in certain conditions, these abrasive grains could remove fine microchips from the workpiece superficial layer;

- *a microcracking process* developed essentially by the sharp and hard abrasive grains pressed on the workpiece surface layer; if the workpiece material is fragile enough, the grains could initiate a microcracking process. The extension and the connection of the microcracks may facilitate the gradual separation of small parts from the workpiece material;

- *a microcavitation process*, consisting in the breaking of the working fluid mass in small particles and their reunion under the action of the ultrasonic vibration. The liquid seems to boil, due to the virtual existence of a certain type of bubbles. The generation and the disappearance of the bubbles are accompanied by processes of increase and decrease of the local pressure, so that another factor able to generate microcracks may be signalized. As in the previous situation, the joining of the microcracks finally determines the material removal from the workpiece as small particles.

As a consequence of such phenomena developed in the work zone, small quantities of material are separated from both the workpiece and tool; if certain specific machining conditions are met, the material removal is more intense in the workpiece surface layer than in the tool active surface layer. To remove the particles detached from tool and workpiece and found in the work gap existing between the machined surface and the tool active surface, usually, a way of the abrasive slurry circulation is adopted. For example, one may take into consideration inclusively the process of pressure increase and decrease as a consequence of periodical approach and removal motions due to the ultrasonic vibrations.

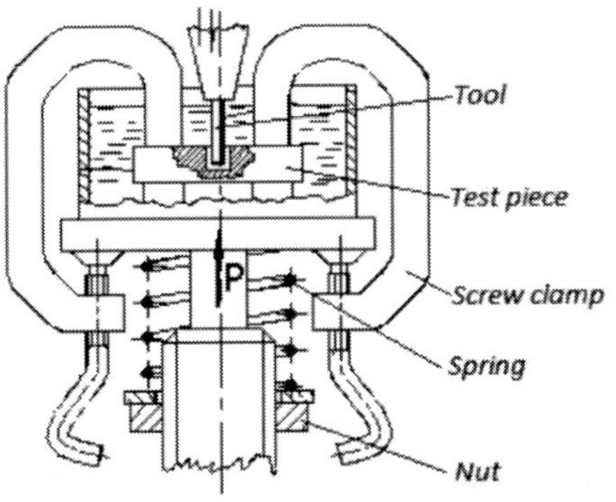

Fig. 3. Device for positioning and clamping the workpiece at ultrasonic machining based on the use of a spring.

In accordance with the general requests valid in the case of a machining technique, as a parameter of technological interest one may consider the material removal rate, the machining accuracy, the roughness of the machined surface, the tool wear etc.

There are some groups of ultrasonic process input factors able to exert influence on the parameter of technological interest valid for the ultrasonic machining:

a) Characteristics of vibration motion: amplitude, frequency, the variation of the amplitude in time etc.;

b) Chemical composition and physical properties of the workpiece material; generally, one appreciates that fragile materials have a better machinability by ultrasonic machining techniques;

c) Chemical composition and physical properties of the tool material; in this case, a certain tenacity of the tool material may increase the tool life;

d) The shape of the tool active surface and the trajectory to be met as a consequence of the relative work motions between tool and workpiece;

f) Characteristics of the working liquid found in the work gap and the chemical and physical properties of the abrasive grains. Thus, small-dimension grains are used in the case of the ultrasonic finishing processes and fine abrasive grains are used in the case of roughing ultrasonic processes when the material removal rate could be considered as an important parameter of technological interest;

g) The pressure exerted between the tool active surface and the workpiece surface to be machined. It is necessary that this pressure has a value between certain limits, to ensure a more convenient development of ultrasonic machining process and simultaneously an efficient of the worn abrasive particles from the work gap. If the pressure is too low, the intensity of the microcracking phenomenon is diminished, while a too high pressure could intensify a possible fracture process able to affect the integrity of the abrasive particles.

The above-mentioned processes specific to the ultrasonic machining highlighted the necessity of determining and applying a certain relative pressure between the tool and workpiece. It is possible that this pressure has specific values for distinct ultrasonic machining processes (distinct machining techniques, distinct dimensions, and shapes of the abrasive grains, distinct workpieces materials etc.). To better understand and apply the abrasive cavitational machining techniques, detailed knowledge concerning the pressure between tool and workpiece in the ultrasonic machining could be necessary; to investigate the possible influence exerted by the relative pressure on the values of the parameters of technological interest, the problem of designing a device able to offer a variable known pressure was stated.

The objective of the research presented in this paper was to use the axiomatic design in order to design and develop a device for investigation of the influence exerted by the pressure between the tool and workpiece in the abrasive cavitational ultrasonic machining.

 https://doi.org/10.1051/matecconf/201822301021

Table 1. *FR*s and *DP*s for the device for generating and changing the values of this machining relative pressure and clamping small dimensions test pieces.

Line no. 1	**Design parameters** **Functional requirements**		*DP*1: **Ultrasonic machining equipment**	*DP*2: **Ring plate**	*DP*3: **Plastic recipient**	*DP*4: **Screw clamp**	*DP*5: **Spring and nut**
Column no. 1	2	3	4	5	6	7	8
3	**Functional requirement of zero level**	**Functional requirements of the first level**	**Design parameters corresponding to each functional requirement**				
4	Design a device for generating and changing the values of this machining relative pressure and clamping small dimensions test pieces	*FR*1	X				
5		*FR*2		X			
6		*FR*3			X		
7		*FR*4				X	
8		*FR*5					X
9		*FR*6					X

3 Functional requirements in the case of a device for the study of the ultrasonic abrasive process

In accordance with the graphical representation from Figure 2, one could consider that to obtain better knowledge concerning the influence exerted by the relative pressure between the tool and workpiece in the ultrasonic process, an adequate device has to be imagined; within the axiomatic design method, this could be *the main customer need*.

In the laboratory for nonconventional machining technologies from the "Gheorghe Asachi" Technical University of Iași - Romania, there is some equipment for ultrasonic machining of small and medium dimension workpieces.

Initially, an older ultrasonic machine was taken into consideration; in such a case, the sonotrode could be vertically moved to ensure the initial contact between the tool and the test piece. The available machining equipment includes a threaded vertical bar, fixed at one end on the machine tool table, while at the other end, a circular massive block table could be placed on the threaded zone of the bar.

The functional requirement of zero order (*FR*0) could be: design a device adaptable on the ultrasonic machining equipment able to ensure possibilities of generating and changing the values of this machining relative pressure and clamping small-dimension test pieces.

If the analysis of the desired device is detailed, one could state the following functional requirements of second order:

*FR*1: Ensure general conditions valid in the case of ultrasonic machining (vibration movement with imposed values of the amplitude, frequency and amplitude change in time), a work movement along an established trajectory and positioning the tool over the workpiece;

*FR*2: Ensure components for positioning of the test piece and which allow the drilling of the test piece;

*FR*3: Ensure the immersion of the work zone including the tool and test piece in the abrasive slurry;

*FR*4: Ensure possibilities of clamping the test piece in the recipient used for immersion of the tool and test piece in the abrasive slurry and, if possible, of simultaneous clamping of the recipient on the machine tool table;

*FR*5: Ensure a subsystem for materializing a variable relative pressure between thin test pieces and tool;

*FR*6: Ensure possibilities of achieving a relative rectilinear work motion between the test piece and tool.

4 Design matrices in the case of two devices for study of abrasive ultrasonic machining

The initial matrix including the functional requirements and design parameters corresponding to the above-mentioned functional requirements is presented in Table 1. One may notice that the solutions adopted for each functional requirement were the following:

*DP*1: existing equipment for ultrasonic machining;
*DP*2: ring plate;
*DP*3: transparent plastic recipient;
*DP*4: Screw clamp (2 such screw clamps);
*DP*5: Spring and nut placed on the threaded bar;
*DP*6: Spring and nut placed on the threaded bar.

The functional requirements and the adequate initial design parameters were included in the matrix represented by the content of Table 1. During the zigzagging activity, one noticed that there is the possibility to use two screw clamps both to clamp the thin test pieces in the plastic recipient and simultaneously the recipient on the threaded bar attached to the machine tool table. Examining the content of Table 1, one may notice that the use of the screw clamps for meeting two functional requirements generated an uncoupled matrix. To eliminate the uncoupled character of the matrix, a joining of the functional requirements no. 5 and 6 could be applied.

Table 2. *FR*s and *DP*s in the case of the device for generating and changing the values of pressure and longer work strokes

Line no. 1		**Design parameters of first order**											
2	**Functional requirements**	**Ring plate**	**Plastic recipient**	**Clip**	**Cylindrical bar and sleeve**	**Screw clamp**	**Plate**	**Bar and sleeve**	**Weights**	**Sleeve moving along vertical threaded column and nuts**	**Flexible cable**	**Guides with balls**	**Base plate**
3 / Column no.1	2	3	4	5	6	7	8	9	10	11	12	13	14
4	**Functional requirements of first order**	**Correspondence between functional requirements and design parameters**											
5	*FR*1	X											
6	*FR*2		X										
7	*FR*3			X									
8	*FR*4				X								
9	*FR*5					X							
10	*FR*6						X						
11	*FR*7							X					
12	*FR*8								X				
13	*FR*9									X			
14	*FR*10										X		
15	*FR*11											X	
16	*FR*12												X

As a result of attempts to solve the functional requirements and adequate selection of the design parameter, finally, the solution presented in Figure 3 was developed [5]. One may remark that in our case, the screw clamps usually used to clamp two parts allowed a certain simplifying of the solution adopted and a creative solving of the stated problem. Rotating the nut that supports the spring, the elastic component is compressed and it is able to generate the necessary pressure between tool and test piece. Since the spring could be compressed by different vertical feeds of the nut, distinct values of the pressure could be obtained. However, the use of the nut and spring to simultaneously meet the functional requirements 5 and 6 generated a certain disadvantage; as the tool penetrated the test piece, the spring relaxes and the value of the pressure diminishes; for this reason, the device could be applied only in the case of low depths of ultrasonically machined holes, when the variation of the pressure could be neglected.

A second approaching of the same problem was necessary to remove or at least to diminish this disadvantage. The new objective was to find a solution able to ensure a constant pressure as the tool penetrates in the test piece.

The principle of interconnected vessels was mentioned during the discussion of persons interested in solving the new problem, but one remarked the difficulties possible to be generated by the necessity of sealing the joining type cylinder – piston, the last part is used both to support the subsystem for positioning and clamping the test piece and the changeable weights used to generate distinct values for the relative pressure

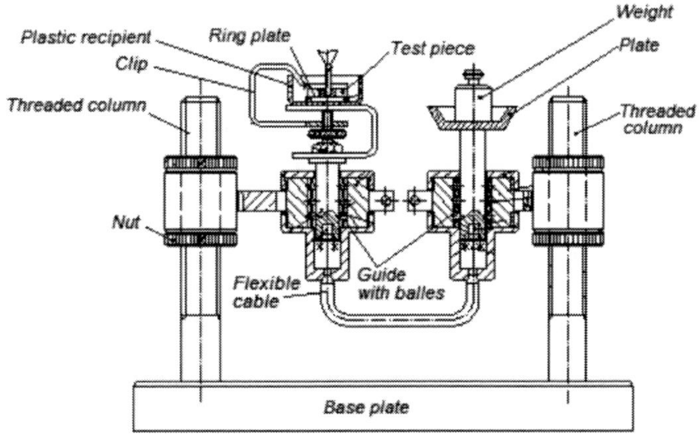

Fig. 4. Device for generating variable relative pressure at ultrasonic machining

involved by the ultrasonic machining process. Somebody remarked a simple solution applied in the case of bicycles, when the brake force is transmitted from the handlebars to the break elements by means of a flexible cable; such a cable or a special flexible cable could also be used to transmit the variable force generated by distinct weights to the part able to support the recipient containing the test piece. Once this idea was outlined, the first principle of axiomatic design could be applied.

In this way, the functional requirement of zero order could have the aspect:

*FR*0: design a device that could be used in the case of ultrasonic machining, able to ensure the change of the value corresponding to the pressure developed between tool and test piece and also possibilities of achieving holes with a higher depth.

As functional requirements of the first order, one may consider:

*FR*1 ensure: positioning and clamping the workpiece;

*FR*2: ensure a possibility of immersing the work zone, including the tool and test piece, in an abrasive slurry;

*FR*3: ensure a plate on which the possible recipient containing the abrasive slurry could be placed;

*FR*4: ensure a bar that could be moved in a sleeve to support the plate;

*FR*5: ensure positioning and clamping the subsystem supporting the test piece along a vertical direction, to contact the ultrasonic tool;

*FR*6: ensure a plate for placing distinct weights, able to generate a certain pressure between the ultrasonic tool and the test piece;

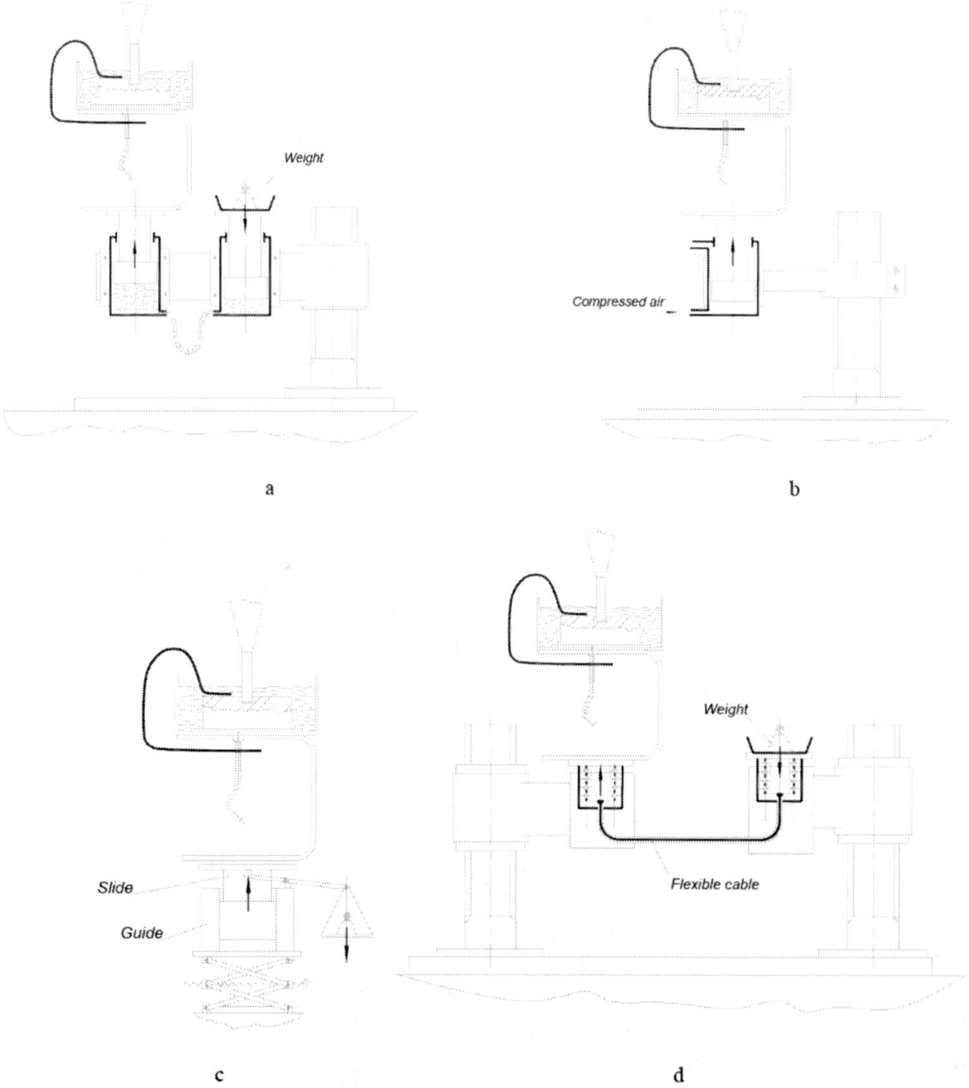

Fig. 5. Alternatives for the ultrasonic machining device: a – device based on the use of *A*1 uses two hydraulic cylinders and a counterweight; b - alternative *A*2, based on the use of a subsystem cylinder – piston and the compressed air; c - alternative *A*3, that uses a mechanism inspired by the solution car jack type mechanism and a lever acted by a counterweight; d - alternative *A*4, based on the use of two pistons connected by a flexible cable and a counterweight.

*FR*7: ensure a bar that could be moved in a sleeve to support the plate with distinct weights;

*FR*8: ensure movement of the plate supporting the weights along a vertical direction, in order to generate the work motion and compensate the penetration of the ultrasonic tool into test piece;

*FR*9: ensure positioning and clamping the subsystem supporting the weights along a vertical direction;

*FR*10: ensure transmitting vertical movement of the subsystem supporting the weights along the vertical direction;

*FR*11: diminish the friction between the parts able to ensure the movement of subsystems supporting the test piece and distinct weights, respectively;

*FR*12: ensure a base piece on which the distinct subsystems could be positioned and fixed.

For each of the above-mentioned functional requirements, using a zigzagging investigation, design parameters *DP*s were identified, analyzed and established. The obtained results were used to gradually elaborate the matrix included in Table 2.

On the base of the considerations concerning the functional requirements and the selected constructive alternative for these requirements, the principle solution presented in Figure 4 was elaborated [6]. One may notice that the matrix corresponding to this version of the device is an uncoupled matrix.

During the elaboration of the solution, other functional requirements were highlighted (for example, one noticed that, probably, due to the vibration phenomenon, an unscrewing of screws and nuts could appear and adequate solving this problem will be considered before approaching the stage of manufacturing the device.

Table 3. Results of comparing the evaluation criteria two by two.

Line no. 1	**Criteria**							
2	**Decision matrix**						**Priority**	**Rank**
3	**Criterion**	***C*1**	***C*2**	***C*3**	***C*4**	***C*5**		
Line no. 4 Co-lumn no. 1	**2**	**3**	**4**	**5**	**6**		**7**	**8**
5	*C*1	1	4.00	5.00	3.00	2.00	44.4 %	1
6	*C*2	0.25	1	1.00	2.00	1.00	14.5 %	3
7	*C*3	0.20	1.00	1	2.00	0.50	12.1 %	4
8	*C*4	0.33	0.50	0.50	1	0.33	8.4 %	5
9	*C*5	0.50	1.00	2.00	3.00	1	20.6 %	2
10	Number of comparisons: 10			Principal eigen value λ_{max}=5,171				
11	Consistency ratio *CR* %=3.8			Eigenvector solution: 4 iterations, *delta*=8.8E-10				

5 Methods of optimal selection

Essentially, the concept of *optimization* refers to a selection of one or many solutions appreciated as maximally convenient among many available solutions.

The optimization could be applied in many fields of the human activity. Over the years, the researchers searched and developed adequate methods for the mathematical solving of the optimization problems.

The current *field of decision analysis* includes a group of methods applicable to select a certain version when there are many available solutions. If the optimal solution is found using a single selection criterion, this situation corresponds to *the monocriterial optimization*, while when the necessity of simultaneous fulfilling of many criteria is stated, there is a problem of *multicriterial optimization*.

Some of the current methods of mono- or multicriterial optimization are: value analysis – *VA*, technique of matrix with two inputs, the technique of the imposed decision, the Technique for Order of Preference by Similarity to Ideal Solution (*TOPSIS*), analytic hierarchy process (*AHP*), digraph-based approach, analytic network process (*ANP)*, data envelopment analysis (*DEA*), preference ranking organization method for enrichment evaluation (*PROMETHEE*), geometrical analysis for interactive aid (GAIA), multi-objective optimization on the basis of ratio analysis (*MOORA*), *Electre* methods (in French, ELimination Et Choix Traduisent la REalité), multi-attribute utility theory (*MAUT*), superiority and inferiority ranking method (*SIR*) method, potentially all pairwise rankings of all alternatives (*PAPRIKA*) etc.

Some of the optimization methods are based on the comparison two by two of the versions previously identified.

Within the method of the matrix with two inputs, this comparison is made taking into consideration the global image of each alternative of problem-solving.

The method of imposed decision achieves initially the evaluation and the weighting of the criteria applicable to find the optimal solution and subsequently the alternatives are evaluated by means of each criterion. A final importance coefficient takes into consideration both the weighting of the criteria and the evaluation of each alternative by means of each evaluation criterion. When comparison of the criteria or of the alternatives is made, only three situations are considered and evaluated by marks: 1-0 when the first alternative is better appreciated, 0-1 when the second alternative is considered as more convenient, and 0.5-0.5 when the two alternatives are considered as of equal importance.

In the case of the analytic hierarchy process (AHP), the comparisons are based on a more detailed analysis, highlighting of how many times an alternative is better by means of marks included between 2 and 9 (the mark 1 is attributed to the situations when the analyzed alternatives are considered as being of equal importance).

 https://doi.org/10.1051/matecconf/201822301021

Table 4. Results of comparison of the alternatives by means of each evaluation criterion.

Line no. 1	**Criterion *C1*: work pressure and motion**						
2	**Decision matrix**					**Priority**	**Rank**
3	**Alternative**	***A1***	***A2***	***A3***	***A4***		
Line 4 Co-lumn 1	2	3	4	5	6	7	
5	*A1*	1	3.00	1.00	1.00	27.9	2
6	*A2*	0.33	1	0.33	0.33	9.3	4
7	*A3*	1.00	3.00	1	4.00	42.3	1
8	*A4*	1.00	3.00	0.25	1	20.4	3
9	Number of comparisons: 6			Principal eigen value λ_{max}=4.29			
10	Consistency ratio *CR* %=9.1			Eigenvector solution: 5 iterations, delta=8.7E-8			
11	**Criterion *C2*: workpiece positioning**						
12	**Decision matrix**					**Priority**	**Rank**
13	**Alternative**	***A1***	***A2***	***A3***	***A4***		
14	*A1*	1	1.00	0.33	2.00	20.1	3
15	*A2*	1.00	1	0.50	3.00	24.8	2
16	*A3*	3.00	2.00	1	2.00	42.5	1
17	*A4*	0.50	0.33	0.50	1	12.5	4
18	Number of comparisons: 6			Principal eigen value λ_{max}=4.175			
19	Consistency ratio CR %=6.4			Eigenvector solution: 5 iterations, delta=4.0E-8			
20	**Criterion *C3*: low friction**						
21	**Decision matrix**					**Priority**	**Rank**
22	**Alternative**	***A1***	***A2***	***A3***	***A4***		
23	*A1*	1	0.50	0.50	0.25	10.8	4
24	*A2*	2.00	1	0.50	0.33	16.4	3
25	*A3*	2.00	2.00	1	0.50	25.6	2
26	*A4*	4.00	3.00	2.00	1	47.2	1
27	Number of comparisons: 6			Principal eigen value λ_{max}=4.046			
28	Consistency ratio *CR* %=1.7			Eigenvector solution: 4 iterations, delta=1.8E-9			
29	**Criterion *C4*: constructive simplicity**						
30	**Decision matrix**					**Priority**	**Rank**
31	**Alternative**	***A1***	***A2***	***A3***	***A4***		
32	*A1*	1	0.33	0.50	0.50	12.0	4
33	*A2*	3.00	1	0.50	3.00	32.8	2
34	*A3*	2.00	2.00	1	2.00	38.3	1
35	*A4*	2.00	0.33	0.50	1	16.8	3
36	Number of comparisons: 6			Principal eigen value λ_{max}=4.046			
37	Consistency ratio *CR* %=1.7			Eigenvector solution: 4 iterations, delta=1.8E-9			
38	**Criterion *C5*: manufacturability**						
39	**Decision matrix**					**Priority , %**	**Rank**
40	**Alternative**	***A1***	***A2***	***A3***	***A4***		
41	*A1*	1	0.33	0.50	1.00	13.9 %	4
42	*A2*	3.00	1	2.00	2.00	41.9 %	1
43	*A3*	2.00	0.50	1	3.00	29.7%	2
44	*A4*	1.00	0.50	0.33	1	14.4%	3
45	Number of comparisons: 6			Principal eigen value λ_{max}=4.046			
46	Consistency ratio *CR* %=1.7			Eigenvector solution: 4 iterations, delta=1.8E-9			

6 Use of *AHP* method

As above mentioned, the AHP is a fine selection method, since there is a large scale of evaluation when comparing the alternatives two by two. The method was proposed by Thomas L. Saaty, architect and professor at the University of Pittsburg.

Some details concerning the stages corresponding to the AHP method used in the case of a device for evaluating the universal lathe university were presented in [7]. In this paper section, a more synthetic presentation of applying the *AHP* method in the case of selecting a device for ultrasonic machining will be made.

As above-mentioned, the problem was to identify a solution for a device for clamping the workpiece on an ultrasonic machining equipment, when a hole of small diameter and length must be obtained. The available ultrasonic machine ensures only the vibration of the ultrasonic tool, so that the work motion and pressure must be achieved by the desired device. In fact, there is a possibility of achieving the work pressure and motion manually acting on a hand wheel.

One supposes that as a result of applying the axiomatic design principles or other methods for the creativity stimulation to find distinct solutions for a constructive problem four engineers individually established the alternatives presented in Figure 5:

- The alternative *A*1 uses two hydraulic cylinders by which the pressure generated by the counterweights is transmitted to the device subassembly intended to press the workpiece on the active surface of the vibrating tool;
- The alternative *A*2 uses the compressed air to move and press the workpiece against the active surface of the vibrating tool;
- The alternative *A*3 uses a mechanism inspired by the solution of a car jack to ensure the positioning coarse of the workpiece and a piston moved in a cylinder as a consequence of acting a lever by means of a counterweight;
- The alternative *A*4 is based on the use of two pistons connected by a flexible cable and whose motions are guided by means of rollers sleeves. The work motion and pressure are ensured also by means of counterweights.

These solutions could be found, for example, by using the method of ideas diagram [8].

If in the case of the alternatives *A*1 and *A*2, a threaded column - nut type subsystem is used for positioning course of the workpiece, in the case of the alternative *A*4 two such subsystems are necessary. A distinct solution was proposed in the case of the alternative *A3*, based on the use of subsystem using the quadrilateral mechanism and a screw-nut mechanism, respectively.

In applying the *AHP* method, five evaluation criteria were used: *C*1 – the way of ensuring the work motion and pressure; *C*2 – the way of achieving the workpiece positioning; *C*3 – the necessity of ensuring as possible a low friction for the moving components of the device; *C*4 – the constructive simplicity; *C*5 – the possibilities of manufacturing the device components using only machining equipment available in the mechanical workshop.

Table 5. Determination of the general composite weight.

Criterion weight Alternative	Criterion					General composite weight %	Rank
	C1 44.4 %	C2 14.5 %	C3 12.1 %	C4 8.4 %	C5 20.6 %		
Column no. 1	2	3	4	5	6	7	8
A1	27.9	20.1	10.8	12.0	13.9	20.48	4
A2	9.3	24.8	16.4	32.8	41.9	21.09	2
A3	42.3	42.5	25.6	38.3	29.7	37.37	1
A4	20.4	12.5	47.2	16.8	14.4	20.95	3

The software proposed in [9] was used to solve the problems corresponding to distinct stages of applying the *AHP* method when selecting the more convenient alternative for the device necessary in the ultrasonic drilling. A synthesis of the calculus developed in these stages is shown in tables 3, 4 and 5.

The content of table 3 highlights the results of comparing the evaluation criteria, in accordance with the principle of AHP and using an adequate software [9]. In table 2, other information obtained as a consequence of applying the AHP method was also included (number of comparisons, principal eigenvalue, consistency ratio, eigenvector solution).

The evaluation of each alternative by means of each criterion is presented in table 2. Thus, in the lines 5-8, the alternatives were evaluated by means of the criterion of the way of obtaining the work pressure and motion, in the lines 14-17 – by means of the criterion of the workpiece positioning, in the lines 23-26 – by means of the criterion of ensuring a low value for the friction coefficient, in the lines 32-35 – by means of the criterion of the constructive simplicity and in the lines 41-44 – by means of the criterion of manufacturability. In this way, for each alternative, a certain priority value was determined by considering a certain criterion.

The information synthetized in table 4 was used to calculate the so-called general composite weight for each alternative but considering the priority values previously determined and highlighted in table 4. The results thus obtained were included in table 5.

The priority size of each alternative was determined to take into consideration the weights of the criteria and of the alternatives by means of each criterion:

$$A1=(44.60\cdot 27.90+14.50\cdot 20.10+12.10\cdot 10.80+20.60\cdot 13.90)/100=20.48\ \% \quad (1)$$

$$A2=(44.40\cdot 9.30+14.50\cdot 24.80+12.10\cdot 16.40+8.40\cdot 32.80+20.60\cdot 41.90)/100=21.09\ \% \quad (2)$$

$$A3=(44.90\cdot 42.30+14.50\cdot 42.50+12.10\cdot 25.60+8.40\cdot 38.30+20.60\cdot 29.70)/100=32.37\ \% \quad (3)$$

$$A4=(44.60\cdot 20.40+14.50\cdot 12.50+12.10\cdot 47.20+8.40\cdot 16.80+20.60\cdot 14.40)/100=20.95 \quad (4)$$

On the base of the above-mentioned weights and the alternatives ranks included in the column no.7 from table 5, one could decide that the most convenient alternative when all the distinct evaluation criteria are considered is the alternative *A*3 that has the maximum general composite weight.

7 Conclusions

One of nonconventional machining techniques that may be used to achieve a hole with distinct transversal sections in difficult-to-cut materials could be the ultrasonic machining.

The ultrasonic machining is a machining method that has a version in which an abrasive slurry is affected by an ultrasonic vibration and the abrasive grains are pressed by the ultrasonic tool against the workpiece surface to be machined. In this way, a gradually material removal from workpiece contributes to the generation of a certain cavity. To investigate some aspects concerning such a non-conventional machining technique, the problem of designing a device able to ensure the changing of the pressure developed between the ultrasonic tool and test pieces was formulated. The analysis of the accessible work conditions by means of the first principle of axiomatic design facilitated initially the elaboration of a device able to ensure the change of the values of the pressure by means of a spring and simultaneously a work movement necessary to achieve a small depth hole. Due to the fact that as the ultrasonic tool penetrates the test piece the spring relaxes and the pressure could decrease up to less convenient values, the analysis was continued by considering a new version of the device, in which distinct weights generate the pressure by means of a flexible cable. In cases of both versions of devices, the elaboration of design matrix highlighted problems whose solving could ensure a better functioning of the devices and innovative ways of identifying and finding solutions for the approached problem. Even in the last case of the device for ultrasonic machining, there was the opinion that new versions of the device could be identified. Thus, one considered that using the axiomatic design or other methods for the stimulation of the technical creativity, four relatively distinct solutions were found. The stages of applying the analytic hierarchy method were used to finally detach another possible convenient solution. In the future, there is the intention to continue the investigation to see if applying other optimization methods, other device versions could be considered as optimal alternatives.

References

1. N. P. Suh, *The Principles of Design* (Oxford University Press, New York, 1990)
2. A. V. Khandekar, S. Chakraborty, Int J Adv Manuf Technol **83**, 529 (2016)
3. D. G. Lee, N. P. Suh, *Axiomatic Design and Fabrication of Composite Structures: Applications in Robots, Machine Tool, and Automobiles* (Oxford University Press, Oxford, 2006)

4. A. Mourão, G. Neştian, L. Slătineanu, A. M. Gonçalves-Coelho, Nonconventional Technologies Review **4**, 50 (2007)
5. L. Apetrei, L. Slătineanu, L., A. Munteanu, O. Dodun, Patent Romania no. 122529 B1 (2006)
6. L. Slătineanu, O. Dodun-Des-Perrieres, M. Coteaţă, D. Uliuliuc, Patent Romania no. RO125894-A2 (2009)
7. L. Slătineanu, O. Dodun, M. Coteaţă, V. Dulgheru, P. Duşa, F. Banciu, I. Beşliu, ICAD 2017, MATEC Web of Conferences 127, 01019 (2017)
8. L. Slătineanu, M. Coteaţă, O. Dodun, A. Toca, Proceedings of the Fifth International Conference on Axiomatic Design (ICAD 2009), The New University of Lisbon, 2009, 79-84
9. K.D. Gospel, http://bpmsg.com/academic/ahp_catchup (2011), accessed: 5.05.2017

Hubcap and ignition switch designs – case studies in Independence Axiom

Hilario (Larry) Oh[1,*]
[1]MIT Park Center for Complex Systems, Cambridge, MA, USA

Abstract. Independence Axiom offers designers a guide to good design. It declares that the design parameters (DPs) conceived for a good design must maintain the independence of the design functional requirements (FRs). Specifically, by relating FRs to DPs through a design matrix [DM] with elements $\partial FR_i/\partial DP_j$, Independence Axiom declares that only designs with diagonal or triangular design matrix can maintain the functional independence of FRs; and that they should be the only acceptable ones.

Starting with the formal definition of functional independence, we derive the criterion for functional independence of FRs as the Jacobian determinant $|J| \neq 0$; where the Jacobian matrix [J] is shown to be identically equal to [DM]. We further show that if and only if $|J| \neq 0$ can the design FRs achieve their target values. Thus the criterion $|J| \neq 0$ substantiates the declaration of Independence Axiom since determinant of a diagonal or triangular design matrix is not equal to zero. It serves as the mathematical basis for teaching and implementing Independence Axiom in design.

Two case studies are presented to illustrate the implementation of Independence Axiom via the Jacobian determinant $|J|$.

1 Introduction

Prior to the introduction of the Independence Axiom, there was no scientific basis to assess the goodness of a design. Assessment is usually done through build and test. In 1979, Independence Axiom was introduced to define goodness of a design and to guide designers through the design process. The axiom is assumed to be self-evident truth for which there is no exception or counter-example. It cannot be proven nor derived from laws of nature [1].

Because of the axiomatic assumption it imposes, Independence Axiom has been rejected by part of the design community. To satisfy the critics and to further advance Independence Axiom as a science in design, we develop in Section 2 a mathematical basis to support the axiomatic assumption. This is followed by two case studies in Section 3. The hubcap case heightens the need for functional independence when functional requirements are opposing. The ignition switch case is a return of the hubcap problem. It is presented to stress the point that design as a science – e.g., Independence Axiom – should be taught so that design mistakes need not be learned again and again.

2 Math basis of Independence Axiom

Usually, a design has multiple functional requirements FRs. These FRs are realized with design solutions that involve physical entities, which we label as DPs the design parameters. The FRs are related to DPs through physical laws which we denote as $f_k(\cdot)$, $k = 1, 2, \cdots, n$:

$$FR_1 = f_1(DP_1, \cdots, DP_m)$$
$$\vdots$$
$$FR_n = f_n(DP_1, \cdots, DP_m)$$

Or in vector form,

$$\mathbf{FR} = \mathbf{f}(\mathbf{DP})$$

In the above and hereafter, bolded quantities denote vectors, bracketed quantities denote matrices and $\mathbf{f}(\bullet)$ denotes vector-valued functions.

Axiomatic Design offers designers two axioms to guide them in the choice of design solutions [1]. In one of the axioms, the Independence Axiom, it directs designers to go for solutions with DPs that maintain the independence of FRs. Specifically, Independence Axiom proposes an equation in the form:

$$\mathbf{FR} = \left[A\right]\mathbf{DP}$$

where elements of the [A] matrix, the design matrix, are:

$$A_{ij} = \frac{\partial FR_i}{\partial DP_j}$$

Considering only those elements "X" that have a strong effect on an FR relative to its tolerance, Independence Axiom declares that only designs with diagonal or triangular design matrix [A] in "X" can maintain the functional independence of FR. They are therefore the acceptable ones. The mathematical basis for such a declaration has been derived in [2]. It is further reviewed here as a lead up to the case studies that follow.

* Corresponding author: ohlarry@yahoo.com

The task in design is to find the root of the equation:

$$\mathbf{FR} - \mathbf{FR}^* = \mathbf{f(DP)} - \mathbf{FR}^* = \mathbf{0}; \qquad (1)$$

that enables **FR** to achieve its target value $\mathbf{FR}^*$.

Usually $\mathbf{f(DP)}$ is nonlinear so that the root $\equiv \mathbf{f}^{-1}(\mathbf{FR}^*)$ cannot be solved analytically. In its place, $\mathbf{f(DP)}$ in Equation (1) is linearized via Taylor expansion:

$$\mathbf{f(DP)} - \mathbf{FR}^* \approx \mathbf{f(DP^k)} + [\,J\,](\mathbf{DP} - \mathbf{DP^k}) - \mathbf{FR}^* = \mathbf{0}.$$

Above equation is then solved iteratively via a succession of linear equations:

$$\mathbf{DP^{k+1}} = \mathbf{DP^k} - [\,J\,]^{-1}\{\mathbf{f(DP^k)} - \mathbf{FR}^*\}.$$

Iteration with k = 0, 1, 2, … ends when $\|\mathbf{DP^{k+1}} - \mathbf{DP^k}\|$ is less than a desired accuracy. At that point $\mathbf{DP^{k+1}}$ serves as the root to Equation (1).

In the above, the matrix [J] is the Jacobian of $\mathbf{f(DP)}$ with element $\partial FR_i/\partial DP_j$ evaluated at $\mathbf{DP^k}$. It is identically equal to A_{ij}, the element of the design matrix [A] defined earlier. If Jacobian determinant | J | = 0, then the inverse of the Jacobian $[\,J\,]^{-1}$ does not exist; iterative root finding cannot proceed and **FR** cannot achieve its target **FR***. This is the crux of design's failure to achieve its target.

Under what condition then is | J | = 0? In the next section, we show this condition to be the consequence of functional dependency among FRs. While the derivation is based on two FRs involving two DPs, similar derivation holds true for *n* FRs involving *n* DPs, *n* >2.

We start with the formal definition of functional dependency. Namely, FR_2 is functionally dependent on FR_1 if it is a function of FR_1:

$$FR_2 = FR_2(FR_1)$$

Applying the chain rule for differentiation, we have

$$\frac{\partial FR_2}{\partial DP_1} = \frac{\partial FR_2}{\partial FR_1}\cdot\frac{\partial FR_1}{\partial DP_1} \qquad (2)$$

$$\frac{\partial FR_2}{\partial DP_2} = \frac{\partial FR_2}{\partial FR_1}\cdot\frac{\partial FR_1}{\partial DP_2} \qquad (3)$$

Subtract $\frac{\partial FR_1}{\partial DP_1}$ x Equation (3) from $\frac{\partial FR_1}{\partial DP_2}$ x Equation (2) to eliminate the product $\left(\frac{\partial FR_2}{\partial FR_1}\right)\left(\frac{\partial FR_1}{\partial DP_2}\right)\left(\frac{\partial FR_1}{\partial DP_1}\right)$, we arrive at the condition for functional dependency:

$$\left(\frac{\partial FR_1}{\partial DP_2}\right)\left(\frac{\partial FR_2}{\partial DP_1}\right) - \left(\frac{\partial FR_1}{\partial DP_1}\right)\left(\frac{\partial FR_2}{\partial DP_2}\right) = 0.$$

Note that $\left(\frac{\partial FR_2}{\partial DP_2}\frac{\partial FR_1}{\partial DP_1} - \frac{\partial FR_1}{\partial DP_2}\frac{\partial FR_2}{\partial DP_1}\right)$ is the determinant

$$\begin{vmatrix} \frac{\partial FR_1}{\partial DP_1} & \frac{\partial FR_1}{\partial DP_2} \\ \frac{\partial FR_2}{\partial DP_1} & \frac{\partial FR_2}{\partial DP_2} \end{vmatrix} \equiv |\,J\,|.$$

Thus, if FR_2 is functionally dependent on FR_1, then

$$|\,J\,| = 0.$$

The converse case also holds true, [2]. If | J | = 0, then

FR_2 is functionally dependent on FR_1.

Combining the above two statements,

If and only if | J | = 0, then FRs are functionally dependent;

So that (FR_1, FR_2) cannot achieve the targets $(FR_1^*,\ FR_2^*)$

By the same token,

If and only if | J | ≠ 0, then FRs are functionally independent;

and (FR_1, FR_2) can achieve targets (FR_1^*, FR_2^*).

As noted earlier, the design matrix [A] is identical to the matrix [J]. Its determinant for a diagonal or triangular [A] is not equal to zero. Thus according to the statement above, the FRs are functionally independent and the **FR** can achieve its target value **FR** *. In other words, Independence Axiom is corroborated by the condition | J | ≠ 0. The | J | criterion thus can serve as the basis to verify compliance with the Independence Axiom.

3 Case studies in Independence Axiom

3.1 Hubcap – a functionally dependent design

This case study was described in [3]. It is reviewed here to elucidate the functional dependency of the design. Figure 1A shows the front view of GM 1986-88 Pontiac 6000 hubcap. Figure 1B is its back view showing three pairs of clips spaced 120° apart such that the 6 clips form a circle of diameter D_{clip}. Figure 1C is an enlarged view of the pair of clips at the 4 o'clock position. The clips are cantilevers fixed at a post. Figure 1D shows the wheel rim with a circumferential ledge, shown in white, onto which the hubcap snapped on. The diameter of the ledge

D_{rim} is smaller than the clip diameter D_{clip}. As the hubcap is snapped on to the rim, the ledge catches the cantilever clips. Wheel retention force is developed via interference fit = $k\delta$; where k is the spring rate of the cantilever and δ is the interference = $(D_{clip} - D_{rim})/2$

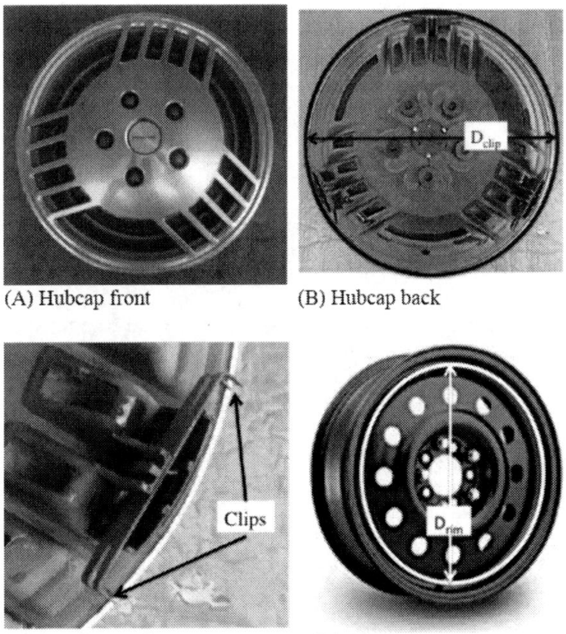

(A) Hubcap front (B) Hubcap back

(C) Cantilever clips (D) Wheel rim

Fig. 1. Attachment of hubcap to wheel rim

There are two FRs for the hubcap design.

FR_1 = retain hubcap on cornering and over road bumps, the larger the retention force the better;

FR_2 = make hubcap removal easier during flat tire repair, the smaller the retention force the better.

Because the two FRs are opposing, the larger the better versus the smaller the better, it is crucial that the design solution adopted can satisfy both FRs independent of each other. If not, there would be conflict. In the above design, the solution adopted is interference fit. So that both FRs are a function of the same variables (k, δ):

$$FR_1 = FR_2 = k\delta.$$

The two FRs are functionally inter-dependent which we confirm by checking if $|J| = 0$:

$$\begin{bmatrix} FR_1 \\ FR_2 \end{bmatrix} = \begin{bmatrix} k\delta \\ k\delta \end{bmatrix}.$$

$$[J] = \begin{bmatrix} \frac{\partial FR_1}{\partial k} & \frac{\partial FR_1}{\partial \delta} \\ \frac{\partial FR_2}{\partial k} & \frac{\partial FR_2}{\partial \delta} \end{bmatrix} = \begin{bmatrix} \delta & k \\ \delta & k \end{bmatrix}$$

$$|J| = \begin{vmatrix} \delta & k \\ \delta & k \end{vmatrix} = \delta k - \delta k = 0.$$

This confirms the design violates Independence Axiom.

To recap, although we set out to define two functionally independent FRs, the solution we choose – interference fit – does not fulfill the intention. It induces conflict between them. Any attempt to satisfy one FR invariably dissatisfies the other. Simply put: one DP, interference fit, cannot satisfy two FRs, retention and removal. The consequence was 25% of hubcaps fell off as the car corners or hits bumps and potholes. And some customers complained about the difficulty in removing the hubcap for a flat tire repair.

Back in 1986, we had to resort to a compromised target value of FR = 32N; and reduce variability around it via robust design optimization as follows, see [4].

Define a (compromised) target: FR_{target};

Identify "noise", the source of variability: δ;

Minimize $\partial FR/\partial \delta$ (=k) sensitivity to noise: $k \rightarrow$ small;

Subject to the constraint that: $k\delta = FR_{target}$.

The results of the optimization are shown in Figure 2. The solution was a compromise. It had limited success because the performance of an ill-conceived design cannot be improved via subsequent optimization.

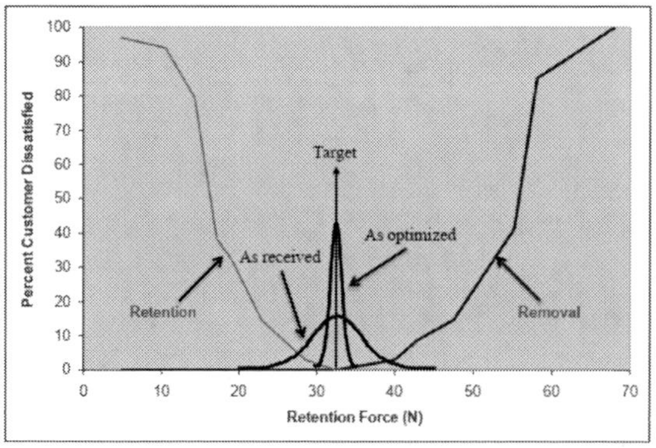

Fig. 2. Customer dissatisfaction versus retention force

In the next case study, we show that the same mistake was committed – coupling of opposing FRs. We further show how to resolve the coupling thereby avoid conflict.

3.2 Ignition switch – resolving coupling in FRs

In the beginning 2001-2002, some Saturn Ion ignition switches exhibited low torque during production testing. From mid-2004 thru late 2005, some Chevy Cobalt and Saturn Ion were reported to "inadvertently turn off" the ignition switches while in motion. From 2006 thru 2014, a series of investigations were undertaken to address the problem including a secret redesign in 2006. The activities culminated with a massive recall in early 2014. For details and timeline of the events, see [5].

The primary issue was the unintended shifting out of the "Run" position that caused the engine to stall, knocking out airbags, power steering, and brakes. We describe below the configuration of the ignition switch, the physics that govern its operation and the flaw inherent in the design.

Figure 3 shows a photo of an ignition switch assembly. On one end of the assembly is the ignition switch and on the other end, the ignition key.

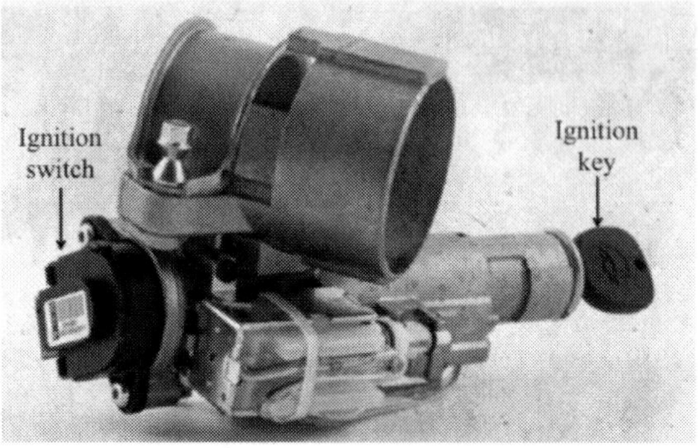

Fig. 3. Ignition switch assembly

Figure 4 shows the top view of the ignition switch. The ignition key rotates the ignition switch by means of a shaft through the slot shown.

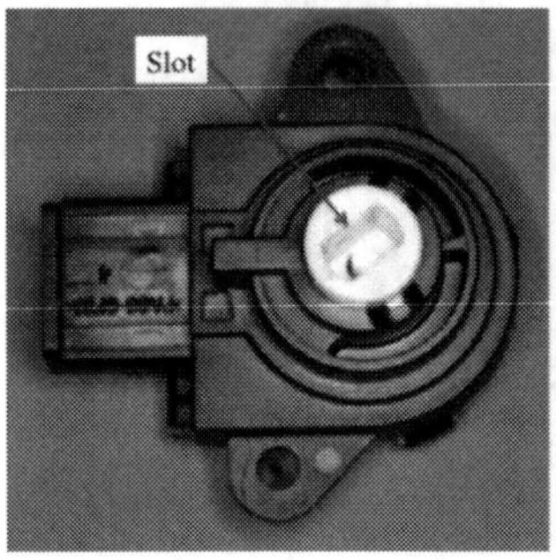

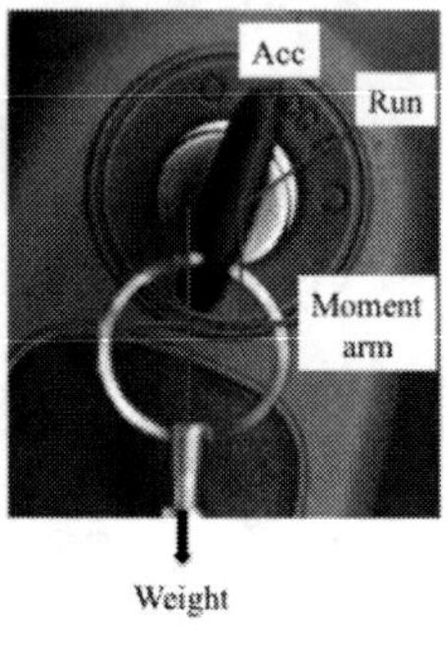

Fig. 4. Top view of ignition switch Fig. 5. The key positions

Figure 5 shows the ignition key in the key cylinder at "Acc", the accessory position. With the key at this position, the engine is off. Another position of interest is the "Run" position at which the engine is on. In a key with wide slot, the weight of the keychain is at an offset to one side. The offset provides leverage for the weight of the keychain to produce a torque that tends to shift the key from Run to Acc thereby stalling the engine.

Figure 6 shows the components inside the ignition switch: the spring-loaded plunger and the switch disc with détentes. Note that the cam profile comprising the two détentes is symmetrical about line A-A equidistant from the two detente positions. For details, see [6].

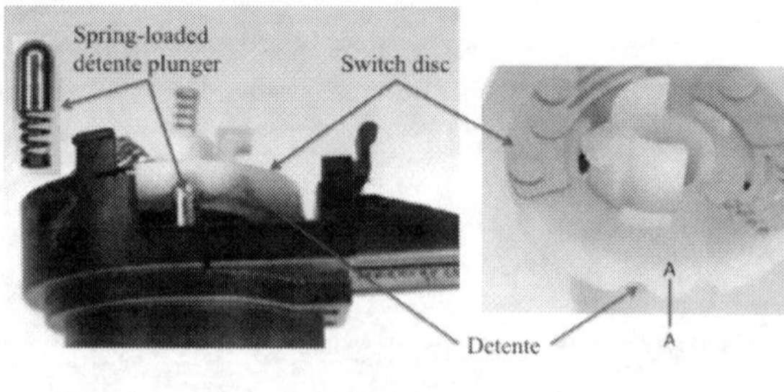

Fig. 6. Components inside the Ignition switch

When the ignition key is turned, it rotates the switch disc inside the ignition switch. As the switch disc with the détentes rotates and glides over the spring-loaded plunger, the plunger retracts out of the Run (Acc) détente and extends into the Acc (Run) detente to hold the switch in Acc (Run) position.

The FRs for the ignition switch are:

FR_1: Prevent unintended shifting from Run to Acc; the larger the resistance to shifting the better.

FR_2: Make the shifting from Acc to Run easy; the smaller the resistance to shifting the better.

Like the hubcap design, the two FRs are opposing. If the design cannot independently satisfy the two FRs, we once again would end up with conflict and compromise.

The resistance to shifting from one détente position to another is proportional to the energy needed to retract the plunger from one detente and extend it into the other. This energy may be derived as follows.

Referring to Figure 7, the cam profile that glides over the plunger is an inverted peak with two valleys. At one valley, the Run position, the plunger is deflected by an amount δ. The associated energy stored is $k\delta^2/2$. As the cam glides over the plunger and the plunger retracts out of the détente to reach the "peak", the plunger is deflected by an amount Δ. The associated stored energy is $k\Delta^2/2$. Thus, the energy "hump" to surmount the "peak" is $k\cdot\left(\Delta^2-\delta^2\right)/2$.

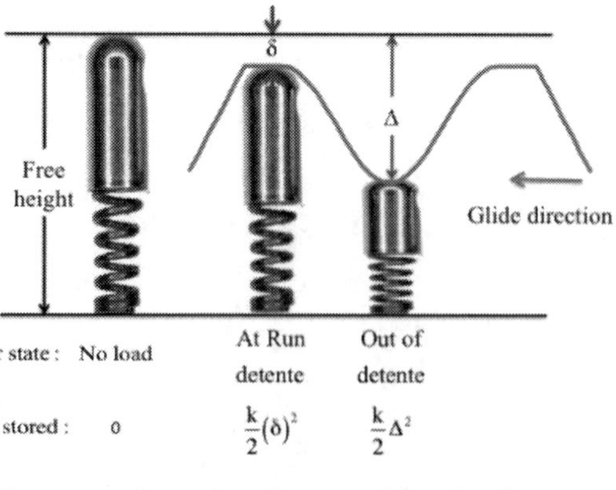

Fig. 7. Energy stored at various plunger positions, Run to Acc.

Since the cam profile is symmetric about the "peak" position, line A-A in Figure 6, the energy hump to surmount from Run to Acc is the same as that from Acc to Run, see Figure 8 below. Namely,

$$\begin{bmatrix}\text{Energy hump}\\ \text{Run}\rightarrow\text{Acc}\end{bmatrix}=\begin{bmatrix}\text{Energy hump}\\ \text{Run}\leftarrow\text{Acc}\end{bmatrix}=\frac{k\left(\Delta^2-\delta^2\right)}{2}$$

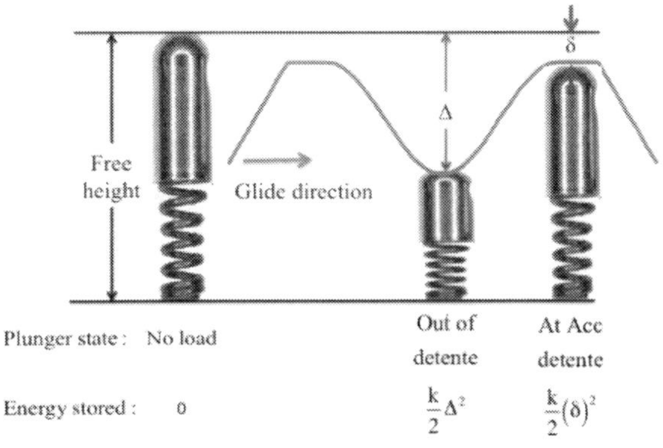

Fig. 8. Energy stored at various plunger positions, Acc to Run.

Given that resistance to shifting from Run (Acc) to Acc (Run) is proportional to energy hump to surmount, it follows that:

$$FR_1 = FR_2 = \frac{k(\Delta^2-\delta^2)}{2}.$$

Thus the two FRs are functionally dependent on the same set of variables. Since FR_1 and FR_2 are opposing, the design cannot satisfy one FR without dissatisfying the other. This is the fundamental flaw of the design.
To confirm functional dependency, we check if | J | = 0:

$$\begin{bmatrix}FR_1\\ FR_2\end{bmatrix}=\begin{bmatrix}\frac{k(\Delta^2-\delta^2)}{2}\\ \frac{k(\Delta^2-\delta^2)}{2}\end{bmatrix} \tag{5}$$

$$[J]=\begin{bmatrix}\partial FR_1/\partial k & \partial FR_1/\partial\Delta & \partial FR_1/\partial\delta\\ \partial FR_2/\partial k & \partial FR_2/\partial\Delta & \partial FR_2/\partial\delta\end{bmatrix}=\begin{bmatrix}\frac{\left(\Delta^2-\delta^2\right)}{2} & k\Delta & -k\delta\\ \frac{\left(\Delta^2-\delta^2\right)}{2} & k\Delta & -k\delta\end{bmatrix}$$

The three Jacobian determinants | J | that can be formed from two out of three columns in the [J] matrix above are all equal to zero.

$$\begin{vmatrix}\frac{(\Delta^2-\delta^2)}{2} & k\Delta\\ \frac{(\Delta^2-\delta^2)}{2} & k\Delta\end{vmatrix}=\begin{vmatrix}\frac{(\Delta^2-\delta^2)}{2} & -k\delta\\ \frac{(\Delta^2-\delta^2)}{2} & -k\delta\end{vmatrix}=k\begin{vmatrix}\Delta & -\delta\\ \Delta & -\delta\end{vmatrix}=0$$

Therefore the two FRs are functionally interdependent.

In view of the functional dependency discussed, we now review the fixes that were made in the past. In 2006, there was a secret redesign involving changes in the plunger length – the free height – and spring stiffness, see Figure 9A. The changes increase the torque resistance to shift from Run to Acc, a desirable safety feature. Due to coupling, however, the changes also increase the torque resistance from Acc to Run, an undesirable customer satisfaction outcome. This coupling is indicated in Equation (5) in which any change in free height and spring stiffness, i.e., (δ, Δ, k), to affect one FR invariably affect the other FR as well. In other words, the secret redesign did not address the fundamental flaw: the coupling of the two opposing FRs.

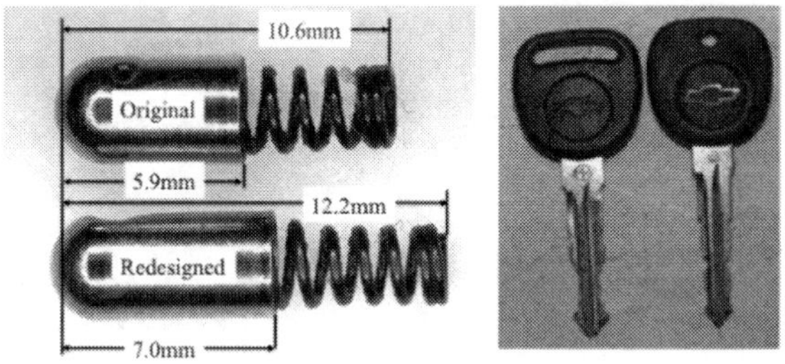

(A) Plunger redesigned (B) Slot converted to hole

Fig. 9. Fixes for the defective ignition switch

Another remedy undertaken, which formed part of the recall effort, was to make the wide slot in the original key into a small hole; see figure 9B. This modification reduces the leverage for heavy key chains to rotate the key out of the Run position. The remedy is a good temporary fix. It reduces the potential torque input that rotates the key out of Run position. However, it still did not address the fundamental flaw of the functional coupling of the two opposing FRs.

As an illustration to removing the design fundamental flaw, one solution – albeit not the only one – is a cam profile shown in Figure 10. With this profile, the torque to shift the key out of Run position will be higher than the torque to shift out of Acc position.

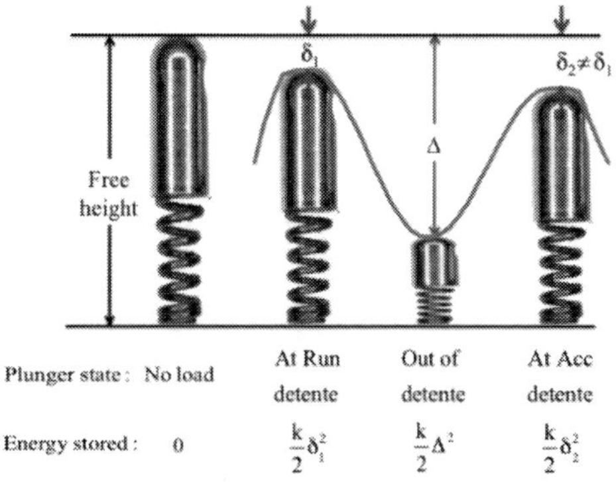

Fig. 10. A cam profile for generating unequal energy humps

The FRs associated with the proposed cam profile are:

$$\begin{bmatrix} FR_1 \\ \\ FR_2 \end{bmatrix} = \begin{bmatrix} \frac{1}{2}k(\Delta^2 - \delta_1^2) \\ \frac{1}{2}k(\Delta^2 - \delta_2^2) \end{bmatrix}; \qquad \delta_2 \neq \delta_1.$$

The Jacobian matrix is:

$$[J] = \begin{bmatrix} \partial FR_1/\partial k & \partial FR_1/\partial \Delta & \partial FR_1/\partial \delta_1 & \partial FR_1/\partial \delta_2 \\ \partial FR_2/\partial k & \partial FR_2/\partial \Delta & \partial FR_2/\partial \delta_1 & \partial FR_2/\partial \delta_2 \end{bmatrix}$$

$$= \begin{bmatrix} \frac{(\Delta^2 - \delta_1^2)}{2} & k\Delta & -k\delta_1 & 0 \\ \frac{(\Delta^2 - \delta_2^2)}{2} & k\Delta & 0 & -k\delta_2 \end{bmatrix}$$

All six Jacobian determinants | J | that can be formed from two out of four columns in the [J] matrix above are not equal to zero.

$$\begin{vmatrix} \frac{(\Delta^2 - \delta_1^2)}{2} & k\Delta \\ \frac{(\Delta^2 - \delta_2^2)}{2} & k\Delta \end{vmatrix} \neq 0; \quad \begin{vmatrix} k\Delta & -k\delta_1 \\ k\Delta & 0 \end{vmatrix} \neq 0;$$

$$\begin{vmatrix} \frac{(\Delta^2 - \delta_1^2)}{2} & 0 \\ \frac{(\Delta^2 - \delta_2^2)}{2} & -k\delta_2 \end{vmatrix} \neq 0; \quad \begin{vmatrix} k\Delta & 0 \\ k\Delta & -k\delta_2 \end{vmatrix} \neq 0;$$

$$\begin{vmatrix} \frac{(\Delta^2 - \delta_1^2)}{2} & -k\delta_1 \\ \frac{(\Delta^2 - \delta_2^2)}{2} & 0 \end{vmatrix} \neq 0; \quad \begin{vmatrix} -k\delta_1 & 0 \\ 0 & -k\delta_2 \end{vmatrix} \neq 0$$

Thus the two opposing FRs are functionally independent of each other. They can be simultaneously satisfied without conflict and compromise.

4 Concluding remarks

The I J I criterion substantiates the Independence Axiom. It provides a formidable proof that non-compliance with the axiom will impede a design from fulfilling its functional requirements.

A design mistake, the hubcap, identified but not taught will reappear, as in the ignition switch, until the lesson is learned. The I J I criterion can serve as the mathematical basis for teaching and implementing Independence Axiom in design so that design mistakes need not be learned again and again.

5 Disclosures

The author was a member of a team that worked on the hubcap design. He was not involved in any way in the recall of the ignition switch. He was therefore not privy to information and data that went into the analyses and redesign for the recall. All the analyses and conclusions drawn by the author about the ignition switch herein were based on publicly available information and data.

6 References

1. N.P. Suh, *The Principles of Design*, (Oxford University Press, 1990).
2. H.L. Oh, *Mathematical underpinnings for achieving design functional requirements*, Proc. CIRP 50, pages 228-233, (2016).
3. H.L. Oh, *Mathematical exposition of the design axioms*, in A.M. Farid and N.P. Suh (eds), Axiomatic design in large systems: complex products, buildings and manufacturing systems, Chapter 2, Springer, (2016).
4. H.L. Oh, "Modeling Variation to Enhance Quality in Manufacturing." *Conf. on Uncertainty in Engineering Design*, NBS, (1988).
5. http://www.autonews.com/section/report01
6. https://docs.house.gov/meetings/IF/IF02/20140401/102033/HHRG-113-IF02-20140401-SD061.pdf

Industrial Feedback on Implementing Functional Decomposition Design Processes for Reliability and Functional Safety

Matt Pallaver[1*], *Ahed* Qaddoura[2], *Sung-hee* Do, Ph.D.[3]

[1]ZD-TRW, Livonia, MI 48150 USA
[2]Schlumberger, Sugar Land, TX 77498 USA
[3]Lexington, MA 02420 USA

Abstract. The value of Axiomatic Design functional decomposition as a design analysis point tool has been widely reported. This paper reports on the implementation of functional decomposition design processes as a system design tool on 23 industrial projects over a 5 year period with product development teams ranging from 6 to 35 engineers. The products developed were systems of systems with mechanical, electrical, firmware, software, and operational interface elements. Functional decompositions ranged from about 200 to 1600 Functional Requirements. A number of these projects are now in commercial production. This paper reviews the process definition and implementation process steps that evolved from these experiences. The paper then reports on the implementation lessons learned and the value propositions noted. Conclusions and recommendations are made. The experiences demonstrated that functional requirement decomposition processes aid in achieving on-time, on-cost and on-specification project development targets. The authors propose this paper summarizes the "Endgame" design process impact that axiomatic design can reasonably expect in industry design practices for system development.

1 Introduction and Overview

We applied Axiomatic Design (AD) processes to concept phase design of software, hardware, electronics and systems of systems. The complete process was referred to as Functional Decomposition analysis. This paper first summarizes the current working process and then discusses lessons learned.

Prior reported applications of AD have established a value of the process as a point tool for the analysis of specific design problems. We are not aware of discussions of large scale applications of AD to system design in industrial design settings.

The implemented process is much larger in scope than traditional AD methods. The matured process presented is based on an AD decomposition backbone. We refer to the process descriptively as a Functional Requirements and Decomposition process producing concept phase Function Models for subsequent analysis and design iteration. We use the FR-DP and zig-zag decomposition terms of AD methods.

Not intended as academic research, this paper assumes a general knowledge of the AD definition of Customer Needs (CNs), Functional Requirements (FRs), Design Parameters (DPs), Process Variables (PVs), Design Matrices, axiom 1 and axiom 2 as well as zigzag decomposition between the FR and DP domains. Terms that are defined in the Key Terms of Appendix 1 are capitalized in this text.

From 2011 to 2017 Functional Requirements analysis, Functional Decomposition processes and analysis of the resulting Function Maps were introduced to 23+ projects. Primarily, the projects involved products developed to perform a variety of functions within oil and gas down-hole exploration. Example functions include pressure sampling, liquid sampling, rock formation sampling, moving and manipulating down-hole process components and making measurements with various sensors of the down-hole rock formations. The products were typically processor controlled systems communicating with the surface and controlling hydraulics, motors, sensors and other active components. The environment is harsh being highly corrosive, having temperatures often in excess of 150 C (300 F) and up to 30,000 psi hydrostatic pressure.

Design teams were composed of trained engineers often at master and PhD levels from some of the finest schools in the world with typically 5 years prior design experience.

The primary need driving us to propose changes to design processes was improvement of functional reliability and safety of the products.

* Corresponding author: Matt@Pallaver.com

2 Implementation Issues

The methods we used evolved considerably over the period of use as we responded to implementation issues. Most process evolution was in the area of integrating Decomposition into other key functions of the company's concept phase processes. Areas of implementation evolution included:

- Definition of Terms
- Stakeholder requirements analysis
- Contractual requirement obligations
- Constraints management
- Product risk assessment
- Functional performance (reliability) risk analysis
- Prior product lessons learned and historic failure modes
- Design verification plans
- End to end traceability
- Fitting functional decomposition into the design V model and Process Assessment Models (PAMs)

2.1 Conflict with Aesthetic Design

We note that Functional Analysis applies to the performance aspect of product. It does not easily apply to design for consumer perception of aesthetics or goodness. Often aesthetic design will dominate the design equation of a successful product.

We further note that Functional Analysis and good functional design is often at odds with aesthetic design. For example, a functional requirement for a reasonable cell phone powered life (perhaps DP = Battery Capacity) conflicts with the aesthetic requirement for a visually slim package.

2.2 Conflict with Success

The authors' experience is there is not a strong correlation between good functional design and product success in many markets.

In part this is because Customers are generally incapable of judging good functional performance or fitness for use and their purchase decisions are more often driven by aesthetics, advertising or celebrity promotion of the product.

As a result the measure of good design and design processes in industry is defined largely by the subsequent product business success.

Thus, it is important to note in implementing a functional performance based design approach that the primary resistance to change in a successful company will be unsophisticated management who are afraid of changing underlying process 'recipes' and that will not see a connection between better functional design and business success.

3 Definition of important terms

Our design projects are often composed of internationally dispersed development teams. For all development projects, to minimize the risk of introducing communication based design and process errors, a common and unambiguous vocabulary is essential and the importance of having good working definitions cannot be overstated. See Appendix 1 for definitions of key terms of our Functional Decomposition and related analysis processes.

4 Summary of current working process

The current operational process is presented graphically in Appendix 2. The Functional Decomposition process passes through the following steps:

1. Process initiated by release of Contractual Requirements
2. Stakeholders Needs Assessment.
3. Requirements analysis.
4. Development of Operational Requirements and Input Constraints.
5. Functional Decomposition of Operational Requirements.
6. Systematic Product Risk assessment.
7. Validation of Input Requirements against the Function Map.

These process steps are discussed in turn.

4.1 Contractual Requirements document

Our overall design process starts with a Contractual Requirements document. A Contractual Requirements document is common industry practice. This document defines the contractual requirements between the development funding source and the development organization. This will typically contain a marketing needs analysis and business justification. The Contractual Requirements define, as detailed as possible considering that the design has not started, the development requirements to deliver on the business justification. In our Functional Decomposition process, this document is a significant source of many business needs.

4.2 Stakeholder Needs Assessment

Stakeholder Needs assessment is composed of determining stakeholders and collecting Stakeholder Needs. This phase has three tasks.

4.2.1 Determine Stakeholders

Stakeholder categories and potential contacts need to be developed. Stakeholder is a broad term which includes traditional people roles, regulatory agencies, interfaces with other systems and significant physical domain constraints. The assessment of whom or what is a stakeholder is driven by the question "With what or whom will our design need to interact during its complete product life cycle from creation to disposal?" The output of this task is a list of stakeholder categories, with specific named stakeholders to be contacted when appropriate, with contact information and assignments of the staff responsible for each category.

4.2.2 Eliciting (human) Stakeholder Needs

The systematic contact and solicitation of stakeholder needs from persons is a qualitative research project, and all the rules of good research apply. Perform data gathering in waves of contacts. Between waves, during processing of prior wave research, adjust questionnaires and methods, and test for data saturation. Stop assessing within a stakeholder category when saturated (no new information is being gained by further research). The primary goal is to assess and reach data saturation within all stakeholder categories.

4.2.3 Collecting other Stakeholder Needs

There exist other 'stakeholder' needs. These include, for example, internal standards, regulatory authorities and interfaces. These need to be researched and documented. Generally these will convert to Input Constraints.

The outputs of the Stakeholder Needs collection tasks are stakeholder statements of need, organized by Stakeholder.

4.3 Requirements Analysis

To analyse the Stakeholder needs statements collected from people we first use K-J analysis [1] to categorize the stakeholder needs into Affinity Lists. Then a single step Quality Function Deployment (QFD) [2] House of Quality (HOQ) is used as a process to develop functional objectives to satisfy the customer needs affinity lists. We use stakeholder pairwise comparison ranking [3] of QFD input needs (typically in the form of Affinity Lists). The outputs of this HOQ task are lists of independent Critical to Quality functional statements with targets and prioritization. These statements are in the words of the analysts, traceable back through the QFD and KJ Analysis to the stakeholder statements of need.

Another key Requirements Analysis step is to analyze the Contractual Requirements. Specific product design performance needs from this document must be identified and extracted. The output of this process step is either a separate requirements document summarizing product needs of the Contractual Requirements, or a summary of which paragraphs are product needs, if the document is suitably structured, that are binding on the product design.

In virtually all companies, there are a series of controlling documents representing various organizational requirements applying to new designs. These will document standard needs for things like supply chain, manufacturing and good design practices. All of these documents need to be researched and included as requirement documents that apply to the current design. These requirements almost universally become Input Constraints and do not affect the Operational Requirements. If structured appropriately, these requirement documents can be appended directly to the Input Constraints document.

Separate from Stakeholders, but significant in establishing functional performance requirements, is an analysis of any prior product history. This is research on potential problems, issues and failure modes of current or past similar products. This is generally a research task of manufacturing and field records. Information discovered will often overlap with needs identified by Stakeholders. This research is reviewed and analyzed to define additional needs to resolve historic issues. The output of this process step is a list of addition needs traced back to the relevant research findings.

4.4 Development of Operational Requirements and Input Constraints

Operational Requirements are the system performance functions that must be met to deliver the required business value. These are not a complete set of requirements. Rather they are the complete set of top level Functional Requirements. These are controlled by the design team. These requirements should be viewed as a design response to the required functionality of the Contractual Requirements. This requirement list is developed specifically to drive Functional Decomposition.

Because Contractual Requirements documents in our experience are universally incomplete assessments of Stakeholder Needs, it is necessary to both conduct Stakeholder Needs analysis and examine this analysis along with the Contractual Requirements in crafting the Operational Requirements.

Operational Requirements come out of inspection and discussion of the Stakeholder's Needs analysis and the Contractual Requirements. This is not a deterministic process and will typically take weeks of work.

Operational Requirements determine important metrics like delivery times, project and product costs. Often, assumptions of cost versus technology performance trade-offs may be required in developing the Operational Requirements. There is a design process tendency to want to start engineering design to verify and de-risk these trade-off assumptions before finalizing Operational Requirements. We found it more useful to carry these trade-off risks through to completion of the Operational Requirements and a reasonable first pass Functional Decomposition. Often we found initial proposals on solutions don't survive the relatively quick Functional Decomposition phase. Thus we avoid spending expensive engineering time analysis of trade-offs that wouldn't survive Functional Decomposition. However, verifying these assumptions which carry significant risk should be the first engineering tasks of the design phase.

Operational Requirements are continually subject to revision, particularly during the early design phase as risks are either confirmed or mitigated resulting in conceptual design iterations.

Contractual Requirements or Stakeholder Needs that were determined to be Constraints and not functions are separated from the Operational Requirements and tracked as Input Constraints.

4.5 Functional Decomposition

Functional decomposition proceeds from the Operational Requirements. If there are N Operational Requirements, then there would be potentially N level one decomposition branches. In practice, not all branches are equal and often we would drop a few if insignificant or risk free.

We defined the Decomposition Node to contain:

- A unique ID to identify the node
- A title description of the FR
- A target FR Performance Measure with tolerances
- A title description of the DP
- A definition of the DP verification test
- An assessment of DP risk

We taught designers to read decomposition, when considering the child FRs of the parent FR-DP Decomposition Node, as "The minimum set of independent child FRs required to enable the parent DP to satisfy the parent FR." FRs are to be solution neutral.

We taught Axiom 1, one DP for each FR, and explained the independence requirement for the DPs.

DPs need to be checked to insure they do not violate any of the constraints of the Input or Derived Constraint lists. The DP verification test, to be used to demonstrate that the DP delivered on the FR, is defined.

In the early phases of decomposition, the DP test needs only to be defined sufficiently such that reasonable staff can agree on its definition. These tests will become more elaborate test specifications written during the design phase.

If the selection of a DP creates a binding constraint on the balance of the design process, the DP is added to the Derived Constraints list.

Completion of all node information is not required initially. We would start with FRs and DPs, perhaps defining the balance of the Decomposition Node information to create clarity if the FR-DP text was not clear. Once FR-DP Decomposition Trees are hashed out, and design starts to feel stable, then a more systematic completion should be done.

Trade studies, when needed, to determine DP selection would be documented, released and then noted on the decomposition node comments.

4.6 Systematic Product Risk Assessment

Risk assessment is presented as a question in the decomposition process at the Decomposition Node level, "How might the DP fail to satisfy the FR?" Risk tracking is implemented using an FMEA format. FMEA actions to mitigate risks resulting in one or more of the following options:

• Acceptance of the risk
• Scheduling of an engineering test during development to assess the design margins of the risk
• Mitigation of the risk by addition of child FRs to address the risk
• Changing of the DP to mitigate the risk.

Systematic risk assessment is a substantial axiom 2 value-add to engineering concept phase development processes. In a 1000 FR decomposition, we can easily add 100 FRs responding to DP risk mitigation opportunities. There will also be easily 200 engineering tests scheduled to evaluate DP performance risk during the engineering development phase. Most of these design phase engineering tests are assessing design margins.

4.7 Verification of Input requirements

When the Functional Decomposition is substantially completed, a quality process of Stakeholder Needs and Requirements verification begins.

Each of the Input Requirements documents, which are composed of the Contractual Requirements, crucial Stakeholder Needs, Prior Product History and Other Design Process Standard documents are systematically reviewed. For each identified need of these documents, the corresponding FR in the Decomposition Tree is identified, and the need traced to the FR.

This full traceability of selected Stakeholder Needs, affinity lists, and other input needs to FR-DP nodes to verification tests is an excellent quality tool to insure completeness of the proposed design. It also supports the management of thousands of system FRs that need to be implemented during the design phase.

If a corresponding FR is not found, then this 'Orphan' need is analyzed and a determination is made on its validity. If the Function Tree is at fault for missing a corresponding requirement, then the FR-DP Decomposition is refactored to include a corresponding FR and the trace link made. Often we find the need was not justified, and we would note this by linking the need to an explanatory summary document of unmet needs.

Politically, important stakeholders, customer and contractual needs were explicitly examined and if not met, more often than not, the Decomposition was revised even if the need was not justified by decomposition.

At this point, a design review is held on the Function Tree as a condition of a full release to begin the design work.

With release, design tasks are scheduled to reflect a priority of work on high risk portions of the design and logical dependencies.

Generally we maintained the Functional Decomposition during the early design phases to track and update the testing plans and track the overall design risk. As the design progresses onto engineering and manufacturing documentation control systems, and the work transitions from planned work to fire fighting, we found little value in maintaining the Functional Decomposition as it could not capture or contribute to the myriad of details and issues of later stage development.

5.0 Process Findings and Lessons Learned

Findings and lessons learned deploying a working industrial functional decomposition process are presented in statements grouped in two sections, Deployment Process and Value proposition. These are presented individually in the general order of the process steps. The findings are contrasted to the general design and development experiences of the authors, not any specific processes of any one organization. The authors share more than 50 years of development experience in software, hardware and manufacturing across more than a dozen organizations.

5.1 Deployment Process Findings

We found that classroom teaching of Functional Decomposition is noteworthy for its ineffectiveness. Then how can we teach the process? We learned what is effective is to require that functional decomposition sessions take place facilitated by staff skilled in the process. People learn by doing.

We learned our toolkits needed to be updated to manage process updates. The Acclaro™ Toolkit [4] was revised to manage the following process issues:

- Management of Aggregate Constraints
- Management of Decomposition Node functional risk.
- Management of the engineering design testing plans (tests, status, traceability)
- Development of an FTA calculation for the Decomposition Tree
- Management of traditional Contractual Requirements and similar documents with full traceability into the Functional Decomposition
- Reporting of design risk mitigation status

Even the best design methods fail when applied to the wrong requirements. Garbage in, garbage out (GIGO) is an expression summarizing how flawed, or nonsense inputs produce nonsense outputs or "garbage" design. In both the spirit and practicality of implementing a Functional Decomposition design process, a design team needs to step up one level above the current design to analyse and understand the driving Functional Performance objectives. Otherwise Functional Decomposition is potentially producing better performing decoupled "Garbage" designs.

In the AD process, with the creation of the Operation Requirements document, our AD vocabulary changes from Needs to Requirements. However, we retained the use of Requirements in early document names, such as the Contractual Requirements, to simply avoid confusion with traditional practice.

We found it is not possible to separate the processes of requirements analysis from concept synthesis. This is primarily because higher level design decisions create lower level requirements that need further design analysis. Historically, organizations often chose to separate the requirements phase from engineering development, putting the requirements analysis function primarily in Marketing and assuming the Contractual Requirements represented 100% of the requirements analysis. In fact, Contractual Requirements are only a minor percentage of the requirements work remaining to be done for a good systems engineering effort. And the requirements work can only be completed in the presence of design analysis and trade decisions.

Additionally, we learned that marketing department driven Contractual Requirement statements are remarkably poor in defining functional requirements. In our experiences we noted that marketing driven requirements consist largely of features to catch up with the competition, marketing's view of new features they perceive customers want to buy, marketing's view of solutions to existing problems of current product and overly optimistic reliability and cost targets needed for management buy-in of the development budget. The majority of actual requirements, functional or otherwise, are assumed, and not explicitly defined.

We discovered, as discussed in section 2.2 Conflict with Success, working with business and marketing to change the requirement analysis paradigm is hard. The conversations would go like this:

Marketing: "I don't understand what you want; Just design the features we need."

Design: "We are looking at the problem from a system point of view and need to develop measures of functional performance for the entire system to best understand how to define the needed engineering performance requirements."

Marketing: "I have already suggested the solution you should use. If you find something better, fine, but I think you are making this too complicated."

Design: "Can we chat with some of our customers to understand better their objective measures of performance of our product."

Marketing: "I respect what you are trying to do, but there is not enough time. We are not going to bother our customers. We are not going to redesign the product. I have given you a budget and defined what we need to do, so now let's get going…"

Even with historic first pass design yields being virtually zero, and not a single project delivering as initially scheduled, it was near impossible to change marketing behaviour, particularly if the company has been financially successful.

Furthermore, we have developed the opinion that it is not even useful to try and educate marketing and sales staff on the skills of requirements analysis. We feel that the most reasonable solution is to place functional requirements analysis processes in the engineering development team. The contribution of marketing should properly be considered the marketing needs input, certainly important, but simply one of many stakeholders.

We found early on that stakeholder needs and Contractual Requirements were insufficient to drive the Functional Decomposition. This drove the creation of the Operational Requirements document (discussed in detail later). Then how do we view the Contractual Requirements and other stakeholder needs? First, these are key inputs in the generation of Operational Requirements. Second, when completed, the Function Map is used to verify that stakeholder needs, Contractual Requirements as well as other input needs are met.

We found that there is a major difference between our Functional Decomposition and historic design processes. In the past, a development team would consider a marketing produced requirements document as the driving design document. With Functional Decomposition we introduce and design to the Operational Requirements and we merely verify against the more traditional Stakeholder Needs driven documents. With our Functional Decomposition approach we found many Stakeholder Needs were dismissed as irrelevant or even counterproductive to delivering on top level performance requirements. In prior design processes these needs would have been incorporated in the design. The magnitude of this difference cannot be overstated. It is a paradigm change. Bottom up "perceived" Stakeholder Needs design is driven by stakeholder experience. And when technology and business needs are changing rapidly, stakeholder experience is more often a handicap than an asset in defining and developing new solutions.

We learned that determining the Operational Requirements have proven to be a most difficult aspect. Stakeholders reliably fail to provide insight into the objective top level functions of the product under development. Instead, stakeholders discuss their needs from a framework of their experiences with current and prior solutions. From a Functional Decomposition process point of view, to determine the Operational Requirements, we had to invariably return to the business and marketing staff to figure out and define the development needs that had to be accomplished in the customer function space. Yet Business and Marketing staff, certain in their opinion of the required solution features, would battle their perceived waste of time to try and define what the solution actually needed to do.

We learned we needed Project Management, Design and Business Analysis skills and participation to complete the Operational Requirements and the subsequent upper level Functional Decomposition.

We found that all applications of Functional Decomposition need Operational Requirements. These are the AD top level functions. The text of Operational Requirements needs to be extensive to capture the performance requirements of a system. These are often statements with multiple paragraphs to define intent, and not simple single statement FRs that are common in axiomatic design papers.

We learned a technique to coach the development of Operational Requirements. Typically these requirements are key performance metrics of product cost, maintenance cost, reliability, and competitive performance functionality. To help staff envisage what top level functions are, we developed the term "Black Box" requirements. We tell staff to imagine they have multiple potential solutions for the marketing and business case requirements, all in black boxes. Staff is not allowed to see the solutions. To determine which of these solutions is best, staff can only ask questions or have the results of tests run on these solutions. What questions and tests would we ask to determine which of the black boxes has the best solution to achieve our business objectives? These questions and tests will correspond to key Operational Requirements.

We found that Functional Decomposition processes enable systematic risk assessment much earlier in the development process than any other process we had knowledge of. In our experience, previous systematic risk reduction processes were composed of table top reviews, design reviews, FMEAs and testing. Most of these traditional risk processes, by their very nature, were later stage exercises around design solution documentation. A Functional Decomposition tree enables a systematic risk review process during the concept phase around FR-DP nodes long before significant design effort has been invested.

We have found that experienced senior designers are often a handicap and a resistance to process change. The typical argument made by experienced staff against active participation is that this new process is clearly not required as proven by their personal past success. Functional Decomposition work is just introducing needless documentation and project delays. We found the only way to deal with this resistance is with +3 level management support. Without such support we would often observe that designers quickly generated their design, documentation and prototypes without systematic risk assessment or design margin analysis or verification to input stakeholder needs. Then, when the incompleteness of the design was established, usually during prototype evaluation, designs were patched, functionality dropped or problems ignored to stay on schedule. The +2 management, often bonus compensated by delivery schedule dates, readily permits delivery of substandard and incomplete product.

We learned, or rather concluded, there are two forms of relevant experience, environmental experience and solution experience. Environmental experience refers to understanding of the environment that the final solution under development needs to function in. This is very valuable, particularly in risk assessment processes. Solution experience refers to an understanding of how the design problem was solved in the past. Knowing prior solutions seemed to limit the ability of a team to identify or accept new superior solutions. Often their reasoning is that proven prior designs had less risk. Yet most staff would admit many new product problems came from past 'proven in use' designs failing under new conditions.

We found that defining good FRs was not difficult if a test driven approach is used. Historically, in AD literature, much is made of vocabulary and structure of forming FR statements. The better defined the FR statement was, the easier to understand the FR to derive the testing to demonstrate the FR is met by the DP. It is much easier to skip the vocabulary exercise and just define the test.

We found that we needed six informational elements in an FR-DP node. These were 1) the FR, 2) the DP, 3) the FR measure and tolerance, 4) the definition of the test used to demonstrate the DP delivers on the FR measure within the tolerance range, 5) a DP risk assessment and 6) a unique FR-DP node identifier. This unique node identifier is not the node numbering system, which will be constantly changing for a give FR-DP pair during Functional Decomposition. As previously discussed, defining the DP verification test and the FR test measurement objective with tolerances effectively backward defines the FR as a function.

We learned a culture of understanding and practicing stakeholder needs analysis is important. Design teams in the concept phase need a business analysis focus with an understanding of the customer needs. In one project, a three month Stakeholders Needs assessment and Requirements Analysis uncovered that 7 of the 8 most important functional needs were absent from the Contractual Requirements. We theorize the reason for these kinds of gaps between true customer needs and the existing Contractual Requirements comes from a marketing culture of dependence on experience, re-use of prior solutions and a healthy dose of process laziness.

We discovered the formal source of customer needs, marketing, would know the current product problems we needed to fix, wish list features that customers had requested, and the features that competition had that we didn't. Marketing and development staff usually did not have a minimal understanding of how the system is used functionally by the customer, or other stakeholders, to meet their internal needs. Functional Decomposition processes reveal these information gaps and forces design engineering into the stakeholder needs analysis process to properly drive Functional Decomposition.

We found the DPs of the upper levels of decompositions are more "subsystem" placeholders than actual solutions (that can be linked to PVs). For example, we have an FR to slow down. The Target Measure might be a deceleration rate with tolerances. The DP acceptance test would be defined. The DP proposed could be "4 independent regenerative braking subsystems from 10mpg to max velocity, friction braking below effective regenerative braking, and friction braking supplement for emergency braking requests." This is a subsystem definition with performance decisions, but not having a detailed technical definition.

We found that Design Parameters (DPs) and Process Variables (PVs) do not feel like distinctly separate domains in our industrial applications. Rather, these are endpoints on an engineering development continuum. In a traditional AD representation of the design domains, initial conceptual solutions are proposed as a DP. Detailed product development work converts the DP to PVs. We found the proposed DP can often be defined directly as a final PV with no further development work required. Or other times the DP decision is just the beginning conceptualization of a multi-step process of development of PV solution during the implementation phase of the design V-model. Development and definition of DPs into PVs represents the bulk of the design effort. In summary we found that:

1. The PV domain didn't have much systematic value in the concept phase. In part, defining and completing the PV domain represents the bulk of the project design work, not the concept work.
2. PV concepts are often not relevant at the higher decomposition levels, where DPs represent more often architectural system and subsystem structures.
3. Practically, during the concept phase, the "PV domain" represented real world constraints on the implementation of selected DPs and contained the knowledge required to complete trade studies between alternative DPs. So a designer would "Visit the PV domain" to study the implementation risks of alternative DPs.
4. There was not a hierarchical zig-zag process between the DP and PV domains. We propose that DP-PV zig-zagging is a misconception in many axiomatic design writings. Instead the linking, if any exists, is one to one or many to one DP to PV (component or process) traceability. We still assume independence of PVs.
5. In the case of specific manufacturing process designs that might justify a zig-zag functional decomposition defining process decisions to implement a DP, we would re-purpose the FR and DP domains in a separate decomposition.

We have found we have virtually no new (from scratch) designs. Most industry design efforts are fixing or updating existing, highly constrained solutions. In part, we feel this is a self-imposed situation as we see many projects try to conserve or reuse "proven" designs from a perception that this practice minimizes development risk. We note that re-use creates coupling, so there is an inherent conflict between industry practice and axiomatic design independence goals.

We found that re-used solutions should be introduced as a DP in the Functional Decomposition. A characteristic of re-use is that typically, particularly with software, numerous independent FRs are all met by this DP 'block of code.' In such a case we would view the re-use risk as extremely high and systematically require design phase testing against the entire set of FRs serviced by the re-use DP.

We found over time that we should only apply Functional Decomposition when there was a structured Requirements Analysis effort. Early on in our efforts, design teams had a garbage-in garbage-out issue in that their requirements are poor, resulting in constant discovery of missed needs (requirements) during the project. This changing of requirements is typically referred to as "Requirements Creep" and explained by project staff as management's tendency to ask for more and more as the project goes on. We dispute this argument from our experiences. Our observations are that requirement creep is a direct consequence of poor requirements analysis. Requirements are not changing so much as they are being discovered late in the project.

https://doi.org/10.1051/matecconf/201822301023

As changing requirements blow the value proposition of any design process out of the water, we feel there is little advantage to introducing new design processes when not practicing rigorous requirements analysis. Functional Decomposition efforts fall flat as they reveal and try to deal with missed, poorly defined or incomplete requirements. Most of the toolkit functionality developed during our efforts was in the area of integrating needs analysis into the Functional Decomposition process.

We found that a traditional axiom 2 explanation of design versus process range analysis was not helpful. Axiom 2 conceptually represents an assessment of the systematic risk that the DP will (will not) deliver within the tolerances of the FR Measure. Axiom 2 does not seem to address random risks. The traditional academic textbook Axiom 2 representations feel simply like six-sigma based manufacturing process risk analysis. Instead we choose to use traditional risk assessment concepts to implement Axiom 2 and do not introduce the concept itself. We teach, using conventional reliability theory, that each FR-DP node needs an assessment of the systematic and random risk failure modes that might prevent the DP from delivering on the FR. How risk assessment is implemented varies between technical domains. Software risk assessment, for example, is different than hardware risk assessment. Traditional risk tools will apply. We implemented an FMEA format to capture these risks and their mitigations with our software toolkit.

We realized after a few projects that Function Maps were valuable largely in the early design and planning stages of a project. However, as the project progressed into the detailed engineering phase, and development staff started reacting to problems with testing and prototypes, Function Maps had decreasing value in design phase problem solving efforts. As such, once the major engineering effort began, we would effectively stop maintaining the Functional Decomposition unless there was a specific area of interest or perhaps a limited redesign effort.

5.2 Value Proposition Findings

We have found the following value propositions applying Function Decomposition process to system design and development as a concept phase process:

Thinking clearly in terms of solution neutral functional requirements rather than traditional features and solutions results in:

- Better requirements definition and clarity resulting in less project risk related to misunderstood, missing or creeping requirements

Function Maps enable excellent requirements and concept phase solution visualization resulting in:

- Increased collaboration and problem identification earlier in the development process which minimizes wasted time on substandard solutions and reduces design iterations.
- More complete hierarchical requirements definition that minimizes lower level design iterations due to unclear and un-reviewed subsystem requirements.

Driving the design top down from Operation Requirements and then verifying the solution against the input requirements results in:

- Functionally leaner designs simplifying the solution and lowering project and product costs

Functional Decomposition enables systematic Product Risk performance analysis structured by functions, resulting in:

- Better performance (less systematic and random risks) as significantly more performance risks are uncovered then testing could ever find.
- Better project delivery and cost metrics as more performance problems are discovered and dealt with systematically in the design phase, rather than appearing unplanned in test or deployment phases of the project.

We note that many AD proponents claim better design through design matrix analysis and decoupling, as an argument for process adoption. We did not observe this value proposition.

We found little overall value of systematic design matrix assessment in our industrial experience and dropped design matrix analysis from our process. Without prejudice as to this value in certain specific situations, why did we not see any value? In part, analyzing and maintaining a design matrix for systems of 500+ FRs that are constantly changing during the concept and early design phase is an intractable problem. Also, mentally practicing axiom 1 during design decomposition along with FR-DP test definition produces largely uncoupled design. Also, design matrix assessment is not reliable as systems evaluated as uncoupled during the concept phase end up being coupled anyway. Also, coupled systems pass the required tests and perform reliably. Finally, we find the level of competitive functional design so poor that designs are commercially competitive merely with sufficient functionality, not the optimal functionality of a fully decoupled design, making delivery, cost, feature set and other factors more important to achieving business goals.

The authors feel strongly that business strategy, process or software designs are more fertile ground than hardware design for applying Functional Decomposition processes. Yet typically staff in these areas is much less receptive to applying design process tools to their decision making. Management in particular, in our experience, resists these concepts. Convincing management that their business or operational strategies should be 'designed' and risk assessed is an incredibly difficult task.

6 Conclusions, Discussion and Recommendations

We found in our development projects that the value proposition of introducing Functional Decomposition processes was an increased first pass yield of designs better fit to deliver the Operational Requirements with increased functional reliability. This would also significantly reduce project costs and delays over the prior process(es).

We conclude, from our personal experiences and observations, Functional Decomposition processes applied during the concept phase and early design phase provide two primary underlying benefits to create this value proposition:

First, Functional Decomposition produces a more complete, internally consistent and mature set of system requirements verified against Contractual Requirements, Stakeholder Needs and other input requirements. This minimizes traditional requirements creep. This avoids errors of requirements omission.

Second, Functional Decomposition enables the earliest possible methodical approach to identification of systematic and random reliability failure modes. This permits a more complete mitigation of functional performance risks that would not traditionally be captured by verification or validation testing.

6.1 Discussion

In our experience virtually 100% of projects fail to deliver against the initial functionality, schedule and cost budget. This acceptance of such a high design process failure rate by industry is interesting. Common sense dictates that early processes will have the most impact on improving this project performance.

Yet we observe industry is only recently beginning to approach normalization of early stage design processes with Process Acceptance Models (PAMs). ISO/IEC 15504 is an example. Yet industry and PAMS focus on deliverables, which are called work products, and not the definition of the underlying processes themselves. This applies particularly to the design synthesis phase. Designers are left to their own devices and experiences, often ad-hoc, on how they develop the solutions to be documented by the work products.

We attribute this lack of interest in developing concept phase design processes to a couple of environmental variables. First, design teams in the concept phase are lulled into complacency as they have lots of time, lots of budget and lots of confidence in their abilities. Supporting these observations, we do not see design processes blamed for failures. In our experience, project failures are typically attributed to technical issues, insufficient time or inadequate design resources. Second, we see a pervasive belief that design, and in particular concept synthesis, is a "Creative" effort that defies structured processes.

Ironically, when projects result in commercial success, we observe that the development teams like to credit their creative and innovative design process skills for their success, even if the development processes technically failed to deliver as planned.

All of these conflicting observations lead us to conclude that it is common to have a lack of organizational process maturity in identifying, documenting and deploying concept phase design processes.

We also note that even with an AD Functional Decomposition framework the design processes to synthesize and propose individual DPs remain undefined and still equally difficult.

This recognition that AD operates a level above the bulk of the DP design synthesis work helps to highlight an interesting aspect of AD Functional Decomposition process implementations. We suggest it is more proper to state that Axiomatic Design is a technique to legitimately compartmentalize the hierarchical requirements architecture of a solution around functions using the independence axiom and functional decomposition. The design synthesis process, itself, as used to generate and select potential DPs, has not been systematized by AD. We invite comments on this observation.

The traditional definition of a quality process is repeatability. We suggest an interesting collaborative academic research project would be to have multiple student design classes independently take on the same design problem. This could be over time within a school, or over geography with different schools. Some efforts should apply AD. Others should be left to their traditional devices. The results should be compared. If AD has true elements of a process, then the AD design outcomes should be converging, and not be a scatter gram of solutions that we might predict with the less systematic non-AD process approaches.

Software design projects benefitted immensely from Function Decomposition processes. It is difficult for programmers to visualize performance requirements at the coding level from feature sets developed bottom up, by business analysts and architects, from stakeholder identified features. A top down functional decomposition with its inherent traceability of FRs makes the performance requirements of code modules very clear. The implementation of functional decomposition into an ISO/IEC 30003 SPICE PRM/PAM is underway.

This paper covers a lot of seminal ground. The topics within many of our brief paragraphs could be expanded into complete papers. Please contact the corresponding author for additional questions or discussion underlying the points made.

6.2 Discussion of Prior Process Reporting

As mentioned above, our paper is reporting on lessons learned from our industrial application. However we can contrast our findings against previous similar academic discussions around potential AD system design implementation processes.

Thompson discussed a requirements process to precede Functional Decomposition in great length [5]. She proposed a unique process for managing Stakeholder Needs analysis. We observe that adapting existing conventional Stakeholder Needs analysis processes worked fine for us.

In addition, unlike the process Thompson suggested, we found no need for hierarchical zig-zag mapping within, between or around Stakeholder Needs and the FR domain. Primarily this is because we found Stakeholder Needs are not hierarchical. Nor did we have to create any new work products to supplement existing conventional Stakeholder Needs analysis techniques.

The significant difference in our process findings compared to prior practice was how we needed to use traditional Stakeholder's analysis to develop a discrete intermediate work product we called Operational Requirements which equates to AD top level FRs and driver of Functional Decomposition.

We also explicitly identified an early quality step of verifying the quality and completeness of the Function Map. We did this by traceability of QFD CTQs, Affinity List items and needs of critical stakeholders (such as management and customers) into the set of FRs of the Functional Decomposition Tree.

Brown and Henley discussed the structure of the FR-DP node and related process steps [6]. Our industrial practice findings were significantly different from the proposals of these authors.

First, interestingly, the authors seem to discuss that the design is the FRs. We suggest that in Functional Decomposition, the design, and the design freedom, is with the DPs. Solution risk, for example, is a characteristic linked to the DP. Constraints on the solution operate on DPs. FRs and their respected measures are the minimal but sufficient set of functions or sub-functions required to ensure the parent DP 'solutions' will deliver on its FR.

As expected and proposed by Brown and Henley, we also agree completeness and independence of the set of child FRs needed to implement a parent DP was a good working quality check of a Node decomposition. We did not find systematic Design Matrix independence checking critical to our value proposition. We attribute this tolerance of less than perfect independence to little need for optimal designs; sufficient designs are adequate. Coupled designs would easily pass required testing. Also, it is easy to see independence (or lack there-of) by examining any duplication of the DP verification tests without a design matrix.

Lastly, unlike the Brown and Henley proposal, we point out that we needed to supplement the FR-DP node with additional attributes of Unique IDs, FR measures, the DP verification test, and DP risks.

In particular, the DP verification test proved useful forcing designers to both understand and define the FR with one (or more) performance measures. This has the effect of eliminating onerous FR definition text. This test attribute is directly from practical test driven development concepts in industry.

Both systematic and random performance risk assessment at the Function Node level introduces Axiom 2 into the working Functional Decomposition process. This early systematic risk assessment is significant. Industrial projects do not reset when problems are found. Delivery target dates do not change easily. Rather than reset or refactor designs when problems are found, the design is usually patched and some functionality and manufacturability lost. Systematically identifying and mitigating risks earlier the design process made Axiom 2 concepts more valuable than Axiom 1 in most projects.

FR Measures were perhaps inherent in prior practice, but to drive good systematic DP selection thinking processes and reliability concepts at the concept phase we needed to make performance targets an explicit aspect of Functional Decomposition nodes.

6.3 Integration into PAMs

As mentioned earlier, Process Assessment Models (PAMs) are being used more often in industry to both define and assess good design processes. PAMs assess a process defined by a Process Reference Model (PRM). See ISO/IEC 33004 for a relevant discussion.

Functional Decomposition is just a small piece of the overall development process from needs elicitation to product retirement specified in these all-encompassing PRMs.

We propose that Functional Decomposition processes create one new process and two new work products that fit into a generic PRM under architectural engineering requirements analysis. They also similarly appear under engineering requirements analysis.

The new process is Functional Decomposition.

The first new work product is the Operational Requirements and Function Model. It will have elements of both traditional requirements analysis and design, in that design processes are required to establish lower level requirements.

The second new work product is the traceability between the FRs of the functional model Function Model back into the Customer Needs and Input Requirements and forward into implementation items. Whereas traditionally customer needs are considered requirements and traceable to design items and their verification steps, we propose that customer needs are traceable to functional requirements of the Function Model, which in turn can be traced to DPs, risks, and verification testing.

We also propose that risk assessment processes typically found in the Management Processes of the PRMs are extended forward in time into the requirements analysis process to take advantage of the Function Model framework's ability to support systematic risk assessment.

6.4 Recommendation

We recommend, particularly in the development of systems that have significant functional performance requirements, such as functional safety or high reliability systems, that design teams develop and implement a structured Functional Decomposition process during concept phase processes. The process focus should be on the benefits of the requirements analysis and process steps needed to create Function Maps and risk assessment and mitigation. The value is created by exercising the process, not by documenting the work products. In practice, Functional Decomposition serves as an integrated requirements analysis, Function Model and risk management process.

References

1. R. Scupin, *The KJ Method: A Technique for Analyzing Data Derived from Japanese Ethnology*. Human Organization. 56. (1997)
2. L.K. Chan, M.L. Wu, *Quality function deployment: A literature review*, European Journal of Operational Research, Volume 143, Issue 3, Pages 463-497, (2002)
3. K.G. Jamieson, R.D. Nowak, *Active ranking using pairwise comparisons*. arXiv:1109.3701v1, (2011)
4. Acclaro Overview, Functional Specs Inc. Retrieved from Http://www.axiomaticdesign.com/products/default.asp (2018)
5. M.K. Thompson. *Improving the requirements process in Axiomatic Design Theory*. CIRP Annals - Manufacturing Technology, 62(62):115-118. (2013)
6. C. Brown, H. Henley, *Metrics for Developing Functional Requirements and Selecting Design Parameters in Axiomatic Design*. The 10th International Conference on Axiomatic Design, ICAD 2016. Procedia CIRP 53 113–118. (2016)

APPENDIX 1: Key Terms Defined

Affinity Lists: The categorized summary lists of Customer Needs produced by KJ Analysis

Aggregate Constraints: See Constraints.

Constraints: Constraints are derived from stakeholder needs that serve to limit the DP solutions that can be considered. (for example, "Product may not contain lead"). Constraints can be further defined into Input Constraints, Derived Constraints and Aggregate Constraints. Input Constraints are identified from stakeholder needs in the initial Requirements Analysis. Derived Constraints are Constraints created during the design process by DPs of the Functional Decomposition decision processes which become binding for the balance of the design effort. Aggregate Constraints represent either Input or Derived Constraints that can only be applied to total system aggregate measures such as weight or product cost. In application, Constraints are systematically checked to verify the acceptability of Design Parameters being considered.

Contractual Requirements: The contractual understanding between the funding source and the development team that exists prior to the start of development. Typically this is a statement of required business and customer needs. Although these are needs in an AD approach, we maintain the convention of calling this a Requirements document. Typically Contractual Requirements includes a list of project (cost, delivery, etc.) needs, proposed design solutions, lower level design features, and numerous Input Constraints of the system to be designed.

Customer: See Stakeholder. We prefer to reserve the term Customer for the specific category of stakeholders involved in the economic purchase of the design under development. But often in industry the term Customer is used interchangeable with Stakeholder.

Customer Needs: (AKA Needs) See Stakeholder Needs.

Customer Needs (CN) domain: This refers to the AD domain space of Stakeholder Needs that represents the gathering and analysis processes related to identifying and converting Stakeholder Needs and other inputs into Operational Requirements.

Decomposition: See Functional Decomposition

Decomposition Node: An FR-DP point on a numbered decomposition tree with 6 fields:

1. A unique node identifier
2. FR description
3. FR Measure
4. DP description
5. DP verification test
6. DP risk assessment

Decomposition Tree: (See Function Map)

Design Matrix (DM): A mapping of the dependencies between specific FRs and DPs when the FRs are mapped to the rows, and the DPs to the columns of an analysis grid. Used to expose and document FR to FR coupling by DPs.

Design Risk: See Performance Risk

Design Parameter (DP): The proposed conceptual design solution to deliver the Functional Requirement (FR) within target tolerances of the FR Measure. A FR-DP pair is defined completely with a DP verification test description and a risk assessment of systematic and random risks associated with the DP.

Design Parameter Attributes: Various measures of the physical characteristics of DPs that need to be tracked to manage an Aggregate Constraints of the total system. For example: weight, cost or power consumption.

Functional Decomposition process (AKA Decomposition, AKA Functional Analysis, AKA Functional Decomposition Performance Analysis): The process of synthesizing a top down hierarchical decomposition of a solution to the design under development in FR-DP pairs applying the rules of axiomatic design to develop a functionally independent, decoupled solution architecture that defines the FRs and DPs at all levels of the design.

Function Map: (AKA Function Tree, AKA Requirements Decomposition Tree, AKA Functional Model, AKA Functional Decomposition) A hierarchical top to bottom decomposition of requirements, starting from Operation Requirements, composed of Decomposition Nodes with parent and child relationships, consistent with Axiom 1 independence rules, is called a Function Map.

Functional Requirement (FR): A solution neutral description of the required functional performance. An FR is defined completely with a Description and a target Performance Measure with acceptable Tolerances.

Input Needs (AKA Input Requirements): The sum total of product needs from which Operational Requirements will be derived and against which the Function Map will be verified. These are composed of Contractual Requirements, Stakeholder Affinity Lists, prior product history and other design and process needs. In an AD perspective, these are Needs, but we will also use the traditional industry term of Input Requirements.

Needs: See Stakeholder Needs

Node: See Decomposition Node

Operational Requirements (AKA Top Level Functions, AKA System Performance Requirements): These are the objective requirements that summarize the expected and required business solution functional performance of the design under development in total absence of any definition of the solution. This defines functional performance requirements, which a subset of the total system requirements.

Performance Risk (AKA Functional Performance Risk, AKA Design Risk): An assessment of the risk that the selected DP will fail to deliver the FR Performance Measure? Systematic and random risks are analysed. Analysis is structured by failure modes in an FMEA format.

Performance Measure: The expected performance of the Functional Requirement. This will consist of a range of acceptable performance (Often a Target and a Tolerance). For example a requirement for weight control will have a target weight with acceptable tolerances.

Prioritization: The process of assigning an ordinal ranking of goodness to options under consideration. Prioritizing is used in trade analysis and QFD needs ranking.

Project Requirements: These are business requirements for the development process such as project costs, delivery dates and required review and approval cycles. These are usually contained within the Contractual Requirements.

Project Risk: Risks related to meeting project goals of delivering required business functionality on time and on budget. In contrast, Product Risk assesses the confidence at all levels of a proposed solution that the DPs will deliver on the FR Target Measure within required Tolerances.

Process Variable (PV) domain: This is referred to as the implementation or manufacturing design space associated with the implementation of a DP. A documented completed design has addressed all the "PV" issues of reliably replicating a solution to deliver on the Operational Requirements.

Requirements: See Functional Requirements

Requirements Analysis: A method of using process tools such as Kano, K-J Analysis, QFD and others to convert Customer Needs into a coherent de-conflicted set of Operational Requirements and Input Constraints.

Requirement Decomposition Trees: See Function Maps

Requirement Reference Numbers: (AKA Unique Node Identifiers) Unique identification numbers associated with FR-DP nodes. These are used in a practical tool to track nodes through edits and traceability.

Stakeholder (AKA Customer): The broad group of people, organizations, regulations, interfaces that place demands upon, and interact with the design under development from which needs for the design under development can be collected.

Stakeholder Needs (AKA Customer Needs, AKA Needs): A 'Voice of the Customer' collection of inputs on requirements (or features) of a potential solution that are essential or very important to stakeholders of the system being created. In Requirements Analysis, these needs are codified by KJ Analysis into summary need statements called Affinity Lists. After the development of Operations Requirements, Needs become Requirements in a vocabulary change.

Trade studies: the process of analysis to determine the preferred Design Parameter (DP) to select from a set of potential DPs

APPENDIX 2: Functional Decomposition process

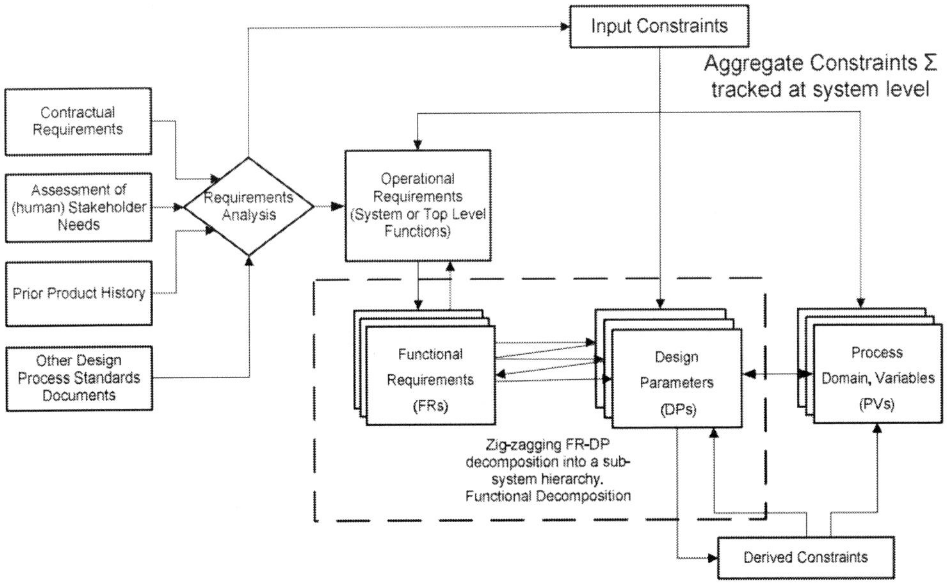

The Complexity of Mapping Customer Needs...

(and the Myth of a Unanimous Customer)

Danielle M. Vossebeld[1,3,*], *Joseph T.* Foley[2], and *Erik* Puik[3]

[1] *University Medical Center Utrecht, Heidelberglaan 100, 3584 CX Utrecht, The Netherlands*
[2] *Reykjavik University, Menntavegur 1, Reykjavik 101, Iceland*
[3] *HU University of Applied Sciences Utrecht, Padualaan 99, 3584 CH Utrecht, The Netherlands*

Abstract. Axiomatic Design and Complexity Theory as described by Suh focus heavily on the coupling often found in functional requirements. This is so fundamental to the analysis of the design that it is the core of the Axiom of Independence which examines the coupling between functional requirements due to chosen design parameters. That said, the mapping between customer needs and functional requirements is often overlooked. In this paper we consider coupling, found due to this mapping, as a possible source of complexity in terms of a user interface to a designed product. We also re-examine the methodology of how customer needs are generated and translated into the other domains to understand how they can give further insight into the customer mindset. Based on this analysis, we believe customer domain complexity should always be examined in design that includes end-user interaction.

1 Introduction

At the initial phase of design, the voice of the customer (VOC) must be transformed into a list of specifications that can then be rendered into a final product. In Axiomatic Design, this is the process of generating customer needs (CN). CNs are mapped to functional requirements (FR), and usually ending with a list of design parameters (DP). This process is inherently complex[1], challenging, and multi-disciplinary, requiring experts in multiple fields to result in repeated success. A great deal of effort has been spent in the technical fields on the process of mapping FRs to DPs, analyzing their interactions, and rendering a solution. However, complexity in the customer needs themselves has not been closely examined. This is an oversight because any vagueness or contradiction inherent in the mapping to FRs is likely to result in challenges to the design.

Before complexity of customer needs and how this might result in complexity elsewhere is examined, the basics of Axiomatic Design and Product Design are explained. This paper is organized as follows: Section 2 outlines and summarizes the basic processes involved in Axiomatic Design, Complexity Theory, and generation of customer needs. Section 3 analyses the cases from the perspective of complexity. Finally, Section 4 discusses the findings and summarizes the findings.

*e-mail: D.M.Vossebeld@umcutrecht.nl

[1]In the traditional Suh [1] sense, which is the inverse probability of meeting the goal

2 Background

To better understand the interplay between customers and requirements, some relevant elements of Axiomatic Design theory are explained.

2.1 Axiomatic Design theory

Axiomatic Design theory is a general-purpose solution-agnostic design methodology developed by Nam P. Suh at MIT in the mid-1980's [3]. More recently, the theory has been generalized to incorporate more modern concepts of 'complexity' into its structure, leading to Suh to develop Complexity Theory [1]. In both cases, the basic premise for evaluating whether a design is good or not is according to two axioms [3, p.47]:

Independence Axiom: Maintain the independence of functional requirements (FRs).

Information Axiom: Minimize the information content of the design.

These axioms are in the order of importance: one should not consider the information content, i.e., the unreliability of meeting requirements, without first considering the coupling between the FRs. Traditionally, functional requirements and design parameters (DPs) are gathered in domains (See Figure 1). A domain is a set of elements bound by a specific characteristic, e.g., 'Functionality' for the FRs and 'Physical Properties' for the DPs. The domains are connected by a mapping process, relating FRs and DPs, structuring how functionality aspects are realized with physical design solutions. A third domain, called the

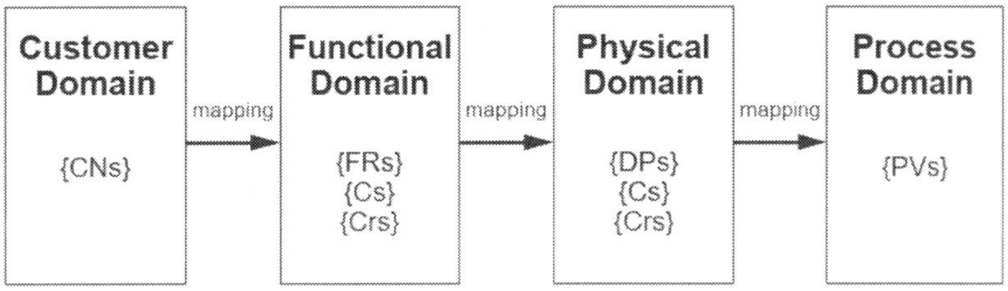

Figure 1: AD Domains and mapping. Items in braces are the lists generated during evaluation of the domain with zig-zagging. Based upon [2, p.11]

'process domain', comparably relates 'process variables' (PVs) to DPs. Domains are not automatically structured and may be in a state of illogical presentation. The understanding of the domains by the designer benefits from a clear organization. Therefore, domains are hierarchically decomposed into parallel lists following the process of zig-zagging.

Zig-zagging refers to the process of structured decomposition between parallel trees of the different domains [2]. The process usually starts with the functional domain. Then the elements in that domain are enumerated with a unique sequential identifier. For a Functional Requirement, this might be FR_1 or FR1. This list is then mapped to a list of elements in the next domain in the sequence. These elements are again enumerated with an identifier for the domain, e.g. DP_1 or DP1. Once this enumeration is complete, the process jumps to the functional domain to decompose each list element into smaller parts as needed. Girgenti [4] pleads for a slightly different procedure; instead of continuing the process of zig-zagging to the next level of decomposition, he first verifies his findings at the same level by reversing the zig-zagging process. He calls this process 'zig-zagging conversely'. The goal is "forcing to self-question whether the problem has been completely dissected or something better and more connected with real customer needs could be found". This verification is usually executed after decoupling of the system and is then called 'Reverse Zig-zagging' [5, 6]. It means that an iterative verification takes place to secure the findings before zig-zagging continues to the next-lower hierarchical level (by self-questioning).

The process of decomposition, with or without verification, should be Collectively Exhaustive and Mutually Exclusive (CEME), a mnemonic developed by Brown [7]. As such, decomposition advances from the higher to the lower level domains. All decomposed elements have IDs that explain the child-parent relationship: $FR_{1.1}$ or FR11 which is mapped to $DP_{1.1}$ or DP11. These are both children of FR_1 and DP_1, respectively. Following the process, the examination of the domains evokes the concept of a 'zig-zag'.The most common zig-zag decomposition is seen between the functional domain (FRs) and physical domain (DPs), eventually process domain (PV) is included.

Inter-domain coupling is evaluated by building a Design matrix: a Cartesian product-transfer-matrix of all the listed elements in the two domains associated with them [8, 9]. Traditionally, this is primarily done with FRs and DPs, but the same can be done with DPs and PVs.

After rearranging the lists to best fit a triangular matrix in traditional linear-algebraic transformations, the design can determine if the design is:

coupled (non-triangular matrix), in which case finding a generalized solution is difficult,

de-coupled or path-dependent (triangular matrix), for which the order in which elements are designed matters,

uncoupled (diagonal matrix) indicating that changes are localized between a single FR-DP pair so the design can be done in whatever order desired.

2.2 Complexity Theory

Axiomatic Design theory was further extended by Suh [1] in order to focus on 'relative' understanding of the system, analogue to the information concept brought up in the Information Axiom. He explores the meaning of complexity, finally settling on "Complexity is defined as a measure of uncertainty in achieving the specified FRs." [1, p.58] This definition is then subdivided into four different types:

time-independent real complexity which is simply the information content of a design: $C_R = I$, where $I_i = -\log_2 P_i$ and P_i is the probability of meeting satisfying FR_i.

time-independent imaginary complexity arises in coupled or path-dependent solutions where the order in which DPs should be addressed is unclear or improperly ordered.

time-dependent combinatorial complexity develops in systems in which operation has a higher probability of going out of specification due to "continued expansion in the number of possible combinations with time". In short, it is systems that progress toward chaotic states over some time period.

time-dependent periodic complexity is similar to combinatorial complexity except that a functional period has been identified over which the system can be reset before it enters an unpredictable state.

These four categories of complexity provide a generalization and quantification of the predicted reliability of a design based upon the operating specifications and analysis of coupling during the design phase. Suh also provides guidelines for reducing these types of complexity: see [1] for a in-depth discussion of this topic.

2.3 Customer Needs

The customer domain is characterized by the needs (or attributes) that the customer is looking for in a product or process or systems or materials. Examples are given for CAs[2] in various disciplines[2, p.12]:

Manufacturing Attributes that customers desire

Materials Desired performance

Software Attributes desired in the software

Organizations Customer satisfaction

Systems Attributes desired of the overall system

Business ROI

Suh [2, p.14] recognizes that finding and developing customer attributes is challenging. He recommends considering quality function deployment [10] and working with customers. He gives the tagline: "The rule is to ask the right questions to the right customers at the right time." Kurniawan et al. [11] also suggest employing: Voice of Customer, Conjoint Analysis, Kano Diagram, Kansei Engineering, and Web-based consumer elicitation as methods to bring out customer needs (or attributes). Once CA lists are developed, Pugh matrix [12], analytical hierarchy process (AHP) [13, 14], Taguchi loss functions [15], and the weighted sum of product attributes are methods for ranking and sub-selecting from the CAs.

Ulrich [16] gives a structured approach for developing these lists of customer needs: an entire chapter of the book focuses on this subject. The overall process is [16, p.75]:

1. Gather raw data from customers
2. Interpret the raw data in terms of customer needs. Organize the needs into a hierarchy of primary, secondary, and (if necessary) tertiary needs.
3. Establish the relative importance of the needs.
4. Reflect on the results and the process.

Gathering data is accomplished through interviews, focus groups, or observing the product in use. A key step during this is to identify and choose the correct customers to focus the more high-effort data collection activities. Helpful questions during interviewing potential end users are:

- When and why do you use this type of product?
- Walk us through a typical session using the product.
- What do you like about existing products?
- What do you dislike about the existing products?
- What issues do you consider when purchasing the product?
- What improvements would you make to the product?

In addition to normal needs, Ulrich [16, p.79–80] emphasizes the need to stay flexible and observe all aspects. Some needs can be identified through interaction and nonverbal expression. In particular, designers should be looking for 'latent needs' which are 'neither fulfilled nor commonly articulated and understood', which is also stressed by Hintersteiner [18]. If these needs can be met, they are excellent product differentiators from competitors in the market.

After collection, the CNs are interpreted by a marketer, designer or engineer. In an example of a screwdriver, Ulrich [16] shows a DP mentioned by a user, namely 'pistol grip', being interpreted as a CN 'comfortable to grip'. This is a combination of an FR of 'holding the screwdriver' and the criterion of 'comfort'. In this case, this criterion could be more extensive as comfort for holding the screwdriver also entails choosing the center of gravity of a tool. In this paper, the focus will be on the term customer needs (CN), as it focuses on the criticality of the request.

If the composition of all CNs in the customer domain is investigated, the essential elements of the system can be recognized, containing the whole range of combinations of FRs, DPs, PVs, nFRs, constraints, and criteria. Brown [19] also mentions the different kinds of elements in the CNs, leaving the sorting to the designer. Based on Ulrich [16], the CNs may be considered as a display of interpretations of typical characteristics of the system.

2.4 Summary

As previously mentioned, the 'customer domain' (Figure 1) is an unorganized source of knowledge about what requirements should be generated. The customer domain is characterized by the needs (or attributes) that the customer is looking for in a product, process, systems, or materials [2, p.10]. As such, the customer domain is a set of elements that the customer associates with a good design. Analogue to the other domains, the customer domain also may lack a clear structure, for the customer himself as well as the designer. Disorganization of the customer domain makes it more difficult to translate the customer's wishes into a clear list of FRs and leads to disorganization of the other domains. As such, any complexity in the customer domain may be forwarded to the other domains. This area that has not been studied in depth in the current literature and is of great interest to the authors.

To be explicit:

How is complexity, coming forth from disorganization in the CNs, forwarded to the functional-, physical-, and process-domains?

[2] Suh applies the term "customer attributes"

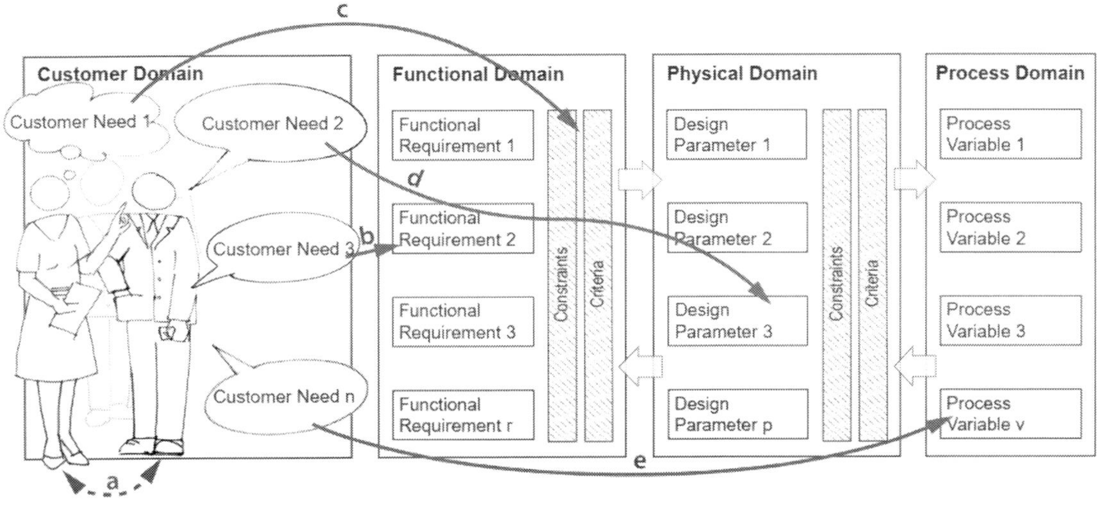

Figure 2: Interpreted CNs may add complexity other domains. (a) different stakeholders, (b) coupled FRs, (c) constraints, (d) coupled DPs, (e) limitations in PVs. Schematic based on [17].

3 Analysis of the complexity in the customer domain

To examine the effect of mapping CNs and the complexity, the nature of the customer domain and the CNs should be examined first. We explore existing literature on product or systems development using Axiomatic Design and also use examples of current research projects, to identify complexity and even the possibility of coupling.

Our presuppositions are that the complexity of effective mapping CNs is caused on five instances, which are annotated in Figure 2

a. Conflicting CNs of different stakeholders.

b. Coupled FRs are similar to (coupled) CNs.

c. Constraints and criteria in CNs cause coupling.

d. DPs in customer domain cause coupling.

e. Limitations due to PVs in customer domain.

These presuppositions will be applied as guidance to explore this subject.

3.1 Conflicting CNs of different stakeholders

The CNs in the customer domain contain (combinations of) FRs, DPs, PVs, nFRs, constraints, and criteria of different stakeholders. The term customer needs is applied for not just the needs of the customer who acquires a product, but also the needs of different parties within this customer as an organization or external parties influencing the needs of this customer. Thompson [20] refers to the CNs as SNs i.e. the stakeholder needs. The consequence of different parties or stakeholders is that they do not necessarily have common needs and can have conflicting requirements according to Thompson [20] (see 'a' in Figure 2 and process in Figure 3). A customer who wants a product developed can have different goals and needs than a manufacturer that has to fabricate it.

Even within the organization that acts as a 'single customer', there can be conflicting needs. Weber et al. [21] refers to an automobile manufacturer with several internal groups with competing demands. He uses color coding in AD to identify the FRs of stakeholders or interest groups. Hintersteiner [18] mentions the well-known difference between the buyer and the user of a certain product. We also see this in our work. Within a hospital, for example, there are many involved parties for acquisition or design of (medical) equipment. Nurses want to register patient data at the bedside, to be able to spend more time on patient care and less on administrative tasks. A possible solution (DP), a computer on wheels (COW), can satisfy the need for registration at the bedside but was not

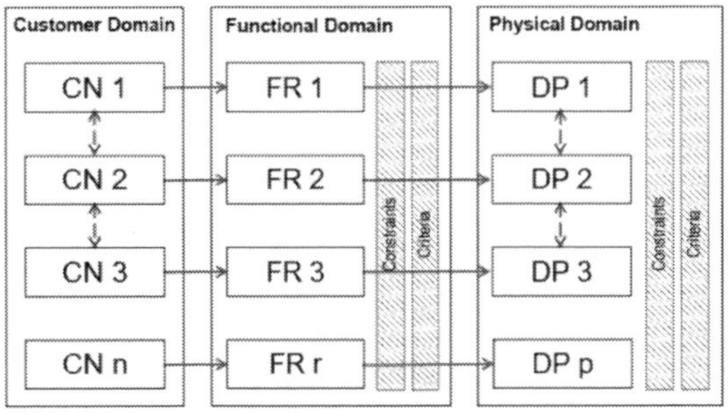

Figure 3: Conflicting CNs of different stakeholders

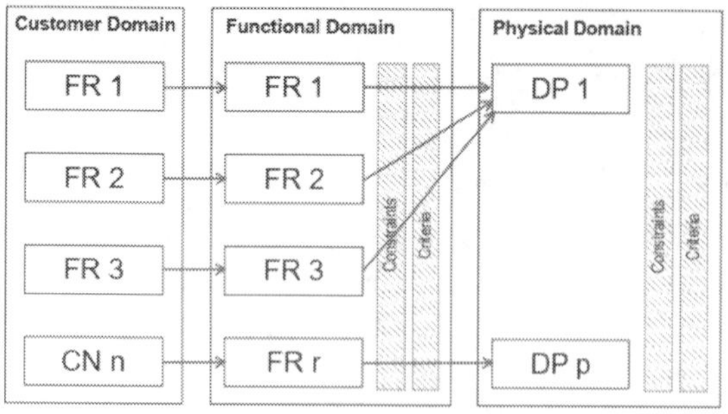

Figure 4: coupled FRs due to (coupled) CNs

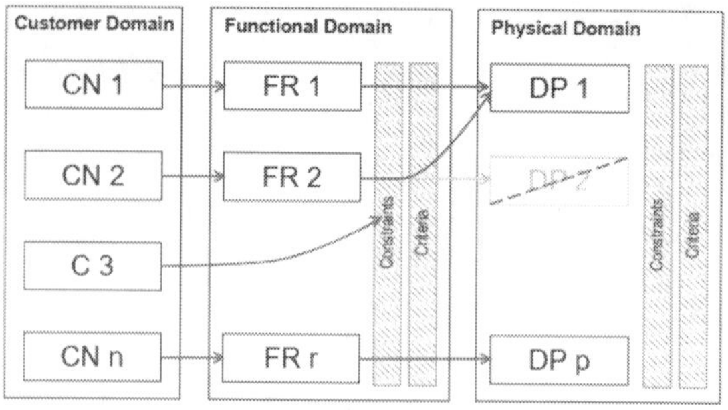

Figure 5: coupling due to C or Cr in CN

allowed in the patient room due to hygiene rules imposed by the hygiene department who focused on infection control. Making the product easy to clean would allow the product in the room if is cleaned after each patient visit. This would take more time, which contradicts with one of the CNs of the nurses. The choice for COWs as a solution is among others based on cost (constraint or criterion) by management. The underlying CN for all parties, or in this case the hospital as one customer, is better patient care. The interpretation of this CN for the different internal stakeholders is conflicting. Due to these conflicts arising from effectively incompatible tolerances, it can be viewed as an instance of Real Complexity. If we also consider the possible changing state of stakeholders, this can also include some elements of Combinatorial Complexity.

3.2 Coupled FRs are similar to (coupled) CNs

Ulrich [16] mentions that CNs should be "largely independent from the product we might develop", thus independent from the DPs, by describing the CNs as what the product should do. This is very similar to Suh's guidance that "FRs should be solution independent" i.e. following the Independence Axiom. If these FRs are coupled with the choice of a single DP for two or more FRs [3], the CNs also may be considered to be coupled. As these CNs are directly mapped to the FRs, no coupling is shown between the customer domain and the functional domain (see 'b' in Figure 2 and process in Figure 4). The inherent coupling leads to Imaginary Complexity; there exists a lack of knowledge that prevents the CNs to be completely understood.

3.3 Constraints and criteria in CNs cause coupling

Suh [3] describes an example of the design of a refrigerator in his book. He emphasizes the choice of independent FRs, but also mentions how "constraints have a limiting effect on design". In the example, he uses the constraint of the maximum cost of a refrigerator door, which can cause coupling of FRs. Thompson [22] also mentions criteria, for ranking choices. A fixed maximum price can be a constraint, a criterion for choosing between alternative solutions can be 'lowest cost'. In both cases, not all DPs will be acceptable as a solution (see 'c' in Figure 2 and process in Figure 5). Suh [3] mentions that the vertical hung refrigerator door "is *not* a good design" according to Axiom 1, due to the coupling of FRs caused by a constraint. Coupling due to more constraints is seen with the design of professional tools, like drills. The company Bosch [23] explains how drills should be made smaller and lighter to fit the build and strength of women. A constraint on the handle would be the size of hands or a maximum lifting power based on ergonomics. This would however also reduce the power of the tool, making the work more time-intensive to finish, which would not be acceptable for a professional tool. A maximum of time spent on a specific task could also be a constraint.

This is a mixture of Imaginary- and Real Complexity. The Imaginary Complexity is due to the confusion about what which needs are the ones to focus on and possible orderings that need to be considered; the FR 'powerful tool' causes coupling with the FR 'easy lifting/gripping'. The Real Complexity comes forth from mis-categorization during the translation process, allowing constraints to become FR and disrupting FR-DP relations.

3.4 DPs in customer domain cause coupling

Bragason et al. [24] describe one of the disadvantages of having an in-domain expert involved in the development process of CNs. Such experts already 'know how to solve the problem' without first going through the separation of function from implementation. The example given is for a non-explosive high-altitude rocket parachute release system developed by Bragason et al. [24] An interview with the rocket vendor interested in developing the project created a long list of CNs with a lot of technical specifications. As a thought experiment, these CNs were translated directly into FRs and an iteration of design completed (see 'd' in Figure 2 and process in Figure 6). It was quickly discovered that the significant coupling that arose in the FR-DP design matrix made finding a suitable design unfeasible. From considering the DP list, it was obvious that the CNs had effectively specified an FR-DP mapping without considering the possible coupling.

The team started over and applied proper FR and DP guidelines [2, 25]:

FRs begin with an action or transformational verb and are verifiable

DPs begin with a noun and can be quantified or compared

This new design matrix had significantly less coupling. A prototype was tested and was found to be unreliable. Further analysis realized this was due to coupling found in the thermally active material and the pressure release mechanism; heat softened the plug, but the release of the gas cooled the plug. This project has continued at Reykjavik University under the guidance of Professor Joseph T. Foley for a new iteration named Plasbar, which is expected to be published this year. In this new design, the coupling has been directly addressed by separating the plug mechanism from the thermally actuated element.

Girgenti [4] also cautions that the voice of the customer (VOC) can lead directly to DPs. He suggests finding the hidden CNs by zig-zagging conversely. In his example, he mentions the FR 'to provide classic Italian racing colors' and the mapped DP 'color red' for a car, with the hidden CN 'sporty feeling'. This is a non-functional requirement (nFR) [22], which applies to several parts of the car, like the body, interior and also the rims. Girgenti translates this to the FR 'to provide a racing experience'. Requirements of this sort are heavily driven by the subjective interpretation of the interaction between the user and the item being designed. This is a very hard requirement to evaluate, appearing in nature closer to the 'Feeling/Experience Requirement' ($\mathcal{FR}$) described in Creative Axiomatic Design by Foley and Harðardóttir[26]. Their strategy for dealing with such requirements is to condense them down to fundamental emotions to help simplify evaluation. To validate such requirements, the designer provides a test environment and surveys what emotions are registered by the participants. In many ways, this is very similar to Ulrich's [16] concept of a latent need: something that is not well expressed. From a practical implementation, nFRs such as these are best implemented as constraints or criteria that have a limited scope to only certain elements of the design. Iino and Nakao [27] address a similar challenge of limited-scope constraints in designs that need electricity for operation. They address it by use of specialized symbols on their design record graph visualization of an FR-DP decomposition; in the case of needing electricity, related FRs and DPs have a battery symbol next to them. This is an example of Imaginary Complexity due to increased coupling.

3.5 Limitations due to PVs in customer domain

Suh [28] mentions that the customer can also suggest PVs, e.g. when existing machines must be used (see e in Figure 2). This limits also the choice for DPs (see 'e' in Figure 2 and process in Figure 7). These CNs *or better* these PVs limit the choice for DPs and as such are considered to be constraints [28]. The underlying need can be a limitation on costs, which is a constraint in the functional domain and process domain. Replacing the PV with this constraint will increase the options for other, more suitable, DPs and PVs. It is an open question of what type of complexity these limitations are, however, due to the conceptual impact it is at least expected to increase Imaginary Complexity.

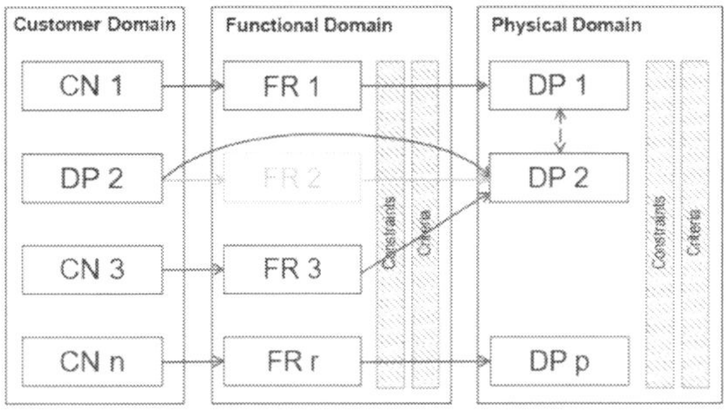

Figure 6: DP in CN causes complexity

4 Discussion

Now that the identified sources of complexity have been inventoried from the perspective of the customer domain, we will discuss to which insights these investigations have led.

4.1 Reducing complexity

The gathering of raw data from the customers or stakeholders is the first step of the designer to get to the essence of the true needs of the system to be developed. During this interpretation, the CNs can be carried over (mapped) or placed in the functional, physical, or process domains. This will give an overview of the project and mentioned needs. All CNs that are placed in the physical or process domain (see (d) and (e) in Figure 2) should initially be analyzed for the underlying CNs, FRs, constraints or criteria. In this interpretation DPs and possible PVs are translated to the underlying needs, or what Girgenti [4] mentions as zigzagging conversely (reverse zig-zagging). A reverse mapping between the domains could be more accurate as it server as an extra verification of potential unsubstantiated assumptions. Thus gained and verified knowledge reduces Imaginary Complexity during the design process and as such reduce the chance of coupling of FRs. Complete elimination of the interactions between the PVs or DPs is not always possible. As a result coupling of FRs may remain.

The reverse mapping from the physical domain to customer domain is similar to a reverse arrow (d) in Figure 2, not passing the functional domain. This is similar to using models and prototypes as DPs for feedback from the customer and also eliciting more (latent) needs.

4.2 Placing the customer in his domain

With reverse mapping, we place the interpreted needs based on given DPs or PVs back in the customer domain. From this mapping, we make an interpretation based on

 https://doi.org/10.1051/matecconf/201822301024

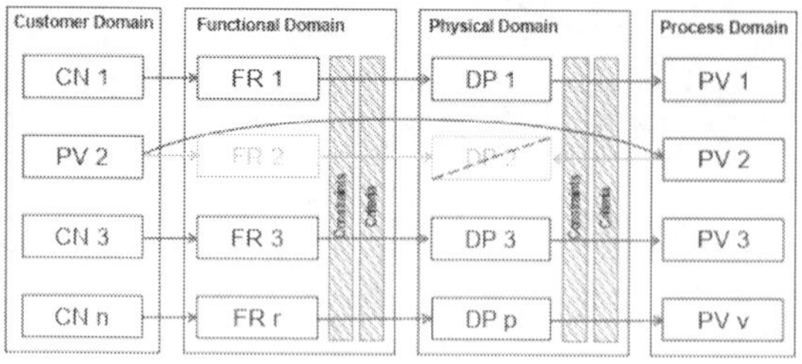

Figure 7: Limitation due to PV in CN

our knowledge of our customers and on the CNs in this domain. These interpreted needs, as a product of reverse mapping, should always be validated with the internal and external stakeholders, as stated needs and also by using prototypes. We want to observe the interaction with the 'living' customers as part of the customer domain.

4.3 Further research

The focus in Axiomatic Design lies on the mapping between FRs and DPs, and DPs and PVs. The customer domain and the mapping between CNs and FRs get less attention. The influence of customers and stakeholders on the development of products and systems can't be overlooked and should get a greater emphasis in Axiomatic Design, also mentioned by Hintersteiner [18]. Further exploration and discussion of how to involve the broad spectrum of (internal and external) stakeholders are needed. Integrating knowledge of other methods like "participatory design", where users are seen as partners in the product development process [29], can also emphasize the importance of the needs of our customers in Axiomatic Design.

4.4 Summary

Identification of CNs is a critical step in design of virtually anything, but the process of eliciting and interpreting them is still unrefined. The customer domain consists of (combinations of) FRs, nFrs, constraints, criteria, DPs, and PVs. These are a collectively exhaustive and mutually exclusive set of preconditions in which the CNs from multiple stakeholders are placed. The multiple stakeholders may have conflicting needs or opinions. The customer domain also contains invisible needs of which we and the customers are not aware of (e.g. hidden or latent needs).

As described in this article, there appear to be three steps:

1. There should be active reverse mapping from the process, physical and functional domain to the customer domain.

2. Customers should be part of the customer domain as persons, not just their interpreted needs.

3. The complexity of customer domain needs further exploration and discussing.

With products that involve many customers or stakeholders and that includes end-user interaction, customer domain complexity should always be analyzed in depth, to maximize independence, minimize information, and also optimize the fit with the customer.

References

[1] N.P. Suh, *Complexity* (Oxford University Press, 2005)

[2] N.P. Suh, *Axiomatic Design - Advances and Applications* (Oxford University Press, 2001)

[3] N.P. Suh, *The Principles of Design* (Oxford University Press, 1990)

[4] A. Girgenti, B. Pacifici, A. Ciappi, A. Giorgetti, *An Axiomatic Design Approach for Customer Satisfaction through a Lean Start-up Framework*, in [30], pp. 151–157, sep. 21–23

[5] E. Puik, E. Smulders, J. Gerritsen, B. van Huijgevoort, *A Method for Indexing Axiomatic Independence Applied to Reconfigurable Manufacturing Systems*, in *Proceedings of ICAD2013 The Seventh International Conference on Axiomatic Design Worcester – June 27-28, 2013* (2013)

[6] E. Puik, *Risk Adjusted, Concurrent Development of Microsystems and Reconfigurable Manufacturing Systems*, in *Doctoral dissertation, PhD thesis manuscript University of Warwick* (Coventry, United Kingdom, 2017)

[7] C.A. Brown, *Teaching axiomatic design to engineers — Theory, applications, and software*, Journal of Manufacturing Systems **24**, 186 (2005)

[8] D.S. Cochran, J.T. Foley, Z. Bi, *Use of the Manufacturing System Design Decomposition for Comparative Analysis and Effective Design of Production Systems*, International Journal of Production Research **55**, 870 (2016)

[9] E.M. Benavides, *Advanced engineering design - An integrated approach* (Woodhead Publishing, 2012)

[10] J.B. ReVelle, J.W. Moran, C.A. Cox, *The QFD Handbook* (J.C. Wiley, 1998)

[11] S.H. Kurniawan, M. Zhang, M.M. Tseng, *Connecting Customers in Axiomatic Design*, in *Proceedings of ICAD2004, The Third International Conference on Axiomatic Design, Seoul* (2004), pp. 1–7

[12] S. Pugh, *Total Design: Integrated Methods for Successful Product Engineering* (Addison-Wesley, 1991)

[13] T.L. Saaty, *The Analytic Hierarchy Process* (McGraw Hill, 1980)

[14] T.L. Saaty, *Decision making with the analytic hierarchy process*, International Journal of Services Sciences **1**, 83 (2008)

[15] G. Taguchi, E.A. Elsayed, T.C. Hsiang, *Quality Engineering in Production Systems*, McGraw Hill Series in Inductiral Engineering and Management Science (McGraw-Hill College, 1988)

[16] K.T. Ulrich, S.D. Eppinger, *Product Design and Development*, 5th edn. (McGraw-Hill, New York, 2012)

[17] D.M. Vossebeld, E. Puik, J.E. Jaspers, M.J. Schuurmans, *Development process of a mobile electronic medical record for nurses. A single case study.*, Manuscript submitted for publication. (2018)

[18] J.D. Hintersteiner, *Addressing changing customer needs by adapting design requirements*, in *Proceeding of ICAD2000, First International Conference on Axiomatic Design, Cambridge* (2000), pp. 290–299, http://ns.axiomaticdesign.com/technology/icad/icad2000/icad2000{_}063.pdf

[19] C.A. Brown, *Elements of Axiomatic Design: a simple and practical approach to engineering design."*, Cazenovia, New York, NY (2006)

[20] M. Thompson, *Improving the requirements process in Axiomatic Design Theory*, CIRP Annals **62**, 115 (2013)

[21] J. Weber, D. Förster, J. Kößler, K. Paetzold, *Design of Changeable Production Units within the Automotive Sector with Axiomatic Design*, Procedia CIRP **34**, 93 (2015)

[22] M.K. Thompson, *A classification of procedural errors in the definition of functional requirements in Axiomatic Design theory*, in *7th International Conference on Axiomatic Design (ICAD 2013)*, edited by M.K. Thompson, CIRP (Axiomatic Design Solutions, Inc., Worchester, MA, 2013), Vol. 32, pp. 1–6

[23] D.M. Vossebeld, *In de prijzen*, Tijdschrift voor Ergonomie **34**, 44 (2009)

[24] G. Bragason, S. Þorsteinsson, R.I. Karlsson, N. Grosse, J.T. Foley, *Heat-activated Parachute Release System*, in *Proceedings of College International Pour La Recherche en Productique (CIRP), 9th International Conference on Axiomatic Design (ICAD)*, edited by M.K. Thompson, A. Giorgetti, P. Citti, D. Matt, N.P. Suh, Procedia CIRP (Elsevier ScienceDirect, Florence, Italy, 2015), Vol. 34, pp. 131–136, sep. 16–18, http://www.sciencedirect.com/science/article/pii/S2212827115008203

[25] D.S. Cochran, J. Li, K. Vanover, J.T. Foley, *A System Design of a Rural Hospital Operating Room*, in [31], pp. 597–603, jun. 15–17

[26] J.T. Foley, S. Harðardóttir, *Creative Axiomatic Design*, in [31], pp. 240–245, jun. 15–17

[27] K. Iino, M. Nakao, *Design Record Graph and Axiomatic Design for Creative Design Education*, in [30], pp. 173 – 178, sep. 21–23

[28] N.P. Suh, *Axiomatic design theory for systems*, Research in engineering design **10**, 189 (1998)

[29] E.B.N. Sanders, P.J. Stappers, *Convivial Toolbox: Generative Research for the Front End of Design* (BIS, Amsterdam, 2012)

[30] A. Liu, ed., *10th International Conference on Axiomatic Design (ICAD)*, Vol. 53, Procedia CIRP (Elsevier ScienceDirect, Xi'an, Shaanxi, China, 2016), sep. 21–23

[31] *26th CIRP Design Conference*, Procedia CIRP (Elsevier ScienceDirect, Stockholm, Sweden, 2016), jun. 15–17

AUTHOR INDEX